AN INTRODUCTION

TO

ENGLISH LITERATURE

BY

HENRY S. PANCOAST

THIRD EDITION, ENLARGED

NEW YORK

HENRY HOLT AND COMPANY

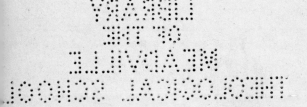

PREFACE

TO THE THIRD EDITION.

Fifteen years ago, Mr. Henry Holt asked me to arrange
a series of representative selections from English literature in chronological order, and to connect them with such
biographical and historical matter as might be found
necessary for an understanding of them, and of their
relation to national and literary history. The result of
this request was a book, *Representative English Literature,*
which appeared in 1892. In this book, owing to the large
proportion of space taken up by selections, the historical
sketch was necessarily very brief, and a few years later,
at Mr. Holt's suggestion, I prepared a second book, *An
Introduction to English Literature,* based on the first, in
which the selections were omitted and the historical outline revised and considerably expanded. Two years later
this second book was enlarged by the addition of further
biographical and other matter. In the present book the
subject is treated with still greater fulness but upon the
same general plan. The first half of the book has been
practically re-written, and the chapters dealing with the
Early and Middle English periods have been considerably

enlarged. Greater space has also been given to the
literature of the Queen Anne and Victorian periods, and
separate lives of Bunyan, Dryden, Steele, Cowper, and
others have been added.

No one who attempts to act as guide in this long journey from Beowulf to Kipling believes himself secure from
error, unless he is very foolish or preternaturally learned.
I can only say, for my own part, that I have tried faithfully to avoid mistakes, that I have, so far as possible,
shunned controversy, and that in matters of opinion I
have honestly set down the truth as it appeared to me.
I am painfully conscious that, in spite of all the labours of
others, it is a difficult, perhaps an impossible, thing to see
the whole origin, growth, and development of English
literature in a just proportion; to see the relation of each
book, each man, each event, to the whole story, to interpret every great writer with equal sympathy and fairness,
and to get at the heart of every great book. One's only
comfort is, that the very vastness, the very impossibility of the undertaking can be urged in mitigation of
one's inevitable shortcomings. Well may the author of
even a short and unpretentious history of English literature say with Chaucer —

> " I have, God woot, a large feeld to ere,
> And wayke been the oxen in my plough."

I have had more friendly help in the preparation of
this book than I can suitably or specifically acknowledge.
Dr. Arthur Adams, of Trinity College, read a great part of
the manuscript and furnished me with much of the
material for the bibliography. Mr. Keith Willoughby
has given many hours of conscientious labour to the prep-

aration of the chronological tables, and I am deeply indebted in various ways to Professor Cecil F. Lavell, Professor Felix E. Schelling, Mr. W. C. Carleton, the librarian of Trinity College, and Mr. George Dana Smith, the assistant librarian of the Watkinson Library, Hartford.

H. S. P.

HARTFORD, *September 3, 1907.*

CONTENTS.

PART III.

THE FRENCH INFLUENCE, 1660 — cir. 1750.

CONTENTS.

PAGE

PART IV.

THE MODERN ENGLISH PERIOD, since cir. 1725.

ENGLISH LITERATURE.

INTRODUCTION.

ENGLISH literature is the expression in memorable poetry and prose of the life and character of the English people.

English literature and English history. In English history we see the character of the people revealed through action. The English people establish a great nation: the English nation founds a great colonial empire. The English extend their language to the ends of the earth: they build up one of the noblest and richest literatures known to history. How have they been able to produce this literature? Not because they were naturally fond of talking, like the Gauls; not because they had any peculiar talent for making verses, or any especial turn for saying graceful or pretty things. English literature, like English history, is memorable and inspiring because it is the genuine expression of a great race. When a brave, earnest man, who has felt, and seen, and done much, tells you his innermost thoughts, he is worth listening to; and when a nation like the English speaks to us out of its heart through its books, its books are worth reading. For more than fourteen hundred years, generation after generation of Englishmen has tried to put something of its life into words. At first the attempts were crude and imperfect; the nation struggled to speak through the rough song of some heroic deed or the brief chronicle of historical events; but as time went on, the soul of the people found a readier and fuller utterance in ballad and drama, and epic and novel, in books on religion, or history, or philosophy. So that at last in that long

succession of books which make up English literature, we
have the record of the inner life of the people, of the loves
and hatreds, doubts and fears, hopes and beliefs of each
succeeding generation; the story of the nation, told by the
nation itself for those who can read and understand.

It is clear that English literature is thus a part of English history, and that any historical event which vitally
changes the life and thought of the people changes their
literature also. Thus, such important events as the introduction of Christianity into England, the triumph of King
Alfred over the Danes, the conquest of England by the Normans, or the loss of Normandy by King John, are turning-
points in the literature as well as in the history. The great

**The chronolog-
ical divisions
of English lit-
erature.** divisions of English history and of English literature are therefore the same. The history of
the literature, reflecting the changes that have
followed each other in the outward or inner life
of the race, naturally divides itself into four main periods of
development:

     I. *The Period of Preparation.*
        About 670 to about 1400.

    II. *The Period of Italian Influence.*
        About 1400 to about 1660.

   III. *The Period of French Influence.*
        About 1660 to about 1750.

   IV. *The Modern Period.*
        Since about 1725.

No exact dates can be given for any of these periods.
Changes in the mental life of a nation, and in the literature
which reflects that life, come gradually, — so gradually that
it is impossible to state the exact year in which such a
change takes place. Yet each of these periods has a character of its own, each has certain traits that distinguish

it from the rest. We all know that childhood differs from youth, and youth from manhood; although we cannot fix upon the precise minute when the individual passes from one of these stages of growth to another. In the same way these periods, or stages in the growth of the nation's literature, are no less real because their limits cannot be precisely defined. We must try to get some general idea of the nature of each of these four periods at the beginning, although their character and meaning will become clearer after we have studied them more fully.

I. The Period of Preparation.

From about 670 to about 1400.

During this long period of more than seven hundred years we find no poets worthy to be compared with Shakespeare, Milton, or Tennyson, no prose writers at all equal to Burke, or Ruskin, or Carlyle. Yet these seven centuries did much to prepare the way for them and for the other writers of the later time. This long preparatory period was a time of national growth and national discipline, in which England was made ready for the work of her maturity, and the foundations of her literature were laid. When it began, England was not one united nation. There was no king who ruled over all England, and the people in different parts of the island spoke different languages, or different dialects of the same tongue. The eastern part of the land was broken up into a number of small Anglo-Saxon kingdoms, often at war among themselves; the western part was held by the still unconquered Britons, the people whom the English called the Welsh. To the north of the English and the Britons lay the land of the Scot, a wild region, comparatively barren and mountainous, thinly inhabited by yet other tribes, bearing some resemblance to the Britons but differing from them; and differing still more from the English in manners and in speech. Small as it was, the island was thus broken up into separate and often hostile communities; on every side there was a conflict of authority, a confusion of race, of tribes, and of tongues.

As there was no nation, and no national language, there could be no truly national literature. Such literature as there was, was *local;* for, as each poet used the speech of the little community in which he lived, many of those who dwelt in other sections could not have understood his poems even if they had heard them. Now one great work of these preparatory centuries, was to make a single and united nation out of these separate or hostile races and tribes; another great work was to make a language capable of expressing the thoughts of a great nation, a language which should in turn become the mother-tongue of the whole people. By the end of the fourteenth century the hardest part of these two great tasks had been accomplished. Although Scotland was still an independent kingdom, England had become a strong and united nation; and, while Gaelic was still spoken in the Scotch Highlands, while Welsh still lingered in Wales, and many dialects were still used in England, the foundations of a national language had been securely laid. At one period in the history of these seven centuries, the Danes had poured into England, bringing with them their own speech; at another, the Normans had conquered the land, and they spoke Norman-French. But the English language, although it was modified by the influence first of the Danes, and then of the Norman-French, held its place against its foreign rivals. By 1400 one especial variety of this modified, or *Frenchified,* English, that spoken in and about London, was already in a fair way to become the national language. The fact that this was the form of English used at the Court, and employed by the Court poets and other writers of the capital, naturally raised it to a position of importance; and it is from this particular dialect, that the English we speak to-day, however enlarged or modified, is directly derived.

In these centuries the way was further prepared for the triumphs of the later literature by the training, the civilising of the English race. The first great agency in this training was the Christian religion. The Christian Church was the earliest civiliser of these untamed English, and she labored faithfully to train and educate men's minds as well as to save their souls. The second great civilising agency was the influence of the Normans, who conquered England in 1066. The Norman was a hard master, but he brought with him from the Continent a higher scholarship and a more courtly and polished civilisation than was then known in England. The Norman brought also his chivalric and romantic literature, as well as his language.

Now the fourteenth century is the time when the mixture of all the various elements, separate and antagonistic at first, begins to be fairly complete. Then, as we shall see, many of these elements in life, literature, and language were combined in the work of GEOFFREY CHAUCER (about 1340–1400), the first great poet of this united England.

II. THE PERIOD OF ITALIAN INFLUENCE
From about 1400 to about 1660.

In this period the thought and imagination of England were wonderfully broadened and quickened by a new spirit that was changing the civilisation of Europe. The great change that took place in the life of Europe during the fourteenth, fifteenth, and sixteenth centuries, is known as the *Renaissance,* or *re-birth,* because in many ways European civilisation seemed at that time to be born again. It was a stirring and adventurous time, when men were full of energy and enthusiasm, and when they claimed a greater

freedom of thought and action. Europe was passing out
of the narrower and more restricted life of the Middle Ages;
Greek and Latin art and literature, long neglected and forgotten, were studied with delight; and the finer minds responded to the influence of new feelings and ideas. Italy,
the first European nation to resume the study of Greek,
was the leader in this "revival" of the old learning, and
she became the teacher and inspirer of Europe. It was not
long before the passion for the "Greek learning" crossed
the Alps. Nation after nation learned the new love of letters, the new delight in life and in beauty, and France,
Germany, and England came under the power of this new
spirit.

The effect of this influence of Italy is deeply impressed
upon the literature of England. At first it made itself felt
chiefly at the universities. At Oxford and Cambridge, the
two great centres of learning, it gave a fresh impulse to
education, it introduced new subjects of study, and it produced scholars of a new type. As we should expect, the
effect of these changes in education and scholarship was
soon apparent in literature, and books were published which
spread the new ideas still more widely. But the influence
of Italian style and culture was not a purely literary
or educational influence. While it began at the colleges,
with the learned men, the teachers, and the writers, it soon
extended far beyond this comparatively small field and
entered into the life of the nation at large. If we study the
state of England in the reign of Queen Elizabeth (1558–
1603), we shall find traces of the popularity of Italian fashions, Italian tastes, and Italian literature, on almost every
side. Architecture, dress, and landscape gardening, showed
the fascination which Italy then exercised over the English
mind. Italy, in fact, had poured into England a new life
as well as a new learning; and this new life was quickened
by the many great things which were then taking place in

Europe and America. During the reigns of Elizabeth and James I, this *Renaissance* spirit found its supreme literary expression in Spenser, Shakespeare, Bacon, and their great contemporaries.

During the seventeenth century the influence of Italy upon England began to decline. A change came over the spirit of the people, and the time and energy of the nation were largely taken up with grave problems in government and religion. Yet these troubled years, when the Puritan fought with the Cavalier, left their mark upon literature likewise. This is the age of Cromwell, the man who worked the will of England with his sword, but it is also the age of Milton, the man who expressed the noblest spirit of England with his pen, and Cromwell and Milton stand side by side.

III. THE PERIOD OF FRENCH INFLUENCE.

From 1660 to about 1750.

After the new thoughts and mighty passions that came with the Renaissance had spent their force, England seemed for the time to have grown tired of great feelings either in poetry or in religion. She became scientific, intellectual, cold, and inclined to attach great importance to the style, or manner, of writing, thinking that great works were produced by study and art rather than by the inspiration of genius. This tendency was encouraged, perhaps originated, by the example and influence of the French. This was during the brilliant reign of Louis XIV, when such writers as *Molière, Racine, Corneille,* and *Boileau,* were making French literature and literary standards fashionable in Europe. Charles II ascended the throne in 1660, after his youth of exile on the Continent, bringing with him a liking for things French; and for a time there was a tendency on the part of some writers to turn to France for their models, and to adopt the French theories of the art of writing. France,

however, exerted no such profound influence as Italy had
exercised during the preceding period. It is true that a
marked change took place in both the form and spirit of
English literature at this time; but this seems to have been
due far more to an altered condition of affairs at home, than
to the influence from abroad. After the Restoration, JOHN
DRYDEN became the leading man of letters in England, and
early in the eighteenth century we reach the so-called
"Augustan Age," when Queen Anne was on the throne, and
POPE and SWIFT, STEELE and ADDISON, lived and wrote.

IV. THE MODERN ENGLISH PERIOD.

From about 1725 to the present day.

In the course of this eventful period, great changes have
taken place both in the social and political condition of
England and in her place among the other nations of the
earth. Old customs and ideas, old ways of living and
methods of government, have been greatly altered or altogether given up, and *Modern England* has come into existence, the familiar England of to-day. While these changes
have been at work at home, the change in England's relations to the world without has been correspondingly great
and important. She has made her power felt far beyond
the limits of Europe: she has built up a vast colonial empire, planting new Englands in the Far East and the Far
West. Countless ships carry her manufactures over almost
every sea; her sons go out to live among strange people;
and her civilisation, her language, and her literature, have
become known in the farthest parts of the earth.

As England has changed, her literature has changed likewise, and her new experiences at home and abroad have
found a voice in her poetry and her prose. It is true that
she has shown from time to time the passing influence of
some foreign literature; but, on the whole, her inspiration

during this period has come from within rather than from without. It is, above all, the *life* of modern England that has produced the *literature* of modern England.

Only a few general features of the literary history of this period need be mentioned here. As the eighteenth century advanced, the scoffing, sceptical, and trifling spirit that had been apparent in the literature of Queen Anne's time, began to give place to a greater depth and seriousness. Tastes, ideas, and habits were changing, and literature both promoted and expressed the changes. A succession of poets taught men to find pleasure in the country, and taught them a deeper love and respect for mankind. Other poets awakened men's interest in the life of the past, and especially in the Middle Ages, the golden time of chivalry and romance. The Scotch poet ROBERT BURNS (1759-1796) was among those who sang of freedom and human brotherhood; WILLIAM WORDSWORTH (1770-1850) was one of the greatest and most original of the interpreters of nature; and SIR WALTER SCOTT (1771-1832) did more than any other writer to create a popular enthusiasm for the Middle Ages and to give the romantic past a place in the popular imagination. Throughout the whole of this period we can see the effects on English literature of this more general diffusion of knowledge, and of that rapid advance of democratic institutions and ideas which is a leading feature in the history of the times. In Europe, as well as in England, the old order of society was being transformed by these new ideas, and the *French Revolution* (1789-1815), the most startling and dramatic outcome of this change, profoundly stirred some of the greatest English writers. This new passion for liberty and equality animates the earlier verse of Wordsworth, and makes itself felt a little later in the poetry of BYRON (1788-1824) and SHELLEY (1792-1822).

Finally the England of Victoria (1837-1900), the England of science and of steam, of social discontent and social reform, of new theories of the universe, and of anxious questionings of the old faith, records in its literature the life of our modern civilisation. ALFRED TENNYSON (1809–1892) remains the most comprehensive and melodious interpreter of this age in poetry; while in prose it can show such illustrious men as Lord Macaulay, Dickens, Thackeray, Ruskin, and Carlyle.

Having gained some preliminary notion of the general trend of literary history in England and of some of the great stages of growth through which the nation has passed, we may now take up these periods at greater length.

PART I.

THE PERIOD OF PREPARATION

(About 670 to about 1400).

CHAPTER I.

FROM THE BEGINNING TO THE NORMAN CONQUEST.

THE great work of this long preparatory period, which stretches from the dim beginning of English literature to the work of Chaucer in the latter half of the fourteenth century, was the uniting of the various elements which are combined in Chaucer and in the literature of England since his time. These elements were at first quite separate, or, in some cases, actually antagonistic. They mixed slowly and reluctantly; but the pressure of circumstances, the course of events, steadily forced them together, and in time each was compelled to contribute its share to the life and the literature of a composite but united nation. Thus we saw, in the brief survey of this period, that during these centuries one race was made by the mixture of many; one language by the mixture, for the most part, of English and French; one literature from the literatures of the English, the Celt, and the Norman, enriched and developed by Christianity, and by the learning and culture of Rome. The enforced mingling of such varied elements introduced, for a time, a great confusion and disorder. There were rival races, rival languages, each with a literature of its own; but all this struggle, hard as it may have seemed at the time, was not without meaning and purpose, for the

Union of different races, languages, and literatures.

11

variety of the elements thus brought together gave extraordinary richness to the language and greater breadth and fulness to the national literature and life. This mixture of elements is now so complete that many of us never realise that the books we read and the words we use every day are silent witnesses to the composite character of our English literature and our English speech. A single illustration will help to make this clear. Let us take the following lines from the song to the water-nymph Sabrina, in Milton's poem of *Comus,* and try to find out some of the elements which have contributed to the making of this one passage.

> " *Sabrina* fair,
> Listen where thou art sitting
> Under the glassy, cool, *translucent* wave,
> In twisted braids of lilies knitting
> The loose *train* of thy *amber*-dropping hair
> Listen for dear *honour's* sake,
> Goddess of the silver *lake,*
> Listen and *save !* " [1]

Now there is probably not a word in this passage that seems to you foreign, or unfamiliar; it is simply our well-known English from first to last. Yet if we were to examine it more closely, if we should look up the history of each of these words in some good dictionary, we should find that some of them were originally not English words at all, but Latin or French. Thus, *honour* is the Old French word *honur,* which is derived in its turn from the Latin *honor,* and which survives in the modern French *honneur.* Now this word is one of the living witnesses to the composite character of our English speech. It reminds us that England was once conquered and ruled by a French-speak-

[1] *Comus,* l. 859. The words printed here in italics are those which have come in from the Latin or the Norman-French. The French language grew out of the Latin, hence the origin of these French words is Latin. Nevertheless they did not come into the English directly from the Latin, but through the medium of the French.

ing people, for it is one of the thousands of words that contact with the Norman brought into the English speech. *Honour* is a word which has come into our language from the Latin through the French. *Translucent* (Latin *translucens*; *trans*, through, and *lucere*, to shine) has been brought in directly from the Latin with only a trifling change. As such words as *honour*, *train*, and *save*, carry us back to the Norman Conquest, and show us that what we know as the English language is in reality partly French, so *Sabrina* takes us back to the Roman occupation of Britain at a much earlier time, for *Sabrina* was the name given by the Romans to the river Severn.[1] By far the larger number of words in the passage, however, are pure English; that is, they are the modern representatives of words in use among the English, or Anglo-Saxons, from a very early time. Thus, *listen* is the modern form of the Anglo-Saxon *hlystan; under* is the Anglo-Saxon *under*, and so on. Yet there are enough French and Latin words mixed with those of pure English origin to suggest to us that our daily speech is a composite language, compounded of English and French.

But as the *language* of this passage is essentially English, so its *poetic form* is essentially un-English, essentially different from the characteristic Anglo-Saxon verse. The early English made *alliteration* the basis of their verse; that is, they systematically introduced into it words beginning with the same letter or sound. With them alliteration was not an ornament, or an accident; it was an absolutely necessary feature of their verse. Now English poets have long since given up the Anglo-Saxon method of writing poetry and adopted another. It is true that they still use alliteration, but they no longer make it an essential part of their

---

[1] Some suppose *Sabrina* to be the Roman form of a Celtic name of the river, and that it means a boundary; but, in any case, the name is a relic of the Roman rule. See *Severn* in *Names and their Histories* by Isaac Taylor.

verse; they employ it as a mere ornamental addition, that they can introduce or leave out as they please. After the Norman Conquest, the form of verse natural to the English was gradually abandoned in favor of a foreign method of writing poetry, an important feature of which was the use of rhyme. This new method was brought in by the Normans. This little poem of Sabrina, based as it is on *rhyme* and *metre* and not on alliteration, bears witness, in its form as well as in its language, to the influence of the Norman; it leads us to think of the extent of that influence upon the great body of English verse.

So far in our study of these few lines, we have found traces of a mixture of English and Norman, with a hint of another great influence in the background,—the influence of the old-world civilisation of Rome. But when we turn from the language and the outward form of these lines and look into their *subject*, we find then the impress of yet another literature and of another race. The story of Sabrina, the guardian nymph of the river Severn, is not English, nor Norman, nor Roman, but Celtic. It belongs to the legendary history of the Welsh, or Britons, the Celtic people who lived in the Island before the English came, and it was told to English readers by a Welshman a great many hundred years before Milton's time.[1] Nor is this all. A few lines farther on in the poem we come upon a number of classical allusions, and see that Milton has not hesitated to mingle Greek and Roman mythology with this old myth of the Celt.

We see, then, that in actual fact, all these elements, the English, the Norman, the Roman, and the Celtic, have united to make this one little song. Of course this is not

[1] It is found, along with many other stories, in a *History of Britain* (*Historia Regum Britanniæ*) by Geoffrey of Monmouth, written about the middle of the twelfth century. The legend won a place for itself in English literature, and it is referred to by Spenser, Drayton, and other English poets.

always the case. All English poems, for example, are not founded upon Celtic legends, although it is likely that many more show the influence of the Celtic spirit and disposition than we might at first be inclined to believe. Nevertheless, it is certain that every one of these various elements is present in different proportions in the great body of our English literature. This fact should be clearly understood in the very beginning of our study of English literature, for the mingling of these different elements has made that literature what it is.

The making of England. What, then, were these elements that went to the making of England, where did they come from, how were they joined together, and what did each contribute to the final result?

The answer to these questions will tell us how the foundations of English literature were laid.

I. THE MAKING OF THE RACE.

The races which have mingled in different proportions to make the modern English are:

a. The *English,* a people of *German* or *Teutonic* stock. They were akin to the great races of Northwestern Europe, — the Germans, the Scandinavians, and the Danes.

b. The *Britons,* who belonged, as we have said, to the *Celtic* race. Among their kindred were the Irish and the Scots.

c. The *Danes,* who were closely related to the English.

d. The *Normans,* the men of the North, or *Northmen* from Scandinavia, who won lands for themselves in the north of France. The Normans came of the same *Teutonic* stock as the English, but they settled in a country where the basis of the population was *Celtic,* and where the civilisation was derived mainly from that of Rome.[1]

It appears from this list, that representatives of the two great races of Northwestern Europe, the *Teutonic* and the *Celtic*, have entered at various times into the composition of that mixed people the modern English. To appreciate what this union of two great race-stocks means, we must know something of the Englishman and the Briton before it took place.

The English.

The English conquerors of Britain were three Germanic tribes, the *Angles* (or *Engles*), the *Saxons*, and the *Jutes*. **The early home of the English.** They came from the Northwestern limits of that great wilderness which the Romans called *Germania*. To the Romans, *Germania*, a vast tract of swamps and forests inhabited by fierce and barbarous tribes, seemed beyond the boundary of the civilised world. The Roman historian Tacitus describes it as "a land hideous and rude, under a rigorous climate, dismal to behold or to cultivate."[2] The English tribes dwelt on the borders of the Baltic and of the North Sea, in one of the bleakest, most exposed, and most gloomy regions of this for-

---

[1] The following table, although based primarily on language, will help to make the position of the English and Britons more plain.

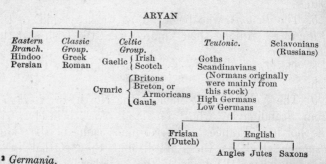

ARYAN

Eastern Branch.	Classic Group.	Celtic Group.	Teutonic.	Sclavonians (Russians)
Hindoo Persian	Greek Roman	Gaelic { Irish / Scotch	Goths Scandinavians (Normans originally were mainly from this stock)	
		Cymric { Britons Breton, or Armoricans Gauls	High Germans Low Germans	

Frisian (Dutch)   English

Angles Jutes Saxons

[2] *Germania.*

bidding land; the Saxons in the low-lying tracts about the mouths of the rivers Elbe and Weser; the Angles and the Jutes in the peninsula (now, in part, Denmark) which lies immediately to the north. The three tribes, while politically distinct, came of the same stock, spoke the same language, and held to the same customs and beliefs. Cheerless and savage as this northern wilderness seemed to Tacitus, beside the unclouded sunshine and soft skies of Italy, it was yet well fitted to be the cradle of a strong race. Fierce storms from the North Sea drove down upon its sunken coasts, then unprotected by dyke or sea-wall, flooding their shoals and winding inlets, and overflowing the desolate island tracts of marsh and pool. Dismal curtains of fog settled down upon it; its tangled forests were soaked and dripping with frequent rains. Here it was a man's lot to suffer cold, hardship, and tempest; here he learned to face and to defy the perils of the sea; here, to live at all he must live bravely and hardily, fighting for his place. So, on land and sea, the English were trained and disciplined in a school for heroes.

These early English were a fierce, rude folk. Hunters, farmers, and sailors, they were, above all, fighters by land and by sea. They were sea-robbers, like **Life and character.** their kinsmen the Danes, and their high-prowed war-ships were a menace and a terror to the richer coast settlements far to the southward. For nearly a century before they actually settled in Britain, they harried and plundered its western coast. Their attacks were often as sudden as they were terrible, for, despising danger, they sometimes landed in the midst of a tempest, so that their approach could not be seen from a distance, and their victims might be caught unprepared.[1] They are likened to eager wolves urged forward by

[1] We are told this by *Sidonius Apollinaris,* a bishop of the fifth century, who lived in the Roman province of Gaul. *Epist.* viii. 6.

the scent of their prey.[1] This comradeship of the English with the sea left its mark upon their early poetry. There we see the sailor at the prow watching in cold and darkness for the dreaded rocks, his feet stiff with the bitter frost; we watch the storm fling the great surges against the cliffs; we hear the scream of the sea-bird; we hear the tern, her feathers crusted with ice, answer the howl of the storm-wind against the rocks.[2] It is almost always the wilder and fiercer aspects of the sea that are brought before us in these descriptions. Not the calm blue depths of the Southern waters, but the very sea that the English Vikings knew and conquered; the dull-hued waste of the Northern ocean, full of perils to be fought and to be overcome.

The English and the sea.

These English were large men, big-boned and muscular, with ruddy faces, fair hair, and blue or grey eyes. They were hard men, with something of the primitive savage yet in them; strong but untamed; huge feeders and deep drinkers; quick to strike; bloody and cruel as well as adventurous and brave. Yet it is a great mistake to think of them as mere barbarians. There was a strain of nobility in them; they were the true forefathers of the men who were to make England. If they had some of the faults of youth, they had also its splendid freshness, vigour, and vitality. We do not really know them until we look beneath the surface of coarse revelry and bloodshed, and find those noble and redeeming traits that lay even then at the base of their national character. They were *loyal*. The *thegns*, or chosen followers of the king or chief, were required to be faithful, and, if needs be, to lay down their lives for their lord. They were *brave* and *self-reliant*; and *honour*, as they

Noble traits in the English character.

---

[1] Sidonius Apollinaris, Carm. **vii.**

[2] See the early poem of *The Seafarer*, given in Morley's *English Writers*, ii. 21.

understood it, was dearer to them than life. Beside the moral corruption of the decaying Roman civilisation their lives stood sound and pure. While they showed no tendency to romantic sentiment, women were given a conspicuously high and honourable place among them. In the old English epic of *Beowulf*, the great Queen passes among the company as the stately and honoured mistress of the household, greeting the young men and distributing gifts.[1] One fragment of early verse, whatever its origin, brings us very close to the gentler and more domestic side of life among these early English, about which, as a rule, their poetry is silent. It tells us of a simple incident in the ordinary life of the humble and the obscure; it shows us not the royal hostess, but the woman, man's true helpmate and the maker of his home; it is the poem of the English fireside.

> "Dear to the Frisian wife is the one whom she welcomes,
> When the vessel reaches the haven — his ship is at hand,
> Her lord is come to his home, he who provideth for her,
> And she summons him in; she washes his sea-stained garments
> And giveth him raiment new. Full pleasant is it for him
> Whose belovèd wife waiteth for him ashore."[2]

We find too in these early English that instinct for *law and freedom* which in the coming generations was to build parliaments and create republics. That which an old chronicler wrote of the Frisians is equally true of the English, their neighbours and kinsmen: "These men been high of body, stern of virtue, strong and fierce of heart; they be free, and not subject to lordship of any man; and they put their lives in peril for the cause of freedom, and would liever die than embrace the yoke of thralldom."[3] English literature and English history are full of this stubborn devotion to liberty, and the same spirit of independence that

[1] See *Beowulf*, l. 2020.
[2] C. B. Tinker in Cook and Tinker's *Translations from Old English Poetry*.
[3] Quoted in *The Anthropological History of Europe*, by J. Beddoe.

we find in the Englishman of the fifth century thrills us in the verse of a great English poet of the nineteenth:

> " We must be free or die, who speak the tongue
> That Shakespeare spake; the faith and morals hold
> Which Milton held." [1]

Religion. The religion of the English appears to have been substantially the same as that of the other Teutonic peoples of Northern Europe. *Woden,* the *Odin* of the Scandinavian, was one of their chief gods. His name survives in our *Wednesday,* or Woden's day; and from him many of the English kings claimed to be descended. Besides Woden, the English had many other gods: *Thunor,* the Scandinavian *Thor,* the thunder-god; [2] *Tiw,* the war-god, a fierce and terrible power, the *Tyr* of the Norse mythology. Among these gigantic impersonations of the spirit of battle and tempest, are gentler deities associated with the creative and kindly forces of nature: *Frea,* the divinity of joy, warmth, and harvests; *Eostre,* the East, the shining goddess of dawn, or of spring, the dawn of the year. The English called April *Eastermonath,* Easter month, and from this goddess of the renewal of life in nature we get our word *Easter.*

Fatalism. But it is not so much their mythology, the outward form of their religion, that impresses us, as it is the essentially religious spirit of the English race. There was depth and earnestness in the English nature as well as a crude strength, and they felt that the strongest hero was helpless in the hands of the mysterious power that ruled the world. A will stronger than man's will was typified for them in the dreaded goddess *Wyrd,* or fate, literally "that which happens," or "that which comes to pass," the embodiment of the thing which must be. Beowulf, the

---

[1] Wordsworth's sonnet, "It is not to be thought of."

[2] *Thunor* is the Anglo-Saxon word for *thunder.* *Donar* is the old German word for thunder, and Donar was their name for the thunder-god Thor.

hero of our oldest English epic, is true to the spirit of his race when he cries before his last fight: "To us it shall be as our Wyrd betides, that Wyrd is every man's lord."[1] The cruelty of this inexorable fate and the passing of all human things, are the chief themes of one of the early English poems, *The Wanderer*. The speaker tells us in his opening words, that he must tread the paths of exile because Fate has decreed it, "Wyrd is full fixed." At its close, after a passionate outcry over the ruin which has overtaken the mighty works of men, and a lament for all the dead joys and glories of the past, he concludes:

"All the realm of earth is full of hardship;
Wyrd's decree changes the world beneath the heavens;
Here wealth passes away, here friend passes away,
Here man passes away, here woman passes away,
All the earth's structure becomes empty."[2]

Again and again in this early poetry the thought recurs, and we feel sure that it is no mere poetical adornment, but the expression of a feeling at the heart of the English nature.

The mighty works of men's hands, the joy of the feast and of the harp, the strong warrior, all these pass into the great shadow and are as though they had not been.[3] The same stoical resignation to fate is found in the literature of the Northern nations akin to the English. The Scandinavian poet sings in the same spirit as his English kinsman: "We have gotten

Continuity of the spirit of English literature.

---

[1] *Beowulf*, l. 2525.

[2] *The Wanderer*, translated by Israel Gollancz in the edition of the *Exeter Book* published by the *Early English Text Society*. Miss Emily H. Hickey's translation, a more spirited but less literal rendering, is given in *Translations from Old English Poetry*, by Cook and Tinker.

[3] This thought recurs in a striking passage in Carlyle: *v.* passage beginning, "That warrior on his strong war-horse," etc. in *Sartor Resartus*, Bk. iii. chap. viii., and cf. Pancoast's *Stand. Eng. Prose*, p. 641, n. 344.

a good report though we die to-day or to-morrow.   No man
can live over the evening when the word of the Norns (Fates)
has gone forth." [1]   From the seventh century to the twentieth, English literature expresses the fundamental traits of
the English character, and we appreciate the full force
of this only when we see for ourselves how the spirit of
these founders of England animates the literature of their
descendants.   The famous lines of an English poet of the
seventeenth century express, though in a more polished
form, the thought of these rude singers of a thousand years
before:

> " The glories of our blood and state
> Are shadows, not substantial things;
> There is no armour against fate;
> Death lays his icy hand on kings." [2]

And indeed it is the same mood that finds its greatest
expression in the words of Shakespeare:

> " We are such stuff
> As dreams are made on, and our little life
> Is rounded with a sleep." [3]

The fact that such a mood was familiar to these heathen
English, reveals to us something of the depth of their
strong and reverent nature.   These men,
Seriousness and reverence in English character. brooding on death and fate, were not mere sea-
robbers, not mere fighters and feasters.   Not-
withstanding all their outward barbarism, they
had within them a profound seriousness, an awe in the
presence of the invisible and unknown.   While they
looked death in the face as "the necessary end," they confronted it steadily and boldly, and with no weak complaint.   Nor did their haunting sense of the shortness of

[1] *Hamdismal* (or the Lay of Hamther) *Corpus Poeticum Boreale,*
vol. i, 59.
[2] *A Dirge,* by James Shirley (1659).
[3] *The Tempest,* Act iv. Sc. 1.

life produce in them the ordinary resolve to enjoy to-day to the full; it rather strengthened their desire to quit themselves like men. The English conscience speaks in such lines as these:

> " This is best laud from the living
> In last words spoken about him: —
> He worked ere he went his way,
> When on earth, 'gainst the wiles of the foe,
> With brave deeds overcoming the devil." [1]

So in studying these early English we look back to the rock from which a great race was hewn. We recognise in them those traits of mind and character that in the centuries to come took shape in the deeds of heroes and the songs of poets. In these half-savage pirate-tribes, with the deep northern melancholy, is the germ of that masterful and aggressive nation which was to put a girdle of English round the world. Of this blood are the sea-dogs who chased the towering galleons of the Spanish Armada, the Six Hundred who charged to their death at Balaclava, or those other English, who declared and maintained their inheritance of freedom in new lands. The spirit of this older England, enriched by time, is alive, too, in the works of Shakespeare, of Milton, and of Browning, as it is in the deeds of Raleigh, of Nelson, of Chatham, and of Gordon.

The Britons.

When the English settled in Britain, the British Isles were possessed by a number of tribes belonging to the Celtic race. Scotland and Ireland were occupied by tribes belonging to one great branch or division of this race, the *Goidels*, or *Gaels*, and the country afterwards known as England by another, the *Brythons*, or *Britons*.

---

[1] *The Seafarer*, Morley's translation, *English Writers*, vol. ii. p. 24.

Mingled with this Celtic population of Britain were the descendants of an entirely different race, whose ancestors the Celtic invaders had found in possession and subdued. But although the inhabitants were not all pure Celts, the Celts were everywhere uppermost, and when the English conquered Britain, they got a foothold in a cluster of islands filled with the Celtic spirit from the western coast of Ireland to the eastern shores of Britain, and from the Hebrides to the Land's End. That conquest, therefore, took the Englishman out of the land of the Teuton, where his neighbors were men of his own race, and set him down in the land of the Celt. The Celtic temperament was very different from the English, and the English people were thus brought under new influences that were destined to enter their life and literature through many channels and to modify them in many ways. It is, therefore, important for us to know something of the race that was thus grafted on the original English stock. Although

English and Celt. the Celts somewhat resembled the English in appearance, the character of the race was very different. The English of to-day are a practical, capable race; they excel in statesmanship, in commerce; they shrink from any open display of their feelings; they are stronger in deeds than in words. These traits they have inherited from their Teutonic forefathers. Now, the Celtic temperament was the very reverse of this, for the Celt was, above all, emotional, a creature of impulse. He had that excitable, sensitive nature, that keen delight in whatever is beautiful or tragic, pathetic or grotesque, which we associate with the poet, the painter, the musician. Swept onward by a rush of feeling, the Celt could be brave to the point of rashness, but when the time for steady endurance came, he lacked the dogged tenacity of the English, the stubborn persistence that so often turns defeat to victory.

The Celts, we are told, would attack the enemy with a reckless fury; but, if repulsed, their retreat often changed quickly into a panic-stricken flight. This sudden change of mood is characteristic of the impulsive Celt. His feelings were violent but transitory, and he passed easily from tears to laughter, or from hope to despair. The French, who are largely Celtic, have a similar lightness and instability of temperament; and the Irish, ready to fight, jest, or weep, show the same lack of steadfastness and self-control. But if the Celts were inferior to the English in certain solid qualities, they were quicker-witted, more fanciful, less ponderous and matter-of-fact. The spirit of the early English resembled those sombre northern solitudes that were the home of the race; but the Celt loved brightness, colour, and sunshine.

Celtic love of colour.

The plaid, with its ingeniously varied combination of colours, is the badge of the Celt, found alike among the Gauls of the Continent, the various tribes of Britain, and the clans of Scotland and Ireland. The Britons loved glittering ornaments; they delighted in *torques*, or collars of twisted gold, in bracelets, and strings of bright coloured beads; their chiefs were glorious in shining helmets, corselets, and shields. This passion of the Celt for brilliant and contrasted colours lights up his literature with a richness and splendour not found in that of the early English. When a Celtic poet wished to bring an object vividly before his hearers, he dwelt on its colour rather than on its form. In the following descriptions, one taken from an early Irish epic, the other from a collection of Welsh stories, we can hardly fail to be impressed with the love of colour and the love of Nature so apparent in both:

"Her soft hands were as white as the snow of a single night, and her eyes as blue as any blue flower, and her lips as red as the berries of the rowan-tree, and her body as white as the foam of the wave." [1]

[1] *Gods and Fighting Men, the story of the Tuatha De Danaan and of the Fianna of Ireland, arranged and put into English by Lady Gregory,* p. 91.

The second description is written in much the same style:

"The maiden was clothed in a robe of flame-coloured silk, and about her neck was a collar of ruddy gold, on which were precious emeralds and rubies. More yellow was her head than the flower of the broom, and her skin was whiter than the foam of the wave, and fairer were her hands and her fingers than the blossoms of the wood anemone amidst the spray of the meadow fountain. The eye of the trained hawk, the glance of the three-mewed falcon, was not brighter than hers. Whoso beheld her was filled with her love. Four white trefoils sprung up wherever she trod." [1]

With this love of colour the love of Nature was closely associated. The Celtic poet and romancer loved the beauty and the brightness of the world about him, the cheerful sunshine, the vivid hues of the flowers, the songs of the birds.

Celtic love of Nature.

In early English poetry, Nature is usually brought before us in her more cheerless and savage moods. We are shown the haunted pool in the depth of the forest,[2] the windy headland, the angry seas; whereas in many of the Celtic poems, as in the following Irish song of love and spring, Nature is beautiful and friendly, and we hear not the "scream of the gannet," [3] but the song of the cuckoo in the spring woods.

"May time, delightful time! *How beautiful the colour!* the black-birds sing their full lay; would that Laighaig were here! The cuckoos sing in constant strains. How welcome is ever the noble brilliance of the seasons! On the margin of the branching woods the summer swallows skim the stream; . . . the sea is lulled to rest, flowers cover the earth." [4]

[1] *Kilhwch and Olwen*, Guest's *Mabinogion*, Dent's ed. p. 127. The poetic fancy at the close is a characteristic touch of Celtic sentiment, and is marked by a delicacy to which the cruder and less pliant strength of the early English could hardly attain.

[2] See the famous description in *Beowulf*, l. 1357, partially paraphrased on p. 40.

[3] *The Seafarer*, see p. 18, *supra.*

[4] This is taken from an early Irish poem of uncertain date. It is quoted by Dr. Hyde in his *Literary History of Ireland*, p. 275.

These two peculiarities, *the love of colour*, and *the love of natural beauty*, continue to mark Celtic literature throughout its later history.

To these traits the Celt added that peculiar delicacy and tenderness of feeling, that fresh and poetic susceptibility to the finer emotions, which is best described by the word *sentiment*. *Sentiment*, according to a great critic, is the distinguishing mark of the Celtic nature. Not only was the Celt emotional, he *delighted in his emotions* with the delight of the artist and the poet. His strong imagination, his deep sense of the wonder of all things, brought him very near to the invisible and the unknown. He lived on the borderland of a world of mystery, and his belief in unseen powers is shown in innumerable myths and superstitions.

Celtic sentiment.

In addition to the greater deities, the Britons recognised a multitude of supernatural beings of an inferior order, such as good and bad fairies, giants and demons. So deeply rooted were these popular superstitions, that in those parts of England which were the last stronghold of the Celt we find some lingering traces of them even to this day.

There were many reasons why the Celts should produce an abundant literature. They were more demonstrative than the English, they had the temperament of the artist, and the power of putting their feelings into words. They loved to tell or to hear stories; and the Bard, or poet, held an honourable and important place among them. It was the Bard who preserved in his songs the memory of the past; it was the Bard who celebrated the great deeds of heroes; and it was through his praise that a man's fame lived on to after times. Each of the three Celtic countries, Ireland, Scotland, and Britain, had an extensive literature both in poetry and in prose, and in the remains of this literature we can see clearly the peculiar genius of the Celt.

Celtic literature.

How far this settlement in the land of the Celt may have modified the English character, is a matter of dispute; but it

Celtic influence on the English. is probable that the influence of the Celt upon the English has been much greater and more lasting than can be easily proved. It is true that during the early stages of the Conquest the mass of the Celtic population was forced slowly westward before the stubborn advance of their conquerors, leaving the eastern part of the island almost entirely English in its population. But it is also true that the west remained Celtic, and that its people preserved the language, literature, and traditions of their race. In some parts of the country, and particularly in that borderland between the Eastern English and the Western Celt, the two races gradually mingled, making a virtually new stock. To what extent this mixture took place is uncertain; but in any case, we know that English and Celt have continued to live within the limits of the same small island for more than fourteen hundred years, and we know that Celtic story and legend, from Ireland and Scotland as well as from Cornwall and Wales, have been absorbed into English literature and have become a part of the spiritual heritage of the English race. We gain some idea of the strength of this unobtrusive and constant influence when we reflect that some of the popular customs and superstitions of the English were borrowed from the Celt. Some of their popular beliefs passed into literature, and were made use of by Chaucer, Shakespeare, Milton, and other great English poets.[1] Celtic poetry and legend have furnished subjects to English writers from a very early period down to our own day. The story of *King Lear*, the theme of one of Shakespeare's sublimest tragedies, was originally Celtic; the story of *Locrine*, like-

[1] For example, Mab, Queen of the Fairies, described by Shakespeare in *Romeo and Juliet*, Act i. Sc. 4, and alluded to by Milton in *L'Allegro*, belongs to Celtic mythology. *Cf.* also the allusion to *Sabrina*, p. 14, *supra*.

wise of Celtic origin, has been retold by Swinburne, one of the great poets of the Victorian age; above all, the stories that cluster about the British *King Arthur* and his knights hold a high place in the national literature of England, and have been selected by Tennyson as the subject of one of his most ambitious poems. Nor is this all. There is good reason to believe that the *spirit of English literature* has been enriched and refined by the spirit of the Celt: fancy has been added to fact, and beauty and romance to moral earnestness and strength.

It is not hard to see why this should have been the case. The union of English and Celt was a marriage of opposites, and the very differences between the **English and Celt.** two races make them peculiarly helpful to one another. Each had something to give the other; each needed the other to complete its character, and the fusion of the two prepared the way for the triumphs of a later time. We can better understand this by remembering that William Shakespeare, the greatest genius of the modern world, was born in a district where the mixture of the two races was especially great, and that, by inheritance as by the quality of his genius, we may think of him as the highest example of the union of the Teuton and the Celt. "It is not without significance that the highest type of the race, the one Englishman who has combined in their largest measure the mobility and fancy of the Celt with the depth and energy of the Teutonic temper, was born on the old Welsh and English borderland, in the forest of Arden." [1]

The Dane and the Norman shared with the Celt the task of making the modern English, but the coming of these invaders and its results belong to a later period in the story of the literature.

---

[1] J. R. Green, quoted in article on "Shakespeare" by Professor T. Spencer Baynes, in *Encyclopedia Britannica,* ninth ed.

II. The Geographical Position of England.

The English people, fitted, as we have seen, by strength, courage, endurance, and integrity, to play a leading part in history, were placed by their conquest of Britain in a situation peculiarly favourable to the growth of their great qualities. Not only were they thus brought in contact with the Celts, a people wonderfully prepared to give them what they most needed, but they also became masters of an island especially fitted to be the centre of a great world-power. The English, when they conquered Britain, were the right race in the right place. Had they remained on the Continent they could hardly have maintained a separate national existence. In all likelihood, these three Low-German tribes, hemmed in by a great Germanic population, must have sooner or later been lost to history, like their neighbours the Frisians, in the life of some larger state. But by their conquest of an island they interposed a strip of sea between them and Continental interference, and that sea became, as Shakespeare has said, "like a moat defensive to a house." Here in their island-fortress, protected, but not entirely exempt from foreign invasion, they were far enough away from Continental influences to live their own lives and embody their own nationality in literature without serious hindrance.

Yet such were the peculiar advantages of the geographical position of England that, while the English were sufficiently cut off from Europe to preserve their individuality and to grow according to the natural bent of their genius, they were not so estranged as to lose the benefit of contact with the European civilisation. We see this more clearly if we contrast the position of the English with that of certain of their Teutonic kindred who established them-

Advantages of England's geographical position.

selves in Iceland and in Northern France some centuries
after the conquest of Britain. The Scandinavian bands,
which early in the ninth century possessed themselves
of Iceland, were set apart in a region too remote from the
centres of the world's life for their fullest development.
That lonely northern island was too isolated, too bleak,
and too barren, to be the seat of a world-power. And as
Iceland was too far, so Normandy, settled in the tenth
century by other roving bands of Teutons, was too near.
In Normandy the Northman almost lost his identity
under the pressure of the strange influences that surrounded him; he learned new things quickly; he adopted
a foreign language, foreign customs and ideas. Moreover,
the land, which the Norman had won, was hemmed in on
three sides by the territories of France; and, shut in by
that great power, the Duchy of Normandy was finally
absorbed by the kingdom of which it was naturally a part.

Nearer than Iceland, yet farther off than Normandy,
the intermediate situation of England preserved her alike
from the disadvantages of isolation and from the dangers
of a too close contact. She has been repeatedly stimulated and enlightened by influences which have reached
her from the Continent, — by Christianity, scholarship,
literature, architecture, and art, — and these influences
have been strong enough at times to make an era in her
intellectual and literary life. Yet, while she has learned
much from the civilisation of the Continent, the strong
original traits of the English character have remained
essentially the same. The genius of England has often
changed what she has received from without into a new
thing; she has been improved but not radically changed
by the world beyond her borders; there has been no serious
interference with the growth of her powers, and she has
kept that independence of mind which has set her apart
from other nations. The geographical position of Eng-

land has consequently been an important factor in the making of her literature; it has helped to make that literature truly national; it has kept the English genius faithful to the past, and forced it, at the same time, to learn from the present; it has given it both opportunity and liberty.

III. THE MAKING OF THE LITERATURE.

We do not know just when or how English literature began. Its foundations were laid in the obscurity of a far-off past, long before Angle, Jute, and Saxon had left their old home on the Continent. We have no knowledge of a time when the English had not their poets and their songs, their myths and their wonderful stories of heroes; and these accumulated stores of popular poetry and legend they brought with them to their new home in Britain. It is true that this mass of song and story was *literature* only in the broadest sense, for it was *unwritten*,[1] and preserved, if preserved at all, only in the memories of the poets and of the people themselves. We must think of this earliest literature of the English not as anything which belonged to one favoured class, not as something locked up in books or parchments, but as the common inheritance of the whole people. Children learned these ancient songs and stories from their parents; and the younger gleemen, or minstrels, sang to the harp many lays that had been handed down to them from the singers who had come

The beginning of English literature.

---

[1] From very early times the English, in common with the Scandinavians, used an alphabet, the letters of which are supposed by some to have been derived from the alphabet of the Greeks. It seems probable, however, that the English only used this runic-writing for the short inscriptions on sword-hilts and the like, and not for any distinctly literary purpose. Their literature was, so far as we know, composed and preserved without the use of letters, and such early English poems or fragments as have survived were reduced to writing at a later time.

before them. These old songs they altered, perhaps, in language or substance, or, it may be, they added new songs of their own; and, then, in their turn, handed both the new songs and the old to their successors. We can easily understand that a poem which has thus grown by frequent repetition through successive generations of singers, has neither author nor date, for it is not the work of any one time. So it comes about that no one can say when or by whom a great part of this poetry of the early English was composed, and so it is that we often find lines that come to us straight from the old world of heathenism and lines that are distinctly Christian side by side in the same poem.

We live in such a different world that it is not easy for us to realise how large a place poetry filled in the daily life of the people. It stirred men to patriotism and to brave deeds, for it kept alive and glorified the memories of the past; and the warrior who heard with pride of the triumphs of his fathers, 1oped that the remembrance of his victories also would survive in song. When the leader sat with his followers in the great feast-hall, when the fire blazed on the hearth, and the cups of mead were passed around, these men rough and roving, and cruel as they doubtless were, loved to listen to the gleeman's celebration of their chieftain's daring, and fight their battles over again in his song.

The large place of poetry among the early English.

Nor was it the gleeman only, the professional poet or harper, who sang; the warrior, the sailor, the farmer, chanted crude verses of war and glory, as the harp was passed from hand to hand that every one might sing in turn. Nor was song invoked only in hours of ease. It is probable that the English, like the other German tribes, raised their harsh, terrifying battle-hymn as they rushed forward to the conflict, increasing the din and confused tumult of sound, as was the German fashion, by holding their shields closer to their mouths that the reverberation might intensify the sound.[1]

Poetry was also closely associated with religion. Indeed, this very song before battle was in part a religious rite, and the soldier saw in it a mystic augury of victory or defeat.

Poetry was part, too, of the every-day labours of peace. The farmer in the field invoked the great creative powers of nature with a solemn song, or hymn:

> "Erce, Erce, Erce, mother of Earth,
>   May the Almighty, the Eternal Lord, grant thee
>   Fields fertile and flourishing,
>   Fruitful and full of vigour.
>   .   .   .
>   Well be it with thee, Earth the mother of men!"[2]

There is a charm to keep bees from deserting the hive; a charm to be used when land had been bewitched or when it was unfruitful. In the same way men joined religion and poetry and called them to their aid in a charm against rheumatic, or other pains, which were supposed to come from the invisible dart or spear of witches.[3] After the English became Christian, the Church changed many of these old heathen charms and songs, or introduced new and entirely Christian poetry in their place. They were so closely associated with the old heathen beliefs that a Canon of the Church in the days of King Edgar, in the latter half of the tenth century, forbade the singing of

[1] Tacitus. *Germania*, Ch. 3. "Adfectatur praecipue asperitas soni et fractum murmur, obiectis ad os scutis, quo plenior et gravior vox repercussu intumescat.

[2] Cook and Tinker's *Trans. from Old Eng. Poetry*, 166–67, gives this and other similar charms. These charms contain Christian elements that belong of course to a later date, but portions of them are evidently survivals of the old heathen rites, and belong to a very early period.

[3] This curious charm is also given in Cook and Tinker, but for an interesting comment on it see Gummere's *Germanic Origins*, p. 372 f.

"heathen songs" on the great religious festivals.[1] Yet much of this poetry was remembered and cherished among the people, and by some at least of the best Christian scholars and teachers. Bede (673–735), the great monk-scholar of Northumbria, was well-skilled in the English songs, and recited some English verses on his death-bed; a contemporary of Bede, Bishop Aldhelm, although he wrote much in Latin did not neglect the native poetry of his own tongue; as a child King Alfred, nearly two centuries later, learned the songs of his people, "which he often heard recited,"[2] and Alfred's children, we are told, learned "especially the Saxon poems;"[3] still later, in the tenth century, St. Dunstan, the famous Archbishop of Canterbury, is reported to have "loved the vain songs of ancient heathendom, the trifling legends, and the funeral chants."[4] So the more closely we look into the matter, the more we are impressed with the important place held by literature, and especially by poetry, in the early life of the English people; we see that poetry was present on the farm, in the battle, at the sick-bed and at the feast; that it was loved by the plain people and the scholars; that children learned it from their parents, and that the aged saint chanted on his death-bed the words of an English song.

But although the national songs belonged to the people and were loved and sung by them, there was also among the English a distinct class of men who devoted themselves to the making or reciting of poetry. There were two kinds of professional poets or singers: first the *scôp*, that is, the *shaper*, or *maker*, of verse;

Gleeman and Scôp.

---

[1] "And we enjoin, that on feast days heathen songs and devil's games be abstained from." Thorpe's *Ancient Laws and Institutes of England*, ii. p. 249.

[2] Asser's Life of Alfred, *Six Old English Chronicles*, Bohn's ed. p. 51.

[3] Ib. p. 68.

[4] Quoted in Gummere's *Germanic Origins*, 470.

and second, the *gleeman*, or *harper*. The *scôp*,[1] as his name implies, was above all the *poet*, that is, the composer or inventor of songs, although he also chanted or recited them: he was generally attached to the household of some king or chieftain, but he sometimes wandered from land to land, a welcome guest at a feast. The *gleeman*,[2] on the contrary, was not distinctly a *maker* but a *singer* or *reciter* of poems, and he consequently held a less dignified position than the scôp. He was the merry-maker, and at an early period of English history, he seems to have been jester, acrobat, and juggler, as well as a singer.[3]

Two very early poems, *Widsith* and the *Complaint* of *Deor*, not improbably of Continental origin, reveal to us

Widsith and the Complaint of Deor.

something of the varying life and fortunes of those early singers. In both of these the poet speaks in the first person and gives us an apparently true account of his own experiences. Widsith, or, as we should say, the *wide-wanderer*, or *far-traveller*,[4] recounts his wanderings through many lands; he tells how he sang in many halls, how he was praised, and how men of high rank gave him rich gifts for his songs. Always, he says, north or south, the singer finds a welcome. Always he finds some one, open-handed in his gifts, who appreciates song, and looks to it to magnify his fame and keep it in lasting remembrance. The *Complaint of Deor* shows us, that then, as now, the artistic life had its bitter disappoint-

---

[1] *Scôp*, from A. S. *scieppan*, to shape, make, or fashion (*cf.* Ger. schaffen), creation being generally recognised as the supreme faculty of the *poet*, or *maker* (Gr. ποιητής = a maker, ποιεῖν = to make).

[2] *Gleeman*, from Anglo-Saxon *Glēoman*, music-man, or harper. *Glēo* means fun, mirth, amusement, as well as music. See the various uses of the modern *glee* in the *Cent. Dict.*

[3] See Strutt's *Sports and Pastimes*, p. 251.

[4] Anglo-Saxon, *wid* = wide, extended; *sith* = going, motion, way, road, etc. The first meaning of Widsith is consequently *a long journey;* the second, one who takes such a journey, a traveller in many lands.

ments as well as its rewards. Deor was not a wandering singer: he belonged to a chief's household, and was "dear to his lord," until supplanted by a rival. The poet schools himself to endure the evil that has come upon him, and fortifies himself by remembering the others who have endured sorrow: "this man," he says, "overcame, and so may I." This is the refrain of the poem and its dominant note. It has the true English ring, for it is the note of a manly fortitude and not of a weak complaint.

Among these relics of Anglo-Saxon poetry, *Beowulf*, a crude but vigorous epic of more than three thousand lines,

Beowulf. easily holds the first place. It has, indeed, more than a national importance, for it is the oldest surviving epic of any Teutonic people, older than the *sagas*, or stories, of the Scandinavians, older than the German epic, the *Nibelungen Lied*, or song of the Nibelungs. Nor is it in Teutonic literature alone that it is remarkable, for it is far older than the great epics and romances of the Middle Ages; older than the *Song of Roland*, the Norman-French *Chanson* (or song) of the great knight of Charlemagne; older than the poem of the *Cid*, the romance which celebrated the valour of the early national hero, or champion of Spain. We may say, therefore, without exaggeration, that *Beowulf* stands in an impressive, if not in an unique, relation to the literature of modern Europe.

Apart from what we can gather or infer from our study of the work itself, we know almost nothing definite about

Origin of the poem. this venerable poem. We do not know who was its author, nor are we certain just when or where it was composed. We need not concern ourselves here with the many speculations to which this uncertainty has given rise; we will confine ourselves to what is apparent or reasonably certain. The poem shows clearly a mingling of different elements. Part of it appears to be purely or largely mythical or legendary, part of it again seems to have grown out of actual history. It is essentially heathen; yet it contains passages that show an acquaintance with the Bible. The monster Grendel, for instance, a demon of the waters and fen, although plainly a creature of the old heathendom, is yet said to be descended from Cain, the first murderer. It seems probable, therefore, that it was not entirely the work of one man; but that it grew by frequent repetition; and that sagas, myths, and historic facts were gradually mingled together and shaped into an epic form. The scene of the poem is laid on the Continent somewhere near the old home of the English, and Beowulf is not an Englishman but the Prince of a Teutonic tribe called the Geats. But the English appear to have shaped the story as we know it, and scholars think that the poem took its present form in the north of England, in Northumbria or in Mercia, sometime during the seventh or eighth centuries.

One thing, at least, seems clear, — the close relation between the literature of the early English which *Beowulf* represents, and that of the Englishman's Teutonic neighbours and kinsfolk. The dwellers in the Scandinavian peninsula, or in the depths of the German forests, were men of the same blood as the English. They looked on life in much the same way; and innumerable similarities, in speech, religion, and manners, show them to be all sprung from the same stock. This similarity, this common origin, is likewise shown in literature. Beowulf is truly an English epic, but in a wider sense it is a Teutonic epic, for it belongs to a group of poems produced by other branches of the same race-stock.[1] The Teuton in Scandinavia, Iceland,

Its relation to other Teutonic poems.

[1] Critics have called attention to the interest which the Anglo-Saxon showed in the heroic sagas of other Teutonic tribes, "a fact which indicates a lively intercourse with the various Teutonic tribes of the Continent:" De La Saussaye, *The Religion of the Teutons*, p. 154.

and Germany, had likewise his stories of heroes, his legends of great fighters like the Icelandic champion *Grettir the Strong*, or Sigurd, whom the Germans called *Siegfried*. *Grettir*, like *Beowulf*, rid a dwelling of a horrible monster, overcoming him by the mighty grip of his bare hands: *Siegfried*, like *Beowulf*, fought and slew a fiery dragon, guardian of a fabulous horde of treasure.[1] The resemblance is not founded merely on a similarity of incident; the early English literature is akin in spirit to the other literatures of the Teutonic north. Beowulf is our English hero-saga. These facts are important; they mean that English literature is in its origin essentially and fundamentally Teutonic. Like the Scandinavian, the Icelandic, it comes out of that wonderland of the north; dark, reticent, and cruel, but deep-hearted, true, and strong, and however softened and enlivened by a mingling with the Celt, however deeply influenced by the Latin civilisation of France and Italy, it remains at heart Northern and Teutonic throughout all its changing history.

Beowulf is a poem of battle; the battle of a man against three monstrous and mysterious incarnations of the powers of evil. The poem naturally divides itself into three parts, the central interest in each part being the life and death struggle between the hero and some supernatural adversary. Hrothgar, a Danish king, builds for himself a splendid mead-hall, Heorot, wherein he sits feasting with his thegns. A fiendish monster, Grendel, lurking in the dark marshes without, is tortured by the sounds of minstrelsy that reach him from the hall. In jealous hate he enters Heorot

The story of the poem.

---

[1] There is also in *Beowulf* a direct reference to the slaying of the dragon by Siegfried, but the adventure is ascribed not to Siegfried but to his father Siegmund. The story is told by a thane, or noble, who knew many old sagas, and who was skilful in telling them. See *Beowulf*, l. 867.

by night and slays thirty sleeping companions of the king. Again and again he comes to destroy, until the splendid hall has to be forsaken. After twelve years Beowulf, a prince of the Geats, or Goths, endowed with the strength of thirty men, comes with his followers in a ship to rid Hrothgar of this scourge. He is made welcome, and that night he and his band occupy the hall. All are asleep save Beowulf when Grendel strides into the hall, his eyes glowing like flames. He snatches a warrior, rends him to pieces, and greedily devours him. Then he attacks Beowulf, and they close in deadly grapple, the hero using no weapon, but trusting solely in his mighty strength. The stanch hall trembles with the fierceness of the contest; the massive benches are splintered; the Danes stand around, panic-stricken. Then Grendel, howling, strives to escape, but Beowulf crushes him with his terrible hand-grip. At length the demon, with the loss of an arm, wrenches himself free, and flies to the fens to die. On the morrow all crowd round Beowulf, rejoicing; but the next night Grendel's mother comes to avenge her son, and carries off one of the thegns. Beowulf resolves to conquer this new foe. With his thegns he tracks the woman-fiend over murky moors, through rocky gorges, and by the haunts of the water-nixies, until he comes upon a stagnant pool, frothing with blood and overhung by gloomy trees. By night the waters are livid with flame. The deer, pursued by dogs, will die on the bank rather than tempt those unsounded depths. It is a place of terror. Beowulf plunges in and fights the water-fiend in her cave under the flood. His sword proves useless against her. Again he trusts to sheer strength. "So it behooves a man to act when he thinks to attain enduring praise; — he will not be caring for his life." Beowulf falls, and the fiend is above him, her knife drawn. Then the hero snatches from a pile of arms a mighty sword, giant-forged, and slays his adversary.   Again there is mirth and praise at Heorot.

In the last part of the poem Beowulf has become King of the Goths and has ruled over them for fifty winters. At this time the land is worried by a dragon, who sets men's homes aflame with his fiery breath.   The dragon's lair is near a wild headland at whose front the sea breaks; here Beowulf seeks him and gives battle, trusting "in the strength of his single manhood."   The old king is again victorious, but is mortally hurt.   He bids a follower bring out the dragon's treasure hoard, and as the glistening gold and jewels are spread on the grass, he gives thanks that he has won them for his people.   So Beowulf dies, and a lofty mound is raised in his honour on the high cliff, which sailors, in voyaging upon the deep, could behold from far.   The poem ends in a requiem of praise:

> "Lamented thus
> The loyal Goths,
> Their chieftain's fall,
> Hearth-fellows true; —
> They said he was,
> Of all kings in the world,
> Mildest to his men
> And most friendly,
> To his lieges benignest,
> And most bent upon glory."

Something of the poem's spirit makes itself felt even through this meagre summary. We catch something of its profound earnestness, its gloom, its simple-minded intensity.   Beowulf, the one central figure, moves before us in heroic proportions.   In his courtesy, his vast strength, his quiet courage, his self-reliance, his submission to fate, he may stand as the pattern of the early English ideal of manhood, as Achilles of the early Greek.   The story is relieved by few gentler touches.   As a background to this life of conflict, Nature

Spirit of
the poem.

rises before us, harsh, sombre, pitiless, alive with superstitious terrors, dreary amid the remoteness and savagery
of the northern solitudes.

The prevailing gloom is hardly ever lifted; there is none
of the Celtic delight in the splendour of glowing colours; no
thought of yielding to ease or pleasure; none of that
supreme delight in beauty which fills so large a place in
the world's art. No story of love, no touch of romantic
tenderness, gives grace or softness to the stern but ennobling record; this is a man's world, and all is tense and
stark. Beowulf, about to set out against Grendel's mother,
comforts Hrothgar in the most matter-of-fact manner and
with a true English reticence in the expression of emotion.
"Sorrow not," he exclaims; "it is better one should avenge
his friend than mourn for him long. Each of us must
abide life's end in this world." [1] It is true that there are
hours of rejoicing; but while the lighted mead-hall echoes
with song and cheer, about it lie the black wastes, the
haunts of demons. Such a tone suits best with the unflinching courage, the uncompromising morality, which
thrill through the poem. Life may not be a pleasant
thing; it may be made a noble thing. "He who has the
chance should work mighty deeds before he die; that is
for a mighty man the best memorial." [2] The ideal embodied in the life of this early English hero anticipates
by a thousand years the spirit of the noble precept of the
great Puritan:

> "Nor love thy life, nor hate; but what thou liv'st
> Live well; how long or short permit to Heaven." [3]

Courage, fortitude, self-sacrifice, these things are preferred to the pleasures of the senses, even to life itself.

[1] *Beowulf*, l. 1384. C. G. Child's trans., *Riverside Literature Series*,
p. 38.
[2] *Beowulf*, ll. 1387–1390.
[3] *Paradise Lost*, Bk. xi. l. 553.

There was good stuff in these English even while they were yet heathen. There is little display of sentiment, but a downright, matter-of-fact heroism; little grace or flexibility, but a sheer if somewhat clumsy strength. As we study *Beowulf*, we see that it is all unconsciously the epic of the origin of a great race; for it shows us the material out of which the English were hewn. This, indeed, is perhaps its highest merit. To some its story may seem commonplace, its characters stereotyped or conventional; but we must all agree that, whatever it may lack, *Beowulf* has a lasting interest and value as a picture of life and manners. Wherever the scene may be laid, wherever the story may have originated, *Beowulf* was shaped by Englishmen, and it reveals the English character and ideals. In it the English of the fifth or sixth centuries still think, and speak, and act: — in the boat, in the fight, or in the hall, "in habit as they lived." This alone would make it a priceless possession, for we can say as we read it, "It was by such men as these that the foundation of England was laid." ✓

Beowulf and the other very early poems are essentially heathen; for the insertion of some Christian reflection or **The effect of** allusion, introduced, perhaps, by some monkish **Christianity** transcriber, does not change their real character. **on literature.** But, at the time immediately preceding the introduction of Christianity, English heathenism seems to have largely consisted in the absence of any vital and definite religious belief. Old superstitions are indeed present in these early poems: we hear of *nickers* (A. S. *nicor*), or water-sprites, *eotens*, or giants, of dragons and demons, but little or nothing of the gods or of a life hereafter. The real ruler of man's life is not *Odin*, or *Thor*, but *Fate*.[1] The truth seems to be that the English had outgrown the crude mythology of an earlier time,

---

[1] See pp. 20-21, *supra*.

that belief in it had become half-hearted or formal. When Christianity was first preached in Northumbria, the chief priest himself advised the king to listen to the new teaching, "for," he said, "I can assure you from my own experience, that the religion we have heretofore professed has no virtue in it." [1] These men were thinkers: they, too, could feel something of the burden and the mystery of a world that they could not understand, and they faced life and death with reverence but without fear. This spirit is often apparent in the early poetry. We find an admirable example of it in the speech of that heathen Ealdorman of Northumbria, in which he likened man's life to a sparrow which flies out of the wintry storm into a hall where men sit at a feast, and tarries but for a moment in the warmth and brightness, and flies out again into the cold and tempest beyond the little circle of light. [2]

The story shows us a man profoundly curious about the deepest questions of life, a man who has apparently put aside as inadequate the old notions of his forefathers about the future life, and who is therefore able to regard the whole matter with a mind open to new ideas. Such, there is every reason to suppose, was the state of mind of

[1] *Bede, Ecc. Hist.* ii. xiii.

[2] The speech is given as follows by Bede in a justly famous passage: "The present life of man in this world, O King, seems to me, in comparison to that time which is uncertain, as if a sparrow, swiftly flying through the room, warmed with the fire in the midst of it, in which you sit at dinner, in the winter, with your friends, whilst the storms of rain and snow prevail outside; the sparrow, I say, flying in at one window, and immediately out again at another, whilst it is within doors does not feel the inclemency of the weather, but, after a very short space of time, vanishes out of your sight, returning from one winter to another. So the life of man here appears for a very short space of time; but of what went before or of what is to follow, we are entirely ignorant. If, therefore, this new doctrine contain something more certain, it seems to deserve our approbation and reception." *Ecclesiastical History,* Bk. ii. chap. xiii.; *v.* also Wordsworth's rendering of this, *Ecclesiastical Sonnets,* Part i. xvi,

many of the English at this time. Deeply religious by nature, their old religion had lost its hold upon them, and they were prepared to welcome something new. This is one great reason why Christianity spread so quickly among them, and why it became such a strong motive force not only in their lives but in their literature. For nearly a century and a half after their first settlement in Britain, the English kept, at least outwardly, to the faith of their fathers. The Christian Church had already been planted in Britain, but the Britons were their enemies. Christian Europe lay to the eastward, Christian Ireland to the west; but the first business of the English was to wrest the land from its owners, slaying them, or forcing them westward. The Jutes, the first of the English tribes to effect a permanent settlement, landed about 449, and they were followed by two more important tribes, the Saxons (c. 477–491) and the Angles. The Britains fought with desperate bravery, but, after about a century and a quarter of conflict, the English had possessed themselves of the best lands, and their mastery of the island was assured.[1] Important as was this work of conquest and settlement, it cannot have materially changed the Englishman's view of life, or widened his mental horizon. So far the civilisation of Europe had touched him no more nearly in his new home than it had in his old. He held, if somewhat less firmly, the old beliefs; he sang, we may assume, the same songs his fathers had made across the sea; or, if the dramatic incidents of the conquest suggested new themes, he sang of new exploits in the old traditional manner. But towards the close of the sixth century

---

[1] That is from 449, the date of the landing of the Jutes, to 577, the date of the battle of Deorham. This was a battle between the West Saxons and the Britons. It was fought near Bath, and threw open the valley of the Severn to the Saxons. The Angles had meanwhile been independently advancing westward, and by 577 the eastern portion of the island was divided up among the various English kingdoms.

there entered England a new force that was to transform the nation and make a new epoch in its literary history. This new force was Christianity, and it reached the English from Rome and from Ireland. The first Christian missionary was sent directly from Rome. In 597 St. Augustine [1] and his band of forty monks, sent by Pope Gregory, landed on the little Isle of Thanet off the coast of Kent, on the very spot where the war-ships of Hengist and Horsa, the first English conquerors of Britain, had landed one hundred and forty-eight years before. Christianity was thus planted in the South of Britain, and the interrupted communication with Rome and its civilization was reëstablished.

The landing of St. Augustine.

But while Rome Christianised the South, the lasting conversion of the North came not from the Roman, but from the Celt. In 635, Aidan, a monk from the Irish mission station at Iona, an island off the west coast of Scotland, settled in Northumbria and became the first great bishop of the North. After twenty years of contest with the old religion, Penda, King of Mercia, "the last champion of heathenism," was defeated and killed in battle (655), and English paganism gave way before the zeal and devotion of the Celt.

Aidan.

With the coming of Christianity a new life began for the English people. It revealed a world of which they had never dreamed; education, culture, literature, and the arts followed in its train. To appreciate this we must remember that in these early centuries, when modern Europe was beginning to take shape, the new nations were absorbing and turning to new

The Church and culture.

---

[1] St. Augustine, or St. Austin, the missionary to the English, must not be confused with the even greater St. Augustine (354–430), the author of the *Confessions*, and one of the four great Fathers of the Latin Church. The St. Augustine, who first brought the Gospel to the English, had been a monk in a Benedictine convent at Rome. He became the first Archbishop of Canterbury, and died in, or about, 607.

uses fragments saved from the culture of the past. The Church was the chief heir and guardian of this classic learning and culture, and upon the Church the gigantic task of educating and civilising the crude populations of Europe had almost entirely devolved. To be outside the pale of Christendom, therefore, was to be cut off from the intellectual traditions, the learning and the art, which Christian Europe had inherited from the Roman Empire. To be a part of Christendom, was to share in that civilisation which represented, however imperfectly, the accumulated results of thousands of years of human progress.

And not only was England admitted to this older and larger world, but the circumstances of her conversion also gave her exceptional advantages, greater perhaps **Celtic Christianity.** than any other nation of Europe then enjoyed. The first of these advantages was England's close relations to Celtic culture. At this time Ireland led Western Europe in scholarship and in her monastic schools, and England's proximity to Ireland was therefore a distinct intellectual gain. Ireland was an important factor in England's education. The earliest monasteries in Northumbria were founded by Irish missionaries, or were the direct outcome of their labours; while Englishmen sometimes journeyed to Ireland to visit her famous teachers and consult her rare manuscripts.[1]

The second of these advantages was the exceptional ability of her teachers sent from Rome. These two teachers were THEODORE OF TARSUS, and ADRIAN, or **Roman Christianity.** HADRIAN, a monk from Africa. Theodore, a Greek by birth, who had studied in Athens,

---

[1] Bede says that " many young noblemen and gentlemen " were in Ireland at the time of the plague of 664, " to improve themselves either in learning or virtue." He adds that they were furnished with books and teaching and accommodation free; one of them returned to England full of learning and became a Bishop. *Ecc. Hist.* Bk. iii, chap. xxvii.

brought with him some flavour of culture older than that of
Rome. He was Archbishop of Canterbury from 668–690,
and he made the school at Canterbury which St. Augustine
had founded, of national importance. Hadrian, "the
fountain of letters and river of arts," as an old chronicler
calls him, was placed at the head of this school, and a great
number of pupils gathered there, some coming from a long
distance. Under these two teachers, Canterbury exerted a
profound and far-reaching influence upon England's intellectual life. Greek, practically lost to Western Europe from
the fifth to the fifteenth century, was taught there, besides
the Bible, poetry, astronomy, arithmetic, and music. The
school at Canterbury was the model of others, notably of
a great school at York (735); and Adrian's pupil, Aldhelm
of **Malmesbury,** became one of the most justly famous
scholars of his time.

The seventh century stands out in English history as an
epoch of great ecclesiastical foundations, and wherever the
The founding Church went fresh ideas and generally some
of monasteries definite provision for education went likewise.
and schools. It was in the seventh century that Hilda, a
grand-niece of King Edwin of Northumbria, founded
her famous Abbey on the cliffs at Whitby; that BENEDICT
BISCOP, or BADUCING (c. 628–690), a Northumbrian noble,
established two associated monasteries near the mouth of
the rivers Tyne and Wear, enriching them with rare manuscripts and precious relics which he had brought back from
Rome. It was in the seventh century that Wilfred, Archbishop of York, introduced a higher standard in architecture
by building at Hexham "the finest church on " the western " side of the Alps." It was in the seventh century that
the walls of great abbeys arose in the fenlands of Lincolnshire, at *Peterborough*, *Ely*, and *Crowland*, and that the
monastery at *Malmesbury*, on the western edge of Wessex,
became a centre of culture through the labours of its Abbot

Aldhelm. These and many other churches, abbeys, and schools, set in the midst of dense ignorance, violence, and coarse brutality, wrought a marvellous change in the life of Englishmen. The century which followed the conversion of England may be justly compared to that educational period which prepared the way for the literary glories of the Elizabethan Age. In both the seventh and the fifteenth centuries England was stimulated and refreshed by the new ideas which reached her from beyond her borders, and, towards the close of both of these receptive or educational periods, the accumulation of fresh thought and emotion found expression in a new literary epoch.

In the seventh century the Church was the parent of the new literature, the earliest English literature unquestionably native to English soil. It began with religious poetry, and its birthplace was the monastery and the monastic school. In a monastery CÆDMON (c. 670), "the first English poet whose name we know," composed that poem which begins the recorded history of English literature in England; it was in a monastery that *Bede* (670–735), the monk-scholar, lived his tranquil life of study and labour; while ALDHELM (640?–709), his great co-worker, was then abbot of a monastery and a bishop. The lives of these three men show us better than any general statement can do how a new life began for literature under the pressure of Christianity and Latin culture.

CÆDMON, as Bede tells us his story, was an inmate of St. Hilda's monastery of Streoneshalh, at Whitby. He was not a monk, but a plain, unlettered man, who took care of the cattle and shared, no doubt, in the practical tasks of the community. For some reason he could not make or recite poetry, although this was a favourite recreation among his companions, and so he was accustomed to steal away from the feast when the harp was passed from hand to hand so that each should sing in turn.

Cædmon.

One night when he had left the feast as usual, and gone to the stables where he had charge of some cattle, a stranger appeared to him in a dream or a vision and said: "Caedmon, sing me a song." "I cannot sing," Cædmon answered, "and that is why I have just left the feast." "You must, however," said the stranger, "sing for me." "What shall I sing?" Cædmon asked, and he was commanded to sing "in the praise of creation." And immediately Cædmon began to sing some verses which he had never heard before in the praise of God the Creator of all things. The matter was brought to the notice of the Abbess; and Cædmon, being taken before her, repeated to her the verses he had composed in his sleep. The Abbess, believing that God had given to this humble man a wonderful gift, induced him to become a monk. He could not read, but the Abbess had the Bible read aloud to him, and Cædmon, ruminating on what he had heard, turned those portions of it that most appealed to him into verse, paraphrasing in this way the Books of Genesis and Exodus, "and many other histories of holy writ."

There is good reason to believe that this story is substantially true, and the more we know about the strange workings of the poet's genius the less we shall be inclined to doubt. Its details may have been coloured by legend, but we can, I think, still discover something of the real Cædmon in this old story; a herdsman-poet, humble-minded, self-distrustful, unlearned, but a good man, whose unsuspected genius, unstirred by the old heathen themes, awoke suddenly under the inspiration of the new religion.

Cædmon was the founder of a new school of religious poetry; he led the way into a new world. Bede says that

The Cædmonian cycle. "many others endeavoured to compose religious poems in English, but none of these could ever equal his." There is an old manuscript volume in the Bodleian Library at Oxford, made up of a number of

Early English poems. Since these poems agree generally in subject-matter and character with the Biblical paraphrases of Cædmon, it was assumed that they were his, and for a long time his reputed authorship of them remained unquestioned. Scholars are now sure that Cædmon did not write all of these poems, and many believe that not even a part of the book was composed by him.[1] Apparently the book is a collection of religious pieces, by various authors, arranged in the order of the Bible narrative. If it is true that not a line of it was actually composed by Cædmon, it is probable that his poems served as a model, or that they were used as the basis of the work.

The poems themselves are of very unequal merit. In some instances we have but a dull, almost mechanical paraphrase; in others a scene or character is revealed to us with that imaginative definiteness which marks the true poet. On the whole, we feel that this religious poetry is close to poetry of the old heathen past; it is the poetry of the scôp, little changed in spirit or in metrical form, but it has found a new theme. When the poet uses his original with the greatest freedom, and gives the fullest scope to his own power, then we feel this resemblance most strongly. Satan is brought before us as a warrior, proud, daring, defiant, a rebellious vassal. He gathers his faithful followers to his cause, as the kings and chiefs among the English were wont to rally their thanes, their chosen body-guard, to their support. "Stand by me strong supporters, firm in strife." After his overthrow he reminds them of the nature of this bond between them, declaring that if he has ever given them

The Cædmon poems.

[1] Competent scholars now generally agree that all we have of Cædmon's writing are the nine lines of his *Hymn*. This is probably the first piece of extant English literature composed on English soil. The lines are found at the end of the Moore MS. of Bede's *Ecclesiastical History*, and were probably copied there in or about the year 737. See the translation in Cook and Tinker's *Select Translations*, p. 77.

princely gifts in the old days in that good kingdom, now is the time to repay him by faithful service. He appeals, then, to the same obligation which is felt by Wiglaf, the thane of Beowulf, in the fight with the dragon: " I mind me, the time we drank the mead, we vowed then to our lord in the beer-hall, who gave us these rings, that we would requite him for our war-gear, the helmets and swords of temper, if this-like need should befall him." [1]

We find, too, especially in the *Exodus*, the true fighting spirit of the Teuton, and a delight in the very pomp and trappings of war. The approach of the host of Pharaoh is thus described:

> "They prepared their arms,
> The war advanced,
> Bucklers glittered,
> Trumpets sang,
> Standards rattled,
>
> . . . .
>
> Among them scream
> The fowls of war,
> Greedy of battle,
> Dewy-feathered,
> Over the bodies of the host
> The dark choosers of the slain;
> The wolves sing their
> Horrid evensong." [2]

The poet sings of these things as a Christian scôp. The battles are English battles, for the singer has taken the Bible story, and translated it by the light of his own understanding or experience.

There are a number of other religious poems besides the *Biblical Paraphases* of Cædmon and his followers. As a rule, these poems are not founded on the Bible, but on some legend of an apostle, martyr or saint. Thus, the *Andreas* treats of the adventures of the apostle St. Andrew, who goes into a land of

Other religious poems.

---

[1] *Beowulf*, Child's translation, p. 72.   [2] Thorpe's translation.

cannibals and sorcerers to rescue St. Matthew; the *Juliana*
is the story of a saint and martyr, who refused to become
the wife of a pagan; the *Guthlac* describes the temptations,
triumphs, and death of Guthlac, an English saint of the
eighth century, who forsook the world and lived the life
of a hermit in the fens of East-Anglia, or Lincolnshire.[1]
Among these religious poems the *Judith*, the *Phoenix*, *The
Dream of the Rood*, and the *Crist*, or *Christ*, are of especial
interest. The *Judith* and the *Phoenix* are strikingly different. The *Judith* is an epic fragment, the greater part
of which is lost. It tells the story of the Jewish heroine
related in the Apocryphal Book of Judith, who slew the
enemies' captain Holofernes to deliver her native town. It
brings before us the Anglo-Saxon battle; the din of shields,
the showers of arms, " the smoke of war," the lean wolf
on the edge of the wood, the black raven, and the eagle
waiting for the prey. Judith, beautiful and terrible, shows
neither fear, hesitation, nor pity; the warriors march grim
and relentless to take vengeance on their enemies bewildered with wine.[2]

While *Judith* is full of heroic daring, of blows and revenge
and the tumult of battle, the poem of the *Phoenix* lifts us
into an ideal region of rest and peace. The *Phoenix* the
wonderful bird of the Eastern fable, which rises into re-

---

[1] St. Guthlac died in 714. Crowland Abbey was built, possibly
by King Æthelbald of Mercia, on the site of Guthlac's retreat.

[2] In his fine poem *Judith and Holofernes* (1896), Aldrich has introduced " a note of tenderness " into Judith's character not found in the
Apocryphal story, or in the Anglo-Saxon poem. Aldrich, for instance,
makes Judith hesitate before she kills the sleeping Holofernes :

> "And Judith looked on him, and pity crept
> Into her bosom. . . .
> O broken sword of proof! O Prince betrayed!
> Her he had trusted, he who trusted none.
> The sharp thought pierced her, and her breast was torn,
> And half she longed to bid her purpose die," etc.

newed life from the ashes of its nest, dwells in a far eastern island. This island is an earthly paradise such as the Celts and the poets of many other races have loved to imagine. The green forests stretch far and wide beneath the skies, and there "neither rain nor snow, nor breath of frost, nor fall of hoar-frost, nor heat of sun, nor ever-during cold, nor warm weather, nor winter shower, works aught of harm. The land is full of flowers, the fruits fail not, and the trees are forever green."[1]

The authorship of most of these religious poems is unknown or conjectural, but it is certain that at least three **Cynewulf.** of them were written by a poet named CYNE-WULF. We know this because Cynewulf has woven his name in runic letters into the text of these poems, the *Elene*, the *Juliana*, and the *Christ*, so as to form an acrostic. There is no other record of this man, who was certainly one of the greatest poets of his time, but he is generally supposed to have been a Northumbrian scôp, who lived in the latter part of the eighth century. Some suppose him to have been the author of the *Andreas*, *Judith*, and a remarkable collection of poetical *Riddles*, and various other poems have been attributed to him. But while history is silent about Cynewulf, there are several remarkable passages in his poems in which he tells us of himself. These passages tell us little of the outward events of his life, but they reveal with sufficient clearness the depths of his inner experience. We gather that in his youth he tasted of pleasure and success as the favourite of the great, and that he had received "the jewel and the

---

[1] *Cf.* Tennyson's description of "the island valley of Avilion,"—

"Where falls not hail, or rain, or any snow,
Nor ever wind blows loudly; but it lies
Deep-meadowed, happy, fair with orchard lawns
And bowery hollows crown'd with summer sea."
— IDYLLS OF THE KING: *"The Passing of Arthur."*

twisted gold in the mead-hall," the reward perhaps of his songs. But sorrow overtakes him, perhaps some definite grief from without, perhaps simply some secret change, some crisis in his spiritual growth, and earthly pleasures seem poor and empty. The disillusionment of age is heavy on him. "Joy has waned, pleasure has decreased with the years; youth has fled, the former pride." An overwhelming sense of the transitoriness of all the things which man delights in takes possession of him; it all passes, and the joy of life slips away like running water. He is tormented by the remembrance of the errors of his careless youth; he speaks of himself as "guilty of misdeeds, fettered by sins, bowed with bitterness, beset with tribulations." But at last his whole view of life is changed; he finds comfort in religion, and the Divine power lifts him out of this depth of despair, unlocks his heart, and grants him again the power of song. So, old and ready to depart by reason of the treacherous house of the flesh, he composes Christian poems, not free from sadness indeed, but full of hope and peace.[1]

His poem of *Christ* is bright with the assurance of a final triumph. The heavens are opened, and we hear the hymning of angels. The voice of God declares in words that seem to scatter the ancient darkness of English heathenism:

Cynewulf's "Christ."

> "Let there be light for ever and ever,
> A radiant joy for each of living men
> Who in their generations shall be born." [2]

The poem treats of "the threefold coming of Christ, his birth, his ascension, and his advent at the last judgment,"

[1] Cynewulf's Rune passages are given in translation in Cook and Tinker's *Translations*, Morley's *English Writers*, vol. ii., and Brooke's *Early English Literature;* but see also Professor Cook's *Introd. to Judith*, and Professor Strunk's *Introd. to Elene*, in *Belles Lettres Series.*

[2] *Christ*, Gollancz' translation.

and its serenity is broken by a terrible vision of judgment. But its final note is triumph, as the poet pictures the happiness of those who have endured and overcome:

> "There is angels' song; the bliss of the happy;
>
> · · · · · · · ·
>
> A gladsome host of men; youth without age;
> The glory of the heavenly chivalry; health without pain
> For righteous workers; and for souls sublime
> Rest without toil; there is day without dark gloom,
> Ever gloriously bright; bliss without bale; ·
> Friendship 'twixt friends forever without feud;
> Peace without enmity for the blest in Heaven,
> In the communion of Saints." [1]

We are ignorant of almost any incident in Cynewulf's life, yet the man himself — apart from the accidents of birth and surroundings — survives in his work. In spite of all the vagueness of his language he is very real to us. The "cry of Cynewulf," as it has been called, moves us to-day after the passage of a thousand years, for it comes out of the depths of a man's soul. It has the directness and truth of that "lyric cry" which misery and disappointment wrung from the heart of Burns. Such a cry interprets the grief that is common to man; and whether it is uttered by King David, by Cynewulf, or by Burns, our human nature responds to it and understands.

The earliest attempts of the English at literary expression were cast in the poetic form. This form was **Anglo-Saxon verse.** very different from that of the poetry with which we are familiar; but, while the Anglo-Saxon verse may sound rough and hard to us, as rendered by the gleeman, it was doubtless both vigorous and inspiriting. In form this Anglo-Saxon poetry may be described as a *rhythmical chant*. Each verse, or line, was composed of two half lines, separated by a pause, or *cæsura*. There was no rhyme, nor was the number of

[1] *Christ*, Gollancz' translation.

syllables in each verse always the same.   Instead of rhyme
the Anglo-Saxon poet employed *alliteration,* that is, he
habitually introduced words beginning with the same
sound; while the regular beat, or rhythm, was given by
emphasising, or accenting, these alliterative words.   It
was usual to have one or two of these emphatic, or accented, words or syllables in the first half of the line, and
only one in the second, thus:

Oft *Scyld Scéfing*   *sceaþena þréatum* [1]
Oft *Skyld Scifing*   from *scathers thronging.* [2]

Probably a strong twang on the harp at the accented
words reënforced the emphasis of the voice and heightened
the marching movement of the rhythm.

When Christianity gave a fresh impulse to English literature, it did not at first change its manner, it simply gave

**Christianity
and litera-
ture. The
monk-scholar.**
it new subjects.   It took the traditional poetic
form, and turned it to a new use.   The chief
centre of this Christian poetry, which is generally thought to have begun with Cædmon,
appears to have been in Northumbria, where the infusion
of Celtic culture was especially strong.   It was not long,
however, before the knowledge of the various branches
of foreign learning introduced by the Church brought
about a new stage of literary development.   Beside
the poet, the *Christian scôp,* who belongs at once to
the old world and the new, there appears the *monk-scholar,*
an Englishman of a wholly new order, the representative
of a class which was destined to guide the intellectual
development of Europe for centuries to come.   This beginning of English scholarship is directly traceable to the Canterbury school of Theodore and Adrian.   From this school,
says Green, "our written literature"—the literature, that

---

[1] Anglo-Saxon character þ = *th.* [2] *Beowulf,* l. 4.

is, of the English in Britain —"took its birth."[1] From this school came Aldhelm, the first Englishman to gain eminence as a classical scholar and teacher,[2] who began in the South a work similar to that which Bede, at a little later date, took up in the North. Aldhelm's learning was gained from Ireland as well as from Rome. His first teacher was *Maildulf*, or *Meldun*, an Irishman who had retired into a lonely spot in the woods of Northern Wessex, which came to be known as Maildulfesburh (Maildulf's-town) or Malmesbury. From Malmesbury Aldhelm went to Canterbury to study under Adrian, returning full of the inspiration of the new learning. After the death of his old teacher, he was made Abbot of Malmesbury, and later Bishop of Sherborne. He died in 709. Aldhelm was a leader in the intellectual awakening of England, and the fame of his learning extended to Scotland and to the Continent. He helped forward the advance of English architecture, and a church which he built at Bradford-on-Avon still stands as a memorial to his labours. Although he wrote much in Latin, both in prose and verse, Aldhelm did not neglect his native tongue, and King Alfred pronounced him the best English poet of his time. A familiar story of him shows his skill as a poet and a musician, as well as his power of being all things to all men. We are told that when he found that the congregation at Malmesbury was in the habit of leaving church before the sermon, Aldhelm disguised himself as a gleeman and stationed himself on a bridge near the town. The people coming from church crowded about him, and when he had gained their attention Aldhelm gradually introduced words of Scripture into his song, and so in effect made his hearers

---

[1] *Making of England*, 326.

[2] Aldhelm, says Professor Stubbs, "was the first Englishman who cultivated classical learning with any success, and the first of whom any literary remains are preserved." *Dict. Christ. Biog.*: "Aldhelm."

listen to a sermon without knowing it. As none of Aldhelm's poems have been preserved, we are too apt to think of him only as "the Father of Anglo-Latin Poetry." He was more than this: his is the earliest name that we know in the English poetry of the South.[1] He had his share in creating the poetry of the people, — how great a share we can only conjecture; but we know that four hundred years after his death Aldhelm's songs were still remembered and sung.

Wide-spread as was Aldhelm's influence upon his contemporaries, after his death learning and literature in Wessex rapidly declined. During the eighth century Wessex was troubled by civil strife; it was menaced by the rival power of the rising kingdom of Mercia; and, finally, it was forced to face repeated Danish invasions. Ignorance increased, literature languished, and Aldhelm is the one Southern writer of any prominence, until we come to King Alfred, nearly two centuries later.

Literature in the South.

Very different was the history of literature and learning in the North. The great kingdom of Northumbria, although it failed to maintain its political supremacy, remained for several generations the intellectual centre of Western Europe. The influences that contributed to this result have already been indicated. The zeal of Irish missionaries, the favour of Northumbrian kings, the spread of Roman civilisation, all worked together towards the same end. The learning of the school at Canterbury mingled with the learning derived from Celtic teachers. The Northumbrian noble, BENEDICT BISCOP, introduced glass from abroad, and brought a collection of books and relics from Rome (cir. 678). The

Literature in the North.

[1] It is not unlikely that Aldhelm's English poems antedated those of Cædmon, who is commonly accounted "the Father of English Poetry."

fame of the school at York spread throughout Europe, while its library was said to have no equal outside of Rome. We have seen that this new culture first found literary expression through poetry, and that less than half a century after the coming of Aidan from Iona (635) Cædmon founded a school of religious verse (cir. 670). The second great outcome of these new intellectual conditions, following hard upon the first, is the rise of a school of Latin, or Anglo-Latin literature, written almost entirely in prose.

Bede.   The greatest and one of the earliest of these Northern scholars was Bǣda, or Bede, the most famous man of letters of his time.

Bede was born in 673 on the Northumbrian coast near the mouth of the river Wear. A year later his birthplace became the territory of the Church, as it was part of a tract of land granted to Benedict Biscop. On this land Biscop built the monastery of St. Peter's (674), and a little later the neighbouring monastery of St. Paul at Jarrow. Bede, early left an orphan, was intrusted to the care of the Abbot Benedict, who placed the child, then seven years old, in the monastery of St. Peter. There, and in the associated monastery at Jarrow, to which he was afterwards transferred, all the rest of his life was passed. Bede himself has summed up the history of his fifty-five years of monastic life in a few words: "I wholly applied myself to the study of the Scripture; and, amidst the observance of regular discipline, and the daily care of singing in the church, I always took delight in learning, teaching, and writing."[1] This is the simple record of a useful and well-ordered life, filled with varied activities, but tranquil and content.

Bede, as his words imply, was a *student*, a *teacher*, a *writer;* indeed, it is hardly too much to say that he was the best scholar, the most influential teacher, and the greatest

[1] Bede, *Ecclesiastical History*, Bk. v. chap. xxiv.

man of letters, in all Europe in his time. His life was a fortunate one. As a student he had opportunities which at that day were open to very few. Not every monastery had an abbot so able and progressive as Benedict, Bede's first teacher, and it is probable that few monasteries in Western Europe were furnished with a library equal to that which Benedict had gathered at Jarrow. Even the site of the monastery was favourable, for it was sufficiently central for Bede to avail himself of the learning of Ireland and of Rome, of Gaul and of Canterbury. [1] With the keen love of knowledge, the unwearied industry, the broadly receptive mind of a great scholar, Bede absorbed from such varied sources nearly all that was best in the learning of his day. He knew Latin and Greek, and had even some acquaintance with Hebrew. Quotations from the classical poets are found in his works. He wrote about forty books, many of them text-books for the use of his scholars, upon a great variety of subjects. His commentaries on the Bible bear witness to the thoroughness of his studies; his little book on natural science

His work as writer. (*De Rerum Naturæ*) shows that he had mastered the popular science of his day. Besides all this foreign learning, he knew and loved the songs of England, and he was above all a student of her history. His *Ecclesiastical History of the English People*, his best known and most valuable book, is the chief authority for the period of which it treats. By this book Bede "was at once the founder of mediæval history and the first English historian." [2] Bede wrote in Latin, as all the scholars of Europe did at that time and for long after, but his last book, the closing words of which he dictated to his scribes almost with his dying breath, was an English translation of the Gospel of St. John.

[1] See Bishop Stubbs's article on "Bede" in *Dict. Christ. Biog.*
[2] J. R. Green.

As a teacher Bede holds an important place in the educational history of Europe. At one time six hundred scholars including strangers from a distance are said to have attended his school at Jarrow. He helped to mould the great school at York. His pupil Egbert became the head of the school, and Egbert's great pupil ALCUIN (735–804) went to the Continent and organised the schools of Charlemagne, "on which the culture of the Middle Ages was based." [1]

His work as teacher.

Bede did a great work, but the man himself was even greater than his books. His life in its simplicity, its singleness of purpose, its lofty aim, has a singular unity and completeness. Gentle, hating a lie, or the least inaccuracy or slovenliness in work, and remarkably free from the prejudices of his age, the character of Bede is exceedingly lovable and noble. In him, as in Cynewulf, the stern submission to an unknown weird is lost in the joyous acceptance of a larger hope. Well might he repeat in his last illness that noble sentence of St. Ambrose: "I have not lived so as to be ashamed to live among you; nor am I afraid to die, because we have a good God." The meaning and influence of such a life grows clearer, as we read in the unaffected words of one of his disciples the story of the Master's death. With failing breath he had toiled through the day, dictating his translation of St. John's Gospel, and as the day closed, his work was done. At twilight, amid his weeping scholars, his face turned towards the oratory where he was wont to pray, with "great tranquillity" his soul went out from among them.

His character.

The conditions which had lifted Northumbria into intellectual leadership, and made Bede the great teacher of the Western world, were not destined to last. Soon after Bede's death (735), dangers began to threaten it from

[1] Bishop Stubbs's *Dict. Christ. Biog.*, art. "Bede."

within and without. The peaceful work of the monasteries, indeed, went on without interruption, and the school at York rose to eminence; but the kingdom became a prey to treason, lawlessness, and plague. Finally, towards the close of the century (cir. 787), came the Danish pirates. These heathen adventurers were a greater menace to learning than civil or foreign war. They came originally for plunder, and they were especially attracted by the riches of the great religious houses. In 793 they plundered the monastery of Lindisfarne; in the year following they sacked and burnt the monasteries at Wearmouth and Jarrow. In the next century they came not only to plunder but to conquer. They captured York (867), and Northumbria became the land of the heathen Dane. The civilisation of the North, which men had been building up for more than two hundred years, perished, for the very sources of literature and learning were destroyed. They sacked abbeys and churches, they burned the libraries, and broke up the schools. Streoneshalh, the home of Cædmon, was demolished, and the place was called by the Danish name of Whitby. " There was not one home of learning left from the Forth to the Humber." [1] Two years later they entered East Anglia, to plunder and destroy Peterborough, Crowland, and Ely, the great religious houses of the fens. The fate of all England hung in the balance, until at last they were checked by the steadfast heroism of King Alfred (battle of Edington, 878). It was after this battle that Alfred made his famous treaty with the Danes, the Peace of Chippenham (878). Under this, although a great tract of England was surrendered to the invaders, Alfred retained all of Southern and part of Middle England. England was indeed saved for the English, but the Dane

The decline of Northumbria, and the coming of the Danes.

[1] Stopford Brooke's *English Literature from the Beginning to the Norman Conquest*, p. 124.

was master from the northern bank of the Thames to the river Tees.

But while learning and civilisation in the North had received a blow from which it took them centuries to recover, in the South they rose into new life under the unflagging and comprehensive energy of Alfred. The intellectual and literary preëminence of Northumbria was due to a happy combination of causes; the sudden rise of Wessex to a position of literary leadership was the work of one man. From his youth Alfred had loved books. When he was called to the throne, England had already lost her place as a centre of European culture, and the Dane threatened to sweep away even the remnants of learning that were left. So utterly had learning fallen away in England, writes King Alfred in a famous passage, "that there were very few on this side of the Humber who could understand their service-books in English, or even put a letter from Latin into English; and I think there were not many beyond the Humber. So few there were of them that I cannot think of even one when I came to the throne." [1] For the first fifteen years of his reign (871–cir. 886), Alfred was occupied in fighting for the very existence of his kingdom, or in providing means for its defence. His first duty was not to encourage civilisation, but to preserve it by the sword. But after he had concluded a second peace with the Danes (886), the king was able to spare more time for his work of reform. He restored the religious houses and founded a monastery at Athelney; he established a school at his court for the education of the young nobles. His children were brought up to use books constantly, and were especially taught "the Saxon" (or English) poems.[2] He laboured for

The revival of learning in the South. Alfred.

---

[1] Alfred's preface to his translation of St. Gregory's *Pastoral Care* (*Cura Pastoralis*), or "Herds-man's Book."

[2] Asser's *Life of Alfred*.

the better training of the priesthood, and was a friend to the monks, although he believed that learning should not be monopolised by the clergy. His ideas on popular education were far in advance of his time. It was his wish that "all the youth now in England of free men who have the wealth to be able to set themselves to it be put to learning while they are not of use for anything else."

Alfred and education. "Those whom one wishes to teach further," he adds, "let them afterwards be taught further in the Latin tongue." These memorable words are the best explanation of the services of King Alfred to literature. Education is to be made as general as is practicable, and the language of the elementary or ordinary education is to be English, the language of the people, not Latin, the language of the ecclesiastical class. One great obstacle to the carrying out of this plan was the dearth of books in English. Latin was the ordinary medium of education; the text-books were in Latin, as well as nearly all of the literature of the time. Alfred saw that the most needful of these Latin books must be translated into English, that learning should thus be made the possession of the people. The king himself knew little or nothing of Latin, but from time to time, after the treaty of Chippenham, he gathered learned men about him and became a pupil. Some of these men were English, but learning had so fallen away in England that he was obliged to seek further help from abroad. Among those who came was Asser, the Welshman, who became the king's biographer. The king inspired these men with something of his own indomitable spirit, but he did even more than this; in spite of the weight

Alfred's translations. of his "manifold cares," in spite of the heavy burden of illness, he undertook the task of translating into English the books "most needful" for his people.

One of Alfred's first works was a translation of the *Shep-*

herd's Model (Regula (or Cura) Pastoralis) of Pope Gregory
the Great. This book, as its name implies, was a hand-
book for the clergy, the shepherds of the people, intended
to guide them in their duties and furnish them with the
model of the ideal priest. The clergy were the teachers of
the kingdom, and on the improvement of the clergy Alfred's
educational reform must be based. A copy of this book
was sent to every bishopric, and the very book which the
king sent to Worcester is now in the Bodleian Library at
Oxford. Alfred also translated the greater part of Bede's
Ecclesiastical History,[1] so that Englishmen might read the
story of their native land in their own tongue. Alfred's
patriotism did not make him provincial. In order that his
people should know something of the world outside, he made
a free rendering of a book which was then the standard manual of general history, the work of *Paulus Orosius*, a Spanish monk of the fifth century. But it is misleading to think
of Alfred as a mere translator. His object was not to give
a literal version of his original, but to adapt it to the popular
use, to edit it, condensing or expanding it as he thought
best. Alfred is therefore an author as well as a translator,
and he has left on many a passage the impress of his own
character. This is especially applicable to his translation,
or adaptation, of Boethius' *Consolations of Philosophy*
(*De Consolatione Philosophiæ*), a famous book throughout the Middle Ages. Boethius, a Roman patrician of the
fifth and sixth centuries, was imprisoned for treason, and in
this book he endeavoured to comfort himself by philosophy.
In paraphrasing and adapting the book of Boethius, Alfred
fills it with his own spirit, until, as **Mr. Frederic** Harrison
says, "it is almost an original treatise." It is full of noble
and lofty thoughts, and nowhere do we get nearer to the

[1] Some think it more probable that Bede's *History* was not translated by Alfred himself, but by one of his priests by the king's command.

soul of the great king. "Alfred took the *Meditations* of Boethius as a standard text-book of moral and religious thought, and he uses it as the basis of his own musings upon man, the world, and God."[1] So far as we know, Boethius was not a Christian, but Alfred transposes his *Consolations of Philosophy* into the consolations of religion. It is Alfred, not Boethius, who writes: "Lift up your hearts to Him when ye raise your hands, and pray for what is right and needful for you, for He will not deny you."[2] "Some sages, however, say that Fate rules both weal and woe of every man. But I say, as do all Christian men, that it is the divine purpose that rules them, not Fate; and I know that it judges all things very rightly, though unthinking men may not think so."[3]

The translations of King Alfred remain one of the great landmarks of literary history. He made them to

Alfred and English prose. fill an immediate and pressing need; but the work, humbly and simply done, had a far wider and more lasting influence than he could

have imagined, for it was the true beginning of English prose. With him begins the stream of English prose that was to broaden and deepen until its waters should cover half the globe. And not only is Alfred "the founder of English prose," but he anticipated also a new stage in the advance of learning, for he was the first English man of letters who was not an ecclesiastic. Theodore of Tarsus, Adrian, Aldhelm, and Bede were priests, and they wrote in Latin, the language of the Church; but King Alfred was a layman, and it was reserved for him to take prose literature out of Latin, the language of the Church, and put it into English, the language of the people.

[1] *The Writings of King Alfred*, by Frederic **Harrison.**
[2] *King Alfred's Version of the Consolations of Boethius*, Trans. by W. J. Sedgefield, p. 175.
[3] Ib. p. 153.

Apart from their influence on English prose, Alfred's writings have no little intrinsic merit. He was far from being a literary artist, or a finished scholar; but many passages scattered through his translations bring us near to a very good and a very great man. He had little need of the refinements of a conscious art, for his style has a dignity and elevation of tone that is the natural expression of the man. He lived in the company of wise and lofty thoughts, and he has told us something of his inner life, his meditations and his hopes, with a transparent sincerity and simplicity. We feel this in that noble sentence from Boethius which is so closely associated with his name. "To be brief, I may say that it has ever been my desire to live honourably while I was alive, and after my death to leave to them that should come after me my memory in good works." [1]

It was during Alfred's reign, and probably under his direct influence and supervision, that the *English Chronicle* was revived and rearranged in a fuller and better form. From very early times it had been the custom in certain monasteries to make a brief record of the most important historical events of each year. This was done in the monasteries in Northumbria, and the same practice was followed at Canterbury and Winchester. It will be remembered that Alfred lived at Winchester, which was then the capital of Wessex, so it was but natural that the Winchester *Annals* should be selected as the basis of the revised history. The old *Annals*, besides being enlarged, were continued so as to include the greater part of Alfred's reign. But the *Chronicle* does not end with Alfred; for two hundred and fifty years after his death the monks went on adding to the wonderful record of England's history, until it finally came to an end with an

The English Chronicle.

[1] *King Alfred's Version of the Consolations of Boethius*, trans. by W. J. Sedgefield, p. 42.

account of the accession of Henry II. in 1154, written by a monk of Peterborough, the last in the long succession of English Chroniclers. The *English Chronicle* covers a period of seven centuries, from the middle of the fifth to the middle of the twelfth century. For the most part, it is, as its name implies, a brief, dry statement of facts, not a finished history. Here, for example, is the record for the year 806: "Here the moon eclipsed on Sept. 1; and Eardwulf, King of the Northumbrians, was driven from his realm; and Eanbert, Bishop of Hexham, died." But in some places, as in an oft quoted description of William the Conqueror, it is fuller, and shows a power of portraying character and a greater literary skill. Occasionally the dry prose record is abandoned for verse. Two poems, one celebrating the battle with the Scots at *Brunanburh* in 937, the other describing the defeat and death of Byrhtnoth in a stubborn contest with the Danes at *Maldon* (991), are alive with the old fighting spirit of the race.

However direct a share Alfred may have taken in the editing of the *Chronicle*, its improvement is naturally related to that elevation of English prose into a literary importance which is one of the glories of his reign. As the history of English poetry reaches back to that great era when Northumbrian scholarship was paramount in the West, the rise of English prose dates from the court of Alfred at Winchester.

Growth of English prose.

The century and a half which lies between the death of Alfred and the Norman Conquest (901–1066) produced little of sufficient value from a purely literary aspect to detain the general reader. Yet certain features of the period must be fixed in the mind if we would not loose our hold on the continuity of England's mental growth. Although the country ceded to the Danes by the Treaty of Chippenham (878)

From Alfred to the Norman Conquest.

was gradually won back under Alfred's successors, Edward the Elder (901–925) and Athelstane (925–940), Wessex and the South retained that literary and political supremacy which Alfred had begun. After the ravages and final settlement of the Danes, the brilliant literary activity of the North seems to have been extinguished, and for more than three centuries after the death of Alcuin (804) the pathetic silence that settles down on Northumbria remains almost unbroken. In the South alone, where the effects of Alfred's practical enthusiasm still lingered, we find the traditions of culture and the signs of some literary activity. This Southern learning and literature was chiefly associated with great religious foundations and with the history of the Church. The men who rise into literary prominence are chiefly ecclesiastical dignitaries: DUNSTAN (924–988), Abbot of Glastonbury, and afterward Archbishop of Canterbury; ÆTHELWOLD (908(?)–984), Bishop of Winchester; ÆLFRIC (fl. 1006), Abbot of Eynsham, or Ensham, near Oxford. The energies of these men, and especially of the two last mentioned, were largely occupied in introducing into the English monasteries, that had become worldly and corrupt, the stricter rule of life which had already begun to prevail in Gaul and Flanders. They were educational and monastic reformers, and the tone of their work is consequently scholarly or theological. Ælfric "is the voice of that great Church reform which is the most signal fact in the history of the latter half of the tenth century." His *Homilies*, or sermons (990–994), are probably the best examples of Old English or Anglo-Saxon prose that we possess. In bulk the extant writings of Ælfric exceed those even of Alfred. The most important of these writings, except the *Homilies*, are his metrical *Lives of Saints;* but he wrote treatises on grammar and astronomy, translated a considerable part of the Old Testament, and was the author of a number of theological works. He is by far the prose writer of greatest importance after Alfred.

On the whole, we observe that while poetry had held a large place in Northumbria during the era of her literary leadership, the energies of Wessex during this later period find their main outlet in prose. The historic prose of the *Chronicle* (broken occasionally by the chant of the war-song), text-books, sermons, or the lives of saints: such is the shape taken by the literary production of this time.

In the four centuries that lie between Cædmon and the Norman Conquest, England had surpassed every other nation of Northern Europe in literary achievement. None of her neighbours in that early time could boast of such famous scholars, such a body of native poetry and prose. But it cannot be denied that toward the end of this period there was an evident loss of creative power, and many other symptoms of decline. In the tenth century the English seemed to be sinking into a narrow insularity and stagnation. The old impulse that had come from Christianity and Roman culture had apparently spent its force, and the nation waited for the breath of a new impulse. This came suddenly with the Norman Conquest.

Decline of literature before the Norman Conquest.

CHAPTER II.

FROM THE NORMAN CONQUEST TO CHAUCER.

(1066–CIR. 1400).

"Thus com, lo! Englonde into Normandies hond."
(Lo! Thus came England into the Norman's hand.)
— ROBERT OF GLOUCESTER'S *Rhyming Chronicle*, cir. 1298.

"The English at that time (i.e., just before the Conquest) appear to have had little spirit of enterprise; they had settled down into a quiet kind of farmer's life, content with holding their own and keeping off their enemies. The Normans were restless and full of ambition. Wherever there were adventures, and fighting was to be had, Normans would be sure to be there. At the present day the people who wander over the whole world are the English: . . . This is due to the Norman fire and energy, which joined itself to the Teuton perseverance and industry. It was like putting the swift spirit of an eagle into the strong body of an ox." — M. J. GUEST.

"Of one self-stock at first,
Make them again one people — Norman, English;
And English, Norman; we should have a hand
To grasp the world with, and a foot to stamp it —
Flat."

— TENNYSON'S *Harold*.

THE Norman Conquest in England in 1066 begins a new chapter in the history of the English language and litera-
The effect of ture. Indeed, so sweeping were the changes
the Norman wrought by the Norman that it seems at first
Conquest. sight as though almost every vestige of the older England had disappeared. The land was helpless in the mailed hand of a strange ruler; foreigners held the chief offices; the country was filled with these strangers, proud, masterful men, un-English in speech, in dress,

in taste, and in character. Numbers of the great estates passed into the possession of these intruders, until the land-owning class was nearly all composed of Normans. England was a conquered country; and the Norman tower, massive, square, and obdurate, was the sign of the Englishman's subjection, the witness to the hated foreign rule.

The Norman was the last in a long procession of conquering races. From a time before the beginning of recorded history, the island appears to have been swept by wave after wave of foreign invasion, and these primitive struggles were followed by the successive conquest of the Iberian, Celt, and Roman, the Englishman and the Dane. Each of these successive conquerors, except the Roman, made some lasting and especial contribution to the national life. Finally, with the coming of the Norman, a new ingredient was added to the wonderful mixture of character and race. We may compare the land of England to a great crucible, or caldron, over which an unseen power presides, preparing a race for its place in history. At the fortunate time, this unseen power throws new elements into the caldron, — new races, new beliefs, new ideas; and these new elements, at first distinct, are gradually mingled with the old, until they are dissolved, and confusion is again succeeded by comparative unity. After such an interval of confusion and ferment, the Norman, too, was to be stirred in and absorbed. In the end he did not destroy the elements which had existed in the England of Alfred or Harold, but he greatly modified them by contributing something new to English life and literature.

Who, then, were the Normans, and what did they contribute to the progress of English literature? The Normans were originally a mixed horde of piratical adventurers from Scandinavia and Denmark who had won a country for themselves in the North of

France (911). They belonged to a restless, adventurous race, which terrorised Western Europe for three hundred years. Enterprising, quick-witted, open to new ideas, this race of born rulers did more than seize upon some of the fairest lands of Europe. Wherever it went, it appropriated much that was best in the civilisation of those it subdued. True to their race, this was just what the Normans did in France. They were rough sea-rovers when they won Normandy; kinsmen of the Danes who had plundered the English monasteries; they were men of the North, sprung from the same race-stock as the English: yet they had been so changed by their contact with the Southern civilisation that when they conquered England scarcely an outward sign of their origin remained. They spoke a language of Southern origin, for, after they had established themselves in Normandy, they had rapidly acquired the corrupt Latin then spoken in their new home, and raised it to the new dignity of a literary language. They became Christians; they showed a liberal spirit towards learning, and they encouraged the great Italian scholars LANFRANC and ANSELM to settle among them. They built splendid castles and cathedrals; their dress was more splendid than that of the English; their manners were more courtly; they were foremost in instituting chivalry. Their poets, or *trouvères*, chanted long, narrative poems of battle and knightly deeds, differing both in style and spirit from the old Teutonic poetry of the North. Such were the people that became the masters of England in 1066.

The Normans brought so many new ideas and foreign fashions into England that, for a long time, there was great confusion and diversity, as many of the Englishmen were slow to give up the old ways. So it happened that for some time after the Conquest there were two races in England, the Norman and English, separate, and yet forced into daily contact;

Diversities in language and literature.

two languages, Norman-French, the language of the ruling class, and English, the language of the people. Moreover, the Norman had his literature, written, of course, in his own tongue; while the Englishman still held to the literature of his fathers. Besides this, many scholars, English as well as Norman, wrote their prose books, and even some of their poetry, in Latin. There were two distinct literatures and three literary languages. Books in Norman-French and in Latin can hardly be called English Literature, but they are so intimately connected with England's literary development that we should know something of their general character.

The Norman Conquest infused new life into the Church; it improved education, and created a revival of learning **The Latin** in England. England had long since lost her **writers.** intellectual leadership; and during the early part of the eleventh century, while learning languished in England, it had made rapid progress in the great schools of Normandy and France. After the Conquest, nearly all the great places in the Church were given to foreigners, men whose scholarship was generally far superior to that of the English prelates they superseded. Thus the famous Italian scholar and writer Lanfranc (cir. 1005–1089) was taken from the monastic school at Bec, then famous for the part it was taking in the intellectual revival of Normandy, and made Archbishop of Canterbury. From Bec, too, came Anselm (1033–1109) to be Lanfranc's successor in the Archbishopric, a man of rare holiness, and one of the leading writers and thinkers of his age. English bishops were replaced by Normans, and the great monasteries were ruled by abbots of Norman, or Continental origin. When we reflect that nearly all the books were written by the clergy, that they were the recognised historians of the nation, and that the entire system of education was in their hands, we can see at once the importance of this change. During the twelfth and thirteenth centuries a great many books were written in England by these foreign scholars and their pupils, — histories, biographies, and learned treatises on theological or even scientific subjects. But these men were scholars and Churchmen, and they wrote in Latin, the common language of scholarship and of the Church throughout Europe at that time. While, therefore, they did much to advance *learning* in England, their immediate effect on English literature, and especially on English prose, was distinctly unfavourable. Two centuries before the Conquest, King Alfred had tried to bring literature to the people by taking it out of Latin, the language of the learned class, and making it English. In this truly great undertaking Alfred had been at least partially successful. But after the Conquest all this was changed. English was only the despised speech of the lower classes; these new scholars wrote for scholars, and Alfred's broadly democratic idea of literature as a possession of the people was utterly foreign to their character and tone of mind.

Among the most important books in the mass of Anglo-Latin literature are those that deal with English history. During the twelfth century, in the hands of the greater Latin historians, history ceases to be a dry and disconnected *chronicle*, and becomes a more orderly narrative, told with no little literary skill. Some attempt is made to show the underlying relation between events and their causes, and greater attention is given to the portrayal of character. WILLIAM OF MALMESBURY (d. 1143?), one of the best of these Latin historians, was also one of the pioneers in this improved method of writing history. He was of mixed Norman and English descent, but he was Norman in his sympathies. He had the advantage of being connected at different times with the two great Abbeys of Glastonbury and Malmesbury.

His history of England is his most important work (*Gesta Regum Anglorum* and its sequel *Historia Novella*). He also wrote a life of Aldhelm, with whom, as we know, the greatness of Malmesbury Abbey began.[1]

Another of these monastic historians was MATTHEW PARIS (d. 1259), who has been called the last and the greatest of them all. He was a monk in the ancient and splendid Abbey of St. Albans, which was noted at that time for its art and learning. Especial attention was given there to the writing of history, and as a young man Matthew was carefully trained in its *Scriptorium*, or room where manuscripts were copied and enriched with painted designs. In time he rose to be the regular chronicler or historiographer of the abbey. Matthew Paris brought his history down to 1259, the year of his own death; and it is one of its greatest merits that in dealing with recent or contemporary events he endeavoured, as far as he could, to get at the facts for himself, by observation, or by conversing with those who had seen or had taken part in the events he describes. He was well known to King Henry III., who often visited the abbey; and he had many friends among the great. Sometimes he left his devotions to witness a great court ceremony. His history is not a mere compilation from the old records; he painted from life, and no doubt it is his knowledge of the great world outside the walls of his monastery that gives to his work its distinctive freshness and charm.

Matthew Paris.

A little apart from these later historians stands a writer whose fictions, put forth as history, produced more effect on literature than the sober truth. This was GEOFFREY OF MONMOUTH (d. cir.–1154), whose fabulous history of the early kings of Britain (1147) gave Europe new subjects for romance, and thus made an epoch in literary history. Geoffrey deals with a period of British history about which,

Celtic influence on English literature. Geoffrey of Monmouth.

[1] See p. 58, *supra*.

as he complains, Bede is silent.   He tells us how Brutus, the descendant of the Trojan Æneas, came to Albion, or Britain, which was then inhabited by giants, and how he built a new Troy by the river Thames.   In Geoffrey's account of the kings which succeeded Brutus, occur names and stories which were destined to become a part of the world's literature.   We find the story of *Sabrina*, the nymph of the Severn; the story of *King Lear* and his daughters; the story of *Ferrex and Porrex*, which was made the subject of the earliest English tragedy; above all, we find the story of *King Arthur*.   In Geoffrey's book these wonderful stories appear in a comparatively brief and prosaic form.   The story of Arthur, in particular, is very different from that with which we are familiar.   As we shall see, it was reserved for others to lift Geoffrey's rather involved and matter-of-fact record into the magical world of romance, and to elevate Arthur into the heroic pattern of mediæval knighthood.   But to Geoffrey belongs the honour of the pioneer.   He was not a great genius, but he wrote in a popular and entertaining style.   He brought these stories out of obscurity; he put them into Latin, the common language of the educated, and so gave them to Europe.

Many things appear to have contributed to fit Geoffrey for such a task.   He himself was in all likelihood of Welsh descent.   He lived in the Welsh Marches, for Monmouthshire did not become an English county until four hundred years after his time.   He was thus at the meeting-place of three races, for here in the southern part of Wales, Englishmen, Norman, and Celt met on common ground.   He lived, too, in one of the districts especially associated with memories of the great British king.   A little south of Monmouth lay Caerleon, Caerleon-upon-Usk, once a famous British stronghold, where tradition said that Arthur held his court.   We do not know how far Geoffrey used these local legends in compiling his "history," but we do know that he lived and wrote surrounded by the romantic associations of a Celtic past, in that border region which was the meeting-place of Welsh fable and Norman culture.

The influence of this Celtic, or partially Celtic, western district on English literature is not seen in Geoffrey of Monmouth alone. Wales, and the shires along its borders, produced several other writers during the latter half of the twelfth century that left an impress on English literary history. From this Celtic West came WALTER MAP (1140?-1210?) and GERALD DE BARRI, or GERALDUS CAMBRENSIS (1146?-1220), both distinguished wits and scholars at the court of King Henry II. Map was a Welshman, and "almost certainly a native of Hertfordshire." He wrote Latin poems, and is thought to have had a share in the building up of the great romance of King Arthur. Gerald de Barri was born in Wales on the south coast of Pembrokeshire. He was of mixed Norman and Welsh descent; indeed, he was the great-grandson of one of the Welsh Princes. Among his works is an account of a trip he made to Wales (*Itinerarium Cambriæ*, 1191) as the emissary of King Henry II. Another more important writer from this Celtic district was Layamon, whom we shall meet later as the author of the first notable poem written in the English language after the Norman Conquest. The importance of the Celtic element in English literature has already been alluded to, and the influence of the Welsh and their literature at this time is a good illustration of this fundamental fact.

To the Norman influence on English literature, there was thus added the influence of the Celt. Without implying that the second of these two influences was equal in importance to the first, we may safely say that, as the coming of the Norman was the feature of English literary history in the eleventh century, the coming of the Celt was the great feature of the twelfth.

There were many other important Latin writers during the twelfth and thirteenth centuries, but they need not be

Summary. mentioned here. The important thing for us to remember is that for three or four centuries after the Norman Conquest the great bulk of the prose literature in England, and even some of the verse, was written in Latin; that all the serious thinkers of the nation wrote in Latin; and that (with the single exception of the English *Chronicle*) hardly one notable piece of English prose was produced between the coming of the Normans in the latter half of the eleventh century and the work of Chaucer and Wyclif in the latter half of the fourteenth.

The poetry as well as the scholarship of Normandy came into England in the train of the Conqueror. This

The Norman-French literature. poetry differed from the Old English poetry in many ways, and both the time and the manner of its introduction worked together to make it widely influential. When it was brought to England, the great period of Old English poetry was over; while, on the other hand, the great period of Norman poetry had just begun. While the spirit that had produced *Beowulf* and the *Creation* seemed spent, the Normans were fast entering upon a period of poetical production. So at the very moment when English poetry was declining for lack of fresh subjects and inspiration, a new poetry, in the vigour of its youth, was sung at court and castle. England was thus joined to a nation which during the next two centuries was to be a leader in the literary development of modern Europe.

Between the eleventh and the fourteenth centuries, the Norman poets composed a great many long, narrative poems. Some of these poems, inspired by the love of "Fair France" and by pride in her triumphs, tell of the deeds of Charlemagne and his knights, — of "Roland and of Oliver;" some of them are founded on classic stories, and go back to Thebes or Troy; while one large and important group, or *cycle*, of poems, deals with the British King Arthur and with the various adventures of his Knights.

Romances. Other long poems of this period were simply histories in verse. The *Roman de Rou* (or Romance of Rollo), for instance, recounts the history of the Normans from the conquest of Normandy by Rollo to the early part of the reign of Henry I. As a rule, these poems, whether they are romances or histories, are of prodigious length, some of them reaching ten, twenty, or even thirty thousand lines. One of them is said to be sixty thousand lines long, or nearly six times as long as *Paradise Lost*. They show the easy flow of words that is characteristic of the Norman and the Celtic genius, but which is distinctly un-English. While they tell the story pleasantly and fluently, these Norman poets have the lightness of the Frenchman and the Celt; their genius is more lively and flexible than that of the English, but it lacks that gloomy intensity, that depth and concentrated power, which is distinctively Teutonic. At first, as in the famous *Song of Roland*, the chief theme of their poems was battle and knightly heroism, but, as the institution of chivalry developed, love entered more and more largely into their themes, and the Arthurian romances are full of that romantic sentiment, that union of *romantic love, religion,* and *chivalric prowess*, which is peculiarly associated with the Middle Ages.

The Arthurian legends furnished a theme well suited to the spirit of the time; and when Geoffrey of Monmouth

The Arthurian legends. showed the way to the rich stores of Celtic poetry and romance, the poets were not slow to follow him. It is said that within twenty years after the appearance of his "history," the British heroes had

become "household names throughout Europe," and that
" by the close of the twelfth century nearly every existing
literature had assimilated and reproduced the story of
Arthur and his knights." [1] Geoffrey's legendary story of
Britain was put into French verse by GEOFFREY GAIMAR, a
Norman *trouvère*. Then WACE, another *trouvère*, retold it
with sundry additions (1155), and presented his book to
Queen Eleanor, the wife of Henry II. At first Arthur's
reign was made merely an episode in the history of Britain;
but writers soon began to confine themselves to the story
of the hero-king and his knights. Mythical and legendary
elements were constantly added, other stories were inter-
woven with the original theme, and the hero-king of Britain became the central figure in a great cycle of romance.
Many elements contributed to its making. The adventurous and chivalrous spirit of the Normans was combined
with that sense of beauty, wonder, and mystery which
distinguishes the Celt. The Arthurian romances do not
show knighthood as it was, — it was too often coarse, brutal, and cruel, — but they do show us the ideal of chivalry,
the pattern of the true knight. We find Launcelot and
Tristram setting an earthly passion before anything else in
life, but we find also the soldier-saint Sir Percival; we find
men whose trade is war starting in search of the Holy
Grail (the cup used at the Last Supper), the mystical sign
of the Divine presence. With such strangely contrasted
elements there are mingled fragments of ancient heathenism, of the old magic and mystery of the Celt; — the white-
bearded enchanter Merlin, the magic sword wrought by
the Lady of the Lake, the mysterious land of Lyonesse,
and Avalon, where Arthur awaits the hour of his return.

English literature was affected, although to a far less

---

[1] Rhys. *The Arthurian Legend*, p. 289.

degree, by the poetry of other parts of France. The love-

Other French poetry. lyrics of the *troubadours*, the poets of the South as the *trouvères* were of the North, were not unknown in England. Richard I. (1189–1199) was himself a *troubadour*, and delighted in the southern or Provence poetry. [1]

Looking at this Anglo-Norman literature as a whole, whether in Latin or in Norman-French, we must remem-

Summary. ber that while it is foreign or un-English in language, a part of it was written by Englishmen, or by men of Anglo-Norman descent. Many of the Latin chroniclers were Englishmen, although they wrote under the influence of the Norman culture, and so late as the fourteenth century we find the English poet John Gower writing a great part of his poetry in French. Many of the French Romances were translated into English prose; while, on the other hand, an English original seems to have been the basis of the French Romance of Havelock the Dane (*Le Lai de Haveloc*). In this way each literature supplied something to the other; and all through this confused period of borrowing and adapting, of translating and retranslating, the romantic sentiment, the chivalric spirit, the foreign poetic forms, of the Norman were being appropriated by the English and gradually made a part of the literary wealth of the whole nation. Politically the Norman conquered England; but in fact, during the two centuries that followed Hastings, England conquered the Norman, absorbing his good qualities without losing her own, taking for her use such materials for her language and literature as pleased her, yet keeping the essence of her language and her national genius essentially unchanged. Chaucer in the latter part of the fourteenth century was

---

[1] Readers of Scott will remember the introduction of the trouvère *Blondel* in *The Talisman*, and the presentation of Richard as a patron of poetry. See especially chap. xxvi.

the heir of this mixture of the Norman and the English, and in his poetry we see that the union of the two races, the two languages and the two literatures, is practically complete.

For nearly a century and a half after the Norman Conquest (1066–cir. 1205) very little of any importance was **Literature in English 1066–1205.** written in the English language. French was the language of the Court, of the great nobles, of polite society; it was taught in the schools, it was used in the law courts; Latin was the language of the learned, and if a man would gain the ear of the upper classes he must write in French or in Latin. The "low men," the great uneducated mass of the people, held to their mother-tongue with a true English tenacity; but some Englishmen not only learned to speak French, but wrote in French and in Latin. Yet while English was very far from holding the first place in England as a literary language, even during the twelfth century it was not entirely crowded out by its more fashionable rivals, but was rather stubbornly holding its own until better times. Thus the twelfth century was more than half over before the old custom of chronicling the nation's history in English was finally abandoned (1154). A few other works in English have come down to us from this time, sermons, or occasional poems, usually of a religious or didactic character. Yet, when we have pieced together such relics of an English literature as a diligent search can discover, the result is meagre enough beside the great volume of French and Latin which were the real literary languages of the time.

The revival of English literature in thirteenth century. But at the opening of the thirteenth century there are signs that the English language is beginning to win back its literary importance. A great change in the political importance of England, at the beginning of that century, marks the beginning of a new epoch. For one hundred and forty years England had been ruled by foreign kings. Now, in 1204, King John lost nearly all his lands on the Continent, a territory comprising three-fifths of modern France. England could no longer be regarded as the dependency of a foreign power; it was the chief, almost the only dependency of the crown, free once more to follow the bent of its own genius. When John lost Normandy, the antagonism between the English and the Normans had already disappeared. For generations they had lived together in the same island; they had intermarried; they had fought side by side against a foreign enemy; many Normans had learned to speak English, and many English could both speak and write in French. Now, cut off from the rest of the world, they were to draw even closer together, and force the *Great Charter* of liberty from their king.

Some time during these early years of the thirteenth century, English poetry, which had showed but little sign of life since the *Song on the Battle of Maldon* (991), suddenly revived in the *Brut*[1] of LAYAMON (cir. 1205). The end of a foreign rule in England and the rebirth of a true English poetry are thus almost exactly contemporaneous. All that we know of Layamon, he tells us himself in the opening lines of his poem. He was a parish priest in North Worcestershire, and dwelt at Earnley (now Ernley Regis) on the banks of the river Severn. There "came to him in mind and in his chief thought that he would of England tell the noble deeds." So he got books, among others the *Brut* "of the French Clerk that was named Wace," and retold in English the legendary history of Britain. Layamon tells us very little about himself,

Layamon.

---

[1] *Brut* = Brutus, who, according to the fabulous accounts of Geoffrey of Monmouth and others, was the great grandson of Æneas and the founder of New Troy or London. The recitals of British legends were commonly given this name (as Wace's *Brut d'Angleterre*), and the word *Brut* came to mean *chronicle.*

yet his few words make him very real and human to us.
No one who loves books will doubt that this country priest
was a true book-lover. He tells us that he had "to take a
wide journey over the land" to obtain "the noble books"
which he "took for a pattern." We may imagine him returning in triumph with his treasures to his quiet home by
the Severn, and settling to work with a tranquil mind.
"Layamon laid down these books and turned the leaves,
he beheld them lovingly. May the Lord be merciful to
him! Pen he took with his fingers and wrote a book skin,
and the true words set together, and the three books compressed into one." Layamon speaks of using three books,
but he relied chiefly on one. His *Brut*, a metrical chronicle of the legendary history of Britain, is
based mainly on Wace's book, as Wace's *Brut* was
based on the history of Geoffrey of Monmouth. There is
a vein of true poetry in it, unwieldy as it seems, and it is
notable as marking the entrance of many famous stories
into English literature. Let us look for a moment at the
significance of this extraordinary poem. From one aspect
it is almost like a voice from the England of Cædmon or
of Cynewulf. Its vocabulary is almost wholly English, as
hardly fifty words of French origin are to be found in its
thirty thousand lines.[1] At times we recognise the true
fighting spirit of the old English battle-song. Yet, from
another aspect, the poem bears witness to the influence of
those foreign elements which had already entered deeply
into English life and literature. Layamon lived near the
Welsh border, and there, where the land of the Englishman
almost touched the land of the Celt, he pondered over a
Norman's version of a Celtic legend. Layamon's chief material is thus not English, but Norman or Celtic; and his

Layamon's
Brut.

[1] This computation was made by Sir F. Madden, the editor of the
standard edition of Layamon, and it is based on an examination of the
earlier of the two extant versions of the poem.

theme is not the glory of English, but of British heroes. It would be hard to find a better example of the singular fusion of languages and literatures. A Norman *trouvère* and an English poet vie with each other in singing the praises of British Kings. The stories, which Wace the Norman had taken from Geoffrey the Welshman, are now retold by Layamon the Englishman. Three men, of three races, recite the *Brut;* each uses a different language, — the Welshman, Latin; the Norman, French; until finally the work is taken up by the Englishman, and this foreign material is made contributory to English literature.

Two other books may be associated with Layamon's poem, as illustrations of this advance of the English language in literary importance. These are the *Ormulum* (cir. 1215), and the *Ancren Riwle*, or Rule of Anchoresses (cir. 1225). The *Ormulum* takes its name from its author, a monk named *Orm* or *Ormi*.

> "Thiss boc iss nemmnedd Orrmulum,
> Forrthi thatt Orrm itt wrohhte."
>
> (This book is named Ormulum,
> For that Orm it wrought.)

It consists of a paraphrase in English verse of those parts of the New Testament that were appointed to be used in the sermons of the Church, followed by a short sermon, also in verse, on each selection. Its author has been led to think that great profit would follow if English folk would learn and follow this service. The Church services were in Latin, and this is but one among many attempts to familiarise the people with the Bible.[1] The *Ancren Riwle* is a manual, or book of good counsel, pre-

---

[1] The *Ormulum* may be compared with Keble's *The Christian Year* (1827). This is a series of poems on the more important services of the English Church throughout the year, arranged in the order of their occurrence.

pared for three nuns who lived in a monastery in Dorsetshire.

We have seen that during the twelfth century nearly
all the poetry in England was French both in language
French lit- and form. During the thirteenth and four-
erature in teenth centuries, a number of these French, or
English. Anglo-Norman, poems were imitated or reproduced in English. Apparently there was an increasingly
large number of people in England, who, while they enjoyed the French Romances, preferred to hear them in
English. In this way the Anglo-Norman poetry, which,
although produced in England, was foreign rather than
national, now became incorporated with English literature.
This absorption of the French, or Anglo-Norman, literature
by the English is one of the features of the literary history
of this time. Just as Layamon at the beginning of the
thirteenth century put the French chronicle of Wace into
English, with certain additions of his own, so a little later
various French romances of the preceding century began
to reappear in an English dress. Some of these English
romances, such as *Havelok the Dane* (cir. 1270–1280), *Guy
of Warwick* (cir. 1300), and *Bevis of Hampton*, are founded
on Norman versions of Danish or English themes. Havelock, Sir Guy, and Sir Bevis are local heroes, and in these
romances the story of their deeds comes back into English
by way of the French. Some romances, on the other hand,
are taken from stories that are French in origin. But
it is not only in the metrical romances that we see the
traces of the French influence; we see it on every side
colouring English poetry with softer and brighter hues, and
moulding it into new forms. *The Owl and the Nightingale* (cir. 1220), a poem in which the two birds dispute
about the merits of their different ways of living, follows
the fashion of a class of poetry then popular in Southern
France. Another poem, *The Land of Cockaigne* (later

thirteenth century), a clever satire on the gluttony and indulgence of the monks, has a cynical wit that suggests the livelier genius of the Norman.

The English songs, too, some of which have a wonderful grace and melody, certainly owe much to French and **English songs.** foreign influences. Some of these are religious; hymns to the Virgin full of a warmth of adoration which is not English but Southern. Some are war-songs, and they show how the people were beginning to make themselves heard and felt after the great contest with the king in the Barons' War. Others, again, are songs of love and springtime, so true and beautiful, that we, reading them after six hundred years, can still feel the quick pulse of youth and gladness beat in them. Perhaps the most beautiful of these love-songs is the one to Alysoun:

> " Between soft March and April showers,
> When sprays of bloom from branches spring,
> And when the little bird 'mid flowers
> Doth song of sweetness, loudly sing:
> To her with longing love I cling,
> Of all the world the fairest thing,
> Whose thrall I am, who bliss can bring,
> And give to me life's crown.
> A gracious fate to me is sent;
> Methinks it is by heaven lent;
> From women all, my heart is bent,
> To light on Alysoun." [1]

These lines have a delicate and dreamy beauty, a grace and sentiment, which we cannot but feel has been learned from England's foreign masters. But on the other hand we must not conclude that all these English songs were but mere echoes of the French. There is good reason to believe that there was a popular poetry among the English

[1] I have preferred to quote Ten Brink's admirable modernised version. The poem is accessible in its earlier form in *The Oxford Book of English Verse*, and Chambers's *New Encyclopedia of Eng. Lit.*

which the coming of the Norman invaders did not destroy.
It is true that those thirteenth-century songs which have
been written down and preserved are not of this popular
character. They are suggestive of the art of the Norman,
or, perhaps, their verse is the echo of some Latin drinking-
song learned by English students at the University of
Paris. Yet even in these songs scholars have found here
and there a strain that seems to have been taken from the
poetry of the people. In one of the thirteenth-century
love-songs, for instance, there is a refrain not easily forgotten, — superior, I think, in grace and melody to all
the rest of the poem:

> "Blow, Northern wind,
> Send thou me my sweeting,
> Blow, Northern wind, blow, blow, blow!"

Now competent scholars believe that this was not in-
vented by the poet, but borrowed from some old popular
song.[1] The famous *Cuckoo Song* (cir. 1250), which is
redolent of the homely, wholesome life of farmyard and
pasture, is thought to echo the refrain of a popular dance-
song:

> "Summer is a-coming in,
> Loud sing cuckoo:
> Groweth seed and bloweth mead,
> And springeth the wood new.
> Sing cuckoo, cuckoo.
>
> Ewe bleateth after lamb,
> Cow after calf calls,
> Bullock sterteth, buck verteth,
> Merry sing cuckoo,
> Cuckoo, cuckoo, well sings the cuckoo.
> So sweet you never knew,
> Sing cuckoo, now sing cuckoo."[2]

[1] Ten Brink: *Early Eng. Lit.* p. 305, Bohn's ed. See also Professor
Gummere's comment on Ten Brink's view in *The Beginnings of Poetry*,
and Chappell's *Popular Music of the Olden Time*, vol. i. p. 24. The song
is given in Wright's *Specimens of Lyric Poetry*, No. 16, and in *The
Oxford Book of Verse*.

[2] Given in its original form in Ten Brink's *Early Eng. Lit.* 1 p. 305.

But after all the really important matter is not whether a certain refrain, or a certain lyric shows the influence of the folk-song; the really vital fact is the exist-

The popular literature. ence at this time of a truly popular literature.

A great literature is built upon the broad and solid basis of a national appreciation. Almost invariably it is the supreme literary expression of thoughts, feelings, and tastes that are very widely diffused. The fact that from an indefinitely early period English literature has such a popular basis, is therefore a matter of real moment; for on this almost unseen foundation the literary triumphs of a later time were largely based. During these centuries that were preparing the way for Chaucer and for Shakespeare, the people of England had their *songs*, their *ballads*, and their *drama*.

Just as the English people — the ploughmen and shepherds, sailors and artisans — held stubbornly to their own mother-English after the advent of the Nor-

The songs of the people. man, so, beyond any reasonable doubt, they sang the old songs of their fathers and made new ones. Their songs were outside the formal bounds of literature, the wildflowers of the field and forest, not the carefully tended plants of the garden. For we must remember that poetry was not then shut up in print, as it now is. Then it was not merely the possession of a cultivated minority, not merely a thing to be read in a library or studied in a school. It was a possession of the people; it was a thing not of the eye merely, but also of the ear. Thousands sang songs, who could not write nor read them, and men and women worked and played to their singing, and danced to it under the open sky. If we would get a true picture of the England of those days, we must indeed imagine the monk in his *scriptorium* bending over his parchments; we must imagine the *jongleur*, in the castle-hall singing his high-flown romances of love and chivalry; but we must not forget the toilers who had little to do with this world of luxury and of art. To complete the picture we must imagine the villagers singing their songs of harvest, the sailors chanting their rhythmic chorus, the women singing at their spinning, and the youths and maidens singing and dancing to welcome the return of spring.[1]

In some of these *dance-songs*, or *ballads*, a simple story was told in a simple and popular form of verse.[2] The word **Ballads.** *ballad* is a vague one, since it includes songs of various kinds. But when we speak of the "old," or "popular ballads," we commonly mean short, narrative poems, adapted to singing, that have grown up among the people. Such famous ballads as *Chevy Chase*, the *Robin Hood* ballads, belong to this class. Now while nearly all the "old ballads" that have been written down and preserved, are probably later than the thirteenth century, at least in the form in which we possess them, there is good reason to think that ballads of the same, or of a similar, character were made and sung by the people of England and Scotland from a very early time. In the words of a very high authority: "There is ample evidence for the antiquity of the popular ballads in England. Indeed, there is no difficulty in proving beyond a reasonable doubt that there were ballads in plenty from the dawn of English history (not to speak of what lies before this epoch) down to the seventeenth century when printed and written documents begin to abound."[3] We must think, then, of the

---

[1] This may seem fanciful, but it is, I believe, not far from the truth. A little *regulated* imagination probably brings us much closer to the facts in this matter than we should get by ignoring or denying everything not susceptible of absolute demonstration. See Wright's *Political Songs of England,* "Preface," x.

[2] *Ballad,* from Low Lat. *ballare* to dance. For the derivation and various meanings of this word, see Cent. Dict., "ballad" and "ball."

[3] Professor G. L. Kittridge's "Introduction" to *English and Scottish Popular Ballads,* Cambridge ed.

ballad as a part of the life of the people in the thirteenth, fourteenth, and fifteenth centuries. Many of these ballads are lost, but we have enough to show that in them the soul of the people struggled for expression. In them were told brief or simple stories of faithful or faithless lovers, of ghosts and fairies, of battle, and of brave exploits. In them we see the epic and romance of the people; we see a sense of the loveliness of nature, and of the wonder, the poetry, and tragedy of human life, uttering itself perhaps crudely or coarsely, but often, if we may judge from those ballads which remain to us, with a remarkable truth and power.

The third form of the popular literature was the religious drama, the *miracle plays*, or *mysteries*. It will be more convenient for us to speak of these plays later on in connection with the after history of the drama, but we must not forget that chronologically these religious plays belong to the period we are now considering. Passing over the earlier plays in French or Latin, we must note here that from the end of the thirteenth and through the fourteenth and fifteenth centuries, these religious plays were made in English, and produced by and for the people. To understand the full significance of this, we must not regard these plays merely as preludes to the Shakespearean drama, as we are so apt to do. To actor and audience these plays were not a preparation for some unimagined drama of the future; they were an end in themselves. We should go back to these centuries in imagination and see these religious plays in their true relation to the *ballad* and the *song*, as one great channel through which the soul of the masses found literary expression.

Even a brief review of literature during the centuries immediately following the Norman Conquest increases our appreciation of the immense importance of that event

in its relations to literary history. Clearly, without the
Summary. Norman the language and the literature of Eng-
The effects land from the twelfth century to the thirteenth
of the Con- would have been entirely different, and almost
quest on lit- certainly poorer, heavier, duller, and more con-
erature and
language. tracted.   This becomes more apparent when we
enumerate the chief effects of the Conquest on literature
and language, and try to review it in its broadest relations
to the nation's intellectual growth.

I. *The Norman Conquest brought England into direct
contact with a Continental and superior civilisation.* For
nearly one hundred and fifty years after William's victory
at Senlac, England was a dependency of one of the most
cultured and progressive nations in Europe. During this
long period of political union, when kings and prelates,
nobles, scholars, and poets, were passing back and forth
between Normandy and England, the language, the art,
the learning, and the literature of the foreigners were being
absorbed by the English and made subservient to their
national growth.

II. *The Norman civilisation was not Teutonic and Northern but essentially Latin and Southern in character. Thus
for the second time England moved forward under the pressure
of Latin culture.* Throughout nearly all its long history
the literary genius of England has been kindled or sustained
by that of two races very different from that of her own,
the Latin and the Celt. The first definite beginning of literature in England, it will be remembered, was a response to
the introduction of Christianity and Latin culture by the
Roman and Celtic missionaries; another period of literary
advance followed a second infusion of Latin civilization.
Great as is the contrast between the two men, there is
one striking point of similarity between the work that St.
Augustine and that William the Conqueror did for England.

III. *The foreign influence brought in by the Norman came*

when England stood in need of a fresh inspiration. Nearly five hundred years stretch between the landing of St. Augustine and the landing of William, and the impulse given to English thought in the seventh century had lost much of its force. As an outlying island, on the edge of Western Europe, England was constantly in danger of falling behind; she was in need of an occasional stimulus of foreign thought to prevent her from lapsing into an intellectual stagnation, or from becoming narrow and insular in mind. As the eleventh century advances, the need of such an intellectual renewal becomes increasingly apparent. The old poetry is worn out and practically abandoned, and the new poetry has not come. Learning and religion languish. Indeed, there is no reason to doubt the substantial truth of William of Malmesbury's words: "Nevertheless, in process of time, the desire after literature and religion had decayed; for several years before the arrival of the Normans, the clergy, contented with a very slight degree of learning, could scarcely stammer out the words of the sacraments, and a person who understood grammar was an object of wonder and astonishment."[1]

IV. *The new impulse given by Latin culture was followed by an advance in learning, art, and literature.* To what has already been said upon this advance, we must add a few words upon the great improvement in architecture that followed in the wake of the Norman. The foreign ecclesiastics, who poured into England in the train of the Conqueror, had a passion for building and a contempt for the ruder work of their Saxon predecessors. During the twelfth and thirteenth centuries, a great many of the old churches and cathedrals were torn down and replaced by new and more splendid structures, until at last, not a single great church of the earlier times was left. In the twelfth century, the Cistercian monks came to England and built

[1] *Gesta Regum Anglorum* (trans. by J. A. Gates, London, 1847).

many beautiful abbeys. A large part of the religious aspiration, the awe, and the love of beauty, was given a tangible form in these great poems in stone. Such noble
buildings as the great cathedrals of Lincoln and Canterbury and Westminster Abbey were the gift of the Norman,
and such great works have long been a part of the spiritual
inheritance of the English people. While we can only
glance at this effect of the Norman Conquest, it is one that
no student of English literature can afford to ignore. Without these great buildings England would have been poorer
in one great incentive to high emotion. For centuries they
have brought into the daily life of the stolid Englishman
the consecration of their beauty and their majestic repose.
And when the soul of the youthful Milton is stirred by the
grandeur of —

> "The high embowed roof
> With antick pillars massy proof,"

or when Wordsworth records his meditations among the
ruins of the Cistercian Abbey of Tintern, we feel that these
things are surface indications of the profound and subtle
influence of great architecture on great literature, an influence which can never be measured.

V. *The introduction of a new poetic form.* English poetry, as has been said, yielded to the influence of the French,
and the romances of the Norman reappeared in an English
dress. Beowulf and Cædmon were forgotten, and new
English versions of the songs of the *trouvères* ruled in their
place. But not only did the French alter the subjects and
spirit of English poetry, but also through them a great
change took place in its outward form and structure. The
old English device of *alliteration* as a necessary part of
poetic form was gradually abandoned for the French fashion of *rhyme*, although the use of the *accent*, a characteristic
feature of the English versification, was retained in a

developed form.   Alliterative poems were written so late as the fourteenth century; and, although it was given up as an essential structural part of English verse after that time, the poets still frequently introduced it at their pleasure, often with brilliant results.   Nevertheless, while some traces of it remained, the system of Anglo-Saxon versification passed away forever under the pressure of Norman fashions, and a new versification took place, formed to a large extent after the models of the Latin and French.

VI.   *The enrichment and modification of the English language by its mixture with the Norman-French.*   Not the least important consequence of the Norman Conquest was the change it made in the national language.   With this change the fortunes of the literature were inseparably connected.   Words are the material with which the literary artist works; they are to the writer what color or stone are to the painter or the sculptor, and the effects produced by the writer must depend to no small extent upon the quality and the resources of the language he has at his command.   The nature of the language at the command of the English writer was practically settled during the three centuries that followed the Conquest, and it was settled for all time.   Was the England of the future to be a French-speaking or an English-speaking nation?   Was the genius of Shakespeare and of Milton, of Wordsworth and of Tennyson, to have as its appointed instrument of expression a language essentially English, or essentially French?   By the end of the fourteenth century the triumph of English was reasonably certain; and the English language, now known and spoken in almost every corner of the earth, had begun to assume its present form.   The result of the struggle between the two rival languages is manifestly so important that we must indicate briefly how it came about.   For some two hundred years after the Conquest, or until the early part of the thirteenth century, the Norman-French and the English remained separate and distinct. French, as we have seen, had at once taken the first place as the language of poetry. To speak French was a mark of social distinction; it was the language of the king and his nobles, as well as of the Norman retainers and domestics, and of innumerable foreign officials. It became the language of the law-courts, and it was employed in the schools. English was despised as the barbarian speech of a conquered race. Many of the English themselves learned to speak French, and indeed a knowledge of it must have been almost indispensable to social standing or political preferment. On the other hand, many of the Normans learned to understand and even to speak English, finding such a knowledge useful in their daily contact with the mass of the people. In this way it came about that there were numbers, both among the English and the Normans, who could speak both French and English, and who adapted their language to those with whom they happened to converse. Meanwhile the original antagonism between the two races rapidly disappeared. Intermarriages, except between the highest classes, became common; and after the accession of Henry II. (1154–1189), or in less than a century after the Conquest, the marked distinctions between Normans and Englishmen had been almost entirely effaced. But while the two races were thus drawing closer together, two circumstances combined to give the French language an increased importance. The first of these was the establishment of the house of Anjou on the English throne. Henry II. and his immediate successors were masters, directly or indirectly, of the greater part of France, and England was thus joined not only to Normandy, but also to many other French possessions. England was by no means the largest part of the king's dominions, and French was the native language of the people in most of the countries over which

he ruled. While the English were thus brought closer to
the foreign nobles and to French-speaking populations of
the Continent, French literature, and particularly French
poetry, was rapidly growing in influence and importance.
The popularity of the French poetry in England, and the
neglect and decadence of the native verse, tended to con-
firm the supremacy of the French language, but, in spite of
all this, the bulk of the English people, with a true British
conservatism, kept doggedly to the use of their mother-
tongue.

When England was joined to the Continent by the Norman Conquest, it was as though a bridge had been laid
across the channel by which French and Latin
culture could pass over; when King John lost
nearly all of his Continental possessions at the
beginning of the thirteenth century, it was as though that
bridge had been broken down. The loss of Normandy
suddenly ended a connection between England and
Europe that had lasted for nearly one hundred and
fifty years. The steady influx of French influence
was thus cut off; insular England was suddenly thrown
once more upon her own resources, transformed at a
stroke from the province of a French-speaking nation
to an independent island power. Henceforth England
was to be "for the English," and such a change was
bound to promote a general adoption of the English speech.
This result, while it was certain to come, came slowly. We
have already seen how during the thirteenth century the
books written in English increased in numbers and in volume, how French romances reappeared in an English dress,
and how the dominant spirit of the time was a defiant
hatred of foreign aggression and of papal interference, of
foreign favourites of the king, and a patriotic devotion to
the liberties of England. "The English were despised like
dogs," wrote a poet after the victory of the people at Lewes,

The triumph of English.

"but now they have lifted up their heads and their foes are vanquished."

Nevertheless the French language retained much of its social and literary importance. It is probable indeed that English was steadily gaining ground; but Robert of Gloucester, writing towards the end of the thirteenth century, could yet declare that "unless a man knows French, he is little thought of. But low men keep to English and their own speech still." [1] During the early half of the fourteenth century this stubborn "holding to English" on the part of the great mass of the population had secured the ultimate triumph of the native speech. The Hundred Years' War against France, begun in 1336 while Edward III. was on the throne, probably helped to bring French into disfavour, and to promote the more general adoption of English. After 1349 English instead of French began to be used in the schools as the medium of instruction. In 1362 Parliament passed an act providing that the pleadings in the law-courts should thenceforth be in English, "because the laws, customs, and statutes, of this realm, be not commonly known in the same realm for that they be pleaded, showed, and judged in the French tongue." The rising spirit of independence that had characterised the thirteenth century, the severance from France, followed by actual war upon her, increased the popularity of the English speech.

Men recognised the claims of English upon their patriotism. One author in the early half of the fourteenth century declares:

> "Right is that Inglishe Inglishe understond,
> That was born in Inglond." [2]

[1] "Vor bote a man conne Frenss, me telþ of him lute;
Ac low men holdeth to Engliss and to hor owe speche yute."
— *Rhyming Chronicle*, cir. 1297.

[2] The metrical romance of *Arthur and Merlin*, cir. 1350.

Another author, probably a contemporary of Chaucer, writes in the same spirit: "Let clerks indite in Latin, and let Frenchmen in their French also indite their quaint terms, for it is kindly to their mouths; and let us show our fantasies in such words as we learned of our own mother-tongue." [1] But while French was being thus given up, there was as yet no one national English established and understood throughout the whole of England. One kind of English was spoken in the north, another in the middle districts, and another in the south, and even these three forms were split up into further dialects. These three dialects are commonly known as the Northern, Midland, and Southern English. During the latter part of the fourteenth century the East Midland English, or that spoken in and about London, which was in the eastern part of the Midland district, asserted itself above the confusion and gradually became accepted as the national speech. Midland English had an importance as the language of Oxford and Cambridge, as well as that of the capital and the court, and its supremacy was further due to its being made the language of literature. The language of Wyclif's translation of the Bible (1380), a variety of this Midland form, is plainly the parent of the noble Bible English of our later versions. The poet JOHN GOWER (1330–1408) gave up the use of French and Latin to write in the *King's* or Court English; and, more than all, it was in this same East Midland English of the court that Geoffrey Chaucer wrote his poems. These works did much towards giving to East Midland English a supremacy that it never lost.

But this triumph of English was a partial triumph; for, when during the fourteenth century a national language

[1] *The Testament of Love*, a poem of uncertain authorship formerly attributed to Chaucer and supposed to have been written before 1388.

began to emerge out of all this confusion of tongues, it was not the purely Teutonic speech of the earlier time.

The French element in English. When Chaucer wrote, the language of the East Midland district was no longer a pure English; there, as elsewhere, the local variety of the native speech had been modified by a large infusion of French. It was a mixed language, still substantially English in its foundations of grammar and construction, but a composite, so far as its vocabulary was concerned, of the two rival tongues. The barriers between the two languages, so long kept separate, had been broken down; and between 1300 and 1350 a vast number of French words passed over into English. Our modern English is thus built out of Teutonic and Romance (that is, French and Latin) elements, and these two elements have contributed about equally to its vocabulary. Yet, in spite of the strength of these foreign influences, the language of Chaucer and of Tennyson is English rather than French. The words brought in from the French have proved a most desirable addition to the language; but, while they add enormously to its dignity and its resources, the French words are, after all, annexed to the English language, and they are a luxury, not a necessity. The little, indispensable words that form the basis of the language, the words that we use the oftenest, are English and not French. We can make ourselves understood if we discard the French element and use words of English origin only, but we can hardly frame an intelligible sentence made up entirely of words imported into English from the Latin or French. Yet, while this Saxon English may suffice for the bare necessities of speech, while at times it may even be amply sufficient, the obligations of both the English language and literature to the Romance element cannot be measured. It is this mingling of Romance with Teutonic, this fusion of two languages, that has given to modern English many of the peculiar virtues of each and made it the richest and noblest instrument of literary expression which men have created for their use since classic times. By virtue of this union of opposites, English can be rugged, strong, terse, simple, and direct, or it can be sonorous, flowing majestic, and melodious. It is as though something soft, sweet, and feminine were united to something full of rough and masculine vigour; and, as a rule, the passages that are the glories of the literature owe their distinctive style to a blending of Saxon elements with the French, and to a conscious or unconscious appreciation of the advantages to be gained from each. The benefit that the language has derived from the assimilation of this Romance element is but another illustration of the deep and various obligations of the English to the Latin genius. It helps to impress us afresh with the conviction that there was something in the quality of that Latin civilisation of the South which the great Teutonic race of the North needed to inspire it, to supplement its deficiencies, and to carry it forward to its full growth.

As we look back to the beginnings of the literature, we see that not only the Latin element but many others had combined in this composite England, and that the way was made clear for a great poet who should record the capabilities of the plastic language, and whose genius should express this union of diverse elements. That poet was Geoffrey Chaucer.

CHAPTER III.

THE AGE OF CHAUCER.

CHAUCER'S CENTURY.

"Forget six counties overhung with smoke,
    Forget the snorting steam and piston stroke,
    Forget the spreading of the hideous town;
    Think rather of the pack-horse on the down,
    And dream of London, small, and white, and clean,
    The clear Thames bordered by its gardens green;

While nigh the thronged wharf Geoffrey Chaucer's pen
    Moves over bills of lading."
                                        —WILLIAM MORRIS.
                                    Prologue to *The Earthly Paradise.*

To get near to Chaucer, to read his poetry with entire sympathy and delight, one must forget our modern world for the time and go back in imagination into that other world of the fourteenth century, in the midst of which he lived and worked. There was much in that world to fire the imagination and to quicken the energies of a great poet. It was a brilliant, stirring, and ambitious time, when life was full of violent and dramatic contrasts. It was peculiarly a time of change. Europe was already restive under the leaven of new ideas. Here and there men were beginning to grow impatient of the old restraints and conventions, and to rebel against long established institutions or accepted modes of thought. The old order indeed yet remained; but, as we look back to the fourteenth century and interpret it by our knowledge of the centuries that followed, we see plainly signs of a new order, a new way of living, and a new conception of life. Europe, still mediæval, was on the threshold of the Renaissance. Chaucer's world was mediæval; he grew up under the influences of mediæval literature and mediæval ideas. Yet it was also the world of the coming Renaissance, shaken and stimulated by new ideas. We cannot study the history of this time without finding traces of the new spirit growing under the old forms, which it will presently break and utterly destroy.

Chivalry, for instance, was a peculiarly mediæval institution, and in the fourteenth century chivalry still flourished Chivalry. in even more than its former pomp and splendour. In England, the reign of Edward III. was marked by a showy magnificence. In that reign the war between England and France, known as the Hundred Years' War, was begun, and this contest between two powerful and chivalric nations was the occasion of a great display of knightly deeds. Then, as Froissart wrote, were many "honourable and noble adventures of feats of arms, done and admired." [1] It was in this reign that Edward, the Black Prince, when a boy of sixteen, won his spurs at Creçy, and that the blind king of Bohemia was guided by his own command into the thick of the battle "that he might strike one stroke with his sword." The heart of the old chronicler Froissart kindles as he recites the names of the gallant knights who fought for England: "they in all their deeds were so valiant that they ought to be reputed as sovereigns in all chivalry." "Also in France at that time there were found many good knights, strong and well expert in feats of arms; for the realm of France was not so discomfited but that always there were people sufficient to fight withal." In England the outward forms and shows of chivalry were yet an accepted part of the nation's life. Edward was a patron of the tournament; he had a Round Table at

[1] Froissart's *Chronicles*, Berner's ed. chap. ii.

Windsor, in emulation of that of King Arthur; he instituted the famous chivalric Order of the Garter.

There are many other things in this England of the four-teenth century to remind us that Chaucer lived in a me-

Chaucer's England.

diæval world. If we have the splendour and romance of the Middle Ages, we have also the dirt and squalor, the crude ignorance and the unspeakable coarseness, which were at least equally char-acteristic of that time. The land itself is in part sheer wilderness. There are great stretches of forest, the haunts of the deer, the grey wolf, the boar, and the wild bull; there are marshes, such as the great fens of Lincolnshire and Somerset, untenanted as yet save by the birds. It is a rough, cruel world; life is none too safe even on the king's highway. The townspeople dwell within walls and shut the gates at curfew. At Newcastle-on-Tyne, near the Scotch border, where marauding bands swoop down, as the Douglas did against the Percies, a hundred armed citizens keep nightly watch upon the walls. London itself, except on the side towards the river, was still a walled town; the houses were chiefly of wood and timber; the streets, nar-row and unpaved, sloped to a gutter or open sewer in the middle, foul with refuse; but the Thames was still clear and beautiful, and beyond the city gates lanes led the Lon-doners through fair meadows, where the tender spring green of the grass was starred by the daisies that Master Chaucer loved to greet and honour. A stone bridge, with houses built on either side of its narrow roadway, connected Chau-cer's London with Southwark on the opposite of the Thames. At Southwark there were fields and gardens, and round wooden buildings for bear-baiting or cock-fighting; there, near the end of the bridge, was the old Tabard Inn, in whose square courtyard motley companies of pilgrims were wont to gather on their way to the shrine of St. Thomas à Becket at Canterbury.

But this strange, picturesque, and narrow world of the Middle Ages was already near its end. Already the new world was beginning to push it aside. While Edward was founding a new order of chivalry, his Knights of the Garter (1344), a new instrument of destruction, the cannon, was being introduced into warfare which was to revolutionise the art of war. Before long this new invention, unimportant at first, was to shatter the solid masonry of the feudal castles and make the armour of the knight a useless encumbrance. Meanwhile the supremacy of the knight was threatened by a new power, the rising power of the English people. There are many signs of this. The battles in the Hundred Years' War are memorable not merely for their display of chivalric courage and courtesy, but also for the great part played in them by the people of England. The truly significant feature of these battles is indeed not the splendid spectacle of knightly gallantry; it is rather the effectiveness of the English yeomen, the archers whose "grey-goose shafts" did so much to turn the day at Creçy and Poitiers. It has been said that this national character of the English army, this triumph of the foot-soldier over cavalry, was "the death-knell of Feudalism."

The popular spirit, asserting itself in unconscious rivalry or in open opposition to the feudal power of king and barons, found at the same time a political expression in the establishment of the Commons as a separate branch of the Parliament. Beneath all the ostentatious magnificence of the early part of Edward's reign, we see the transfer of the real power from the king to the people; and, by a singular irony, Edward parts with some of his royal privileges that he may carry on the contest with France. The chivalric pride of Edward's army was thus sustained by an increase in the rival power of the people. Finally, in the "Good Parliament" of 1376, we find the "Commons" united against their feudal superiors, the Baronage and the King.

Many things combined to produce a popular demand for liberty and equality that was curiously modern. The old manorial system of land tenure was being abandoned for one which secured greater independence to the labourer, but the chief causes of this popular uprising were probably the unsettled state of labour, the bitter discontent and the growing importance of the working-classes, which followed the successive visitations of a terrible plague called "The Black Death." It is difficult for us who live in a world made comparatively clean, comfortable, and decent, to imagine the abject misery to which the English people were reduced by this loathsome and often fatal disease. The first of this awful series of pestilences reached England from Southern Europe in 1348, two years after the brilliant victory of Creçy, and from that time until nearly the end of the century the land was desolated by periodical recurrences of the disease. The number of deaths was very great, for, besides those who died of the plague, many more perished miserably from want and hunger. Famine followed the pestilence, as some farms had been left untilled, some had but scanty crops, and on others, for want of labourers, the harvests rotted in the fields. The land was filled with vagrants, driven by illness and starvation to beggary or theft. The organisation of labour was unsettled, and the very foundations of society seemed shaken. The people, thus laden with a burden that seemed almost too heavy to bear, were called upon to pay a heavy tax to defray the cost of the French war. The poor were arrayed against the rich; they questioned and scoffed at the class distinctions that were so inseparable a part of the feudal society, and rose in armed revolt. The age of the courtly Froissart is thus also the age

The Black Death.

of a peasantry pushed forward by new economic conditions
to fight against the old order of society. While the
French chronicler celebrates the glories of Knighthood,
the English people are singing the crude rhyme:

> "When Adam delved and Eve span,
> Who was then the gentleman?"

This feeling found a spokesman in the revolutionary
teachings of John Ball, "the mad Priest of Kent."

The new democracy. Crowds gathered about Ball in the cloisters of
Canterbury Cathedral, and "many of the mean
people loved him" and affirmed that "he saith
truth." Inside the great cathedral was the rich shrine
of St. Thomas à Becket, the goal of many a mediæval
pilgrimage, but outside in the cloisters the voice of the
preacher seems to be the voice of the modern world.
"What have we deserved, or why should we be kept
thus in servage? We be all come from one father and
mother, Adam and Eve: whereby can they say or show
that they be greater lords than we be, saving by that
they cause us to win and labour for that they dispend?
They are clothed in velvet and camlet furred with grise![1]
and we be vestured with poor cloth; they have their wines,
spices, and good bread, and we have the drawing out of
the chaff and drink water: they dwell in fair houses, and
we have the pain and travail, the rain and wind, in the
fields; and by that that cometh of our labours they keep
and maintain their estates."[2] Ball's teachings were socialistic: he declared that "everything should be common;"
and many, while they stopped short of this extreme,
shared in his democratic feeling and in his demand for
a social reform. In the *Vision* of William Langland,
the poet of the people, the Plowman warns the Knight

---

[1] Grey: here the grey fur of the squirrel or rabbit.
[2] Froissart's *Chronicles*, chap. ccclxxxi.

that the class distinctions, of which men then thought so much, were but temporal things, of but little moment beside the eternal difference between the good and the evil. "And if thou ill-use not thy bondman thou mayest speed the better; though he be here thy underling, in heaven it may well hap that he be set higher and in greater bliss than thou, except thou do better and live as thou shouldest; *Amice, ascende superius*;[1] for in the charnel house at the church it is hard to know churls, or a knight from a knave; know this in thine heart."[2]

In religion, too, we notice signs of a coming change. Mediæval Christianity was still supreme; the Church

Religion.

was enormously wealthy and powerful; prelates dressed richly and lived in ostentatious luxury; her services were splendid and impressive. In England Westminster Abbey was being enlarged; noble cathedrals were being erected; the great builder, William of Wykeham, was busy at Winchester. But the forces of disruption were already active. The Church no longer inspired that devotion which we find in the days of the earlier crusades. In 1309 the Pope removed from Rome to Avignon, and the reverence and awe with which he had been regarded were greatly lessened when men saw him made the political tool of the growing power of France. Englishmen resented the Pope's interference in the affairs of their kingdom; they refused (1366) to pay the tribute which England had paid the Pope since the reign of King John. The sale of pardons, and the multiplying corruptions and abuses in the Church, the sordidness and lack of spirituality in many of its clergy, moved

---

[1] "Friend, go up higher."   St. Luke, xiv. 10.

[2] Langland's *Vision of Piers the Ploughman*, ed. by Kate M. Warren, p. 91.   *Cf.* Shirley, "A Dirge:"

> "Sceptre and crown
> Must tumble down," etc.

earnest men to scorn and satire. The Church of the Middle Ages, like the feudalism of the Middle Ages, was shaken by the modern spirit, and the Reformation was at hand.

The old educational system, the scholastic learning of the Middle Ages, was still intrenched at Oxford and Cambridge. Two Oxford scholars, DUNS SCOTUS (d. 1308), and WILLIAM OF OCCAM (d. cir. 1349), are among the last of the mediæval schoolmen. The Oxford *Clerk* in the *Canterbury Tales* delighted in Aristotle, an author of the first importance in the old education of the monastic schools. Yet a "new learning" had already arisen in Italy; a liberation of the intellect had already begun in which Chaucer himself shared. Twenty years before Chaucer's birth Dante, the first supremely great poet since the classic writers, had died in exile at Ravenna, leaving behind him in his *Divine Comedy*, the supreme expression of the world of Mediæval Christendom. When Chaucer was a year old, Petrarch, poet and scholar, and the great pioneer in the new way of thinking and feeling, was crowned with laurel at Rome. Boccaccio was pointing out in the prose tales of his *Decamerone*, the fresh and careless pleasure in love, laughter, and the beauty of this world, that was to characterise the Italy of the Renaissance.

The new learning.

Art, too, guided by the same new impulse, was freeing itself from mediæval restrictions. Sculpture was advancing in the work of such men as *Niccola Pisano* and *Ghiberti*, and in painting *Giotto* (1276–1337) stands at the beginning of a new and mighty era in the history of art. In England, these social, religious, and intellectual changes, which marked the breaking up of the mediæval and the beginning of the modern world, found expression in three great writers, *William Langland, John Wyclif,* and *Geoffrey Chaucer*.

LITERATURE IN THE FOURTEENTH CENTURY.

Literature in fourteenth-century England shows that diversity in language, that confusion of traditions and ideals, which characterised the time. When the century opened, London had not yet taken its place as the literary centre of the nation; literature was still local, and writers of the North, South, or middle West still used the dialect, or form of English, peculiar to their section. Before the century closed, a comparative order and unity had emerged from the confusion; the East-Midland dialect had won the ascendency, and a truly national literature had been begun. The part played by Langland, Wyclif, and Chaucer in this memorable transition cannot be understood without some knowledge of the provincial or minor literature of the time.

The earlier writers of the century took up and carried forward the work of their immediate predecessors without any marked break or change. In the latter half of the thirteenth century, Northumbria, the old home of poetry and culture, had given promise of a literary revival; and during the first half of the century following, several remarkable works were produced in the North. Among them the *Cursor Mundi* (cir. 1320–5), a poem of nearly thirty thousand lines, on the course of human history, holds an important place.[1] The author of this vast work, nearly three times as long as *Paradise Lost*, is unknown; but it is thought to have been written in the diocese of Durham. Like the paraphrases of

Literature in the North.

---

[1] *Cursor Mundi*, so-called because it runs over the history of the world. At the beginning of one of the many manuscripts of the poem an unknown hand has written:

"This is the best boke of alle,
The cours of the werlde men dos hit calle."

See TEN BRINK, *Eng. Lit.* i. p. 289.

Cædmon and his school, the *Cursor Mundi* is based on the Bible; but the author has also drawn from other sources, and introduced many mediæval legends and traditions into the original narrative. The occasion for poems of this character in the Middle Ages is apparent. To make the Bible intelligible to the masses, it was necessary to render it into the vulgar tongue; and in those days, when the people were densely ignorant and slow-witted, men sought to make the chief events of Bible history vivid and interesting to the populace. The *Cursor Mundi* is thus obviously connected with the miracle plays, and especially with the so-called *Collective Mystery*, which presented the course of the sacred narrative in a series of dramatic scenes.

Among this group of Northern writers is the strange figure of RICHARD ROLLE, the Hermit of Hampole. This man, Richard Rolle, of Hampole. eccentric as he may appear to modern eyes, was one of the influential and typical personages of his time. Born at Thornton in Yorkshire about the end of the thirteenth century, he came as a youth to study at Oxford, at this time the rival of the University at Paris as a school of learning. But the hard logic of the Schoolmen failed to satisfy the emotional side of his deeply religious nature, and at nineteen Rolle left Oxford and returned home, resolved to become a hermit and give himself up to prayer and contemplation. He made a hermit's habit for himself out of two of his sister's kirtles, one white and the other grey; and, slipping his father's cloak over this improvised costume, he retired to a neighbouring wood. Shortly after he preached a sermon which so impressed the Squire, Sir John Dalton, that he supplied the youthful hermit with a more appropriate dress and the means of subsistence. Rolle was a true mystic, a man to whom the invisible seemed very real and near, but he did not spend all his life in an ecstasy of meditation. He believed in good works also, and wandered through Northern Yorkshire, preaching to the people. He made a metrical version of the Psalter, and wrote many religious works both in prose and verse. He settled finally in Hampole, in Southern York-shire, where he died in 1349, the year of the first pestilence. Whether we view him as a man or as an author, Rolle amply repays our study. He is a mediæval saint and mystic, yet he rebels against the fetters of scholasticism, and he speaks to the common people in plain English with the zeal of a Protestant reformer. In this abandonment of Latin for English he anticipated Wyclif, and in his recognition of the importance of good works he resembled Langland. From one aspect he represented the spirit of the past, from an-other he seems the herald of the future. Rolle's work marks a forward step in the advance of English prose. Earnest and devout, he rises at times to a true eloquence, and in some purely narrative passages his style is strong, simple, and clear. He bears witness to those abuses of the time which a little later called forth the invective of Lang-land, and the following passage reads like a prose version of *Piers the Plowman*. Dread, describing the torments of the sinful, says that he saw in hell — "Riche men with their servants that the poor harmed; Doomsmen that would not doom, but it were for mede; — Workmen that falsely swynkis (work) and take full hire; — Prelates that have care of men's souls, that neither chastise nor teach them."[1] Besides his prose Rolle made a metrical version of the Psalter, and composed a long poem, called *The Prick of Conscience*, and a number of religious lyrics. In these poems, as in Rolle's other work, rhapsodies of devotion alternate with gloomy reflections on the horrors of death and corruption, the instability of earthly glories, and the pitiful weakness and wretchedness of man's earthly lot.

[1] *Richard Rolle of Hampole;* Yorkshire Writers, i. 153. Passage quoted has been modernised.

He has a mediæval contempt for the body; he broods on death and the grave with a morbid intentness:

> "For in is world es nane swa witty,
> Swa fair, swa strang, ne swa myghty,
> Emperour, kyng, duke, ne caysere,
> Ne other at bers grete state here,
> Ne riche, ne pure, bond ne fre,
> Lered or lawed,[1] what swa he be,
> That he ne sal turne at the last oway,
> Til poudre and erthe and vyle clay;
> And wormes sal ryve hym in sondre." [2]

Trite as these reflections are, they are noteworthy because the mood is so characteristically English. In spite of all those alien influences with which England has been saturated, influences from which Rolle himself was by no means exempt, there remains the substratum of English seriousness and English religion. Here in this fourteenth-century mystic is the spirit which produced that unknown Anglo-Saxon's poetic meditations on the Grave,[3] the spirit that speaks in Raleigh's famous apostrophe to Death, the spirit that moves Hamlet to a curious interest in the business of the gravedigger, and prompts him to say to Yorick's skull, "Now get you to my lady's chamber and tell her, let her paint an inch thick, to this favour she must come." *The Prick of Conscience* (c. 1340), Rolle's most important work, is a sombre, distressful poem, addressed to the unlearned, "that can ne Latyn understand," and intended, by its dreadful picture of death and judgment, to prick the reader's conscience, so that he may "work good works and flee folly."

With these religious poets we may mention LAWRENCE MINOT, who wrote patriotic lyrics in commemoration of the

---

[1] Learned or ignorant (lewd).

[2] *The Prick of Conscience*, l. 880 f.

[3] This poem is given (in translation) in Morley's *English Writers*, II. 333.

foreign victories of Edward III. Next to nothing is known
of Minot, but he is supposed to have come from the border

region between the South-Midland district and
Lawrence Minot. the North. His songs are of no great poetical
merit, but Minot sings the deeds of his heroes
with the enthusiasm of an old-time gleeman celebrating
the triumphs of his chief, and his lyrics at least suggest
to us the rising spirit of national pride.

Fourteenth-century England had also a rich inheritance
in the world of ballad and romance. Marvellous tales of
magic and knightly adventure, which the Eng-
Romance. lish had appropriated from Wales and Ireland,
from Normandy and Brittany, had become a popular
possession. Wandering minstrels still rehearsed the old
stories of romance. Jugglers still made mirth in the
castle-hall, and in the farm or village ballads were made
or sung. Men still believed in marvels; they were capable
of fear, wonder, and awe in the presence of the unseen;
and the land was "fulfilled of fayerye." In the middle
years of the century, probably about 1370, when Chaucer
in London was just entering upon his poetical career, a
poet in the Welsh Marches wrote one of the most beautiful
of English romances, *Sir Gawayne and the Green Knight*.
Of this poet absolutely nothing is known; some are inclined to think that he lived in Cheshire. In any case,
the dialect in which his poem is written indicates that its
nameless author came from somewhere in that border
region, the country of Geoffrey of Monmouth and of Layamon, which was a meeting-place for the genius of the English and the Celt. The story of *Sir Gawayne* need not be
told here, for no summary could do justice to its peculiar
and fantastic charm. It is enough to say that the hero,
the brave and noble Knight of earlier legend, not the
light-minded and dissolute Gawayne of Tennyson's
Idylls, sets forth alone upon a dangerous enterprise;

that he is sorely tempted, and that, though he does not come through scathless, he yet succeeds in preserving his knightly honour essentially pure and unstained. A moral purpose runs through the story. Gawayne, seeking to save his own life, stoops to deceit, and is wounded because of his lack of perfect openness and loyalty. He owns his fault with a frank humility, declaring that he will henceforth wear the green girdle (which he had trusted would protect him by its magical virtue), not as a charm, nor for its jewels and samite, but as a sign of his transgression, that he may remember his weakness in prosperity, when he "rides in renown." There are traces in *Sir Gawayne* of French and perhaps of Celtic sources, but its freshness and originality are far more important than its relation to the past. This unknown poet was no servile imitator of foreign models; he could appropriate foreign material, and use it in his own way. There is, moreover, a blending of native and foreign elements which is highly significant. It suggests the close of the long period of apprenticeship to French masters; it suggests that the native English genius, having "spoiled the Egyptians," is about to pass out of the land of bondage. In *Sir Gawayne* the old fashion of alliteration is revived, although the old metrical form is not preserved. Moreover, the author evidently saw Nature for himself; and instead of the conventional landscape of the French romances, with its soft grass, its buds and flowers, we find the cliffs and forests of the Welsh mountains. Instead of the traditional May morning, we meet with pictures of the bleaker and rougher aspects of nature that recall the sterner note of the Anglo-Saxon. Gawayne journeys in winter through a harsh and forbidding wilderness. He scales cliffs, he fords streams, he sleeps in his iron harness on the naked rocks. At last he approaches his destination:

"At morn by a mountain he merrily rideth,
  Through a forest full deep that was wondrous and wild,
  High hills on each hand, with a wood stretching under
  All full of hoar oaks, a hundred together;
  The hazel and hawthorne, entwined in a tangle,
  The rough, ragged moss on every side streaming,
  And birds sitting sadly perched on the bare branches,
  Most piteously piped for pain of the cold.[1]

There is also an appreciation of the various aspects of
Nature remarkable in that early time. Three hundred
years before Thomson published the *Seasons*, the poet
of *Sir Gawayne* packed into thirty lines the germ of Thomson's poem. The changes wrought by the successive
seasons are brought before us by a few suggestive details.
We follow the course of the "revolving year" until

— "All ripens and rots that bloomed at first,
  And thus runneth the year into yesterdays many,
  And winter winds round again as the world asketh."

With the romance of *Sir Gawayne* we may associate
three other poems, *Cleanness, Patience,* and *The Pearl.*
Cleanness,   These have been handed down to us in the
Patience, and same manuscript as *Sir Gawayne,* and are writ-
The Pearl.   ten in the same dialect. This has led many to
conjecture that all four poems are the work of the same
nameless author. Both *Cleanness* and *Patience* have a
distinctly moral purpose, being intended, as their titles
imply, to enjoin the duty of purity and of submission to
the Divine will. The beautiful elegy of *The Pearl,*[2] "our
earliest *In Memoriam*," teaches the same lesson of resig-

[1] *Sir Gawayne and the Green Knight,* l. 740. In modernising the
above passage an attempt has been made to preserve as far as possible
the spirit of the original at the expense of a literal accuracy.

[2] It is proper to say that Professor Schofield of Harvard dissents
from the usual interpretation of *The Pearl.* He contends that it is
not an elegy, the expression of grief for a personal loss, not the lament
of a father for the loss of his child, but a theological disquisition. See
his interesting paper in the publications of the Modern Language Association.

nation. A father, overcome with grief at the death of his little daughter, is taught to rise above the merely earthly view of his loss, and to accept it with faith and patience. The poet in the true mediæval spirit has treated this theme in the form of an allegory. He tells us that he has lost a precious jewel in his arbour, a spotless pearl, that has slipped from the grass into the ground. To this arbour he comes mourning on a day in August, when the corn is cut with the sickle, and falls asleep above the grassy spot where his lost pearl lies. Then, while his body sleeps, his soul leaves the earth and comes, by God's grace, to a far country, very strange and beautiful. He sees hills crowned with shining cliffs of clear crystal, with a wonderful forest near by, in which the tree-trunks are azure and the leaves are gleaming silver. Surrounded by such beauty he forgets his grief. He follows a path through the woods until he comes to a broad river, whose banks gleam as the beryl stone. Jewels gleam from its dark depths, as stars glimmer in the sky on a winter night when weary men sleep. He longs to cross this stream, but cannot. At length, filled with longing, he sees a little maid, clad in glistening white and more radiant than gold, standing in the sunshine on the farther shore, and she is adorned with pearls. She comes nearer, and he speaks to her:

> "'O Perle,' quoth I, ' in perles pyght,
> Art thou my perle that I haf playned
> Regretted by myn one, an nyghte?
> Much longeyng haf I for the layned,
> Sythen into gresse thou me aglyte; —
>
> . . . .
>
> What wyrde has hyder my juel wayned
> And don me in del and gret daunger?
> Fro we in twynne wern towen and twayned
> I haf been a joyles jueler.'"

Then the child rebukes and comforts him. She tells him that his pearl is not lost, but safe; that the treasure he lost was no jewel, but a rose that like all roses had to bloom and fade, and that now this rose had become a pearl of great price. The father is finally granted a sight of the Heavenly City, and he sees his child among the glad and shining train, his pearl that he had loved and lost.

So far in this survey of this period, we have seen during the early half of the century, the signs of literary activity in the North, followed by a remarkable development of alliterative poetry in the West-Midland district. But during the latter half of the century, London, the birthplace and residence of Chaucer, the greatest poet that England had yet produced, became for the first time the literary centre of the country. Up to this time London, notwithstanding its size and political position, had been of no literary importance. The educational, intellectual, and literary activities of the nation had centred now at Canterbury, or Jarrow, now at York, or Winchester, at Oxford or the Welsh border. But with the advent of Chaucer and his fellow-poet the learned John Gower (1330–1408), the geographical centre of England shifted once and forever, and London became the literary capital of the whole people. From that time to this, from Chaucer to Shakespeare, from Shakespeare to Pope and Johnson, from Johnson to Carlyle, the scene of England's literary history is laid in the streets and theatres, the taverns, clubs, and coffee-houses of the city of London.

London becomes literary centre.

The effect on language of this ascendency of London and the East-Midland district has been already noticed; its effect on poetry was of a similar character. The East-Midland dialect, the language of Chaucer, obtained precedence over the various local forms of speech; while Chaucer's manner and verse-forms were copied by his poetical successors. English poetry followed in the

wake of the great Londoner, and the revival of the alliterative verse along the Welsh border was but a local and
temporary outbreak of a form which was soon to pass
away. One other great alliterative poem which we must
consider separately, Langland's *Vision of Piers Plowman*,
was indeed written presumably by a native of the West
Midlands, but with it the native verse-form practically
passes out of the literature.

The period which is marked by the rise of London to
literary importance is also memorable in the history of
The rise of English prose. English prose. The work of Alfred in behalf of a
native prose-literature had been so effectually
undone by foreign ecclesiastics that, from the
middle of the twelfth to the latter part of the fourteenth century, only a few specimens of vernacular prose
emerge from the great stream of Latin. English prose
was much slower than English poetry in regaining its
freedom; but early in the reign of Richard II. (1377–
1399) it begins to reassert itself, and before the end of the
century it has made a decided advance. This advance
was not due to any one writer, it was rather a manifestation of national conditions, social, political, and religious.
It is connected, of course, with the ever increasing importance of the English language, and it is nearly related to
that rise of the people which is one of the great historic
features of the time. Underneath the violence and
clamour of the popular uprisings, men felt, if vaguely, the
appearance of a new social force. The people were thus
to be reckoned with, to be appealed to, argued with,
persuaded; and to reach the people, the scholar must
abandon Latin and the scholastic phrase, and address
them in simple English prose.

This was the course adopted by JOHN WYCLIF (cir.
1324–1384), "the last of the Schoolmen, the first of the
Protestant reformers," and the most famous English

scholar of his time. Like Rolle, Wyclif had come to Oxford from his native Yorkshire. But Wyclif was

Wyclif. made of sterner stuff than his emotional predecessor. A man of strong and subtle intellect, he mastered the scholastic philosophy. At a comparatively early age he was made Master of Balliol College, and he soon became prominent as a daring thinker and a skilful controversialist. At first, like the Schoolmen before him, he wrote in Latin; but if his language and manner were mediæval, his spirit was modern. The new note of independence, the disposition to examine into the basis of authority, sounds in his works. He counselled England to refuse to pay the tribute demanded by the Pope. He opposed the interference of the Church in matters of state, for the temporal as well as the spiritual power was derived from God. As the controversy progressed, Wyclif's position became more radical and revolutionary. His sympathies were with the poor; the vast wealth of the Church aroused his hostility; he did not spare even the Pope himself, but declared that as the Vicar of Christ he should be poor and meek as his Master was, and the servant of all.[1] Over against the authority of the Church and the priesthood, he set the authority of the Bible, the right of every man to read it for himself, and the direct relation of every man to God. Such a position forced Wyclif to turn to the people, and to reach the people the great scholar must abandon Latin and speak to them in a language all could understand. If the Bible was to be a guide for the individual conscience, it must be made the book of the people. About 1378, therefore, Wyclif, with the aid of Nicholas Herford and

[1] *Sermon*, xvi. *Select Eng. Works of Wyclif*, i. 40. Arnold's ed. See also Wyclif's famous reply to the Pope's summons (1384), in Arnold's ed. *supra*, ii. 504–6, or *Translations and Reprints*, ii. 5, University of Pennsylvania.

John Purvey, began to translate the entire Bible into English (completed 1383). Wyclif also sent out his followers, his "poor priests" as they were called, to spread his doctrines; while he himself spoke to the people in innumerable sermons and tracts, teaching them in plain and homely phrase. Memorable as these tracts and sermons are, the position of Wyclif's Bible in the history of English prose is probably even more important.

It is safe to say that the English translation of the Bible is the greatest monument of our prose literature. Its influence on prose literature has been incalculable. Many of the greatest masters of English prose have drawn from it as from a great storehouse, so that biblical illustrations and biblical phrases have been wrought into the very fabric of the literature. The style of our English Bible has a dignity, simplicity, and force that have seldom been approached and never excelled. Now the basis of the English Bible was Wyclif's translation. Later translators corrected, modernised, and improved upon his version; but Wyclif was not merely the pioneer, his work was the model for all that came after.

Wyclif is called "the Father of English Prose," but in reality this later English prose was growing up through the labours of a group of writers of which Wyclif was one. **Other prose writers.** Chaucer belongs to this group, although his superiority as a poet makes his prose comparatively unimportant. It should be remembered, however, that of his *Canterbury Tales* "The Parson's Sermon" and "The Tale of Melibeus" are in prose, and that he made English prose versions of Boethius' *Consolations of Philosophy* (cir. 1382) and a treatise on the *Astrolabe* (1391). Another of these latter fourteenth-century prose-writers was JOHN OF TREVISA, vicar of Berkley in Gloucester, who translated a number of works from Latin into English. His best known work

(1387) is an English rendering of the *Polychronicon* of Ranulph (or Ralph) Higden, a formidable survey of general history. Still more notable is *The Voyages and Travels of Sir John Mandeville,* the English version of which dates from about this time or a little later. This entertaining book purporting to be an account of a journey to the Holy Land, was intended (so the author tells us) as a guide for those who "will visit the Holy City of Hierusalem, and the places that are thereabout." But in reality it is not, like the *Travels of Marco Polo,* the record of an actual journey, but a medley, partly compiled from popular legends and travellers' stories, and partly pure invention. The book is thought to have been written originally in French by a physician named Jean de Bourgogne; Sir John Mandeville "was as purely a fictitious person as Gulliver or Robinson Crusoe." The maker of the English version is not known. But this book of marvels, recounted in a rather matter-of-fact fashion, as though noted by the quick eye of an observant traveller, did much to enlarge the borders of English prose, and take it beyond the narrow limits of history and theology. We travel into a far country, a land of the imagination, where all things are possible: we read of diamonds which grow when wet in May-dew; of men who have but one foot, that one of such a size that they lie on their backs and hold it up as a shelter from the rain and heat; of men with heads like hounds, and of men who have no heads at all, with eyes in their shoulders; of griffins, and of giants. Mandeville's *Travels* was a book for the people: we are told in the preface that it was translated "out of French into English that every man of my nation may understand it." Whoever the translator may have been, he helped to prepare the way for later English prose.

So far in our general survey of the literature of the fourteenth century, we have considered some of its local manifestations, and have noted the beginning of a more national poetry in London, and the renewal of English prose. We must now consider two of the representative poets of the period at somewhat greater length.

WILLIAM LANGLAND.

(Cir. 1332–cir. 1400.)

> "Langley, that with but a touch
> Of art hadst sung Piers Plowman to the top
> Of English songs, whereof 'tis dearest, now,
> And most adorable."
> — Sidney Lanier: *The Crystal.*

> "And on the vision he lay musing long,
> And o'er his soul rude minstrel-echoes throng,
> Old measures half-disused; and grasp'd his pen,
> And drew his cottage-Christ for homely men."
> — Francis T. Palgrave: *The Pilgrim and the Ploughman.*

"The vehement and passionate England that produced the great rising of 1381, and the heresy of Wyclif, that later on will give birth to the Cavaliers and Puritans, is contained in essence in Langland's work; we divine, we foresee her." — J. J. Jusserand.

Of the outward circumstances of Langland's life almost nothing is now known. Chaucer, his great contemporary, was a protégé of the court; he had a powerful patron, he held public office, and had a share in great events; and at least the outlines of Chaucer's life can be gathered from a careful study of the public records of his time. But Langland, the poet, as he has been called, of "*The Divine Comedy* of the poor*,*" lived and died apart from these things, an obscure, solitary man, not rich certainly, nor looked upon with favour by the wealthy or the noble. He would have been clean forgotten long ago if he had not put his truest self, his answer to the puzzle of human life, into his poem. That is his memorial; and, while our knowledge of how and when he lived is vague and fragmentary, he reveals himself in his work so that, knowing only this, we know what manner of man he was.

His story — so far as it is known or conjectured — is soon told. He is supposed to have been born about 1332, at Cleobury-Mortimer, in Southern Shropshire. He certainly came from somewhere in that region of the Welsh border which had already given more than one name to literature, for he wrote in a western form of English, and he was evidently familiar with the beautiful scenery of the neighbouring Malvern Hills. It is among these hills that he falls asleep by a brookside, as he tells us in the beginning of his poem, and over these hills he wanders brooding over his dream.[1] Whatever his situation in life may have been, he did not grow up without education, probably gained at some monastic school.

> "When i yong was, quod I, manny zer hennes,
> My fader and my frendes founden me to scole
> Til i wiste withturli what holy writ bi-menede
> And what is best for the bodi as the bok tellethe." [2]

Yet this schooling seems to have left him with a great longing for a wider knowledge.

> "Alle the sciences under sonne and all the sotyle craftes,
> I wolde I knewe, and couth kyndely in myne herte." [3]

But he had a gift that no schools or universities can give, and he had a learning that was not to be found in the wisest books of his day. He had that rare gift of vision, by which he could see the men and women about him as they were; and he had, what is still rarer, the gift of a great pity for the sins and miseries of the world. Like most really great writers, he looked at the world for himself and not through the medium of books; and he knew how the poor lived, what they ate, how they dressed, and how they talked, — he identified himself with them as even Chaucer,

[1] *The Vision of Piers Plowman*, Prologue, l. 1 ff. and Pass. viii. l. 130.

[2] *Vision*, text C, Pass. vi. l. 35.

[3] *Vision*, text B, Pass. xv. l. 48, quoted by Jusserand, *Literary History of the English People*, i. 377.

who lived among the great, could not do. Langland entered into the full stream of life by this poet's insight; he knew, as few could have done, the suffering, rebellious England of his day, in which the old forms were rent and shaken in a painful struggle with the new thought. And yet all the while he seems to have been in the world and yet not of it, to have looked on as an outsider at the strange medley of human existence; observing it with a singular impartiality, as one who viewed it from a height.

Apparently Langland lacked either the art or the wish to push his own fortunes, and his lot was a humble if not a wretched one. He became what was known as a clerk (*clericus*), that is, he was included among the clergy, but only in a minor capacity and not as a priest. He settled in London, we do not know how or when, and acted as chorister in the *chantries* (or memorial chapels), singing *dirges* and *placebos* in the masses held for the repose of the dead. There is a kind of pitiful irony in the fact that Langland, who believed that the divine forgiveness could not be bought for money, and that men were saved by their good deeds, should have been compelled to make his living by such a means. Yet this, if we are to take Langland's words literally, was all that he could do, since he had not the strength to labour with his hands, and he was forced to live by that labour "he had learned best." In his poem he alludes to his wife Kit, or Catherine, and tells us that he lived in a cottage near Cornhill, clothed like a "loller," or, as we should say, a vagabond, or "tramp." He has no fellowship with the rich, the prosperous, and the thoughtless, but thrusts his way through the gaily dressed crowds of the street, a silent, self-contained, poverty-stricken man, filled doubtless with his own melancholy and bitter thoughts. He is not one to court favour, or to fawn on the great; he scorns to salute those with gold collars, or to say "God save you"

to the proud nobles. The crowd looked at him in wonder, as it has looked at many another prophet who has
sought to make the world better, and called him a fool and
a madman. In some such fashion, surely, Dante, who
had seen a yet more fearful vision, passed among the
women and children at Ravenna, gaunt and terrible in
that solitude which is so often the price exacted from
the great.

But underneath this show of calm or indifference,
Langland's heart was hot within him. The sight of
that world which Chaucer accepted with such easy good-
humour aroused in Langland a passion of pity, indignation, and bitter scorn. He found in his poem a constant
refuge from loneliness, misunderstanding, and neglect;
and so in him as in that other prophet of old, the fire
kindled, and he spake with his tongue.

For thirty years or more Langland laboured at his
poem, struggling to give a fit expression to his thought.
He is supposed to have completed his first
Langland's version of it in 1362, when he was still a
Vision. comparatively young man; but apparently it
was always in his mind, and from time to time he re-wrote
and enlarged it. With all his effort he could not make it
a finished or coherent work of art. It remains rough-hewn,
confused and fragmentary; the style is rambling, often
crude and unmusical, and hard to follow. But the more
we read it, the more clearly we see its great redeeming
qualities. The man who wrote it was not so much an
artist as a prophet; he was no idle singer in ladies' bowers;
he had eaten his bread in sorrow, and he spoke with a
bitter earnestness and sincerity out of the perplexity and
trouble of his spirit.

In the opening of the *Vision*, the poet lies down by a
brookside, among the Malvern Hills. He has gone far
and wide through the world, and he is "weary of wan-

dering," so, as he listens to the cheerful murmur of the water, he falls asleep and dreams a dream. He finds himself in a strange wilderness. On the top of a hill to the eastward rises a great tower,—the Tower of Truth; opposite is a deep valley in which is a dungeon, the abode of the Father of Falsehood. Between Tower and Dungeon there stretches a vast plain, crowded with people, the scene of the great human drama, acted out between Truth and Falsehood, between Right and Wrong. Representative figures from the England of Langland's time are gathered on this plain. There are plowmen who play full seldom, and gluttons who waste the fruit of the plowman's toil. Ascetics, who renounce the pleasures of this life for the hope of another, and pleasure-lovers who dress themselves gaily, and minstrels who make mirth for gold. There are friars who preach for their own profit, a Pardoner selling indulgences, sergeants-at-law who will not open their mouths without money; there are workmen of many trades; and there are "cakes and ale" too, for in the hostelries the cooks are crying out, "Come and dine," and the "taverners" praising their wines. "Holy Church" tells the dreamer the meaning of his vision. She tells him that truth is the best of all treasures, and that the way to heaven is through love.

But what is truth? After various episodes, in which Langland satirises the abuses of the time, and personifies in the richly dressed Lady Meed that spirit of worldly rewards which seduces men everywhere by her tempting gifts, the search for truth becomes the chief theme. Conscience preaches to the people, assembled in the "fair field" of this world, and bids pilgrims to seek not the "saints at Rome" but "St. Truth, for he may saven you all." [1] So the world makes a pilgrimage to seek Truth, and finds a guide in Piers, a plowman at work in the

[1] *Vision*, Pass. vs. v. Skeat's ed.

fields. He tells them the way to Truth in an allegory, which is a striking anticipation of Christian's journey in *Pilgrim's Progress*, but declares that he himself must stay and finish ploughing his half acre. Finally he is persuaded to lead them. By *Truth* Langland appears to have meant a heavenly wisdom which should teach men how to live rightly, and it becomes plain as the poem proceeds that the way to truth is through humility, unfeigned goodness, and honest labour. Work is the poet's great remedy for the social disorders that were about him. He denounces the wasters and the beggars: he scorns those who, while Piers toils at his half acre, help him by singing "Hey! trolly-lolly!" over their ale. High or low, all should work according to their vocation; if they shirk, Hunger must compel them. Meanwhile Truth, having heard of the pilgrimage, bids Piers to stay at home and till the earth; she also sends a pardon to him and his helpers, and to those who cannot work through age or illness, and who bear their sufferings meekly. This pardon, which the priest thinks no pardon at all, is nothing more than this: "Do well, and have well, and God shall have thy soul; and do evil, and have evil, and hope thou no other but that after thy death-day the devil shall have thy soul." Without questioning openly the Pope's pardons or the efficacy of prayer and penance, the poet solemnly warns them that are rich in this world that at the Day of Doom, though they come with a bag full of pardons and have indulgences double-fold, yet unless their good deeds shall help them he would not give for all their pardons "a magpie's tail."

Langland has no novel remedy for the world's healing. He bases his poem on scriptural texts; he is under the guidance of the Church. Truth reveals to the pilgrim only the old doctrine that to fear God and keep his commandments is the whole duty of man. But, if the teachings of the poem are neither new nor revolutionary, they were at least sound and wholesome. Visionary as he was,

The poet and his teaching. he was also a close and accurate observer, and a practical reformer. Spenser in his *Faërie Queene* transports us into dreamland; but Langland shows us under the guise of a dream his England of the fourteenth century, peopled by real persons sometimes as vividly described as the characters of Chaucer himself. And he sees this world fairly. He does not cry out, like John Ball, that all things must be in common, nor lay all the blame upon the upper classes. He scorns indeed the follies and extravagance of the rich, but he rebukes with equal severity the idleness and improvidence of the poor. His shortcomings, as a poet, lie on the surface. Plainly he lacked Chaucer's skill in the poet's craft, the ability to tell a story well, the ease, and grace, and charm. But, lacking them, he had a far greater intensity, and a rugged, uncouth, but unmistakable power. Langland, indeed, was English, and the English earnestness, the English sincerity, the English conscience, speak through him. He preaches, too, with the true English awkwardness and bluntness; his verse is the old alliterative measure of his race; his style untouched by any of the refinements of French or foreign art. To those who think that the manner is the only important part of poetry, Langland may hardly seem to have been a poet at all; but in any case, he had in large measure those qualities which have done so much to make England and her literature great. For the force back of the native genius of the English is not so much artistic as religious and moral. It excels, not because it has a turn for fine phrases, a trick of style, a delight in beauty for beauty's sake, but because it faces life steadily and seriously, and tries honestly to know what it is and what it means. There are a few elegant triflers among the ranks of England's writers of genius; but, as a

rule, the greatest — Spenser, Milton, Bunyan, Wordsworth, Tennyson, Carlyle, Ruskin, Browning — are
teachers, earnest men, bent upon teaching some gospel.
Shakespeare himself, although his message may seem less
definite, is, beneath all his wit and laughter, tragically
serious and profoundly moral. Whatever Langland's deficiencies as an artist, however rude, abrupt, and disjointed
his verse, he is yet one with this immortal company by
virtue of his moral earnestness, his passion for righteousness, his intensity of purpose.

There is force in him; unpolished as his lines are, the
strength of his character dominates us; here is a man who
thinks and makes us think, who feels and makes us feel,
who sees and makes us see; and we listen to him, as the
world did to Piers, the plowman in the field.

GEOFFREY CHAUCER.

(Cir. 1340–1400.)

"The pupil of manifold experience, — scholar, courtier, soldier,
ambassador, — who had known poverty as a housemate, and been the
companion of princes, he was one of those happy temperaments that
could equally enjoy both halves of culture, — the world of books and
the world of men." — Lowell: Essay on *Chaucer.*

"His, to paint
With Nature's freshness what before him lies:
The knave, the fool: the frolicsome, the quaint:
His the broad jest, the laugh without restraint,
The ready tears, the spirit lightly moved;
Loving the world and by the world beloved."

F. T. Palgrave: *Visions of England.*

Chaucer is the first-born of the greater poets of England; the predecessor of Spenser, Shakespeare, Milton,
and the rest of the royal line of the English rulers of song.
He was not indeed as some of his earlier disciples igno-
rantly thought him, "the Father of English Poetry," for

England, as we have seen, had produced a long succession of poets before his time; but he was the first great poet who wrote in an English which presents but little difficulty to the modern reader; he was "the finder of our fair language." Chaucer marks the point of departure from old precedents and traditions. If he is not "the Father of English Poetry," he is the founder of a new dynasty, the first great exemplar in England of a poetry that in form and spirit was, in a large measure, neither Anglo-Saxon nor Celtic, but foreign. This departure on Chaucer's part from the older poetry was not a deliberate rejection of it, but a natural result of the poet's education and of all the varied experiences which combined to mould his genius and direct its course. It is true that poets are born, not made, but the work of even the greatest poets is to some degree coloured and shaped by the influences which surround them. To understand the direction taken by Chaucer's genius, we must therefore know something of his life.

Chaucer was both a poet and a practical and sagacious man of affairs, both a student and a courtier, a dreamer Chaucer's life. and a man of the world. Scholars have learned something of the outward and public events of his life from various contemporary records; the story of his inner life, and of the development of his genius, must be largely a matter of inference or conjecture. In studying his life we must endeavour to view it from this double aspect; to remember that he was the "pupil of manifold experience," and that, while he lived and learned in the world of courts and camps, he withdrew at other times into that other world of thought and imagination.

Geoffrey Chaucer was born in London in or about 1340. His father, John Chaucer, a prosperous wine-merchant on Thames Street, was purveyor to Edward III. and had attended the King and Queen in an expedition to Flanders and Cologne (1338). The name *Chaucer* (which some derive from the French *chaussier*, shoe, or stocking, maker, and others from *chauffecire*, one who makes wax seals for legal documents) suggests that the poet was sprung from Norman stock. These few facts are significant. The poet, who was to leave behind him such lively and brightly coloured pictures of mediæval life, dress, and manners, was born in the nation's capital, the focus of England's political, social, and commercial life. The narrow, crooked streets of the old town were a wonderful school for the painter of contemporary life, but the dweller in the London of the Plantagenets was not wholly cut off from the influence of very different surroundings. Chaucer was to be the lover of nature as well as the poet of man; in mediæval London, the sky was not yet obscured by soot and smoke, and the open fields and the hedge-rows were not very far away. Poet of nature and of man, Chaucer was also to be the poet of the upper classes and the court, and the conditions of his life led him naturally to this likewise. Norman, we may presume, by descent, and sprung from a well-to-do family of the merchant class, his father's relation to the King must have made the court less remote than it would ordinarily have been to a child of Chaucer's comparatively humble station. Into this life of the court which his father may often have described to him, Chaucer himself was destined to enter, for, when he was about seventeen, he was made page to Elizabeth, Countess of Ulster, the daughter-in-law of Edward III. This early introduction

Page to Countess of Ulster c. 1357. to the court atmosphere is a crucial point in Chaucer's career. While the native English spirit was beginning to assert itself throughout the country, the tone of the court at this time was still foreign. French literature was in fashion: "French poets and 'menestrels' were in the service and pay of the English

King." [1] Queen Philippa and her ladies amused themselves with French poetry and romance. It was a brilliant, comfortable world too, adorned with a splendid ceremonial, stirred by the echo of chivalric deeds, for the King had just won the battle of Poictiers (1356). At an age when life is very new and wonderful to an eager and susceptible youth, the boy-poet Chaucer was transported to the midst of this foreign atmosphere, this little world of fair ladies and great lords, of French singers and French tastes. Outside in the country was the greater world of England, a plague-stricken and miserable land where the people toiled and hungered, enduring "wind and rain in the fields." But circumstances had shut the young Chaucer away from this world of the poor; his training was that of a gentleman's son; his world, the world of chivalry, of romance, and of the court.

Besides this courtly training and worldly experience, Chaucer gained in some way a knowledge of books. He learned Latin, and he was probably familiar with French from his earliest years. Like Shakespeare he was a lover not only of men but of books; and, possessing the industry and enthusiasm of the student, he was doubtless his own best teacher. His poems are almost always founded upon books; many of them are translations or paraphrases of other men's work, and he is fond of introducing reminiscences of his reading. More than one passage reveals his delight in study, and shows us that in the midst of a busy life he turned to books for rest and refreshment. Sad and wakeful he turns to a book —

Chaucer the student.

> "To rede, and drive the night away;"

preferring his romance to a game "at chesse or tables." [2]

---

[1] Ten Brink: *English Literature*, ii. 38.   Robinson's trans.
[2] *The Dethe of Blaunche the Duchesse.*

He describes the poor student's love of his library with a sympathy that is suggestive of a kindred taste.

> "For him was levere have at his beddes heede
> Twenty bookes, clad in blak or reede,
> Of Aristotle and his philosophie,
> Then robes riche, or fithele, or gay sawtrie." [1]

He tells us that when he was busy in the London Custom House, after he had finished his day's work, instead of seeking rest and diversion, he would go home and sit over another book than an account book as "dombe as any stoon." [2] The character and scope of Chaucer's reading were such as his training and opportunities would lead us to expect. He was a child of foreign influences. Trained in a court where the King could hardly speak an intelligible English sentence, where the names and the language of Cædmon and Cynewulf were unknown, Chaucer's literary inheritance was not English but Latin and French. He studied the Latin literature of the twelfth and thirteenth centuries, — Monmouth's *Historia Britonum*, or the caustic verse of Walter Map; he knew Vergil's *Æneid* and Ovid's *Metamorphoses*, and he had some acquaintance with other classical works. But his mother-literature was the French. He read the *Romaunt de la Rose*, the lengthy allegory of the French *trouvères* Guillaume de Lorris and Jean de Meung; he was influenced by the lyrics of his French contemporaries, Guillaume de Machault (1284?–1370?) and Eustache Deschamps (1320–c. 1400). These men were Chaucer's masters; and, when he began to write, addressing, as he did, a courtly audience whose literary sympathies were French, he naturally followed the French manner.

But reading and poetry formed but a part of Chaucer's eventful and many-sided career. Before he was twenty

---

[1] "Prologue" to *Canterbury Tales*.
[2] *The House of Fame*.

he saw something not only of the court but of the camp and of the field, for he was with the English army in the

In the French war, 1359. French campaign of 1359, probably as a member of Prince Lionel's suite. While this campaign was marked by no brilliant military exploits, there must have been much to stir the imagination. In those days war was magnificent with that "pomp and panoply" in which poets delight, and Chaucer saw such spectacles as poets dream of with his bodily eyes. As the King's host moved through France, says Froissart, it seemed to cover the country, and the soldiers "were so richly armed and apparelled that it was a wonder and great pleasure to look at the shining arms, the floating banners." [1] And in this mighty army were the King, the Black Prince, Sir Walter Manny, and others of the greatest knights and captains of the age. Chaucer learned something too of war's reverses, for he was taken prisoner by the French and ransomed by the King for £16. After his return from the French campaign, Chaucer entered the service of the King. In 1367 he was granted a pension of twenty marks as "valet of the King's chamber" (*valettus cameræ regis*), and somewhat later he rose to the position of *esquire*. In 1369 he again took part in a campaign in France, and before 1379 he had been employed in no less than seven diplomatic missions to various places on the Continent.

But, while Chaucer was thus making his way as courtier, soldier, and diplomatist, he had already begun his work

Early poems. as a poet. He wrote love-lyrics in the French manner, — "Balades, Rondel, and Virelayes," — most of which have been lost. He translated the *Romance of the Rose* (1360–65 ?). Several poems usually assigned to this early period of his work, allude to a disappointment in love, and are pervaded with a gentle sad-

[1] Buchon's *Froissart*, i. 416.

ness. But we cannot be sure that such passages are the outcome of a personal experience. Thus the *Compleynte to Pitie* is the lament of a despairing lover, who complains that Pity is dead, sundered from Love and Truth, and that Cruelty is enthroned in her stead. One of these early poems, *The Dethe of Blaunche the Duchesse* (1369), was called forth by the death of Blanche of Castile, the wife of John of Gaunt, the poet's patron. The love of Nature, in her milder and fairer aspects, — of the soft grass, the birds, the flowers, and the green woods, — and a deep and reverent appreciation of the beauty of womanhood, these two traits so characteristic of Chaucer's maturer work, are already apparent in this poem. It is here that we find that melodious and charming description of happy girlhood, which takes its place beside the work of the great masters:

> "I saw hir daunce so comlily,
> Carole and singe so swetely
> Laughe and pleye so womanly,
> And loke so debonairly,
> So goodly speke and so frendly,
> That certes, I trow that evermore
> Nas seyn so blisful a tresore."

Meanwhile — the exact date is not known — Chaucer had married a lady whose first name was Philippa. This lady **Marriage.** is supposed to have been Philippa Roet, a sister of the third wife of John of Gaunt.

The King and his advisers appear to have found Chaucer a trustworthy and competent agent, for in 1372 he was **First visit** sent on a diplomatic mission to Italy. He was **to Italy,** abroad nearly a year, visiting Florence and Genoa, **1372.** and possibly meeting Petrarch, who was staying near Padua at the time. This journey to Italy, and a subsequent visit to Lombardy (1378–79), had a profound effect upon the development of Chaucer's genius. The French were no longer the literary leaders of Europe; the age of *troubadour* and *trouvère* was already passing. Italy had turned away from the Middle Ages, and was entering into a new world of the spirit. Chaucer's ability in practical affairs had secured for him, plain merchant's son as he was, an opportunity of entering this Italy of the early Renaissance. He passed from his Northern island into that wonderful land of the South, once the mistress of the civilised world; from the land of mailed knights, to the land of the artist and the scholar; from the old world of the *trouvère*, to the new world of Petrarch and Boccaccio. In the midst of the fragments of an old civilisation, there were already signs of the awakening of a new art and culture. The devotion to beauty, characteristic of the coming era, showed itself in wonders of architecture, in paintings and frescoes; a new literature, inspired by enthusiasm for the masterpieces of antiquity, had already declared itself. Chaucer was the first great poet of England to feel that spell which Italy has exercised over so many English writers from Shakespeare to Browning. His work testifies to the profound impression made upon him by his Italian journeys. In his literary apprenticeship he is the imitator and translator of the French poets; then, brought close to another descendant of the same Latin civilisation, he draws a fresh inspiration from Italy.

After his return to England from this memorable first visit to Italy (1373), Chaucer received various marks of the Royal favour. He was made Comptroller of **Return to England.** the Customs on Wool and Hides for the Port of London, granted a pension by John of Gaunt, and sent from time to time on missions to France and elsewhere. In 1382 he became Comptroller of the Petty Customs at London, and in 1386 he was returned to Parliament as one of the Knights of the Shire for Kent. About this time (1385–8), Chaucer may have actually gone upon a pilgrimage to Canterbury, and found in his experience a hint for the setting of his *Canterbury Tales.*

But Chaucer, like Shakespeare, possessed the rare power of keeping the ideal and the practical side of life in an even **Troilus and** balance, and during these active and prosper-**Cressida, and** ous years study and poetry were not neglected. **other poems.** Shut in his house above the gate of Aldgate he lived in a world of imagination and reminiscence.. "There," writes M. Jusserand, " all he had known in Italy would return to his memory, campaniles, azure frescoes, olive groves, sonnets of Petrarch, poems of Dante, tales of Boccaccio; he had brought back wherewithal to move and enliven 'merry England' herself." [1] A number of poems bear the impress of his Italian studies. One poem contains a reproduction of the triple rhyme of Dante's *Divine Comedy ;* another, left unfinished, is translated in part from the *Teseide* of Boccaccio. A long and important poem, *Troilus and Cressida* (c. 1380–1383?), is based on Boccaccio's *Filostrato*, while the uncompleted *Hous of Fame* shows the influence of Dante. In his masterly version of the story of Troilus, the lover, and the beautiful but faithless Cressida, Chaucer is the precursor of the modern novelist. The chief characters are drawn with a subtle understanding of men and women; and, though something of the prolixity of the old romance still remains, the story is told with a consummate delicacy and skill that make it worthy of the great masters of English narrative verse.

But a change in Chaucer's fortunes was at hand. So far his success as a courtier had given him many opportuni-**Chaucer** ties which proved of advantage to him in his art. **becomes** He had learned from prosperity, he was now to **poor, 1386.** feel the discipline of another teacher. In 1386, the same year in which he had entered Parliament, he was suddenly reduced to comparative poverty. Edward III.,

* *A Literary History of the English People,* i. 290.

who had done so much for Chaucer, had died some years before this; and, during the minority of Richard II., now one and now another of the young king's uncles gained the chief power. In the absence of Chaucer's steady patron, John of Gaunt, the Duke of Gloucester gained control of affairs; and Chaucer was among those who lost their government positions as a result of this political change. Among Chaucer's minor poems is a group of ballads in which he meditates upon the fickleness of Fortune, upon contentment in adversity, on the vanity of wealth without nobleness, and on kindred themes. It is highly probable that we have in these poems an indication of the spirit in which Chaucer met his misfortunes. The tone of these ballads is brave, sensible, and manly; they bring before us a man of sweet and kindly nature, sustained by religion, philosophy, and a sense of humour, who is able to take "fortune's buffets and rewards" with "equal thanks." So Chaucer defies ill fortune, refusing to sing, "I have lost my all, my time and my labour," at her bidding;[1] so, deprived of his offices, he declares philosophically that —

"Gret reste stant in *litel besinesse.*"[2]

No man, he says, is wretched unless he chooses to think himself so,

"And he that hath himself hath sufficiance."[3]

The little poem the *Ballad of Good Counseil*, or *Truth*, seems to bring Chaucer very close to us:

"That thee is sent, receyve in buxumnesse,
 The wrasling for this worlde axeth a fal.
Her nis non hoom, her nis but wildernesse:
  Forth, pilgrim, forth! Forth. beste, out of thy stal!
  Know thy contree, look up, thank God of all;
Hold the hye wey, and lat thy gost thee lede:
And trouthe shal delivere, hit is no drede."

---

[1] *Balades de Visage sanz Peinture.*
[2] Truth — ("*Fle Fro the Presse*").
[3] *Balades de Visage sanz Peinture.*

In these years of financial stress and "litel besinesse" Chaucer is supposed to have turned his leisure to good account and found "rest" in composing the greater part of his *Canterbury Tales* (1386–91?), the crowning work of his life. The *Canterbury Tales* consists of a number of separate stories supposed to be told by the various members of a company of pilgrims, journeying together to the tomb of St. Thomas à Becket at Canterbury. In a general prologue we are told how these pilgrims met at the Tabard Inn in Southwark, the district opposite to London on the other side of the Thames; how they agreed to be fellow-travellers; how the jolly innkeeper, "Harry Bailly," proposed that] each pilgrim should tell two tales on the way to Canterbury and two returning. There are, by way of interlude, prologues to the several stories thus told, which bind the whole series more firmly together and recall to us the general design. The idea of stringing distinct stories on some thread of connection is not an uncommon one. Boccaccio in his *Decamerone* linked together a collection of stories by a very simple expedient. A number of gay lords and ladies leave Florence during the plague, and, sitting together in a beautiful garden, they amuse themselves by telling the tales that form the main part of the work. Chaucer's work is founded on a pilgrimage, one of the characteristic and familiar features of the life of the time. With rare tact he has selected one of the few occasions which brought together in temporary good-fellowship men and women of different classes and occupations. He is thus able to paint the moving life of the world about him in all its breadth and variety; he can give to stories told by such chance-assorted companions a dramatic character and contrast, making Knight, Priest, or Miller reveal himself in what he relates.

The chief interest of the Prologue lies in the freshness

(margin note: The Canterbury Tales.)

and truth with which each member of the little party of pilgrims is set before us. As one after another of that immortal procession passes by, the intervening centuries are forgotten, and we ourselves seem fourteenth-century pilgrims riding with the rest. It is a morning in the middle of April as we with the jolly company, thirty-two in all, with our host of the Tabard, Harry Bailly, as "governour," pass out of the square courtyard of the inn and take the highroad toward Canterbury. The freshness of the spring is all about us; showers and sunshine and soft winds have made the budding world beautiful in tender green, and the joy of the sweet season in the hearts of innumerable birds makes them put their gladness into song. This time, when the sap mounts in the trees, and the world is new-charged with the love of life, fills us with restless desires and the spirit of adventure.

"Thanne longen folk to gon on pilgrimages."

Our little company is made up of men and women of many sorts and conditions. There rides a Knight, a good type of all that is best in the chivalry of the time, who has fought bravely in fifteen mortal battles. His dress is stained, for he has just returned from a voyage; even the trappings of his horse are plain. In his bearing he is as meek as a maid. His son is with him, a gay young Squire with curled locks. He is a boy of twenty, over-flowing with life and happiness, splendid in apparel, and expert in graceful accomplishments. After the Knight and the Squire rides their attendant, clad in the green of the forester. He is the hero of the new order, as the Knight is the hero of the old. A very different figure is Madame Eglantyne, a coy and smiling Prioress, a teacher of young ladies, whose table manners are a model of deportment, whose French smacks of the "school of Stratford atte Bowe." She is so sensitive that she weeps to

see a mouse caught in a trap. Though pleasant and
amiable, she affects court manners, and holds herself on
her dignity that people may stand in awe of her. There
ambles the rich, pleasure-loving Monk, "ful fat" and
ruddy; one of those new-fashioned Churchmen of the
day who have given up the strict monastic rule of an
earlier time. He cares neither for learning nor to work
with his hands, but delights in hunting. The corruption
of the Church is also to be seen in the next pilgrim, a
brawny, jolly Friar, licensed to beg within a prescribed
district. The Friar has no threadbare scholar's dress; his
short cloak is of double worsted. His cowl is stuffed with
knives and pins, for he is a pedlar, like many of his order.[1]

After the Merchant, sitting high on his horse, and
always solemnly talking of his gains, comes the Clerk with
his lean horse, and threadbare cloak. He is a philosopher;
he has not prospered in the world,

> "For he hadde geten him yit no benefice
> Ne was so worldly for to have office."

Then the Sergeant-at-Law, who seems always busier
than he is; the Franklin, or farmer, with his red face and
beard white as a daisy; he keeps open house, the table
standing always covered in his hospitable hall.[2]

Various occupations are represented by the Haber-
dasher, the Dyer, the Tapicer, or dealer in carpets and
rugs, the Cook, who can "roste and sethe, and boille and
fry," and make "blankmanger" with the best. The

---

[1] Wyclif writes of the friars: "They become peddlers, bearing
knives, purses, pins, and girdles, and spices, and silk, and precious
pellure, and fouris for women, and thereto small dogs." Quoted in
Jusserand's *English Wayfaring Life*, p. 304.

[2] The Franklin held his land directly from the King and free of
feudal service. In the fourteenth century the dining-tables were
usually boards placed on trestles, and were taken away after each
meal. The Franklin's was "dormant," i.e., permanent. See Wright's
History of Domestic Manners and Sentiments in England, p. 139.

weather-beaten Shipman, whose beard has been shaken by many a tempest, seems not quite at ease on horse-back. The Doctor of Physic is a learned and successful practitioner, who knows the literature of his profession, and studies the Bible but little. He keeps all the gold he made in the pestilence:

> "For gold in physic is a cordial
> Therfor he lovede gold in special."

Among all there is the buxom, dashing Wife of Bath, gaily dressed, with scarlet stockings, new shoes, and a hat as broad as a shield, and, in sharp contrast, the Parish Priest, the "*poure persoun* of a town," reminding us that, in spite of luxurious monks and cheating friars, the Church was not wholly corrupt.

> "Benigne he was, and wonder diligent,
> And in adversitee ful pacient.
> . . . .
> He wayted after no pompe and reverence,
> Ne maked him a spyced conscience,
> But Cristes lore, and his apostles twelve,
> He taughte, but first he folwed it him-selve."

The party is made up by the Ploughman, the Reeve, or steward, the Miller, who carries a bagpipe, the Summoner, an officer of the law-courts, the Pardoner, or seller of indulgences, his wallet full of pardons, the Manciple, or caterer for a college, and last, the Poet himself, noting with twinkling eyes every trick of costume, and looking through all to the soul beneath.

In this truly wonderful group the moving and varied life of Chaucer's England survives in all its bloom and freshness, in the vital power of its intense humanity. Student of books as Chaucer was, and teller of old tales, we see here and elsewhere the shrewd observer and interpreter of life and character, the man with the poet's gift of fresh and independent vision. As we have said, the several stories in the *Canterbury Tales* are dramatic studies as well as masterpieces of narrative, as each narrator unconsciously reveals something of his own character in the tale he tells. Thus the *Knight's Tale* is steeped in the golden atmosphere of chivalry. Theseus, journeying homeward with his bride, Hippolyta, leaves her, as a true knight should, to champion the cause of woman in distress. The whole story revolves about the supreme power of love, a doctrine dear to the heart of mediæval chivalry.

> "Wostow nat wel the olde clerkes sawe,
> That ' who shal yeve a lovere any lawe?'
> Love is a gretter lawe, by my pan,
> Than may be yeve to eny erthly man." [1]

At the call of this great and mighty god of love, the life-long friendship and affection of Palamon and Arcite are changed in an instant to rivalry and hatred, the solemn oaths which bind them to each other unhesitatingly disregarded. The story is rich and glorious in heraldric blazonry; the gorgeous description of the tournament sparkles and glitters with the lustre of that romantic and knightly world. Yet the *Knight's Tale* is not wholly mediæval. It was founded on the *Teseide* of Boccaccio, and its very origin reminds us that Chaucer touched the new world of the Renaissance, as well as the vanishing world of the Middle Ages, and the luxurious beauty of the description of the temple of Venus seems to breathe the spirit of beautiful and pagan Italy, which was to find its English reflex in the delicious verse of the *Faërie Queene*. The Knight takes us into his world of the gentles; so the drunken Miller, a consummate example of obtuse vulgarity, brutally strong and big of brawn and bones, incidentally acquaints us with life as he knows it; while the dainty Prioress, speaking from her sheltered nook of

---

[1] *Knight's Tale*, l. 305, etc.

pious meditation, tells her tender story of a miracle, and, as we listen, we seem to hear the clear, young voice of the martyred child ring out fresh and strong. Among the most beautiful of the tales are those told by the Clerk and the Man of Law, two stories that in some respects may be placed together. Both reveal Chaucer's deep reserve of gentleness and compassion; both reveal his reverential love of goodness; both bring before us, as the central figure, a patient and holy woman, unjustly treated, and bearing all wrongs and griefs with meek submission. In the *Clerk's Tale* the unselfishness and wifely submission of Griselda is placed in sharp contrast with the selfishness of her husband. The one gives herself up first to her father and then to her husband, making her bed "ful harde and no thing softe." The other gives himself over wholly to present self-indulgence, even hesitating to take a wife because he rejoices in his liberty that

"Selde tyme is found in mariage."

When two such natures are brought together, the more unselfishness yields — the more selfishness takes. The ideal of womanhood revealed in Griselda is eminently mediæval, and Chaucer admits that he does not expect women of his time to follow her humility, adding that he tells us the story to show that

"Every wight in his degree
Sholde be constant in adversitie
As was Griselde."

Fortitude may likewise be taken as the patron virtue of the *Lawyer's Tale*, as indeed the name of the heroine, Constance, seems to imply. But the story also shows the divine care of innocence in adversity. Over and over again is Constance placed in peril, only to be rescued by the Divine hand. She stands on the sea-shore, betrayed, and about to be set adrift with her new-born child.

Even in the face of this deadly peril her faith remains unshaken:

> "He that me kepte fro the false blame
> While I was on the lond amonges yow,
> He kan me kepe from harm, and eek fro shame .
> In salte see, al thogh I see noght how;
> As strong as evere he was he is yet now.
>
> . . . .
>
> Her litel child lay wepying in her arm,
> And knelynge, pitously to hym she seyde,
> 'Pees, litel sone, I wol do thee non harm!'
> With that hir kerchef of hir heed she breyde,
> And over hise litel eyen she it leyde,
> And in hir arm she lulleth it ful faste,
> And in-to hevene hire eyen up she caste." [1]

Words cannot be more simple or more tender, nor pathos more profound. We see all as in a picture: the sobbing country people crowding about the fair woman kneeling in their midst; the sacred beauty of motherhood, of suffering, of heroic faith; the boat ready at the water's edge, and, in melancholy perspective, the receding background of the waiting sea. In such passages we feel the truth of Mrs. Browning's words:

> "Chaucer, with his infantine
> Familiar clasp of things divine." [2]

The *Man of Lawe's Tale* may be set beside Milton's *Comus* as the story of that virtue which can be "assailed, but never hurt." "Great are the perils of the righteous, but the Lord delivereth him out of all;" this may be said to be the text of the story of Constance.

In the Middle Ages it was not customary to invent new plots, and Chaucer, like many another poet, translated or adapted old stories gathered from many sources — French, Italian, or Latin. Critics have discovered the sources of

---

[1] *Man of Lawe's Tale.*
[2] Mrs. Browning's *Vision of Poets.*

many of the *Canterbury Tales,* and it is quite possible that none of them were entirely original with Chaucer. But the literature of the world belongs to the supreme poet by right of eminent domain; and Chaucer, the teller of the *Canterbury Tales,* was not an imitator or translator, but a new creative force. Chaucer's originality became more pronounced as his genius matured. As we read his masterpieces we feel that he painted from life, and that, whether he borrowed from France or from Italy, he made a style of his own, breathing into it the breath of his own spirit.

On the accession of Henry IV. in 1399, the son of Chaucer's old patron, John of Gaunt, the poet's fortunes again improved. Chaucer lost no time in bringing his poverty to the notice of the King, by sending him a humourous little poem, the *Complaint of his Empty Purse.* It was evidently in response to this appeal that Henry promptly granted a pension of forty marks a year to his father's old protégé. But Chaucer had nearly done with pensions and Court favour. He died on the 25th of October, 1400.

Chaucer's last years.

Chaucer's relation to literary history has been already indicated. Through him those foreign influences which for three centuries had been enriching the civilisation of England found expression in English poetry. He begins his work as "an English *trouvère*" as the spiritual descendant of such poets as De Lorris and Machault. Ignorant of the poetry of the Anglo-Saxon, Chaucer's work marks a final break with the literary traditions native to the English people. Not only is he un-English in manner, but he also has a lightness of touch, an easy cheerfulness, grace, and humour, very different from the sombre earnestness and ponderous strength of the Anglo-Saxon. He is indeed sensitive to suffering, quickly touched by the sadness "in mortal things;" but, like a light-hearted child, he turns away

Chaucer and his work.

from this aspect of life with relief. In his own phrase, he is "so weary for to speke of sorwe." Arcite dies in the strength of his youth, and Chaucer accepts the fact with characteristic philosophy. It is tragic, but why should we cry over spilt milk? Can he thank us if we make ourselves miserable? "Nay, God woot, never a del." Let his rival and sworn brother be sensible. Why should he wish to die also? has he not "gold enough and Emely?" In such passages there is an avoidance of painful reflection, a Gallic gaiety foreign to the natural bent of the Teutonic mind.

But we must not think of Chaucer as a mere transmitter, or Angliciser of foreign influences. His genius had another side. He chooses to write in the English language, while his contemporary, John Gower, composes the greater part of his poetry in Latin and in French. If he began by translating French romance, he became before he died the great painter of the contemporary life of England. His foot was firmly planted on English soil, and few poets of any age have surpassed him in his power to observe and reproduce the external aspects of the world around him. His genius is objective; he has a strong grasp of plain fact. He has no touch of morbid grief or of maudlin sentimentality. He hates shams; he is eminently frank, robust, and wholesome. Dryden called him "a perpetual fountain of good sense." Now in these things Chaucer seems essentially English. In his frank realism, his appreciation of human nature, he resembles Shakespeare and Scott; his broad humour, free from malice or restraint, suggests the robust presence and hearty laughter of Fielding. Chaucer, then, is neither Norman nor Saxon, but a mixture of both. He united the Norman spirit of romance with English solidity and common sense. His very language, a fusion of French and English, shows that in him a long process of amalgamation is nearly completed, and that once separate elements are being welded into one.

Nor must we forget that Italy, as well as France and England, contributed to the full development of Chaucer's

Chaucer and the Renaissance.

powers. Dante, the first great poet of Modern Europe, stands at the end of the Middle Ages: Chaucer, born three-quarters of a century later, stands at once at the close of the mediæval and at the beginning of the modern world. The inheritance of the past and the promise of the future mingle in his work; and, like his century, he marks both the end of an old order and the beginning of a new.

Genius is often associated with the excessive or abnormal development of a single faculty. In such cases one

Chaucer as poet.

side of the man's nature grows at the expense of the rest. From this besetting weakness of genius, Chaucer is conspicuously free. The artist in him did not warp or spoil the man; the varied life of the man contributed to the triumph of the artist. Perhaps the most remarkable fact about Chaucer is his ability to keep each of the diverse elements that make up life in its proper place, and his ability to use all, while he prevented any one from gaining an undue ascendency. As we have seen, he lived with men, with books, and with nature; he was busy and successful in life's practical activities, and a poet; he was a man of this world and a dweller in that other world of art. Chaucer's healthy contact with life and his marvellous equipoise of character give a sane, wholesome, normal quality to his work. In his power to harmonise the ideal and the practical, he resembles Shakespeare and Walter Scott. He is truthful, setting down what he sees honestly and naturally; he can enjoy life with almost the frank delight of a child, capable of laughter without malice; and, boisterous or coarse as he may sometimes seem, he is at heart surprisingly gentle and compassionate. If he is the poet of the Wife of Bath, he is also the poet of Griselda and Constance. He reveres a good woman; he writes of little children with a wonderful tenderness. He is not bitter, rebellious, or complaining, but accepts what life gives him with a cheerful courage and manly resignation. There is something natural, almost childlike, in his delight in birds and grass, in flowers and sunshine, in "Maytime and the cheerful dawn." He is among the greatest comic writers; the father of English humour, he has a Shakespearean sympathy with the follies or the absurdities which he describes. When Chaucer wrote, our English language, with its more frequent vowel sounds, was softer and smoother in men's mouths, and Chaucer, the master of this melodious English, is one of the most musical of English poets. When we compare the line,

> "And smale fowles maken melodie,"

with

> "And the small birds make melody,"

or some such modern equivalent, we see that the English of Chaucer's day, as he used it, could rival the liquid flow of the Italian.

Chaucer added to these varied gifts, the power of telling a story in a clear, rapid, and effective manner. He was a great narrative, as well as an excellent descriptive, poet. He could reveal his characters through action, interest us in their adventures, and bring before us striking scenes or situations with vividness and dramatic force. The *Pardoner's Tale* is a good example of his narrative and dramatic skill. This gift is rare among the English poets; and the strength of some of even the greatest, — Spenser, Milton, and Wordsworth, — lies rather in other directions.

With all this comprehensive excellence, there were aspects of life that Chaucer touched lightly or ignored. He pictures men and women of various social conditions, from the knight to the miller and the ploughman, but he shows

Poet of the Court. breadth of observation rather 'than breadth of sympathy for the miseries or wrongs of the poor. The laureate of the Court, something of the courtier clings to him, and he remains the poet of a feudal society, the outcome of the voice of chivalry in its class distinctions and exclusiveness, as well as its splendour. His easy-going nature has in it no touch of the reformer, the martyr, or the fanatic. He takes the world as it is; he loves the good, but the sight of the evil stirs in him no deeps of moral indignation; on the contrary, he often regards grossness and vulgarity with an amused tolerance. He painted Mediæval life in its outward aspects, while Dante, revealing its soul, probed to the centre. He seems to dwell at his ease in his broad, sunshiny world of green fields and merry jests; but if he took life and its graver issues lightly, this buoyant good-humour is not only his limitation but also his enduring charm.

PART II.

THE PERIOD OF THE ITALIAN INFLUENCE.
(About 1400 to about 1660.)

CHAPTER I.

THE FOLLOWERS OF CHAUCER AND THE DECLINE OF MEDIÆVAL LITERATURE.

In following the course of English literature from its obscure beginnings, we are conscious, as we reach the fifteenth century, of an unmistakable loss or suspension of our interest. There is a pause in the action of the great drama, and the tension is suddenly relaxed. The stage seems empty, deserted as it is by those typical and striking characters on whom our attention has so lately been fixed. When the century opens, Wyclif has been dead some fifteen years, and the Government has already set itself to undo his work and to suppress his followers. Langland and the poet of *Sir Gawayne* have ended their labours, and, above all, Chaucer is just dead, "the maister dere and fadir reverent," and his death is lamented as an irreparable loss to poetry.[1] Chaucer indeed has successors, facile and industrious writers who can turn out a prodigious quantity of verse; but most of them bring no strong original impulse to poetry; they are imitators; and their productions, huge as they are, cannot fill the void left by the master's departure. The very fact that these poets are copyists places them at a disadvantage, for it

[1] See Occleve's tribute to Chaucer in the Prologue to his *Gouvernail of Princes.*

forces us to compare their inferior work with that of their great model. Some beautiful and vigorous work was indeed done in Scotland where the poetry of Chaucer took root in a fresh and fertile soil, but the English successors of the great master are hardly more than names to the reader of to-day.

One of these poets, THOMAS OCCLEVE, or HOCCLEVE (cir. 1370–c. 1450), a clerk in the Exchequer, appears to have known Chaucer personally, and came directly under the elder poet's influence. His tribute to Chaucer, in the Prologue to the *Gouvernail of Princes*, shows both admiration and affection for his friend and master. But the greater part of Occleve is dreary reading, and we have no difficulty in believing him when he says:

> "My dere maister — God his soule quyte —
> And Fader Chaucer, fayne would have me taught,
> But I was dulle, and lerned lytle or naught." [1]

JOHN LYDGATE (cir. 1370–1451) was another of this Chaucerian school. He was a monk at the Benedictine Monastery of Bury St. Edmund, in Suffolk; a learned man, and a pitilessly prolific writer. He tells us that Chaucer helped him with some of his early poems, amending the work of his "rude penne," and, like Occleve, he calls Chaucer "maister." He employed Chaucer's favourite metres, but missed the great poet's smoothness and melody. Indeed, he realised the deficiencies of his own versification, and in one of his poems, written after Chaucer's death, he regrets the loss of his master's help. "I had no guide," he says, and so, —

> "I toke none hede nouther of shorte nor longe." [2]

His *Complaint of the Black Knight* is an imitation of

---

[1] Prologue to *Gouvernail of Princes* (*De Regimine Principum*), Occleve's longest and principal work.
[2] *History of Troy* quoted in *Social England*, vol. ii. 378.

Chaucer's *Dethe of Blaunche the Duchesse*, and his *Story of Thebes* was intended as an addition to the *Canterbury Tales*.

Lydgate appears to have set himself seriously to the writing of poetry about 1420, when he was already some forty years old, and it is estimated that he bequeathed one hundred and fifty thousand lines of verse to posterity. *Stephen Hawes* (d. cir. 1520-30), who was Groom of the Chamber to Henry VII., carried this French or Chaucerian poetry on into the sixteenth century. He addresses Lydgate, "the most dulcet spryng of famous rethoryke," [1] as his master; but his long and tedious allegory, mis-named *The Pastime of Pleasure*, takes us back to the *Romaunt of the Rose*. This poem deals with the educa-tion of the perfect knight, and in its subject and purpose dimly foreshadows Spenser's *Faërie Queene*. Fifteenth-century England produced many other poems in the Chaucerian manner, some of which were long attributed to Chaucer himself. *The Cuckoo and the Nightingale* (between 1403-1410), which Milton admired enough to imitate, is slight but very graceful and pleasing. It is attributed to SIR THOMAS CLANVOWE, a courtier in the reigns of Richard II. and Henry IV. and a friend of "Prince Hal." [2]

At last men began to tire of the established poetic form and manner and to seek for something new. In the early years of the sixteenth century a restless search for novelty in metre and style is exemplified in the rude dog-gerel rhymes of JOHN SKELTON (1460?-1529). This eccen-tric and enigmatical poet was a clergyman in Norfolk. He was a noted scholar, and was at one time tutor to Henry VIII., but in his later life he gained a most un-

---

[1] *The Pastime of Pleasure*, canto xiv.

[2] This poem is included in Skeat's *Chaucerian and Other Pieces*. Some account of its author is given in the *Introduction*. The poem of Milton's referred to above (to which Professor Skeat calls attention) is the sonnet *To the Nightingale*.

savoury reputation. In the early part of his career he wrote some poems of a rather conventional character, such as his *Dirge on the Death of Edward IV.* (1483); but he abandoned this tamer manner for the extraordinary and more original style with which he is chiefly associated. The characteristic *Skeltonic verse* is short-lined and highly alliterative; it is full of double rhymes, and bristles with fragments of Latin and French. We are overwhelmed by a rapid, rattling discharge of words that strike us in quick succession like the pelting of hailstones. There is, moreover, a reckless and breathless volubility which at times approaches positive incoherence. Singular as was his manner, Skelton attacked some grave abuses with boldness and vigour, and he warns us that a serious meaning is under this grotesque exterior:

> "For though my rime be ragged,
> Tattered and jagged,
> Rudely rayne beaten,
> Rusty and moothe eaten,
> If ye talke well therewith
> It hath in it some pith."

His *Boke of Colin Clout,* that is of the simple rustic, the representative, like *Piers Plowman,* of the moral sense of the nation, from which the lines just quoted are taken, is a general indictment of ecclesiastical corruption. Another satire, *Why Come Ye not to Court ?* is a daring assault upon Cardinal Wolsey, then "in the plenitude of his power." Perhaps his best known work is his whimsical *Boke of Philip Sparrow,* which celebrates the death of a pet bird. This has undoubted merit, but it suffers from that elaborate verbosity characteristic of his style. Skelton has been compared to Rabelais and to Dean Swift, and undoubtedly, while inferior to them in ability, he had some traits in common with those great men. His work on the whole is coarse and earthly, with hardly a gleam of poetic beauty; but, while his verse has little intrinsic value, he at least helped poetry to break its bounds.

But while a large amount of verse was composed in England, under the dominant influence of Chaucer, if we would find the most brilliant and original development of his poetry we must cross the Scottish Border.

Chaucer in Scotland.

So far the Scotch had contributed very little to English literature; but now, for a hundred years or more, the Scotch poets surpassed their English rivals. A partial explanation of this striking fact is found in the conditions of Scotland at this time. Early in the fourteenth century the Scotch had won their independence at Bannockburn (1314) after a hard and glorious struggle. A little later the intense patriotism of the Scot, and the pride of national independence, found expression in JOHN BARBOUR's poem of the *Bruce* (cir. 1375), which chronicles the trials and final victory of the nation's hero. The fire of the old poet breaks out in that passionate and excellent apostrophe to Freedom which can stir men's hearts to-day:

> "A! Fredome is a noble thing!
> Fredome mayse man to haif liking;
> Fredome all solace to man giffis,
> He livis at ese that frely livis!"

Scotland, it is true, was still an unsettled, and in the remoter portions an almost barbarous country. It was full of discordant and warring elements. But it was free, its patriotism had already found a voice through poetry, and the best minds of Scotland were ready to appropriate and respond to the stimulus of foreign culture. At this critical time, KING JAMES I. (1394–1437) returned to Scotland after eighteen years of captivity in England. The king was one of the most accomplished and highly cultured princes of his time. He knew something of law and of philosophy, he was expert in all knightly exercise, he excelled in manly sports, and he was a skilful musician. He loved poetry, and he looked up to Chaucer and Gower as his masters in the art, pronouncing them "superlative as poetis laureate." When he came back to Scotland in 1424, he accordingly brought with him the best culture and the prevailing poetic taste of the South. And James was himself a poet.[1] In his *King's Quair* (King's Quire, or Book), he tells the story of his love for the Lady Jane Beaufort, his future bride. Coming to the window of his prison-tower to hear the song of the nightingale, he sees a lady at her orisons in the garden below, so beautiful that from henceforth he becomes her willing "thrall." Or, in Rossetti's words,

> "— the nightingale through his prison wall
> Taught him both lore and love." [2]

In its poetic form the *King's Quair* is highly artificial. Not only are there obvious reminiscences of Chaucer, but the hackneyed conventions of the French love-poets are freely employed. But with all this the *King's Quair* is not merely a frigid poetical exercise. When we get beneath the conventional dress and trite reflections, we reach the real lover. It is true that the prince may not have seen the lady at the precise place and time he describes, — the situation is indeed suspiciously poetical. But the important matter is not when he saw her, but that he loved her, and that his book is the genuine record of that love. Imitator as he was, we feel that the deepest source of the poet's inspiration was not Chaucer but Lady Jane Beaufort.

ROBERT HENRYSON (1425?–1506?), the next notable name in this line of Scottish Chaucerians, surpassed his royal

Henryson.   predecessor in originality and native force. Little is known of him beyond the fact that he was "a schoolmaster in Dunfermline." So far as is known, his

---

[1] It is proper to say that modern scepticism has denied that James wrote the *King's Quair*, or any other poems.

[2] Rossetti, *The King's Tragedy*.

Robyne and Makyne, a very human and simple little piece, is the earliest English pastoral. His *Testament of Cresseid,* a continuation of the story of Chaucer's *Troilus and Cressida,* shows appreciation of Nature, a gift of vivid description, and not a little tragic power. The faithless and once beautiful Cressida has become a leper, driven to beg in company with others who suffer from that terrible disease. Troilus sees her as he rides by. Something in the wretched outcast vaguely reminds him of Cressida, and he throws her an alms. After her death when the news of her fate is brought to Troilus, his words have a tragic restraint, a compressed passion, not unworthy of Shakespeare:

> "I can no moir,
> She was untrue, and wo is me thairfoir!"

On her tomb he puts this inscription:

> "Lo! fair ladyis, Cresseid of Troyis town,
> Sumtyme countit the flour of woman heid,
> Under this stane, late lipper, lye's deid!"

But Henryson did more than reproduce the romantic poetry of the past. He was an independent observer, and in his *Fables* he delineated the every-day and humble aspects of life with insight and a kindly humour.

The third in this succession was WILLIAM DUNBAR (1460? – 1520 ?), who is commonly considered the greatest poet **Dunbar.** of the British Isles "in the interval between Chaucer and Spenser." Dunbar is the true predecessor of Burns. He has the same power of graphic portraiture; the same coarse wit; the same delight in mingling the homely, the vulgar, the horrible, and the grotesque. Nor do the two poets seem to have been unlike in character. Dunbar appears to have been a man of strong and conflicting passions. He is by turns a bitter satirist and a lover of natural beauty. He is religious, and a master of coarse and scurrilous invective.

He shows an uproarious delight in the things of this life, and he is oppressed by the sadness and emptiness of existence. Now, in the spirit of Chaucer's *Good Counsel*, he bids us to "be blythe in heart for any aventure," and again the fear of death takes hold of him, and he declares that "all earthly joys return in pain." The little that is known of his life is in keeping with his vigorous and complex character. Born, as is supposed, in the East-Lothian district, in the middle years of the fifteenth century, he became a begging friar of the Franciscan Order. But he was unsuited to a friar's habit; and (as he says), he "made good cheer in every flourishing town in England betwixt Berwick and Calais." The friar's life seemed to him full of deceit, and he accordingly left the Order, and attached himself to the Scottish Court. One of his poems, *The Thistle and the Rose* (1503), celebrates the marriage of his royal patron James IV. with the Princess Margaret, the sister of Henry VIII., a marriage which united the Scotch thistle and the English rose. His masculine and vigorous genius is shown in his *Dance of the Seven Deadly Sins*, a gruesome vision which reminds the reader of the witches' revel in *Tam o' Shanter*. Among his shorter poems his *Lament for the Makers* is probably the best known. It was written in a time of sickness, and is a meditation on the universal conquests of death. After lamenting the fate of Chaucer, Gower, and other poets whom death had already taken, Dunbar declares that he will be the next to be summoned. Familiar as is its theme, the *Lament* is an impressive and dignified requiem, and its solemn refrain,

"*Timor Mortis conturbat me,*"

reverberates through the poem like a bell tolling for the departed.

Although Dunbar was the chief "maker," the poet

laureate, at the court of James IV., he was by no means the only poet of the time. He lived in a "Golden Age" of Scottish poetry; an age of intellectual activity and of general progress, when Scotland was assuming a more im-

Scottish literature. portant place among the powers of Europe. But this progress does not begin with James IV. In spite of frequent lapses, Scotland had been growing more law-abiding and more enlightened ever since the iron rule of James I. (1424–1437); and indeed the whole period, from the end of the fourteenth to the beginning of the seventeenth century, was a memorable one in the history of her literature. This literature lies beyond our present limits, but certain facts in regard to Scottish literature as a whole ought to be briefly noted. Unlike the early literature of Wales, Scottish literature, as the phrase is commonly used, is not distinctively the product of the Celt. It is composed within the political limits of Scotland, but it is not written in Gaelic but in the local form of English. It is true that there were poets in the wild regions of the North, in the outlying islands and the places comparatively inaccessible to English influence, who recited in Gaelic the legends of the Celt. But this Gaelic poetry lies outside the boundaries of the national literature, as we do not look to the Orkneys or the Hebrides for the national poets of Scotland, but to the Lowlands — the country of Scott or of Burns. Clearly the civilisation and literature of Scotland begin in the Lowlands, in that part of the country nearest to England; and from the Lowlands, civilisation pushes northward, gradually displacing the Gaelic by the English speech. The eastern Lowlands, the historic border-country north of the Cheviot Hills, was a source and a centre of civilisation. This beautiful region of the Lothian, and of "Ettrick and Teviotdale," of the Hills of Lammermuir and the Valley of the Tweed, is associated with the vague beginnings of Scottish (or Anglo-Scottish) poetry, for here are the Eildon Hills where, according to tradition, THOMAS THE RHYMER was held captive by the Queen of the Fairies. And this Lothian district has been the literary centre of Scotland almost from that time until now. It was the birthplace of Dunbar, John Knox, Hume, James Thomson, Walter Scott, and many of the greatest Scottish scholars and men of letters. It is the seat of Edinburgh, the city which was called "the modern Athens." Now this region was from its situation, not only peculiarly open to English influences, it had once been English ground. In Saxon times it was included in the Anglian Kingdom of Northumbria, which stretched as far north as the Frith of Forth. The region which was to be the heart of Scotland was thus peopled and ruled by the compatriots of Cædmon, Bede, and Alcuin, and Edinburgh itself was the capital of an English kingdom long before it was the capital and the literary centre of a Scotch one. When, nearly five centuries after the establishment of Northumbria, this region was included within the limits of Scotland, it remained substantially English in manners, language, and population. Speaking broadly, Scottish literature is thus the product of the Lowlands, where the English elements are the most pronounced, and it is in that part of Scotland where the English influences are the strongest and where the English race has the greatest ascendency that nearly all its greatest triumphs have been won.

Having traced the outcome of Chaucer's influence in Scotland and noted its culmination a century after Chaucer's death in the poetry of Dunbar, we must **English literature of the fifteenth century.** go back and take up the story of literature in England. We have seen that poetry in England after the death of Chaucer showed no spirit of progress. The poets are unable to take the old materials and transmute them into something new. "They are no longer able to discover new ways; instead of looking forward as their master did, they turn, and stand with their eyes fixed on him, and hands outstretched towards his tomb."[1] To make matters worse, these poets do not seem to have realised the superiority of their master's greatest work. Chaucer himself outgrew his dependence on French models; but his English successors often chose to follow him in his earlier manner, and in doing this they were struggling to keep alive poetic conventions that were worn out and doomed to pass away. This French poetry and culture had done a great work for England; but now its force was largely spent, and France for the time had nothing more to give. *Troubadour* and *trouvère* belonged to a world that was already growing antiquated; and Italy, not France, was becoming the intellectual leader and inspirer of Europe. But while bookish writers like Occleve and Lydgate drew little inspiration from the life that was within and around them, and so became conventional and pedantic, true poetry survived among the people in ballads and songs. The existence of this popular poetry from a very early period has been already alluded to, and nothing further need be said here upon the much discussed question of its origin and growth. It is enough to say that the fifteenth century was a great ballad-making epoch, that from about the middle of this period, some of the ballads were written down, and that in the beginning of the sixteenth century they found their way into print. Something may appropriately be said here, however, about this ballad poetry as a whole.

We are accustomed to speak of the naturalness and simplicity of the old ballads; but we must remember that the ballad has its settled conventions, its distinguishing poetic form and style. It has its own "poetic diction,"

[1] Jusserand: *A Literary History of the English People,* i. 495.

as well marked as that found in poetry of the most highly
wrought and artificial character. There are
certain stock phrases, certain tricks of verbal
repetition, certain refrains, which were the common property of the ballad-makers, and they recur in
ballad after ballad with little or no variation. More than
this, there is a general similarity of tone and method, the
same outlook on life. The union of all these and other
characteristics puts ballad poetry in a class by itself. The
ballads create for us a world of the imagination, less uni-
formly noble and majestic than the ampler world of the
epic, but with a fascination peculiarly its own.

**The old
ballads.**

And, in spite of what has just been said about the conventions of ballad poetry, this fascination comes largely
from the artlessness and simplicity of the ballads and from
their essential truth to human nature. The stereotyped
phrases are not stuck in as meaningless ornaments, they
are used to help out the imperfect art of the narrator.
They are convenient formulæ for the improviser, or for
the poet whose range of expression is small; but through
them, or in spite of them, the genuineness and integrity of
the poet's feeling makes itself felt or tears its way. And
so it happens that in reading the ballads we often come
upon jets of pure poetry, in the midst of comparatively
crude or uninspired verse, that show the force of the
central fires. Such an outburst is the revulsion of feeling
in *Edom o' Gordon* as he looks on the woman he has slain:

> "Then wi' his spear he turn'd her owre;
>   O gin her face was wan!
> He said, ' Ye are the first that e'er
>   I wish'd alive again.'

> .   .   .   .

> 'Busk and boun, my merry men a',
>   For ill dooms I do guess; —
> I cannot look on that bonnie face
>   As it lies on the grass.'"

Such is the cry of Margaret to her dead lover in *Clerk Saunders:*

> "'Is there ony room at your head, Saunders?
> Is there ony room at your feet?
> Is there ony room at your side, Saunders,
> Where fain, fain, I wad sleep?'"

And such are the three beautiful stanzas, beginning with a sustained and musical lyric movement and passing to a more retarded and solemn ending, which form the conclusion of *Sir Patrick Spens.*

These ballads then, rough and coarse as they often are, are securely based on nature. In Carlyle's phrase, they have "got the grip of it." They have one essential of great poetry, a true and deep sense of the wonder and pathos, the heroism and the tragedy, of human life. The *Twa Corbies* is a tragic masterpiece, abrupt, vivid, ghastly; Browning's *Last Duchess* is not more wonderful in concentration or in its power to suggest a story which is left half told. *The Nut-Brown Maid*, charming and musical from first to last, holds an assured place in the love-poetry of the literature.[1] In these ballads too we find the old fighting spirit of the race:

> "For Witherington my heart was wo,
> That ever he slain should be;
> For when both his legs were hewn in two,
> Yet he kneeled and fought on his knee."

And while there are no traces of that more subtle "feeling for nature" so common in modern literature, there is yet a robust and wholesome satisfaction in the "merry greenwood" and the free life out of doors. There is something charming in the refrain —

> "And the birk and the broom blooms bonnie,"

and there is a breath of the woods in the familiar lines —

---

[1] Professor Gummere points out that *The Nut-Brown Maid*, although commonly classed with the ballads, is rather a lyrical dialogue.

"When shaws been sheene, and shradds full fayre,
   And leves both large and longe,
   Itt is merrye walking in the fayre forrèst,
   To hear the smalè birdes songe."

As we should expect, the magical and the mysterious too, have their place in this world of the ballad. In the ballads there is a road to "fair elfland," the ghosts of dead loves appear at midnight, witches have "power to charm," and mermaids can wreck sailors. Among much that is gruesome, we find at times that lavish splendour, and that superiority to sordid fact, which helps to create the glamour of fairyland. What a ship this is for a maiden to sail in to seek for her "true love" —

"Her mast was cover'd wi' beaten gold
   And it shone across the sea;
   The sails were o' the grass-green silk,
   And the ropes o' taffatie."

The fact that the fifteenth century was a great ballad-making epoch is significant. The accredited representatives of English poetry at this time might seem uninspired, and poetry, even to their eyes, might seem fallen into a decline, but while the people made ballads and songs and listened to them with delight, the power to create poetry and to love it was still in the nation, and sooner or later under favourable conditions that power might be expected to make itself felt.

Meanwhile, and more particularly from about the middle years of the century, English prose was slowly gaining in range and effectiveness. Theological contro-
Fifteenth-century prose. versy is represented by REGINALD PEACOCK'S *Repressor of Overmuch Blaming of the Clergy* (c. 1455), a vigorous attack upon the Lollards; law, by SIR JOHN FORTESCUE'S *Difference between an Absolute and a Limited Monarchy*; and history, by sundry chronicles. But the noblest prose-work of this time is a work of pure

romance, the *Morte d'Arthur* of Sir Thomas Malory. The *Morte d'Arthur* was written in 1470, in the reign of Edward IV. It was mainly compiled out of certain French romances, translated and pieced together so as to form a tolerably consecutive narrative, "a most pleasant jumble and summary of the legends about Arthur." But we should not think of Malory as a mere translator and compiler; in combining and retelling these old stories he had produced a classic. Malory's *Morte d'Arthur* is the greatest prose-romance of our literature, the accepted version of the national legend. These stories had been often told, but Malory's version of them superseded all others for the great majority of English readers. It is Malory who gathers and preserves the spirit of Romance and hands it on to a later time. Little or nothing is known of him. Recent researches make it probable that he was an adherent of the Earl of Warwick, involved, like so many others, in the civil strifes of the time. But we are at least sure that the man who gave us this "noble and joyous book" of chivalry, lived in a base and cruel age,

> "That hover'd between war and wantonness,
> And crownings and dethronements." [1]

Never before had the nobility of England fallen so far from the old ideals of knightly honour as in this miserable epoch of political assassinations, duplicity, and broken faith. Yet it was a knight of this age, which saw the destruction of the feudal baronage of England, who transmitted to later times the chivalric ideals of the past. It is to Malory's book that the English poets turned in the romantic periods of the literature. In the sixteenth century, Spenser, the poet of chivalry, read it; and, in the nineteenth century, Tennyson made out of it his *Idylls of the King*. It was published by Caxton, the father of printing in Eng-

[1] Tennyson's *Idylls of the King*: Epilogue "To the Queen."

land, in 1485; and six editions of it had appeared between that time and 1634. To the first printer it seemed to teach a lesson, — the same lesson that Spenser afterwards taught in the *Faërie Queene.* "I have set it down in print," Caxton wrote, " to the intent that noble men may see and learn the noble acts of chivalry, the gentle and virtuous deeds that some knights used in those days, by which they came to honour, and how that they that were vicious were punished, and oft put to shame and rebuke; — Do after the good, and leave the evil, and it shall bring you unto good fame and renown."

When we look at this fifteenth-century literature as a whole, we see that it is almost a mere continuation of that which has gone before. Malory's *Morte d'Arthur* was probably the most memorable and permanently important book of the period, yet even Malory's work was a remnant of the Middle Ages made up out of fragments of the past. Good work was done, but it must be admitted that, while the fifteenth century may have been somewhat extravagantly abused, it cannot fairly be included among the great creative periods of the literature. One reason for this has already been pointed out: England stood in need of a new inspiration, and at the same time adverse conditions combined to delay its coming. Having followed the course of English literature during this interval and noted that it sprang mainly from French and mediæval sources, we must now glance at the progress of the new culture in Italy and then consider its entrance into England.

General survey.

CHAPTER II.

THE BEGINNING OF THE ENGLISH RENAISSANCE.

THE enthusiasm for art and letters, already apparent in Italy in the time of Chaucer, had since then continued to increase. The leading minds among the Italians began to turn from the logic and theology of the Middle Ages to the great writers of antiquity. Petrarch, "the Columbus of the new spiritual hemisphere," led the way to the classics, and inspired men with a new spirit. Petrarch himself lived before the revival of the study of Greek, but it was not long after his death before a knowledge of Greek life and literature stirred Italy with the power of a fresh revelation. About 1395, *Manuel Chrysoloras*, who had been an ambassador to Italy from Constantinople, began to teach Greek in Florence, and the study of classical antiquity became a passion. For a time Italy had the monopoly of this "new learning": then students came from beyond the Alps to sit at the feet of her great teachers, and in the fifteenth century she was the university of Europe. Art and learning found rich and powerful patrons. This is the century of *Cosmo di Medici* (1389–1464), the great banker-prince, who fostered the culture and destroyed the liberties of Florence; the century in which his grandson *Lorenzo the Magnificent* (1448–1492) was the centre of brilliant and eager representatives of the new culture. In painting, it was the century of the Pre-Raphaelites, of *Fra Angelico, Botticelli,* and *Ghirlandajo*; in sculpture, of *Ghiberti, Donatello,* and *Lucca della Robbia.* And it was the century in Italy of a growing moral cor-

The revival of learning in Italy.

ruption, which Savonarola tried in vain to cure. In the very citadels of the Church the spirit of a revived paganism was gaining the ascendency, and men were forsaking the Christian ideals, for the worship of beauty, pleasure, culture, and philosophy. At the end of the century Alexander Borgia, a man of revolting wickedness, was in the Papal chair. Italy was thus vibrating with life, agitated and confused by the opposition of rival ideals, swept on into the wildest excesses; she was at once a nursery of vice, and the centre of that love of beauty and culture which it was her mission to dispense. This culture was to be built into the fabric of modern European civilisation; it was to reinvigorate the genius of England, and help to promote there the greatest creative epoch of her literature.

In our general survey of the state of England during the fourteenth century, we saw that the institutions and ideals inherited from the Middle Ages were already beginning to be supplanted by a more modern spirit. In the fifteenth century, this contest between the old and the new order was fought out to its conclusion; and before its close England had passed out of the Middle Ages, and entered upon a new stage of growth. During this interval of transition, the old feudal organisation of society was destroyed, provision was made for a more general education by the foundation of schools and colleges, the printing press was established, the "new learning" was introduced, and signs of a spiritual awakening in matters of religion became apparent. These radical and comprehensive changes were not accomplished by a gradual and peaceable process of growth. In many instances the old order passively or actively resisted the progress of the new, and in the early part of the century the forces of conservatism gained a temporary and partial advantage. The strength of this reactionary spirit is shown in the attitude of the authorities towards the liberal ideas of Wyclif and his followers. Henry IV. supported the claim of the Church to absolute authority in matters of belief, and in 1401 an act was passed, *De hæretico comburendo,* which provided that heretics should be burned to death. This was the first law of this character ever enacted in England. Henry V. (1413–1422) set himself to stamp out the Lollards, who were still very numerous; and by 1417, when their leader Sir John Oldcastle was executed, their influence was practically at an end. This hostility towards freedom of thought was a drag on the progress of the Universities, and especially at Oxford, the source of most of the nation's intellectual life. The old scholastic learning, like the old poetic conventions of the French, was worn threadbare; yet, while the old curriculum handed down from the monastic schools no longer satisfied men's needs, the new learning had not yet come. It was one of those vacant and depressing intervals when men stand irresolute —

Religious persecution.

The decline of learning at Oxford.

> "Between two worlds, one dead,
> The other powerless to be born."

The new vigour which Wyclif had poured into Oxford had been stifled, and for one hundred years after the death of the great innovator, Oxford remained sunk in an intellectual torpor. The Bible was no longer regularly studied there. She produced no great and original thinkers, and by 1438 the decrease in the number of her students had become a matter of public concern. We have associated this decline of learning with the suppression of free thought, but it was also due in part to the condition of the country, unsettled by the frequent political disturbances that characterised this time. What with foreign war and civil dissensions, from the beginning of the century to the accession of Henry VII. in 1485, England was hardly ever at rest. The usurpation of the crown by Henry IV. had brought a long succession of evils in its train, and one revolt against the royal authority followed another until we reach the brutal and bloody period of the civil wars (1455-1485). War is not necessarily disadvantageous to literature; it may even be an incentive to literary production. Towards the end of the sixteenth century Shakespeare made this brutalising civil strife between York and Lancaster the main theme of his great series of English historical dramas. But, while the Wars of the Roses hastened the end of the Middle Ages in England by the destruction of the powerful nobles, the total effect of the foreign and domestic conflicts of this period was unfavourable to the progress of learning and literature. To a great extent, men became depraved and brutalised by this continual bloodshed; and the factional quarrels in which no great principle was at stake increased the demoralisation of the nation and tended to destroy or debase its ideals. The greatest patrons of learning were drawn into the vortex of political discussion. In Henry VI.'s reign, Humphrey, Duke of Gloucester, who though a wily and selfish politician was the most prominent advocate of Italian culture, was arrested for High Treason, and died a few days later. The death of Lord Rivers, the brother-in-law of King Edward IV., was an even greater loss to learning. This accomplished and cultured gentleman, the friend and patron of Caxton, and the translator of the first book printed in England, was executed in 1483. He died in the prime of an honourable and useful life, a victim to the ambition of Richard III. But of all these noble and unfortunate patrons of learning the scholarly and infamous JOHN TIPTOFT, EARL OF WORCESTER (1428?-1470), is probably the most typical. Tiptoft visited Jerusalem and studied in Italy under Guarino of Ferrara, a great teacher of the "new learning." He had a genuine interest in things of the intellect, and won great praise for a Latin oration which

he made before the Pope. He presented valuable manuscripts, which he had brought from the Continent, to the
University of Oxford. He translated several of the Latin
classics into English, and he was beyond doubt one of the
greatest pioneers of the new culture in England. Intel-
lectually eminent, he was also morally depraved, a combination often found in the Italian patrons of art and learning
at this time. His great abilities were largely given to
politics, and he was executed for political reasons in 1470.
Tiptoft represents in his life and character the conflicting
tendencies, the good and evil of his contradictory time;
his death is another illustration of the way in which the
factional quarrels of the period obstructed the advance of
English scholarship. "What great loss it was," wrote Fuller, "of the noble, virtuous, and well-disposed lord, the
Earl of Worcester! The axe did then at one blow cut off
more learning than was in the heads of all the surviving
nobility."

We may then conclude that the progress of the "new
learning" in England was somewhat retarded by the peculiar conditions of the time. In the fourteenth century the influence of Italian culture
is apparent in the later works of Chaucer, and
the spirit of the Reformation was anticipated by
Wyclif; but these men were far ahead of their
time, and it was not until towards the end of the fifteenth
century, when the long struggle for the crown had been
ended by the accession of Henry VII., that the Italian influence began again vitally to affect England, and a great
religious teacher arose again at Oxford in John Colet.

But even before this there were many indications that,
in spite of adverse conditions, a change was at hand. Although the old educational methods were still followed,
and although the study of Greek was not introduced
until the last quarter of the century, the material equip-

*The prepara-
tion for
the "new
learning"
in England.*

ment for education was steadily increased.   Three universities arose in Scotland between 1410 and 1494.   Three
colleges and a Divinity school were founded at Oxford
between 1429 and 1458, and four colleges were founded
at Cambridge between 1437 and 1473.   In 1440 the
gentle and unfortunate Henry VI. established the great
school at Eton known as Eton College.   All this provision
for education was rather a continuation of the work of the
preceding century than the direct result of any fresh stimulus from Italy; yet it helped to prepare the way for the
revival of letters.   From the early years of the century
there are signs that this revival was at hand.   Humphrey,
Duke of Gloucester, the patron of Occleve and other men of
letters, encouraged learning and the study of the Latin
classics, much as rich and powerful men were doing in Italy;
and as early as 1418, Cardinal Beaufort induced Poggio
Bracciolini, a distinguished Florentine scholar, to visit
England.   During the middle years of the century ambitious students began to repair to Italy from the English
Universities, especially from Oxford, to pursue their studies
at Ferrara, Florence, or Bologna.   After their return to
England several of these men rose to high positions in the
Church; they brought back collections of books, which
often went to enrich the college libraries; and more than
this, they brought back something of the spirit of Italian
scholarship.   Thus, through many channels, the New
Learning was slowly beginning to irrigate English soil.

Meanwhile, in the troubled reign of Edward IV. (1461-
1483), the new invention of printing books from movable
type was brought into England.   WILLIAM CAXTON (1422-
1491), who had learned this wonderful art of printing in
the Low Countries, returned to England in 1470 and set
up his press in a house near Westminster Abbey, "at the
sign of the Red Pale."   Here he published the *Dictes and
Sayings of the Philosophers* (1477), translated from the

French by Lord Rivers, the first book printed in England. Caxton was no mere tradesman; he had a genuine love for literature. His press gave England the best he knew — Chaucer's *Canterbury Tales*, Gower's *Confessio Amantis*, Malory's *Morte d'Arthur*, and an English translation of Vergil's *Æneid*. He was himself an industrious translator, and the prefaces which he wrote for a number of his publications are clearly and simply written. He won the favour of the great; "many noble and divers gentlemen" discussed literary matters with him in his humble workshop; even kings took an interest in his work. King Edward died, and Caxton's sometime patron, Richard of Gloucester, usurped the throne; but while England was torn by the strife of factions, the old printer worked on with a steady industry, lamenting at times in his prefaces some scholarly patron cut off by the violence of the times.

Having spoken of the preparatory stage of the "new learning" in England, we must now turn to its definite establishment by a remarkable group of scholars known as the Oxford Reformers. The leaders of this little group were WILLIAM GROCYN (1440?– 1519), THOMAS LINACRE (cir. 1460–1524), JOHN COLET (1467?–1519?), the great Dutch scholar DESIDERIUS ERASMUS (1467–1536), and SIR THOMAS MORE (1478–1535). In 1491 Grocyn returned from Italy, where he had studied under two of the greatest classical scholars of the day, and inaugurated the regular public instruction in Greek at Oxford. He was soon joined by his friend and fellow-student Linacre, a learned physician, then fresh from his studies in Italy, and the two worked together at Oxford, teaching the language which had become the badge of the new learning. Among Linacre's pupils was Thomas More, then an attractive and quick-witted youth who already seemed likely "to prove a marvellous man." By 1497,

The "Oxford Reformers."

Oxford had acquired such a reputation as a school for the classics that Erasmus, too poor to go to Italy, came to England instead, to study under Grocyn and Linacre. And Erasmus found Oxford, lately inert and uninspiring, so full of "polish and learning" that he hardly regretted his change of plan. "When I listen to my friend Colet," he wrote, "it seems like listening to Plato himself. Who does not wonder at the wide range of Grocyn's knowledge? What can be more searching, deep, and refined than the judgment of Linacre? When did nature mould a temper more endearing and happy than the temper of Thomas More?" Under these men and their associates Oxford became the first centre of the new learning in England. Cambridge soon joined in the educational revival; in Henry VIII.'s reign, the influence of the Italian culture reached the Court, and finally became a part of **Humanism** the nation's life. One trait of these Oxford **in England** reformers can hardly fail to impress us; they **and Italy.** were men of lofty character, and their work bears the stamp of a deeply serious and often distinctly religious spirit. The scepticism, the levity, the worship of beauty, the riot of sensuality, which were then degrading Italy, had no place in the lives or the books of these English scholars. Almost from the first the tone of the new learning in England was spiritualised by the inherently moral and religious temper of the English character. The knowledge of Greek which Colet gained in semi-pagan Italy he applied to the study of the New Testament, and his first work after his return to Oxford was to infuse new life into the interpretation of the Bible by a course of lectures on the *Epistles of St. Paul.* He boldly attacked the covetousness and self-seeking then prevalent in the Church; and, quiet scholar as he was, he dared to stand up before an assembly of the greatest prelates of England and rebuke them for their corrupt and worldly lives. He devoted a considerable part of his fortune to the establishment of the free Grammar School of St. Paul in London (1510–12); and in this school (although great attention was given to the classics), the image of the child Christ was set up above the Head Master's desk, with the inscription, "Hear ye Him." Both Erasmus and More were at heart profoundly serious, having indeed caught much of Colet's spirit. Under the keen satire of the one and the playful wit of the other was the reformer's earnestness of purpose. More jested with his executioner on the steps of the scaffold, but he willingly died for his faith. Like Colet and Erasmus, More was keenly alive to the existing imperfections in both Church and State. In his account of the imaginary commonwealth of *Utopia* (1516), he set before Europe a picture of an ideal state, — a picture which suggests in almost every detail the shortcomings and evils of the reality. The social changes which More thus indirectly advocated were both radical and comprehensive, for in almost everything More's *Utopia* is the precise opposite of More's England. In this dream of the future, the old ideals of the Middle Ages find no place; but that modern spirit, which had already manifested itself in Wyclif and Langland, reappears — if in a different aspect — in More's vision of a new earth.

The difference between these English humanists (as the disciples of the new learning were called) and many of their Italian contemporaries is more than personal, it is national also. It helps us to understand why the Renaissance in England was a different thing from the Renaissance in Italy. While Englishmen did not remain altogether untouched by the lower influences in Renaissance Italy, England on the whole was proof against them. The Renaissance in England produced no Raphael, no Michael Angelo; but it produced no Borgia or no Machiavelli.

The Renaissance in Italy, which embodied in colour and stone a love of beauty, produced no such mighty intellect as that of Bacon, it produced no Shakespeare. The attraction of Italy for the English is the attraction of opposites. The profound racial differences between the Teuton of the North and the Latin of the South, modified or transfused the influences of Italy, and made the Teutonic Renaissance not merely a revival of letters but a religious reformation.

While the touch of Greek beauty and philosophy, restored and immortal after their burial of a thousand years, was thus reanimating Europe, the horizon of the world was suddenly enlarged by a series of great discoveries. In 1486 Diaz discovered the Cape of Good Hope; in 1492 Columbus penetrated the sea of darkness and gave to civilisation a New World; in 1498 Vasco da Gama rounded Africa and made a new path to India. England shared in this fever of exploration; and in 1497 the Cabots, sent by Henry VII. "to subdue land unknown to all Christians," saw the mainland of America. We can hardly overestimate the impetus given to the mental life of Europe by such a sudden rush of new ideas. The opportunities for life and action were multiplying: man's familiar earth was expanding on every side. The air was charged with wonder and romance; the imagination of explorers was alive with the dreams of a poet; and cities shining with gold, or fountains of perpetual youth, were sought for in the excitement of sensation which made the impossible seem a thing of every day.

The discovery of the New World.

In the midst of all the new activity, Copernicus (cir. 1540) put forth his theory that, instead of being the centre of the universe, round which the whole heavens revolved, the solid earth was but a satellite in motion round the central sun. While this conception, so

Copernicus.

startling to men's most fundamental notions, was slow to gain general acceptance, it was another element of wonder and of change.

The Church was quickened by the currents of this new life. Men chafed at its corrupt wealth and narrow

The Reformation. mediæval views. The Bible was translated and made the book of the people. Luther, the type of the unfettered, individual conscience, faced Pope and Cardinal with his "Here I stand, Martin Luther; I cannot do otherwise: God help me." This mighty upheaval shook England as well as Germany. The year 1526 saw the introduction of Tyndale's translation of the Bible, and eight years later the policy of Henry VIII. withdrew the Church in England from the headship of the Pope.

Thus England came to share in the diverse activities of the Renaissance, intellectual, maritime, and religious;

Summary. in the revival of learning, the discovery of the world, and the Reformation. In the fifteenth century she had absorbed and stored up many vital influences; early in the sixteenth century these slowly accumulated forces, these new emotions and ideas, began to find an outlet in the work of a new class of writers, and we reach the threshold of the Elizabethan Era, the time when the Renaissance found utterance in English literature.

CHAPTER III.

THE ENTRANCE OF THE NEW LEARNING INTO LITERATURE.

(Cir. 1509–1579.)

With the reign of Henry VIII. (1509–1547), we enter upon a new stage in the progress of the English Renaissance. During this period educational reform spreads from the Universities to the grammar schools, while the influence of Italian art and culture affects many of the great nobles and becomes apparent at Court. England is beginning, in a somewhat halting and experimental fashion, to use the new material she has received. The New Learning, having passed beyond merely academic limits, is beginning to be converted into a new literature.

New Learning at Court.

The new scholarship had naturally started at the Universities; the new literature naturally began at the Court. In spite of those faults which later assumed such terrible proportions, the young Henry VIII. was well qualified to be the patron of art and learning. He was enormously wealthy, open-handed, high-spirited, and remarkable for his frank bearing, manly beauty, and varied accomplishments. He was probably the most learned and cultured prince in Europe: he encountered Luther in controversy, and he wrote songs, composing both words and music. He was a lavish patron of art. He had that love of magnificence, that delight in luxury, beauty, and colour, so characteristic of the men of the Italian Renaissance. Brutal egoist and tyrant as he was at heart, Henry's intellectual sympathies, his love of art, his fondness for gorgeous masques and pageants, combined to promote the new culture. Erasmus went so far as to complain that the love of learning had left the clergy and "gone from them to the secular princes, the court and the nobility." Some of the courtiers made verses which were circulated in manuscript among their friends. The chief among these "Courtly makers," as an old writer calls them, were SIR THOMAS WYATT (1503–1542), and his poetical

Wyatt and Surrey. disciple HENRY HOWARD, EARL OF SURREY (1517 ?–1547). Without great poetic genius, these two courtiers made an epoch in literary history. Indeed, their influence upon the course of English poetry seems out of proportion to their abilities or to the intrinsic merit of their work. Wyatt and Surrey were men of cultivated taste. They read the Latin classics, they were imbued with a love of Italian poetry, especially of the sonnets of Petrarch, and a large part of their work consists of translations or imitations of foreign models. But, while they did not originate a new order of poetry, they were the first to introduce new verse-forms and a new style of poetry into England. Italian scholarship entered England through Grocyn and his colleagues, Italian poetry through Wyatt and Surrey. In this important work, Wyatt, who was about fifteen years older than Surrey, was the leader. Wyatt, like Chaucer, was at one time esquire to the King. When about twenty-three he travelled in Italy, and was afterwards sent on several diplomatic missions. He introduced the sonnet into England, and he is said to have been the first English writer of "polished satire." He often shows an imperfect mastery of metre; but he has left a few lyrics which are a worthy prelude to the great chorus of Elizabethan song. Surrey carried forward the work which Wyatt had begun. His versification is smoother than

that of his master, his touch is more assured. He wrote
sonnets in the Petrarchian manner, made translations
from several Latin poets, and above all, in his translation
of a part of Vergil's *Æneid* he introduced blank verse into
England. The benefit of these innovations to later English poetry is as striking as it is obvious. The sonnet is one
of the recognised glories of English poetry, while blank verse,
used in the first English tragedy, improved and developed
by Marlowe, Shakespeare, and Milton, is the metre of our
greatest dramas and our greatest epic. The publication, in
1557, of the *Songs and Sonnets* of Wyatt, Surrey, and other
authors in a work commonly known as *Tottel's Miscellany*
(the forerunner of many similar anthologies), introduced
this new poetry to a wider audience. Surrey perished at
thirty, a victim to the tyranny of Henry VIII.: his work
was but begun, and, for some time after his death the
poetical reforms which he and Wyatt had inaugurated
made no apparent progress. Indeed, from the publication
of *Tottel's Miscellany* to the appearance of Spenser's *Shepherd's Calendar*, twenty-two years later, the progress of
English literature was slow, difficult, and uncertain. The
two really notable poets between Surrey and Spenser are
THOMAS SACKVILLE, LORD BUCKHURST (1536–1608), and
GEORGE GASCOIGNE (1536?–1577). With Sackville, as with

Sackville. Wyatt, Surrey, Sidney, Raleigh, and many other
aristocratic authors of their century, literature
was but one among many varied duties and pursuits. By
birth, wealth, and personal abilities, Sackville was well
fitted to take an active part in court life and public
affairs. He enjoyed the favour both of Elizabeth and
James I., and he led the active life of a successful
diplomatist, courtier, and man of affairs. He succeeded
Burleigh as Lord High Treasurer, and he died sitting
at the Council Board. But, if circumstances made
Sackville a statesman, Nature made him a poet. As a

young man he was one of the contributors to *The Mirror for Magistrates*, a lengthy poem by various authors. This work was designed to be a *mirror* in which *magistrates*, or those that are great in this world, could see by the example of others how "unstable" is "worldly prosperity" and with "what grievous plagues" the vices of great princes are punished. Its purpose was the same as Lydgate's *Fall of the Princes*, of which it was designed to be a continuation. Sackville's contribution to this poem consisted of a general preface, or *Induction*, and the *Complaynte of Henrye Duke of Buckingham*, in which the shade of that nobleman appears and tells the story of his fall. In the *Induction* we are told how the poet, meeting with *Sorrow*, is led by her into the region of the shades that he may see the spirits of the fallen princes and hear them tell their own stories. This seems but the repetition of an old theme; the thought, the verse, the imagery, all seem taken from the past; but Sackville has vitalised these old thoughts and images by his fresh creative power and made them a new thing. The sombre tone which pervades the noble *Induction*, gives it an impressive and artistic unity. The melancholy mood of the poet, the forlorn and dreary aspect of nature, the bitter cold, the gathering darkness, conduce, as in certain stories of Poe, to produce an harmonious effect. In the midst of this gloom and decay, appear the allegorical figures of Sorrow, Old Age, and the rest, presented with a remarkable vividness and force. It is safe to say that no English poet, from the death of Chaucer to the advent of Spenser, equalled Sackville in elevation, dignity, and force. Sackville was rather the precursor of a new poetry than the follower of the old; and his continuation of Lydgate's *Fall of the Princes*, is in reality the precursor of Spenser's *Faërie Queene*.

In the period of uncertainty and experiment which immediately preceded the great age of Elizabethan litera-

Gascoigne. ture, George Gascoigne is a typical and important figure. It was a time of transition. The
language was changing, and its vocabulary was being
rapidly enlarged. The laws of English prosody were still
unsettled; the possibilities of the sonnet and other novel
verse-forms had yet to be explored. The world of mediæval poetry had been overthrown, and men were trying in
some confusion to set up a new world in its stead. Gascoigne, a man of restless energy and adventurous life,
holds a foremost place among the literary experimenters
of this time. He was versatile and clever, a ready writer,
and a shrewd critic of his time. He wrote the first prose-
comedy in English (*The Supposes*, 1566, a translation of
Ariosto's *Gli Suppositi*); he was part-author of one of the
earliest English tragedies (*Jocasta*, 1566, modelled upon an
Italian adaptation of Euripides); he composed lyrics, tried
his hand at blank verse, and was in many directions the
pioneer of the coming age. Probably his best known work
is *The Steel Glass* (1576), a satirical poem on the evils and
follies of the time, in which he pictures the ideal state
somewhat as More had done in his Utopia.

While poetry was thus preparing the way for new triumphs, English prose was steadily gaining in variety and

The growth of English prose. in literary importance. In this advance, however, English had to contend against the time-
honoured prestige of Latin, and Latin was still
a formidable rival. Even ROGER ASCHAM (1515–1568), although he wrote in English, lamented the inferiority of his
native tongue to Greek and Latin. He thought that it was
more creditable to an author to write in Latin, and declared that in English everything was done "in a manner
so meanly, both for the matter and handling, that no man
could do worse." [1] Nevertheless, changing conditions were

---

[1] *Toxophilus, the schole of Shootinge* (1544).

making the triumph of the national language inevitable. Learning was no longer shut up in cloisters, and Ascham, mindful of the need of "the many," wrote "in the English tongue for Englishmen," and addressed his first book "To all Gentlemen and Yeomen of England."[1] We can gain some notion of the progress of English prose from the accession of Henry VIII. to the middle years of Elizabeth's reign by enumerating a few of the representative books and authors of that time. Much was done in the field of history to increase the Englishman's knowledge and appreciation of England and her past. Sir Thomas More's *History of King Richard the Third* (1513?) is a landmark in the history of English historical prose. It is not a great book, like the *Utopia*, but the story is told simply, clearly, and almost without comment. The historians, on the whole, found it difficult to emancipate themselves from monastic and mediæval methods, and the ponderous Chronicles produced at this time, are quaint, laborious, and respectable, rather than brilliant or profound. FABYAN's Chronicle (*Concordana of Histories*, printed in 1515) is a general survey of the nation's history; HALL's Chronicle, which was completed by GRAFTON (1548), treats of the period of the Wars of the Roses; while the important Chronicle of HOLINSHED and his co-workers (1577), furnished Shakespeare with the material for some of his greatest plays.

The labours of JOHN LELAND (cir. 1506–1552), "the father of English antiquaries," are a further proof of the interest then excited by the nation's past. GEORGE CAVENDISH (d. cir. 1562) wrote a life of his master, Cardinal Wolsey, which is said to be "the first separate biography in the English tongue," while *The Boke Named the Governour* (1531) of SIR THOMAS ELYOT (1490–1546) is "the earliest English treatise on moral philosophy." Froissart was translated into English by LORD BERNERS (1523), and More's *Utopia* by

[1] *Toxophilus, the schole of Shootinge* (1544).

Ralph Robinson (1551). Roger Ascham, at one time tutor
to Elizabeth, and one of the most eminent representatives of the new learning in England, wrote his *Toxophilus* (1544) in praise of archery. Ascham writes in an
agreeable, discursive style, relieving his instructions on the
use of the bow with allusions to Plato and the classics and
with reflections on the problems of education. Ascham
explained his theory of education in *The Schoolmaster* (1570).
His chief argument in this book is "that young children
should rather be allured to learning by gentleness and love,
than compelled to learning by beating and fear." [1] The
sermons of Ascham's contemporary HUGH LATIMER (1485?–
1555), the sturdy reformer, who was burnt at the stake,
are notable for their plain, vigorous, idiomatic English.
The son of a yeoman, Latimer was a man of the people, as
well as a scholar. Although he came "to stand before
kings," he spoke with earnestness, courage, and simplicity,
enforcing his teachings with homely and amusing stories,
often drawn from his own experience. It was in this period that English took the place of Latin in the services of
the Church. The first complete English Prayer Book, compiled and arranged by Cranmer and his assistants from the
old Latin Service Books, was authorised and published in
1549. Before this (1525), the *New Testament* had been
translated into English by WILLIAM TYNDALE, and before the
close of the century several translations of the entire Bible
had appeared. The *English Bible* not only influenced the
course of history; it did much, as has already been said, to
shape and settle the standards of English prose.

But the more distinctly æsthetic features of this period
should not be left unnoticed. These years of growth
The work   led England to Spenser, Shakespeare, and
of the   Bacon, as well as to Milton, Bunyan, and
translators. Cromwell; for "every breeze was dusty with the
golden pollen of Greece, Rome, and Italy." [2] · The sermons

choolmaster, Bk. i.   [2] Lowell's *Essay on Spenser*.

and death of Latimer, the English Prayer Book and Bible, suggest the presence of those moral and religious elements in the English Renaissance which gave it a peculiar seriousness, vitality, and elevation: the numerous translations from Latin, Greek, and Italian, which date from about the beginning of Elizabeth's reign, bear witness to the growing influence of Italy, and the progress of the movement in the sphere of taste, beauty, and passion. By these translations, the spirit of the new culture, which had already spread from the scholars to the nobility and the Court, was extended in ever widening circles to the people and became a living part of the nation's literature. Not only did the learned Lady Jane Grey linger "with much delight" over the Greek of Plato, while the others took their sport in the Park, not only did the Princess Elizabeth herself begin the day by reading the Greek Testament and the tragedies of Sophocles, the translators also did their part. It was for them to give the new thought a wider currency, and to make the great classics the common quarry for all who could read the English tongue.

During the latter half of the sixteenth and early part of the seventeenth centuries, Vergil's *Æneid*, Ovid's *Metamorphoses*, numbers of Seneca's plays, and Homer, in the famous translation of Chapman, were thus made English literature. The Elizabethan writers delighted in a somewhat ostentatious display of this newly acquired learning, and their works are often filled with classic allusions which we should now consider commonplace. But as a quickening power their effect was incalculable. Shakespeare's use of Sir Thomas North's translation of Plutarch's *Lives* admirably illustrates the way in which the translator supplied material for the author. Out of North's version Shakespeare built his *Julius Cæsar, Coriolanus, Antony and Cleopatra*, and, to some extent, *Timon of Athens.* The literature of Italy was likewise thrown open to the English reader. Harrington translated Ariosto's *Orlando Furioso* (1591), Fairfax translated Tasso's *Jerusalem Delivered* (1600), while hundreds of Italian stories were for sale in the London bookstalls clustered about old St. Paul's.

CHAPTER IV.

THE CULMINATION OF THE ENGLISH RENAISSANCE.

(From the Advent of Spenser, 1579, to the Death of Ben Jonson, 1637.)

The great age of Elizabethan literature, one of the most illustrious in human history, began with startling abruptness. For nearly two hundred years, from the death of Chaucer to the appearance of Spenser, the culture of Italy had been slowly forcing its way in England, — interrupted or retarded in its progress by many obstacles. During this long preparatory period of education, growth, and experiment, England had received much, but produced little. Suddenly, with the advent of Spenser, the earliest of the great Elizabethan writers, we pass into a period of the most lavish and amazing creative energy. The lean years, in which England could hardly produce a poet, are followed by a period of plenty; a period marked by a superb vitality, crowded with great works and great men. This period of performance, following as it does after two centuries of promise, extends to about the time of Ben Jonson's death in 1637, or for some sixty years. Indeed, the greatest work of this extraordinary epoch can be found, with a few exceptions, within an even shorter space. Broadly speaking, the literature which we commonly call Elizabethan, was the work of a single generation. Many of the foremost of the Elizabethan writers were born within a few years of each other; while Ben Jonson, the last of the Elizabethans, was only some twenty years younger than Spenser, who may be styled the first. This means that the great age of Elizabethan literature began with the almost simultaneous appearance of a number of remarkable men, and that with the passing of these men it came to an end. Compared with the length of the preparatory period, this literary culmination of the English Renaissance seems almost as brief as it is brilliant.

We cannot hope to account for such an epoch with scientific exactness. Such a sudden and impressive manifestation of latent power was probably the result of a fortunate conjunction of many causes, some of which are unknown or but imperfectly understood. A partial explanation, however, is to be found in the social, political, and educational conditions of the time. In Elizabeth's reign, and especially during the latter half, there was much to stimulate genius and encourage literary production.

In the two preceding reigns much of the national force had been spent in religious controversies. Edward VI. **Freedom from religious persecution.** (1547–1553) had forced Protestantism upon a nation not, as a whole, fully prepared to accept it; Mary (1553–1558), with a religious zeal as pathetic as, in our eyes, it was cruel and mistaken, had striven to persecute the people back into Roman Catholicism. In Elizabeth's reign we pass out of the bitterness and confusion of this warfare of religions into a period of comparative quiet. The religious and political difficulties which beset Elizabeth, on her accession in 1558, slowly sank out of sight under her firm and moderate rule. Patience and toleration did much to soften the violence of the religious parties; the fierce fires of martyrdom which had lit up the terrible reign of Mary, were cold, and the nation, relieved from pressing anxieties, was comparatively free to turn to other issues. The very year in which Shakespeare is supposed to have come up to London to seek his fortune (1587) saw the final removal of a threatened danger by the execution of Mary

Queen of Scots, while the year following England struck down the haughty menace of the Spaniard by her defeat of the Armada.

But the reign was more than a period of relief from past struggles or persecution; it was marked by a rapid advance *Prosperity* in national prosperity and by a widespread in- *of the* crease in the comforts and luxuries of life. *people.* Among the people there were many causes of contentment. Improved methods of farming doubled the yield per acre; the domestic manufacture of wool greatly increased, and homespun came into favour. In many little ways, by the introduction of chimneys, of feather beds, pillows, and the more general use of glass, the conveniences of living were greatly increased. The sea, as well as the land, yielded a large revenue. Not only did the English fishing-boats crowd the Channel, but hardy sailors brought back cod from the Newfoundland banks, or tracked the whale in the vast solitudes of the polar seas.

England was laying the foundations of her future commercial and maritime supremacy. Her trade increased with Flanders and with the ports of the Medi- *Growth of* terranean, and her merchant ships pushed to *Commerce.* Scandinavia, Archangel, and Guinea. In 1566 Sir Thomas Gresham built the Royal Exchange in London, a hall in which the merchants met as the Venetians in their Rialto. Toward the end of the sixteenth century the famous East India Company was established. The *The exten-* progress of popular education under the com- *sion of* bined stimulus of the Revival of Learning *education.* and the Reformation exercised an obvious and important influence upon the literature of Elizabeth's time. The dissolution of the monasteries by Henry VIII. (1535–39) had put an end to the monastic schools, which with a few exceptions had been antagonistic to the new learning. This was followed by a rapid increase in the number of free grammar schools, and through them, widely distributed as they were throughout the country, some tincture of the new classical learning spread to the middle classes. Green says that the grammar schools founded in the reigns of Edward VI. and of Elizabeth constituted " a system of middle-class education which by the close of the century had changed the very face of England." [1] With this spread of the new classical learning, we naturally connect a notable change in the literary conditions of the time. Before the great literary outburst in Elizabeth's reign, the literature of England had been almost entirely written by ecclesiastics or by men of the aristocratic class. The people of course had their rude, religious plays, their songs, ballads, and folk-lore; but apart from these they had been silent. It is a notable fact that in the great literary era of Elizabeth's reign the middle and lower-middle classes are represented for the first time in the history of England. Spenser, for instance, was the son of a cloth-weaver; Shakespeare, of a provincial dealer in hides and wool; Marlowe, of a shoemaker. All these, and many others, came from a class which hitherto had almost no part or place in the making of the representative literature of the nation; and all these men, like many of their followers, began their education at one or the other of the free grammar schools. Before the coming of Spenser, all the principal English poets of the century belonged to the noble or upper class. Wyatt and Surrey were noblemen and courtiers; Sackville, Lord Buckhurst and Earl of Dorset, was Lord High Treasurer of England; Turberville, the translator of Ovid, belonged to an old and distinguished family in Dorsetshire; Gascoigne was the descendant of a Chief Justice. But after Spenser, while there are still noble and aristocratic authors, such as

[1] *History of the English People*, ii. 86.

Sir Philip Sidney, Lord Bacon, and Sir Walter Raleigh, there are also the sons of the people, of the traders and cobblers and weavers; new men who have come up from the grammar schools or universities charged with new ideas. This is the rise of the people in the Kingdom of Letters; the appearance of the "third estate." And it is to these men of the "third estate" that the glory of Elizabethan literature is largely due; it is almost wholly to them that we owe the Elizabethan drama. While the sudden appearance of this new class of writers was by no means the only cause of the sudden greatness of Elizabethan literature, we can hardly doubt that it contributed to this result.

With the ease and wealth that sprang from this increasing prosperity came that delight in beauty, that half-pagan pleasure in the splendid adornments of life, which characterise the Italian Renaissance.

The splendour of life.

Life, no longer shut within the heavy masonry of the feudal castle, ran glittering in the open sunshine. Stately villas were built, with long gable roofs, grotesque carvings, and shining oriels, and surrounded with the pleached walks and the terraces, the statuary and the fountains, of an Italian garden.

The passion for colour showed itself among the wealthier classes in a lavish magnificence and eccentricity of costume. The young dandy went "perfumed like a milliner," [1] and often affected the fashions of Italy as the Anglo-maniac of our own day apes those of England. In its luxury of delight in life and colour, the nation bedecked itself

Dress.

> "With silken coats, and caps, and golden rings,
> With ruffs, and cuffs, and farthingales, and things;
> With scarfs and fans, and double change of bravery,
> With amber bracelets, beads, and all this knavery." [2]

[1] *King Henry IV.*, Act i. Sc. 3.
[2] *Taming of the Shrew*, Act iv. Sc. 3.

Moralists and Puritans bitterly denounced the extravagance and absurdities of the rapidly changing fashions. "Except it were a dog in a doublet," writes an author of the time, "you shall not see any so disguised as are my countrymen of England."[1] But ridicule and reproof were alike powerless to check the nation's holiday mood. Men put off their more sober garments to rustle in silks and satins, to sparkle with jewels; they were gorgeous in laces and velvets; they glittered with chains and brooches of gold; they gladly suffered themselves to be tormented by huge ruffs, stiff with the newly discovered vanity of starch.

Shakespeare, whom we cannot imagine over-precise, is fond of showing such fashionable vanities in an unfavourable light, and from more than one passage we may suppose him to have felt an intense, country-bred dislike for painted faces and false hair. On the other hand, when we read his famous description of Cleopatra in her barge, we appreciate how all this glow of colour appealed to and satisfied the imagination of the time.[2] The same spirit showed itself in the costly banquets; in the showy pageants or street processions, with their elaborate scenery and allegorical characters; in the revels like those with which Queen Elizabeth was received at Kenilworth (1575); in the spectacular entertainment of the mask, a performance in which poet, musician, and — as we should say — the stage manager, worked together to delight mind, eye, and ear. Milton has this splendour in mind when he writes:

> "There let Hymen oft appear
> In saffron robe, with taper clear,
> And pomp, and feast, and revelry,
> With mask and antique pageantry,
> Such sights as youthful poets dream
> On summer eves by haunted stream."[3]

[1] Harrison's *Elizabethan England*, Camelot Series, p. 108.
[2] *Antony and Cleopatra*, Act ii. Sc. 2.
[3] *L'Allegro.*

But the Elizabethan passion for dress and ornament is but a surface indication of the immense delight in life **Elizabethan** which characterises the time. If we would **delight** appreciate the vital spirit of this crowded and **in life.** bewildering age, we must feel the rush of its superb and irrepressible energy, pouring itself out through countless channels. England was like a youth first come to the full knowledge of his strength, rejoicing as a giant to run his course, and determined to do, to see, to know, to enjoy to the full. Shakespeare spoke for his age, when he declared that:

"Home-keeping youth have ever homely wits." [1]

The noble and wealthy sons of England crowded to Italy: they "swam in a gondola," [2] they plunged into the riotous and luxurious pleasures of Venice. The fever of adventure burned in men's veins. "We cannot denie," wrote one of Sir Walter Raleigh's companions, "we cannot denie that the chiefe commendation of virtue consists in action: we truly say that *otium* is *animæ vivæ sepultura*." [3] The thrill of this youthful zest in action, the allurement and mystery of the yet unconquered world, are in Shakespeare's lines:

"He wondered that your lordship
Would suffer him to spend his youth at home;
While other men of slender reputation,
Put forth their sons to seek preferment out:
Some, to the wars to try their fortune there;
Some to discover islands far away." [4]

Drake sailed round the world (1577–1580); the tiny ships of Hawkins, Frobisher, Gilbert, and the rest, parted

[1] *Two Gentlemen of Verona*, Act. i. Sc. 1.
[2] *As You Like It*, Act iv. Sc. 1
[3] *De Guiana Carmen Epicum*, quoted by Jusserand, *Literary History of the English People*, vol. ii. part i. p. 275.
[4] *Two Gentlemen of Verona*, Act i. Sc. 3.

the distant waters of unploughed seas. The buccaneers
plundered and fought with the zest and unwearied vigour
of the viking. When Sir Walter Raleigh was taken
prisoner in 1603, he is said to have been decked with four
thousand pounds' worth of jewels; yet, courtier and fine
gentleman as he was, he could face peril, hunger, and
privation, in the untracked solitudes of the New World.
With an insatiable and many-sided capacity for life typical
of his time, Raleigh wrote poetry, boarded Spanish galleons, explored the wilderness, and produced in his old age
a huge *History of the World*. In their full confidence of
power, men carried on vast literary undertakings, like
Sidney's *Arcadia*, Drayton's *Polyolbion*, or Spenser's
Faërie Queene, the magnitude of which would have daunted
a less vigorous generation. Nothing wearied, nothing
fatigued them; like Raleigh they could "toil terribly."
The young Francis Bacon — lawyer, philosopher, and
courtier — wrote to Cecil with an inimitable audacity:
"I have taken all knowledge to be my province."

The centre of all this full and active life was London.
It was there that not only all the great dramatists, poets,
and courtiers met, but there too came the famous travellers after their long and perilous voyages to take their ease at their inns. At the old
Mermaid Tavern in Bread Street gathered the great men
of the age. Here Shakespeare, Jonson, Raleigh, and the
rest drank their Malmsey and Canary, and smoked with
wonder the newly introduced tobacco, discussing, doubtless, the newest play or poem, or listening eagerly to travellers' tales of the splendours of Italy or the marvels of the
New World.

*Shakes-
peare's
London.*

We must remember that Shakespeare's, like Chaucer's,
London was a walled town, and that its great gates were
still used. Just outside of the wall to the north lay open
fields, dotted occasionally with houses and windmills.

There was Spitalfield, Smithfield or Smoothfield, then a grassy plain where tournaments were held, and where, under Mary, Protestants had been burned. Much of the ground about the city was thus uninhabited. The population of London at this time is placed at about a hundred and fifty thousand people, so that while the city was already pushing out into the country in some directions, the great bulk of the people could still be accommodated within the walls.

The streets were narrow and ill-paved, and unhealthy from refuse and bad drainage, but they were gay with the bright and varied costumes of the people. Along the Strand, which stretched beyond the city wall parallel with the Thames, stood some of the finest houses of the great nobles, — York House, where Bacon was born; Durham Place, where Raleigh lived; Somerset House, Baynard's Castle, and the Temple, with its gardens.

The majority of houses were built chiefly of wood, although brick and stone were beginning to be used. They were turreted, and had many gables and overhanging upper stories. All the handsome places on the Strand, whose beautiful gardens sloped to the Thames, had terraces and steps leading down to the water, and every great establishment had its own barge and watermen. Indeed, by either night or day the Thames was a beautiful sight, for the river then ran clear and sparkling, while on it floated snowy swans, and brightly trimmed boats, filled with a gay company, skimmed over its surface.

The same old London Bridge, which we noted in Chaucer's time, was still standing, but many houses and shops had been added to those it then contained. These were built with their rear overhanging the water, which rushed through the arches beneath them with great rapidity. The tower which stood before the drawbridge had been elaborately rebuilt by Elizabeth and called Nonesuch House, and on its battlements was now displayed a ghastly row of the heads of traitors and criminals.

But to make our mental picture complete, we must repeople these scenes with the rush of life; the nave of St. Paul's is filled with gossiping throngs, the Thames with its pleasure-seekers, the theatres packed with noisy spectators. If we can but make all this alive again in our imagination, we shall realise that to live in Shakespeare's London was to touch at every point all the crowded activities of the time.

And all this young life, with its varied spheres of action, was still further quickened by a deep national pride in the growing greatness of England, and by a feeling of chivalric loyalty to the Queen. Religious differences gave way before a common bond of patriotism. The men that faced "the Great Armada" were united by a common hatred of Spain, a common devotion to England and to her Queen. The destruction of this huge armament removed a great weight of apprehension and left men free to turn to other interests; it became a moving power in the literature of the time. We feel the exultant thrill of this triumph in those stirring words in Shakespeare's *King John:*

> "This England never did, nor never shall,
>   Lie at the proud foot of a conqueror,
>   But when it first did help to wound itself.
>   Now these her princes are come home again,
>   Come the three corners of the world in arms,
>   And we shall shock them. Nought shall make us rue,
>   If England to itself do rest but true.

And the centre of this new nationality was the Queen. Capricious, vain, and fickle as Elizabeth was, she awakened a devoted loyalty denied to the gloomy and relentless Mary, or to the timorous and ungainly James. She

[1] *King John*, Act v. Sc. 7.

SKETCH MAP OF

Based on contemporary maps and showing appro
the chief

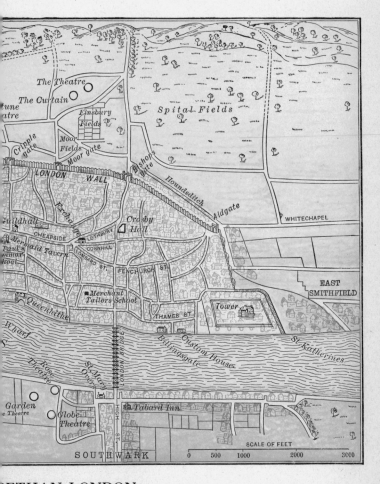

The Theatre

The Curtain

...tune
...atre

Finsbury
Fields

Cripple
gate

Moor
Fields

Moor gate

Spital Fields

LONDON   WALL

Bishops
gate

Houndsditch

Aldgate

WHITECHAPEL

...undhall

CHEAPSIDE

...er
...aul's
...mmar
...ool

Mermaid Tavern

Crosby
Hall

Threadneedle St.

LOTHBURY

CORNHILL

LOMBARD ST.

FENCHURCH ST.

EAST
SMITHFIELD

Queenhithe

Merchant
Tailors School

THAMES ST.

Tower

...Wharf

Rose
Theatre

St. Mary Overy

HIGH ST.

LONDON BRIDGE

Billingsgate

Custom House

St. Katherines

...Garden
...e Theatre

Globe
Theatre

Tabard Inn

SOUTHWARK

SCALE OF FEET

0   500   1000   2000   3000

...BETHAN LONDON

...e sites of the principal theaters, etc., and some of
... suburbs.

was too parsimonious to be a liberal patron to struggling authors, but she had a quick and practical sympathy with

Loyalty to the Queen.

the new intellectual and literary activities of her time. The first regular tragedy was produced before her, and her interest helped the development of the struggling drama. "The versatility and many-sidedness of her mind enabled her to understand every phase of the intellectual movement about her, and to fix by a sort of instinct on its highest representative." [1] As we review the achievements of Elizabethan England we can see that the same magnificent energy which made England prosperous at home and tri-

Summary.

umphant upon the seas is the motive power back of the greatest creative period of her literature. Looking at this great time as a whole, we must see England as "a noble and puissant Nation rousing herself like a strong man after sleep and shaking her invincible locks — as an eagle mewing her mighty youth and kindling her undazzled eyes at the full midday beam." [2] Elizabethan literature is but one outlet for this imperious energy; it is the new feeling for life that creates the drama as well as discovers kingdoms far away.

[1] *Green's History of the English People*, vol. ii. p. 319.
[2] Milton's *Areopagitica*.

EDMUND SPENSER.

(1552–1599.)

"Here next to Chaucer Spenser lies; to whom
In genius next he was, as now in tomb."
CAMDEN'S *Version of Spenser's Epitaph.*

"Our sage and serious poet Spenser, whom I dare be known to think
a better teacher than Scotus or Aquinas."
— MILTON'S *Areopagitica.*

"Sweet Spenser, moving through his clouded heaven
With the moon's beauty, and the moon's soft pace,
I called him Brother, Englishman, and Friend."
— WORDSWORTH'S *Prelude.*

"The gentle Spenser, Fancy's pleasing son:
Who, like a copious river, pour'd his song
O'er all the mazes of enchanted ground."
— THOMSON'S *Seasons.*

"The love of beauty, however, and not of truth is the moving
principle of his mind; and he is guided in his fantastic delineations by
no rule but by the impulse of an inexhaustible imagination."
— HAZLITT'S *Lectures on the English Poets.*

Many of those diverse elements which went to the
making of this varied, impetuous, and romantic time,
found expression in the genius of Spenser, the successor
to Chaucer, the forerunner of Shakespeare in the imperial
line of English poets.   Spenser began his work at a critical
moment in the intellectual and spiritual life of England.
For nearly a century the nation had been stirred by desires and ideals which were distinct and, to some extent,
antagonistic.   Englishmen had felt the allurement of
Italy, the spell of that strange magic which seemed to
the worthy Ascham like "the enchantment of the Circes";
and England, like Germany, had passed through a momentous period in her spiritual and religious life.   The Revival
of Letters and the Reformation, thus entering England
at almost the same time, had produced confusion and

antagonism. Some men were tempted to forget everything in the pure joy of life and in the passion for beauty; while others, in the zeal of their protest against the delights of the senses, condemned art altogether, and grew more rigid and uncompromising in their morality. Men found it hard to reconcile Beauty with Righteousness; and the growing separation between the æsthetic and the ethical ideal, reënforced by political dissensions, divided England in the seventeenth century into Cavaliers and Puritans. Spenser wrote before the lines were thus sharply drawn, while men were yet confused by the jumble of new impressions and ideas, and Spenser is the representative of this time. He represents its incongruities — its conflicting ideals. He was at once an English Puritan and an Italian Humanist: he was a lover of the ideal philosophy of Plato, and he was the poet who brought into English verse the soft music and sensuous beauty of the Italian romance. To Milton he was the "sage and serious Spenser — a better teacher than Scotus or Aquinas." To Hazlitt, a brilliant critic of a later time, "the love of beauty and not of truth" seemed the moving principle of Spenser's mind. We need not attempt to reconcile these opposing views; each has a large measure of truth. Spenser, standing for his time, was the child of the Renaissance and the child of the English Reformation. He was the lofty moralist, and the "Rubens of English poets."

Edmund Spenser was born in London in 1552. The same year saw the birth of Walter Raleigh in a village in Devonshire, and two years later Philip Sidney began his short and glorious life in his family's splendid country-house at Penshurst. Spenser belonged to a respectable Lancashire family. His father is believed to have been a journeyman cloth-maker, who came up to London shortly before the poet's birth. What-

Spenser's
life.

ever his ancestry may have been, Spenser's family had apparently but little means, and he was forced to make his own way in the world. After attending the Merchant Taylors' School, then just opened in London, as a "poor scholar," he entered Pembroke College, Cambridge, as a *sizar*, in 1569.[1] His first published poems, translations from Du Bellay and Petrarch, appeared in the same year in a curious miscellany called the *Theatre for Worldlings*. The work is smooth and creditable, but the especial value of the poem is its indication of Spenser's early interest in the French and Italian literatures. While at college Spenser became acquainted with Edward Kirke (who afterwards wrote an introduction to the *Shepherd's Calendar*), and with Gabriel Harvey, who figures in the literary history of the time as a learned if somewhat formal and narrow-minded critic, deeply interested in the development of English poetry. Spenser left Cambridge after taking his master's degree, in 1576, and spent two years in the north, probably with his kinsfolk in Lancashire. About 1579 he settled in London, where he became acquainted with Sir Philip Sidney, the mirror and pattern of the English gentleman of the time. Tradition has it that Spenser wrote his *Shepherd's Calendar* during a stay at Penshurst, Sidney's country-place. The poem received immediate recognition as a work which marked the coming of a new and original poet. It is an eclogue, or pastoral poem, in twelve books, one for each month. Spenser weaves into its dialogue some of his recent country experiences, including his unsuccessful suit of a lady he calls Rosalind. He asserts his Puritanism, condemns the laziness of the clergy, and pays the customary tribute to the vanity of the Queen. In Elizabeth's time the great avenue to success was through the royal favour,

---

[1] A *sizar* is "an undergraduate student, who, in consideration of his comparative poverty usually receives free commons."— *Century Dict.*

and Spenser tried to push his fortunes at court through his friend Sidney and the Earl of Leicester. It was probably through the influence of these powerful patrons that Spenser was appointed secretary to Lord Grey de Wilton, the new deputy to Ireland; and in 1580 the young poet left the brilliant England of Elizabeth, with its gathering intellectual forces, for a barbarous and rebellious colony. In this lawless and miserable country he spent the rest of his life, except for brief visits to England; "banished," as he bitterly writes, "like wight forlorn, into that waste where *he* was quite forgot."

Lord Grey was recalled in 1582, but Spenser remained in Dublin about six years longer as clerk in the Chancery Court. We find an unintentional irony in the fact that the former incumbent, from whom Spenser purchased the post, a certain Ludovic Briskett, wished to "retire to the quietness of study." Spenser was rewarded for his services by a gift of the castle of Kilcolman, part of the forfeited estate of the Desmonds. There Sir Walter Raleigh found him

> "Amongst the coolly shade
> Of the green alders of the Mullae's shore," [1]

and heard from the poet's own lips the first three books of his masterpiece, the *Faërie Queene*. Raleigh, a poet himself, was filled with admiration. He prevailed upon Spenser to go with him to Court and bring his poem to the attention of the Queen. There was more than one reason why Elizabeth should look with favour upon the work. It was glorious poetry, and it was perhaps the most voluminous and elaborate compliment ever presented by a poet to his sovereign. Not only was it dedicated to "The most high, mighty, and magnificent Empress," Elizabeth, "to live with the eternity of her fame;" it was in itself a stupendous monument of flattery. The *Faërie Queene* her-

---

[1] Spenser's *Colin Clout Come Home Again.*

self was both the type of Glory and the special revelation of it in the person of the poet's "most excellent and glorious Sovereign." Moved by the merits of the poetry, or by the extravagance of the praise, Elizabeth rewarded Spenser with a pension of fifty pounds a year (which he is said to have found great difficulty in collecting), and the first instalment of the *Faërie Queene* was published in 1590.

Spenser remained in London about a year, learning the miseries of a suitor for princes' favours, and then returned in bitter indignation to his provincial seclusion. His keen sense of disappointment and neglect found utterance in a passage in *Mother Hubbard's Tale* (1591), which brings us near to the inner life of the poet himself.

> "Full little knowest thou, that hast not tride
> What hell it is, in suing long to bide:
> To loose good dayes, that might be better spent;
> To wast long nights in pensive discontent;
> To speed to-day, to be put back to-morrow;
> To feed on hope, to pine with feare and sorrow;
> To have thy Princes' grace, yet want her Peeres;
> To have thy asking, yet waite manie yeeres;
> To fret thy soule with crosses and with cares;
> To eate thy heart through comfortlesse dispaires;
> To fawne, to crowche, to waite, to ride, to ronne
> To spend, to give, to want, to be undonne.
> Unhappie wight, borne to desastrous end,
> That doth his life in so long tendance spend!"

It is not often that we are permitted to get so close to Spenser as in these words. They give us a glimpse into the true meaning of his experience. We feel how he hated his exile in Ireland, when we see how deeply his failure to leave it for England had wounded him, and we can estimate more justly the effect of that dreary banishment on Spenser and his work. Shut out from all the excitement and rush of life that crowded Shakespeare's London, he turned from the repulsive coarseness and violence about him, to delight his soul in the languor and beauty of the Italy of the Renaissance. He lived in the dream-world of Ariosto and Tasso, and carried their gorgeous fancies into his *Faërie Queene*.

After his return to Ireland in 1594, he married Elizabeth Boyle, "an Irish country lass," and paid her a poet's tribute in his *Amoretti*, or love sonnets, and in the splendid *Epithalamion*, or marriage hymn, a poem filled with a rich and noble music. Here also, besides writing several minor poems, he completed six of the twelve books that were to make up the first part of the *Faërie Queene*. About 1595 Spenser again visited London, and in the following year published his *Prothalamion*, or song before marriage.

It would appear from this poem that Spenser, in his longing to return to England, had again become an unsuccessful suitor at Court. He alludes to the death of his former patron, the Earl of Leicester, and speaks sadly of his own "friendless state." He speaks of his vain "expectation of idle hopes," of his "long, fruitlesse stay in Princes Court," and of the sullen care and discontent which afflict him. Ireland seems to have been Spenser's doom, and in 1598 he returned to that misgoverned and perilous country which necessity had made his home. Shortly after, the miserable natives again rose in rebellion, and hordes of desperate men ravaged Munster. Spenser's castle was sacked and burnt. Although Spenser and his wife managed to escape, according to Ben Jonson, their new-born child perished in the flames. Spenser soon afterward went to London as bearer of despatches. Here he died a few weeks later (January 16, 1599) in a lodging-house, a ruined and broken-hearted man. Ben Jonson wrote: "He died for lack of bread in King Street, and refused twenty pieces sent to him by my Lord of Essex, saying that he had no time to spend them."

Spenser stands alone. He is the one supremely great

undramatic poet of a play-writing time. In youth he had, indeed, composed nine comedies, now lost, but the quality of his genius was widely different from that of Marlowe or Shakespeare. With a wonderful richness and fluency of poetic utterance, with the painter's eye for colour and the musician's ear for melody, Spenser lacked the sense of humour, the warm human sympathy, the feeling for life and action, indispensable to the successful dramatist. Chaucer possessed the dramatic instinct, and to it his triumphs as a story-teller are largely due; the absence of this quality in Spenser retards the movement of the *Faërie Queene* and tends to make it vague and unreal. While that marvellous poem has a greatness of its own, it is not a masterpiece of narration; it is, as some one once called it, "a gallery of pictures." Although he lived in a time of action, Spenser's genius is pictorial; and in the *Faërie Queene*, while we take but a languid interest in what happens, we are fascinated by the beauty, splendour, gloom, or grotesqueness, of the slowly moving pageant which passes before our eyes.

Spenser as a poet.

Spenser's avowed object, however, was not to satisfy the eye with colour, or the ear with melodious sound: in the *Faërie Queene*, and in several of his other poems, he aimed to be a teacher. England, as has been said, was then a battlefield of rival ideals and contending faiths; she stood at the parting of the ways; and in the *Faërie Queene* Spenser proposed to show, in the form of an allegory, this conflict between truth and falsehood, right and wrong, self-indulgence and self-control. The contending virtues and vices are represented by the different personages of the story, and the general purpose of the poem is "to fashion a perfect gentleman" by exhibiting a pattern of noble manhood and by showing the beauty of goodness and its final triumph. In the first book Falsehood, or

Duessa, is overthrown, and the Red Cross Knight, the "righteous man," is united to Truth, or Una. The remaining books are devoted to man's conquest of himself; to the conflict between his higher and his lower nature. But besides showing the general warfare between good and evil, which is common to all classes, Spenser aimed to portray the specific form which that conflict had taken in his own age. The allegory is thus confused and complicated by the introduction of contemporary issues. Thus the struggle between the saintly Una and the dissembling Duessa represents both the eternal warfare between Truth and Falsehood and the contemporary struggle between the Church of England and the Church of Rome. From time to time we dimly perceive the image of some great personage under this double veil of allegory, — of Mary Queen of Scots, of Lord Grey, or Sir Philip Sidney, — until, in pure bewilderment, we often abandon all attempt to follow the poet's inner meaning and wander careless and delighted as in a world of dreams. For the time at least Spenser the poet, the lover of beauty, dominates Spenser the Puritan, the preacher of righteousness. We are led to enjoy without question the beauty which delights the eye, or the rhythmical undulations of a verse which satisfies the ear. Moral purpose and allegory are alike obscured by the intricacies of a story, which, as we advance, reminds us of a river scattering its divided forces through countless channels, until it ends choked in sand.

It would be a mistake to infer from this that Spenser was not in earnest, or that his moral purpose was introduced merely as a convenient framework for his poem. Among all this delicious and enervating beauty we come suddenly upon passages that sound like trumpet-calls to duty and to high endeavour, passages full of a lofty enthusiasm and of a deep spiritual insight. Spenser revels in his magic world of shining knights and distressed damsels, of dragons, fairies, and enchanters; but he feels at heart, as Shakespeare did, that the substantial world itself is but "an insubstantial pageant."[1] He takes refuge in the thought of a Divine Energy, eternal and immutable, working above and in this shifting pageant of our world, the Master of the dissolving scenes. After all these entrancing visions Spenser's weariness of the mutable shows which surround us, finds expression in the last stanza of his unfinished *Faërie Queene:*

> "Then gin I thinke on that which Nature sayd,
>   Of that same time when no more Change shall be,
>   But stedfast rest of all things, firmely stayd
>   Upon the pillours of Eternity,
>   That is contrayr to Mutabilitie;
>   For all that moveth doth in Change delight;
>   But thence-forth all shall rest eternally
>   With Him that is the God of Sabaoth hight;
> Ol that great Sabaoth God, grant me that Sabaoth's sight!"

But while the noble spirituality of Spenser is present in the *Faërie Queene*, it reveals itself almost entirely in isolated passages. Spenser's claim to be considered a great ethical teacher must rest not upon what he intended to do but upon what he actually accomplished. The soul of the *Faërie Queene* does not spiritualise the whole body of the work. The moral purpose can only be perceived by deliberate and conscious effort of the intellect; it does not force itself irresistibly upon us through the emotions. In *Macbeth* the lesson of the degeneration of a soul through sin is the essence of the play; it is not deduced by the intellect, it is felt by the heart. But Spenser was compelled to furnish us with a prose explanation of his allegory; it does not explain itself like *The Pilgrim's Progress*.

---

[1] *Cf.* Prospero's speech, "Our revels now are ended," etc., in *The Tempest,* Act iv. Sc. 1.

Nevertheless, after all this is admitted, the imperishable charm of the poem remains independent of its story or of its declared purpose. No poet before Spenser had called out such sweet and stately music from our English speech, and none had so captivated by an appeal to the pure sense of beauty. Spenser was a high-minded Englishman, a student of the ideal philosophy of Plato, with a touch of Puritan severity; but he had, above all, the warm and beauty-loving temper of the Renaissance. In his solitary Kilcolman, amid the insecurity, pillage, and misery of unhappy Ireland, he felt the full fascination of Italy. In the *Faërie Queene*, the half-pagan and gorgeous beauty of the Italian Renaissance finds its most perfect expression in English poetry, modified and restrained by Spenser's serenity and spirituality and by his English conscience. With him we are not, as with Chaucer, admitted to the mirth and jolly fellowship of the common highway; rather, like Tennyson's Lady of Shalott in her high tower, we see in a glass only the passing reflection of knight and page. There are moods when this rests and satisfies; then, again, we look down to Camelot at life itself, and the mirror cracks from side to side.

THE ENGLISH DRAMA BEFORE SHAKESPEARE.

Shakespeare is so much a part of our English civilisation, we accept his gift to us so easily, and are so familiar with his greatness, that it is well to remind ourselves of his place as the king of all literature.

Elizabethan drama.

Thomas Carlyle wrote of him: " I think the best judgment, not of this country only but of Europe at large, is pointing to the conclusion that Shakespeare is the chief of all poets hitherto; the greatest intellect who, in our recorded world, has left a record of himself in the way of literature;" [1] and Emerson says, speaking for our own branch

[1] *Heroes and Hero Worship; The Hero as Poet.*

of the English people: "Of all books dependent upon their intrinsic excellence, Shakespeare is the one book of the world. Out of the circle of religious books, I set Shakespeare as the one unparalleled mind." [1] Criticism cannot explain how or why the country-bred son of a Warwickshire trader should have possessed this supreme gift; it is the miracle of genius; but we can partly understand how surrounding conditions favoured the expression of Shakespeare's genius through a dramatic form. It is beyond our philosophy to analyse the nature of the mysterious force shut within a seed, although we may appreciate the conditions which help its development. Let us look at Shakespeare in the light of some of those surroundings in which his genius worked.

Shakespeare did not create that dramatic era of which he was the greatest outcome; he availed himself of it. He lived in the midst of one of the world's few great dramatic periods — a period equalled only, if equalled at all, by the greatest epoch in the drama of Greece. The Elizabethan drama was more than a national amusement. More fully than any other form of literary or artistic expression, it interpreted and satisfied the craving of the time for vigorous life and action. The theatre was then, as in classic Greece, a national force, and a means of national education. An immense popular impulse was back of the Elizabethan dramatist. The wooden playhouses were daily filled with turbulent crowds, and scores of playwrights were busy supplying the insatiable public with countless dramas. Shakespeare was sustained by a hearty, if not always discriminating, appreciation; he was stimulated by the fellowship, or rivalry, of a host of competitors. The number of readers was still small; there were few bookbuyers outside of a little coterie of noblemen and scholars.

Shakespeare part of a dramatic period.

[1] *Representative Men:* Shakespeare.

Under these conditions it was impossible to make a living by writing unless one wrote for the stage. It was the dramatist who enjoyed the public patronage, the dramatist who received the most substantial rewards, and an almost irresistible current impelled young literary aspirants, the clever, impecunious Bohemians, the men of genius and the men of talent, to choose the dramatic form. As Mr. Symonds has said, "Dramatic composition . . . was a trade, but a trade which, like that of sculpture in Athens, of painting in Italy, of music in Germany, allowed men of creative genius to detach themselves from the ranks of creditable handicraftsmen. Shakespeare stands where Michelangelo and Pheidias stand, above all rivals; but he owed his dexterity to training."[1]

At first sight, this dramatic activity may seem to have sprung suddenly into being in answer to a new popular demand. The first regular tragedy was produced about the time of Shakespeare's birth, and he was twelve years old before the first regularly licensed theatre was erected in England (1576).

The preparation for the Elizabethan drama.

But the passion for life and action did not create the Elizabethan drama out of nothing; it rather transformed and adapted to its use a drama which had for centuries been an important part of the nation's life. This drama had its origin in religion: it dealt (if we except its latest developments) exclusively with religious or moral themes. At first it was in Latin, and entirely under the control of the Church, but gradually it passed out of the hands of the clergy, and it was no longer written in Latin but in English; it was acted by professional players and by the people, and it became a popular possession and amusement. What, then, was the general character of this drama, and what were the principal stages in its growth?

[1] *Shakspere's Predecessors in the English Drama*, p. 61.

This religious drama grew up on the Continent out of the need felt by the clergy for some effective means of popular religious instruction. The services **The Liturgi-** of the Church were in Latin, an unknown tongue **cal Drama.** to the great majority of the congregation; the people were not only unlettered, but grossly ignorant and narrow-minded. On certain important festivals of the Church, therefore, the clergy arranged in the chancel an actual representation, or *tableaux,* of the event commemorated on that day, that the services might be more intelligible and impressive. On Good Friday, for instance, the crucifix was taken down and solemnly buried, and on Easter it was brought from the tomb and replaced with elaborate ceremonies. Or, on Christmas Day, the Shepherds might be represented as coming to worship the infant Saviour. From very early times these scenic representations were accompanied by music and a brief dialogue between the principal personages, and the ceremony thus became more dramatic in character. As these dramatic ceremonies were introduced into the services, or liturgy, of the Church, they are commonly called the *Liturgical Drama.*

Out of such beginnings, plays founded on various incidents in the Bible, or on some legend of the saints, gradu-**The Miracle** ally took shape. On the Continent the plays on **Plays.** biblical subjects were called *Mysteries,* and those dealing with saintly legends *Miracle Plays,* but in England only the latter name appears to have been employed. Miracle plays were brought into England by the Normans. It is probable that they were introduced with many other foreign customs very soon after the Norman Conquest, but the first miracle play in England of which we have any record was given by the pupils in a school near St. Albans about 1100–1119. This was a play in honour of St. Katharine. It was produced under the direction of a Norman clerk, who had come from France to take charge of the Convent-school at St. Albans. The miracle play soon became domesticated in England. At first, plays were produced in the churches, or in some ecclesiastical institution, then (as in the play of *Adam and Eve*, c. 1150) on a scaffold at the church-door, then in the church-yards, and at length on the village green, or in the town's streets. Gradually they passed altogether out of the hands of the clergy, and became English plays, acted by and for the people in the vulgar tongue. It became the custom to arrange a number of these biblical plays in a series, or *cycle*, so as to present the chief events of the scriptural narrative from the Creation to Doomsday, in a dramatic sequence. Towards the end of the thirteenth century such *cycles* were acted by the Guilds (or incorporated associations of various trades and crafts) in some of the towns. Miracle plays were often produced on a movable platform called a *pageant*. It resembled a huge box on low wheels, and it was divided into two stories, or tiers. The lower story was commonly enclosed by curtains and used as a dressing-room; the upper, which was open at the sides, was the stage. The spectators assembled in groups at various places in the town, at the street-corners, the town-cross or elsewhere, and the pageants were drawn from group to group. Each pageant performed only one play in the series, and as one pageant followed another in regular succession, each group of spectators would, by remaining in the same spot, see the whole series of plays. Some times scaffolds were used instead of the movable stages. Four *cycles* of these plays have been preserved, — the cycle of *York*, of *Towneley* (so-called because the manuscript once belonged to a family of that name), of *Coventry*, and of *Chester*. These *cycles* contain in all nearly one hundred and forty plays. The people as they watched the production of one of these cycles, saw the most dramatic episodes of sacred history enacted before their eyes. They saw the Garden of Eden, the first sin and the loss of Paradise; they saw the quarrel between Cain and Abel, the first murder, the Flood; they followed the story of man's destiny through the New Testament, or, perhaps, to the terrors of the Day of Doom. Crude as these plays were, enlivened as they were at times by a coarse and incongruous humour, they were the result of an honest effort to make a great theme real and living to simple and ignorant audiences. With such an audience, unaccustomed as it was to mental effort, the occasional introduction of a comic element must have been a necessity, and in all likelihood the mediæval mind saw nothing irreverent or absurd in the quarrel of Noah and his wife before they entered the ark, or in the rough pranks of the shepherds on the plains of Bethlehem. These crude playwrights could form no notion of an oriental background; they had to make the shepherds English shepherds, for they knew no other. This introduction of a comic element and this necessity for a certain truth or realism, had evidently an important bearing on the development of the drama.

Not only did the laity need to know the Bible and the legends of the saints, they also needed to be instructed in **The Moral Plays.** Church doctrine and in conduct. To answer this need another kind of play, called the *Moral Play*, or *Morality*, grew up side by side with the miracle plays. The earliest extant *moral* plays date from the reign of Henry VI., but mention is made of some still earlier. The main theme of the moral play is " the contest between the personified powers of good and evil . . . for the possession of man's soul." [1] In other words, the object of the moral play was to teach a moral lesson by showing in the form of an allegory everyman's lifelong struggle with the various temptations which are

---

[1] Pollard's *English Miracle Plays*, Introduction, xliii.

the common enemies of mankind. Thus, in *The Castle of Perseverance*, the earthly life of man in its successive stages of infancy, youth, manhood, and old age, is brought before us in the person of the hero, the representation, or type, of mankind (*Humanum Genus*). We see this typical man attended by a good and an evil angel; we see him yielding to various temptations, — personified as the World, Pleasure, Folly, and the like, — and finally saved through repentance and confession.[1] In such a play, in spite of all its artistic shortcomings, we find that conception of life as a spiritual warfare which is the basis of the *Faërie Queene*. The moral play of *Everyman* forces home upon the mind and conscience of the hearer a conviction of the shortness of human life and of the vanity of merely earthly interests. A sense of the imminence of death and judgment dominates the play. The profound impression which this play made upon modern audiences, when it was revived a few years ago, shows that the *moral* play at its best has that truth to the fundamental facts of human life, that power in presenting them, which give greatness and permanence to art. The almost unequalled power of this play consists in the universal importance of its theme. The experience of Everyman is, or will be, ours; each hearer moves towards the grave with him, and sees in his struggles and shortcomings the image of his own.

Judging from the specimens which we possess, the morality plays as a whole suffer from the sameness of their theme; on the other hand, we see that in them the drama, once restricted to biblical or legendary subjects, passes beyond these limits toward a wider field.

A further step was taken by JOHN HEYWOOD (cir. 1500–

---

[1] *Cf.* the allegory running through the successive contests of **Gareth** with *Phosporus, Meridian, Hesperus, Nox,* and *Mors* in Tennyson's *Gareth and Lynette.*

1565) in the composition of the *Interlude*.[1] These *inter-*
Interludes.   *ludes* of Heywood's were short, comic scenes,
intended, apparently, to be played between
(*inter ludo*) the courses of a banquet, or immediately
after its conclusion.   The speakers in these witty conversations are not personifications as in the morality
play, they are characters taken from real life, as *Johan
the husband* and *Tyb his wife*, a *Pardoner*, a *Friar*, or
a *Curate.* Heywood, like his contemporary Skelton, was
a satirist; and in his best known work, *The Four P's*, — a
dialogue between the *Palmer*, the *Pardoner*, the *Poticary*,
and the *Pedlar*, — neither the clergy nor the laity escape
his keen ridicule.

We have now traced the beginnings of the English
drama from the time of the Conquest to John Heywood,
Relation of   who died in 1565, — almost to the time of
miracle and Shakespeare.   The last performance of the
moral plays to
Elizabethan York miracle plays took place in 1579; the
drama.   Chester plays were acted until the end of the
century. So the miracle play did not die until the end
of Elizabeth's reign. It had overlapped the noblest period
of the English drama, but it had long since ceased to have
any direct and vital influence. At first sight the relation
of the miracle and morality plays to the Elizabethan
drama may seem fanciful or obscure, but in fact it is very
real and vital. We find allusion to this older drama in
Shakespeare and other Elizabethan playwrights, and here
and there we come upon an actual thread of connection.
The *Vice*, who, dressed as a Court fool, supplied the comic
element in the morality plays, survives in a more elevated
form in Shakespeare's clowns and jesters. The drunken
Porter in *Macbeth* is believed to be a reminiscence of the

---

[1] Mention is made of *interludes* as early as 1464, but the *interlude*
as the term is commonly used appears to have been the creation of
Heywood.

porter of the gates of Hell in a certain miracle play. At times we seem to discern a less superficial connection, as when Marlowe's *Faust* stands like *Humanum Genus*, between his good and bad Angel, or when, like the wicked in the miracle plays, he is carried off by devils to eternal torments. In truth, the miracle and morality plays, with all their uncouthness and deficiencies, were sustained and elevated by their stupendous themes; they dealt with issues so universal, that later dramatists could hardly escape treating them again, although in a different form. *Macbeth* is, after all, but a glorified miracle play. The scene, the time, and the actors are changed, but there in the Scotch Highlands, as in the Garden of Eden, we again see enacted the old drama of man's temptation, his fall, and his spiritual exile. But above all we must remember that for hundreds of years before Marlowe and Shakespeare, this religious drama fostered and kept alive a love of playgoing among the English people. It made the drama a national amusement, a popular possession. This drama, essentially serious and moral, changed and supplemented as it was by the new ideas and fresh inspiration brought by the Renaissance, was a basis for the drama of the later time.

Through the Interlude, as we have seen, the drama became less religious and didactic; by the substitution of real characters for personifications, and by the satirical treatment of contemporary abuses, it drew nearer to life in its more familiar and every-day aspects. All that was needed to transform the Interlude into a comedy was the introduction of a more fully developed plot. In making this transition, England was helped by the example of the classic, and particularly the Latin, writers. It had become customary to produce plays at some of the schools; and the schoolmasters, the schools, and the Universities, had an important share in the establishment

The beginning of the regular drama.

of the regular drama, at this early stage of its growth. The first regular comedy, *Ralph Roister Doister*, was written about 1552 by NICHOLAS UDALL (1505–1556), who was at one time headmaster of Eton College and afterwards headmaster of Westminster School. This comedy shows the influence of the Latin comic dramatist, Plautus. Another early comedy, *Gammer Gurton's Needle*, was played at Christ's College, Cambridge, in 1566. This comedy, unlike Udall's, is not a classical imitation, but a coarse and graphic study of rustic life. This fact is a significant one. It suggests to us that, in spite of the strength of the classical influence, there was a native force and originality in the English nature which would give to the English drama a character of its own. Nevertheless, in tragedy as well as in comedy the English dramatists began as pupils of the Latin. The first regular English tragedy, the *Gorboduc*, or *Ferrex and Porrex*, of Sackville and Norton, while it dealt with a subject in the legendary history of England followed the style of the Latin tragic poet Séneca. Indeed, the numerous translations from Seneca are a proof of his influence and popularity.[1]

Among the native forces thus shaping a new drama out of mediæval miracle plays or classic adaptations, was the intense patriotic pride which, in the days of the Armada, stirred England to more widespread interest in her history, and to a warmer pleasure in the image of her triumphs. The Chronicle histories of England were ransacked for subjects, and her past reviewed in dramas which were the forerunners of Shakespeare's great series of English historical plays. Among the early works of this class are, *The Famous*

Influence of patriotism on growth of drama.

---

[1] Between 1559 and 1566 five English authors applied themselves to the task of translating Seneca. Ten of his plays, collected and printed together in 1581, remain a monument of the English poets' zeal in studying the Roman pedagogue.

Victories of Henry V., acted before 1588, *Sir Thomas More*, about 1590, *The Troublesome Raign of King John*, printed in 1591, and *The New Chronicle History of King Leir and his Three Daughters, Gonerill, Ragan, and Cordella*, acted two years later (1593). The influence of classical study also, was apparent in the choice of subject. Thus, there is an early tragedy on the story of *Appius and Virginia* (cir. 1563), and a *Lamentable Tragedy Mixed Ful of Pleasant Mirth, Conteyning the Life of Cambises King of Percia* (cir. 1569–70).

We can better estimate the power of this patriotic spirit in moulding the drama if we turn for a moment to its influence on other forms of contemporary literature. We have already alluded to the labours of such antiquarians and historians of this time as Leland, Stowe, and Holinshed, and we have spoken of Holinshed's relation to the dramatic presentation of English history.[1] Side by side with this historical prose we find an enormous quantity of verse inspired by the same patriotic interest in the England of the present or the past. William Warner set forth the history of England from the Deluge to the time of Elizabeth in a much read poem of ten thousand lines (*Albion's England*, 1586); Samuel Daniel dealt with English history in his *Civil Wars* (1595); later Michael Drayton wrote his *Heroical Epistles*, his splendid ballad, the *Battle of Agincourt*, and his gigantic poem *Polyolbion* (1613–1622). The last named, a "strange Herculian toil" as Drayton appropriately calls it, is a poetical description of England in thirty books, containing in all about one hundred thousand lines. All these writers were bidding people to

> "Look on England,
> The Empress of the European isles,
> The mistress of the ocean, her navies
> Putting a girdle round about the world." [2]

[1] Page, 187 *supra*.   [2] Massinger, *The Maid of Honour*, Act i. Sc. 1.

From the historical plays already named we pass easily to a higher order of drama in the *Edward II.* of Christopher ✗ Marlowe, Shakespeare's great predecessor, until we reach the climax of England's patriotic drama in the work of Shakespeare himself.

About 1580 we find the drama rapidly taking form in London through the work of a group of rising dramatists, **Shakespeare's predecessors.** many of whom brought from the universities a tincture of the new learning. Many of these playwrights lived in a wild, Bohemian fashion, haunting low taverns, and consorting with the vilest company. Some of them, like the dissipated and unfortunate Greene, were beyond the pale of respectable society. Their means of living were precarious, for literature was not yet a recognised profession. Some of them wrote romances, poems, or pamphlets, as well as plays. They were, as a class, mere literary adventurers: scholars acquainted with the London slums, the associates of actors, then a despised class, if not actors themselves, and struggling to live by their wits as best they could. Prominent among these shapers of the Elizabethan drama were JOHN ✗ LYLY (1553–1606); THOMAS KYD (1558–1595), whose *Spanish Tragedy* was frequently referred to by Shakespeare and the later dramatists,[1] GEORGE PEELE (cir. 1558–cir. 1598); and ROBERT GREENE (1560–1592).

[1] The recent discovery of the precise date of Kyd's birth proves him to have been about six years older than Marlowe and Shakespeare. Some critics argue from this that he probably began his work before Marlowe, and contend that, in consequence of this probable priority, his share in the development of English tragedy is more important than was formerly supposed. Whatever conclusion we may adopt, Kyd was beyond all question an important force in the shaping of English tragedy. His *Spanish Tragedy* (written, perhaps, before 1588, and performed with great success in 1592) was enormously popular; according to a high authority "the most popular play of the entire age outside of Shakespeare." Like *Titus Andronicus,* it "reeks with blood," but the plot is skilfully developed, and there are evidences of dramatic and poetic power. Poetically, it is distinctly inferior to the work of Marlowe. *V.* Prof. Schick's preface to his edition of *The Spanish Tragedy.*

The work of this remarkable group of playwrights must be passed by here with only the briefest mention. Lyly was an Oxford man. He aspired to be Master of the Revels,[1] and he knew the delays and disappointments of the unsuccessful suitor for Elizabeth's favour. "A thousand hopes," he wrote bitterly in 1593, "but all nothing; a hundred promises, but yet nothing." Lyly's plays were produced by two companies of child-actors known as "the children of Paul's" (i.e. the choristers of St. Paul's Cathedral) and "the children of the Chapel" (i.e. the choristers of the Royal Chapel at Whitehall), and they were undoubtedly acted before the Queen. Lyly was not a writer of great depth or power, but his comedies, though slight, are fanciful, lively, and entertaining. The dialogue, as in parts of *Alexander and Campaspe*, is often clever and animated. His light touch fitted him to excel in the lyric, and at least one of his songs, "Cupid and Campaspe," has long been generally known and admired. Lyly first became famous by his two stories, *Euphues, the Anatomy of Wit* (1579), and *Euphues and His England* (1580). These books, which mark the beginning of the Elizabethan romance, were written in a curiously elaborated and artificial form. This highly mannered and pedantic style soon found imitators and was known as *Euphuism*.[2] Lyly used this style again in his dramas. George Peele, like

---

[1] The Master of the Revels was an officer selected to direct the amusements of the Court, or of the household of a great nobleman. In Henry VIII.'s reign the Master of the Revels was made a permanent Court official. He took charge of the masks and costumes used in the public entertainments, and had various other duties connected with the Court amusements and Royal Progresses.

[2] Euphuism is thus defined by Dr. Furness in Preface to *Love's Labour's Lost*. "This style, when examined, discloses as marked characteristics constant antitheses not only in words, but in balanced sentences, and the antitheses are then rendered more noticeable by alliteration; to this is added a profusion of illustrations drawn from 'unnatural Natural History,' to use Collier's happy phrase."

Lyly, was a graduate of Oxford. He came to London about 1581, where he led a reckless and riotous life as poet, dramatist, and actor, and died miserably in 1597–98.

His historical play of *Edward I* contains a fine tribute to "Illustrious England, ancient seat of Kings," and his pastoral, *The Arraignment of Paris,* a very simple and pleasing song, "Fair and fair and twice so fair." Peele had possibly less influence on the drama than either Lyly or Greene, yet his verse kindles at times into true poetry. There is a fervid and noble eloquence in his *Farewell to Sir John Norris,* and the sonnet "His golden locks Time hath to silver turned," is worthy of the beautiful setting which Thackeray has given it in the *Newcomes.*[1] Greene, who left behind him the story of his pitiable life in his singular tract, *A Groat's Worth of Wit Bought with a Million of Repentance,* is probably at his best in his comedy of *Friar Bacon and Friar Bungay.* The scene is laid in the country, and there is a freshness, a wholesomeness, about the play, a suggestion of open air and sunshine, which contrast pathetically with Greene's stifling and sordid surroundings. But, greater than all these in the tragic intensity of his genius and the swelling majesty of his "mighty line,"

Marlowe. was CHRISTOPHER MARLOWE (1564–1593), the immediate forerunner of Shakespeare. When Marlowe began to write, the form of the English drama was still unsettled. Under the influence of its classic models tragedy was inclined to be stiff, stilted, and formal; while in contrast with the work of the scholarly and somewhat artificial writers there were rude, popular interludes in jingling rhymes, full of rough, clownish tricks and jests, and without unity and proportion. Marlowe's fine touch did much to reduce this confusion to order. His verse is the finest before Shakespeare's; and stormy and riotous as was his life, his work shows the true artist's unselfish de-

[1] *The Newcomes,* vol. ii. chap. xxxviii.

votion to a high and beautiful ideal. Marlowe was the son of a Canterbury shoemaker, and was born two months before Shakespeare. He graduated at Cambridge and came to London in 1581 to plunge into the vortex of reckless and lawless life that circled round the theatre. Passionate, unquiet, ambitious, Marlowe was spoken of perhaps unjustly as an atheist and a blasphemer. He dies before he reaches thirty; stabbed, we are told, with his own dagger in a low tavern at Deptford. The touch of the unknown, which he thirsted for like his own *Faustus*, stops him in the midst of his doubts, his passionate longings, his defiance, his love-making, and his fame — and at length he is quiet.

Marlowe's earliest play (*Tamburlaine*, First Part before 1587, Second Part 1590) portrays the insatiable thirst for power, the spirit of the typical conqueror longing for "the sweet fruition of an earthly crown." Another of Marlowe's tragedies, *The Jew of Malta*, is generally thought to have furnished Shakespeare with some hints for his Shylock in *The Merchant of Venice*. *Edward II.* drew more firmly the lines of the English historical drama, while *Dr. Faustus*, with its magnificent bursts of poetry and the accumulating terror of its tragic close, is full of that overmastering longing for the unattainable which seems to have been the strongest characteristic of Marlowe's restless nature. In these famous lines from *Tamburlaine*, Marlowe himself seems to speak to us:

> "Nature, that framed us of four elements
> Warring within our breasts for regiment,
> Doth teach us all to have aspiring minds;
> Our souls whose faculties can comprehend
> The wondrous architecture of the world,
> And measure every wandering planet's course,
> Still climbing after knowledge infinite,
> And always moving as the restless spheres,
> Will us to wear ourselves and never rest —."

Plays were acted in England before any theatres were built. The *Interludes*, or the early dramas, were often

played before the Queen or before some great noble on a
platform, at one end of the huge halls, perhaps at a great banquet or festival. When plays became a popular pastime they were often performed in the open court-yards of the inns. These square inn-yards, overlooked by the galleries or balconies which ran around the enclosing walls of the inn, are supposed to have furnished the model for the regular theatres. The growing delight in play-going seems to have produced a general demand for more permanent and commodious accommodations. In 1576 a building known as "The Theatre" was erected in Finsbury Fields, in the outskirts of London, for the regular production of plays. A second play-house, "The Curtain," was opened a little later. From this time the play-houses rapidly increased, and when Shakespeare came up to London (about 1587) a number were in active operation. Shakespeare's own theatre, "The Globe," built 1599, lay across the Thames from London in the "Bankside," a part of Southwark close to the river. Other famous theatres of the day were "The Fortune," "The Rose," and "The Curtain," at the last of which Marlowe is known to have acted. The theatres were of two kinds, public and private. The first were large six-sided wooden buildings, roofed over above the stage and thatched; the pit, or yard, being without shelter from the sun or rain. Galleries ran round the walls, as in the inn-yards. The stage projected into the pit, which was alive with disorderly crowds who stood on the bare ground, joking, fighting, or shoving to gain the best places. There was little attempt at scenery; in the old plays we find such significant stage directions as these: "Exit Venus; or, if you can conveniently, let a chair come down from the top of the stage and draw her up." [1]

---

[1] In Greene's *Alphonsus* — quoted by Collier, *Annals of the Stage,* vol. iii. p. 357.

In more than one place in the choruses of *Henry V.*
Shakespeare seems to be impatient of the slender resources
of his stage-setting, as when he asks:

> "Can this cock-pit hold
> The vasty fields of France? or may we cram
> Within this wooden O the very casques
> That did affright the air at Agincourt?"[1]

And in the wonderful description that precedes the battle
of Agincourt he complains:

> "And so our scene must to the battle fly;
> Where (O for pity!) we shall much disgrace
> With four or five most vile and ragged foils,
> Right ill-disposed, in brawl ridiculous —
> The name of Agincourt.   Yet, sit and see,
> Minding true things by what their mockeries be."

The private theatres were smaller and more comfortable
than the public.   They had seats in the pit and were entirely under roof.   Performances were given by candle or
torch light, and the audiences were usually more select.
The following description by Mr. Symonds gives us a vivid
notion of the performance of a play in Shakespeare's time:

" Let us imagine that the red-lettered play-bill of a new tragedy
has been hung out beneath the picture of Dame Fortune [i.e. at
" The Fortune " Theatre, the great rival of Shakespeare's Theatre,
" The Globe "] ; the flag is flying from the roof, the drums have
beaten, and the trumpets are sounding for the second time.   It is
three o'clock upon an afternoon of summer.   We pass through the
great door, ascend some steps, take our key from the pocket of
our trunk hose, and let ourselves into our private room on the first
or lowest tier.   We find ourselves in a low, square building, not
unlike a circus; smelling of sawdust and the breath of people.
The yard below is crowded with simpering mechanics and 'prentices in greasy leathern jerkins, servants in blue frieze with their
masters' badges on their shoulders, boys and grooms elbowing

[1] Chorus to *Henry V.* Act i.   [2] Chorus to Act iv.

each other for bare standing ground and passing jests on their neighbours. Five or six young men are already seated before the curtain playing cards and cracking nuts to while away the time. A boy goes up and down among them offering various qualities of tobacco for sale and furnishing lights for the smokers. The stage itself is strewn with rushes; and from the jutting tiled roof of the shadow supported by a couple of stout wooden pillars, carved with satyrs at the top, hangs a curtain of tawny-coloured silk. This is drawn when the trumpets have sounded for the third time, and an actor in a black velvet mantel, with a crown of bays upon his flowing wig, struts forward, bowing to the audience. He is the Prologue.

" The Prologue ends.

" The first act now begins. There is nothing but the rudest scenery ; a battlemented city wall behind the stage, with a placard hung out upon it, indicating that the scene is Rome. As the play proceeds this figure of a town makes way for some wooden rocks and a couple of trees, to signify the Hyrcanian forest. A damsel wanders alone in the woods, lamenting her sad case. Suddenly a cardboard dragon is thrust from the sides upon the stage, and she takes to flight. The first act closes with a speech from an old gentleman clothed in antique robes, whose white beard flows down upon his chest. He is the Chorus. . . The show concludes with a prayer for the Queen's Majesty uttered by the actors on their knees." [1]

*1 *Shakspere's Predecessors in the English Drama*, chap. viii.

WILLIAM SHAKESPEARE.

(1564–1616.)

"I loved the man, and do honour his memory, on this side idolatry, as much as any. He was indeed honest, and of an open and free nature; had an excellent phantasy, brave notions, and gentle expressions, wherein he flowed with that facility that sometimes it was necessary he should be stopped."

— BEN JONSON.

"But Shakespeare's magic could not copied be,
Within that circle none durst walk but he."
— JOHN DRYDEN.

"The stream of time, which is continually washing the dissoluble fabrics of other poets, passes without injury by the adamant of Shakespeare."

— DR. SAMUEL JOHNSON.

"The greatest genius that perhaps human nature has yet produced, our *myriad-minded* Shakespeare."

—SAMUEL TAYLOR COLERIDGE.

" Others abide our question. Thou art free.
We ask and ask — Thou smilest and art still,
Out-topping knowledge. . . . .

. . . .

And thou, who didst the stars and sunbeams know,
Self-school'd, self-scann'd, self-honour'd, self-secure,
Didst tread on earth unguess'd at." . . . . .

— MATTHEW ARNOLD.

There is on Henley Street, in Stratford-on-Avon, Warwickshire, an old house, with gabled roof and low-ceil-

His youth. inged rooms, which every year is made the object of thousands of pilgrimages. Here William Shakespeare was born, on or about the twenty-third day of April, 1564. His father, John Shakespeare, the son of a small farmer in the neighbouring village of Snitterfield, added to his regular business of glover sundry dealings in

wool, corn, and hides, and possibly the occupation of
butcher. His mother, Mary Arden, the daughter of a
wealthy farmer near Stratford, was connected with one
of the oldest and most distinguished families in Warwickshire. The Ardens came of both Norman and Saxon
blood, and thus represented "the two great race elements
that have gone to the making of the typical modern Englishman." [1] The influences about Shakespeare's youth
were such as growing genius instinctively appropriates
to its use. Then, as now, Warwickshire was full of that
Warwickshire. abundant and peaceful beauty which has
come to represent for us the ideal English
landscape. In Shakespeare's day its northern part was
overgrown by the great forest of Arden, a bit of primeval
woodland like that which we enter in *As You Like It;* while
southward of the river Avon, which runs diagonally across
the county, stretched an open region of fertile farm-land.
Here were warm, sunny slopes, gay with those wildflowers that bloom forever for the world in Shakespeare's
verse; low-lying pastures, where meditative cows stand
knee-deep in grass, and through which wind the brimming
waters of slow-flowing and tranquil streams. Stratford
lies in this more southern portion; but in Shakespeare's
day the forest of Arden reached to within an easy distance of it for an active youth. Near his native town the
young Shakespeare could loiter along country lanes, past
hawthorn hedgerows or orchards white with May, coming
now and then on some isolated farmhouse or on the cluster
of thatched cottages which marked a tiny village. There
was Snitterfield, where he must have gone to visit his
grandfather; Shottery, where he wooed and won Anne
Hathaway. There, in the midst of this rich midland
scenery, was his own Stratford with its low wood-and-

[1] *V.* article on "Shakespeare," by J. Spencer Baynes, in *Encyclopedia Britannica*, ninth edition.

plaster houses and straggling streets, its massive grammar school, where, as a boy, he conned his Lilly's Latin Grammar. A little apart, by the glassy Avon, stood old Trinity Church, its lofty spire rising above the surrounding elms. There is abundant evidence that Shakespeare loved Warwickshire with a depth of attachment that nothing could alter. These early surroundings entered into and became a permanent part of his life and genius, and his works are full of country sights and sounds. He shows us rural England in such scenes as that of the sheep-shearing in *The Winter's Tale ;* he contrasts the free woodland with the court in *As You Like It ;* he defines for us the essence of the ideal shepherd's life;[1] and in many a song, written to be sung in crowded London theatres, his imagination escapes to the fields and flowers of his native Warwickshire.

And Shakespeare's Warwickshire added to natural beauty the charm of local legend and the traditions of a splendid past. Within easy reach of Stratford lay Warwick, with its fine old castle, once the home of the great king-maker of the Wars of the Roses. The whole region was bound by tradition and association to that great civil strife which is one of the chief themes of Shakespeare's plays on English history. Near by was Kenilworth, the castle of Elizabeth's favourite, the Earl of Leicester, where the Queen was received (1575) with those magnificent revels, at which the boy Shakespeare may have been present. Travelling companies of players seem to have visited Stratford during Shakespeare's early years, whose performances he doubtless witnessed. He may even have gazed at the wonders of a miracle play at Coventry, a town some twenty miles distant, where these plays were frequently produced by the Guilds.

[1] Lines beginning, "To sit upon a hill," 3 *Henry VI.,* Act ii Sc. 5.

Besides all that he gained from such surroundings and experiences, Shakespeare had the advantage of some Stratford instruction at the town grammar school, which Grammar he probably entered in 1571, when he was School. seven years old. The old school at Stratford had been suppressed along with many others when the monastic system of education was broken up, and the school which Shakespeare attended had been recently established by Edward VI. on the old foundation. The religious upheaval of the early part of the century, and the impulse of the New Learning, were thus felt in that provincial town, and the influence of this great change touched Shakespeare even in his youth. Latin was the chief study, and it is reasonably certain that Shakespeare, who remained at school about six years, gained a fair elementary knowledge of the language, although long after, the learned Ben Jonson spoke slightingly of his friend's scholarship. By 1577 John Shakespeare, who had been prosperous and respected, was already pressed for money, and about this time Shakespeare was taken from school. The boy, then about thirteen, may have helped his father in the business. According to an old account he was "apprenticed to a butcher." However this may have been, it is practically certain that he made himself useful in some way, and that his school life was interrupted because his help was needed at home. Just how the young Shakespeare earned his bread at this time, is, after all, comparatively unimportant; our real interest is in the boy himself. But as soon as we pass beyond the few recorded facts of Shakespeare's life and try to reach the secret of his personality, we enter the doubtful region of theory and conjecture. We can only infer or imagine what he was, thought, felt, or aspired to, during those years of youth and early manhood. We cannot "pluck out the heart of his mystery": we are still, in

Emerson's phrase, "out of doors." The most we can do is to fancy ourselves in Shakespeare's Warwickshire; to picture its country life, its remoteness from the great world, the oddities of its rustics (reproduced, perhaps, in the clownish artisans of *A Midsummer Night's Dream*), and the narrow self-importance of its local magnates. We may feel sure that the marvellously receptive mind of Shakespeare was not insensible to these things. We may feel sure that with his deep and delicate apprehension of human life and of the world of Nature, he was quick to respond to the beauty, the pathos, the comedy, and the tragedy, that lay around him. This was his school: his simple neighbours, his homely duties, his rustic pleasures, gave him his first materials for his art. Here he first strove to spell out the meaning of that great volume which he afterward spoke of as "Nature's infinite book of secrecy." [1]

Nevertheless, all that we know of Shakespeare leads us to imagine that he was not merely the dreamy and meditative spectator of life at this time, but rather one who flung himself into its varied experiences with the zest of an abounding vitality. We are rather led to think of him in these early years as hot-headed, passionate, even, perhaps, as a trifle lawless, as "a man whose blood is warm within." [2] In 1582, when he was only eighteen, and in spite of his father's straitened circumstances, he married

Marriage. Anne Hathaway, a woman eight years older than himself. Three or four years later he left his wife and children and went to London to wrestle with Fortune; coming "as others do" to try against the great "General Challenger" the strength of his youth. [3] According to an old tradition, the immediate reason for

[1] *Antony and Cleopatra*, Act i. Sc. 2.
[2] *Merchant of Venice*, Act i. Sc. 1.
[3] *As You Like It*, Act i. Sc. 2.

Shakespeare's leaving Stratford was his quarrel with Sir Thomas Lucy, a neighbouring landed proprietor. "He had," writes the chief authority for the story, "by a misfortune common enough to young fellows, fallen into ill company, and, among them, some, that made a frequent practice of deer-stealing, engaged him with them more than once in robbing a park that belonged to Sir Thomas Lucy of Charlecote near Stratford." "For this," says the original authority for the story, "he was prosecuted by that gentleman [Lucy], as he thought, somewhat too severely; and, in order to revenge the ill-usage, he made a ballad upon him. And though this, probably the first essay of his poetry, be lost, yet it is said to have been so very bitter that it redoubled the prosecution against him to that degree that he was obliged to leave his business and family in Warwickshire for some time and shelter himself in London."[1] This story is probably not without some foundation; but, in any case, Shakespeare's establishment in London is exactly what his circumstances would lead us to expect. In 1585 he had a wife and three children to support, his father's money affairs had gone from bad to worse, and Shakespeare, strong as we may imagine in the hopes and confidence of youth and genius, had every reason to feel provincial Stratford too cramped for his powers.

> "The spirit of a youth
> That means to be of note, begins betimes."[2]

When Shakespeare reached London (1587 ?) the drama was rapidly gaining in popular favour; clever young playwrights were giving it form, and Marlowe had recently produced his *Tamburlaine*. We know nothing of Shakespeare's life during his first few years in London. There is a story that he was first em-

Shakespeare in London.

---

[1] Nicholas Rowe, *Life of Shakespeare*.
[2] *Antony and Cleopatra*, Act iv. Sc. 4.

ployed at a theatre in holding the horses of those who rode to the play, and that he had a number of boys to assist him. This, however, is generally distrusted. We do know that Shakespeare became an actor and that he made a place for himself among the crowd of struggling dramatists, arousing the envy of Greene by his rapid advance in favour.

He became a member of a leading company of players, the "Lord Chamberlain's Company," and by 1592 he had fairly entered upon a prosperous career.[1] In some way he commended himself to the young Earl of Southampton, to whom he dedicated his first poem, the *Venus and Adonis*, in 1593. Shakespeare seems to have begun his work as a dramatist by adapting and partially rewriting old plays. *Titus Andronicus*, a coarse and brutal tragedy, was probably one of the plays thus touched up by Shakespeare in his 'prentice period. His arrangement of *Henry VI.* (Part I.) was brought out in 1592, and seems to have done much to bring him into notice. Among these earlier plays (written before 1598) were *The Comedy of Errors*, in which Shakespeare joins the imitators of Plautus; *The Two Gentlemen of Verona*, *Love's Labour's Lost*, into which many characteristic features of the Italian comedy were introduced, and the poetic fantasy of *A Midsummer Night's Dream*. Thus we see that Shakespeare, like the other dramatists of his time, turned at the very outset to classic models and contemporary Italy. This early work of Shakespeare thus includes a tragedy, an English historical drama, and a number of comedies. Three forms of dramatic composition are here represented, and in each of

Early work.

---

[1] At this time actors of any standing were organised in companies. These companies were licensed, and many of them bore the name of some great nobleman. Thus there was the Earl of Leicester's company, the Lord Admiral's company, etc. The Queen's company had obtained its license from the Queen herself.

these three branches of his art Shakespeare afterwards became supreme. The tragedy and the history may be passed over here as mere adaptations. They tell us something of the state of the drama when Shakespeare began his work, but they are not really *his*, and we find little trace of his genius in the blood and rant of the one, or in the monotonous dulness of the other. The comedies are amusing, witty, and graceful; but on the whole, they are slighter than Shakespeare's maturer work. Compared with the master's later creations, the characters are shadowy and indistinct; we miss too that strong grasp of fact, that intensity of passion, those passages of deep philosophic insight so characteristic of Shakespeare's more fully developed genius. Yet these comedies remind us of the preliminary sketches of a great artist, and they stand in a direct and evident relation to that which is to follow. Certain incidents or situations in these comedies were used again by Shakespeare in a slightly modified form. If many of the characters seem a trifle nebulous, two or three at least are distinctly human and substantial. Theseus in *A Midsummer Night's Dream* has an heroic largeness of stature, a nobility which leads us to place him with Shakespeare's great men of action. Launce with his inseparable dog, in *The Two Gentlemen of Verona*, is the worthy precursor of Launcelot Gobbo in *The Merchant of Venice*, and of a glorious procession of clowns and jesters. Here too is Bully Bottom, the incarnation of invincible, arrogant, and uncomprehending common sense, the complacent British Philistine solidly established in the midst of Shakespeare's filmy and gossamer world of imaginations and dreams. Indeed, *A Midsummer Night's Dream*, which is commonly thought to have been the latest of those early comedies, easily rises above them all in breadth of conception, imagination, beauty, and suggestiveness. Incongruous as a dream, it has yet an essential unity. Through all the whimsical happenings of the play we are led to perceive that the world of external phenomena is for each one exactly what his imagination "bodies forth." For us, in Hamlet's phrase, it is "thinking makes it so." The ideal and the so-called fact are placed in sharp juxtaposition in this play, but we are taught to see that the imagination interprets or transforms the fact, makes a bush into a bear, or "sees Helen's beauty in a brow of Egypt."[1] In *A Midsummer Night's Dream*, unreal as it seems, we find the germ of *Hamlet* and *The Tempest*.

From this world of high imagination and homespun fact, Shakespeare turned to the story of England's past. In 1594 he produced *Richard II.*, and the other plays of his great English historical series followed in quick succession. Begun a few years after the defeat of the great Armada, these plays reflect the triumphant patriotism of the time. In them, too, Shakespeare holds his faithful mirror up to the contrasted aspects of England's life. These plays are not merely nobly patriotic, they are, above all, broadly human. They show us the usurper Henry IV. sleepless in his lonely power, and the jolly roisterers in the taverns of Eastcheap; the aspiring Hotspur, who would "pluck bright honour from the pale-faced moon;"[2] and the fat, comfortable, companionable Jack Falstaff, the bulky incarnation of materialism, glorified by kindliness and humour, to whom "honour" is but a word.[3] He shows us two royal failures: the incapable Richard II. with his strain of poetry and sentiment, and the saintly but ineffectual Henry VI. He shows us also his hero-king Henry V., the doer of great deeds.

After the completion of this series of historical studies,

The English historical plays.

---

[1] *Midsummer Night's Dream*, Act v. Sc. 1.
[2] *Henry IV.*, Part i, Act i. Sc. 3.
[3] *Henry IV.*, Part i, Act v. Sc. 2.

Shakespeare turned for a time to comedy. The witty and brilliant *Much Ado About Nothing*, with its inimitable Dogberry and its touch of tragedy, the woodland pastoral *As You Like It*, and *Twelfth Night* were written during this time. Meanwhile, so far as his worldly affairs were concerned, Shakespeare had steadily prospered. In these active and hard-working years he grew in fortune as well as in reputation; he showed himself a practical and capable man of business as well as a transcendent genius, and by his character he won the love and respect of his fellows. By 1597 he was able to buy a home for himself in his beloved Stratford. In 1599 he was one of the proprietors of " The Globe Theatre," built in that year. In 1606, a further purchase of one hundred and seven acres of land at Stratford is made by William Shakespeare, *Gentleman*. Thus, while he is adding to the treasures of the world's literature, the thoughts and ambitions of this country-bred Shakespeare seem to return and centre about the Stratford of his youth.

Comedies.

Worldly prosperity.

Up to this time, Shakespeare's success had been in comedy and in the historical drama. He had, indeed, written *Romeo and Juliet*, that rapturous and romantic tragedy of ill-fated love, and, in scattered passages, had given hints of his power to sound the depths of yet profounder passion. But toward the close of the sixteenth century a change begins to be apparent in the spirit of Shakespeare's work. As early as 1594–1595 he had already composed a number, perhaps the greater part of his *Sonnets*, poems in which, as some contend, he "unlocked his heart." We cannot tell whether these *Sonnets* are dramatic studies or whether they are the veiled revelation of Shakespeare's personal experience. In either case, they show us that while he was still writing his joyous comedies, Shakespeare's mind was already turning toward deeper and more tragic issues. The general tone of the *Sonnets*

The Sonnets.

is sombre. They are full of unrest; of gloomy reflections, darkening into despair. We read of a conflict between love and duty, of the passing of youth, of the death of friends, "hid in death's dateless night," of a profound disgust for a world in which evil is captain over good.[1] We find here the cry of one, who, like Hamlet, is tired of such a flat and unprofitable world.

However we may choose to interpret these sonnets (or whether we believe them to be a riddle that cannot now be solved), we cannot but see in them a foreshadowing of Shakespeare's tragic mood. *Twelfth Night*, although written a little later than the greater part of the *Sonnets*, is a rollicking comedy, alive with the spirit of reckless, almost defiant enjoyment. The solemn, Puritanic Malvolio is the butt of the jolly, drunken Sir Toby and the quick-witted Maria, yet even in this play the mirth is not wholly careless. The note of warning mingles with the clown's song: "What's to come is still unsure;" love is not "hereafter," seize it now, for —

> "Youth's a stuff will not endure."

The words at least seem prophetic. So far as we can judge from the character of his work, Shakespeare's own youth was to endure no longer. In the same year in which he wrote *Twelfth Night* (1601), he began in *Julius Cæsar* that great series of plays which won him a place among the supreme tragic poets of the world. In play after play we now find him turning from the humourous and gayer side of life to face the ultimate problems of existence, and to sound the depths of human weakness, agony, and crime. Some

---

[1] See especially the *Sonnet lxvi.*, "Tired with all these, for restful death I cry." *Sonnet xxx.*, "When to the sessions of sweet, silent thought," etc. *Sonnet lxxiii.*, "That time of year thou mayst in me behold," and consult *inter alia Sonnets cli., cxliv., cxxix., xxix., cx., cxi.*

think that these great tragedies were wrought out of the
suffering and bitterness of Shakespeare's own experience.
Some connect them with the death of his only son in 1596,
some with the loss of his father in 1601, some with a painful experience which they believe to be recorded in the
Sonnets, some with the death of the Earl of Essex, 1601.
These theories are more or less probable, but they are mere
theories, incapable of exact proof. Shakespeare's more
earnest and searching mood may have originated in some
troubles without, or it may be that "midway in this mortal
life," having come to the fulness of his powers, he was
forced by the very greatness and intensity of his nature to
probe life to the centre. When he wrote *Julius Cæsar*,
he was about thirty-six, he was still young in years, and he
had won both money and reputation. It may be that
having gained the immediate objects of his ambition, his
thoughts turned elsewhere. The vital thing is, that, from
whatever cause, Shakespeare appears to have passed through
a period of spiritual conflict. Most thinking men have
faced some such crisis of doubt and questioning; perhaps
only the greatest souls have known its full bitterness.
"Name it as we choose: with or without visible Devil,
whether in the natural Desert of rocks and sands, or in the
populous moral Desert of selfishness and baseness, — to such
Temptation are we all called." [1] Obviously the scope and
meaning of the great tragedies of this period cannot be put
into a few sentences; *Hamlet* and *Lear* cannot be reduced
to a formula. Yet it is evident that the thought of Shakespeare in these plays is largely occupied with the great fact
of sin; sin, not in its remote and possible origin,
nor even in its relation to a life hereafter, but
sin as it is in this present world. Whatever form
it assumes, — covetous ambition, envy, malice, ingratitude,
— sin is represented as an ulcer at the heart of life, poison-

Shakepeare's
studies of sin.

[1] Carlyle's *Sartor Resartus*, Bk. ii. chap. ix. v. also Bk. ii. chap. vii.

ing its very source, and bringing with it a train of miseries which confound alike the innocent and the guilty. In *Macbeth* we are present at the ruin of a soul, standing irresolute at the brink of the first crime and then hurrying recklessly from guilt to guilt; in *Othello* we see the helplessness of a "noble nature" in the hands of fiendish ingenuity and malice; Ophelia, the "fair rose of May," and Hamlet, perish with the guilty King and Queen; the outcast Lear, "more sinned against than sinning," and the spotless Cordelia fall victims to a monstrous wickedness:

> "Not the first
> Who with best meaning have incurred the worst.

The stress and turmoil of these mighty tragedies culminates in *King Lear*. In *Hamlet*, terrible as is the protest against the depravity and inadequacy of the world, it is to some extent the protest of the philosophic observer, the idealist in the first bitterness of disillusion; in *Othello* we are largely absorbed by the immediate pathos of the drama, and all general considerations are forgotten in the pure "pity of it;" in *Macbeth* the gloom deepens, until finally in *Lear* the tempest of revolt rises to its greatest height. One sufferer after another seeks to solve the riddle of human misery by some despairing or impious theory. Men's destinies are governed by the stars; by an "opposeless" and inscrutable will; they are the victims of a malicious power:

> "As flies to wanton boys are we to the gods;
> They kill us for their sport." [1]

Shakespeare does not seek to evade or to palliate, he faces the worst, and he reports honestly with that fearless sincerity which is characteristic of his genius. He shows us the worst, and yet he makes us feel that human

---

[1] *Lear*, Act iv. Sc. 1.

society, with all its imperfections, rests securely on the basis of a moral order. He shows us that there is nothing so loathsome and noxious as sin, nothing so beautiful as goodness. He shows us that high endeavour, greatness, and innocence cannot really fail so long as they remain true to themselves, because they are their own exceeding great reward. He makes the good suffer, but he shows us that to the good the uses of adversity are sweet. "Throughout that stupendous third act (of *King Lear*)," says a recent critic, "the good are seen growing better through suffering, and the bad worse through success." [1] Good is not "captive" in the hands of Ill, it is free and invulnerable. It is enough that Brutus was "the noblest Roman of them all," though he lie dead for a lost cause under the gaze of the conquering Octavius. Worldly success may mean spiritual ruin; worldly ruin, spiritual success. Shakespeare does not explain the dark riddle of life; he does say with unequalled earnestness: "Woe unto them that call darkness light, and light darkness; that put bitter for sweet, and sweet for bitter."

Shakespeare is no apologist for error; in his plays sin is laid bare in all its repulsive baseness and deformity, a root of bitterness fouling the sweet springs of life.

His reverence for goodness. The great moral distinctions which — more than differences of class, or race, or intellect — separate soul from soul, are everywhere sharply and firmly drawn. If Richard III., or Iago, or the two woman fiends in *Lear*, reveal the spirit of wickedness incarnate, in no poet are virtue and holiness more lovely and divine. Our conceptions of the worth and dignity of humanity are raised, our ideals purified and ennobled, by the contemplation of the heroic in Shakespeare's world. Cordelia, Virgilia, Miranda, Portia, elevate and sanctify our thoughts of womanhood by their loveliness and purity. The knightly courage of Henry

[1] Bradley's *Shakespearean Tragedy*, p. 327.

V., the faithfulness of Kent, the blunt honesty and loyalty of Faulconbridge, the Roman constancy of Horatio, all inspire us with a generous admiration for manly virtue. "Shakespeare," says Coleridge, "is an author, of all others, calculated to make his readers better as well as wiser." Yet with all his uncompromising morality, his stern condemnation of sin, Shakespeare pours out over the faults and frailties of the erring creatures he has made, the fulness of a marvellous tenderness and pity. The humility of a great nature under the sense of its own shortcomings, the recognition of an ideal of excellence so stainless that all fail alike in attaining it, these personal traits, it seems to us, shine out through Shakespeare's lessons of forgiveness and of charity. Throughout all of Shakespeare's work, this compassion for human weakness, this large-hearted sympathy with human failures and mistakes, sheds a gracious and kindly light, but in two plays, *Measure for Measure* and *The Merchant of Venice*, the need of mercy is given an especial prominence. In the first, Isabella, imploring mercy for her condemned brother, exclaims:

> "Alas! Alas!
> Why, all the souls that were, were forfeit once;
> And He that might the vantage best have took
> Found out the remedy. How would you be,
> If He, which is the top of judgment, should
> But judge you as you are?" [1]

And in the same spirit, Portia declares:

> 'That in the course of justice none of us
> Should see salvation; we do pray for mercy,
> And that same prayer doth teach us all to render
> The deeds of mercy." [2]

[1] *Measure for Measure*, Act ii. Sc. 2.
[2] *Merchant of Venice*, Act iv. Sc. 1.

Thus Shakespeare, hating and condemning sin, teaches us that our human weakness requires another law than that of rigid justice. Neither in our heavenly nor our earthly relations dare we "stand upon our bond." Shylock, intrenched in the support of a lower and earthly law, fails to see upon what compulsion he "*must*" be merciful. But Shakespeare, through Portia, points to the obligation of the higher law; he tells us that there is something not "nominated in the bond," — even charity; the grace of a mutual forbearance without which human life would be literally unlivable. He enforces in his way the parable of the unmerciful servant, "Shouldest not thou, also, have had compassion on thy fellow-servant, even as I had pity on thee?"

His charity.

Toward the close of his life, Shakespeare passed in his art out of his tragic mood to write some of the loveliest of his comedies, with undiminished freshness and creative vigour. The imagination which at the beginning of Shakespeare's work budded forth in *A Midsummer Night's Dream*, the fairy-land of Oberon and Titania, gives being to the dainty spirit Ariel, speeding at the command of Prospero, or cradled in the bell of the cowslip; while in *The Winter's Tale*, the stress of tragedy over, we can fancy ourselves back again in Warwickshire with Shakespeare, breathing its country odours and gazing on the

Last plays.

> "daffodils,
> That come before the swallow dares, and take
> The winds of March with beauty." [1]

As Shakespeare's fortune and engagements permitted him, he seems to have spent more and more time in his native place; and he appears to have returned there about 1610 or 1612. He had said his last to the world; for a few silent years that appeal profoundly to our imaginative interest, he lived in the

Retirement to Stratford.

[1] *Winter's Tale,* Act iv. Sc. 3.

midst of the scenes and associations of his boyhood, and then, on the 23d of April, 1616, the fifty-second anniver-⟨ sary, it is supposed, of his birth, he closed his eyes on the world.

Shakespeare speaks to all times and nations for the English nature and genius. He gathers and sums up the best

Shakespeare and the English genius. that has gone before him — the Celtic wit, fancy, and deftness; the Teutonic solidity and sincerity, its earnestness, morality, and reverence for the unseen. To this capacious nature, drawing its forces from the genius of two races, awakened Italy gives her tribute; and through it the English Renaissance finds its supreme poetic utterance.

A great lyric poet, a consummate if at times a negligent or careless artist, a man of commanding intellect and of comprehensive sympathy, perhaps the greatest single characteristic of Shakespeare is his union of righteousness with charity. The greatest voice of the English Renaissance testifies to the strength of moral fibre in the English, to the power of the English conscience. It is not only as a genius that Shakespeare compels our homage; our instinct tells us that, in addition to all his gifts as a poet, but inextricably associated with them, he was a great man. We are sure that his works, mighty as they are, are but the partial expression of a wise, opulent, and kindly nature; and when Ben Jonson, moved to unwonted tenderness, declares: "I loved *the man*, and do honour his memory on this side of idolatry as much as any," we know that his tribute was just. This man, then, stands for the English people, a king over them for all time. "Here, I say," Carlyle writes, "is an English king whom no time or chance, Parliament or combination of Parliaments, can dethrone! This king, Shakespeare, does he not shine in crowned sovereignty over us all as the noblest, gentlest, yet strongest of rallying-signs; indestructible; really more valuable in that point of view than any other means of appliance whatsoever? We can fancy him as radiant aloft over all the nations of Englishmen a thousand years hence. From Paramatta, from New York, wheresoever, under what sort of parish constable soever, English men and women are, they will say to one another: 'Yes, this Shakespeare is ours; we produced him, we speak and think by him; we are of one blood and kind with him.'" [1]

ELIZABETHAN PROSE.

The greatest names in Elizabethan literature are those of the dramatists and the poets, yet the intellectual advance of the time showed itself also in a rapid devel-

Elizabethan prose. opment of prose. Literary criticism springs into life in such works as Sidney's *Defence of Poesy* (1580–1581), or Puttenham's *Art of English Poesy* (1589). Prose fiction is represented by Sidney's elaborate romance, the *Arcadia* (1590), and by countless shorter stories from the rapid pens of Peele, Greene, and other struggling dramatists. Besides all this we have, in the reigns of Elizabeth and James, an abundant prose literature of history and travel, and innumerable pamphlets on the questions of the day. Two men, RICHARD HOOKER and FRANCIS BACON, tower above the other Elizabethan prose-writers by their intellectual force, and by the broad and comprehensive character of their thought. Personally, the shy country clergyman and the ambitious Lord Chancellor had little in common; but far apart as they were in character and in their aims, they were alike in their capacity for broad generalisation, and in their philosophic breadth and spaciousness of mind.

---

[1] "The Hero as Poet," *Heroes and Hero Worship,* by Thomas Carlyle.

RICHARD HOOKER.

(1553–1600.)

Hooker. Richard Hooker, a man of humble origin, was by nature a thinker and a student. He was born near Exeter in 1553. His family could not afford to give him a University education, but at school the boy's beauty of character and his aptitude for study were so apparent that the Bishop of Salisbury, through the exertions of the local schoolmaster, procured his admission to Oxford. Here he remained for more than twenty years, becoming in time a tutor and a fellow of his College. He entered holy orders in 1581. Hooker was not only a profound student, he had that wide range of intellectual interests which distinguished the great men of the Renaissance. He knew something of music and poetry, and was not "a stranger to the more light and airy parts of learning." [1] He had the placid temper of the student content to live in the world of thought. No worldly ambitions broke the tranquillity of his simple scholar's life, and when he was at last called to other duties he declared that he had lost the freedom of his cell.[1] After a few years in a country parish in Buckinghamshire, where he was found by two of his former pupils reading Horace and tending the sheep, he was called to London in 1585, to be Master of the Temple.[1]

It was a time of angry and violent controversy in matters of religion. The Reformation had left many things unsettled, and England was filled with the wrangling of contending sects. Many of the clergy were eager for battle, and Hooker, who loved peace, found himself involved in a doctrinal controversy with a certain Mr. Travers, the afternoon lecturer at his own church. The situation was so intolerable to one of Hooker's tempera-

[1] Izaak Walton's *Lives*, "The Life of Mr. Richard Hooker."

ment, that he asked the Archbishop to give him some country parish where he could work undisturbed. "Indeed," he wrote, "God and Nature did not intend me for contentions, but for study and quietness." He had his wish, and in 1591 he became rector of Boscombe, in Wiltshire; there he completed the first four books of his great work on Church government, the *Laws of Ecclesiastical Polity*, which appeared in 1594. The remaining years of Hooker's uneventful life were spent away from London, where he could "see God's blessings spring out of the earth and be free from noise." During the intervals of his parochial labours he worked on his book. In 1595 he became rector of a small parish about three miles from Canterbury, and there died in 1600.

We must not regard the *Ecclesiastical Polity* merely as a contribution to current theological controversy. It is not a controversial tract, increased in size and preserved to posterity by the majestic eloquence of its style; but something widely different. Even Milton, in the heat of party warfare, became an eager and bitter controversialist, so far forgetting himself as to assail his enemy with undignified abuse. But Hooker writes as one who is above the wrangling of factions. He is not a disputant, but a philosopher. His tone is dispassionate and judicial. He does not write to irritate or confound his opponents, but to conciliate, to enlighten, to persuade. His freedom from personal rancour, his calmness, do not spring from timidity or even from a mere love of peace. He was above a narrow partisanship, because he was able to view his subject in its large relations to the human society and to the world of Nature. The Puritan, assuming that the Bible contained the only revelation of God, rested his argument on his interpretation of Scriptural texts. But Hooker believed that God had not revealed himself in the

Bible alone, but in the entire scheme of creation; he believed that the Universe was but a "manifestation" of "the eternal law of God." The order, which we, through reason, discern in creation, is a Divine order; the laws of Nature are but the expression of God's will. The largeness and sublimity of Hooker's conception places him with the great spirits of his time. Bacon felt the reign of law in the world of matter; Shakespeare recognised the presence of a great moral order, of a spiritual law, in the world of man; Hooker sees God revealing Himself in the Bible, in Nature, and in human society, manifesting Himself in part through those laws which are the expression of His will. This is the feeling which inspires Hooker's famous tribute to the majesty of law: "Wherefore that here we may briefly end, of law there can be no less acknowledged, than that her seat is the bosom of God, her voice the harmony of the world, all things in heaven and earth do her homage, the very least as feeling her care, and the greatest as not exempted from her power, both angels and men and creatures of what conditions soever though each in different sort and manner, yet all with uniform consent, admiring her as the mother of their peace and joy." [1]

Hooker's style, though often cumbrous, involved, and difficult, is worthy of the greatness of his theme. In the stateliness, the dignity, the sonorous march of his ponderous sentences, he is the precursor of a long succession of great masters of English prose. It has been said that "he first revealed to the nation what English prose might be." There had indeed been great prose-writers before him, but it would be difficult to name one who attained to Hooker's especial kind of excellence. To find his peers we must turn to his successors and compare him with Raleigh, Jeremy Taylor, Milton, and Burke.

[1] End of First Book of *Ecclesiastical Polity.*

FRANCIS BACON.

(1561–1626.)

Francis Bacon was born in London, January 22, 1561. His father was Sir Nicholas Bacon, Lord Keeper of the Great Seal, and one of the most trusted of the early statesmen of Elizabeth; a yet more famous statesman, Lord Burleigh, was his uncle by marriage. From his earliest years, Bacon was thus connected with the court and with public life. When he was eighteen, his prospects were greatly changed by the sudden death of his father. Bacon, who was the younger son, was thus left insufficiently provided for, and was compelled to make his own way in the world. He accordingly entered upon the study of the law, and although Lord Burleigh showed no disposition to assist him, his advance was exceedingly rapid. He was made a barrister in 1582, Solicitor-General in 1607, Attorney-General in 1613, and Lord Chancellor in 1617. From this brilliant public success we get no idea of Bacon's inner life and deepest aspirations. He declared, in a letter to Lord Burleigh, written at the outset of his career, "I confess that I have as vast contemplative ends, as I have moderate civil ends; for I have taken all knowledge to be my province." He early resolved that he would strive to benefit the race by the discovery of truth; and, although he seems at times to have been diverted by worldly necessities or worldly ambitions, he was always true at heart to his lofty purpose. From his inability to reconcile contending interests — the love of place and power, with the unselfish devotion to knowledge — springs the tragedy of Bacon's life. In 1621 Bacon's worldly ambitions were overthrown at a stroke. He was accused of having taken bribes in his office of Lord Chancellor. He piteously confessed the charge, and was henceforth a ruined man in reputation and in fortune. Bacon spent the remainder of his life in the composition of some of the great philosophical and scientific works on which his fame chiefly rests. With Bacon, the philosopher and scientist, however, the student of English literature is not directly concerned. The story of his closing years is pitiable. "The Lord Chancellor," said his former patron, the young favourite, Buckingham, "is so sick that he cannot live long." He still showed a brave front to the world, and moved about with a courtly retinue, like the shadow of his former self, so that Prince Charles said of him: "This man scorns to go out in a snuff;" —yet he must have felt the burden of debt, disgrace, and dishonour. He caught cold from exposure, while engaged in a scientific experiment, and died a few days later, April 9, 1626.

Bacon is generally considered the greatest man of the Elizabethan age, with the single and inevitable exception of Shakespeare. Dean Church calls him "the brightest, richest, largest mind but one, in the age which had seen Shakespeare and his fellows." Yet, speaking strictly, Bacon holds a place in English literature almost by accident, and in spite of himself. He deliberately chose to be a Latin rather than an English writer, having no confidence in the stability of his own language, and believing that it would "at one time or another play the bank-rowte [bankrupt] with books." He even went so far as to have his *Advancement of Learning* translated from English into Latin, so convinced was he of the superiority of the latter tongue. This book in its original form, the *Essays*, *The History of Henry VII.*, and a fragment, *The New Atlantis*, are substantially all that English prose can claim out of the great mass of Bacon's writings.

Yet, while Bacon thought little of his work as an English writer, and threw the weight of his immense energy in other directions, it is his English works that have best held their own. In Raleigh's prose we encounter more impassioned and noble eloquence, as in those rare places in the *History of the World,* where he seems to suddenly leave the ground and soar in the celestial spaces; but Bacon's style has a more even excellence. Incidental and slight as Bacon's connection was with the literature of his own language, a high critical authority has recently pronounced him "one of the greatest writers of English prose before the accession of Charles I." [1]

Incredible as it would have seemed to Bacon, it is by the *Essays* that he is best known to the general reader. By an "essay," Bacon meant the first trial, or weighing, of a subject, as distinguished from a finished treatise.[2] His *Essays* are pithy jottings on great subjects, informally set down, with no attempt to carry the thought to its full or natural conclusion. They read like the note-book of a profound thinker, a shrewd observer of life, a politic and active man of affairs. They are brief, suggestive, without an ornament, but closely packed with thought. They give us the concentrated results of Bacon's experience, and are often comparable to the proverbial sayings in which wise men have delighted since the days of Solomon. Often they go to the heart of the matter with one quick thrust, as in the famous sentence: "Prosperity is the blessing of the Old Testament, adversity is the blessing of the New, which carrieth the greater benediction and the clearer revelation of God's favour." [3]

Bacon's own account of the object of the *Essays* is that he "endeavoured to make them not vulgar, but of a nature whereof much should be found in experience and little in books; so that they should be neither repetitions nor fancies;" and he desires that they should "come home to men's business and bosoms."

His Essays.

---

[1] Saintsbury's *Elizabethan Literature,* p. 209.

[2] *Essay* = assay = a test, or examination of metals, O. F., *assai;* Lat., *exagium.* See Skeat's *Etymological Dictionary.*

[3] Essay on "Adversity."

Three editions of the *Essays* were published in Bacon's lifetime; the first in 1597, the second in 1612, and the third in 1625. The first edition contained only ten essays, but by the third edition the number had grown to fifty-eight.

We are apt to undervalue these essays on the first reading, and it is only through long familiarity that their wisdom and depth really reveal themselves. Some of them, such as the essay "Of Great Place," exhibit the high purposes of Bacon in strange and melancholy contrast to his actual performance. His life was a tragic contradiction, and in such declarations we ought not to believe him deliberately insincere. In thinking of his shortcomings we should remember, also, the nobility of his ideals. "If ever a man," says Dean Church, "had a great object in life and pursued it through good and evil report, through ardent hope and keen disappointment to the end, with unwearied patience and unshaken faith, it was Bacon, when he sought for the improvement of human knowledge, for the glory of God and the relief of man's estate." [1]

SUMMARY OF ELIZABETHAN LITERATURE.

We have seen England, lifted by the common wave of thought and emotion, find an outlet for her richer and deeper experience in the creation of innumerable works in every department of literature. To the careful student of history, the vast possibilities, the latent powers of the English nature are apparent from the first; the genius of Chaucer strengthens his confidence in the correctness of his estimate, and he sees in the supreme literary greatness of England, under the kindly influence of the Renaissance, the splendid confirmation of this view.

We have approached this many-sided and inexhaustible period, chiefly through the study of three of its greatest men, Spenser, Shakespeare, and Bacon. The first is su-

[1] Church's *Life of Bacon*.

preme as a poet of dreamland, the second supreme among all poets, the last is the great thinker who stands at the gateway of our modern science. These men are indeed pre-eminent, but other writers crowd about them, each great enough to stand first in a less abundant time. The extent and richness of Elizabethan literature has made our study most limited, for so "spacious" is the time that on every hand are beautiful regions which we cannot even pretend to explore. For instance, there is all the literature of criticism, the books in which Sir Philip Sidney, William Webbe, and George Puttenham discuss the art of poetry; there is the literature of travel, books such as Hakluyt's *Voyages* (1589), in which the narratives of great navigators like Sir Humphrey Gilbert or Sir Walter Raleigh were collected; there are all the books of short poems, Tottel's *Miscellany*, *England's Helicon*, *The Paradise of Dainty Devices*, and the like, which tell us how prodigal the country was in song in that full time when England was "a nest of singing birds." Then, too, there are series of sonnets, such as those of Spenser, Sidney, William Drummond (1585–1649); the last perhaps the most Italian in tone and among the most beautiful of them all. We have spoken briefly of the drama, but only extended study can make us realise its power and richness, the great host of busy playwrights and their extraordinary vigor and productiveness. We have alluded to the prose-writers, but we must pass by the work of historian, theologian, romance-writer, and antiquarian, almost without mention. We are forced to leave these regions behind us unexplored, but it will help us to a firmer hold on this revival of learning period, if, before leaving it, we fix in our minds certain points of chronology that rise like milestones along the way. In doing this we must remember that such arbitrary divisions of literature are convenient, but not always exactly true, for literary periods are not in reality thus sharply defined.

First (cir. 1491–cir. 1509). We may associate the last ten years of the fifteenth and the first nine or ten years of the sixteenth centuries with that band of teachers and educational reformers who may be called the missionaries of the new learning. This period reaches from about 1491, the year when Grocyn lectured on Greek at Oxford, to about 1509, the year of the accession of Henry VIII. Conspicuous in this time are Grocyn, Erasmus, Linacre, Colet, and, in his young manhood, Sir Thomas More.

Second (1509–1557). During this time the influence of Italy begins to be apparent in English poetry. Henry VIII. is a patron of learning. More publishes his *Utopia*, Heywood his *Interludes*, Roger Ascham his *Toxophilus* (1544), Coverdale and Cranmer their *Translations of the Bible* (1535 and 1537). Phaer's *Virgil*, Heywood's *Seneca*, and other translations of the classics appear. We note in *Ralph Roister Doister* the beginning of regular comedy. On the whole, the new learning is making itself apparent in literature, and the time is full of the signs of promise.

Third (1557–1579). This period may be remembered as beginning with the publication of Tottel's *Miscellany* and ending with that of Spenser's *Shepherd's Calendar*. During this interval the coming of a mighty outburst draws nearer, the work of preparation goes on in the publication of numerous classical translations; Sackville writes his *Induction to the Mirror for Magistrates* (1563); short poems and ballads appear in extraordinary numbers; the first regular tragedy is written, and innumerable Italian stories become popular. It is a time of growth, of preparation, and of expectancy.

Fourth (1579–1637). Between these years is the high noon of the English Renaissance. The period begins with the *Shepherd's Calendar*, the decisive entrance into literature of the greatest poet England had produced since Chaucer. The ten years succeeding are marked by the rapid advance of the drama under Lyly, Peele, Greene, Lodge, and Marlowe, the immediate precursors of Shakespeare. In 1590, with the first instalment of the *Faërie Queene* and the advent of Shakespeare, we are at the opening of twenty of the most glorious years in the whole twelve centuries of the literature. From about 1613, when Shakespeare ceased to write, we note the slow decline of this creative energy, and in 1637 two events occur which emphasise for us the ending of the old and the beginning of the new. In that year Ben Johnson died, the greatest surviving representative of the glory of the Elizabethans, and in that year also there was published the *Lycidas* of the young Puritan, John Milton. Thus the old order was changing, yielding place to the new.

CHAPTER V.

THE DECLINE OF THE RENAISSANCE.

THE ENGLAND OF MILTON.

ALTHOUGH Shakespeare and Milton are familiarly linked together in our ordinary speech as the two greatest poets of England, in the whole spirit and nature of their work they have hardly anything in common. It is not merely that they are, for the most part, distinguished in separate provinces of poetry; that Shakespeare is above all the dramatic, and Milton the epic poet of the literature; the difference lies much deeper, and declares itself unmistakably at almost every point. Now, this is not entirely due to an inborn, personal difference in the genius of these two representative poets; it is due also to the difference in the spirit of the times they represent. For in a sense even Shakespeare was "of an age," as well as "for all time." [1] So far as we can guess from his work, he seems to have shared the orthodox politics of the Tudor times, distrusting the actions of the populace, and stanch in his support of the power of the king. In the true spirit of the Renaissance, Shakespeare's work is taken up chiefly with humanity in this world, rather than with its relations to any other; his dramas are alive with the crowding interests and activities which came with the Revival of Learning. But the England in which Milton lived and worked was stirred by far different emotions; its finest spirits were inspired by far different ideals. Milton

Shakespeare and Milton express the spirit of different times.

---

[1] "He was not of an age, but for all time." From Ben Jonson's poem "To the Memory of Shakespeare."

interprets and expresses the England of Puritanism, as Shakespeare does the England of Elizabeth; and to understand the difference in the spirit of their poetry, we must turn to history and grasp the broad distinction between the times they respectively represent.

At first sight the change from the England of Shakespeare to that of Milton seems an abrupt one. In point of actual time the two poets are close together, for at the death of Shakespeare Milton was eight years old. But little more than half a century lies between that England in which loyalty to queen and country so triumphed over religious differences that Romanist and Protestant fought the Armada side by side, and that England which hurried Charles I. to the scaffold, or in which Cromwell declared: "If I met the King in battle I would fire my pistol at the King as at another." Yet in reality this change of the nation's mood was not hasty or unaccountable, but the natural result of a long and steady development.

Elizabethan and Puritan England.

We spoke of the Renaissance as the rebirth of the religious as well as of the intellectual life of Europe, and we saw that while in Italy the new life of the mind took form in what we call the Revival of Learning, in Germany the new life of the spirit had its outcome in that religious awakening we call the Reformation. If in Italy the Renaissance meant freedom of thought, in Germany it meant freedom of conscience. The Revival of Learning and the Reformation entered into England almost side by side. If the enthusiasm for the new learning, the luxury of colour, and the "enchantments of the Circes," had entered England from Italy, something also of the awakening of conscience and the protest against Romanism had come from Germany, to find a deep response in the kindred spirit of Teutonic England.

In our study of the Elizabethan period we have been

occupied chiefly with the first of these two influences. Let us look for a moment at the second. The Oxford scholars — scholars who were chiefly instrumental in bringing the new learning to England — were animated, as we have already seen, with moral earnestness and religious zeal, as well as with an interest in classical studies. They were scholars, but they were social and religious reformers also. Great events conspired to force these questions of religious reform upon the life and conscience of the nation. In the century which saw the independence of the Anglican Church; the uprooting of great ecclesiastical institutions, which had been the growth of centuries; the horrors of religious persecution; men and women could not have forgotten questions of religion even if they would. It was the century, too, in which the interrupted work of Wyclif was accomplished — the century which gave the nation the English Bible. Just as the introduction of the study of Greek at Oxford changed the horizon of the English mind, so the introduction of Tyndale's translation of the Bible was an incalculable spiritual force. "If God spare my life," Tyndale had said to a learned opponent. "ere many years I will cause that a boy that driveth the plough shall know more of the scripture than thou dost." And year after year the inestimable influence of an ever-widening knowledge of the Bible was at work in thousands of English households.

Beginning in the upper stratum of society, the new learning had worked downward until it touched the people. But the changes wrought by direct The English contact with the English Bible, if slower, were Bible. even more vital and more extended. The Bible became the literature of the people, telling the poorest and plainest of the essential things of life in words which all could understand. If we find a typical picture in the crowd of London shopkeepers and 'prentices crowding the pit of the "Fortune" or the "Globe," we find one no less typical in the eager throngs gathered about the reader of the Bible in the nave of St. Paul's. "The disclosure of the stores of Greek literature had wrought the revolution of the Renaissance. The disclosure of the older mass of Hebrew literature wrought the revolution of the Reformation." [1]

With this new idea of religious liberty, the idea of political liberty became closely associated. Stimulated

Religious and political liberty closely connected.

and emancipated by greater intellectual and religious freedom of inquiry, men began to scrutinise and discuss the whole theory of government. They grew restless under the arbitrary rule of the early Stuarts, as their minds rose to the conception of their supreme obligation to a higher law; to a Power above the will of the king in the state, above the will of man in the kingdom of God. In the early part of the seventeenth century many things combined to call out and develop these new feelings. The middle classes had advanced greatly during Elizabeth's reign, in prosperity, influence, and intelligence; the danger from Spain was at an end, and men were free to give themselves up to matters at home. But the natural growth of the nation toward a greater political and religious freedom was met by petulant opposition. Elizabeth had been wise enough to know when and how to yield to the will of her Parliament and people, but it was characteristic

Arbitrary rule of the early Stuarts.

of the Stuarts to take a wrong position and hold to it with an obstinate and reckless tenacity. The unkingly James (1603–1625) flaunted what he considered the "Divine Right" of his kingship in the face of an exasperated England. In the early years of the following reign (Charles I., 1625–1649), the growing Puritan sentiment was outraged by brutal persecution,

[1] Green's *History of the English People*, vol. iii. p. 11.

the rising spirit of liberty insulted by flagrant violations of the long established and sacred political rights of Englishmen. Thus the England that rose up in protest against the severities of Archbishop Laud and the tyranny and duplicity of Charles, was on fire with other interests and other aspirations than that of Elizabeth; its energies were centred upon two great issues — politics and religion. In the one, it was determined to "vindicate its ancient liberties;" in the other, it "reasoned of righteousness and judgment to come." Among its great leaders in politics were Eliot, Hampden, Pym, and Cromwell; in literature it spoke in the strong, simple, biblical prose of John Bunyan, a poor tinker; its poet was John Milton.

LATER ELIZABETHAN LITERATURE.

The Drama.

But while the new ways of looking at the deepest questions of life, which for years had been agitating the Puritan element in England, were thus coming to the surface in history and in literature, during the early part of the seventeenth century many continued to write in the general manner and spirit of the Elizabethans. This later Elizabethan literature lies outside our present plan of study, but it cannot be passed over without a few words.

To form any just conception of the commanding genius of Shakespeare, we must measure his altitude by that of his contemporaries. We must imagine him, also, in his daily human relations with men of his own class and calling: we must think of him as an actor among actors, as a theatrical manager, as one of that immortal group at the Mermaid Tavern which included Ben Jonson, Francis Beaumont, and John Fletcher. Shakespeare, said Hazlitt, "towered above his fellows, 'in shape and gesture

proudly eminent,' but he was one of a race of giants." [1]
Some knowledge of Shakespeare's contemporaries or
immediate successors in the drama, is absolutely necessary
if we would see either Shakespeare or his time in proper
perspective; but the number of these dramatists is so great,
their total production so enormous, that the subject can
be treated here only in the most general terms. We can
do little more than enumerate some of the most important names, and attempt to gain some general understanding of the chronology of the period.

The dramatists immediately preceding Shakespeare (see
p. 222) were followed by a number of men of genius, who
had the advantage of writing at a time when the theatre
was a more recognised institution, and when the general
form of the drama had been fixed by successful experiment.
A number of these men began their work during the closing years of the sixteenth century. BEN JONSON (1573–
1637), a big-framed, aggressive, dominant man, whose
learning was not free from pedantry, produced his first
play, the comedy of *Every Man in his Humour*, in 1598,
and the earliest plays of GEORGE CHAPMAN (1559–1634),
THOMAS MIDDLETON (1570–1627),THOMAS DEKKER (c. 1570–
1637), THOMAS HEYWOOD (1581?–1640), and JOHN MAR-
STON (1575–1633) date from within a few years of this
time. During the early years of the seventeenth century,
while Shakespeare was still writing, FRANCIS BEAUMONT
(1584–1616), JOHN FLETCHER (1579–1625), JOHN FORD
(1586–1640), and JOHN WEBSTER began their work. The
first play of PHILIP MASSINGER (1584–1640), *The Virgin
Martyr* (written with Dekker), was brought out a little
later (1622). Among all these men Ben Jonson, while
probably inferior to some of the others in his purely poetical gifts, predominated by the solidity of his understand-

[1] *Lectures on the Dramatic Literature of the Age of Elizabeth.*
Lecture I.

ing, the vigour of his work, and by the sheer strength of his personal ascendency. For some years before Jonson's death, the Elizabethan drama had shown symptoms of decline, and when he died in 1637 the force and production of this extraordinary dramatic period were nearing their end. Plays were indeed written after that time in which something of the old glory survived, but these are but the echoes of a greater age. At last with JAMES SHIRLEY (1596–1666), the greater part of whose work was done between 1625–1655, these last echoes of the Elizabethan drama die away.

Looked at as a whole, the Elizabethan drama, even apart from Shakespeare, in its magnitude, its intensity, its beauty, its variety, its snatches of exquisite song, is one of the most astonishing achievements of the English in literature. In attempting to form any general estimate of it, we must remember that these dramas were, as a rule, not carefully elaborated literary productions, but acting plays, hastily put together for immediate use. Play-writing was an art, but it was a business also. The demand for plays was great, the price (especially before 1600) was comparatively trifling.[1] Under these circumstances, the dramatists naturally saved time and invention by appropriating such material as could serve their turn. They ransacked the literatures of Italy, Spain, or France; they borrowed from foreign novels or dramas; they worked singly, or in partnership like Beaumont and Fletcher; they

General survey.

[1] "The writer of a play usually sold it to the theatre, but sometimes to a kind of broker who stood between players and authors, buying from the one, and selling, so as himself to profit by the transaction, to the other. Such was *Philip Henslowe*, a dyer, a pawnbroker, theatrical lessee and speculator, who during the years of Shakespere's authorship had many dramatic poets in his pay. His diary still exists, and from it we learn that the highest price given by him for a play before the year 1600 was £8; the lowest sum is £4; while for an embroidered velvet cloak no less than £16 is given, and £4 14s. for a pair of hose. After 1600 the price of a play rose to £20 if the dramatist was one of repute." — DOWDEN: *Shakespere Primer*, pp. 11–12.

translated, they made new plays, they adapted or furbished up old ones. We can form no definite idea of the number of these plays; many of them are doubtless irretrievably lost. Only twenty-three of Thomas Heywood's plays have been preserved, yet he declared in 1633 before his adventurous career was over, that he had "an entire hand, or at least a main finger," in the composition of no less than two hundred and twenty plays. Work produced under such conditions is naturally of very unequal merit, yet even in the poorer plays we are liable to stumble upon a passage that shows us that the lesser men could catch for a moment the accent of the masters. As Sir Walter Scott has so justly said: "The dramatic poets of that time (i.e. the early seventeenth century) seem to have possessed as joint-stock a highly poetical and abstract tone of language, so that the worst of them often remind you of the very best." [1]

Ben Jonson stands apart from this crowd of playwrights as unmistakably as Shakespeare rises above them. Independent, overbearing, and combative, prone to despise others, and upheld by an unfaltering confidence in himself, Jonson was not made for a follower, he was one to conquer and rule over a kingdom of his own. He doggedly fought his way to the front in the face of many obstacles. As a youth he was set to lay bricks, a "craft" which, he said, "he could not endure." He was a soldier in the Low Countries, where he killed an enemy in single combat "in the face of both the camps." By 1597 he was established in London as actor and dramatist. About a year later he fought a duel with another actor at Shoreditch-in-the-Fields, and killed his antagonist. He was tried for homicide, but escaped the extreme penalty of the law. He wrote comedies and tragedies, and during the reign of James I. he composed numerous masks for the entertainment of the Court. That learned monarch

Ben Jonson.

[1] Scott's *Journal*, for August 1st, 1826.

made him Poet Laureate, and is said to have offered him knighthood, which he declined. He asserted himself in the choice company of wits gathered at the Mermaid, or the Falcon Tavern, engaging in many "wit-combats" with Shakespeare himself. After Shakespeare's death Jonson was the most prominent man of letters in England. He was the literary dictator of London, and was surrounded by admiring disciples who were said to be "sealed of the tribe of Ben." His last years were darkened with illness and embittered by disappointment. He had outlived his popularity, the taste of the time had changed, the visitor had out-stayed his welcome, and "told the jest without the smile."

The differences between Jonson and Shakespeare are obvious and fundamental. Jonson's work as a whole is barer, more prosaic, more learned, and more laboured than Shakespeare's. Shakespeare, while he remains true to life, yet contrives to invest his mimic world with a magical atmosphere of beauty and romance. But Jonson is a realist. He presents the life of his time, but especially the low life of Elizabethan London, with a hard, dry literalism. His object in his comedies was didactic. He thought that the poet's mission was to paint a moral and to reform society. He ridiculed the abuses and fashionable follies of the time by making the persons of his dramas represent the peculiar hobbies or "humours" of men, but in doing this his drama lost in faithfulness to life through a method which inclined him to make the mere caricature of what we call a "fad" take the place of a character. The method of Jonson, great as he was, was thus a distinct falling off from that of Shakespeare. Jonson's tragedies, *Sejanus* and *Catiline*, are massive, scholarly, and painstaking, but they lack the warmth and humanity which distinguish Shakespeare's treatment of classical themes, and one is apt to read them with respect and with profit rather than with delight.

But there was another side to Jonson's rugged nature. Ponderous as he often seems, he could write the lightest and most charming of lyrics. Songs such as the "Hymn to Diana," "Drink to Me only with Thine Eyes," or "See the Chariot at hand here of Love," are among the treasures of English poetry, while his charming pastoral drama, *The Sad Shepherd* (1637), is filled with an unexpected tenderness and beauty.

Beaumont and Fletcher, "the great twin brethren of the stage," follow Shakespeare and not Jonson. The plays

Beaumont and Fletcher. which pass under their joint names are full of romance, beauty, and passion; there are melodies in them — as in the lyrical passages in *The Faithful Shepherdess* —which invite comparison with Shakespeare. But beautiful as these plays are, they lack the wholesomeness, the masculine vigour, the depth of thought, the firm grasp of human character, which delight us in Shakespeare. They are softer, sweeter, more relaxing, and we feel that in them the sharp distinctions between right and wrong are blurred or obscured. So the work of Beaumont and Fletcher, like that of Ben Jonson, shows in its own fashion that the decadence of the drama has begun.[1]

So far we have associated the decline of the drama with a perverted theory of art and with a moral deterioration.

Puritan hostility to the stage. But we must remember that in addition to any decline in its original power, to any failure that came from within, the drama was forced to contend with the bitter attacks of the Puritans from

---

[1] Among the most notable plays of this period (exclusive of those of Shakespeare) are *Philaster* and *The Maid's Tragedy* of Beaumont and Fletcher; *The Duchess of Malfi* and *The White Devil* of John Webster; *The Changeling* (at least in parts) of Thomas Middleton; *A New Way to Pay Old Debts* of Philip Massinger; and *The Broken Heart* of John Ford. Cyril Tourneur (1575?–1626) wrote two lurid and horrible tragedies, *The Revenger's Tragedy* (printed 1607) and *The Atheist's Tragedy* (printed 1611).

without. In the early seventeenth century this hostility to the stage increased; unsuccessful attempts were made (1619–1631–1633) to suppress the Blackfriars Theatre, and the representation of plays on Sunday was prohibited. Many of the more respectable people stayed away from the theatres altogether, while those who came demanded plays of a more and more depraved character. Finally, about the beginning of the Civil War (1642) the theatres were closed altogether, and the drama almost ceased until the Restoration (1660).

The Poets of the Early Seventeenth Century.

From the Death of Spenser, 1599, to the Restoration, 1660.

The poetry of the early half of the seventeenth century is largely a continuation or a development of that of the greater Elizabethans. As we have just seen, many of the rising generation of writers were united by a personal loyalty to Ben Jonson, and by a reverence for his critical opinions. Other poets took Spenser for their model, drawing inspiration from his pastoral rather than from his chivalric poetry, and following him chiefly in his more serious moods. Others, again, imitated the poetic mannerisms of John Donne, another Elizabethan of wayward but powerful genius, of whom we have not yet spoken. England at this time was a house divided against itself, and the religious and political dissensions which rent and racked the nation, divided the poets also into sharply contrasted groups. Some, like the saintly George Herbert, expressed in poetry much that was best in the Church of England; others, like Milton, stirred by different ideals, represented the militant and reforming spirit of Puritanism. But great as this difference may seem between the Anglican and the Puritan, it is insignificant to that which separates the *Cavalier poets* — the gay, elegant triflers of the Court, like Carew and Lovelace —

from those poets who, apart in some respects, are at least united by a devotion to high ideals and by a lofty spirituality of nature. The variety of these schools, or groups, into which the poets of this time may be divided, the irreconcilable differences in feeling, and in the general attitude towards life, are characteristic of the confusion of the time. This diversity, we must remember, is not wholly due to the inevitable differences in human character, it is also national, for it is the literary expression of those conflicting beliefs and ideals which were fought out in the Civil War.

Spenser, "the poet's poet," exercised a profound and important influence on English poetry, both in his own and succeeding times. When he died, his work unfinished, England was just midway in an illustrious era, and in the full tide of literary production. But while many great poets survived him, Spenser's loss was deeply felt, and his effect upon the poetry of the early seventeenth century was probably greater than that of any other Elizabethan, not excepting Shakespeare himself. Apart from his general and less definite influence, Spenser's effect on some of his successors was direct and specific. The chief of these disciples of Spenser are the brothers GILES and PHINEAS FLETCHER, first cousins of JOHN FLETCHER the dramatist, and WILLIAM BROWNE. The Fletchers are certainly a remarkable trio. Southey, indeed, goes so far as to assert, that "no single family" ever produced three such poets in one generation. Giles and Phineas Fletcher were both clergymen. Their uncle was Bishop of London; their father, a man of learning and distinction, had himself published a volume of poems. Giles Fletcher's chief work, *Christ's Victory and Triumph in Heaven and Earth over and after Death*, was published in 1610. The poem is divided, as the title suggests, into four parts. It is written in a modification of Spenser's stanza, and it retains "much of his

The Spenserian School.

melody and luxuriant expression." Giles Fletcher's master-piece, although now but little read, is a remarkable and in places a truly noble poem. Through this poem, Fletcher was at once the successor of Spenser and the precursor of Milton. On the one hand, Fletcher's description of the Bower of Vain Delight takes us back to Spenser's descrip-tion of the Bower of Bliss in the *Faërie Queene,* while, on the other hand, his account of Christ's temptation in the wil-derness carries us forward to Milton's treatment of the same theme in *Paradise Regained.* Fletcher's work is thus a link between two of the greatest poems of the literature. Phineas Fletcher's chief claim to be remembered rests on his singu-lar poem, *The Purple Island; or, The Isle of Man* (1633). This is one of those ill-advised attempts to combine science and poetry, and, although the work of a true poet, it suffers from the unpoetical nature of its subject. The Purple Island is not an "enchanted isle" of the imagination, but the human body; and the poem is an allegorical treatise on human anatomy and what we should now call psychology. Fletcher chose a pastoral setting for his work, and the introduction of allegorical disquisitions on physiology into Arcadia increases the singularity of the poem. Yet there is genius in *The Purple Island* as well as eccentricity and bad taste. In places we forget science in the charm of the Arcadian atmosphere, and some of the descriptions of Na-ture and of country life are full of quiet and beauty. One stanza from a description of the happiness of the shepherd's life, will show how charmingly Fletcher could treat a well-worn theme:

> "His bed of wool yields safe and quiet sleeps,
>   While by his side his faithful spouse hath place:
> His little son into his bosom creeps,
>   The lively picture of his father's face:
> Never his humble house or state torment him;
> Less he could like, if less his God had sent him;
> And when he dies, green turfs, with grassy tomb, content him." [1]

[1] *The Purple Island,* Canto xii.

William Browne was a Devonshire poet, and his loosely constructed but often pleasing poem, *Britannia's Pastorals* (1613), contains some admirable descriptions of the beautiful scenery of his native country. At times — as in his description of some boys chasing a squirrel — his pictures of country life are unusually spirited, fresh, and natural.

While these Arcadian poets thus follow "Divinest Spenser"[1] looking up to him as their "Colin, whom all the Graces **John Donne.** and all the Muses nurs'd,"[2] others were led in a very different direction through the example of the great but eccentric poet JOHN DONNE (1573–1631). Donne was a man of intense and "highly passionate" nature, possessed of that abounding vitality, that capacity for strong emotions, which makes great saints or great sinners, and drives men to extremes. In his youth he showed that delight in action, travel, and adventure, characteristic of so many of the great Elizabethans. He was a hard student, but also a lover of pleasure. He was with Essex in 1596 in an expedition against Spain, in which the English destroyed the Spanish fleet and pillaged Cadiz. He took a trip to the Azores. He wandered through Spain and Italy, spending his fortune, it is said, in his travels and in "dearbought experience." After his return to England he became chief private secretary to Sir Thomas Egerton, a distinguished lawyer and Lord Keeper of the Great Seal, but a clandestine marriage with his patron's niece in 1601 ruined, for the time, his prospects of advancement. The marriage proved a happy one, but years of struggle and poverty followed. After much hesitation he resolved to take orders, and was ordained in 1615. His wife's death two years later appears to have wrought a great change in him. He was one to "contend to the uttermost for his life's set prize," and his thought now became concentrated upon spiritual things.

[1] Browne's tribute to Spenser in *Britannia's Pastorals*, Bk. ii. Song 1.
[2] Fletcher's *Purple Island*, Canto i,

Now that his wife was "removed by death, a commensurable grief took as full a possession of him as joy had done," and "his very soul was elemented of nothing but sadness." [1] He held various ecclesiastical positions, and in 1621 was made Dean of Saint Paul's. Donne had enjoyed and suffered greatly, and that same intensity that had urged him into youthful excesses, helped to make him one of the greatest preachers England ever produced. He was, wrote Izaak Walton, "a preacher in earnest; weeping sometimes for his auditory, sometimes with them; always preaching to himself, like an angel from a cloud, but in none." [2] In these latter years he was noted for his saintliness of life, given to "continual study" and to good works. He died in 1631.

One of the most obvious facts about Donne is the sharp contrast between the worldliness and impetuosity of his youth, and the saintliness and asceticism of his age. His life is naturally divided into two periods, the one before and the other after his wife's death in 1617. Donne's poetry was almost all written during the first of these two periods,—probably by the close of the sixteenth century; in the second period he expressed himself chiefly through his sermons. As a poet, Donne is thus strictly an Elizabethan, although his followers belong to the reigns of James and Charles.

Donne's poetry.

Yet while Donne was a younger contemporary of the greatest Elizabethan poets, he was independent of them. He was an "innovator," and in his own generation he stood alone in England in his conception of poetry, and in his difficult, fantastic, and at times harsh and repellent style. Donne's style, difficult and peculiar as it seems, is not only similar to that of certain European poets of this period, it is also related to that tendency to literary affectations which had already shown itself in England.

[1] Walton's *Life of Donne*.　　　[2] Walton's *Life of Donne*.

Donne's singularities are in keeping with that delight in far-fetched comparisons and extravagant "conceits," as they were called, which had found expression in the euphuistic extravagances of Lyly, or in the elaborate similes of Sidney's *Arcadia*. Even the greatest Elizabethan poets are not free from a similar extravagance and over-ingenuity of expression, although the niceties of style are by no means their chief concern. The tendency to find an intellectual satisfaction in the whimsical, the abstruse, and the unexpected, in verbal quibbles, and novel analogies, found its exponent in Donne. What the love of beauty was to Spenser, the love of ingenuity, the delight in intellectual subtility, in verbal dexterity, was to Donne. He was the poet of "wit." According to Dr. Johnson's famous definition, wit consists in "a combination of dissimilar images, or discovery of occult resemblances in things apparently unlike." [1] This ingenuity of Donne must be dwelt upon, because his mannerisms were imitated by certain younger poets, and became the distinctive feature of a group of poets commonly known as the "Metaphysical School." But it would be a great mistake to think of Donne as a mere master of paradoxes, or a mere intellectual gymnast. Donne's peculiarities, as Saintsbury justly says, obscure his beauty. His poems are alive with suggestion, close-packed with thought, and lit up by an occasional felicity of expression which the greatest poets hardly surpass.

Traces of Donne's over-elaborated and often deplorable manner are found in the works of many of his successors. **The influence of Donne.** Such traces often seem like "the trail of the serpent," but they sometimes produce an effect that is rather pleasing. One of the most notable of his followers was ABRAHAM COWLEY (1618–1667), whose great contemporary reputation was so short-lived that fifty years after his death his poetry was already neglected.

[1] *Lives of the Poets:* "Cowley."

Cowley's prose-essays, written in a pleasant and simple style, are a grateful contrast to the studied complexity that mars much of his verse. Traces of Donne are also obvious at times in the quaint but often beautiful religious poetry of GEORGE HERBERT (1593-1633), RICHARD CRASHAW (1613-1650?), HENRY VAUGHAN (1621-1695),[1] and FRANCIS QUARLES (1592-1644). Crashaw rises at rare moments to great heights of beauty and eloquence, but his verse in general is weighed down and disfigured by "conceits." Herbert and Vaughan, while not free from the same tendency, write more simply, and their poems are full of sincere religious feeling. Indeed, their poetry is so tranquil, so lifted into the serene air of holy meditations, that it seems a place of sanctity in the midst of a turbulent age. The circumstances in which these two poets wrote were in keeping with the remote and unworldly atmosphere of their work, for Herbert was a country parson and Vaughan a village doctor in Wales. Herbert sprung from the younger branch of a distinguished family, was a courtier in his youth, and thought of devoting himself to a public career. His birth and spirit, he tells us, entangled him in a world of strife, and inclined him towards —

"The way that takes the town."[2]

But, after some hesitation, he resolved to take orders. He was influenced at this critical period by Nicholas Ferrar, a retired merchant, whose peaceful and religious household at Little Giddings has been described by Shorthouse in *John Inglesant*. In 1630, Herbert became vicar of Bemerton, a village about a mile from Salisbury. Here

[1] *Thomas Traherne* (b. 1636) was another of this group. His work resembles that of Herbert and Vaughan, and as he was younger than either of those poets he presumably owed much to their example. His poems were recently discovered in manuscript, and first published in 1903.

[2] Herbert's *Poems:* "Affliction."

he wrote his poems, and here he died three years later. The English country parson, immortalised by Chaucer and by Goldsmith, is, at his best, one of the most attractive types of manly goodness that England has produced. Herbert had not the simplicity of Goldsmith's hero, for he had seen and known the world, but he had the goodness, faithfulness, and spirituality. He was, to paraphrase Walton, lowly in his own eyes and lovely in the eyes of others, and both the beauty of his nature and the religious seclusion of his surroundings shine through his poems. "It is his quiet religion, his quaint, contemplative, vicarage-garden note of thought and scholarship, which pleases most, and will always please, the calm piety of England." [1] Vaughan, Herbert's disciple in sacred poetry, fell below his master in art but surpassed him in depth and originality. Born in Wales of an ancient Welsh family, Vaughan left London shortly after 1646, and settled down for the rest of his life as a country doctor in his native Brecknockshire. Living out his secluded life in the quiet valley of the Usk, Vaughan saw God revealed not only in the services of the Church, but also in the living world of Nature, in the holy innocence of childhood, and in the "immortal longings" of his own spirit. He gazes on a gilded cloud or a flower, and finds in them some "shadows of divinity;" searching himself, he comes upon strange hints of man's Divine origin, he discovers "some rills" from the Eternal source of being,

" With echoes beaten from the eternal hills." [2]

To Vaughan, man's life on earth is a brief exile from that eternal existence from which he came, and to which, when he rises above his temporal limitations, he longs to return. The light of man's spirit is a spark of the Divine light.

[1] Stopford Brooke: *Primer of English Literature.*
[2] Vaughan's *Poems,* "Vanity of Spirit."

> "For each enclosed spirit is a star
>   Enlight'ning his own little sphere;
> Whose light, though fetch'd and borrowed from far
> Both mornings makes and evenings there."

The Retreate, Beyond the Veil, and *Childhood,* are among Vaughan's most beautiful poems. The reader will have no difficulty in discovering there, and in many other places in Vaughan's work, a striking anticipation of some of Wordsworth's favourite ideas.

Meanwhile at Court a group of aristocratic poets composed their slight, but often charming love-songs to Celia, or Lucasta. Their thoughts are given to the pleasures of this world as frankly as those of Vaughan and Herbert are centred on the next. Among these are THOMAS CAREW (1598–1639), RICHARD LOVELACE (1618–1658), and SIR JOHN SUCKLING (1619–1641). Each of these holds an assured, though minor place, in literature by virtue of comparatively few poems; yet each has contributed to it at least one lyric which has become a classic. ROBERT HERRICK (1591–1674), a Devonshire vicar, while he shares in the mood of these light and graceful amourists, rises above them in vigour and charm, and in the fine quality of his lyrical gift. His limpid and altogether charming verse is troubled by no depth of thought or storm of passion. The greater part of his verse reflects the pagan spirit of those who lie at ease in the warm sunshine; content to enjoy, they sigh that life is but a day, and lament as the lengthening shadow draws near. The closing verse of his poem, *Corinna's going a-Maying,* is a good example of his familiar mood: the inevitable chill of regret creeps into the sunshiny lyric of May day, and his laughter ends in a sigh:

> "Come, let us go while we are in our prime,
>   And take the harmless folly of the time!
>   We shall grow old apace, and die
>   Before we know our liberty.

(The Cavalier Lyrists.)

> Our life is short; and our days run
>   As fast away as does the sun;
> And as a vapour, or a drop of rain
> Once lost, can ne'er be found again:
>   So when or you or I are made
>   A fable, song, or fleeting shade;
>   All love, all liking, all delight
>   Lies drowned with us in endless night.
> Then while time serves, and we are but decaying,
> Come, my Corinna! come, let's go a-Maying."

There is a captivating naturalness and freshness in Herrick's note; the rural England of his time is green forever in his verse, the hedgerows are abloom, the Maypoles gay with garlands. He sings

> "Of brooks, of blossoms, birds and bowers.
> Of April, May, of June, and July-flowers." [1]

England was racked with civil war, but neither the strife of religions nor the tumults in the state are able to shatter his Arcadia; while king and Parliament are in deadly grapple, Herrick sings his dainty love-songs to Julia and Anthea, and babbles "of green fields."

In his youth, Herrick was one of those genial spirits who gathered round Ben Jonson, and in 1647, deprived of his living by the Puritans, he left Devonshire and returned to London. In 1648 he published a book of poems, "both Humane and Divine," containing the *Hesperides* and *The Noble Numbers*. For even Herrick wrote what he styled "pious pieces," and a few of these are very quaint and charming. In one of them, he laments the license of his verse, and asks forgiveness for his "unbaptized rhymes." But it is not likely that his penitential moods were very deep or lasting. His natural temper seems to have been light and earthly. Enjoy your May-day, gather your rose-buds, "Let's now take our time ;" such were the gay songs he flung defiantly in the face of sober, Puritan England.

[1] *Hesperides.*

In the midst of this poetry of self-indulgence there rose
the mighty voice of Milton. In *Lycidas*, which may be

Herrick and Milton.

said to conclude the poems of his earlier period,
Milton, too, asks the pagan question, "Seeing
that life is short, is it not better to enjoy?"
but only to meet it with triumphant denial. This famous
passage becomes of especial interest when we think that
it was probably written with such poets as Carew and
Herrick in mind; when we recognise in it the high
seriousness and religious faith of Puritanism, squarely
confronting the nation's lighter mood:

> "Alas! what boots it with uncessant care
> To tend the homely, slighted, shepherd's trade,
> And strictly meditate the thankless Muse?
> Were it not better done, as others use,
> To sport with Amaryllis in the shade,
> Or with the tangles of Neæra's hair?
> Fame is the spur that the clear spirit doth raise
> (That last infirmity of noble mind)
> To scorn delights, and live laborious days;
> But the fair guerdon when we hope to find,
> And think to burst out into sudden blaze,
> Comes the blind Fury with th' abhorrèd shears,
> And slits the thin-spun life. 'But not the praise,'
> Phœbus replied, and touched my trembling ears:
> 'Fame is no plant that grows on mortal soil,
> Nor in the glistering foil
> Set off to the world, nor in broad rumour lies,
> But lives and spreads aloft by those pure eyes
> And perfect witness of all-judging Jove;
> As he pronounces lastly on each deed,
> Of so much fame in heaven expect thy meed."[1]

[1] *Lycidas*, ii. 64–84.

JOHN MILTON.

(1608–1674.)

"Three poets, in three distant ages born,
Greece, Italy, and England, did adorn.
The first in loftiness of thought surpass'd;
The next in majesty; in both the last.
The force of Nature could no further go;
To make a third, she join'd the former two."

— DRYDEN.

"Thy soul was like a star, and dwelt apart:
Thou hadst a voice whose sound was like the sea:
Pure as the naked heavens, majestic, free,
So didst thou travel on life's common way
In cheerful godliness; and yet thy heart
The lowliest duties on herself did lay."

— WORDSWORTH.

" . . . He died,
Who was the sire of an immortal strain,
Blind, old, and lonely, when his country's pride
The priest, the slave, and the liberticide
Trampled and mocked with many a loathèd rite
Of lust and blood, he went, unterrified,
Into the gulf of death; but his clear Sprite
Yet reigns o'er earth, the third among the sons of light."

— SHELLEY.

"His sympathies with things are much narrower than Shakespeare's.
Shakespeare was not polemical: Milton was polemical altogether."

— CARLYLE.

"An appreciation of Milton is the last reward of consummated
scholarship."   — MARK PATTISON.

"God-gifted organ voice of England."

— TENNYSON.

Shakespeare, the poet of man, was born in rural England; John Milton, into whose remote and lofty verse
humanity enters so little, was born in Bread Street in the
heart of London, December 9, 1608.

His early years were passed in a sober and orderly
Puritan household among influences of refinement and

culture. His father, John Milton, was a scrivener, an
Boyhood at London, 1608-1624. occupation somewhat corresponding to the modern conveyancer, but he was also well known as a musical composer. The younger Milton's faculty for music had thus an opportunity for early development; a fact of especial interest when we recall the distinctively musical character of his verse.

Milton was early destined "for the study of humane letters," and given every educational advantage. He had private instruction, and about 1620 was sent to the famous Grammar School of St. Paul. Here, to use his own expression, he worked "with eagerness," laying the foundation of his future blindness by intense application. He began to experiment in poetry, and we have paraphrases of two of the Psalms made by him at this time.

In 1624 Milton entered Christ's College, Cambridge, where he continued to work with the same steady and regulated
Cambridge. 1624-1632. enthusiasm. His youth was spotless and high-minded, with perhaps a touch of that austerity which deepened as he grew older. His face had an exquisitely refined and thoughtful beauty; his soft light-brown hair fell to his shoulders after the Cavalier fashion; his figure was well-knit but slender; his complexion, "exceeding fair." From his somewhat delicate beauty, and from his blameless life, he gained the college nickname of " the Lady." The year after he entered college he wrote his first original poem, *On the Death of a Fair Infant Dying of a Cough,* and to this period also belong the resonant *Hymn to the Nativity* and other short pieces.

After leaving Cambridge Milton spent nearly six years at his father's country house at Horton, a village near
Horton, 1632-1638. Windsor, and about seventeen miles from London. Here he lived with books and Nature, studying the classics and physical science, and leaving his studious quiet only for an occasional trip

to town to learn something new in music or in mathematics.

Milton's *L'Allegro* and *Il Penseroso*, composed at this time, reflect both the young poet and his surroundings.

L'Allegro and Il Penseroso. Rustic life and superstitions are there blended with idyllic pictures of the Horton landscape. In *L'Allegro* we hear the ploughman whistle at his furrow, the milkmaid sing at her work; we see the

> "Meadows trim, with daisies pied,
> Shallow brooks, and rivers wide,"

or mark the neighbouring towers of Windsor

> "Bosomed high in tufted trees."

In both poems we detect Milton himself, a refined and serious nature, exquisitely responsive to whatever is best in life, with a quick and by no means narrow appreciation of things beautiful. The poems suggest to us a youthful Milton dreaming of gorgeous and visionary splendours in the long summer twilights, delighting in the plays of Jonson and Shakespeare, and spending lonely midnights in the loftiest speculations of philosophy; a Milton whose beauty-loving and religious nature was moved by the solemn ritual of the Church of England under the "high embowèd roof" of a cathedral. In these poems, especially *L'Allegro*, Milton is very close to the Elizabethans. In their tinge of romance they remind us of Spenser, who, according to Masson, was Milton's poetical master, while in their lyrical movement they strikingly resemble certain songs of Fletcher in his pastoral drama, *The Faithful Shepherdess*.[1] But

Comus. *Comus* (1634), Milton's next work, shows the decided growth of a new and distinctly Puritan spirit. In its form indeed, *Comus* belongs to the earlier

---

[1] See the beautiful lyric, "Shepherds All and Maidens Fair," in Act ii. Sc. 1, and "Song of the River God," in Act iii. Sc. 1, of this play.

age. It is a mask — one of those gorgeous dramatic spectacles which Renaissance England had learned from Italy, the favourite entertainment at the festivals of the rich, with which Ben Jonson so often delighted the court of James. *Comus* has music and dancing, and it affords the requisite opportunity for scenic effects, yet there breathes through it the growing strain of moral earnestness. It shows us how purity and innocence can thread the darkest and most tangled ways of earth, unharmed and invincible, through the inherent might of goodness. In noble and memorable words Milton declares that if we once lose faith in this essential power of righteousness, and in the ultimate triumph of good over evil which that power is destined to secure, the very foundations of the universe give way:

> "... Against the threats
> Of malice or of sorcery, or that power
> Which erring men call Chance, this I hold firm:
> Virtue may be assailed, but never hurt,
> Surprised by unjust force, but not enthralled:
> Yea, even that which Mischief meant most harm
> Shall in the happy trial prove most glory.
> But evil on itself shall back recoil,
> And mix no more with goodness, when at last,
> Gathered like scum, and settled to itself,
> It shall be in eternal restless change
> Self-fed and self-consumed. If this fail,
> The pillared firmament is rottenness,
> And earth's base built on stubble." [1]

We see the powers of Heaven descend to protect beleaguered innocence, and in the parting words of the attendant spirit, we find both the practical lesson of the mask and the guiding principle of Milton:

> "Mortals, that would follow me,
> Love Virtue; she alone is free.
> She can teach ye how to climb
> Higher than the sphery chime;
> Or, if Virtue feeble were,
> Heaven itself would stoop to her." [1]

[1] *Comus.*

In his next poem, the pastoral elegy of *Lycidas* (1637),
the space between Milton and the Elizabethans continues

Lycidas.   to widen. From the enthusiasm for virtue, he
passes to an outburst of wrath and denuncia-
tion against those in the Church whom he considered the
faithless shepherds of the flock.

> "The hungry sheep look up, and are not fed,"

but the hour of retribution is at hand; already the

> "two-handed engine at the door,
> Stands ready to smite once, and smite no more." [1]

The first thirty years of Milton's life had thus been lived
almost wholly "in the still air of delightful studies." [2] In-

Travels,   dustrious and select reading was part of his
1638–1639.   systematic preparation for the life-work he set
himself. Up to this time he wrote little, although
that little was enough to give him an honourable place
among the poets of England; but already he was full of great
designs, writing in 1637, "I am pluming my wings for a
flight." To all he had learned from books he now added
the widening influences of travel.

Leaving England in April, 1638, he passed through Paris
to Italy, meeting many learned and famous men, among
the rest the old astronomer Galileo, to whom he refers in
the early part of *Paradise Lost.*

Meanwhile the civil troubles in England seemed gathering
to a crisis, and Milton resolved to shorten his trip, because,
as he wrote, "I considered it base that while my fellow-
countrymen were fighting at home for liberty, I should be
travelling abroad for intellectual culture."

---

[1] *Lycidas.* For full analysis of this passage see **Ruskin's** *Sesame
and Lilies.*

[2] Milton, *The Reason of Church Government*, Int., Bk. ii.

We learn from the *Epitaphium Damonis*, a beautiful Latin elegy written at this time (1639), that Milton was already planning a great epic poem, but this project was to be rudely interrupted. England was on the brink of civil war, and after long years of preparation Milton put aside his cherished ambitions and pursuits, and freely gave up his life and genius to the service of his country. Except for occasional sonnets, the greatest poet in England forced himself to write prose for more than twenty years. Most of this prose was written in the heat of "hoarse disputes," and is often marred by the bitterness and personal abuse which marked the controversies of that troubled time; but this is redeemed in many places by earnestness and a noble eloquence.

Prominent among the works of this prose period are the *Tractate on Education* (1644), and the splendid *Areopagitica*, a burning plea for the liberty of the press, of which it has been said: "Its defence of books, and the freedom of books, will last as long as there are writers and readers of books." [1]

Meanwhile (1643), Milton had taken a hasty and unfortunate step in marrying Mary Powell, a young girl of less than half his age, of Royalist family, who proved unsuited to him in disposition and education. After the execution of Charles I. (1649) Milton ranged himself on the side of those who had taken this tremendous step, in a pamphlet on *The Tenure of Kings and Magistrates*, and a month after its publication, was made the Latin, or foreign, Secretary to the newly established Commonwealth. His pen continued to be busy for the state, until in 1652 his eyes failed him through over-use, and he was stricken with total blindness. In this year his wife died, leaving him with three little girls. In 1656 he married Katherine Wood-

[1] Stopford Brooke, *Milton*, p. 45, Classical Writers Series.

cock, who lived but little more than a year, and to whom he paid a touching tribute in one of his sonnets. [1]

In these later years of Milton's life, during which he suffered blindness, sorrow, and broken health, the cause **The later** for which he had sacrificed so much was lost, **poetic period** and England brought again under the rule of a **1660-1674.** Stuart king. Milton had been so vehement an advocate of the Parliament that we wonder at his escape; but, from whatever reason, he was not excepted from the general pardon put forth by Charles II. after his return (August 29, 1660). In the riotous years that followed, when England, casting off decency and restraint, plunged into "the mad orgy of the Restoration," Milton entered in earnest upon the composition of *Paradise Lost*, singing with voice

> "unchanged
> To hoarse or mute, though fallen on evil days;
> On evil days though fallen, and evil tongues,
> In darkness, and with dangers compassed round,
> And solitude." [2]

In his little house in Bunhill Fields, near the London in which the pleasure-loving king jested at faith and honour, and held his shameless court amid

> " . . . the barbarous dissonance
> Of Bacchus and his revellers," [3]

the old poet lived his life of high contemplation and un-daunted labour. At no time does Milton seem to us more worthy of himself; he is so heroic that we hardly dare to pity him. But wherever the fault lay, his daughters, whose privilege it should have been to minister to him, greatly increased his burdens. They are said to have sold

[1] "Methought I saw my late espousèd Saint
  Brought to me like Alcestis from the grave," etc.
[2] *Paradise Lost*, Bk. vii.   [3] *Paradise Lost*, Book vii.

his books without his knowledge, and two of them counselled his maidservant to "cheat him in his marketings."

When we reflect that the oldest daughter was but fourteen at the Restoration, and that the education of all had
been neglected, we are inclined to judge less hardly, but
we can scarcely wonder that Milton should have sought
some means of relief from these intolerable discomforts.
This he happily found through his marriage with Elizabeth
Minshull in 1663. Yet even when matters were at the
worst, Milton seems to have borne them with a beautiful
fortitude, "having a certain serenity of mind not conde-
scending to little things." His one faithful daughter,
Deborah, speaks of his cheerfulness under his sufferings
from the gout, and describes him as "the soul of conversation." In the spirit of his sonnet "On His Blindness,"
he was content to "only stand and wait," sending up the
prayer out of his darkness,

> "So much the rather thou, Celestial Light,
>   Shine inward." [1]

The words of one who visited him at this time help to
bring Milton before us, dressed neatly in black, and seated
in a large arm-chair in a room with dark-green hangings,
his soft hair falling over his shoulders, his sightless eyes
still beautiful and clear.

Paradise Lost was published in 1667, to be followed
in 1671 by *Paradise Regained*. With the latter poem
appeared the noble drama of *Samson Agonistes* (or the
Wrestler), and with it Milton's work was ended. He died
on November 8, 1674, so quietly that those with him
knew not when he passed away.

> "Nothing is here for tears, nothing to wail
>   Or knock the breast; no weakness, no contempt,
>   Dispraise, or blame; nothing but well and fair,
>   And what may quiet us in a death so noble." [2]

[1] *Paradise Lost*, Bk. iii.   [2] *Samson Agonistes*, l. 1721.

We are stimulated and thrilled by the thought of Milton's life, as at the sight of some noble and heroic action. Obviously it is not free from our common human shortcomings, but in its whole ideal and in its large results, we feel that it moves habitually on the higher levels, and is animated by no vulgar or ordinary aims. It is much that as a great poet Milton loved beauty, that as a great scholar he sought after truth. It is more that, above the scholar's devotion to knowledge, Milton set the citizen's devotion to country, the patriot's passionate love of liberty; that above even the employment of his great poetic gift, he set the high resolve to make his life "a true poem," and to live

Milton's ideal of life.

> "As ever in my great Taskmaster's eye." [1]

He has accordingly left us an example of solemn self-consecration to a lofty purpose, early undertaken, and steadfastly and consistently pursued. Milton's life was lived at high tension; he not only set an exacting standard for himself, he was also inclined to impose it upon others. He is so sublime that some of us are inclined to be a trifle ill at ease in his presence, or are apt to be repelled by a strain of severity far different from the sweet companionableness of Shakespeare. In Milton's stringent and austere ideal we miss at times the saving grace of Shakespeare's charity, or we are almost moved to exclaim with Sir Toby:

> "Dost thou think, because thou art virtuous, there shall be no more cakes and ale?" [2]

In *Samson Agonistes,* when Delilah pleads before her

---

[1] Sonnet "On his Arriving at the Age of Twenty-three."
[2] *Twelfth Night,* Act ii. Sc. 3,

husband that she has sinned through weakness, she is
met by an uncompromising reply:

> ". . . If weakness may excuse,
> What murderer, what traitor, parricide,
> Incestuous, sacrilegious, but may plead it?
> All wickedness is weakness: that plea, therefore,
> With God or man will gain thee no remission." [1]

From such a rigorous insistence on condemnation in
strict accord with the offence, our minds revert to Portia's
inspired plea for mercy,[2] or to Isabella's searching question:

> "How would you be,
> If He, which is the top of judgment, should
> But judge you as you are?" [3]

However we may appreciate these differences in the
spirit of two great poets, we do Milton wrong if we fail to
honour and reverence him for that in which he
was supremely great. We must remember that
this intense zeal for righteousness was a master
passion in the highest spirits of Milton's time, and that
it is hard to combine zeal with tolerance. It is but natural
that in the midst of the corrupt England of the Restoration, the almost solitary voice of the nation's better self
could not prophesy smooth things. This Puritan severity
is especially marked in the three great poems of Milton's
later life. As a young man he had chosen a purely romantic subject for his projected epic — the story of Arthur;
his maturer interests led him to abandon this for a purely
religious and doctrinal one; he treated of the fall of man
and the origin of evil, that he might "justify the ways of
God to men." *Paradise Lost*, with its sequel, *Paradise
Regained*, constitutes the one great contribution of the
English genius to the epic poetry of the world. The style
of these great works alone shows genius of the highest

*Paradise
Lost.*

---

[1] *Samson Agonistes*, l. 831.   [2] *V. supra*, p. 243.
[3] *Measure for Measure*, Act ii. Sc. 2.

and rarest kind. By the incomparable dignity and majesty of the verse, with its prolonged and solemn music, and the curious involution of its slowly unfolding sentences, we are lifted out of the ordinary or the trivial, into the incalculable spaces of that region into which it is the poet's object to transport us. In *Paradise Lost*, caught in the tremendous sweep of Milton's imagination, we see our whole universe, with its circling sun and planets hanging suspended in the black abyss of chaos,

> "In bigness like a star."

Heaven, "the deep tract of Hell," and that illimitable and chaotic region which lies between, make up the vast Miltonic background, where legions of rebellious angels strive with God, and wherein is enacted the mysterious drama, not of men, but of the race of Man.

The attitude of Shakespeare toward that unseen and mysterious region which lies beyond the limits of our human experience, was that of the new learning. He places us in the midst of our familiar world, and there we only catch at times the half-intelligible whisper of voices coming out of those blank surrounding spaces which no man can enter. Hamlet, slipping out of this little earthly circle of noise and light, can but whisper on the brink of the great blackness of darkness, that

Milton and Shakespeare.

> "The rest is silence."

But Milton, with the new daring of Puritanism, took for his province that "undiscovered country" beyond the walls of this goodly prison, as Shakespeare, through Hamlet, called the world. At the beginning of his great epic he invokes "The Heavenly Muse,"

> "that on the secret top
> Of Oreb or of Sinai, didst inspire,
> That shepherd who first taught the chosen seed,
> In the beginning how the heavens and earth
> Rose out of chaos." [1]

[1] *Paradise Lost.* Bk. i.

He looks to the Hill of Sion,

> "and Siloa's brook, that flowed
> Fast by the oracle of God," [1]

rather than to Parnassus, and by Celestial guidance intends to soar "above the Aonian mount," and to pursue

> "Things unattempted yet in prose or rhyme." [1]

SEVENTEENTH-CENTURY PROSE.

Our study of Milton has carried us beyond the date of the Restoration, but before we leave Elizabethans and Puritans, and enter that new England which began with the return of Charles II., we must turn back to the opening of the seventeenth century, and note some salient features in the history of prose. While the deep emotions, high imaginations, and poetic fancy which possessed Renaissance England, found their fullest and their earliest expression through poetry and the drama, from the close of the sixteenth century they began to ennoble prose also. We have already noted the beginning of a more sustained and majestic prose-style in Hooker; we must now glance at the further development of prose in the hands of some of his greatest and most representative successors. Raleigh's *History of the World* (1614), tedious and discursive as it is, is illuminated by many noble and poetic passages. Raleigh had known the world as few men know it, its ambitions, its rivalries, its heroism, its splendid successes, its cruel humiliations and defeats, and — imprisoned in the Tower at the close of his life, crowded with great exploits — he undertook to write a survey of the course of

[1] *Paradise Lost*, Bk. i.

human history. When we put aside all that seems pedantic or absurd in Raleigh's *History*, when we pass beyond the parade of a now antiquated learning, and reach the heart of his book, we see that it is the verdict on human life pronounced by a man who had known life well. Shut out at last from an active share in the world's life, Raleigh, the courtier, the soldier, the statesman, the colonist, the freebooter, the explorer, the poet, the philosopher, sits down at last in quiet, and asks what does this world mean, and what is its worth. The book, useless or ridiculous as history, is memorable as the personal revelation of a restless and splendid personality. It has the deep religious feeling and the deep melancholy of the English nation: it begins with a noble apostrophe to God, "The Almighty Mover" who "has been pleased to make himself known by the work of the world," and it ends with that passage on the emptiness of earthly ambitions, that tribute to Death the Conqueror, which is one of the glories of English prose: "O eloquent, just, and mighty Death! whom none could advise, thou hast persuaded; what none hath dared, thou hast done; and whom all the world hath flattered, thou only hast cast out of the world and despised Thou hast drawn together all the. far stretched greatness all the pride, cruelty, and ambition of man, and covered it all over with these two narrow words, *Hic jacet!*"

In such passages, and others which fall but little short of this high level, we see how in the seventeenth century the passion and poetry of the Elizabethans shone out through the less transparent medium of prose. JEREMY TAYLOR (1613–1667), called by Coleridge the "most eloquent of English divines," was one of the greatest masters of this poetic, or impassioned prose. Read, for instance, this passage on the shortness of man's life, and see how he invests a familiar comparison with freshness and beauty creating out of old materials a prose-poem not unworthy

to stand beside many a familiar lyric on the same theme.[1]
"But so have I seen a rose newly springing from the clefts
of its hood, and, at first, it was fair as the morning, and full
with the dew of heaven, as a lamb's fleece; but when a
ruder breath had forced open its virgin modesty, and dis-
mantled its too youthful and unripe retirements, it began to
put on darkness, and to decline to softness and the symptoms of a sickly age; it bowed the head and broke its stalk;
and, at night, having lost some of its leaves and all its
beauty, it fell into the portion of weeds and outworn faces.
The same is the portion of every man and every woman." [2]

There was also a quaint scholastic air in some of the sev-
enteenth-century prose-writers, analogous to the extravagances of Donne or his followers in verse. This musty
flavour of odd learning permeates the *Anatomy of Melancholy* (1621) of ROBERT BURTON (1577–1640), and enters
into the fascinating style of SIR THOMAS BROWNE (1605–
1682). Burton, "that fantastic great old man," as Charles
Lamb called him, spent the greater portion of his life in the
studious seclusion of Oxford. Many, we are told, "accounted" him "a severe student, a devourer of authors, a
melancholy **and humorous** person." [3] His *Anatomy* (or
analysis) *of Melancholy*, heavily freighted with the spoils of
his wide and curious reading, impresses us as an unconscious
revelation of **the humorous** personality of the man. Sir

[1] Many of these lyrics, however, urge that, — life being short, — we
should gather rosebuds while we may. Many examples will occur to
the reader: Herrick's *To the Virgins to make much of Time*, and
To Daffodils; Waller's *Go, lovely Rose*; Spenser's song (translated
from Tasso) in the *Faërie Queene*, Bk. ii. Canto xii. ("Ah, see the
Virgin Rose, how sweetly she," etc.), and Giles Fletcher's variation
of Spenser's Song in *Christ's Triumph on Earth. Cf.* also Ausonius'
"De Rosis Nascentibus," ll. 49–50, and Ronsard's *A Cassandre
(Mignonne, allons voir si la rose,* etc.). Taylor naturally uses the comparison to point an orthodox moral. *Cf.* the various biblical passages
in which man's life is compared to a "flower," "grass," etc.

[2] *The Rule and Exercises of Holy Dying,* chap. i. § ii.

[3] Anthony à Wood: *Athenæ Oxonienses.*

Thomas Browne's style, like Burton's, is that of an old-time scholar, full of recondite allusions and fragments from the classics, but it mounts into loftier regions of poetry and imagination. Browne was a learned and busy physician, who, after taking his degree abroad, settled down at Norwich in 1637, to the practice of his profession. He loved to investigate the odd and the mysterious, and delighted in curious speculations. He was a scientist, but he was above all a poet and a mystic. The ostensible object of his *Enquiries into Vulgar and Common Errors* (1646) is to dispel certain popular superstitions by the light of reason and common sense, but his real interest is with the things which never can be proved. To him there are not "impossibilities enough in religion for an active faith." "I love," he writes, "to lose myself in a mystery; to pursue my reason to an *O altitudino!* "[1] Browne's first book, *Religio Medici* (1642–1643), shows a detachment from the present and the temporal, a nearness to the unseen, which strongly reminds us of Vaughan. He counts the world "not an inn but an hospital, and a place not to live but to die in." He loses himself in the contemplation of God, and in his "solitary and retired imaginations" he remembers that he is not alone. Like Vaughan he finds a divine spark in his own nature: "There is surely a piece of divinity in us — something that was before the heavens and owes no homage unto the sun."[1] This mystical exaltation is united with a quiet, contemplative melancholy. He surveys the world as from a height; he sees the past in a long retrospect, and he speculates upon the endless procession of generations. He meditates on death and on the life after death, and even the burial rites of various nations and the visible signs of mortality have an interest for him. The discovery of some ancient sepulchral urns containing human bones, in a field in Norfolk, stirs his imagination, and furnishes

[1] *Religio Medici.*

him with a theme for his *Hydriotaphia,* or *Urn Burial,* one
of the most eloquent and characteristic of his works.   The
thought of "these dead bones" hid a yard underground in
their "thin walls of clay," and quietly resting "under the
drums and tramplings of three conquests," is the inspiration of one of the noblest passages of English prose.[1]   The
Urn Burial was published in 1658, the year of the death of
Oliver Cromwell.   But if from one aspect Browne seems remote and withdrawn from the agitations of his time, from
another he is as truly the spokesman of its lofty spirituality
and melancholy contemplation.   He wrote when the vigorous, mundane activity of the Elizabethan era had been
succeeded by a more mature and meditative mood.   This
solemn tone, like the stillness of an autumn twilight after
a day of action, pervades some of the noblest spirits of his
age.   It was in Raleigh when he wrote his *History of the
World;* it was in Donne, when, after his fevered and passionate youth, he preached and meditated on death and
the hereafter.   Indeed, there are passages in Donne's sermons which might well have been written by Browne.
When we look deeply, we see that Vaughan in his Welsh
village, Herbert at Bemerton, Nicholas Ferrar at Little
Giddings, and Browne at Norfolk, were in spirit not far
apart.

The seventeenth century was a memorable one in prose,
but we must confine ourselves to a passing mention of some
of the most notable names.   THOMAS FULLER
(1608–1661), a genial, shrewd, and delightfully
humorous author, wrote, among many other
books, a *Church History of Britain* (1656), and a fascinating
book on *The Worthies of England* (1662).   LORD CLAREN-
DON'S *History of the Great Rebellion* (after 1660), the work
of a great actor in the events he describes, is written with
vigour and vividness, and a certain stateliness and dignity

*Other prose-
writers.*

---

[1] *Hydriotaphia,* chap. v.

of style. Before Clarendon set down his impressions of
the great struggle of the century, IZAAK WALTON (1593–
1683), a London linen-draper, had found in country
scenes and by the borders of a quiet stream, inspiration of
a widely different character. Walton's kindly, worldly
nature, his quiet goodness, his simple pleasure in Nature
and in country sports, shine through his books and make
him one of the most restful, and companionable of writers.
His *Lives*, short, sympathetic sketches of Donne, Hooker,
Herbert, and other notable men, while not always free
from partiality, are in other respects models of brief biography. His *Complete Angler* (1653) is so wholesome, so
full of wise thoughts and innocent enjoyment, so idyllic
in its country atmosphere, that it has long held a secure
place among the masterpieces of English prose.

Finally, we must not forget that Milton, whose work
has been already alluded to, holds a high, perhaps the
highest, place among the prose-writers of this time.
Many of Milton's prose-works deal with the theological
or political controversies of his day. They were addressed primarily to the men of his own generation;
written to gain some immediate and definite result. Works
of this character inevitably lose something of their vitality by the mere lapse of time; for future generations, busy
with their own problems, are apt to take but a languid
interest in these dead issues of the past. Yet, in at least
some of his prose, such as the immortal *Areopagitica*,
Milton's greatness, his passion for truth and liberty, his
comprehensive scholarship, his sonorous, majestic, and
subtly-musical style, his instinct for the felicitous and
memorable phrase, triumph over anything that is temporal
in his subject and purpose, and a work addressed to his
own age becomes the delight and admiration of later times.

JOHN BUNYAN.

(1628–1688.)

"Was there ever yet anything written by mere man that was wished longer by its readers, excepting *Don Quixote, Robinson Crusoe*, and *The Pilgrim's Progress*"? — DR. SAMUEL JOHNSON.

> "Ingenious dreamer! in whose well-told tale
> Sweet fiction and sweet truth alike prevail;
> Whose humourous vein, strong sense, and simple style,
> May teach the gayest, make the gravest smile;
> Witty, and well employed, and, like thy Lord,
> Speaking in parables his slighted word."
>
> — COWPER.

"We are not afraid to say, that, though there were many clever men in England during the latter half of the seventeenth century, there were only two minds which possessed the imaginative faculty in a very eminent degree. One of those minds produced the *Paradise Lost*, the other the *Pilgrim's Progress*." — LORD MACAULAY.

Raleigh, Browne, Burton, Milton, and many other great prose-writers of the seventeenth century, were children of the Revival of Learning. It is true that they were imbued with the religious, serious, or meditative spirit prevalent in their own time, but they had been trained up and steeped in those classical studies which had come in with the Renaissance, and their works were the outcome of the new culture.

Bunyan's spiritual inheritance was a mighty but a restricted one. He "never went to school to Aristotle

Bunyan the child of the Reformation. and Plato;"[1] he had no share in that world of classical culture, of art and beauty, which had enriched the lives of so many of the greatest Elizabethans. He was not the child of the New Learning, but of the Reformation; the child of that long period of religious struggle and experience, which began when the plain, unliterary people of England — the shopkeepers, artisans, and plowmen — could first read the Bible

[1] *Doctrine of the Law and Grace Unfolded: Epistle to the Reader.*

for themselves. A few years before the publication of
Pilgrim's Progress, Milton had put the doctrine and the
spirit of Puritanism into his great epic, but Milton had the
varied scholarship and the beauty-loving temperament
that marked the men of the Renaissance. He was master
of almost every language and every literature then known
to European scholars; he was literally "the heir of all the
ages," and he made royal use of his vast inheritance.
But Bunyan sprang from and belonged to the great mass
of the people. His father was of "that rank which is
meanest and most despised of all the families of the land." [1]
While Milton had all; Bunyan had only the torments of
his strange spiritual conflict, the enforced leisure of his
long imprisonment, his genius, and the English Bible.
And it is the comparative narrowness of Bunyan's inheritance, the obscurity of his station, the commonplace
character of his surroundings, that make him, more truly
than the cultured Milton, the representative of the great
body of English Puritans, — of the earnest, simple-
minded men and women who had no library but the
English Bible, and to whom religion was a vital and absorbing reality.

John Bunyan was born on the outskirts of Elstow, a
village about a mile from Bedford, in 1628. His father
Life. was a brazier, or tinker, a patcher of old cans
or kettles, — and Bunyan was bred to the
same humble calling. There was nothing exceptional in
his situation, or especially striking in his surroundings.
He was a poor man's child in an English village, "brought
up . . . in a very mean condition, among a company of poor
countrymen." The country about Elstow is restful and
pleasing, rather than bold or romantic; near by, the river
Ouse flows tranquilly through broad stretches of flat and
open meadows. The land is fertile. It is a place where

---

[1] *Grace Abounding.*

one would expect to find comfort, dulness, and content. Bunyan was given some elementary instruction, but he afterwards forgot most of the little he had ever learned. When he was in his seventeenth year he served for a short time in the Parliamentary army (1644–1647). But at the close of the Civil War, after this experience of the world outside his village, he returned to Elstow, married a woman as poor as himself, and began a life apparently destined to be undisturbed, monotonous, and respectable.

Bunyan was no pale, hysterical fanatic, no weakling, no over-wrought student; he was a sturdy, big-boned, florid-faced, English tinker, every inch a man, yet there was something in him that set him apart from his neighbours. In the midst of those peaceful, commonplace surroundings, he was tortured by a sense of his own wickedness, by doubts, by temptations to utter terrible blasphemies, by despair. Living, to all outward appearance, the most ordinary of lives, Bunyan's soul became the battlefield of that fierce conflict which he has himself described in *Grace Abounding to the Chief of Sinners*. This book is the autobiography of a man's spirit. No one can read it without feeling that the foundation of Bunyan's character, as well as the chief source of his power, is his intense and direct relation to the unseen. We cannot explain this; but as truly as Napoleon had a genius for war, or Watts for scientific invention, Bunyan, like Dante or St. Francis of Assisi, had a genius for religion, and things which to others seem vague and remote, were to him immediate and sometimes terrible realities. As a child he had been affected with fearful dreams and terrible visions. Once, when he was nine or ten years old, an awful despair overcame him in the midst of his play. As he grew older these visions left him, until that strange conflict began within him not long after his return to Elstow. This spiritual conflict lasted about four years. Once when he was playing tip-cat, a voice from heaven darted suddenly into his soul, asking him if he would leave his sins. Burdened with a sense of his guilt, he gave up his favourite amusements one by one. He gave up the delight of ringing the bells in the church-tower: he gave up dancing on the village green. But Bunyan, though given to swearing in his youth, had never been what the ordinary man would call wicked. His struggle was not the ordinary battle with the grosser temptations; what he desired was not outward respectability, not outward conformity to the conventional standards of those about him, it was a state of inward certainty and peace. He was "in a flame to find the way to heaven," but for him the way seemed barred. One day he sat down on a settle in the street of a neighbouring town and brooded upon his condition. "I lifted up my head," he writes, "but methought I saw, as if the sun that shineth in the heavens did grudge to give light; and as if the stones in the streets, and the tiles upon the houses, did bend themselves against me. Methought they all combined together to banish me out of the world."

To men of a colder and more materialistic temperament, this violence of emotion seems merely morbid, unnecessary, or absurd. It is as incomprehensible to them as the raptures of a poet to one whose nature is hopelessly prosaic and matter-of-fact. But to understand Bunyan, or his greatest book, we must follow him through the agonies of his spiritual experiences, with sympathy and imagination. We must realise that in those years of inward torment Bunyan — poor, narrow-minded, perplexed, but magnificently and utterly in earnest — was making his own painful pilgrimage from the City of Destruction to a City of Peace.

At last he found it. In 1653 he joined a little community of dissenters, presided over by a certain John Gifford, and after a time he began to preach. After the Restoration he was arrested for preaching in unlicensed conventicles and thrown into the Bedford gaol. He refused to make the promise to give up preaching which would have given him liberty. "If you let me out to-day," he said, "I will preach again to-morrow." He remained in the gaol for eleven years, supporting himself by making "long-tagged thread laces," preaching to his fellow-prisoners, and writing *Grace Abounding* and several other books. In 1672 the Declaration of Indulgence was passed, an act granting religious liberty both to Roman Catholics and Nonconformists, and Bunyan was released. But three years later on the repeal of this act, Bunyan, who had resumed his preaching, was again imprisoned. It was during this second imprisonment, which lasted three years, that he began to write *Pilgrim's Progress*. The first part of this marvellous book was published in a cheap and unostentatious form in 1678, the same year which saw the appearance of the great John Dryden's tragedy on the story of Antony and Cleopatra, entitled, *All for Love and the World Well Lost.*

Bunyan wrote many other books after this; The second part of the *Pilgrim's Progress, The Life and Death of Mr. Badman,* and *The Holy War,* the last of which Macaulay declared to be, *Pilgrim's Progress* alone excepted, "the best allegory that ever was written." In these last years Bunyan rose to great influence among those of his own sect, and was popularly called "Bishop Bunyan." In 1688 exposure to a rain-storm while he was engaged in a work of mercy, resulted in a sudden illness, and he died in a few days.

The popularity of the *Pilgrim's Progress* was long confined to readers of the lower and middle classes. It was written for the people by a man of the people. The Pilgrim's Progress. It was written by a dissenter at a time when dissenters were persecuted and despised, and its distinctly religious purpose, as well as the humble station of its author, combined to place it outside the conventional bounds of literature. The polite world disdained it; the critics ignored it, or failed to take it seriously. But in the course of a hundred years the power of the book began to impress the literary and fashionable classes, and when Macaulay wrote his sketch of Bunyan in 1854, the "educated minority" had "come over to the opinion of the common people."[1] To-day the fame of Bunyan's masterpiece is probably greater than it has ever been before. It has been translated into many foreign languages, and it stands with those few supreme books which, like *Robinson Crusoe* and *Gulliver's Travels*, remain the delight and admiration of the high and the low, the young and the old, the ignorant and the cultured. What is there in the unpretentious work of "the inspired tinker" that has obtained for it the permanence and the universality of the great classics?

In the first place, Bunyan, sectarian as he was, chose for his allegory a broad and vital theme. In *Paradise Lost*, Milton was concerned with some of the deepest mysteries of theology. When we pass beyond all the splendid poetry, the magnificent imagery in which he has clothed his purpose, we see that Milton's primary object is to reconcile the existence of sin in the world with the wisdom, goodness, and omnipotence of God, and that his ultimate appeal is to the intellect. In *Pilgrim's Progress*, Bunyan is not occupied with such abstract and philosophical speculations; his purpose is purely practical, and his appeal is not to the head but to the heart. Milton's aim, to "justify the ways of God to men," is general: the key-note of Bunyan's book is the cry of the individual conscience; it is heard in the question of Christian at the very beginning of the allegory, "What shall *I* do to be saved?" Bunyan's appeal is thus direct and personal, for Christian, the pilgrim, is a repre-

[1] "Life of Bunyan" in *Encyclopedia Britannica*.

sentative man, corresponding, in many ways, to the hero
of the old Moralities; he is a type of the race. Christian's
journey, it is true, is not every man's journey through this
world; it is the story of a pilgrimage "from the City of
Destruction to the City of Zion;" but the general treatment of this theme is so broadly human, that Christian's
pilgrimage becomes the living and dramatic record of
man's spiritual progress, the type of the battle fought by
every thinking man whose hopes and aspirations are not
wholly earthly and material. This largeness of view is
one of the most surprising features of Bunyan's book, and
one of the reasons for its perennial interest. Froude's
views on theological questions were widely different from
those of Bunyan, yet Froude wrote: "The religion of *Pilgrim's Progress* is the religion which must be always and
everywhere, as long as man believes that he has a soul and
is responsible for his actions." [1]

And this theme of fundamental and almost universal interest is not presented in an abstract, or doctrinal, form,
it is made extraordinarily real by the intensity of Bunyan's
earnestness, extraordinarily picturesque and dramatic by
the vividness of his poetic imagination. Christian's experiences are real to us because they were real to Bunyan;
because Bunyan himself had sunk in the Slough of De-
spond, climbed the Hill of Difficulty, and fought his own
fight with Apollyon. He had lived in the presence of the
invisible; he still bore the scars of his own awful conflict,
and the powers of evil had for him a positive and objective
reality. He could describe these things from bitter experience; he could describe them poetically because he had
that power of imagery which distinguishes the poet. He
turns instinctively to imagery when he describes his torments in *Grace Abounding*. Describing one of his periods
of doubt and depression, he wrote: "I found myself in

[1] *Life of Bunyan.*

a miry bog, that shook if I did but stir." In another place he speaks of his "tumultuous thoughts, that did use, like masterless hell-hounds, to roar and bellow, and make an hideous noise within me." It is this inborn power to conceive of the invisible and the intangible, in objective forms, that makes the allegory in the *Pilgrim's Progress* so spontaneous, so free from any suggestion of artifice. Bunyan, moreover, was not a mere sublime visionary, oblivious of the vulgar realities around him; he was a shrewd observer of human life and character, and his intensely spiritual nature was well ballasted with humour and solid common sense. Although *Pilgrim's Progress* purports to be a dream, Bunyan does not transport us to cloud-land. Christian travels through our familiar and every-day world, meeting many very substantial human beings in the course of his journey. The very names of Bunyan's characters are often miracles of characterisation. Mr. By-Ends alone, whose judgment always happened to coincide with his worldly advantage, shows Bunyan's satiric humour, his insight into human nature, and his power of dramatic portraiture. In this hold on real life, *Pilgrim's Progress* resembles Langland's *Piers the Plowman*, and differs very widely from the *Faërie Queene*.

To such enduring qualities in *Pilgrim's Progress*, we must add the remarkable strength, simplicity, and beauty of its style. Like many another Puritan, Bunyan had read and re-read the Bible, until the strong, vigorous, and musical English of King James' Translation had become a part of his mental as well as his spiritual life. His style was formed, his images were often taken from this great model, and his prose has much of the grandeur and restraint of his original. This reticence is characteristic of Bunyan's style; he says what he means with directness and precision, and produces the impression he desires without the introduction of one superfluous word. In one place

Bunyan's style.

the inhabitants of heaven are briefly described as "the shining ones," but the phrase seems to light up the page. This is Bunyan's description of the entrance of Christian and Hopeful into the heavenly city: "Now I saw in my dream, that these two men went in at the gate; and lo! as they entered, they were transfigured; and they had raiment put on that shone like gold. There were also that met them with harps and crowns, and gave them to them; the harps to praise withal, and the crowns in token of honour. Then I heard in my dream, that all the bells in the city rang again for joy, and that it was said unto them, 'Enter ye into the joy of your Lord.'"

Such, then, are some of the great qualities which have made a book, written without conscious art and with no thought of literary fame, a great classic. When Bunyan wrote, the fine gentlemen of the Restoration, the professional authors, and critics, were bent on reforming the language, and busy declaring the true principles of the literary art. The tinker in Bedford gaol knew nothing of these matters. He had something to say, he was constrained to give his message as best he could, but to him the message was the important matter, not the words in which it was delivered. "I could also," he says in *Grace Abounding*, "have slipped into a style much higher than this in which I have here discoursed, and could have adorned all things more than I have seemed to do; but I dare not. God did not play in convincing of me; the Devil did not play in tempting of me; neither did I play when I sunk as into a bottomless pit, when the pangs of Hell caught hold upon me: wherefore I may not play in relating of them, but be plain and simple, and lay down the thing as it was." Here in brief is the main source of Bunyan's power.

There are few more dramatic contrasts than that between such a man and John Dryden, the poet laureate of the

England of the Restoration. He had great abilities, scholarly training, social position, and a share of the royal favour. He won immense reputation in his own age, and he holds an assured place among the great writers of England, but he wrote nothing that so moved and moulded the world as *Pilgrim's Progress*. He had no particular message unless it was that in literature the words are more important than the thought. His judgment, like that of Mr. By-Ends, often agreed with his worldly advantage. The difference between Dryden and Bunyan is fundamental. It is the difference between the practical man of letters, the finished craftsman who knows his public and aims to give it what it wants, and the man of genius, who, strong in a vital conviction, tells the world simply and strongly the thing he believes. But when Milton composed *Paradise Lost*, in blindness and solitude, when Bunyan wrote *Pilgrim's Progress* in prison, the age of Puritanism was passing, the age of Dryden and the men of the Restoration had already come.

PART III.

THE FRENCH INFLUENCE.

(1660–Cir. 1750.)

CHAPTER I.

THE ENGLAND OF THE RESTORATION.

(1660–1700.)

> "We conquer'd France, but felt our captive's charms;
> Her arts victorious triumphed o'er our arms;
> Britain, to soft refinements less a foe,
> Wit grew polite, and numbers learn'd to flow.
> Waller was smooth; but Dryden taught to join
> The varying verse, the full-resounding line,
> The long majestic march, and energy divine."
>
>   — POPE。

THE Restoration of the Monarchy under Charles II. is one of the great turning-points in the history of England.

The results of the Restoration. It is more than a change in government: it marks the beginning of a new England in life, in thought, and in literature. How is this seemingly sudden change to be explained? The King's return promoted but did not cause it: it was rather this change in the feelings of the nation that led it to bring back the King. The Puritan had attempted a splendid, but impossible, task — and had failed. The pure passion for liberty had ended in a military despotism. The zeal for religion had fallen, in too many cases, into cant and hypocrisy. The fire of enthusiasm which had burned in

Hampden, Cromwell, and Milton had grown cold; men had become suspicious of high aims, they wanted ease. The Puritan had set up a fixed pattern of righteousness, lofty indeed, but formal, uncompromising, and severe, and had thought to compel men to come up to his standard. He had made "Merrie England" a dismal England; he had forbidden dancing, and made Christmas a fast-day; he had dreamed that because he was virtuous there should "be no more cakes and ale." Then came the day of reckoning. There was something of the healthy savage still in the race. They had been pent in, and hectored, and drilled through a long session, but now school was out, and the reign of the schoolmasters was over. What wonder, then, that joyful crowds greeted the King when he landed at Dover; that his journey to London was a triumphal progress through shouting multitudes; that the bells were set ringing, and the flags flying, — the King had come to enjoy his own again, and his people were in the right mood to enjoy it with him.

Over-strictness naturally leads to over-indulgence, and for the time the violence of the reaction transformed the **The protest against the Puritan.** nation. The May-poles were set up again; the Puritan Sabbath was disregarded; the brutal sport of bear-baiting revived. The sombre dress, solemn face, and scriptural phrase of the Puritan had become detestable and ridiculous in men's eyes; and many a gay Cavalier, despising this as mere hypocrisy, took pains to show by the openness of his vices, that he at least was no hypocrite. While Milton, unmoved in adversity, was composing *Paradise Lost,* the ideals of Puritanism were travestied in the clever but vulgar verse of SAMUEL BUTLER. Butler had been clerk to a Puritan gentleman, and *Hudibras* (Part i. 1663) is a coarse burlesque of the Puritan and his cause. It is rough, lively doggerel, keen and quotable, and it delighted the people and the King. The Church did little to check the wickedness of the time, and the Court did much to increase it. The King, witty, good-humoured, and gifted with an easy charm of manner, was a selfish voluptuary, without shame, patriotism, or honour, and his Court became a centre of evil influences which corrupted society and defiled literature. Gay, dissolute courtiers, like LORD ROCHESTER and SIR CHARLES SEDLEY, wrote lyrics which, although not without lightness and lyrical charm, often show only too clearly the moral depravity of the time. The King was a patron of the drama; and the theatres, which had been practically shut for nearly eighteen years, were soon crowded with fashionable audiences, demanding to be amused. The day of the romantic comedy, of *Twelfth Night* and *As You Like It*, had passed; and a new kind of comedy took form, light, witty, cynical, immoral, — suited to the taste of the time. In tragedy, too, in deference, it is said, to the taste of the King, dramatists turned from the Elizabethan masters, and sought their models in France. Like the French tragedies, these *heroic plays*, as they were called, were in rhyme, the *heroic couplet* being substituted for the traditional blank verse of the English stage. In these tragedies, the poetry, passion, and intense humanity of the Elizabethan drama, were too often replaced by mere rant and pompous declamation, as though the writer sought to hide his lack of feeling under his high-sounding lines.

But we must be careful to note that this reaction was not so sweeping as it seems. There were those who were not swept away with the current, nor was the work of Puritanism altogether undone. It was after the Restoration that Milton, standing apart from the riot of London, produced his greatest poems; that Izaak Walton wrote his life of George Herbert (1670),

The survivors of the older literature.

and John Bunyan his *Pilgrim's Progress* (1678–1684) and *Holy War* (1682); that we hear in James Shirley and Thomas Otway, some echoes, however faint, of the drama of Elizabeth.

Such men, however, belonged to an older generation, and represented a kind of writing which was rapidly pass-
The French influence. ing out of favour. To understand the course of literary history after the Restoration, we must rather study the men who introduced or popularised a new style of writing, and left behind them works which became the models of a succeeding generation.

What, then, was the spirit of this age, and what did its great writers accomplish for literature? To understand the state of England after the Restoration, we must realise that it was not merely a time of reaction from Puritanic restraints, but a time when the higher energies of the nation were temporarily exhausted. Ever since the influ-ence of the Renaissance first stirred the depths of the English nature, and enabled it for the first time to express its full force in literature, ever since then the nation had been living under the strain of strong excitement and heroic endeavour. There had been something large and heroic in the Elizabethan Age; the nation had poured out its strength in great achievements; in literature, it had shown a lavish creative energy; and, following hard upon the age of Shakespeare and the Armada, there had come years no less intense and exacting, of religious ardour and civil conflict, of warring principles and of high ideals. The Restoration found England emotionally exhausted; men had grown suspicious of great emotions; they doubted the wisdom of sacrificing comfort to lofty aims; their tem-per was cold, worldly, and prosaic, and they forsook enthu-siasm for reason and "good sense." Right or wrong, Charles I. gave his life for a principle. Charles II., believ-ing in the same principle, did not think it worth the sac-

rifice of his comforts, and preferred to make any base con-
cession rather than to "start out on his travels again."

Now this hard, prosaic temper is apparent in the altered
style of writing, and in the prevailing theories of literary

Signs of the time in literary style. art. Even before the Restoration we find in
some writers a tendency to abandon the fan-
tastic and extravagant comparisons or "conceits" for a clearer but less exalted style. And now at
the Restoration, when a great creative and imaginative
period had come to an end, men turned instinctively to
literary criticism; inspiration was failing, and they naturally began to insist upon a greater attention to the rules of
art. "Nothing," said Dryden, the representative writer
of the age, "nothing is truly sublime that is not just and
proper." Many felt that the English poets of the past,
however great their genius, had fallen short because they
neglected, through ignorance or indifference, the established rules of composition; and THOMAS RHYMER (1641–
1713), a noted critic of the day, ridiculed Shakespeare's
tragedies and sneered at *Paradise Lost*. There was a feeling that the literature of Shakespeare and of Milton needed
to be reformed, and that the remedy for the lawlessness
of the past lay in an application of classic rules, and the
greatest attention to the form of expression. It was in
accordance with this spirit that Horace's *Art of Poetry*, a
classic manual of precepts for the poet's guidance, was
translated by the Earl of Roscommon (1680). It is in com-
mending this translation, that EDMUND WALLER (1605–
1687), a poet who was looked up to as the great refiner of
language and versification, thus expresses the characteristic opinion of the time·

"Horace will our superfluous branches prune
  Give us new rules, and set our harp in tune;
  Direct us how to back the Wingèd Horse,
  Favour his flight, and moderate his force.

Tho' Poets may of inspiration boast,
Their rage, ill-governed, in the clouds is lost." [1]

The results of all this may be briefly stated. The aim
of this new school of writers was to be clear, precise, well

Effects of the new style on literature. balanced, and moderate, and in this they may
be said to have succeeded. They gave to
English prose a style, which by its strength,
simplicity, and directness, was admirably adapted for all
ordinary every-day needs. And similarly by their handling
of the heroic couplet they gave to English poetry a form of
expression which was lucid, concise, and epigrammatic,
a medium skilfully adapted to description, argument, or
moral teaching, and a marvellous instrument for satire.
So far this new manner was a distinct gain to literature,
but it was a gain that brought a great loss with it, for this
new style became so supreme that, for a time, it almost
altogether replaced the old. The serious limitations of
Dryden and his followers, their deficient sense of beauty,
their lack of spiritual vision, are reflected in their style,
excellent for certain useful purposes, but totally inadequate
for higher needs. When men exchanged the noble eloquence of Jeremy Taylor for the sensible pedestrian gait
of Dryden, when they replaced the rich and complex harmonies of Milton with the thinner melody and measured
stroke of the rhymed couplet, they were like men who
should cease to cultivate the rose, because the potato is a
useful article.

This critical study of writing as an art, this care in
regard to style, was partly due to the example and the

French influ-ence on Eng-lish style. influence of France. In the early years of the
Renaissance, Italy had been the guide and in-
spirer of Europe in scholarship and art. But
by the seventeenth century she was no longer the centre of
culture; her influence on literature had sensibly declined

[1] *Upon the Earl of Roscommon's Translation of Horace, De Arte Poeticâ.*

throughout the whole of Europe, and, at this time, was being partially replaced by that of France. Early in the seventeenth century the French poet *Malherbe* (1555–1628) had begun a so-called reform of poetic language and style, similar to that which took place in England under Dryden and his successors. Malherbe, who was called "the tyrant of words and syllables," strove to banish the warmer, more highly coloured style, for one more fixed and restrained. In this he was followed by *Boileau* (1636–1711), a poet who became the literary law-giver of the day. In his *Art of Poetry* (1673), Boileau urged poets to leave glittering rhapsodies to the Italians, and endeavour always to write with "good sense." When these doctrines were put forth, France stood high in the eyes of Europe, and Louis XIV. (1643–1715), the most splendid living embodiment of despotic kingship, had gathered a brilliant group of writers at his court. It was the "Classical Age" of French literature, a time when men felt bound to follow the rules and practices of the past, but a time splendid nevertheless with great names in poetry and in prose. For the time, French literature dominated Europe, and it was but natural that England, in common with other nations, should have responded to her influence. But there was also an especial reason why English literature should have come under the influence of the French. Charles II. had spent a great part of his exile in France, and while there he had gained some acquaintance with French literature, and acquired a liking for the French style. "He was in France," says a writer of the time, "at a time when they were most set on reforming their language," and so, he adds, he approved certain preachers whose style was "clear, short, and plain."

It is thus plain that all these forces, the changed temper of the nation, the influence of France, and the personal taste and influence of the king, were pushing English literature in the same direction.

JOHN DRYDEN.

(1631–1700.)

The changes in literature after the Restoration, in both its spirit and its style, were seen most perfectly in the work of John Dryden, a man of cold, logical intellect, and, in his own province, one of the great masters of our English tongue. Few men have so perfectly represented their age or so manifestly determined the course of literary history. From the Restoration to the end of the century, Dryden dominated English letters, "the greatest man of a little age;" and long after his death the student of literature sees in both prose and poetry the impress of his powerful personality and literary skill.

John Dryden was born at Aldwinkle, a small village in the northeastern part of Northamptonshire, in 1631. He came of a highly respectable Puritan family, some of his relations both on his father's and his mother's side being active supporters of the Parliamentary cause. But little is known of his early years. He went to Westminster School, London, and in 1650 he entered Trinity College, Cambridge. After leaving the University in 1657, he is supposed to have attached himself to the Puritan household of his cousin, Sir Gilbert Pickering, a favoured follower of Cromwell. Before he left Westminster, Dryden had contributed some verses to a book of elegies, published in memory of one of his schoolfellows, Lord Hastings. Unmeasured in their flattery, these verses are cold, artificial, and insincere. It is evident that the young poet has regarded the event as an opportunity to display his rhetorical dexterity, and the perverted ingenuity and false taste of his "conceits" outdo the worst extravagances of Donne and his followers. The poem is a boyish effort, but it shows some traits in the character of the man, an

Dryden's life.

ability to comply with a prevailing literary fashion, a tendency to substitute rhetoric for genuine feeling, and a mastery of the art of adulation.

Dryden was naturally among the poets who lamented the death of the Protector, and his *Heroic Stanzas on the Death of Cromwell* (1659) show a gain in moderation and sincerity. The poem is skilfully constructed, and impresses us with a sense of Cromwell's greatness. At times we recognise, as in the strong line, —

Early poems.

" Fame of the asserted sea through Europe blown," —

a fulness of utterance which suggests the future master of the "majestic line." This tribute to the great Puritan was followed, a year later, by the *Astræa Redux*, an effusive welcome to Charles II. upon his "happy restoration and return." "Church and State," the poet declares, have groaned for the king's absence; age has been in despair —

" To see the rebel thrive, the loyal cross'd," —

but now the Golden Age returns. The "blessed saints" lean from their stars in "joyful wonder" to see General Monk restore the exiled king, and the chalk-cliffs of Albion, clad in the white of penitence, advance to welcome the returning monarch. All this sounds strange from the late eulogist of Cromwell, yet it must be remembered that many Puritans honestly believed at this time that the hope of the nation lay in the king's return. Dryden may have been honest in his sudden conversion; nevertheless, his poem, with its elaborate rhetoric and its strain of absurd flattery, carries with it no conviction of sincerity. The *Astræa Redux* is otherwise noteworthy as affording the first example of Dryden's use of the heroic couplet, the verse-form which became so effective in his hands, and which he, with Pope his great successor, made the standard metre of English poetry for a hundred years.

If we are ignorant of the motives which led Dryden to change his political faith, the reasons which led to his next step are only too clear. In spite of his ancestry, he was entirely lacking in that uncompromising independence which was so conspicuous a trait of the Puritan character. Milton felt that the true poet was God's prophet, bound to speak the truth delivered to him: but Dryden made writing a trade; he was quick to feel what the public wanted, and he showed no scruples in adapting his wares to the popular demand. After the Restoration, play-writing was the most lucrative branch of literature; and for about eighteen years (1663–1681) Dryden gave up nearly all of his time and energy to writing plays, although he felt that in so doing he was sacrificing his higher success to a transient popularity. He writes frankly: "I confess my chief endeavours are to delight the age in which I live. If the humour of this be for low comedy, small accidents and raillery, *I will force my genius to obey it, though with more reputation I could write in verse.*" [1]

As dramatist.

Dryden carried his complaisance so far that, in his efforts "to delight" his age, he produced some comedies whose license was remarked even in that lax time. It is characteristic of him, that the coarseness which disfigures so many of his plays, was rather a bid for popular favour than an expression of his own inclination: in Dr. Johnson's words, it was "his trade rather than his pleasure." [2] Personally he seems to have preferred virtue, yet he did not scruple for his own profit to encourage the moral corruption which surrounded him. While he traded in vice, he kept a touch of the Puritan's conscience. In one of the most beautiful of his poems, he cries out in a rare burst of genuine feeling:

[1] Preface to *The Indian Emperor* (1665).
[2] *Lives of the Poets*, "Dryden."

"O gracious God! how far have we
Profaned thy heavenly gift of poesy!
Made prostitute and profligate the Muse,
Debased to each obscene and impious use,
Whose harmony was first ordained above
For tongues of angels and for hymns of love." [1]

And towards the close of his life, he meets the fierce attack
of Jeremy Collier, who wrote a famous book upon the
Immorality and Profaneness of the Stage (1698), with a
manly acknowledgment of his fault. This episode has
been dwelt on here, because perhaps more than any other,
it shows us the man, John Dryden, as he was. Amiable,
kindly, and not without good impulses, we see in this weak
compliance with the public taste the spirit of the time-
server, of a man willing to sacrifice principle to a worldly
expediency. He was one of those who are resolved to
"delight" their age at any cost, and the judgment on such
men is summed up in the saying that —

" Those who live to please must please to live." [2]

One poem, the *Annus Mirabilis* (1667), broke this long
period of dramatic activity. It deals with two great

Annus Mirabilis. events of the *wonderful year* 1666, the war with
Holland, and the great fire of London.

From the worldly point of view, Dryden did
not serve the stage for naught. His plays are now never

Worldly Success. acted, and but seldom read; but he won a foremost place among the dramatists of his day.

In 1670 he was made Poet-Laureate, with a
salary of £200 a year, and in 1677 he made an advanta-
geous contract to furnish plays to the King's theatre.

[1] *Ode to Mistress Anne Killigrew.*
[2] Dr. Johnson's *Prologue at the Opening of the Theatre Royal*, 1747.
The student would do well to consult this poem for its strictures on
the Restoration drama, and its attack upon the playwright who strove
to please the depraved taste of the age.

At fifty, Dryden had made but a slight impression as a poet: his reputation rested almost entirely on his plays.

Satires.   Yet at fifty, he entered suddenly upon the most splendid period of his career. All England had watched the struggle between the Earl of Shaftesbury, a brilliant but dangerous politician, and the Crown. Shaftesbury had schemed to secure the succession to the Duke of Monmouth, and in 1681 the climax was reached in the arrest of the Earl and in his indictment for High Treason. Dryden seized the dramatic moment, and spoke to the nation while it hung breathless on the issue, in his satirical allegory, *Absalom and Achitophel* (1681). The revolt of Absalom, aided by his evil counsellor Achitophel, against his father, David, becomes in Dryden's satire, an allegory of the ambitious desires of Monmouth and Shaftesbury against the King. After years of apprenticeship, Dryden had come to his own, and we feel at last those distinctive qualities in which he has been seldom approached and never excelled — the impetus of the rapid verse, the keen, discriminating intellect, the epigrammatic brilliancy, and the tireless vigour that animates the whole. The story is but a slight background for a pitiless delineation of character. The men whose names were in every mouth, Shaftesbury, Buckingham, and the rest, are pilloried in passages which are marvels of characterisation, for all England to see. Other satiric masterpieces followed, among which *Mac-Flecknoe* (1682) is perhaps the best known. In it, Dryden ridicules Thomas Shadwell, then leading poet and dramatist of the opposite political party. Shadwell is derisively styled *Mac Flecknoe* (or the " son of Flecknoe "), that is, the poetical successor as ruler of the realm of Nonsense, of a certain Richard Flecknoe, an obscure and unfortunate poet who had lately died.

Dryden did not entirely abandon the drama after his success in satire, but his energies were chiefly spent in

other directions. He showed his extraordinary power of
Other works. arguing in verse, in the *Religio Laici* (1682),
and the *Hind and the Panther* (1687). The first
is a declaration of faith in the doctrines of the Church of
England, the second an elaborate argument in behalf of the
doctrines of the Church of Rome, Dryden having changed
his religion after the accession of the Roman Catholic,
James II. The "milk-white Hind" represents the Church
of Rome, the Panther the Church of England, and the two
oddly assorted beasts engage in a lengthy theological
argument. But, in spite of the manifest absurdity of its
scheme, the poem has great melody, charm, and intellectual
power, and shows us Dryden at his best.

The accession of William and Mary and the triumph of
Protestantism was a heavy blow to Dryden's fortunes. He
Later years. did not again change his religion, and in consequence lost his pension and the laureateship,
his old enemy Shadwell being appointed in his place. This
single act of constancy stands out in the midst of all the
fluctuations of Dryden's career, and at no time of his life
is he so worthy of our respect as in the years that followed.
He toiled manfully for his support; he wrote plays, translated Vergil and other classic poets, modernised Chaucer,
and told some stories from Boccaccio in charming verse. He
toiled, — as he tells us a few years before his death, —
"struggling with want, oppressed with sickness," and
"curbed" in his genius, yet steady to "his principles" and
not "dispirited with" his afflictions.[1]

Tradition pictures him as sitting in the sunny bow window of Will's Coffee House, a red-faced, portly, grey-haired
old man, the literary law-giver of the young wits and rising authors, who loved to gather about him and listen to
his stories of the past. He died in 1700, and was buried
at the feet of Chaucer in Westminster Abbey.

[1] "Postscript to the Reader," in his *Dedication of the Æneis*, 1697.

In his strength and in his weakness Dryden is the representative of his time. He lived in an age when the critical faculties were stronger than the creative, and he is the father of modern literary criticism, the master of clear thought and forcible expression. He was not the inspired poet, but the conscientious literary workman, toiling for years to gain the mastery of his craft. His work is unequal, experimental; he acquires his art slowly. His first poem is disfigured by the very faults that he is afterwards to expel from literature; his heroic plays are full of the rant and exaggeration which he was afterwards to condemn. He succeeded by the sheer force of a vigorous intellect, and by an instinctive response to the spirit and needs of his time. He simplifies and strengthens his style, until he is able to produce models for his successors. His poetry has obvious merits, and as obvious defects. He is the greatest satirist in the range of English poetry; his verse has clearness, ease, and a vigour which at times is almost brutal; he can be smooth and swift, majestic and sonorous. But in reading Dryden we feel the spiritual limitations of his time; everything seems material and earthly, with no redeeming touch of the divine. He shows little love of nature, little sense of beauty, little real religion; tenderness, pathos, compassion, and a sense of the "mystery of things" are almost entirely absent from his works. In reading him we often feel the great gulf that divides rhetoric from poetry, and the splendid resonance of some of his odes seems but sounding brass beside the finer music of Collins, Keats, or Shelley. But we must remember that there are many kinds of poetry, and that in his own province Dryden is supreme.

In prose Dryden's work was almost equally important. He introduced a plainer style of writing, better adapted to the daily needs of our modern world than the more eloquent, poetical, and involved manner of some of his predecessors.

Character and work.

In this he performed a distinct service; for, while we may prefer the loftier and fuller style, the practical usefulness of a more direct and simple mode of expression is self-evident.

Dryden's prose is important for other things besides style. He is one of the masters in English criticism; and the critical prefaces to his plays and poems, as well as his famous *Essay of Dramatic Poesy*, are among the most interesting and valuable of his works.

Something of Dryden's character has been already shown in the brief story of his life. We have seen him catering to the weaknesses and vices of his time; changeable in his opinions; fulsome in his flattery of the great and powerful. He studied the nation's moods, and was skilful in appealing to the popular interest by treating of the topic of the hour. How far he was sincere we cannot tell; it is not unlikely that he lacked depth of conviction, and so easily persuaded himself that the truth lay on the winning side. Thinking of him we realise that, to attain the highest success in literature or in life, something more is needed than all the powers of the intellect, or all the skill of a practised writer, — something worthy of the name of greatness, — loftiness of character and nobility of life.

OTHER RESTORATION WRITERS.

The Drama.

Among the chief writers of tragedy at this time besides Dryden, were THOMAS OTWAY (1651–1685) and NATHANIEL LEE (1653–1691). In Otway's best verse something of the glory and passion of the Elizabethan tragedy yet lingers. His life was that of the adventurer, varied, dissipated, and unhappy. The son of a country clergyman, he left Oxford in 1672 and tried his fortune on the London stage. For a time he was a soldier; but, forced to abandon the army, he returned to

Restoration tragedy.

London to write for the stage. His greatest plays are *The Orphans* (1680), and *Venice Preserved* (1682), which has been called "the best tragedy of the Restoration." [1] He lived in poverty and died miserably at thirty-four. The following description of morning in the country, which shows a true feeling for Nature unusual in the poetry of that time, will give some idea of Otway's best style.

MORNING.

"Wished morning's come; and now upon the plains
  And distant mountains, where they feed their flocks,
The happy shepherds leave their homely huts,
  And with their pipes proclaim the new-born day.
The lusty swain comes with his well-filled scrip
  Of healthful viands, which, when hunger calls,
With much content and appetite he eats,
  To follow in the fields his daily toil,
And dress the grateful glebe that yields him fruits.
  The beasts that under the warm hedges slept,
  And weathered out the cold, bleak night, are up,
  And, looking towards the neighbouring pastures, raise
The voice, and bid their fellow-brutes good-morrow.
  The cheerful birds, too, on the tops of trees,
Assemble all in choirs, and with their notes
Salute and welcome up the rising sun."

There is a melancholy resemblance between the career of Nathaniel, or "Nat" Lee, and that of his contemporary Otway. Like Otway, a clergyman's son, he also sought his fortune in London, and, after failing as an actor, became a playwright. His life was vicious, drunken, and darkened by insanity, and he died miserably at thirty-seven. Lee has been called "a vulgar Marlowe." His plays have touches of true poetry and genuine pathos, but they are often marred by a declamatory frenzy and extravagance. At his best he has an almost Elizabethan fervor; at his worst his violence and his rhetoric carry him beyond that fatal line that separates the sublime from the ridiculous.

N. Lee.

[1] *A History of Eighteenth Century Literature*, by Edmund Gosse.

The general character of the Restoration comedy has been already indicated (p. 307). It is distinctly English,
Restoration comedy. although the plots were often drawn from Spanish or French sources; its merits are its wit and its living pictures of the fashionable town-life of the day; its greatest blot is its airy contempt for all moral laws. Among the most famous comic writers of the Restoration were WILLIAM WYCHERLEY (1640–1715), a "fine gentleman" and a favourite of Charles II.; WILLIAM CONGREVE (1670–1729), courted, flattered, and famous; SIR JOHN VANBRUGH (1666–1726), and GEORGE FARQUHAR (1678–1708). Among these Congreve holds the first place, the acknowledged master in English of "the comedy of repartee," the comedy, that is, conspicuous for the witty thrust and parry of its dialogue, rather than for its delineation of humours after the manner of Jonson. Besides *Love for Love* (1694), *The Way of the World* (1700), and other sparkling comedies, Congreve wrote *The Mourning Bride* (1697), a tragedy of no little poetic beauty.

Other Writers.

In the philosophy of JOHN LOCKE (1632–1714) with its strong grasp of facts, its plain common sense, its conviction that reason is the best and surest guide to truth, we see another side of the reaction against the Puritan spirit. This sense of the value of facts, ascertained by observation and experiment, and interpreted by reason, is further shown in the great development of science.

The interest in scientific inquiry extends even to the gay and versatile Duke of Buckingham, who dabbled in chemistry, and to the flippant King. The foundation of The Royal Society in 1662, for the promotion of scientific research, is one of the signs of the time; nor must we forget that this age of Dryden and Pope is also the age of one of England's greatest scientists, SIR ISAAC NEWTON (1642–1727).

CHAPTER II.

THE AGE OF POPE.

(CIR. 1700–1750.)

"In tea-cup times of hood and hoop,
  Or while the patch was worn."
          — TENNYSON: *The Talking Oak.*

While the death of Dryden removed a great personality
from the literary and social life of London, much of the
spirit and manner of Dryden and his contemporaries lived on in the work of their successors.
In Dr. Johnson's phrase, Dryden had "enriched
his language" with a great "variety of models,"
and after these "models" much of the best work done by
the succeeding generation was formed. Dryden, Cowley, and
Waller were thought to have begun a new and better era
in literature, an era of smoother versification, and greater
propriety and correctness of expression. The writers immediately succeeding Dryden, therefore set themselves to
carry forward the literary movement thus begun, to apply
the principles laid down, to copy and if possible to improve
upon the "models" bequeathed to them. The immediate
reasons for this were the strong personal influence of Dryden, and the brilliancy of his work; but another and deeper
cause is found in the fact that there had been no great
change in the capital or in the nation since Dryden's time.
In the age of Pope, Dryden's great successor, London life
was much the same as in the age of Dryden, and so it came
about that literature, the voice of that life, was much the
same also. The influence of the French writers increased.

Dryden's suc-
cessors con-
tinue his
work.

Pope speaks of Boileau as "the first poet of the French, as Virgil of the Latin," [1] and declares that he sits on the throne of Horace as a law-giver to poets.[2]   The tendency to follow the French in attaching the highest importance to a perfection of literary form, increased likewise, and lucidity, elegance, and propriety of expression became the poets' ideal.   Thus Addison, the most charming prose-writer of the period, declares in the spirit of Boileau "that wit and fine writing doth not consist so much in advancing things that are new, as in giving things that are known an agreeable turn."   While Pope himself declares that:

> "True wit is nature to advantage dressed,
>   What oft was thought but ne'er so well expressed."

In accordance with this tendency, Pope gives the heroic verse of Dryden a greater smoothness and a finer finish, **Pope and the heroic couplet.** although in his hands it loses something of its exuberant strength and fire.   In his boyhood, Pope was urged to make correctness "his study and aim," and he took the advice to heart.[1]   His own lines, written long after, embody the spirit of his early counsellor and express the prevailing critical doctrine of his time.

> "Late, very late, correctness grew our care,
>   When the tired nation breathed from civil war,
>   Exact Racine, and Corneille's noble fire,
>   Showed us that France had something to admire.
>   Not but the tragic spirit was our own,
>   And full in Shakespeare, fair in Otway shone:
>   But Otway failed to polish or refine,
>   And fluent Shakespeare scarce effaced a line.
>   Ev'n copious Dryden wanted, or forgot,
>   The last and greatest art, the art to blot." [3]

As the result of all this thought for style, a manner of verse was elaborated which reflects with striking exactness the merits and the limitations of its careful builders.   It is

---

[1] Spence's *Anecdotes*.   [2] *Essay on Criticism*.
[3] *Satires:* Book ii.   First Epistle.

generally clear, fluent, and flexible, often clever, often epigrammatic; it can express a trite thought, or
moral precept, in a neat and easily remembered
couplet; it can describe a game of cards or a
muddy London street after a shower, with vividness and accuracy. But we feel that there is something
about it which is formal, mechanical, artificial; that it does
not speak for humanity, but for the literary and social London of Queen Anne; that it moves on the easy level of the
worldly and the conventional, incapable of comprehending
the tragic depths of man's anguish, or the heights to which,
at rare moments, his spirit can ascend. Limited as it was
in thought and emotion, this verse became a convenient
medium for the treatment of a great variety of themes.
As style was thought the essential factor, the most commonplace and prosaic subjects were treated in verse,
apparently on the theory that they could be made poetical
by the outward adornments of rhyme and rhythm. One
poet discusses the raising of sheep, the treatment of their
diseases, and the details of the manufacture of woollens;
another, the *Art of Preserving Health;* while another sets
forth the advantages of fresh air and exercise; and in this
way the distinction between poetry and prose is too often
lost. Indeed, it was "an age of prose," and its verse
is often little or nothing but prose disguised in rhyme.

Merits and limitations of the pre- vailing style.

Literature in the age of Pope was, in every sense, a
literature of the town, born in the town, written mainly
for the town, and often portraying the life of
the town to the minutest detail. The London
of Pope is even more wonderfully alive to us
through literature than the London of Shakespeare. We
can see its ill-paved streets with their narrow sidewalks
and their running gutters; we know Grub Street where
obscure authors fought with debts and starvation; the
Fleet; the gay boating party on the Thames; the pleasure-

The literature of " the town."

gardens where society drank and flirted, listened to the music, and exclaimed at the fireworks. All that restless, gay, animated life is still before us; the beauty in her sedan chair, the beau with his lace ruffles and his flowing wig; and we can imagine the courtly presentation of the snuff-box, or the flutter of the fan. But this brilliant surface was but a thin veneer, and beneath it life was vulgar, vicious, and cruel.

The age which prided itself on its polish and politeness indulged in bull-baiting and cock-fights; its young aristocrats, wandering in drunken frolics through the ill-lighted London streets, habitually committed the most shocking outrages on inoffending passengers. Drunkenness, says a high authority, "became for the first time a national vice." [1] It was confined to no class of society, and there is hardly an author of the so-called Augustan Age who was entirely free from it. Its underlying brutality and coarseness of thought and action stain the pages of its literature; its misanthropy, its petty spites, and literary rivalries, break out in slanderous abuse, and bitter, mirthless satires. On every side are indications of a low moral tone. At the beginning of the century the Church was lifeless and worldly, and its great places were intrigued for and sought after as political spoil. Public life was debased, and bribery was regarded as a regular feature in the conduct of government. Many of the greatest men of the time, disgusted with the mercenary spirit and low aims which surrounded them, lost confidence in human virtue, and expressed — sometimes with terrible power — their cynical contempt for man, and their hatred of his petty world. Yet even at this time the higher and nobler elements of the English character were struggling to reassert themselves, and long before the death of Pope, the spiritual redemption of England had begun.

---

[1] Lecky, *England in the XVIII. Century*, I. 516.

ALEXANDER POPE.

(1688–1744.)

"He [Dryden] died, nevertheless, in a good old age, possessed of the Kingdom of Wit, and was succeeded by King Alexander, surnamed Pope.

"This prince enjoyed the crown many years, and is thought to have stretched the prerogative much farther than his predecessor."

— FIELDING: *The Covent Garden Journal*, No. 23.

Pope was beyond all question the most eminent and the most representative poet of his time. He directed and satisfied the poetic taste of his contemporaries; he expressed the predominant thought and sentiment of the men about him, and he won for himself a central place among the wits, philosophers, and statesmen of a brilliant age. "Glorious John Dryden," portly, florid, easy-going, and kindly, is gone, and in his place there reigns this new King, "Alexander, surnamed Pope," a nervous invalid, small, fragile, misshapen, his thin face drawn as if with pain, and yet alive with an eager intellect, and lit with the large, brilliant eyes of the poet.

In many ways Pope's story is both painful and pitiable. He himself spoke of his life as "a long disease," [1] and he spoke truly. A few men, like Robert Louis Stevenson, can keep the sound mind in the unsound body; their characters are untouched by invalidism, their sympathies healthy and normal. Pope, unhappily, was not among these few. His delicacy of constitution, his nervous sensibility, affect his whole life and character; and we cannot help feeling the narrowness, bitterness, and irritability of the invalid in his work. Yet there was lodged in his weak and deformed body a spirit of indomitable persistence and courage; and, in a brutal time that spared neither the weak nor the unfortunate, he won and kept the headship of British letters.

[1] *Epistle to Dr. Arbuthnot.*

Only those who have worked stubbornly on under the weight of pain and weakness, who by sheer force of mind and will, and in spite of physical infirmities, have beaten the strong man in the race, can imagine the cost of Pope's fight for fame, and fairly appreciate his triumph.

Alexander Pope was born in London in 1688. When he was about twelve years old his father took a house at Bin-

Pope's life. field, a village near Windsor Forest in Berkshire. In this beautiful retreat, then much wilder and more thickly wooded than at present, the greater part of Pope's early years were spent. The family were Roman Catholics, and in the years immediately following the deposition of James II. the feeling against persons of that faith was very strong. Almost from the first, therefore, Pope's religion set him apart, and stood in the way of his worldly advancement. Most of the great thinkers and writers of England have been regularly educated in accordance with the established English system; that is, they have gone to Eton, Harrow, Westminster, or one of the other great public schools, and thence to the university. Such was the training of Spenser, Milton, Dryden, Gray, Byron, Shelley, and many others. But Pope, included on account of his religion among a "hated minority," grew up entirely outside of the regular educational system of his country, and separated from the youth of his own age, who would have been his natural companions. His education was accordingly desultory and superficial. He had some instruction from a priest, and studied for a short time at a Roman Catholic seminary near Winchester. Here he is said to have begun his career as a satirist by writing a lampoon on the master. The better part of his education he gained for himself. A sickly, lonely, and precocious child, he found his resource and delight in books, and especially in poetry. He read, according to his own account, without any design but that of pleasing himself, "like a boy gath-

ering flowers in the fields just as they fell in his way."[1]
Very early he began to write verses himself; he made
metrical translations of the classics, and composed a tragedy
and an epic poem of four thousand lines. His reference to
his precocious facility has become almost proverbial:

> "As yet a child, nor yet a fool to fame,
> I lisped in numbers, for the numbers came." [2]

But in fact the "numbers" seem to have come less spon-
taneously than this passage would lead us to suppose. The
truth is that by hard and careful study and by incessant
practice Pope was making himself a master of his art.
When Pope was about sixteen (cir. 1704), he made the acquaintance of Wycherley, then an elderly man about town,
following him with all the devotion that a bookish boy with
literary aspirations naturally feels towards a successful man
of letters. In a short time he had become known to Steele,
Addison, Swift, and other great authors of the day. His
first literary venture was the publication of the *Pastorals*

The Pastorals. (1709), a series of eclogues, treating of the
four seasons. Pastoral poetry had long since
become hopelessly artificial, and Pope's pastorals were no
exception to the rule. According to classic precedent *Strephon* and *Daphnis* contend in song, and *Thyrsis* mourns
the death of Daphne. Heathen gods and goddesses are
domesticated in England, and Apollo is to be gladdened by
the sacrifice of a "milk-white bull" near the banks of the
Thames. But the really notable thing about the *Pastorals*
is not their artificiality, — which is only what might have
been expected, — but the even flow of the verse. This venture seems to have been favourably received, and

Essay on
Criticism. Pope's next publication, *The Essay on Criticism*
(published 1711), took London by storm. It is
a didactic poem in which many of the established rules of

---

[1] Spence's *Anecdotes*.   [2] *Epistle to Dr. Arbuthnot.*

composition are restated in a terse and clever fashion. It was, as has been said, an age of criticism, an age when men sought to write according to the classic precedents, and Pope's poem was in accord with the mood of the time. This spirit had already shown itself in a similar manner: one writer had composed an *Essay on Satire*, another an *Essay on Translated Verse*, and it is to poems of this class that the *Essay on Criticism* naturally belongs. Pope's work resembles these in subject, but has merit which places it far above them. The ideas seem now somewhat trite, the argument is not always convincing; yet the poem possesses at least one characteristic merit, it is quotable. All through it we find couplets in which an idea, often commonplace enough, is packed into a form so terse, striking, and remarkable that it has become firmly embedded in our ordinary thought and speech. Through his power to translate a current thought into an almost proverbial form, Pope has probably enriched the language with more phrases than any other writer save Shakespeare:

> "A little learning is a dangerous thing;
> Drink deep, or taste not the Pierian spring."

> "To err is human, to forgive divine."

> "For fools rush in where angels fear to tread."

Such quotable bits as these are used by thousands who are entirely ignorant of their source.

In 1712 Pope published the first version of *The Rape of the Lock*, a poem so graceful, delicate, cynical, and witty, that it seems to embody not only the peculiar flavour of his genius, but the light tone and shifting colours of his time. We should probably be right in pronouncing *The Rape of the Lock* the most representative poem of its age; but, in saying this, we must be careful to remember that after all it depicts and expresses only a

The Rape of the Lock.

fragment of the nation's life. Chaucer's Pilgrims represented fourteenth-century England, from the knight to the
plowman. *The Rape of the Lock* introduces us to a little
world of frivolity and fashion, busy with its pleasures, its
dressing, flirting, and card-playing, in the old London of
Queen Anne. It is true that the life of the passing hour
is here made immortal in art; yet that life is not the life of
the nation, but of a little group of idlers in the town. Yet
Pope was representative in this very narrowness. In
those days, fashion, wit, literature, and politics met in
London. There — men thought — was the life of England; outside lay a vague region, little thought of and seldom visited; a dull place with stupid squires, and muddy
roads, where every one was behind the times. Town was
supreme; and Pope, the poet of the town, represented its
supremacy.

The Rape of the Lock literally grew out of that artificial
society which it depicts and satirises, for it was suggested
by an actual occurrence in the fashionable world. Lord
Petre, a young nobleman of twenty, possessed himself of a
lock of hair belonging to a famous beauty of the day,
Mistress Arabella Fermor. The result was a serious misunderstanding, and Pope was asked to write a poem that
should put the whole incident in an absurd light and restore
good-humour. Pope acted on the suggestion and produced
the most perfect mock-heroic poem in the literature of
England, if not in the literature of the world.

The Rape of the Lock is the story of a day in the life of a
London beauty. We see Belinda luxuriously slumbering
on till noon, when her lap-dog Shock awakens her. We
are present at her toilet, and watch the progress of "the
sacred rites of pride." We see her with a gay party on its
way up the Thames to Hampton Court, smiling impartially
upon the "well-dressed youths" that crowd about her, the
very type of liveliness, tact, and coquetry. We follow the

party through the game of ombre, and the coffee, until we reach the tragic catastrophe of the severed curl. Where can we find so light, so poetical, a treatment of things which we think of as trivial or ordinary? Here is the epic of the frivolous: true to Pope's world, but true also with a little change of dress and scene to the world of the pleasure-seeker in Babylon, Rome, or New York. Pope suggests to us the vanity and shallowness of this life; and, by celebrating its inanities with the lofty dignity of the Homeric epic, he insensibly leads us to measure this petty world by the large standards of the heroic age. Yet the poem is not only a satire on the trivial; it affects us also as a travesty on the sublime, and its wit consists largely in placing the sacred or the admirable on a seeming equality with the trifling or the absurd. We are amused because all ordinary standards are changed, because we hear in the same breath of the State-counsels and the tea-drinking of a Queen, of the deaths of husbands and of lap-dogs, of the neglect of prayers, and the loss of a masquerade. In the *Gulliver's Travels* of Swift, Pope's great contemporary, we are entertained by the upsetting of our fixed ideas of physical relations; we see a man become a giant among pygmies, a pygmy among giants; in *The Rape of the Lock* we are entertained by a similar reversal of our moral and spiritual ideas, and in its tolerant cynicism the petty becomes great, the great petty.

The Rape of the Lock was followed by *Windsor Forest* and other short poems; and about 1713 Pope settled down in earnest to the great task of his middle life, the translation of Homer. We cannot but admire the spirit which prompted this undertaking. Pope's father was old, and the family fortunes were not prospering; so the poet turned from original work to the more profitable task of translation. At first he was depressed by the magnitude and difficulty of his undertaking; and

Translation
of Homer.

it shows the force and endurance of the man that, in spite of a frail body and a very imperfect knowledge of Greek, he should have pushed it through to a successful conclusion. Every one knows the verdict on this work of the great scholar Dr. Bentley: "A very pretty poem, Mr. Pope, but not Homer." In repeating this, we are too apt to forget that the first part of the criticism is as true as the last. Quite apart from its value as a translation, Pope's Homer is "a very pretty poem," and thousands have read it with delight.

Pope made about five or six thousand pounds by his translation of the Iliad alone, a very large sum for those **Twickenham.** days; and he determined to invest a part of this money in a house and grounds at Twickenham, on the bank of the Thames, about twelve miles above London. There were woods and a lawn sloping to the river; and the poet delighted to cultivate and adorn his grounds, and to dress nature "to advantage." He built a tunnel under the public road that ran through his place and called it his "grotto." On the walls and roof of this "grotto" were stuck shells, "pieces of looking-glass," bits of spar, and fragments of ores and lava. He had also a temple "wholly composed of shells in the rustic manner." [1] In this famous retreat at Twickenham, where nature was polished by art, and incrusted with glittering ornaments, this poet of the artificial held his court. Here came John Gay, the poet, and the great and terrible Dean Swift; here, Pope tells us, the brilliant Lord Bolingbroke, "nobly pensive," meditated in his "Egerian grot." [2]

For more than ten years (cir. 1713–1725), Pope had given his time and effort almost entirely to his work as transla-

[1] Pope: Letters.

[2] See his poem On his Grotto at Twickenham Composed of Marbles, Spars, Gems, Ores, and Minerals.

tor and commentator.[1] His long task faithfully done, came
to an end in 1725 with the completion of his translation of
the Odyssey, and the appearance of his edition of Shakespeare. At thirty-seven he had made his fortune and his
reputation, and he was in a position to write what he
pleased. But Pope's success had excited the envy of less
fortunate authors; his disposition, and in part his religion,
had made him many enemies; while he, on his side, with
his insatiable vanity and his high-strung organisation, was
easily touched to passionate resentment. Unfortunately,
one of the first uses he made of his liberty was to attack his
The Dunciad. adversaries, many of whom were beneath notice, in his famous satire of the *Dunciad*, or,
Epic of the Dunces. In its plan the *Dunciad* bears some
resemblance to Dryden's *Mac Flecknoe;* but it shows more
personal spite, and less careless power. Dryden regards
his victim with an air of assured superiority and amused
unconcern, but Pope shrieks out his unsavoury abuse as
one who engages in a street-fight on equal terms. He pitilessly uncovers the miseries of the obscure literary hack,
starving in his garret; "he revels," says Thackeray, "in
base descriptions of poor men's want." [2] "What paving-
stones," exclaims Taine, "to crush flies!" [3] If Pope's
enemies were as contemptible as he would have us believe,
why was it necessary to put forth so much strength against
them? The question suggests to us the inherent weakness
of the poem; it employs satire rather as an instrument of
revenge in a private quarrel than as a corrector of any public wrong. As Dr. Johnson very sensibly observes: "Whom

[1] Pope writes of this with regret:

"Gay dies unpensioned, with a hundred friends;
Hibernian politics, O Swift! thy fate;
And Pope's, ten years to comment and translate."
Dunciad, end of Bk. iii.

[2] *English Humourists*: "Prior, Gay, and Pope."
[3] *History of English Literature*, Bk. iii. p. 352. (Van Laun's trans.)

did it concern to know that one scribbler or another was a dunce?"[1] A poem "on *dunces,*" the great doctor once said contemptuously, and then turned to poor Boswell and added: "It was worth while being a dunce then. Ah, sir, hadst *thou* lived in those days!"[2]

The closing period of Pope's literary career contains some of his strongest and maturest work: his philosophical poem, **Last poems.** *The Essay on Man, The Moral Essays,* the *Imitations of Horace,* and *The Epistle to Dr. Arbuthnot.* These poems are full of apt sayings; they show the poet's wonderful instinct for the memorable phrase. Pope was not a profound, consistent, or original thinker; but he had something which may fairly be called wisdom, — the wisdom of a close, if superficial, observer of life and manners, as he knew them in the club, the drawing-room, and the street.

In Pope this practical wisdom of the man of the world is touched at times with a true nobility; and among much that is misanthropic and cynical we come upon thoughts like these:

"Honour and shame from no condition rise;
  Act well your part, there all the honour lies."[3]

"Worth makes the man, and want of it the fellow;
  The rest is all but leather or prunella."[4]

Even nobler than these is that beautiful rule of life, in which he tells us that we should keep the equal mind —

"Never elated when one man's oppress'd;
  Never dejected while another's bless'd."[5]

The chief work of Pope's last years was the addition of a fourth book to the *Dunciad,* which is justly celebrated for

---

[1] *Lives of the Poets,* "Pope."
[2] Boswell's *Johnson,* vol. ii. p. 96 (B. Hill's edition).
[3] IV. Epistle of the *Essay on Man.*
[4] IV. Epistle of the *Essay on Man.*
[5] IV. Epistle of the *Essay on Man.*

its magnificent close. His feeble frame was shaken by illness and the end was at hand. He died quietly in his villa in 1744, and was buried in the Twickenham church near the monument he had erected to his parents.

It is almost impossible for readers and critics of this generation to be fair to Pope, either as a poet or as a man. To most of us he is the spokesman of a dead time, separated from ours by the most fundamental differences in its ideals of literature and of life. So absolutely is he bound up with that time that we must try to enter it in imagination if we would understand and sympathise with its typical poet. He set its world of fashion before us in *The Rape of the Lock*, he unveiled the jealousy, recriminations, and wretchedness of its literary class in the *Dunciad*, he made himself the mouthpiece of one of its leading philosophers in the *Essay on Man*. He illustrates its desire for perfection of style, its cynical disbelief in the possibility of virtue in man or woman. His world was narrow and ignoble; but, such as it was, he interpreted it with the minuteness and truth of a great artist. We must not forget that the wide world of poetry includes many different kinds of excellence, and that there is room in it for Juvenal, the satirist of corrupt Rome, as well as for Dante, the seer and the prophet. So we must grant to Pope his place and his praise; not because he wrote the noblest or the highest kind of poetry, but because he fills his own place, and does his own work honestly and well.

When we turn from Pope's writings to the man himself, we hesitate between contempt and pity. He was greedy for praise, inordinately vain, and painfully sensitive to criticism; when his self-love was wounded he retaliated with petty malice, rare even in the history of genius. He resorted to equivocations, or direct falsehood, to advance his reputation; he delighted in underhand methods and small intrigues, so that, in the famous phrase, "he hardly drank tea without a stratagem." Yet he was neither cold-hearted nor selfish; he did many acts of kindness; he had loyal friends; he loved his parents and tended them with a touching and beautiful devotion.[1] He had a brave, independent spirit; he fought, an invalid, against the world, a cripple, but with the heart of a soldier. There is much in his life that cannot be tolerated or defended, but there is also something to admire. We are very gentle over the diseased and puny body — shall we fail in pity for the warped nature, the morbid soul?

SOME MINOR POETS OF POPE'S TIME.

Three poets, MATTHEW PRIOR (1664–1721), JOHN GAY (1688–1732), and THOMAS PARNELL (1679–1717) were more or less closely associated with Pope and his circle of wits. In two of them at least, Prior and Gay, we find that levity of disposition and easy good-humour which distinguish their time.

Matthew, or "Matt" Prior, as he was familiarly called, was of humble origin. As a boy he acted as assistant **Matthew Prior.** in his uncle's wine-house in London, and there attracted the attention of the Earl of Dorset by his fondness for Horace. Through the kindness of the Earl, he was placed at school at Westminster; and after graduating from Cambridge, he made his way in the world as courtier, diplomatist, and poet. He was a man of slight, worldly nature, not inclined to let any devotion to a prin-

[1] This is beautifully expressed in these famous lines at the close of his *Epistle to Dr. Arbuthnot:*

> "Me, let the tender office long engage,
> To rock the cradle of reposing age,
> With lenient arts extend a mother's breath,
> Make languor smile, and smooth the bed of death,
> Explore the thought, explain the asking eye,
> And keep awhile one parent from the sky."

ciple or a party stand in the way of his own advancement, and he was merry in good company. With no depth of feeling, he took life lightly and superficially, enjoying its pleasures. But Prior had the true artist's gift of expression. As a man he was probably no better than many another flippant trifler of his day; but he was a poet, with a poet's power of telling the world what he felt and saw through art. Nearly all of his best poems are the expression of that gay, cynical, easy-going philosophy which would avoid anything that is serious, or would turn life into a jest. In the one instance in which he tried to be serious and sublime, in his ambitious work, *Solomon on the Vanity of the World*, he became dull and tedious; and we feel that the laborious verses are forced and perfunctory. But in his wayward, fanciful poem of *Alma; or, The Progress of the Mind* (1718), a careless, rambling, clever dialogue on the relations of soul and body, the real man, "Matt" Prior, seems revealed to us; and we are charmed with that inimitable union of ease and grace, liveliness and cynicism, with which he delights us in his happiest moods. This neatness and finish of execution make him a master of the epigram, and give to many of his slight verses on every-day themes an unmistakable tone of elegance and distinction. This, indeed, is Prior's peculiar excellence. He had, as the poet Cowper long ago pointed out,[1] the happy faculty of being familiar and colloquial without descending to the level of the commonplace or the prosaic. By virtue of this rare gift, he is one of the greatest masters in English of the lighter forms of verse.

John Gay was a friend of Pope, Swift, and Bolingbroke, who treated him, according to Dr. Johnson, "with more

John Gay. fondness than respect."[2] He loved comfort and good eating; he was indolent and kindly, or, in Dr. Johnson's words, "a soft and civil companion."[3]

---

[1] Letter to Rev. William Unwin, Jan. 17, 1782.
[2] *Lives of the Poets,* "Gay."   [3] *Lives of the Poets,* "Gay."

Pope describes him as a man "of a timid temper and fearful of giving offence to the great." [1] As we should expect, the poetry of this good, easy man is not of the highest order. His *Fables* (1727), short moral stories in smooth and easy verse, are often clever and amusing. In this he is the follower of the French poet La Fontaine; and, while he does not equal his original, he has probably produced the best work of this order in English literature. Two of his songs have been much admired, " 'T was when the seas were roaring," and "Sweet William's Farewell to Blackey'd Susan." The first of these is distinctly superior to the second, but neither is worthy to be placed with our best lyrics. Probably Gay is at his best in his description of certain outward aspects of the life about him. He was a close observer, with a quick eye for trifles; he did not see beneath the surface, but he has given us wonderfully minute and vivid pictures of his world as it appeared to the passer-by. He has the same careful, uninspired fidelity to commonplace facts, which some old Dutch painters show in their pictures of the interior of a butcher's shop or a tavern. His poem of *Trivia, or the art of walking the streets of London* (1715), is a perfect treasure-house of information for the student of dress and manners; and, even in his pastoral poem *The Shepherd's Week* (1714), we come upon a careful and interesting account of certain rural customs and superstitions. But Gay, like Pope and most of the great writers of the time, was only accurate within certain narrow limits, for we cannot really see those things which lie beyond the range of our understanding and our sympathy. So restricted were men's sympathies in this age, so contracted was their field of vision, that they saw and described most clearly the frivolous or the trivial, the artificial or the base. Pope, Gay, and Prior were marvellously truthful to the facts they saw, but there was a world

[1] Spence's *Anecdotes.*

outside of these facts of which they knew nothing. So, **Realism in Pope and Wordsworth.** when Pope writes of the beauty of Nature, he relies on books, and is affected and conventional; but, when he describes a game of cards, he paints from the life. We may then properly inquire, not only whether a poet describes facts truly, but also what kind of facts he describes. When Wordsworth, the great poet of Nature, writes:

> "The silence that is in the starry sky,
> The sleep that is among the lonely hills," [1]

he reveals something to us about Nature that, obvious as it may seem, could only have been learned through sympathy. Such were the facts this poet saw and described. In the following passage in *Trivia*, Gay is equally accurate and far more specific:

> "If when Fleet-ditch with muddy current flows
> You chance to roam; where oyster-tubs in rows
> Are ranged beside the posts; then stay thy haste,
> And with the savoury fish indulge thy taste:
> The damsel's knife the gaping shell commands
> While the salt liquor streams between her hands."

Such were the facts that the eighteenth-century realist delighted to describe.

Thomas Parnell, an Irishman of good family, was, like Gay, the friend of Pope, Swift, and the other great writers of his time. He died at thirty-nine, and nearly **Thomas Parnell.** all of his best work was composed during the last six years of his life, the years during which he had the advantage of Pope's advice and encouragement. He wrote but little, and even within these narrow limits he is seldom at his best. Yet some of Parnell's poems, *The Hermit*, *A Night Piece on Death*, *A Hymn to Contentment*,

[1] *Song at the Feast of Brougham Castle.*

and perhaps a few others, show the spirit of a true poet; and we find in them traces of a higher mood and a deeper feeling than in all the verse of Gay or Prior. A greater seriousness, an appreciation of natural beauty, slight as it may seem compared with the Nature poets of a later time, make us feel that Parnell stands apart from his greatest poetic contemporaries, anticipating, if only in a faint and hesitating way, the spirit of the age which is to come.

AUTHORSHIP IN THE AUGUSTAN AGE AND THE RISE OF THE NEW PROSE.

One of the important features in the literary history of England, during the latter seventeenth and early eighteenth centuries, is the change which took place in the position of the man of letters. Before this time it had been almost impossible to make a living by writing, unless one wrote for the stage. Marlowe, Shakespeare, Ben Jonson, nearly all the writers who supported themselves entirely by the pen, were dramatists, while those who were not dramatists were not entirely dependent on what they earned by their literary work. Thus Hooker was a clergyman, Sir Thomas Browne a physician, Izaak Walton a linen-draper; while Wyatt and Surrey, Sidney and Raleigh, represent the large class of courtiers and gentlemen to whom literature was not a profession but an occasional pursuit. Even in the latter half of the seventeenth century, Dryden felt himself forced to write plays for a livelihood, although convinced that his talents lay in another direction. The explanation of this is very simple; writing did not pay as a profession, because there were so few readers; play-writing paid, because many crowded to the theatres who would not or could not read a book.

After the Revolution of 1688, authorship offered far greater chances of worldly advancement; and it became possible for a writer to make a career for himself through literature, without being compelled to write for the stage. This was not because the number of readers had begun to increase, although this was in fact the case; it was because the government, finding literature useful in guiding or forming public opinion, employed authors to write in its service, and rewarded them with a pension, an embassy, or some public office. This practice may have been partly due to the example of Dryden, who had showed by his political satires and by his timely advocacy of the Roman Church, how strong an influence literature could exert on the public mind; but it was largely brought about by the political condition of affairs after the Revolution had placed William and Mary upon the throne. It will be remembered that these sovereigns and their successors did not rule by a "Divine right," as the Stuarts had claimed to do, but derived their authority from the will of the Parliament. Under such circumstances, it is not surprising that the power of the crown declined, and that the control of affairs passed more and more into the hands of the great political leaders and their followers. The result was an eager contest for power between the two great political parties, the Whig and the Tory. Each looked to the public for support, and each realised that capable writers could do much to win the public to its side. Such a state of things could not but bring about a great change in the author's position. Men of letters had their share in the work of the government; they were brought into frequent contact with the governing class; and the successful writer, treated as an equal by great nobles and leading statesmen, obtained a comfortable income through official patronage. This alliance of literature and politics was particularly marked in the reign of Queen Anne (1702–1714), and men of letters were so

Effect on authorship of the Revolution of 1688.

highly honoured that men compared this brilliant and
favoured period to the Golden Age of Latin literature under
the Emperor Augustus, and called it proudly the "Augustan Age." Among many authors rewarded by the government at this time, were the poet Prior, who was
connected with various diplomatic missions; Swift, who was
made Dean; and Addison, who rose to the high post of
Secretary of State.

But, while literature was thus largely dependent upon
political patronage, or the favour of some distinguished
The growth patron to whom the struggling author dedicated
of the read- his book, the increase in the reading-class was
ing public. already preparing the way for a yet greater and
more lasting change. Ever since the Restoration the
wealth of the nation had steadily increased. Trade with
the Colonies grew rapidly; and, as the commercial class
became wealthier, it gained in social and political importance. Dean Swift remarked that the political power
which used to be monopolised by the great land-owners
"had gone over to money," and Dr. Johnson declared that
"an English merchant was a new species of gentleman."
Formerly there had been very few readers outside of the
aristocratic or scholarly circles, but now, as the commercial
class increased in wealth and consequence, the number
of those who bought and read books increased also. This
gradual widening of the popular intelligence was in time
to make the author independent of both the state and the
patron, and enable him to look directly to the great mass of
readers for recognition and support.

Other influences besides the spread of education were
slowly and silently adding to the great army of readers.
The freedom The establishment of the freedom of the press,
of the press, in 1695, opened the way to a fuller and freer
1695. discussion of public questions, and led to the
foundation of numerous newspapers and periodicals, read

by many who never opened the larger and more formidable
works. London was the natural centre of this
The Coffee-
houses.
intellectual activity; and in London the Coffee-
houses, the meeting-places of statesmen, wits,
merchants, and fashionable idlers, did much to quicken
and enlarge the mental life of the town. The first Coffee-
house in England had been started about the middle of
the seventeenth century, and by Queen Anne's time,
Coffee-houses had become an established and important
feature of London life. One writer estimated that in 1708
there were nearly three thousand of these Coffee-houses in
London alone. The Coffee-house resembled the modern
club; but it was less expensive, less exclusive, and less
luxurious. There the Londoner gossiped with his friends,
read and wrote his letters, and enjoyed his coffee and his
pipe. We can imagine the effect of the incessant dis-
cussions, daily, almost hourly, carried on in these thousands of places of public resort. In these Coffee-houses,
writes a foreign observer, "you have all manner of News;
you have a good Fire, which you may sit by as long as
you please; you have a Dish of Coffee, you meet your
friends for the Transaction of Business, and all for a penny,
if you don't care to spend more." [1]

All these conditions, political, commercial, or social,
favoured the rise of a new kind of prose literature, and
tended to give prose a wider influence. The
The rise of the
new prose.
professional writer, no longer tied to the drama,
was free to devote himself to prose; and it was
prose, in its shorter, lighter, and more amusing forms, that
the new public found the easiest and most entertaining
reading. So, as we shall see, periodicals were started, containing brief essays, sketches, and sometimes stories; and
these pleased the taste of the town. Sometimes these essays
pictured, in a few numbers, some aspect of the life of the

[1] Misson, a French traveller, who visited England in 1713 (?).

day; sometimes they caught the floating talk of the clubs and Coffee-houses, and gave it a brief, graceful, and witty literary form. In the hands of great writers this new prose became a powerful social and educational force; but to appreciate this better we must turn to two of the great masters of the essay, Addison and Steele.

SIR RICHARD STEELE.

(1672–1729.)

"He was unswerving in his loyalty to his friends; he was the most loving of fathers; and, in days when marriage was a lighter tie than now, his devotion to his wife may be called romantic. There have been wiser, stronger, greater men. But many a strong man would have been stronger for a touch of Steele's indulgent sympathy; many a great man has wanted his genuine largeness of heart; many a wise man might learn something from his deep and wide humanity. His virtues redeemed his frailties."

— AUSTIN DOBSON.

"If Steele is not our friend, he is nothing. He is by no means the most brilliant of wits nor the deepest of thinkers; but he is our friend: we love him as children love their love with an A, because he is amiable."   — THACKERAY.

Thackeray spoke truly when he called Steele "our friend." With Goldsmith, he is one of the most lovable of English authors. He had his weaknesses, although they have been greatly exaggerated; but they were the faults of a warm-hearted, heedless nature, essentially high-minded and noble, and full of a sincere and beautiful humility of spirit. It is easy to love Steele, but men are just beginning to see that even this is not enough; they are beginning to see more clearly how great a work this man did for England, careless and easy-going as he seems; what a depth of love and tenderness there was in him, how lofty was the purpose which animated his life from first to last; and, as they see this, they know that there is something in him that not only wins our love, but commands our respect and admiration.

Richard Steele, or "Dick" Steele, as his friends called him, was born in Dublin in 1672, the year of the birth of Addison, the great writer whose name was to be so closely associated with his own. The Steeles were English, and it may be that he inherited his excitable, generous, and loving nature from his mother, who is supposed to have been of Irish descent. When he was very young he was left an orphan, and was cared for by an uncle, who secured his admission to the Charterhouse School in London. In one of his essays Steele tells of the impression his father's death made upon his childish mind. He was then too young to realise what had happened, but some vague "instinct of sorrow" reached him through his mother's grief; this, he writes, "seized my very soul, and has made pity the weakness of my heart ever since." [1]

From the Charterhouse, where he began his long friendship with Addison, Steele went to Oxford; but left, before taking his degree, to enlist in the Horse Guards. According to his own account, he lost the succession to "a very good estate" in Ireland, by this step, sacrificing, as always, his prospects to the inclination of the moment. By 1700 he was Captain Steele, had published verses, and had made the acquaintance of some of the wits of the town. The life was full of temptations, especially for a young officer of an improvident and emotional disposition and high spirits, and these temptations Steele did not always successfully resist. His life in truth was far better than that of many of the men about him; but, unlike many others, he was quick to repent of a fault, and ready to confess it with a singular frankness. So, he tells us, "he writ for his own private use, a little book called the

Steele's life. (side note)

---

[1] *Tatler*, No. 181, June 6, 1710.

Christian Hero, with a design principally to fix upon his own

His Christian Hero.

Mind a strong Impression of Virtue and Religion, in opposition to a stronger Propensity towards unwarrantable Pleasures." [1] This book was designed to show "that no Principles but those of religion are sufficient to make a great man." [2] Many of the noblest traits of Steele's character are unconsciously revealed in the book, but it did not add to his popularity. It was inconvenient, moreover, if he indulged in "the least levity" to be accused of falling below the standard which he had set up. To counteract this, and "to enliven his character,"

His Comedies.

he wrote a comedy called *The Funeral,* which was followed by several other plays. These plays are not without merit, and some of them were at least fairly successful in their day; but it is not by his dramas that Steele holds his place in literature. One feature of these comedies, however, can not be altogether passed over, if we are to rightly estimate the ruling spirit of their author's life; they are the work of a man who has set himself to purify the thoughts and correct the vulgarity and wickedness of his age. Steele's life-long purpose is to separate wit from immorality, to show that a good

Social reformer.

man is neither a milksop nor a sanctimonious hypocrite, and that it is possible to be decent without being dull. This purpose is apparent in his comedies, which are pure and wholesome compared to those of Wycherley, Congreve, or the other dramatists of the Restoration. He did not condemn the stage outright, as some reformers then did; but he tried to elevate it, believing, as he wrote, "that a good play, acted before a well-bred Audience, must raise very proper Incitements to good Behaviour, and be the most quick and

---

[1] *Mr. Steele's Apology for Himself and His Writings; Occasioned by his Expulsion from the House of Commons,* 1714.

[2] Title-page to the *Christian Hero.*

prevailing method of giving Young People a Turn of Sense and Breeding." "I own myself," he adds, "of the Society for *Reformation of Manners.*" [1] But to this needed reform Steele, like his great co-worker Addison, brought not merely enthusiasm, but taste, humour, and the experience of the man of the world. Since the accession of William and Mary the better side of the English nature had been fighting against the moral corruption which had disfigured society after the Restoration: associations had been formed for the *Reformation of Manners*, and Collier had filed his sweeping indictment against the stage. But now vice and folly were to be arrested by two writers whose weapons were to prove more effective than the angriest invective, writers whose playful humour could make frivolity ridiculous, whose kindly satire provoked no resentment, and insensibly enlisted the readers' sympathies on the side of virtue.

In 1707 Steele was put in charge of the *Gazette.* This newspaper was the official organ of the Government, through which it gave the public such news as it thought expedient, and Steele's position was consequently a government post. In 1709 he started

Periodicals. The Tatler.

a periodical of his own, the *Tatler*, an event which we look back upon as the beginning of a new era in the history of English prose. The conditions which favoured the rise of newspapers and periodicals at this time have been already alluded to (p. 342). The first successful daily newspaper, the *Daily Courant*, had been begun in 1702; and in 1704 Daniel De Foe started a paper called the *Review*, which began as a weekly, and which, besides articles on such serious subjects as books and politics, devoted some space to lighter topics and the social gossip of the town. Besides these papers there were many others; the power of the press and the demand for news was increasing, and there

---

[1] *Tatler*, No. 3, April 14, 1709.

was a great opportunity for the writer who could satisfy this demand and lift journalism to a higher level. Steele was the first writer to seize this opportunity. The *Tatler* was so far in advance of any of its predecessors that we now look back to it as the first of those famous eighteenth-century periodicals which were to become a distinctive feature in the literary history of the century. If we could place a copy of the *Tatler* beside one of our huge, well-printed dailies, this famous periodical would look almost ridiculously mean and insignificant. It consisted of but one folio sheet, with double columns; and was published three times a week, on Tuesdays, Thursdays, and Saturdays, the days when the mail left London for the country. It was sold for a penny, and, in addition to the theatre notices and current news, it contained an essay which often treated lightly and good-humouredly of some folly or affectation of the time. Shabby as this little paper would seem to us now, it did a wonderful work in purifying the town; and it gave us essays which have kept their charm and freshness for nearly two hundred years, while the wisest and cleverest articles in our imposing modern journals hardly outlast the day. The success of the *Tatler* was immediate; Queen Anne read it at the breakfast table; and it was said to have attracted more customers to the coffeehouses "than all the other News Papers put together."[1] Before long Steele's old friend Addison began to write for the *Tatler*, and after it had run for about a year and a half, became a regular contributor. Thus the two greatest essayists and reformers of the day, sharing the same high purpose, and united by an almost life-long friendship, came to work side by side. The *Tatler* was discontinued January second, 1711; and on the first of the following March, Addison and Steele started a yet more famous periodical, the *Spectator*, which appeared every day except

[1] This was said by John Gay in 1711. See Dobson's *Steele*, p. 124.

Sunday. As we shall have something to say about the *Spectator* in our study of Addison, we may return now to the story of Steele's life. He was an ardent Whig; and, like many of the leading writers of his day, he took an active part in politics. We need not follow him into this region of political controversy; it is enough to say that from about 1713 not a little of his life and energy was absorbed by political affairs, or taken up with attempts to extricate himself from money difficulties in which he was continually involved. He had stoutly defended the succession of the House of Hanover, and when George I. came to the throne he was knighted (1715) and rewarded with several lucrative offices. But sanguine, careless, and improvident, he struggled with debts to the end.

Political activity.

In 1724 he left London and retired to a country-place in Wales, broken in health. Since he had left Oxford some thirty years before, he had lived in the thick of the contest, playing his part in that world of the capital, in which the activities of the whole nation were focussed. He had been soldier, dramatist, government official, editor, politician, and theatrical manager; he had been intimate with the greatest Englishmen of his time; he had known success and disappointment, praise and abuse; and he had fought a brave fight, not always wise or prudent, but true, on the whole, to high ideals; and, in some wonderful way he had kept his hopeful spirit and kind heart through it all. The last glimpse that we get of him at the close of his hurried and bustling life is very beautiful. "I have been told," wrote one of his friends, "that he retained his cheerful sweetness of temper to the last; and would often be carried out in a summer's evening, when the country lads and lasses were assembled at their rural sports, and, with his pencil, give an order on his agent, the mercer, for a new gown for the best dancer." [1] So the quiet

Retirement and death.

[1] *Original Letters, Dramatic Pieces, and Poems*, by Benjamin Victor, i. p. 330.

hour was given him at the end of the day. He died in 1729.

In Steele's writings, and especially in his letters, we see the man as he was. He wrote frankly and carelessly, and **Character.** he was transparently honest and direct. His unaffected goodness, his large-hearted human sympathy, shine out through his works. We see in them a man of a sincerely religious nature, who loved his fellows, who had a chivalric reverence for women, who was tender towards suffering, devoted to his wife and children, loyal to his friends. He had high standards, and was quick to blame himself when he fell below them. His faults were those of a generous and impulsive nature; and we must not make too much of them, but remember that he confessed frankly what many a man would have tried to conceal. "I shall not carry my humility so far as to call myself a virtuous man," he writes, "but at the same time must confess that my life is at best but pardonable." How many are there who could not truly say so much, what truly good man would dare to say more?

His writings are unequal, and every one agrees that they lack the peculiar charm and finish of Addison's; but their **Steele's work.** purpose is as high, their pathos at times warmer and deeper. It was Steele, moreover, who led the way in which Addison followed, who originated what Addison brought to perfection. Steele himself has told us in no measured terms how much he owed to Addison, and critic after critic has repeated his generous words; but we must not forget the debt that Addison owed to Steele, that it was Steele who gave Addison the greatest opportunity for distinction, and Steele who enabled Addison to give the world his best. We may then respect Steele, knowing what he did and what he was. When Pope sneered and Swift railed at men with a savage hatred, Steele passed through a rough world with an overflowing charity, striving to make men better. "As for my labours," he writes, "if they wear but one impertinence out of human life, destroy a single vice, or give a morning's cheerfulness to an honest mind; in short, if the world can be but one virtue the better or in any degree less vicious, or receive from them the smallest addition to their innocent diversions; I shall not think my pains, or indeed my life, to have been spent in vain." [1]

JOSEPH ADDISON.

(1672–1719.)

"He has restored virtue to its dignity, and taught innocence not to be ashamed. This is an elevation of literary character, above all Greek, above all Roman fame. . . . Whoever wishes to attain an English style, familiar but not coarse, and elegant but not ostentatious, must give his days and nights to the volumes of Addison."

— DR. JOHNSON.

Joseph Addison, one of the most charming of English prose-writers, and one of the wisest and most kindly of social reformers, was born at his father's rectory at Milston, Wiltshire, in 1672. His father, who became Dean of Lichfield Cathedral, was a kindly scholar of some literary ability, and Addison's earliest impressions of life were gained in a loving, refined, and happy home. He went to the Charterhouse School, where he formed his memorable friendship with "Dick" Steele, and thence to Oxford, where he obtained a scholarship at Magdalen College through some Latin verses on King William the Third. He had a liking for Latin literature; and his fellow-students are said to have thought him shy, studious, and reserved. The Church seemed the natural career for a young man of Addison's position and character, but an unforeseen opportunity turned the course of his life in another direction. He had written some verses to Dryden

Early years.

[1] The _Tatler_, No. 89.

(1693), which had pleased the old poet, then in the height of his fame; and shortly after he was brought to the notice of two leaders of the Whig party, Charles Montague, afterwards Lord Halifax, and John (afterwards Lord) Somers. These two statesmen, anxious no doubt to secure a promising young writer for the party, obtained a pension for Addison, which he was to use in foreign travel in preparation for a public career. Accordingly, in 1699 he left for the Continent, visiting France, Italy, and Switzerland, writing a little and observing much. But the political changes which followed the King's death in 1702 lost Addison his pension, and he returned home in the following year with no certain prospects, and, as Dr. Johnson quaintly says, "at full leisure for the cultivation of his mind." [1] But it was not long before Addison's opportunity came. In 1704, Marlborough, the most brilliant soldier of the age, won the battle of Blenheim; and Lord Godolphin — then Lord High Treasurer — asked Halifax, Addison's old patron, to recommend some poet to him who could fittingly celebrate the victory. At Halifax's suggestion Addison was selected; and the man who was acting as the head of Her Majesty's government sent the Right Honourable Chancellor of the Exchequer to wait on the poor author in his garret, [2] and ask him to write the poem.

The Campaign.

Remember that at this time Addison's friends were out of power; that he was miserably poor and almost unknown. Could there be a more impressive illustration of the way in which politics turned to literature, or of the respect which the author was beginning to command? *The Campaign*, the poem which Addison wrote in response to this request, pleased Lord Godolphin and the public. It was through his poetry that Addison had first attracted the

[1] *Lives of the Poets*, "Addison."

[2] Pope says that Addison was lodged up three pair of stairs, over a small shop in the Haymarket. See Spence's *Anecdotes*.

attention of the Whig leaders and laid the foundations of his fortune, and now poetry came a second time to his aid. As a reward for his services to the party, he was made one of the Commissioners of the Excise, that is of the domestic taxes (1704), and from this time until 1710, when the Whigs went out of office, he held various government posts.

Shortly before this, as we have seen, he became a contributor to Steele's new enterprise, the *Tatler*, finding through his friend a fresh and congenial field for his talents, and entering on what was to prove his most brilliant and useful sphere of work. In the succeeding periodical, the *Spectator* (1711), his fine qualities are seen at their best.

Writes for the Tatler.

The wonderful essays in these periodicals, and in a few others of their kind, performed for the English of the eighteenth century the same service which Hamlet said the players did for the sixteenth; they were the "abstract and brief chronicle of the time." The world read them, and saw itself reflected in the mirror of art. Others had held up mirrors to life, — Chaucer the poet, to his world of the fourteenth century; Shakespeare the dramatist, to his world of the sixteenth; and now in the early eighteenth-century world come the essayists also, holding up in their turn their mirror to the human comedy about them. And that world remains; reflected in these little essays, slight and trifling as they seem, not only for the men of the generation that produced them, but for us also, if we read them with sympathetic understanding. It is full of men and women more real to us than many of the great personages of history: the immortal country squire, the amiable and eccentric Sir Roger de Coverley; Will Honeycomb, the elderly man of gallantry; Sir Andrew Freeport, the representative of the rising merchant-class; and poor, aimless, idle Will Wimble. There, too, is Ned Softly, haunting the coffee-houses for a chance to read his verses; Tom

The periodical essays.

Folio, the pedantic bibliographer, the type of those who glorify the outward details of scholarship, while incapable of appreciating its spirit; and Addison himself, the *Spectator*, the shy, silent man, who sits by and watches and records it all.   There are all these and many more painted with such truth and distinctness that, like the pilgrims of Chaucer's worthy company, they remain the living representatives of their time.   And it is to be observed that the typical characters brought before us in these essays

Town and country in the De Coverley papers.

are chosen and presented so as to represent the life of the country as well as that of the town. Indeed, the Sir Roger de Coverley series is so cleverly planned that it constantly suggests to us the ever widening differences between town and country life and ideas in Addison's time.   We see the Londoner, the Spectator, visit the country, and we view it through his eyes; we see the country squire, Sir Roger, come up to town and appreciate by his old-fashioned dress, and his ludicrous mistakes, how swiftly the capital has moved away from the simple-minded, narrow, conservative world that surrounds it.   So the whole thing is a skilful and vivid study in contrasts.   Such studies of life and character were varied by essays of other kinds; critical essays, such as the famous series on *Paradise Lost;* reflective essays, such as the *Meditations in Westminster Abbey;* or stories and allegories, such as *Hilpa and Shalum* or the *Golden Scales.*

We are to note also that both the *Tatler* and the *Spectator* were directly and consciously addressed to the growing

Addison and the reading public.

public of readers, or, as Addison says, to the "great audience" that "I have raised to myself." Especial care was taken to reach and interest women, whose claims were then generally ignored.   "There are none," says Addison, "to whom this paper will be more useful than to the female world;" [1] and his words tell us

---

[1] *Spectator,* No. 10.   See entire paper.

that the spirit of Restoration England, where women were flattered and despised, is passing away. Addison does not flatter; he shows the fine women of fashion how vain and ignorant they are, how empty and frivolous are the lives they lead; but we feel that his severity is inspired by his belief that woman was made for higher things.

With the production of his ponderous tragedy of *Cato*, in 1713, Addison reached the summit of success in his fortu-

Cato. nate career. By singular good luck, *Cato*, which lacked almost every quality of a good acting play, achieved an extraordinary success. It was brought out in a moment of feverish political excitement, and both the Whigs and the Tories claimed to see in it a confirmation of the justness of their respective views. We find it intolerably dull and sententious, and it is forgotten except for a few well-known lines; nevertheless, in the eyes of his contemporaries it was the crowning triumph of its author, and the great Frenchman, Voltaire, pronounced it a masterpiece.

Addison's last years show us what a great social and political eminence a man of high character, sound judgment,

Last years. and literary ability could then attain. In 1716 he married the Dowager Countess of Warwick, and in the year following he became Secretary of State. Failing health soon compelled him to resign this great office, and he died in 1719.

Almost universally popular and respected in his lifetime, Addison remains one of the most honoured of English writers.

Character and works. His poetry, except a few of his hymns, was commonplace and uninspired; his once famous tragedy is little short of a failure; but his best essays have a humanity, a grace, and a sympathetic humour which neither time nor the change in literary fashions has been able to impair. And Addison is still honoured, not only for what he wrote, but also for what he was. He lived in the midst of literary warfare, of contending factions in politics, and bitter animosities in religion; he had his enemies — what man in such a time has not? — yet he lived out his prosperous, well-ordered life undisturbed by these things, a man of stainless honour, wise, benevolent, dignified, and serene. He was a shy man, silent, and, it is said, even stiff and awkward among strangers; but when he was at ease with his friends he is reported to have been "the best company in the world."[1] Even to this day we feel this touch of chill in his dignified reserve, and we should not dare to claim him for our friend as we did Steele. We are attracted to Steele by his frank humility; we have an uncomfortable impression that Addison knew how much better he was than the rest of us. His hero, Cato, is the essence of self-complacent superiority; he thus instructs one of his followers:

"Dost thou love watchings, abstinence and toil, laborious virtues all? learn them from Cato."[2]

Addison himself taught the world after a very different fashion; he would never have *said* this, but we are inclined to suspect that he also felt the comforting assurance of superior virtue. But, if Addison calls forth our respect rather than our affection, we must not fail to do full justice to the nobility of his character and his life. When we reflect upon the great work that he performed for English society, and the way in which he accomplished it, even the slightest disparagement of him seems ungrateful and unimportant; we remember him only as Macaulay truly described him, as "the unsullied statesman; the accomplished scholar; the great satirist who alone knew how to use ridicule without abusing it; who, without inflicting a wound effected a great social reform, and who reconciled wit and virtue after a long and painful separation, during

---

[1] Lady Mary Wortley Montagu.
[2] *Cato*, Act ii. Sc. 4.

which wit had been led away by profligacy, and virtue by fanaticism."[1]

THE HISTORY OF THE NOVEL.

We can understand why it was that this unideal and unromantic epoch, with its growth of prose, its prevailing common sense, its firm grasp of the things which can be seen and handled, should have brought one especial kind of fiction to a higher development than it had yet known in England. The hard, practical intelligence of the time, weak in high emotions and in its sense of the mystical and the unseen, was correspondingly strong in the power of closely observing and faithfully reproducing the passing aspects of every-day life. Such conditions favoured the rise of the novel of domestic life and manners, which, in the hands of Defoe, Richardson, and Fielding, became virtually a new literary form. Yet the novel, while one of the most original and important contributions which the eighteenth century made to literature, was not a wholly new creation, but rather a new form given to a very ancient kind of writing by the changed temper of the times. In part, at least, it grew out of the earlier romances and short stories, just as the Elizabethan drama grew out of, yet differed from, the earlier dramatic forms. To make this clear, it is necessary to speak briefly of the history of English fiction before this time.

The love of a story is so wide-spread and deep-seated that it seems natural to the race. We delight in stories before we are out of the nursery, and the world has loved to tell and hear them since its childhood. Many of the noblest stories of early times were in verse, such as the *Iliad* and the *Odyssey*, the latter perhaps the most fascinating story of antiquity. To this

Origin of the novel.

---

[1] Macaulay, *Essay on the Life and Writings of Addison*. The only exception that could be justly taken to this splendid and famous tribute is that Steele is given no credit for his share in this reform.

class our own *Beowulf* belongs. We may thus think of the epic poem as a kind of exalted precursor of the novel, supplying, after its own fashion, the same deep, human need. Besides the great stories in verse, there was, of course, an immense mass of myth and folklore, and some of these world-stories have never ceased to delight children down to our day.

After the classic epics, we reach another stage of development in the mediæval romance. This, in its original meaning, was a narrative poem in one of the Romance dialects, as Old French or Provençal. These romances may be thought of as a mediæval form of the epic; they embodied the chivalric ideas peculiar to the time, and marked an important step towards the creation of the novel.

We have seen how these romances came into England with the Norman Conquest, passing from French to English paraphrases in the metrical romances of the thirteenth century. Another step to-wards the novel is taken when some of these stories are retold in English prose: Malory's *Morte d'Arthur* may be taken as an example of this important change in form. The revival of learning infused new life into English story-telling, as it did into almost every other form of literary art, and in the sixteenth century the romances increased in number and importance. Besides the romances produced by English writers, great numbers of Italian, French, and Spanish stories were translated or paraphrased, and, put forth separately or in collections, became widely popular. Paynter's *Palace of Pleasure* (vol. i. 1566), a good example of such collections, contained stories from Boccaccio, "and other italian and french authours." From Spain came the famous romance, *Amadis de Gaul.* Through such channels a flood of foreign romance poured in upon the English. Romantic stories piled on the London

The romance in England.

bookstalls, and eagerly bought and read, furnished plots
and suggestions to the English dramatist and story-teller.
Shakespeare used them, and Sidney modelled his *Arcadia*
in part upon the *Amadis de Gaul.*

The general tone of the Elizabethan stories was poetic
and fanciful: many of them were pastoral or chivalric
in character. It is true that both Greene and Nash wrote
stories, "the main object of which was to paint, to the life,
ordinary men and characters," but most of the famous
stories of the time were as remote from the prosaic realities
of existence as a Watteau shepherdess. Thus More's
Utopia, if we choose to consider it a romance at all, introduces us to a world that exists only as an ideal; John
Lyly's *Euphues* is couched in a highly-wrought and
affected style, elaborately artificial, although close enough
to the strange humour of the time to become a passing
affectation of the court. Lodge's *Rosalind* — the original
of Shakespeare's *As You Like It* — is a pastoral idyl,
where shepherds and shepherdesses utter high-flown
sentiments, and sing madrigals and "pleasant eclogues"
under the boughs of Arden Forest. The very title of Sidney's *Arcadia* takes us into this land of pastoral romance,
where the shepherd boy pipes "as though he should never
be old." [1] Such works aimed less at the lifelike delineation
of character, than at the creation of a world transfigured
by the light of a chivalric or idyllic atmosphere. Yet
such stories, however alien to the life of our day, were far
less removed from that of the Elizabethan. Then the
spirit of chivalry lived, and the imagination was liberated
and quickened by the swift advance, the stir and strangeness, of the time. The Elizabethan romance is the true
child of the age which produced such works as *Faustus,*
As You Like It, The Tempest, The Faithful Shepherdess,
and the *Faërie Queene.*

[1] *Arcadia,* Bk. i.

During the seventeenth century the romance, instead of advancing toward truthfulness and simplicity, became more full of false and extravagant heroics, and farther removed from actual life. French romances were immensely popular, in the original, or in the translation; and in spite of a few attempts to stem the current, the general tone was pompous and inflated. Jusserand says of this period: "The hundred years which follow Shakespeare's death are, therefore, taken altogether, a period of little invention and progress for romance literature. The only new development it takes consists in the exaggeration of the heroic element, of which there was already enough in many an Elizabethan novel; it consists, in fact, in the magnifying of a defect." [1] For the time, farther progress in the old lines of romance-writing became impossible. After the Restoration the rhapsodies of a pseudo-chivalry became more and more out of keeping with the open-eyed, practical, and comparatively modern temper of the time. Prose was discarding its ponderous, or elaborately affected manner, and becoming plainer, more serviceable, and more direct. Under these conditions a new form of story-telling, distinguished by its skill in the delineation of character, its simple style, free from factitious embellishments, its sharp and clear-cut presentations of ordinary life, gradually took form. It is true that this kind of fiction had been partially anticipated at a much earlier period. As far back as the Elizabethan days, Thomas Nash, the forerunner of the realistic novelists, had introduced his readers to well-defined types of contemporary character. In *Pierce Penniless*, for instance, he describes, among many other characteristic personages, "the prodigal young master" who falls in a quarrelling humour with Fortune, because she made him not "King of the Indies;" who swears that

[1] *The English Novel in the Time of Shakespeare*, p. 412.

"neither father nor brother will keep him under;" that
he will go to sea, "and teare the gold out of Spanish
throats, but he will have it, by'r ladye." [1]

Ben Jonson introduced similar character-sketches into
his *Cynthia's Revels* (1600), and in the seventeenth century several books were published, consisting entirely of
short character-studies, unconnected by any framework
of narrative. Among these, one of the best known is the
Characters of SIR THOMAS OVERBURY (pub. 1614), a courtier and minor poet. Other "character-writers" of the time
were JOSEPH HALL (*Characters of Virtues and Vices*, pub.
1608) and JOHN EARLE (*Microcosmography*, 1628). Thus,
while in the tedious and drawn-out stories of the romance-
writer, the depiction of character was commonly neglected,
a form of prose became popular, in which character was
the sole interest. But these character-writers portrayed
a type rather than an individual; and the general characteristics of this type, or class, were exhibited merely by
the dry enumeration of peculiarities of life, dress, or
manners.

A further step was taken toward the modern novel of
character when Steele and Addison, in their periodical
essays, depicted a type of contemporary life,
The essay and not by a formal enumeration of qualities, but
the novel. through living men and women shown acting
and conversing in the midst of their daily surroundings.
In the De Coverley papers, with their fresh and faithful
pictures of English town and country life, with their grasp
of character, their amusing or pathetic scenes and incidents, we have all the elements but one of the modern
novel. Here, indeed, is a novel held in solution. Had
these elements been united by a regularly constructed plot,
bringing an added interest, and binding scene to scene, and
character to character, by a closer and more inevitable

[1] *Works of Thomas Nash*, Grosart's ed. ii. p. 29.

sequence, we should have had a story to set side by side with the *Vicar of Wakefield*. Here and there, in the De Coverley essays, are persons and situations almost identical with those which were soon to find a place in the master-pieces of English fiction. The ingenuous comments of Sir Roger at the play may be compared with the provincial criticisms of Partridge on Mr. Garrick's *Hamlet* in Field-ing's *Tom Jones*. Sir Roger himself may be appropriately placed beside the contrast-study of Squire Western in the same novel. If, on the other hand, we compare these charming sketches of Addison's with what has preceded them, we realise that the "Country Gentleman" in Over-bury's *Characters* is a mere aggregation of qualities, while Sir Roger, representing the same class, is no type or ab-straction, but a veritable man, whose little oddities we know and understand — a friend we love and mourn for.

Having advanced thus far, we have reached the very boundaries of a new development in the story-writer's art. But into this region Addison and Steele did not enter. The next great step toward the modern novel was left for a man whom Addison scorned, one of the most brilliant, indomi-table, and enigmatical of English writers, Daniel Defoe.

DANIEL DEFOE.

(1659?–1731.)

"De Foe is our only famous politician and man of letters, who represented, in its inflexible constancy, sturdy resolution, unwearied perseverance, and obstinate contempt of danger and tyranny, the great middle-class English character."   — JOHN FOSTER.

"One of these authors (the fellow who was pilloried, I have forgot his name) is indeed so grave, sententious, dogmatical a rogue, that there is no enduring him."   — JONATHAN SWIFT.

"He that will help you, must be hated and neglected by you, must be mobbed and plundered for you, must starve and hang for you, and must yet help you. And thus do I."   — DANIEL DEFOE.

Defoe's life is charged with the spirit of adventure. He was "ever a fighter;" and, although he was the most prolific English writer of his time, he was no scholarly recluse, but first and last a practical man, who took an active and not unimportant part in the daily work of the world. The spirited stories of life and adventure with which, towards the close of his career, he captivated his readers, were the work of one whose own experience was won outside the walls of a library or a university, one who had known riches and poverty, success and failure; one who had stood in the pillory, and had been two years in prison; who had owned a splendid mansion and kept his pleasure-boat and his coach; a man who had been at one time the trusted adviser of a grateful King, and at another an object of hatred, abuse, and contempt. He was one who could write of himself:

His busy and stirring career.

> "No man has tasted differing fortunes more,
> And thirteen times I have been rich and poor;" —

one who could say: "In the school of affliction I have

learned more philosophy than at the academy, and more divinity than from the pulpit, — I have seen the rough side of the world as well as the smooth."

Daniel Foe, or Defoe as he afterwards called himself, was born in or about 1659, in the parish of St. Giles, Crip-

Early years. plegate, London. Socially, his position differed from that of his greatest contemporaries in literature. By inheritance and conviction he was a Dissenter in religion; by occupation he belonged to the trading, or merchant class. His father, James Foe, was a butcher, and appears to have been well-to-do and respected; but we must remember that England had not yet learned the hard lesson of religious toleration, and that Defoe belonged by birth to a persecuted minority. The controversy waged over questions of religion was one of the disturbing political issues of the time; and, in Defoe's childhood, while Roman Catholics were feared and hated, Dissenters, who refused to conform to the services of the Church of England, were oppressed and despised. Defoe, born a member of this dissenting middle-class in such an age, was by that very fact forced into a life of struggle and controversy if he remained true to his standard. James Foe wished his son to enter the ministry, but the boy's tastes lay in other directions. When he was about eighteen, he left school, and, after some years of preparation, set up for himself in the hosiery business. We need not attempt to follow his changing fortunes during these early years. He took a keen interest in politics and in social and public questions, and held decided views; he is supposed to have taken part in the rebellion of the unfortunate Duke of Monmouth; and he became known as an effective pamphleteer. He cannot be called a poet, in any strict, or high sense; but he showed himself master of verse of a certain order, plain, vigorous, sensible, and convincing. On the accession of William and Mary (1689), he became a

strenuous supporter of the government. A few years later
he failed in business, perhaps because his energies had been
so largely given to literary and political pursuits; and after
a time he became connected with a brick and tile manufac-
tory at Tilbury, a little town on the Thames below London.
This has been called "the most prosperous and honourable
period of his life." He was honestly in accord with the
Government, and an enthusiastic admirer of the King, to
whom he had become personally known. He did the King
good service by a pamphlet in defence of a standing
army (1697), and by some vigorous verses, *The
True-born Englishman*, which greatly increased
his reputation.[1] The occasion of this vigorous
production was the growing unpopularity of the King, and
the violent attacks which had been made upon him and
his Dutch followers because of their foreign birth. Defoe
confronted the storm of popular feeling with a splendid
audacity, and belaboured the whole English nation with
no light hand. He pointed out that those who proudly
claimed superiority on the ground that they were "true-
born" Englishmen were themselves of mixed descent.
There was no "true-born" Englishman, for the whole
English nation, as then constituted, was the result of a
mixture of various foreign elements.

> "For Englishmen to boast of generation
> Cancels their knowledge and lampoons the nation;
> A true-born Englishman's a contradiction,
> In speech an irony, in fact a fiction."

Defoe's brief interval of prosperity was suddenly brought
to an end by the King's death in 1702. Under the new
sovereign, the High-Church party was uppermost; there
was much violent talk against the Dissenters, and their

---

[1] According to Defoe's estimate, eighty thousand copies of this
poem were sold in the streets.

position in the state became one of the questions of the hour. Defoe's contribution to the matter was an anony-

The Shortest mous pamphlet, *The Shortest Way with Dissen-*
Way with *ters* (1702), in which, instead of arguing against
Dissenters. intolerance, he affected to take the side of his opponents, and tried, by stating their position in the extremest and most brutal fashion, to arouse a feeling against them. The result was almost farcical, for Defoe had assumed the tone of the extremists so cleverly that both sides took the tract literally. The Dissenters were furious, and some Churchmen delighted; but, when the real nature of the pamphlet became apparent, both sides, angry at being deceived, turned on Defoe. He had pleased nobody, and, as he says, the whole "world flew at him like a dog with a broom at his tail." He was condemned by the authorities to stand in the pillory at Temple Bar, and imprisoned for nearly two years in Newgate. But misfortune and imprisonment were powerless to tame his indomitable spirit or check his restless energy. He kept up the fight within the walls of his prison, writing controversial pamphlets, and starting a new periodical, his famous *Review.* If

Defoe's we needed any proof of that vigour, courage,
Review. and versatility for which Defoe is distinguished, any demonstration of his almost unequalled readiness and fluency as a writer, we could find it in the pages of this periodical alone. In his *Review,* Defoe aimed to set forth and discuss the current news not of England only but of a great part of Europe. To compare the *Review* with a modern newspaper would be plainly unfair. When we reflect that Defoe not only wrote his paper himself, but prepared it without those aids and appliances which modern journalism finds indispensable, we must pronounce it a most extraordinary performance. For over nine years (February, 1704, to June, 1713) Defoe actually carried on this vast undertaking single-handed; and, enormous as was the

labour it involved, the *Review* was but an incident in his life of incessant literary production.[1]

After Defoe was released from prison in 1704, his course became less open and straightforward. He was employed **Secret agent for the government.** on sundry secret missions by the government, sometimes, he tells us, "running as much risk as a grenadier on a counterscarp." The dependence of the author upon the politician, which has been already referred to, had its temptations and its drawbacks as well as its advantages. It was a time of political uncertainty and of rapid change. Now the Whigs were in power, now the Tories; and the struggling author whose very livelihood was largely dependent upon the favour of the party in power had strong, if selfish, reasons for transferring his services to the winning side. Defoe had shown that he could be bold in the defence of an unpopular cause; but he was a master of the art of deception, and his character seems to have been a singular mixture of courage and duplicity. When the Whigs were in control, he served the Whigs, and when the Tories took their place, the Tories; and in doing this he stooped in one instance to a deception which it is certainly hard to defend. Yet it would be a great mistake to think of him as habitually willing to sacrifice his principles to his personal advantage; nothing could be farther from the truth. Addison called him a "false, shuffling, prevaricating rascal;" but, under all his tricks and disguises, there was a basis of conscience and of stubborn integrity. His position was often equivocal, his actions ambiguous; but on the whole he worked consistently for the promotion of civil and religious liberty, the cause in which he believed; he changed his party, but he remained

---

[1] "This [the *Review*] was his largest, if not his most important, work, embracing in over five thousand pages essays on almost every branch of human knowledge; during the same nine years he published eighty distinct works, with 4,727 pages." Chambers's *Cyclopedia of English Literature* (new edition), vol. ii. p. 150.

essentially loyal to his principles; and, while he did not scruple to employ falsehood, he used it in the service of what he honestly believed to be the truth. One can sail under false colours in order to deceive the enemy without being a traitor to one's country, and it is probable that Defoe looked upon double dealing as a legitimate part of the game of politics.

Such was the general character of the first sixty years of Defoe's life, years of change, struggle, and almost incredible toil. Up to this time he had made no great and permanent contribution to his country's literature. He had written much, and he had profoundly influenced the men of his own time; but a great part of his writings had been devoted to questions of the hour, and intended only to serve some present need. All his toil seemed to have brought him but little. Many regarded him with suspicion or contempt; he was a hanger-on of politicians, excluded from the select coterie of the great writers, and a mark for the shafts of Addison and Swift; yet, at sixty, this journalist and political agent of questionable character published *Robinson Crusoe* (1719), a story which promises to delight the world so long as the spirit of manly adventure and the love of the marvellous survive in the heart of man. It may seem strange to us that such a man should be able to turn aside at sixty from the tangles and turmoils of political disputes, and, by sheer force of imagination, to put himself in the place of a poor sailor, cast away on a solitary island in the Caribbean Sea; but, in reality, some of Defoe's past work had, all unknown to him, been a preparation for his great task. Even in his *Shortest Way with Dissenters*, he had shown his ability to assume, for the time, another man's point of view; and in his work as a purveyor of news he had cultivated that power which he naturally possessed in so large a measure, — the power of making fiction look like truth. He had the in-

Robinson Crusoe.

stinct of the journalist rather than the spirit of the old-time scholar; the quick perception of what was likely to interest and amuse his readers, and an adroitness which enabled him to turn any passing sensation to good account. He was expert in making a "good story," as a modern newspaper reporter would call it, out of an especially destructive storm, an earthquake, or the dying confession of a famous criminal; and in these stories truth and invention were sometimes so cunningly mingled that they became inseparable. Now, *Robinson Crusoe* is but a reporter's "story" in a more expanded and a more purely imaginative form. It has a basis of fact, for it was founded on the adventures of Alexander Selkirk, an English sailor, who, in 1704, was abandoned by his companions on the island of Juan Fernandez. After about four years of solitary exile, Selkirk was rescued, and on his return to England became an object of public interest. Steele wrote of his singular adventures in *The Englishman*; and Defoe — who is said to have visited him at Bristol — found in them the suggestion for a narrative which has made the imaginary Crusoe seem real and substantial, while Selkirk, the actual man, is but little more than a name. But while we can in part explain how it came to be written, the production of such a book as *Robinson Crusoe* remains one of the marvels of literature. Out of the fret and partisanship of an artificial time, when Pope and the rest are treating of the fashions and follies of the town, there comes suddenly the story of a far-away world; the story of a man in an almost primitive relation to nature, shut away from kings, or party squabbles, or political institutions, and set face to face with the first vital problem of the race, the problem of wresting food and clothing and shelter from the earth and the sea by the ingenuity of his mind and the labour of his hands. The success of *Robinson Crusoe* diverted Defoe's energies into a new channel, and he wrote a number

of other stories which make his later years the most brilliant
literary period of his life.   Among these "secondary novels," as Lamb called them, *The Memories of a*
Secondary novels. *Cavalier, The Life of Captain Singleton, Moll
Flanders,* and *The History of Colonel Jack,* are
perhaps the best known.   As a whole, none of these stories
is equal to their great forerunner; yet they are full of
marvellous bits of descriptive writing, and contain single
scenes of great dramatic and narrative power.   With
Robinson Crusoe, these stories laid the foundations of
English realistic fiction.

Among these works of Defoe's last years, *The Journal of
the Plague Year* (1722) holds a place by itself.   It is probably the most wonderful example of Defoe's
The Journal of the Plague Year. power of mingling fact and invention, and of
imparting to the whole the appearance of
simple truth.   It is a minute, and apparently exact and careful account of the Great Plague which desolated London in
1665; and it professes to be the Journal of an eye-witness,
a saddler, who remained in the city during the pestilence.
It is not a story as we commonly understand the word, for
it can hardly be said to have a plot; it is, to all appearance,
but the simple, ghastly record of death, and terror, and
sorrow, set down by an ordinary citizen who has lived
through the experiences he describes.   There is no display
of emotion; nothing but hard, awful fact.   We do not think
of it as a work of art; it is nature, our daily commonplace
life in its hours of tragic crisis, in those unexpected dramatic situations which seem beyond the fancies of the
romancer.   We hardly realise at first that Defoe's imagination has created this, and that to produce such a perfect
illusion demands the finest and most finished art.   Defoe
lacked many qualities which other great masters of fiction
possessed; but, when he is within his own province, as in

this *Journal of the Plague*, he has been seldom approached and perhaps never surpassed.

When he published *Robinson Crusoe*, Defoe was in easy circumstances; but towards the close of his life he became again involved in difficulties, and even his strong

Closing years.

and brave spirit was at last shaken by repeated misfortunes. Beset by poverty and troubles, he writes the year before his death: "I am so near my journey's end, and am hastening to the place where the weary are at rest; be it that the passage is rough and the day stormy, by what way soever He please to bring me to the end of it, I desire to finish life with this temper of soul in all cases — *Te Deum Laudamus*." His magnificent vitality which had brought him through so much now at last broke, and he "died of a lethargy" in a London lodging-house in 1731. He was buried in a famous Non-conformist cemetery in Bunhill Fields, London; here John Bunyan and Isaac Watts lie also, and his grave is now marked by a monument erected to the author of *Robinson Crusoe* by the children of many lands.

JONATHAN SWIFT.

(1667–1745.)

"To Dr. Jonathan Swift, the most agreeable companion, the truest friend, and the greatest genius of his age."
— Addison's dedication of his *Travels in Italy*.

"Swift was a wild beast who worried and baited all mankind almost, because his intolerable arrogance, vanity, pride, and ambition were disappointed." — Horace Walpole.

"By far the greatest man of that time, I think, was Jonathan Swift. . . . He saw himself in a world of confusion and falsehood; no eyes were clearer to see it than his." —Thomas Carlyle.

"A cynic and a misanthrope in principle, his philosophy of life is ignoble, base, and false, and his impious mockery extends even to the Deity." — John Churton Collins.

"When a shallow optimism is the most living creed, a man of strong nature becomes a scornful pessimist." — Sir Leslie Stephen.

Jonathan Swift, the greatest of English prose-satirists, is the most powerful, most inscrutable, and most tragic figure in the literary history of his century. Born in Dublin in 1667, Swift, like Steele and Goldsmith, was of English descent. But the morose and vindictive spirit in which he faced the world presents a sharp contrast to the loving-kindness and good-humour which helped Steele and Goldsmith to travel a rough road with uncomplaining lips and light hearts. Swift's lot was not, in itself, an exceptionally hard one; indeed, in many ways it was more than usually fortunate; by far the greater part of his troubles were due not to his circumstances but to himself, to his angry resentment when things did not go to his mind, and to a selfish, grasping and imperious temper, which exacted a subservient

Character and early years.

homage to his great powers. He chafed at poverty; he rebelled against college discipline and neglected his studies; his dependence on what he considered the grudging charity of his uncle galled him, and he hated his benefactor. Forced to take refuge in England by the Irish disturbances which succeeded the Revolution of 1688, he became secretary to his mother's kinsman Sir William Temple, a retired statesman of literary tastes. Most men in Swift's circumstances would have considered this position a stroke of good fortune, as Temple showed an interest in his young kinsman's career by acts of substantial kindness. But Swift saw a slight in every careless word. His mind was fixed upon what was due to him, rather than on what he owed to others, and (as he said defiantly in later life) he would not "be treated as a schoolboy." A speck which a healthy man would not notice will inflame a raw wound. A man of Swift's unhappy nature, placed in a position of dependence, sees occasions for offence in trifles, and broods bitterly over imaginary wrongs. Swift had, indeed, a most base and contemptible kind of pride. Smarting under a sense of obligation, he did not reject a kindness, but, to soothe his pride, he accepted it with ingratitude. He availed himself of Temple's good offices and repaid them with petulance and suspicion.

Young, brilliant, ambitious, and inordinately fond of power, Swift's natural bent was towards a political career; but circumstances, if not inclination, led **Enters the Church.** him to turn to the Church, and he was ordained in 1694. The Church was one of the great avenues to advancement, but Swift's choice of a profession seems to have been a miserable error. It is true that he performed his clerical duties with scrupulous fidelity; he held frequent services; he identified himself with the Church of England as a political institution, fought for her privileges, and believed in her as a promoter of sound morals. He gave freely out of his little to the poor, and did many an unostentatious act of kindness; but his nature was earthly and essentially unspiritual, his ruling passion was for worldly power, and as he grew older he came more and more to hate and despise his fellow-men.

Swift was nearly thirty before he showed the world the strength that was in him. During his stay at Sir William Temple's, he had tried his hand at poetry and failed miserably; his success was to be won in other fields. He had written and burned much when, between 1696 and 1698, he wrote two prose works which suddenly revealed to the full the vigour, the ingenuity, the ease, and the robustness of the great satirist. These works, which were not published until 1704, were *The Tale of a Tub* and *The Battle of the Books*. In old times a rambling or fictitious story was sometimes called "a tale of a tub." Swift adopts this old expression for his title, explaining that as seamen sometimes throw an empty tub to a whale to divert his attack from the ship, so he throws out this idle story — this "tale of a tub" — to divert the attention of the wits, or sceptics, from their attack upon the ship of state. The book is a satire upon the corruptions and abuses which have crept into Christianity, and upon the differences and disputes which divide Christendom. Its avowed purpose was to show the superiority of the Church of England, but we feel that the satire has a wider application. These petty religious squabbles (so Swift seems to imply) are but one of the manifestations of the pettiness and inherent depravity of man. At the heart of the book is the truly awful belief that the very springs of life are tainted at their source, that even those feelings which we are accustomed to regard as the glory of man are rooted in selfishness and corruption. It is better not to know the truth, Swift declares with bitter irony; the only happiness is in being deceived, so shall you be "a fool among knaves." Shakespeare, with his deeper and wider vision, could write that there was "a soul of goodness in things evil." Swift in his malevolence would reverse this saying, and thus take away our hope and our reverence and destroy for us the worth and dignity of human life. *The Tale of a Tub* is a great satire, one of the greatest utterances of an unspiritual and unbelieving time; it has marvellous wit, force, and ingenuity; but with all its extraordinary merits, it is the work of a great intellect rather than of a good man.

In *The Battle of the Books*, Swift took his share in a current controversy on the comparative merits of the literature of the classic and modern times. It tells of a contest between the ancient and the modern books in the King's Library, and is a clever burlesque in prose of the Homeric or epic style. *The Battle of the Books* sneers at the shams of pedantry; *The Tale of a Tub* at shams in religion; Pope's *Rape of the Lock* at the shams of fashion.

The Battle of the Books.

Shortly after the death of Sir William Temple in 1699, Swift was given a parish at Laracor,[1] a small village about twenty miles from Dublin. His income was small, his congregation often but "half a score," his church "dilapidated," and his parsonage miserably out of repair. It was indeed a dreary and contracted sphere for an ambitious man of genius; and Swift was not content to settle down at thirty into the humble routine of an obscure country parish. He came often to London, and joined in the political and literary life of the capital. Taken into favour by the Tory leaders, Harley and Bolingbroke, who came into power in 1710, he gained a consideration and influence which show both his ability and

Laracor.

[1] Two other small livings were associated with Laracor, yielding him in all about two hundred pounds a year,

his imperious power over men. Dr. Johnson said of him that "he predominated over his companions with very high ascendency, and probably would bear none over whom he could not predominate." [1] His very looks struck terror; he loved to intimidate weakness and show his power even over the great. "I used them like dogs," he writes, "because I expect they will use me so." [2]

But these years of his triumphs, when he carried his head high among the highest, are also the years in which

Journal to Stella.

the gentler and more playful side of his complex nature is revealed in his *Journal to Stella*. This is made up of letters in the form of a journal, written to his former pupil Hester Johnson, whom he had met as a child in the household of Sir William Temple. He called her "Stella," the "star" of his darkness. Scribbled hastily, with no thought beyond the desire to give pleasure to "Stella" and the little group of friends in Ireland, these letters move us, as no other writings of Swift do, to tenderness, awe, and pity. They warn us that even Swift had "two soul-sides," [3] and remind us that when we cannot understand we should be cautious how we judge.

In 1713 Swift was rewarded by the deanery of St. Patrick's, Dublin; but, in the year following, the downfall of the Tory Government was followed by the

Political reverses.

deaths of Harley and the Queen. Swift's political fortunes went down in the general wreck; nothing remained to him but what seemed a life of weary exile in his deanery, and the bitterness of disappointment and disgust. "What a world is this," Bolingbroke wrote to him after the crash came, "and how does fortune banter us!"

The effect of this sudden plunge into comparative obscurity, from a place of power in the political and

---

[1] Johnson's *Lives of the Poets*, "Swift."
[2] Letter to Stella.   [3] V. Browning's "One Word More."

literary circles of the capital, can be readily understood.
Swift wrote with morbid sadness that there his life was
"no soul's concern," and that those about him would follow his hearse "without a tear." [1] "The best and greatest
part of my life," he declared, "I spent in England; there
I made my friendships and there I left my desires." [2] It
was during those years of loneliness, bitter with brooding
over disappointed hopes, that Swift wrote *Gulliver's
Travels* (published 1726). Swift says in one of
his letters that its chief purpose was to show his
hatred of that detestable animal, man; certainly
he poured into it that *sæva indignatio*, that fierce wrath at
life and his brother-men, which had tormented him in his
hours of darkness. Aside from its deeper purpose, *Gulliver's
Travels* is first of all a fascinating story; wonderful in the
originality and ingenuity of its conceptions, and in the
surprising naturalness which the skill of a great artist has
given to the whole. The most pitiless of satires, it is also,
with some omissions, "the most delightful children's book
ever written." Unbelievable as it is, we are almost
persuaded that it must be true. Simply as a story, it
marks another great advance in the progress of eighteenth-
century fiction; and we feel that these strange adventures
of Lemuel Gulliver, ship's surgeon, have that air of careful
veracity which places them with the adventures of Robinson Crusoe, mariner of York. But while, in Defoe's
romance, we hear the warnings of the preacher, the practical morality of the middle-class Englishman of the day,
in Swift's we hear the fallen politician railing at the
pettiness of statecraft and at all the vaunted glory of man.
"From what you tell me of your country," says the
gigantic King of Brobdingnag to Gulliver, "I cannot but

Gulliver's Travels.

[1] Verses "In Sickness" (1714), Sheridan's ed. of Swift, vol. vii.
p. 142.
[2] Swift's *Letters and Journals*, edited by Stanley Lane Poole, p. 191.

conclude the bulk of your natives to be the most pernicious race of little odious vermin, that nature ever suffered to crawl upon the surface of the earth." [1] This is the motive passion of the book. It is not merely a satire on the passing phases of English politics, or particular systems, or persons; beyond all this it is a satire on our race, on "that hated and detestable animal called man." As the book advances, this rage against mankind grows more rabid and more malignant. Man's knowledge is foolishness; his reason, which to Shakespeare seemed the attribute of a god, is held up to contempt; his instincts are proclaimed brutish and vile. We find here the hopeless, faithless doctrine of *The Tale of a Tub* reiterated and reaffirmed after thirty years.

Swift's life went down in loneliness and darkness. Esther Vanhomrigh, whose love he had slighted, died; Hester Johnson, who had called out the best he had to give of love and tenderness, died also, and one of the strangest and most tragic of the world's love stories was at an end. Once he had written vindictively that he was doomed to die in obscurity "like a poisoned rat in a hole;" now his life drifted on helplessly toward a pitiable and awful close. In loneliness, in failing health, and in what inward and unspeakable anguish we can only conjecture, the shadows of insanity closed in on Swift's clear and splendid intellect; and he sank into a mindless apathy from which he seldom roused. He died in 1745. "An immense genius," writes Thackeray; "an awful downfall and ruin. So great a man he seems to me, that thinking of him is like thinking of an empire falling." [2]

Insanity and death.

Some may ask why this man, the clearest intellect of his age, saw all the world awry. Why could he find no gleams

---

[1] *Gulliver's Travels:* "A Voyage to Brobdingnag," chap. vi.
[2] *English Humourists,* "Swift."

of Divinity in man? Why did he put darkness for light,
and pass over that which was beautiful and
noble, and fasten on the repulsive and the vile?
No one can fully answer such questions, but
they are answered in part by the state of England in
Swift's time. There was actually much in the world, as
Swift knew it, to make a man of earnest and melancholy
nature despair of his kind, much to provoke cynicism and
contempt. Vice indeed was less open and defiant than it
had been a generation or two earlier, and an awakening
sense of decency and order was beginning to make itself
felt; but the wild license of the Restoration had left behind
it a cynical disbelief in virtue. A mocking spirit, the
spirit of denial, infected the moral atmosphere. Men had
sneered at enthusiasm; they had worshipped the reason
and the intellect, and slighted and despised those feelings
which are the true glory of man. They had obscured their
higher nature, and they were then tempted to complain
that there was no higher nature in man. The sins of the
fathers were indeed visited on the men of Swift's generation. Pope had his word of contempt for man; the easy-
going Gay says lightly that "life is a jest;" [1] but to the
man of deeper and stronger nature life was both a farce and
a tragedy. Yet Swift, while he denounced his time,
failed to rise above it. His ambition appears to have
been as earthly, as material, and as selfish, as that of the
men he satirises. He railed at the fools who contended
for the world's trumpery prizes; but few pursued those
prizes more eagerly, few were more bitterly disappointed
than Swift when they slipped from his grasp. There is no
reason to doubt his sincerity when he says of himself:
"All my endeavours from a boy to distinguish myself were

Swift and his time.

---

[1] "Life is a jest, and all things show it;
I thought so once, but now I know it."
— GAY: *My Own Epitaph.*

only for want of a great title and fortune, *that I might be used like a lord.*" Swift then is himself an actor in the farce he satirises; he not only hates his time, but he belongs to it through his life as well as his works. He shares in its vulgarity of aim, he is the strongest expression of its misanthropy and its materialism, and he is the truly awful example of its errors. "We live," said the poet who did so much to restore this lost delight in man and Nature, "we live by admiration, hope, and love." [1] Swift, carrying out to the uttermost the tendency of his age, is a man who tried to live by contempt, by hate, and by despair, and the soul of man cannot live by these things.

OTHER PROSE-WRITERS OF THE EARLY EIGHTEENTH CENTURY.

Among the features of the early eighteenth-century literature, we have mentioned the rise of a clear and effective prose-style, and an extension of the influence of prose as a literary form. We have studied this prose-literature through some of its great masters, —Steele, Addison, Swift, Defoe, —but in order to form any true idea of its variety and importance, we must realise that these representative writers lived and worked among a host of others, philosophers, scientists, essayists, theologians, pamphleteers. Nor is this great host a mere crowd of obscure or "minor" authors; it includes some of the most learned, conspicuous, and brilliant men of the time. We must content ourselves with the merest mention of some of these men; but we must remember that the searching and restless intellect of this age, showed itself in the number of writers and in the sheer amount and range of their productions; and that much must be omitted in our brief enumeration of a few great names. Some of these men

Abundance of prose-literature.

[1] Wordsworth: *The Excursion*, Bk. iv.

indeed, won distinction outside of the strict limits of literature; they were great scholars, or great philosophers rather than simply men of letters; a few are more remarkable for the intellectual stimulus they exerted on the men about them than for the permanent value of their own work, but each helped in his own fashion, to determine the tone and character of his time. Thus DR. JOHN ARBUTHNOT (1667–1735) is now remembered rather

Dr. John Arbuthnot.

for his high character, his friendship, and his personal influence upon some of the greatest writers of his generation than for his own contributions to literature. He was a Scotch physician who settled in London towards the close of the seventeenth century and devoted himself to science, literature, and the practice of his profession. He became physician to Prince George of Denmark, and in 1705 was made physician extraordinary to the Queen. He was on intimate terms with Pope, Swift, and other great writers; and, if we trust the opinion of his friends, was one of the kindest and most lovable as well as one of the ablest of men. Pope wrote of him with gratitude and affection, and addressed one of the best and most famous of his *Epistles* to him. Swift said of him: " He has more wit than we all have, and his humanity is equal to his wit." " If the world," he wrote to Pope, " had but a dozen Arbuthnots in it, I would burn my *Travels.*" Dr. Johnson pronounced him " the first man " among the great writers of his age. " He was the most universal genius, being an excellent physician, a man of deep learning, and a man of much humour." Dr. Arbuthnot was singularly indifferent to his own literary reputation, but in the face of such testimony we cannot doubt that his mere personality was a literary force. He wrote several learned and scientific works; but in literature he is remembered chiefly by two works of satiric humour, somewhat in the manner of Swift — the *Memoirs of Martin Scriblerus,* a travesty on pedantic learning; and *The His-*

tory of John Bull (1712), a satire directed against the Duke of Marlborough and the continuance of the war with France.

Although his works are now but seldom read, HENRY ST. JOHN, LORD BOLINGBROKE (1678–1751), was one of the most brilliant and conspicuous figures in the literary, political, and social life of his age. At first sight he seems destined for distinction, endowed with all the gifts which lead men to greatness and power. He came of an old and noble family; his means were ample; he had extraordinary personal beauty, great charm and elegance of manner; and he was one of the best talkers in London at a time when London was full of clever men. He had an almost unfailing memory, stored with the wisdom of the classic writers; a clear, vigorous intellect, quick and active, if not solid and profound. When not occupied with politics or the pursuit of pleasure, he amused himself with literature and philosophy; and his prose — unconstrained, spirited, and effective — has given him no mean place among the masters of English style. Besides all these advantages, he was possessed of extraordinary eloquence; and his splendid presence, his mastery of language, his charm of voice and manner, made him, by common consent, the greatest orator of his day.

With all these varied talents, Bolingbroke longed for distinction, — distinction not in one direction but in all. He was distinguished among a corrupt, dissipated aristocracy by the wildness of his excesses; distinguished among statesmen by the splendour of his abilities; distinguished among authors and philosophers by his liberal patronage and by his cultivated tastes. He is a great figure in literary as well as in political history, and we probably think of him more often as the friend of Pope than as the antagonist of Sir Robert Walpole. He was the honoured companion of the greatest wits. Swift was his political ally, and employed his unrivalled powers of satire and abuse in Bolingbroke's cause. If you would know how Pope admired him, read over again those famous lines at the close of the *Essay on Man*, in which the poet calls Bolingbroke his "guide, philosopher, and friend," and addresses him as the "master" and inspirer alike of the poet and the song.[1]

The dramatic story of Bolingbroke's career must be read elsewhere. Almost at the height of success, and while he was still a young man, he lost almost at one

Fall of Bolingbroke. stroke all that he had played for; and the most brilliant statesman of England was an exile and a fugitive. For thirty-six years he had been a spoiled child of fortune, fed with pleasures and power; he was to live on for thirty-seven years more, cut off from the triumphs in which he had delighted, an envious, discontented man, left to console himself with philosophy as best he could. Debarred from other avenues to distinction, he turned to authorship, the only road left open. Swift, whose political fortunes were wrecked with those of his leader, sneered at the pettiness and folly of human ambitions; Bolingbroke (whether to console himself, or to deceive others) affected a lofty superiority to ill-fortune. The disappointed place-hunter snarling at the fools who sought for preferment, the disappointed politician in France, declaiming on the advantages of seclusion and contemplation, what a theme was this for Swift's bitter mockery, if the great satirist could only have viewed it with an impartial mind. In

Reflections upon exile. his *Reflections upon Exile* (1710), Bolingbroke pictures himself as the philosopher, serene in the midst of adversity, and able to meditate upon its uses to the wise and virtuous. "Far from the hurry of the world, and an almost unconcerned spectator of what passes in it, having paid in a public life what you owed to the present age, pay in a private life what you owe to posterity. Write

---

[1] Bolingbroke furnished Pope with much of the philosophy of the *Essay on Man*, and Pope dedicated the work to him.

as you live, without passion; and build your reputation, as you build your happiness, on the foundations of truth."

This is a dignified and lofty resolve, nobly uttered; but unhappily, when we compare it with the facts, it only suggests to us the fatal flaw in Bolingbroke's life and works. With all his showy talents, his character had no adequate "foundations of truth." He was the child of his age; resplendent in surface adornments, but wanting in a substantial basis of sound morals and honest conviction. Under these fine phrases there is this taint of insincerity, characteristic of the man. "Few people," said Lord Hervey, "ever believed him without being deceived, or trusted him without being betrayed." Discredited as a statesman by the men of his own generation, and neglected as an author by posterity, his great reputation has suffered because it rests so largely on a foundation of pretence; for one of the virtues which give permanence to literature is truth.

Bolingbroke's *Letters to Sir William Wyndham* (1717), a defence of his political career, is usually regarded as his
Other works. masterpiece in point of style. Among his other works, the *Idea of a Patriot King* (1749) and the *Letters on the Study of History* (1752), are probably the best known. The best works of Bolingbroke, at least, should be studied, if only for their style; for he excels his contemporaries in courtly dignity and elevation, and at times in eloquence. It is the style of the orator, very different from the strong simplicity of Swift and Defoe, or from the grace and almost conversational ease of Addison; and in this Bolingbroke may be regarded as the forerunner of Burke and of Gibbon.[1]

Every one agrees that Bolingbroke represented his age,

[1] On this point consult *Bolingbroke*, by J. C. Collins, p. 14. Mr. Collins's position, however, seems to me somewhat extreme; for he claims that English prose "owes more to Bolingbroke than to any other single writer."

that many traits and tendencies then characteristic of English life and thought were united in his character and apparent in his career. But we must remember that when we speak of the character or "spirit of an age" in general terms, classifying it as religious or sceptical, practical or romantic, we are simply attempting to indicate its most ordinary and apparent traits. All the men of an age are not made after the same pattern; there are always many exceptions to the "spirit of the age," — base men in noble times and high-minded dreamers in the midst of the most practical and sordid societies. Such a pure and lofty spirit was GEORGE BERKELEY (1685–1753), one of the subtlest thinkers and noblest men that England has produced. Against the dark background of the time, his character shines with a clear, unwavering radiance. He remains devout among sceptics; reverent among scoffers; unworldly and unselfish, when every man seems bent upon snatching the prizes of life from his neighbour. As a thinker he squarely opposed the "spirit of the age." In the midst of a coarse materialism, when men held fast to "common sense" and distrusted anything which seemed spiritual or ideal, Berkeley put forth his philosophy of *idealism*, according to which we can only know that which we call *matter* or *substance*, as an *idea in the mind*. The true reality, therefore, was not matter, but thought or spirit. This theory seemed very visionary and absurd to the men of that substantial generation, and Dr. Arbuthnot and many others had their jokes at the philosopher's expense. But they were good-natured jokes; for Berkeley's unaffected goodness, his genuine learning and enthusiasm, made him a favourite even among the scoffers. Born in Ireland, when Berkeley came to London in 1713, after a long residence at Trinity College, Dublin, he was welcomed by the leading men of letters. Swift, his fellow-countryman, showed him much

Bishop Berkeley.

kindness; Pope declared that he was possessed of "every virtue under heaven;" and Francis Atterbury, the well-known bishop and writer, said of him: "So much learning, so much knowledge, so much innocence and humility, I did not think had been the portion of any but angels, till I saw this gentleman." Berkeley's writings are chiefly devoted to the exposition of his philosophical system. His philosophic dialogues (*Hylas and Philonous*, and *Alciphron*) follow the manner of Plato or of Cicero, and have, in addition to their other merits, a decided literary charm. But most of us associate the name of Berkeley chiefly with those verses in which, almost despairing of England, — lost (as she seemed to him) to all that had made her glorious in the past, — he looked forward to a better age in the new world of the West.

> "The Muse, disgusted at an age and clime
>   Barren of every glorious theme,
>   In distant lands now waits a better time,
>   Producing subjects worthy fame.
>
> .   .   .   .
>
> In happy climes, the seat of innocence,
>   Where nature guides and virtue rules,
>   Where men shall not impose for truth and sense
>   The pedantry of courts and schools, —
>   There shall be sung another Golden Age,
>   The rise of Empire and of Arts,
>   The Good and Great inspiring epic rage,
>   The wisest heads and noblest hearts.
>
> .   .   .   .
>
> Westward the course of Empire takes its way;
>   The first four acts already past,
>   A fifth shall close the drama with the day: —
>   Time's noblest offspring is the last."

But low as England had sunk, her state was not so hopeless as Berkeley feared. His very discontent was itself a good omen; even when he wrote, a subtle spirit of change was in the air, and before he died that great spiritual transformation which may be called the redemption of England had definitely begun.

Richardson and Fielding.

While in the hands of Defoe and Swift the novel had come to share in the realistic spirit of the time, it still remained distinctly the novel of adventure; its interest resting mainly, although not entirely, upon the presentation of the more stirring and exceptional side of life. Both Defoe and Swift employed the autobiographical form, and in Defoe's work the supposed narrator was often beyond the pale of respectable society.

Between 1740 and 1750, a new form of fiction came into existence, connected with, and yet distinct from, all

The novel of domestic life. that had gone before; this was the story of ordinary domestic life and manners. To the dramatist, indeed, this world of every day was not unknown, but in appropriating it to his use the novelist was virtually gaining a new world for his art. Like most great discoveries, the thing seems obvious enough when once it has been done; yet Defoe had thought it necessary to drag his readers into obscure and unsavoury places, or to transport them to the ends of the earth, overlooking the artistic possibilities of a world which lay at his feet. In a century and a half this new form of fiction has grown to astonishing proportions, until it is possibly the largest, if not the most important, element in our mental life. The cause of its great and continued popularity is both obvious and fundamental. The vast majority of us are interested first in ourselves, and second in our next-door neighbours. The domestic novel shows us our own familiar life, the life of average, every-day humanity, but invested with an added interest and dignity by its translation into art.

> "For, don't you mark we're made so that we love
> First when we see them painted, things we have passed
> Perhaps a hundred times nor cared to see." [1]

[1] Browning's *Fra Lippo Lippi*.

To see this world of our daily life in the pages of fiction, is to see ourselves and our neighbours; to find our gossip and our daily newspapers given a depth and meaning which we are too shallow and too conventional to perceive. The group of writers who first claimed this world for English fiction make an era in the history of art.

In 1740 SAMUEL RICHARDSON (1689–1761), a London printer, short, plump, ruddy, and prosperous, began this new era by the publication of *Pamela, or Virtue Rewarded*, the story of a "virtuous serving maid." Richardson seems a strange leader for a new movement. Up to this time he had done nothing in literature, and the fact that this shy, demure, and highly estimable printer should, at the age of fifty, suddenly blossom into the novelist of sentiment, into a master in the intricate analysis of human passion, seems even more surprising than Defoe's late incursion into the realm of adventure. The fact is partly explained by Richardson's early and unconscious preparation for his task. In all his novels the story is told in a series of letters. Richardson stumbled into fiction through his marked facility in letter-writing, as Defoe passed into it from journalism by almost imperceptible steps. When only a boy of thirteen, the future author of *Pamela* was intrusted by three young girls of his native town in Derbyshire with the delicate task of composing their love-letters, each confiding in him "unknown to the others;" "all," he tells us, "having a high opinion of my taciturnity." During his apprentice-ship to a London bookseller, he kept up a voluminous correspondence with a gentleman of cultivation who was greatly interested in him. The episode of the love-letters is one of especial significance in its bearing on his later work. Boys of thirteen are not usually distinguished by their warmth of sympathy with sentiment, but we should resist the natural temptation to look only at the ludicrous side of the situation, and see in it a proof of that intimate understanding of women which is one of the distinctive marks of Richardson's work. In Richardson there is a notable absence of that weakness and unreality in the women's characters, so often found in the best work of masculine novelists, which arises from an inability to appreciate the feminine point of view. On the contrary, the character of Clarissa Harlowe, in his greatest work, is admittedly a triumph of portraiture. There was some-- thing in Richardson that invited feminine confidences, and the creator of Clarissa Harlowe gathered around him from boyhood to old age an admiring circle of women. "As a bashful and not a forward boy," he writes, "I was an early favourite with all the young women of taste and reading in the neighbourhood; " and long after he was described by Dr. Johnson as one who "took care to be always surrounded by women, who listened to him im- plicitly and did not venture to contradict his opinions."

Richardson's object in his novels was avowedly a moral one. *Pamela* was the result of a suggestion on the part of some of his friends that he should treat of **Richardson's novels.** the concerns of common life in a series of familiar letters, prepared so as to be of use to "country readers, who were unable to indite for themselves." He announces on the title-page that the work is "Published in order to cultivate the Principles of Virtue and Religion." Richardson's three novels, *Pamela* (1740), *Clarissa Harlowe* (1748), and *Sir Charles Grandison* (1753), deal respectively with life in the humbler, higher, and aristocratic circles. In the first two the central character is that of the heroine; in the last, Richardson, whose chief male characters had before this been despicable and unprincipled, attempts to make amends by manufacturing a fine gentleman, com- posed of all the virtues, and devoid of any redeeming grace of human weakness. An impossible aggregation of the virtues is not a character, and Richardson's hero is one with whom imperfect humanity cannot sympathise. Yet Grandison has come to stand so perfectly for a kind of buckram hero, the apotheosis of stately deportment, tediousness, moral platitudes, and ruffles, that his very name has become a useful part of our vocabulary. Critics agree that one of Richardson's greatest merits as a novelist is his profound knowledge of the human heart, and one of his greatest defects the length and diffuseness of his books. He took infinite pains to produce the effect at which he aimed, elaborating with the artistic carefulness of a Meissonier. Reading page after page, volume after volume, these minute but skilful touches gradually impress us with a cumulative force. Readers of to-day find the eight large volumes of his masterpiece too severe a demand on time and endurance, but the world has recognised his genius and his far-reaching influence on literature.

It was the publication of *Pamela* that turned the genius of HENRY FIELDING (1707-1754) to the writing of novels, but the spirit which moved the second great novelist of this epoch was not the admiration of a follower, but the instinctive protest of a born antagonist. With the mild and diminutive Richardson, sentimentalist, water-drinker, and vegetarian, the boisterous, easy-going, masculine Harry Fielding, with his big frame and high spirits, his keen sense of the ludicrous and his healthy hatred of affectation, could have but little in common. Richardson subsisted on weak tea and feminine adulation. Fielding, according to Lady Mary Wortley Montagu, "forgot everything when he was before a venison pasty, or over a flask of champagne." Yet, in spite of his debts, his extravagance, and the dash of the Bohemian in his youth, Fielding was a sound, sterling bit of manhood, of that sturdy, genuine type which we think of as emphatically English. Such a man was quick to detect a strain of false sentiment in *Pamela*, which its author was too serious or too conventional to perceive. So *The Adventures of Joseph Andrews* (1742), a "virtuous serving man," supposed to be a brother of Pamela, was begun as a parody. But as the book grew, Fielding's interest carried him far beyond his primary intention, and the result was a great and original contribution to fiction. Fielding **His literary form.** differed from his predecessor in literary form as well as in spirit. Instead of employing either the autobiographical or the epistolary form, he wrote his novels in the third person; introducing, from time to time, introductory chapters in which he talks with his readers face to face. Fielding's novels were intended to be a kind of comic prose-epic, his purpose being to show the life of the time, especially on its ridiculous side, with the breadth, but not the dignity, of the epic manner. He was aptly called by Byron "the prose-Homer of human nature." Fielding's work is eminently natural; while we miss in him many of the subtler and finer qualities, in his grasp of fact, his manliness and solidity, he is manifestly the fellow-countryman of Chaucer, of Shakespeare, and of Browning. He hated cant and Pharisaism, and his large heart was very tender toward womanhood and goodness. The creator of the simple-hearted Parson Adams, of Amelia, with her woman's power to love and forgive, had under all outward roughness a reverent and genuine nature.

Roderick Random, the earliest work of TOBIAS SMOLLETT (1721–1771), the third novelist of the epoch, appeared in **Tobias George Smollett.** 1748, and *Tom Jones*, generally considered Fielding's masterpiece, in the year following; so that, within ten years from the publication of *Pamela*, the foundations of the new novel were securely laid.

The realistic school of fiction thus begun continued uppermost until well toward the end of the century. But the pressure of a new spirit of romanticism, which gained ground during the latter half of the century, showed itself at intervals, as in the publication of Walpole's *Castle of Otranto*, in 1764. About **1790,** the advent of mediævalism in the romances of Mrs. Radcliffe showed that the wave of the Gothic revival had invaded fiction, and from this time to the coming of Miss Austen, the supremacy of the romance was assured.

PART IV.

THE MODERN ENGLISH PERIOD.

(Since cir. 1725.)

CHAPTER I.

THE BEGINNING OF MODERN LITERATURE.

(Cir. 1725–1830.)

THE history of England during the greater part of the eighteenth century is the history of rapid and comprehensive changes in almost every department of the nation's life — industrial, religious, political, social, and intellectual. As we advance, the England of Pope and Addison, now well-nigh as remote from our daily life as that of Shakespeare or Milton, recedes with wonderful swiftness, and through a rapid succession of changes we pass into the England of to-day. As we near the middle of the century the political corruption, the coldly intellectual temper, the studied repression and brilliant cynicism, melt before the fervour of a rising spirituality, and new generations, actuated by diametrically opposite ideals of life, crowd forward to displace the old. This fresh national life utters itself in new forms of literature, and with the rise of Modern England we reach the beginning of a literary period surpassed only by that of the Elizabethans.

We may relate many of these changes to one great motive cause. We have watched that mood of dissolute levity which immediately succeeded the Restoration pass into an era of comparative decency and frigid "good sense." Then

393

Addison utters his kindly but somewhat superficial strictures on fashionable follies; then Pope is before us, with his little vanities and complaisant optimism; and Swift, savage, morose, and terrible, is intriguing and place-hunting like the rest, but with the bitter inward protest of contempt and scorn of such a world. Now the nation was too inherently emotional and religious for such a mood to long endure; the higher side of men's nature began to reassert itself; and those human hopes and longings which the "freezing reason" cannot satisfy began to stir and claim their due,

> "And like a man in wrath the heart
> Stood up and answer'd, 'I have felt.'"

So in the drought of the desert men felt the gathering rush of new feelings, and as their hearts were again moved with pity, enthusiasm, and faith, they felt within them the great longing of the prodigal to arise and return.

The new enthusiasm and faith are seen in a great wave of religious feeling that is associated with the rise of Methodism. In the midst of the cold intellectual speculations of Bolingbroke, and the scepticism of Hume, we are startled by the passionate appeal of Whitefield and Wesley to the conscience and the heart. By 1738 the work of these men was fairly begun, and their marvellous eloquence and intense conviction struck deep into the souls of thousands. In his *Analogy of Religion, Natural and Revealed, to the Constitution and Voice of Nature* (1736), Bishop Butler relied for his support of Christianity on close and definite reasoning, but the preaching of Whitefield made the tears trickle down the grimy faces of the Bristol colliers. This influence went far outside the ranks of the Methodists themselves. In the early years of the century, the Church of England shared in the prevailing coldness and unspirituality; the filling of its offices was tainted by political intrigue, while its clergy were idle and often shamefully lax in manners and morals. Methodism, starting within the limits of the Church, helped to infuse into it, and into society at large, a new moral and spiritual earnestness.

The effects of this revival of a more spiritual life in the midst of a jovial, unbelieving, and often coarse and brutal society, are seen in the growth of a practical charity, and in an increasing sense of human brotherhood and of the inherent dignity of manhood.

Deeper sympathy with man.

English history contains few things more truly beautiful than the story of this awakening of tenderness and compassion. The novel sense of pity became wide and heartfelt enough to embrace not men only, but all wantonly hurt and suffering creatures. Bull-baiting gradually fell into disfavour, and the cruel sport known as bull-running was finally suppressed at Tutbury in 1778. The poet Thomson commends the labours of the "generous band,"

> "Who, touched with human woe, redressive searched
> Into the horrors of the gloomy jail." [1]

John Howard endured the noisome horrors of the English prisons (1775–1789) that he might lighten the unspeakable sufferings of the captives; and Wilberforce, Clarkson, and Pitt laboured for the abolition of slavery.[2] The criminal was no longer dragged through crowded London streets to be hanged at Tyburn, a holiday spectacle to jeering or admiring throngs; the rigours of the code which condemned wretches to death for a trifling theft were gradually softened. So, in these and countless other ways, the social revulsion against brutality and violence

---

[1] *The Seasons*, "Winter," l. 358. Thomson is speaking of a jail committee of 1729. See this whole passage from l. 332–388, as a good instance of the new humanity in poetry.

[2] Clarkson and Wilberforce began their anti-slavery agitation about 1787, enlisting the aid of Pitt. The Emancipation Bill was passed in 1833.

which marked the rise of a new England unmistakably declared itself.

To some extent we may even associate this fuller power to feel with the rise and astonishing progress of modern **Handel.** music, the art of pure emotion, both in Germany and England. Händel settled in England in 1710. He struggled for years against popular neglect and misunderstanding to win, toward the middle of the century, conspicuous recognition. It is significant to contrast the fashionable audiences that, lost to common decency, had once applauded the immoral wit of Wycherley or Farquhar, with that assembly, swept by a common wave of enthusiasm and worship, which rose with one consent and stood through the singing of the "Hallelujah Chorus." [1]

A comparison of England under Walpole and under Pitt helps us to realise the growth of the power of enthusiasm and imagination. The administration of Robert **Walpole and Pitt.** Walpole (1721–1742) was an interval of profound peace, during which the energies of England were largely given to trade and the development of her internal resources. Through the increase of the Colonial trade, and from other causes, the commercial and business side of life assumed a new importance.[2] The peace left men free to devote their energies to money-making; the merchant gained in social position, and wealth rapidly increased.[3]

Walpole, the guiding spirit of this prosperous period,

[1] The famous chorus of praise in Händel's *Messiah*. The performance referred to was in 1743.

[2] See Green's *History of the English People*, vol. iv. pp. 126–160.

[3] In the *Spectator* Sir Roger de Coverley stands for the landed gentry, and Sir Andrew Freeport, the city merchant, for the rising merchant class; *v. Spectator*, No. cxxvi.; *v.* also Scott's *Rob Roy* for contrast between the Tory squire, who stands by Church and King, and the new commercial magnate; *v.* Gibbin's *Industrial History of England*, p. 145, for reference to Scott's *Rob Roy*, etc.

was the embodiment of its prosaic and mercantile character. Country-bred, shrewd, and narrow-minded, he had great business ability, but was incapable of approaching life from its ideal or imaginative side. Openly corrupt in his political methods, and openly incredulous as to the possibility of conducting practical politics by other means, he laughed at appeals to man's higher nature as "schoolboy flights," and declared that men would come out of their rhapsodies about patriotism, and grow wiser. Such traits are characteristic of the early eighteenth-century England; we rightly associate that low estimate of human nature on which Walpole habitually acted with Pope's sneering contempt and Swift's fierce and appalling misanthropy. But, as we advance toward the middle of the century, those higher impulses which were manifesting themselves in so many different directions were at work in politics also. Before the fall of Walpole loftier and purer political ideals had already begun to take form in the so-called Patriot party, and by 1757 William Pitt, the animating spirit of the new government, was virtually at the head of affairs. A great historian has observed [1] that Pitt did a work for politics similar to that which Wesley was, at the same time, accomplishing for religion. He believed in his countrymen, and England responded to his trust. Instead of debauching public morals by open corruption, he made his passionate appeal to patriotism. The interests of England, seemingly narrowed in Walpole's time to insular limits, expanded before men's eyes, as, about the middle of the century, the nation entered upon that great duel with the rival power of France which was to raise her from an island monarchy to a world empire.

The expansion of England.

Clive's victory at Plassey in 1757 laid the foundation of her supremacy in India. Wolfe's capture of Quebec in

[1] S. R. Gardiner, *Encyclopedia Britannica*, title "England."

1759 established her dominion in America. Two worlds, the rich civilisation of the ancient East, the vast and undeveloped resources of the new West, were almost at the same instant within her grasp. "We are forced," said Horace Walpole, "to ask every morning what victory there is, for fear of missing one."[1] Men's hearts were warm with a glow of patriotic pride and a sense of England's mighty destiny. Meanwhile, exploration as well as foreign war was helping to direct the thoughts and transfer the interests of Englishmen to distant and almost unknown lands. In 1744, Anson, a commander in the Royal Navy, returned to Europe after a perilous and brilliant voyage around the world. His account of the expedition, which appeared in 1748, was extraordinarily popular. In 1770, an even more famous navigator, Captain Cook, explored the east coast of Australia, and took possession of it in the name of Great Britain. Eighteen years later the first permanent English settlement was made on the site of the present city of Sydney, and the British colonial empire was definitely extended to these far-off waters of the Pacific. The story of Cook's various voyages (1773–1777–1784), like the records of the explorers of Elizabeth's time, brought home a new world to the imagination, and as the vigour of the nation found an almost world-wide scope for its activities, Englishmen looked upon the most distant parts of the earth with a sense of possession. This more cosmopolitan spirit, this sense of the wonder and variety of the world's life, finds utterance in the literature. In Coleridge's *Ancient Mariner* the ship penetrates the solitudes about the South Pole, or lies becalmed in the awful loneliness and remoteness of the Southern Ocean. A widening horizon, a more cosmopolitan spirit, finds its way into literature. In Southey's *Curse of Kehama* we enter the world of the East, with

[1] See Green's *History of the English People*, vol. iv. p. 193.

its unknown gods; in Moore's *Lalla Rookh* we journey with a marriage cavalcade through the Vale of Cashmere, surrounded by all the splendours of the Orient; in Byron's *Childe Harold* the scenic background to the sombre figure of the pilgrim is Europe itself, brought before us with a sympathetic breadth and truth unmatched in the history of the literature.

While patriotism and imagination were thus quickened by the great part that England began to play in the world-wide drama of human destiny, at home a silent revolution was transforming the aspect of life and the very structure of society. From the building of the first canal by James Brindley in 1761, new facilities for transportation and new methods of manufacture follow quickly on each other, until the agricultural England of old times becomes the industrial England of the nineteenth century, and the "workshop of the world." Following hard on these changes are those problems of labour and capital which confront our modern world.

And side by side with all these new things are the initial steps in one of the greatest historic movements since the Renaissance, the rise of modern democracy. With the conviction of human brotherhood, with the passionate sense of the worth and dignity of individual manhood, come the blood and violence of those social upheavals which usher in our modern world. Men are possessed with a fever for the "rights of man;" they dream of a wholesale re-organisation of society, and the coming of an idyllic Golden Age; they struggle to convert Rousseau's gospel of a "return to nature" into a practical reality. In America, a Republic is established on the foundations of human freedom and equality; in feudal France, after generations of dumb misery, the people lift their bowed backs from labour to wreak on their rulers the accumulated vengeance of centuries. The finest spirits of England are thrilled and exalted by this flood of enthusiasm for the cause of man, the word "liberty" sounds as a talisman in men's ears, and the spirit of revolution controls and inspires the best productions of the literature.

We have noted the working of new forces in English society in Wesley and Pitt during the earlier half of the eighteenth century, or from about 1740. Modern England, thus beginning to take shape even during the lifetime of Pope and Walpole, had a literature of its own; but the older literary methods and ideas by no means came to an end with the beginning of the new. Accordingly, after the rise of this new literature, or from about 1725, we find the literature of England flowing, as it were, in two separate streams. The one, marked by a mode or fashion of writing which began definitely with Dryden, may be traced from Dryden on through Pope, its most perfect representative, through Samuel Johnson, until its dissipation in the time of Wordsworth; the other, springing from a different source and of a different spirit, its purer and more natural music audible almost before that of Pope has fairly begun, flows on with gathered force and volume, and with deepening channel, almost to our own time. We have traced the first of these streams until the death of Pope; we must now indicate the general direction of its course after that event. Many of the features which had characterised this Restoration literature in the reign of Anne were prolonged far into the century, and some writers modelled their style on Pope and Addison until toward the century's close. The prosaic spirit, in which intellectual force was warmed by no glow of passion, continued to find a suitable form of expression in didactic and satiric verse. In the protracted moralisings of Young's *Night Thoughts* (1742–1745), and in Blair's *Grave* (1743), a shorter but somewhat similar poem, we detect a general resemblance

Literature after the death of Pope.

to the *Essay on Man;* while Henry Brooke's poem on *The Universal Beauty* (1735), and Erasmus Darwin's *Botanic Garden* (1791), obviously echo the favourite metrical cadence of Pope. In the two works last named, poetry is called in to expound science instead of theology or philosophy, but the tone is none the less didactic; and it is worth noting that in *The Botanic Garden* the Rosicrucian sylphs and gnomes of *The Rape of the Lock* reappear as personifications of the elemental forces of nature.

But there is something more important for us to notice than such single instances of the survival of the early literary spirit. For forty years after the death of Pope, the greatest personal force in English literature and criticism, the dominant power in the literary circles of London was SAMUEL JOHNSON (1709–1784), a man whose sympathies lay with the literary standards of the earlier part of the century, and who had but little comprehension of the new spirit which, in his lifetime, was beginning to displace them. Johnson, the son of a poor bookseller in Lichfield, came up to London in 1737, with three acts of a play in his pocket, and the determination to make his way through literature. For many years his life was one of terrible hardship, but he bore his privations manfully, with unflinching courage, and with a beautiful tenderness toward those yet more unfortunate. He obtained employment on a periodical, *The Gentleman's Magazine*, and soon afterward made a great hit by his satire of *London* (1738), a poem which attracted the favourable notice of Pope. He wrote another satire, *The Vanity of Human Wishes* (1749), conducted *The Rambler* (March 20, 1750, to March 14, 1752) and *The Idler* (April, 1758, to April, 1760), papers similar in design to *The Tatler* and *The Spectator*, and in 1755 published his *English Dictionary*. Shortly after the accession of George III. Johnson's burdens were lifted by the grant of a pension of three hundred pounds a year.   During the remainder of his life he ruled as the literary autocrat of London.   He was the leading spirit in a Literary Club founded by him in 1764 in conjunction with the painter, Sir Joshua Reynolds.   Burke, Goldsmith, Garrick, Fox, Gibbon, and Sheridan were members of this club, yet among such men Johnson maintained his supremacy.   Macaulay says that the "verdicts pronounced by this conclave on new books were speedily known all over London, and were sufficient to sell off a whole edition in a day, or to condemn the sheets to the service of the trunkmaker and the pastry-cook." [1]   After writing several other prose-works, Johnson died December 13, 1784, full of years and honours.   While Johnson's works are now comparatively little read, he remains one of the most familiar and strongly marked personages in the literature.

Personal peculiarities. "The old philosopher is still among us in the brown coat with the metal buttons and the shirt which ought to be at wash, blinking, puffing, rolling his head, drumming with his fingers, tearing his meat like a tiger, and swallowing his tea in oceans.   No human being who has been more than seventy years in the grave is so well known to us.   And it is but just to say that our intimate acquaintance with what he would himself have called the *anfractuosities* of his intellect and of his temper serves only to strengthen our conviction that he was both a great and a good man." [1]

While Johnson wrote some strong, quotable verse, he was preëminently a prose-writer in an age of prose.   We

Johnson the prose-writer of an age of prose. have seen how, during the greater part of his century, the uninspired temper of the time found prose a congenial medium; how the close adherence to fact found a new vehicle of expression in the realistic novel; but apart from this the century witnessed a remarkable growth of prose — in history, theol-

[1] Article on "Johnson," *Encyclopedia Britannica.*

ogy, philosophy, political economy, and in law. During its middle years DAVID HUME (1711–1776), WILLIAM ROBERTSON (1721–1793), and EDWARD GIBBON (1737–1794) brought the art of historical writing to a higher excellence than it had yet attained in England. Although Gibbon is the only member of this group whose work remains as a really lasting contribution to historical literature, the histories of both Robertson and Hume had an important influence on historical writing. Gibbon, one of the great historians of the world, gave his life to a single mighty work, his *History of the Decline and Fall of the Roman Empire* (1776–1788), and built the massive structure of his masterpiece with such minute attention to accuracy of detail, and such a comprehensive genius for the symmetry and grandeur of the general plan, that his work remains unrivalled. While an era was thus made in historical writing, SIR WILLIAM BLACKSTONE, in his *Commentaries on the Laws of England* (1765), performed an unparalleled service for English jurisprudence, ADAM SMITH, in his *Wealth of Nations* (1776), re-created the science of political economy, and a great political literature grew up under the genius of Burke. Yet in such an age Johnson remains a central figure. He was remotely connected with the development of the novel by his didactic story of *Rasselas* (1759); his *Lives of the Poets* (1777–1781), while by no means free from characteristic limitations, is probably his most lasting contribution to literature. Yet Johnson belonged to a time that was passing. His poems of *London* and *The Vanity of Human Wishes* follow the satiric style made popular by Dryden and Pope, a style greatly in vogue when Johnson began his literary career; and are as obviously modelled after Pope in their versification and manner. *The Rambler* is as plainly imitated from *The Tatler* and *The Spectator*, although through Johnson's ponderous, many-syllabled style it follows them, in the clever phrase of Lady Mary Wortley

Montagu, "as a pack-horse follows a hunter." Yet while
Johnson thus stands as the bulwark of the old order, both
by his own work and by his critical verdicts on that of
others, all about him new agitations were already rife.
Absolute as was his literary dictatorship, his throne was
reared on the verge of that revolution which begins the
modern period of our literary history. The industrial and
social England, the rise of which we have suggested, was
taking shape between Johnson's arrival in London in 1737
and his death in 1784; new feelings utterly opposed to
many of his traditions and prejudices, and alien to his understanding and habits of thought, were quickening into
life around him. While he held steadily to the ancient
ways, those changes in literary standards had already
begun which have led to the reversal of nearly every important dictum uttered by this great literary law-giver in
matters of criticism.

The changing spirit of England expressed itself through
literature as it did through religion, politics, and social
life. This new spirit in literature which from
about the first quarter of the century became
increasingly apparent, was at once a result of
those wide-spread changes which characterise the
time, and also one of those forces which altered men's outlook on life and helped to push England on a new path.
Before speaking of some of the authors prominent in this
movement, it will be helpful to gain some idea of its chief
characteristics.

The characteristics of the new literature.

I. The new literature concerns itself distinctively with
the country, as the old literature did with the town. Pope,
Addison, Gay, and Swift had given London the
gossip of the Coffee-houses, the miseries and
malignities of Grub Street, the gay, petty world
of fashion, or the current politics and philosophy. The new
poetry led men's thoughts away from these things into the

The return to Nature.

sunshine and the open fields; it transported the inveterate Londoner into a world which he had half forgotten, or never really known, a world of plough-land and sheep-fold, of mountain, lake, and glen; a world that beside the eagerness and noise of the city, seemed quiet, self-sufficient, and remote. This increasing fondness for country subjects is usually spoken of as "the return to Nature." It was even more than this, it was *the discovery of Nature.* These poets did something more than come back to the old world of earth and sky; they gradually discovered and established a new relation with them; they gave them a new part in man's spiritual life, so that the nature-poetry in which these feelings found its most complete expression is an embodiment of a new view of Nature rather than the return to an old one.

II. This new literature was distinguished by a deeper and a more comprehensive love of man. That deep feeling, which, as the eighteenth century advanced, prompted men to turn from the artificial life of society to the world of Nature, was closely associated with a sympathetic interest in the lives of the country-folk and the poor. The representative writers of Queen Anne's time had despised and satirised humanity. We have seen Pope's low estimate of it, his malice towards men, his ingrained disbelief in women; we have seen Swift's fierce and cynical misanthropy. In a long succession of writers from James Thomson to Wordsworth, we observe that sympathy for human misery and misfortune, that ever deepening admiration for human nature, that love of liberty, and that belief in human brotherhood, which we have already seen in the social development of this time.

The new sympathy with man.

III. This deeper humanity, that was making literature more gentle and compassionate, also declared itself in a sympathy with children and with the home. In the writings of the great representatives of the Classical School childhood has no place. But as poets came to view life with a greater tenderness and a deeper understanding, their hearts were touched by the helplessness and loving dependence of little children, and they felt that childhood had in it something wonderful and sacred. This conviction, more or less vaguely present in the poetry of Blake, finds a definite and philosophical expression in Wordsworth's great *Ode on the Intimations of Immortality from Recollections of Early Childhood*. During the latter part of the century a number of notable stories for children were composed by MARIA EDGEWORTH, THOMAS DAY, and others, and authors wrote for children as well as about them. The quiet and secluded life of the home also found its interpreters in Gray, Burns, Wordsworth, and many other poets of the new school. Nor was this sympathy restricted to humanity or to the world of inanimate Nature; it stooped to the creatures below man, to the hare, the field-mouse, the water-fowl, even to the very worm beneath our feet. This feeling is particularly evident in the poetry of Cowper and of Burns.

IV. We notice in this new poetry an increasing tendency to revert both to the manner and the spirit of the great English poets who preceded Dryden and Pope. The supremacy of the heroic verse, the decasyllabic couplet, popularised by Dryden and perfected by Pope, was disputed, and here and there poets began to take Milton and Spenser as models of poetic form. When Milton chose blank verse as the metre of *Paradise Lost*, he did so in deliberate opposition to the prevailing fashion and the best critical taste of the time. But by the beginning of the eighteenth century the despised verse had its admiring imitators, and as the century advanced it became a favourite metre of the poets of the new school. Milton's influence is also apparent in the eighteenth-century imitations of his *L'Allegro* and *Il Penseroso*. Some of the poets of the new order who were trying, whether consciously or not, to free themselves from the rule of Pope, turned naturally to Spenser, the poet who was in almost every respect Pope's opposite, and in their hands not only Spenser's stanza but his romantic spirit were revived.

V. With these new tendencies we must associate a longing to escape from the world of commonplace fact and every-day experiences, into some strange, untried region of the imagination, remote from the prosaic and the familiar. The supremacy of "common sense" was passing; a love of strong or strange emotions began to manifest itself, and men found pleasure in a poetry which inspired feelings of wonder, awe, horror, melancholy, or mysterious fear. Men found various avenues of escape from that prosaic atmosphere which they now felt to be stifling and confined. But the original impulse of this whole movement was the desire to break down the bars which the writers of the Classical School had so carefully set up; to get out of doors, to get away from the town, to break through the conventions, to experience new sensations, to find a wider area for feeling and imagination. Just as men realised that there was a world outside of London, they realised that there was a world outside of England, and the same impulse which drove the poets from Grub Street to the fields, drove them to seek for new subjects in far-off and unfamiliar lands, or in remote and less artificial times. Some sought fresh pastures in the East: William Collins wrote some so-called *Persian Eclogues* (1742); Bishop Percy translated a Chinese romance; Goldsmith wrote his Chinese Letters (1760). James Macpherson was attracted by the long-neglected poetry of the Celt, and published his version of the old legend of Ossian, the great traditional poet of the Gael. Gray turned to the almost equally forgotten poetry and mythology of Iceland and the North, or introduced into one of his great odes a Bard of Celtic Wales. William Beckford wrote his oriental romance of *Vathek*. Others again collected or imitated the ballads of the common people, which had been long disregarded as outside the bounds of literature. To turn away from poetry of a more academic and literary order, and to come back to these ballads, filled as they were with primitive passions, with primitive and superstitious fears, was, in a very real sense, to come back to Nature. And, moved by this desire to escape from the commonplace, men entered the enchanted ground of chivalry and romance. It was but natural that writers in search of "beauty with strangeness," of something picturesque, heroic and unfamiliar, should find in the Middle Ages something particularly suited to their needs. It was natural that in their recoil from a time which seemed to them flippant, sceptical, and prosaic, men should take shelter in those ages of romance and knightly heroism, of wonder and of faith. So, during the latter half of the eighteenth century, there was a growing interest in everything belonging to this special period of the past: in its costume, its architecture, its manners, its literature. This delight in the Middle Ages, which is commonly called the *Mediæval Revival*, found its greatest interpreter in Sir Walter Scott.

These varied and comprehensive changes were not brought about by any one man, nor were they effected in a single generation. To appreciate the gradual transition from the old literature to the new, from the Age of Dryden and of Pope to the Age of Wordsworth and of Shelley, we must now turn to some of the writers who led the way into the new land.

One fact impresses us at the outset: the important part taken by Scottish men of letters in this reaction from the restrictions of the Classical School. The return of poetry to Nature definitely begins with ALLAN RAMSAY and JAMES

THOMSON, both of them children of the Scottish Lowlands. Ramsay, born in 1686, was familiar in his boyhood with the picturesque and mountainous scenery of Lanarkshire. When he was about fifteen he was sent to Edinburgh, where he became a prosperous and popular wig-maker and book-seller. Ramsay was a man of cheerful temper, and as he was interested in books and fond of a jest, his shop became a favourite place of literary and social resort. He was neither an heroic figure nor a great poet, but the influence on poetry of this short, amiable, plump little book-seller was greater than that of many a greater man. He had a liking for the old popular literature, and he published two collections of early Scottish songs and poems (*The Evergreen*, 1724, and *The Tea Table Miscellany*, 1724). He was thus one of the pioneers in that revival of interest in the popular lyrical poetry which prepared the way for Robert Burns. Ramsay's best and most ambitious work, *The Gentle Shepherd* (published in its complete form in 1725), appears to have been intended as a deliberate protest against the unreality of the prevailing style of pastoral poetry. *The Gentle Shepherd* has no great poetical merit, but when compared with the sham pastorals of the artificial school, it shows a genuine appreciation of natural scenery and of country life. If it does not altogether escape the conventional, it is at least a notable attempt to picture the Scotch rustic as he was. Instead of the classic Damon and Daphne, those thin shadows of a shade, instead of Strephon promising to sacrifice a milk-white bull to Phœbus on the banks of the Thames,[1] we have plain Patie and Roger, we have a simple picture of domestic life:

> "At e'en when he comes weary frae the hill,
> I'll hae a' things made ready to his will.
> In Winter, when he toils thro' wind and rain,
> A bleezing ingle, and a clean hearth-stane;

[1] See Pope's *Pastorals*, "Spring," l. 45.

> And soon as he flings by his plaid and staff,
> The seething pat's be ready to take aff;
> Clean hag-a-bag I'll spread upon his board,
> And serve him wi' the best we can afford." [1]

In such lines as these we feel that poetry has already found a new source of beauty and of power; we see that it has got back to something primary and fundamental, and our thoughts revert to that description of a Frisian household, written perhaps a thousand years before Ramsay's time, which tells us how a sailor's wife welcomes her husband home. This trait of domesticity apparent in Ramsey, reasserts itself in Gray's *Elegy*, and even more strongly in *The Cotter's Saturday Night* of Burns.[2]

James Thomson, whose name we have associated with Ramsay's as a pioneer of the new poetry, was a man of far greater influence and importance, and in him **Thomson.** the tendencies of the new literature were much more distinctly manifest. He was born in 1700, the year of the death of Dryden, at Ednam, a village a few miles from Kelso, in the beautiful valley of the Tweed. A year later his father removed to Southdean, near Jedborough, a retired spot on the slopes of the Cheviot Hills. Here, in the most picturesque and romantic surroundings, the future poet of Nature passed his boyhood. His fondness for poetry showed itself very early, and in 1725 he left the University of Edinburgh without taking his degree, and came to London. His poem of *Winter* appeared in the following year. Encouraged by its success, Thomson published *Summer*, *Spring*, and *Autumn*, and in 1730 the four poems appeared together under the title of *The Seasons*. *The Seasons* begins a new era in the **Nature-poetry of** England, and possibly of Modern Europe. In Ramsay, the

---

[1] *Gentle Shepherd*, Act i. Sc. 2.

[2] *Cf.* especially the stanza in the *Elegy:* "For them no more the blazing hearth shall burn," and "th' expectant wee-things, toddlin', stacher thro'," etc., in *The Cotter's Saturday Night*.

descriptions of nature are merely incidental, and the land-scape is made a mere background to the rustic drama. But in Thomson, Nature herself, seen under the changing aspects of the four seasons, is the chief theme. The traditional practice of the poets is reversed, and while in *The Seasons* we come upon harvesters, sheep-shearers, or youthful lovers, they are hardly more than picturesque features in the landscape, subordinate to that majestic world in which they play their little parts. Thomson, while he wrote with the power of a fresh inspiration, is often stilted and even tedious. But while he does not entirely escape from the artificiality of the prevailing poetic diction, *The Seasons* in the breadth and originality of its conception, and in the essential truth of its descriptions, is both a great and a memorable poem. He had opened men's eyes and showed to Londoners the way to the fields. Dr. Johnson, that inveterate Londoner, has defined the nature of Thomson's great achievement in one memorable sentence: *" The reader of The Seasons wonders that he never saw before what Thomson shows him, and that he never yet has felt what Thomson impresses."* [1] The mission of the new poetry could hardly be more briefly or more happily defined.

We cannot dwell here on other aspects of Thomson's work, on his enthusiasm for liberty, his distrust of cities, his sympathy with man, but we note his appreciation of England's widening power. In 1740, the year of the fall of Walpole, when war had recently been declared with Spain, Thomson foreshadowed the greatness of England's destiny as a sea-power in verses which became the National Song:

"When Britain first, at Heaven's command,
　Arose from out the azure main,
This was the charter of the land,
　And guardian angels sang this strain:
Rule, Britannia! rule the waves!
Britons never will be slaves."

[1] *Lives of the Poets:* " Thomson."

From the time of the publication of *The Seasons* we find a growing delight in nature and a further departure from the poetic style and spirit of Pope. In 1726, the year of the appearance of Thomson's *Winter*, JOHN DYER, a native of a wild and beautiful region of Southern Wales, published his descriptive poem of *Grongar Hill*. Dyer, like Ramsay and Thomson, had learned to know and to love nature in his youth, and in *Grongar Hill* and in his later poem of the *Fleece* (1757), he drew men's thoughts away from the city and helped them to see and to feel. Thus "from remote Scotland and from Southern Wales came a gift to English poetry which neither Grub Street nor Twickenham could bestow." As the century advanced, this departure from the older poetic standards found many representatives until it finally passed from an instinctive divergence into a complete and conscious revolt. We find some of the characteristics of the new spirit in Somerville's *Chase* (1735), a vigorous poem on the delight of hunting, and in Shenstone's *Schoolmistress* (1737). Towards the middle of the century (1746), we reach the delicately musical *Odes* of WILLIAM COLLINS, and the immortal *Elegy in a Country Churchyard* of THOMAS GRAY (1751). The poetry of both Collins and Gray is remarkable for lyrical melody, exquisite finish of workmanship, and sentiment. Collins had the finer and rarer lyrical gift. Gray, while always fastidiously correct and restrained, is less ethereal than Collins, and less remote from ordinary human feelings and interests. Both men turned from the world of the prosaic. Gray explored old myths, or sought some quiet scene, congenial to contemplation. Collins was attracted by mystery and splendour. Collins, writes Dr. Johnson, "delighted to roam through the meanders of enchantment, to gaze on the magnificence of golden palaces, to repose by the waterfalls of Elysian gardens." [1]

Gray, Collins, Dyer, etc.

---

[1] Life of "Collins" in *Lives of the Poets*.

It is this quest for the mysterious and the remote which is evident in Collins's *Ode on the Popular Superstitions of the Highlands of Scotland,* a poem which illustrates that aspect of the romantic revival which has been called "the Renaissance of Wonder." Gray in the *Elegy,* and Collins in the *Ode to Evening,* are the poets of twilight, and Collins especially contrives to invest the darkening landscape with dreaminess and unreality. Other poets of the time paint Nature in her varied aspects, if in a less subtly poetic mood. In Goldsmith's *Traveller* (1764), we look down on the life on the earth, on —

"Lakes, forests, cities, plains extending wide,"

and contemplate Nature in all her variety as the theatre of human activity. In his *Deserted Village* (1770), as in Gray's *Elegy,* we read "the short and simple annals of the poor."

In the *Minstrel* (Bk. i. 1771), JAMES BEATTIE (1735–1803) shows us a youthful poet whose genius was nourished and inspired by the influence of mountain, sea, and sky. This poetry of natural description was continued by GEORGE CRABBE (1754–1832), whose work, written in an unaffected and somewhat homely style, possesses vigour, earnestness, and truth. Cowper, Burns, and others contributed to this nature-poetry, until it found its greatest prophet in William Wordsworth.

These poets of "the discovery of Nature" were almost equally poets of the spirit of a widening humanity. Gray's **The new poetry of Man.** *Elegy* is more than a charming rural vignette, more than a meditation on life's "inevitable end," it is above all a testimony to the essential value of obscure and humble lives. *The Deserted Village* is an indignant protest against the wealth and luxury which encroach upon the simple happiness of the peasant, and in such lines as these we hear the voice of the new democracy:

> "Ill fares the land, to hastening ills a prey,
> Where wealth accumulates, and men decay:
> *Princes and lords may flourish or may fade —*
> *A breath can make them as a breath has made —*
> But a bold peasantry, their country's pride,
> When once destroyed can never be supplied."

Crabbe brought the realism of the earlier part of the century to the painting of the homely and often repulsive life of the country poor. In the opening lines of *The Village* he scorns the artificial pastoral of the older school, and declares —

> "I paint the cot
> As Truth will paint it, and as Bards will not." [2]

The delight in nature, the renewal of a religious fervour, the sense of human brotherhood, the love of animals, all find expression in the life and work of Cowper. Essentially the same feelings are the motive power in the poetry of Blake, and Burns, and Wordsworth.

This change in the subjects and in the spirit of poetry was accompanied by a corresponding change in poetic form. During the years when the French influence was uppermost, the decasyllabic couplet was employed in longer poems, almost to the exclusion of any other form of verse. Dryden sought to substitute it for the blank verse of the Elizabethans. Milton's refusal to use it in *Paradise Lost* was in such flagrant defiance of the critical canons of the day that sundry well-meaning admirers of the substance of that great epic paraphrased it in the sovereign metre to remove its harsh irregularity in form. [3]

The changes in poetic form.

We find one explanation of the extravagant popularity

[1] *The Deserted Village*, l. 51, etc.
[2] *The Village*, Bk. i. See the entire opening passage.
[3] See article in *Andover Review*, January, 1891, "Some Paraphrasers of Milton."

of this verse in its perfect adaptability to the poetic needs of the time. The heroic couplet, as employed by Pope, by its pauses falling with a somewhat monotonous recurrence at the end of the line, lent itself to that clear, terse, and epigrammatic manner in which the age delighted. Instead of the slow evolution of the Miltonic sentence, complex in structure, with the "sense variously drawn out from one verse (i.e., line) to the next," we have sentences so broken up and packed in handy packages of two lines each, that one can snatch up a couplet almost anywhere, and carry it off for quoting purposes. But from about 1726 the sovereignty of the heroic couplet was broken, and the reviving influence of the Elizabethan poets showed itself in a recurrence to their poetic manner. Lowell has aptly dubbed Pope's favourite metre, "the rocking-horse measure," and doubtless people began to weary of the monotonous regularity of its rise and fall. In *The Seasons*, Thomson not only turned to Nature, he abandoned the heroic couplet for blank verse. The Spenserian stanza,[1] which had been discarded except by a few obscure experimentalists, grew in favour, and was employed in Shenstone's *Schoolmistress* (1742), Thomson's *Castle of Indolence*, Beattie's *Minstrel*, and in a number of minor poems. Meanwhile Collins's *Odes* marked the advent of a poet with the fresh, inborn lyrical impulse. By virtue of this incommunicable gift of song, Collins mounts above the monotonous levels of didactic verse that stretch about him. Admirable poetry had been produced in England since the death of Milton, but its excellence was chiefly of a kind that could be subjected to a critical analysis and accounted for. The means, rhetorical

---

[1] *V.* Beers's *English Romanticism — XVIII. Century*, chap. iii., and the chapter on the Spenserian revival, in Phelps's *Beginning of the English Romantic Movement;* also Appendix I. of the same book, for list of Spenserian imitators.

or otherwise, employed by Dryden and Pope to produce a given effect, are, to a great extent, comprehensible to us, while we applaud the result as a triumph of premeditated art. But in the refined and gentle charm of Collins, in the subdued and softened beauty of his colouring, and the lingering and delicate grace of his lyrical movements, we encounter excellence of a wholly different order; we are aware of an indefinable poetic quality the presence of which, unlike the excellence of Pope, can only be fully recognised by the artistic sense, inasmuch as it is, by its very nature, incapable of proof. Thomson wrote of Nature with surprising minuteness and accuracy, but Collins with the inspired touch of a higher sympathy. Swinburne says of him: "Among all English poets, he has, it seems to me, the closest affinity to our great contemporary school of French landscape painters. Corot on canvas might have signed his *Ode to Evening*. Millet might have given us some of his graver studies, and left them, as he did, no whit the less sweet for their softly austere and simply tender gravity." [1]

In the last quarter of the century WILLIAM BLAKE (1757–1827) holds an important place in the advance of the new school of poetry. This singular man, richly gifted as painter as well as poet, was eccentric to the very verge of madness. Indeed, most of his work seems to hover on the dubious border-land between insanity and reason, yet so wonderful is it that we are uncertain whether we should attribute its strangeness to the poet's wildness, or to our conventional dulness of perception. Nevertheless, in certain important particulars, Blake's poetry was strongly expressive of the tendencies of his time. He, too, takes up again the interrupted strain of the Elizabethans, recalling not merely their disused metre, but their gusts of passionate intensity and bold flights of imagination. Thus the

[1] Critical essay in Ward's *English Poets*, vol. iii. title "Collins."

spirited dramatic fragment *Edward III.*[1] is instinct with the lavish and vaulting energy of Marlowe.[2] On the other hand, many poems of Blake's are remarkable for a limpid and inspired simplicity which made him the predecessor of Wordsworth. In his love of children and of animals, in his profound sympathy with suffering, in his lyrical beauty, and in his feeling for Nature, he represents the best tendencies of his time.

While in literature the influence of the Elizabethans was thus overcoming those foreign fashions which for a time had superseded it, on the stage the greatest productions of Shakespeare were being brought vividly home to the popular life and imagination. Acting, like literature and life, threw aside some of its burden of stiffness and artificiality, and, after the conventional mannerisms and declamation of such actors as Macklin and Quin, the comparative truth and naturalness of Garrick took London by storm. Garrick's great London triumph dates from his performance of *Richard III.* at Drury Lane in 1741, after he had won recognition in the provincial theatres. His influence on the popular taste may be conjectured from the fact that he played in no less than seventeen Shakespearean parts, and produced twenty-four of Shakespeare's plays during his management at Drury Lane. Garrick retired in 1776.

Garrick and the Shakespearean revival.

Mrs. Siddons, one of the greatest of tragic actresses, whose *Lady Macbeth* and *Queen Katherine* are among the proudest traditions of the English stage, won her first success in London in 1782, her brother, John Kemble, appearing the following year. Through these mighty

[1] "Blake imitated Spenser, and in his short fragment of *Edward III.* we hear again the note of Marlowe's violent imagination." — Brooke's *Primer English Literature*, p. 165.

[2] According to Gilchrist this fragment was "printed in 1783, written 1768-1777." — Gilchrist's *Life of Blake*, i. p. 26.

actors the stage fell in with and helped forward the revolution against the taste and standards of the critical school.

The labours of a succession of Shakespearean editors and critics had preceded this noble interpretation of his dramas on the stage. In 1709, NICHOLAS ROWE published the first critical edition of Shakespeare. This edition contains the earliest formal account of Shakespeare's life. Nearly a quarter of a century had passed since the publication of the last collected edition of Shakespeare's plays, the so-called *Fourth Folio* of 1685, but after the appearance of Rowe's work one edition of Shakespeare followed another in comparatively rapid succession. The unparalleled greatness of Shakespeare was more and more fully recognised. Critical patronage of him as an untutored genius, a prodigy handicapped by his lack of art, changed into unqualified admiration and homage, until his preeminence as an artist as well as a poet was revealed in the criticisms of Coleridge and Hazlett.

With this growing appreciation of Shakespeare, we may connect the publication of Robert Dodsley's *Collection of Old Plays* in 1744, a book which did much
Dodsley's Old Plays. to revive interest in the Elizabethan drama and make "an epoch in æsthetics."[1]

The last feature of this new literature which we have to consider is the revival of a sympathetic interest in the
The Mediæval Revival. Middle Ages. This, as has been said, was not an independent or unrelated movement, it was but another outward sign of the fundamental and reactionary change which was taking place in the spiritual life of the nation. Like those other phases of the new literature which we have just considered, this Mediæval Revival was an outcome of the Renaissance of feeling, imagination, wonder, and faith. To understand

[1] Lowell, Essay on "Gray."

the emancipation of English literature from the time of Ramsay to the time of Wordsworth, we must grasp the essential unity that underlies all its superficial variety, and see that in all its phases it is but a part of the emancipation of England herself.

The revival of interest in Gothic architecture, chivalry, and the world of the Middle Ages, did not take definite shape in England until about 1750. It was in this year, or shortly after, that Horace Walpole began to build himself a "little Gothic castle at Strawberry Hill." Walpole, the son of the great Prime Minister, was a leader of wit and fashion. He dabbled in authorship, had the reputation of being a connoisseur, and his Gothic castle stocked with relics of the days of chivalry helped to make mediævalism popular. The movement was helped forward by the publication of *Richard Hurd's Letters on Chivalry and Romance* (1762), a book designed to show the superiority of Gothic to classic subjects for poetical purposes. In 1764, Walpole published his extravagant little romance *The Castle of Otranto*, the precursor of many a ghastly story of blood and mystery, and that famous collection of old ballads, Bishop Percy's *Reliques of Ancient English Poetry*, appeared in the same year. Percy's *Reliques* was one of the influential books of the century. It did more than any previous collection to promote an interest in the preservation of the old ballads, and it fostered a love of the ballad poetry. It was the pattern for many similar collections (Herd's *Ballads*, 1769, Scott's *Minstrelsy*, 1802–1803, Motherwell's *Ancient Minstrelsy*, 1827, etc.), and poets began to take the old ballad form as their model. By far the most noteworthy of these early imitations are the ballads of THOMAS CHATTERTON (1752–1770), amazing poems which their boy-author professed to have copied from some ancient manuscripts. Chatterton, the child of a subchanter in the Bristol cathedral, grew up under the spell of antiquity. He was born in Bristol, almost within the shadow of the beautiful old Church of St. Mary Redcliffe; he learned his alphabet from the illuminated letters on some old manuscript music. He would lie on the graves, gazing on the slender, soaring spire of St. Mary's, re-creating the world of mediæval Bristol in his imagination. As Ramsay, Thomson, and Wordsworth were children of the world of Nature, brought up on the green lap of the earth, so Chatterton, drawn to the past by the intuition of genius or by some mysterious tendency of his age, surrounded by the relics and survivals of the past, was a child of the Middle Ages. Such was the popularity of Percy's *Reliques* that the influence of the old ballad poetry became wide-spread. Thus, Goldsmith wrote his simple ballad *The Hermit* (1765),[1] and Shenstone, *Jemmy Dawson* (1745).

Coleridge's *Ancient Mariner* and *Christabel* are a noble outcome of the old ballad literature, and from it also sprang the best poetry of Walter Scott.

When we classify and arrange all these stupendous changes in the external conditions of men's lives, and in **Summary.** men's mental and spiritual estimate of life's meaning and purpose, the great and peculiar place of the eighteenth century in history begins to take shape in our minds. We see that it bears a relation to our modern civilisation similar to that which the fourteenth century held to the Renaissance. Looked at from the external or material side, we are able to feel the force of Mr. Frederic Harrison's words: "Every one can state for himself the hyperbolic contrast between the material condition we see to-day and the material condition in which society managed to live over two or three centuries ago, nay, ten,

---

[1] Goldsmith was accused of taking the idea of this ballad from "The Friar of Orders Grey" (Percy's *Reliques*), which appeared in the same year (1765). He claimed to have read *The Hermit* to Bishop Percy before the publication of the "Friar."

or twenty, or a hundred centuries ago. . . . The last hundred years," that is, since about 1770 or 1780, "have seen in England the most sudden change in our material and external life that is recorded in history."[1] When we endeavour to grasp this transition period, not only externally, but from every side, we see that its beginning dates from the last years of the administration of Walpole, or from about 1730 or 1740. To that decade we have referred the rise or growth of a new spirit in religion, politics, literature, and even music. Its close is marked by England's entrance upon her long struggle with France for the prize of half the world. Between 1755 and 1765 we find those improvements in transportation and manufactures which begin the "industrial revolution," and at the end of this decade Watt's utilisation of steam adds its tremendous impetus to the movement. From about this time the advance toward democracy becomes more rapid and apparent. We enter the era of a bold opposition to authority in John Wilkes and the *Letters of Junius;* of the admission of reporters to the House of Commons and the consequent increase in the power of the press; of the American and French Revolutions, and of the outburst in literature of the revolutionary spirit. From this time also we date the beginning of the Mediæval Revival. Finally, we may group many of these changes about two centres: (a) that longing for a more simple and natural life and the revolt against accepted standards which accompanied a renaissance of the more religious and ideal elements in society; (b) that feeling of compassion for suffering, that sense of the worth of the individual, which we associate with the growth of democracy.

The two great historic movements of the century define themselves as:

[1] Essay on "The Nineteenth Century," in *The Choice of Books*, p. 424, etc.

1. The expansion of England into a world power.
2. The rise of democracy, with all those industrial and social changes which accompany and forward it.

The effect of these movements on literature has been great in the past, and is likely to be enormous in the future.

OLIVER GOLDSMITH.

(1728–1774.)

Goldsmith's relation to the literary and social movements just sketched is both interesting and important, yet so great is the purely human attraction of his life and character that our thoughts instinctively turn first to the man himself. There are few men in the annals of English literature with whom we have a greater sense of companionship. His very "frailties," as Dr. Johnson compassionately called them, his heedless extravagance, his harmless and childlike vanity, but stir our sympathies and endear him to us the more. Blundering, inconsequent, and pathetic as his life is, it is illuminated by a purity and simple goodness of nature which no hard experiences were able to soil or impair. Careless for himself, he cared — if often impulsively and inconsiderately — for others. He had a wonderful power of loving, and Thackeray has ventured to pronounce him "the most beloved of English writers." To know and love Goldsmith is to strengthen our own love of goodness; to increase our confidence in human nature; to grow more gentle and pitiful toward weakness and error. Moreover, to know Goldsmith is to increase our appreciation of his works, for his works are but a partial expression of the man himself.

Although his family is said to have been originally of English stock, Oliver Goldsmith was Irish in disposition as well as by birth. He was born in November, 1728, at Pallas, an insignificant village in County Longford, remote from the main highways of travel, where his father, the Rev. Charles Goldsmith, was curate. When Goldsmith

Life in
Ireland.

was about two years old, his father became rector of a parish in Westmeath, and removed to the village of Lissoy, in the southwestern part of that county. When William Howitt visited it, in the early half of the last century, Lissoy consisted "of a few common cottages by the roadside, on a flat and by no means particularly interesting scene,"[1] yet life there seems to have been sturdy, wholesome, and good-humoured. Goldsmith looked back to its placid pleasures with a pathetic fondness, and memories of it mingled with his description of Auburn in *The Deserted Village*.

No doubt Goldsmith grew up under much the same conditions as those of thousands of his contemporaries. At school he was thought "impenetrably stupid," and something — which seems to have stuck to him through life — made him the butt of his companions. He was thickset and ugly, his face disfigured by an early attack of smallpox, and the consciousness of his personal defects doubtless increased the shyness and morbid sensitiveness of his disposition. Yet his ordinary experiences, and the kindly life of his father's simple household, gave Goldsmith the materials for enduring works of art. The guilelessness, charity, and unworldliness which draw our hearts toward Dr. Primrose in *The Vicar of Wakefield* were characteristic of the Goldsmith family, as they were of Goldsmith himself, and it is beautiful to think that this kindliness, which took no thought for the morrow, should at length have come to have its share in the creation of some of the most perfect and lovable characters in the literature. In after years, Goldsmith's early recollections of his father were embodied in his description of the "preacher," in *The Deserted Village*, the man who

---

[1] *Haunts and Homes of British Poets*, "Goldsmith."

"ran his godly race," "remote from towns," "more bent
to raise the wretched, than to rise;" they entered into his
sketch of "The Man in Black" in *The Citizen of the World*,
and, above all, they found a yet fuller expression in *The
Vicar of Wakefield*.[1]

At seventeen Goldsmith entered Trinity College, Dublin,
as a "sizar," or free scholar. At this time the "sizars"
were virtually part student, part servant, and Goldsmith
suffered many humiliations which his sensitive nature
found it hard to endure. Here he was idle and fond of
pleasure, and spent much time in playing on the flute.
After his graduation in 1749 he returned to the country to wander in easy aimlessness from the house of one
relative to another, while his family were debating what
was to be done with him. In 1752, one of his relatives
Edinburgh having declared that he would "make a good
and the medical man," he left for Edinburgh to study
Continent. medicine. Becoming restless, after about eighteen months, he embarked for a tour on the Continent,
with the ostensible purpose of continuing his studies.
Here he led a wandering life, learning little medicine,
but gaining that knowledge of European countries which
he was to make use of in *The Traveller*. When he left
Leyden he wandered with his flute through the country
districts of Flanders, France, and Switzerland, playing
"merry tunes" that often set the peasants dancing and
gained him food and lodging. In Italy, where the musical
taste seems to have been too exacting for his powers, he is
supposed, like the wandering scholars of the Middle Ages, to
have gained a dinner and a bed by disputing on questions
of philosophy at the universities and convents. After a
year of this strolling life he landed in England in 1756, with
no prospects and with a few half-pence in his pocket.

[1] *Cf.*, also, the character of Honeywood in *The Good-natured Man.*
As an instance of the impression left by early recollections, see Goldsmith's tribute to his brother Henry in *The Traveller.*

On arriving in London Goldsmith was face to face with the problem of keeping himself alive. He is supposed to have been usher in a school; he was an apothe-

Goldsmith in London. cary's assistant, but gave up the place to invest in a second-hand velvet coat and set up as a medical practitioner. At last, driven by his necessities, he became a bookseller's drudge. He laboured anonymously at whatever task was set him, publishing among other works his *Enquiry into the State of Polite Learning in Europe* (1759). From this time until his death Goldsmith's life was chiefly given up to task-work for the publishers, interspersed with those masterpieces which are the more spontaneous utterances of his genius. In spite of his desultory education and lack of exact learning, he had great qualifications for success; a varied experience, fine powers of observation, a sympathetic nature, and, above all, a style of extraordinary ease and charm. He did foolish things, but often wrote wise ones, showing on paper, as in many places in *The Citizen of the World,* a breadth and justness of thought with which he is not always credited. After the publication of the *Enquiry* his fortunes gradually improved. In 1761 he made the acquaintance of Dr. Johnson, who became his literary friend and helper. The appearance in 1760 of *The Citizen of the World* added to his reputation, which was still further increased by the publication of his first important poem, *The Traveller,* in 1764. He was taken into the exclusive literary circles, and, with Johnson, Reynolds, and Burke, was one of the original members of the Literary Club. As his expenses continually outran his earnings, his writing consisted largely of work done to order. He was neither an historian nor a naturalist, yet he wrote histories of Rome, Greece, and England, which won great popularity, and a book on Natural History. The secret of the success of these works was their charm and attractiveness of style. His epitaph in Westminster Abbey declares that he touched nothing he did not adorn. "He is now writing a Natural History," said Johnson, "and he will make it as agreeable as a Persian tale." Yet it is on work of another class that his reputation really rests. From time to time he turned from his drudgery to add a classic to literature — his idyllic *Vicar of Wakefield* (1766), *The Good-natured Man* (1768), *The Deserted Village* (1770), and *She Stoops to Conquer* (1773). These works brought him fame, but he was continually worried by money difficulties, and toward the last the strain told even on his easy-going and buoyant temperament. In the midst of the worries, gaieties, and honours of his life in London, Goldsmith's thoughts would go back longingly to the peaceful and sheltered obscurity of his early village life. Such feelings seem to have prompted many passages in *The Deserted Village*. In fair Auburn he sees Lissoy again as through a golden mist of distance, and he confides to us his desire to return after all his wanderings and his "long vexations" and "die at home at last." His life was to have no such peaceful close; his "vexations" only thickened about him toward the last. Overwhelmed by debts, worried by creditors, struggling to the last to free himself of his burdens by his pen, he was seized at forty-six with illness. His last words were an admission that his mind was not at rest. He died in April, 1774, owing two thousand pounds — a big bill at his tailor's among the rest; but let us remember, too, that, when he lay dying, the staircase leading to his room was filled with poor outcasts whom he had befriended.

When we reflect upon the erratic and ill-ordered character of Goldsmith's life, and upon the amount of hackwork that he was forced to do to pay for his luxuries or quiet the demands of importunate creditors, we are astonished at the high excellence he actually attained in many departments of literature. He takes high rank **Goldsmith's work.** among the essayists of his century; he gave us two of the most charming poems written in England in his generation; he infused into the novel a new sweetness and purity, producing in *The Vicar of Wakefield* a kind of prose-pastoral which Carlyle pronounced "the best of all modern idyls;" and finally, in his two comedies, *The Good-natured Man* and *She Stoops to Conquer*, he not only made a lasting contribution to literature, but led a reaction against a less natural and more sentimental school of comedy and helped to make a new era in the history of the English drama. This wide range of Goldsmith's best work connects him closely with many of the most important literary movements which were going on about him. When he entered upon his work, England had already begun to escape from the ascendency of Pope, and evidences of that wide-spread national change which has been before described were yearly increasing. Yet during the fifteen years of Goldsmith's literary activity, from 1759 to 1774, his friend Johnson, who stood upon the ancient ways, was the literary autocrat of London. The work of Goldsmith stands midway between the writers of the new **His place in literary history.** school and of the old, belonging wholly to neither, sharing in the qualities of both, and, in some cases, admirably illustrating the transition from the one to the other. Thus in *The Bee*, a series of short essays which originally appeared in periodical form, he is one of the many followers of Addison and Steele. In *The Citizen of the World*, supposed to be the correspondence between a Chinese philosopher on a visit to England and his friend at home, the divergence from *The Spectator* slightly widens. Finally, in *The Vicar of Wakefield*, Goldsmith leaves the essay for the novel, and thus exemplifies a transition which was an important feature in the literary

history of his century. *The Vicar of Wakefield* lies close
to the new rural spirit of its time, and may be
appropriately contrasted with *The Rape of the
Lock*. It is of the country, as Pope's masterpiece
is of the town. Goldsmith preaches virtue, simplicity, and
contentment; Pope displays the world of fashion, extravagance, and artifice. In Goldsmith's story the air is fresh
and wholesome; the misanthropy of Pope and Swift is
left behind, and, as Walter Scott declared, "we bless the
memory of an author who contrives so well to reconcile us
to human nature." In their spirit Goldsmith's two most
famous poems, *The Traveller* and *The Deserted Village*, are
close to the new literary and social England, but in form
they continue the heroic couplet of the older school. The
fact is significant of Goldsmith's general relation to the
history of English poetry; he filled the old bottles with new
wine. *The Traveller,* indeed, retains some of the didactic
flavour of the older school, but it sets us in the midst of a
wide expanse of nature, it looks down on the nations from
the mountain-peak, and bids us realise that the inequali-
ties in the lot of man are less great than we suppose. The
poem shows that cosmopolitan temper, rare in the insular
English, which is remarkable in *The Citizen of the World*.

In *The Deserted Village* the new spirit is yet more apparent.
We are in a world that Pope knew not, or else cared not to
depict; the little, contracted world of the village,
where life if narrow, is simple, natural, and
happy. There the preacher and the schoolmaster fill a large place; there too are those rollicking country sports, in which Goldsmith himself once loved
to share. The picture may be partly an ideal one, yet the
description is full of details, suggested by actual experiences,
which give to the whole an astonishing solidity and reality.
There may not have been such a village in the British
Isles, but Auburn exists for us in the world of art. In

The Vicar of Wakefield.

The Deserted Village.

L'Allegro, Milton invested rural England with a softened and poetic charm. Herrick gave us a glimpse of Yuletide frolics, and of merry countryfolk among the hawthorn hedgerows of May Day; but Goldsmith's Auburn is more than a beautiful idyllic fancy; it is a deliberate protest against the oppression of the poor, against luxury and the evils which follow in its train.[1] Although Goldsmith's life was hardly in accordance with his doctrine; although he loved to trick out his homely person with finery — too often, alas! unpaid for, — he seems to have had at heart a longing for that "plain living" that Wordsworth was not to preach, merely, but to practise. Two things were mingled in his life as in his art; he is a follower of the earlier England, yet he belongs by nature to that newer England that was near at hand. His place in literature is not the highest, but it is secure. He did not compete for the greatest prizes, but what he attempted he accomplished, and the things that he did best could hardly be done better. His ideals are sweet and wholesome; his humour gracious and free from malice ; his work full of ease and naturalness, and pervaded by an indefinable and enduring grace and charm.

EDMUND BURKE.

(1729–1797.)

Five years before Goldsmith settled in London after his wanderings on the Continent, another young Irishman, Edmund Burke, had come to the capital, to begin there an even more memorable career. It is interesting to study the lives of these two men together, for, while in many ways they were widely different, Burke's broad relation to the political movements of the time is similar to that which Goldsmith holds toward its literary

Burke and Goldsmith.

[1] *Cf.* what is said of this poem on pp. 413, 414.

history. Like Goldsmith, Burke represents a time of transition, belonging both to the old order and to the new. More than he realised, he helped forward the political changes which marked his time, yet one of his strongest feelings was his reverence for the past.

Edmund Burke was the son of a Dublin attorney, and was born in that city in 1729. He entered Trinity College, **Burke's life.** Dublin, at fourteen, two years before Goldsmith, who was, it will be remembered, about a year his senior. In 1750, after taking his bachelor's degree, Burke came up to London and began the study of the law. He afterward expressed great respect for the law as a science and means of mental discipline, but from his boyhood he had showed a fondness for literature, writing verses at college, and being pursued with what he called the *furor poeticus*. His interest in literary matters, when legal studies were supposed to be his first object, so displeased his father, who was high-tempered and bent on seeing his son a barrister, that he cut off, or greatly reduced, Burke's allowance. Thus in or about 1755, the year before Goldsmith began his battle with London, Burke was left to push his own way in a city which was none too kindly a nurse to struggling authors. We know little of the details, for Burke maintained a dignified reserve in regard to his early struggles, but we know the difficulties and the results. "I was not," he said afterward, ". . . swaddled, and rocked, and dandled into a legislator. '*Nitor in adversum*' is the motto for a man like me."

Burke's career as an author began in 1756 with the publication of a cleverly written essay, *A Vindication of Natural* **Career as author.** *Society,* followed in the same year by *A Philosophical Inquiry into the Origin of our Ideas of the Sublime and Beautiful.* The first purported to be a posthumous publication of Pope's friend, Lord Bolingbroke, and is a skilful imitation of Bolingbroke's manner. The arguments its supposed author had advanced against revealed religion are here employed against the organisation of society, with the intention of showing that as they are obviously unsound in the political sphere, they are equally so in the religious. Both of these works show promise, but neither is among Burke's greatest efforts.

Launched into authorship, Burke naturally began to take his place in the literary life about him. He met Johnson and his followers, and when the Literary Club was started, in 1764, was one of its founders.[1] Meanwhile his studies were turning from purely literary and artistic matters to history and the existing problems of society and government. The changed direction of his thoughts is shown by the publication of a work on the settlement of America, and of an *Annual Register* of the most important public events of each year (1759–1788). Such work was an admirable preparation for a successful Parliamentary career. In 1765 Burke definitely entered politics by becoming secretary to Lord Rockingham, who had just succeeded Grenville as Prime Minister. The difficulty with the American Colonies was one of the gravest questions the new ministry had to face, and Burke, who had obtained a seat in the House of Commons (1765), won immediate distinction by a speech on the repeal of the Stamp Act. It was the beginning of a long and impressive public career, extending over nearly thirty years. It was a period to call out the full powers of an orator, the wisest judgment of a statesman. The people were restive under the arbitrary rule of George III., and the contest over the right of Wilkes to a seat in Parliament showed that Parliament itself was rather an instrument of tryanny than a safeguard of liberty. In these years India was won, America was lost; Warren Hastings was impeached for misgovernment of India in one of the most imposing and dramatic

Literature and politics.

---

[1] See **pp.** 402 and 425, *supra.*

trials in English annals; the French Revolution was begun, and Europe witnessed the Reign of Terror. On nearly every one of these subjects Burke has given us a masterpiece. The troubled times of John Wilkes were the occasion of his *Thoughts on the Present Discontents* (1770), a restrained and well-reasoned discussion of the dangers which then threatened English liberty. It warns men that **Thoughts on the present discontents.** arbitrary power may disguise itself under the very forms of free government, and that a Parliament which has become the servant of the king instead of the representative of the people, is, in fact, an instrument of servitude. The clear perception of the truth that liberty lies deeper than laws and institutions is characteristic of Burke's power to strip off the formal and conventional, and lay hold of the vital truth. The dispute with America called forth three of Burke's best **Speeches on America.** speeches, and placed him with the greatest supporters of the Colonists. In his *Speech on Conciliation with America*, perhaps the finest of the three, he brushes away the legal question of the right of England to tax the Colonies, and rests the argument on the broader ground of expediency and common sense. The legal right to do a certain thing does not prove that the thing should be done. "The question with me is not whether you have a right to render your people miserable, but whether it is not your interest to make them happy." [1]

An English statesman and critic goes so far as to say that these speeches of Burke on American affairs "are almost the one monument of the struggle on which **Trial of Hastings.** a lover of English greatness can look with pride." [2] Burke's advocacy of liberty in the rising colonies of the West was followed by his championship of justice and

[1] *Conciliation with America;* Burke's works.
[2] John Morley; article on Burke in *Encyclopedia Britannica*, ninth edition.

humanity in the newly won dependency of India. In the trial of Warren Hastings before the House of Lords, the burden of the impeachment rested mainly on Burke. He declared that "the cause of Asia" was "being tried in the presence of Europe;" and there is a breadth and largeness in his treatment which lifts us to the height of that great argument. We feel that it is even more than the cause of Asia; it is the cause of that new humanity which was growing stronger in the England of Burke's time. These distant Orientals, whose wrongs and sufferings had been unknown or unregarded, were thus brought into the range of the nation's imagination and sympathy. They too were men, with men's rights; and Burke impeached Hastings in the name of the "eternal laws of justice which he had violated," and "of human nature itself." [1]

On these three great occasions Burke was on the side of liberty and justice; but with a genuine devotion to what he called "a well-regulated liberty," he was by nature a conservative, with an innate veneration for the British Constitution and a love and reverence for the past. John Morley has said that Burke believed in government for the people, but not by the people. The overthrow of social order by the Revolution in France, its violence, its abstract, and, as he thought, visionary doctrine of human rights, shocked and alarmed him, and at the outbreak of the Revolution, he threw the full force of his vast powers into a book — *Reflections on the Revolution in France* (1790) — which remains one of the literary monuments of the time. While Burke could not see far enough to discern the ultimate outcome of the Revolution, he detected, as many enthusiasts about him failed to do, the signs of weakness and disaster, and foretold that failure which, to him, was its only apparent consequence. "Believe me, sir," he wrote, "those who attempt to level

Burke's conservatism.

[1] Impeachment of Warren Hastings. Opening Speech: Fourth Day.

never equalise." He looked back upon the cherished ideals and institutions of historic Europe, and felt that their very existence was hanging in the balance. "People," he declared, "will not look forward to posterity who never look back to their ancestors." In the insults offered to the beautiful and unhappy Marie Antoinette he saw the signal of the death of chivalry. "The age of chivalry is gone. That of sophisters, economists, and calculators has succeeded; and the glory of Europe is extinguished forever." [1]

The conclusion of the trial of Hastings in 1794 was followed by Burke's retirement from Parliament. In the same year he was prostrated by the death of his son, a blow from which he never fully recovered. His grief utters itself in words that read like the lament of David over Absalom: "The storm has gone over me. . . . I am alone. I have none to meet my enemies in the gate. . . . They who ought to have succeeded me are gone before me." Burke's health was broken, but in his *Letters on a Regicide Peace* (1796–1797), written almost in the presence of death, he declaimed with impassioned and almost frantic energy against any truce with France, which he called a "pretended republic of murderers, robbers, and atheists." He solemnly declared that his words, though they might have the weakness, had at least the sincerity, of a dying declaration. He died soon after, at his country-place at Beaconsfield, July 9, 1797.

The fame of the man of letters and that of the statesman, the orator, or even the political writer, are usually entirely

Burke as a man of letters. distinct. Even a great writer's permanent place in literature is seldom based on his contributions to contemporary politics, however effective and popular they may have been at the time. To this Burke is a singular exception. Nearly all his works are political, while his few contributions to other subjects have made no material

[1] For all these passages, *v. Reflections on the French Revolution.*

addition to his fame. He is, perhaps, the only great English statesman who is recognised as a great author because of the permanent value and literary interest of his political writings and speeches alone. To some degree this striking fact may be due to the historic importance and the dramatic interest of many of the subjects with which Burke's genius was engaged. It is due, moreover, to the fact that Burke brought to the discussion of these subjects distinctly literary gifts and a feeling for style which made him one of the great masters of English prose. He was capable of restrained, lucid, and dispassionate argument and exposition, as in the *Thoughts on the Present Discontents,* and of gorgeous descriptions or passionate outbursts of pathos or denunciation. The majestic flow of his eloquence, with its full, rounded sentences, gives to some of his orations an epic volume and grandeur. In this, and in the beauty and variety of his historical and literary allusions, Burke seems, in his loftiest moods, a prose Milton. The tribute to Marie Antoinette,[1] the description of the destruction of the Carnatic by Hyder Ali,[2] the picture of the ambassadors of Europe waiting to present their suit for peace to the "bloody ruffian" Carnot,[3] such passages are celebrated in the history of English prose style. But beyond all this, the enduring fibre in Burke's writings lies in their philosophic thought. In his treatment of current politics he is not merely the orator, the poet, the master of style; he is preeminently the thinker, able to rise above purely contemporary interests. He was the reverse of a political theorist, but he combined with a quick eye for the immediate and practical exigencies of a situation a profound insight into the principles on which the foundations of society rest. His works are rich in a political wisdom,

As political thinker.

---

[1] *Reflections on the French Revolution.*
[2] *Speech on the Nabob of Arcot's Debts.*
[3] *Letters on a Regicide Peace,* i.

in maxims and observations that reach far beyond the particular existing conditions which called them forth. Particular cases are viewed in the light of some general truths, and become illustrations of those secret forces which produce and sustain the social order. Hence Burke has been called the greatest thinker, with the single exception of Bacon, "who has ever devoted himself to the practice of English politics."[1]

WILLIAM COWPER.

(1731–1800.)

The life of Cowper is one of the strangest and the saddest in literary history. A man of shy, gentle nature, shrinking instinctively from the rough conflicts of life, it was his lot to live in a time of struggle, excitement, and change. Born in the high noon of the Age of Pope, and dying after the Age of Wordsworth and Coleridge had definitely begun, Cowper's life covers nearly the whole of that period of transition, that era of national adjustment to new conditions and ideals, which we have endeavoured to describe. While Pitt, Wesley, Burke, Warren Hastings, Captain Cook, James Watt, and many another man of action, were making modern England, while English industry, pluck, and enterprise were determining the destiny of half the world, Cowper led one of the most outwardly uneventful and monotonous of lives. More than half of his days were spent in the quiet seclusion of an English village. From this "retreat," environed by placid country scenes, shut in by the narrow interests of a provincial society, he looked out on the great world from "a safe distance." He saw in imagination the stir of the "great Babel," but he did not "feel the crowd."[2] Yet so marvellous a gift is genius, this timid recluse was not

---

[1] Buckle's *History of Civilisation in Europe*, chap. vii.
[2] See *The Task*, beginning of Bk. iv.

a mere idle spectator; shut away from the world, he was the interpreter of that spirit of change which was guiding the course of history.

William Cowper was born in 1731 in Great Berkhampstead, an ancient and picturesque town in Hertfordshire. His father, Rev. John Cowper, came of an old and honourable family; his mother was related to the poet Donne. Cowper was granted a few years of happiness before he began his long struggle with himself and with the world. Towards the close of his life he looked back with regret and tenderness to "the pastoral house," as he called his father's rectory, and recalled the trivial incidents of his early childhood there, with a pathetic clearness of recollection.[1] But sorrow came to him very early. He was acutely sensitive, and of an affectionate and clinging nature. His father, an upright gentleman, was too preoccupied, or, perhaps, too rigid and unimaginative, to understand or sympathise with such a son. All his child-life centred in his mother, and, when he was six years old, his mother died. To lose his mother was, to a child in Cowper's situation, to be left alone. More than half a century after his mother's death he still remembered the smile that had comforted his childish griefs, and longed to hear his mother's voice.

> "O that those lips had language! Life has passed
> With me but roughly since I heard thee last."[2]

It is hardly too much to say that Cowper's loss made him homeless as well as motherless, since from this time his life was almost entirely passed away from his father's house. Very soon after his mother's death he was "taken

[1] See passage beginning —

    " Where once we dwelt, our name is heard no more,"
    — in *Lines on the Receipt of My Mother's Picture.*

[2] *Lines on the Receipt of My Mother's Picture.*

from the nursery" and entered at a neighbouring school.
Here, the timid, gentle child of six, the memory of his
recent grief still fresh within him, was an easy prey for
the young barbarians, too common at that time in the
schools of England. His chief tormentor was a brutal
bully of fifteen; and poor Cowper, who did not dare to
lift his eyes to the face of his persecutor, said in after
life that he "knew him better by his shoe-buckles than
by any other part of his dress." [1]   At ten Cowper was sent
to the great school of Westminster, where Warren Hastings, the future ruler of India, and Charles Churchill,
the satiric poet, were among his schoolfellows. Cowper's
second experience of school-life seems to have been more
fortunate than his first, for in one of his poems he speaks
with evident sympathy of the Englishman's pleasant recollections of his school days:

> "Be it a weakness, it deserves some praise,
> We love the play-place of our early days;
> The scene is touching, and the heart is stone
> That feels not at that sight, and feels at none." [2]

At eighteen Cowper left Westminster and began the
study of the law, for which he had little aptitude. He
led an idle, aimless existence, apparently careless of the
future, and spending more money than he could afford.
He loved harmless gaiety and fine clothes; he wrote
verses, and became an occasional contributor to the *Connoisseur*, a periodical of the approved eighteenth-century
pattern. But Cowper had a deep-seated tendency to
melancholy, and his high spirits began to be interrupted
by intervals of depression. In 1763, through the influence of his uncle, Cowper had the opportunity of obtaining an excellent government post. To do this, he
was obliged to pass an examination before the House of

[1] Cowper's *Memoir*.
[2] Cowper's *Tirocinium; or, a Review of Schools*.

Lords. To Cowper, this examination, which was often, in fact, a merely formal matter, seemed a terrible ordeal. He struggled frantically to prepare himself, but he could neither face the trial with composure, nor, in justice to his uncle, decline the appointment. The strain was too great for one of Cowper's nervous temperament, and his over-wrought mind gave way.

After two years in an asylum for the insane, Cowper was sufficiently restored to be set at liberty, but all hopes of a successful career for him were at an end. He had had his chance, and lost; and at thirty-four he seemed a beaten man, weak in body and in mind. He was accordingly established at Huntingdon, a quiet old town near the river Ouse, in 1765. He was, to use his own comparison, "a stricken deer" who had "left the herd." The "great Babel," as he called London, had become terrible to him, and he found in those placid country-scenes among which the remainder of his life was passed, a hiding-place and a shelter. He loved to wander along the banks of the Ouse, —

> "Low winding through a level plain
> Of spacious meads with cattle sprinkled o'er."

He loved to watch the labourers at their wholesome tasks, and all the simple, natural sights and sounds about him, brought healing to his mind.

Soon after he came to Huntingdon he went to live with a family named Unwin, and found in their house a true home. The Unwins were gentle, amiable, and devout, and in their quiet household Cowper led the life of a religious recluse. After Mr. Unwin's death in 1767, Cowper and Mrs. Unwin moved to Olney, a village in Buckinghamshire inseparably associated with his memory and his walks. Cowper's friendship for the Unwins was one of the controlling influences of his life. He became the poet of the home; he pictured in *The Task*, the family gathered contentedly around an English fireside on a winter's evening, and a new sense of the worth and sacredness of family life arose in men's minds. We owe this picture of "home-born happiness" to Mrs. Unwin, who gave Cowper, a lonely and half distracted man, almost the only home that he had ever known. She gave him years of sympathetic companionship; she was the "dear companion" of his walks; she watched over him in health, and she nursed him with the tenderness of a mother when the awful night of insanity again darkened his spirits.

Before he left Huntingdon, Cowper had made the acquaintance of the Rev. John Newton (1725–1807), a curate at Olney, who was prominent in the religious revival begun by Wesley. Newton induced Cowper to write hymns, in the belief that some mental occupation might be of benefit. But nothing could avert the return of Cowper's malady, and a second attack of his disease left Cowper shattered in body and mind. Tormented by the belief that he had been doomed to eternal punishment, he tried to find a temporary relief and distraction in trifles. He worked in his garden; he diverted himself with the antics of his pet hares, Puss, Tiney, and Bess, as some condemned prisoner watches the spider in his dungeon. He tried to amuse himself with birds, with his dog, with a squirrel, with carpenter-work, with drawing — with making verses. Cowper, although he had written hymns and occasional verses before this, was about fifty years old when he finally entered upon his work as a poet. But this middle-aged and broken man, who at first experimented with verse-making for his diversion, proved to be one of the most charming and probably the most representative poet of his generation.

The superiority of Cowper's later work has caused these

earlier poems to be unduly neglected. They are moral

essays in verse on some abstract topic, — *The Progress of Error, Truth, Hope, Charity,* — and they follow in general the manner of Pope and his school. But the newer, more unconventional spirit is present in them also, struggling to break through the restrictions of the prevailing poetic form. Cowper saw that this form, however excellent it may have been in the hands of such an artist as Pope, had outlived its usefulness; that Pope's style had raised up innumerable imitators until "every warbler" had the master's "tune by heart." [1]

The success of these early poems was sufficient to encourage Cowper to continue his labours, and in 1785 he

published *The Task*, the greatest of his longer poems. *The Task* was written at the suggestion of Cowper's cheerful and witty friend Lady Austen, who had urged him to try his hand at blank verse. Cowper was at a loss for a subject, and Lady Austen, anxious that he should make a start, said, "Oh! you can write upon anything — write upon this sofa." Lady Austen was right. The important thing was to get Cowper fairly at work; his genius needed this external incentive, and the poem begun as a task soon became a pleasure. Once over the initial difficulties, he poured out in rambling, inconsequent, but charming verse, those nice observations of life and nature that he had accumulated in years of quiet and contemplation. For *The Task*, deficient as it seems in definite plan or structure, has yet an artistic unity, because, from first to last, it is a revelation of Cowper himself. The group about the fire on a winter's night; the woodsman, crossing the snow to his day's work, his lean cur at his heels, or frolicking in the powdery drift; the waggoner, breasting the driving storm beside his reeking team; the quiet return of even-

---

[1] *Table Talk, q. v. passim* for an expression of Cowper's views on this subject.

ing; the still waters of the Ouse, shining like "molten-glass" in the green fields; the square church-tower; the clipt hedge-rows, and all the ordered beauty and repose of the English landscape; — these things Cowper had seen and loved, and his simple, faithful descriptions of them are entirely free from self-consciousness or artifice.[1] And side by side with these idylls of an English village, are the poet's thoughts on life in its wider aspects; on the special problems that the men of his generation were then but just beginning to perceive. Recluse as he was, timid as he seems, he was a leader, a precursor of Wordsworth, a man who helped to bring in the ideals of our modern world. He was the poet of that awakened religious fervour which was then cleansing and uplifting society; the poet of the new love for humanity, that rose above the artificial barriers of nation or of class:

> "My ear is pained,
> My soul is sick with every day's report
> Of wrong and outrage with which earth is filled.
> There is no flesh in man's obdurate heart;
> It does not feel for man." [2]

He is the lover of human freedom, the champion of the slave; the poet of the simple, natural life, who declared that

> "God made the country, and man made the town."

His heart goes out to the helpless and the weak; to all living things. Even the worm seems to him to have his rights in the world.[3] *The Task* established Cowper's fame, and Southey has pronounced him "the most popular poet of his generation." After its publication he devoted himself

---

[1] He says truly in *The Task*, addressing Mrs. Unwin:

> "Thou knowest my praise of Nature most sincere,
> And that my raptures are not conjured up
> To serve occasions of poetic pomp,
> But genuine, and art partner of them all."

— Book II.

[2] *The Task*, Bk. ii. 1–5.   [3] *The Task*, Bk. vi.

systematically to literary work. He made a translation of Homer, and wrote some of the best of his shorter pieces, but completed no other long or great poem. But his life was a tragedy. In his last years the darkness closed over him, and in 1796, after the illness and death of Mrs. Unwin, his mental condition became pitiable in the extreme. He could struggle no longer. He believed himself beyond the reach of mercy, and his poem of *The Castaway*, written during these last despairing years, is the cry of one who is sinking forever into a black abyss. He died in 1800, and "never," said Southey, "was there a burial at which the mourners might, with more sincerity of feeling, give their hearty thanks to Almighty God, that it had pleased him to deliver the departed out of the miseries of this sinful world."

While he could not entirely rid himself of the worn-out conventionalities and the prosaic spirit of the older school. Cowper's poetry possesses certain great and obvious merits. It is great because it expresses with absolute truthfulness, and simplicity of feeling, an essentially noble and loving disposition, and because it records with a delicate exactness the results of a close observation of nature and of men. His imagination does not carry him beyond the limits of his own experience; he cannot enter into and reveal to us the souls of other men; but he reveals his own, and (as his friend Hayley said of him)

"His virtues formed the magic of his song."

If he is limited, he is genuine. It is the unmistakable accent of truth in his *Lines on My Mother's Picture*, that makes it one of the most heart-breaking poems in literature. It is not the skill of the poet which impresses us, but the grief of a man. We feel this unmistakable accent of truth in the poem *To Mary*, in *The Castaway*, and in his finely etched pictures of country-life. And to sincerity, we must add simplicity, that final virtue which the most finished artists sometimes fail to attain. The power of Cowper's poem *On the Loss of the Royal George* is chiefly due to its restraint and directness, to its inspired simplicity. And besides these qualities, Cowper was gifted with a sense of humour, so quick, so playful, and so free from malice, that it only helped to bring him into closer and more human relations with the world. Cowper's letters are among the treasures of the literature, and are worthy to hold a place beside his verse. "Two men of mark in English literature, Southey and Alexander Smith, have called Cowper 'the best of English letter-writers,' and few will be found to challenge this opinion." [1]

Loving and lovable, with all his weakness, it was given to him to see and to understand, through the power of sympathy, and through a kindly humour, and to tell the world truthfully and simply, and often with a peculiar, unobtrusive charm, the things he saw.

ROBERT BURNS.

(1759–1796.)

The soul of the new England, its moving tenderness, its breadth of charity, its deepening notes of lyric passion, throb in the songs of the Scotch ploughman, Robert Burns. The lives and struggles of the mass of men that toiled and died about him were utterly outside the range of Pope's narrow sympathies and understanding; his genius lights up for us only that fashionable, frivolous, or literary world in which he moved, leaving all without in darkness. The scholarly Gray had written of the poor with refinement and taste, surrounding them with a certain poetic halo; but Burns spoke not about, but for them, by his birthright and his heritage of poverty and labour. The

[1] R. W. Benham, "Introduction" to *Letters of William Cowper*.

young democracy hurrying on the day through the labours
of Brindley, the mechanic; Hargraves, the poor weaver;
or Watt, the mathematical instrument maker's apprentice, finds its poet-prophet in a farmer's boy of the Scotch
Lowlands. The natural music, the irresistible melody of
Burns's songs, was learned not from the principles of
literary lawgivers, but from the songs of the people. In
their captivating *lilt*, their rich humour, their note of
elemental passion, is revealed the soul of the peasant
class. "Poetry," wrote the great poet who preached a
little later the superiority of inspiration to artifice, "poetry
comes from the heart and goes to the heart." [1] This is
eminently true of the poetry of Burns, whose best songs
have that heartfelt and broadly human quality which
penetrates where more cultured verse fails to enter, and
which outlasts the most elaborate productions of a less
instinctive art. Burns himself assures us:

> "The Muse, nae Poet ever fand her,
>   Till by himsel' he learned to wander,
>   Adown some trotting burn's meander,
>   An' no think lang:
>   O sweet, to stray an' pensive ponder
>   A heart-felt sang." [2]

Born out of his own experience, Burns's poems are racy
of the soil, as frankly local in subject as in dialect. He
is not ashamed to paint the homely and every-day aspects
of the life about him, and he does this with a boldness
and freedom which mark genius of an independent and
original power. "The rough scenes of Scottish life, not
seen by him in any Arcadian illusion, but in the rude
contradiction, in the smoke and soil of a too harsh reality,
are still lovely to him . . . and thus over the lowest provinces of man's existence he pours the glory of his own

[1] William Wordsworth.   [2] " To William Simpson."

soul." [1] The family group, after their week of toil, gathered in patriarchal simplicity about the cotter's hearthstone; the blazing ingle of the country tavern, where the drunken cronies, "victorious o'er all ills," sing their jolly catches, oblivious of the storm without, or the wrathful wife at home; the current controversy between the Auld and New Lichts in the kirk; a wounded hare, or a flock of startled water-fowl, — such are the homely materials ready to his hand, from which his poems are fashioned. We find in them that high gift which cannot be gained by a study of any *Art of Poetry*, of seeing with a fresh and penetrating insight. For while in one sense Burns's poems are local, they are none the less for all the world, so instinctively does he fasten upon those features of the life about him which best reflect in little some general human experience, and so appeal to the common heart of mankind. The spirit of Tam o' Shanter, defying care and the morrow, is the spirit of Sir Toby in *Twelfth Night*, rousing

"the night-owl with a catch."

Set to a more heroic key, it is that of Antony when he exclaims, while the sword hangs over him:

"Come,
Let's have one other gaudy night: call to me
All my sad captains; fill our bowls once more.
Let's mock the midnight bell." [2]

And more, what is this but an expression of that imperative desire to snatch the present joy which, in greater or smaller measure, is in us all. The poet who can look through the vesture in which life clothes itself, and find beneath the abiding human significance, who can enter into and immortalise those elements of pleasure,

[1] Carlyle, "Essay on Burns."
[2] *Antony and Cleopatra*, Act iii. Sc. 11.

pain, and passion which make the substratum of our human comedy, that poet has shown us the universal in the local.

Robert Burns, the son of a small farmer in Ayrshire, was born January 25, 1759. His family were poor, so that Burns could get but little regular education, and he remained "a hard-worked ploughboy." Through all his labour he was a great reader, having a ballad-book before him at meal-times, and whistling the songs of Scotland while guiding the plough. On the death of his father in 1784, Robert and his brother and sisters took a farm together, but it proved unprofitable. By this time he had written numerous songs, and had gained by them considerable local reputation. His affairs were so involved that he thought of leaving the country, but changed his mind on receiving an invitation from a Dr. Blacklock, who had heard of his poetical ability, to visit Edinburgh. At Edinburgh, Burns, with his genius and flavour of rusticity, his massive head and glowing eyes, became the reigning sensation. In 1788 he leased a farm in Dumfriesshire, married Jean Armour, and spent one of his few peaceful and happy years. In 1789 he was appointed exciseman, that is, the district inspector of goods liable to a tax. From this time the habit of intemperance gained on him. His health and spirits failed, and bouts of reckless drinking were followed by intervals of remorse and attempted recovery. His genius did not desert him, and some of his best songs were composed during this miserable time. He died July 21, 1796, worn out and prematurely old at thirty-seven, one of the great song-writers of the world.

In spite of those weaknesses which cut off a life "that might have grown full straight," Burns's poetry is unmistakably the utterance of a sincere, large-hearted, and essentially noble nature, pleasure-loving and full of laughter as a child, yet broken by a man's grief; a nature with more than a woman's tenderness, and with the poet's soul quivering at the throb of pain.

> "Still thou art blest, compared wi' me,
>   The present only toucheth thee;
>   But och! I backward cast my e'e
>   On prospects drear!
>   An' forward, tho' I canna see,
>   I guess and fear."

Here in the midst of the lingering affectations of the time vibrates the anguish of Burns's *lyrical cry*, quivering with the unmistakable accent of human suffering. This is the universal language of passion not to be learned in the schools. Hence Burns's love-songs, from the impassioned lyric flow of *My Luve is Like a Red, Red Rose*, or *O, Wert Thou in the Cauld Blast*, to the quiet anguish of *Ae Fond Kiss and then We Sever*, or the serene beauty of *To Mary in Heaven*, are among the truest and best in the language.

In *The Cotter's Saturday Night*, as we enter the dwelling and identify ourselves with the daily life of the poor, we feel for ourselves that touch of brotherhood which in other poems it is Burns's mission to directly declare. Never perhaps since Langland's *Piers Plowman* has the complaint of the poor found such articulate expression:

> "See yonder poor, o'erlaboured wight,
>   So abject, mean, and vile,
>   Who begs a brother of the earth
>   To give him leave to toil;
>   And see his lordly fellow-worm
>   The poor petition spurn,
>   Unmindful though a weeping wife
>   And helpless offspring mourn."

When Burns wrote that —

> "Man's inhumanity to man
>   Makes countless thousands mourn,"

he expressed what thousands were coming to feel; when
he wrote —

> "A king can make a belted knight,
>   A marquis, duke, and a' that;
> But an honest man's aboon his might,
>   Guid faith he maunna fa' that,
>
> For a' that, and a' that,
>   Their dignities and a' that,
> The pith o' sense and pride o' worth
>   Are higher ranks than a' that,"

he gave to the world the greatest declaration in poetry
of human equality and the glory of simple manhood.
But, like that of Cowper, Burns's comprehensive sympathy
reaches beyond the circle of human life. He stands at
the furrow to look at the "tim'rous" field-mouse, whose
tiny house his plough has laid in ruins, and his soul is broad
enough to think of the trembling creature gently and
humbly as his

> "Poor earth-born companion
> An' fellow-mortal."

Like Byron, he was a poet of the revolution, but he distinguished more clearly than Byron between the shams
and conventionalities which he attacks, and that which
was enduring and worthy of reverence. Merciless and
daring in his satire upon the cant and hypocrisy of those
who, as he thought, used religion as a cloak for wickedness,
he had himself a deeply reverential and religious nature
which never confused the abuse of the thing with the
thing abused. He is the poet of Nature as well as of man;
he would make the streams and burnies of Scotland shine
in verse with the Ilissus and the Tiber, and

> "Sing Auld Coila's plains and fells;"

and finally in his stirring songs of Bannockburn he is the
poet of patriotic Scotland. "Lowland Scotland," it has

been said, "came in with her warriors and went out with her bards. It came in with William Wallace and Robert Bruce, and went out with Robert Burns and Walter Scott. The first two made the history; the last two told the story and sung the song."

WILLIAM WORDSWORTH.

(1770–1850.)

Toward the close of the eighteenth century we reach, in the French Revolution, the most stormy and critical period in the history of modern Europe. Toward this consummation Europe had been rapidly moving. Poet and philosopher had gone before it, while to the toiling masses, starved, overtaxed, oppressed, the burden was becoming intolerable. Now, during the early acts of that terrible drama, the cloud-land visions and lofty speculations of poet and philosopher, looking for the coming of a Golden Age of peace and brotherhood, seemed to many to be passing out of the region of speculation into the world of substantial fact. Cowper in *The Task* had cried out against the Bastile as a shameful "house of bondage:"[1] four years later it fell before the fury of a Parisian mob (1789). Then

> "France her giant limbs upreared,
> And with that oath which smote earth, air, and sea,
> Stamped her strong foot and said she would be free."[2]

Europe looked on breathless, as the whole glittering fabric of French feudalism, rotten at the base, suddenly crashed into ruin. The ancient barriers of custom and authority were swept away as in a night; the floods were out; the Revolution begun. Blake walked the streets of London wearing the red cockade of the Revolutionists, and the pas-

[1] *The Task*, Bk. v. V. the whole passage.
[2] Coleridge, *France, an Ode.*

sionate hopes for the future of the race broadened far beyond the old national limits, to embrace the whole family of man. Even the great statesman Pitt sympathised with the Revolutionists, and Fox is said to have exclaimed, on hearing of the destruction of the Bastile, "How much is this the greatest event that ever happened in the world, and how much the best!" Edmund Burke, indeed, stood aloof from the rest, a solitary and impregnable tower of conservatism; and in Edinburgh the young Walter Scott, whose intense sympathy with that chivalric past was to revive its glories in the pages of poetry and romance, looked on at the fury of demolition with characteristic disapproval. But for the most part the hopes of youth, and of all the ardent and enthusiastic spirits of the time, went out toward the Revolutionists in a great torrent of exultation. The imagination of the youthful poets William Wordsworth, Samuel Taylor Coleridge, and Robert Southey, all in the impressionable years of opening manhood when the Revolution began, was fired by the idea that the world was being made anew. They trod the earth in rapture, their eyes fixed upon a vision of the dawn. Looking back upon this time one of their number wrote:

> "Bliss was it in that Dawn to be alive,
> But to be young was very heaven."[1]

A spirit of change was in the air which showed itself in many ways. In England it expressed itself in a more positive reaction against much that was hollow and artificial in the life and literature of an earlier time. The longing for something natural and genuine became the master passion of the new leaders of thought. Not only does the new love of Nature and of man inspire the poetry of Wordsworth and of Coleridge, they are the leaders of a deliberate attack

---

[1] Wordsworth, *The Prelude*, Bk. xi.

on the artificial poetic manner exemplified in the poetry of Pope. Wordsworth came determined to destroy the old "poetic diction" and set up a simpler and truer manner in its stead. Another but later expression of this longing for what is genuine is found in the works of the great prose-writer Thomas Carlyle (1795–1881), who fiercely denounced all "shams," railed against the eighteenth century as an era of fraud and unbelief, and preached that men "should come back to reality, that they should stand upon things and not upon the shows of things." In these, and in many similar ways, the period at which we have now arrived was an *era of revolution*. In many spheres of thought and action the old order was changing, yielding place to new.

William Wordsworth, one of the great leaders in this era of change, was born April 7, 1770, at Cockermouth, a little village on the river Derwent in the county of Cumberland. His father, the law-agent to Sir James Lowther, was descended from an ancient family of Yorkshire landowners, while his mother's ancestors had been among the landed gentry of Cumberland since the reign of Edward III. On both sides, therefore, the poet came of a family stock deeply rooted in the country soil, and he may well have inherited from this long line of provincial ancestors that sympathy with the country, and with the simple incidents of country life, which is a principal element in his verse. Cumberland, a singularly lovely region of lake and mountain, was then far more remote than at present from the activities of the outside world. Wordsworth was gifted with a wonderful susceptibility to natural beauty, and the serenity and grandeur of his early surroundings entered deep into his life to become the very breath of his being. In his daily companionship with Nature he seems to have felt at first a kind of primitive and unreasoning rapture, to be changed in later years for a more profound and conscious love. His more regular education

William Wordsworth.

was obtained at Hawkshead School, in Lancashire, and at Cambridge. But college and the fixed routine of college studies failed to touch his enthusiasm, and he is said to have occupied himself before coming up for his degree in reading Richardson's novels. He graduated in 1791, but, as may be supposed, without having distinguished himself. On leaving Cambridge he spent some months in visiting London and elsewhere, finally crossing to France, where he caught the contagion of republicanism, and was on the point of offering himself as a leader of the Girondist party. His relations, alarmed for his safety, stopped his supplies, and in 1792 lack of money compelled his return. On reaching England he found himself with no profession and without definite prospects. After three years in this unsettled condition he was unexpectedly placed beyond actual want by a timely legacy of £900 from his friend Raisley Calvert, who had discerned in Wordsworth the promise of future greatness, and who wished to make him free to pursue his chosen career. Shortly before this he had made his first public ventures in poetry (*An Evening Walk*, 1793; *Descriptive Sketches*, 1793). After the receipt of Calvert's legacy he took a cottage at Racedown in Dorsetshire with his devoted sister Dorothy, resolved to dedicate himself to poetry. From this time Wordsworth's life was of the most studiously simple, severe, and uneventful description, an example of that "plain living and high thinking" in which he believed. It was lived close to nature, in the circle of deep home attachments, and in the society of a few chosen friends, but it resembled that of Milton in its solemn consecration to the high service of his art, and in its consistent nobility and loftiness of tone. Leaving Racedown in 1797, Wordsworth settled at Alfoxden, near Nether Stowey, Somersetshire, where his genius rapidly developed under the stimulating companionship of his friend Coleridge. Here the two poets worked together, and in 1798 published the

Lyrical Ballads, a collection of poems to which each contributed. This work, by its deliberate departure from the outworn poetic manner, marks an era in the history of English poetry. It is in his preface to the second edition of this work (published 1800) that Wordsworth made his famous onslaught upon the school of Pope, declaring, among other things, that poetry was not to be made by rules, but that it was "the spontaneous overflow of powerful feelings." After this Wordsworth worked steadily, holding to his own notions of poetry in spite of the ridicule of the critics and the neglect of the body of readers. In the winter of 1798–1799 he visited Germany. On his return he settled in Westmoreland, in the Lake District, living first at Grasmere (1799–1813), and finally removing to Rydal Mount. In 1802 he married his cousin Mary Hutchinson, also a native of Cumberland. Miss Hutchinson, like Wordsworth's beloved sister Dorothy, had a rare appreciation of poetry. He had thus the devotion and sympathy of two gifted women, both capable of entering into his finest emotions and aspirations. The poet, his wife, and sister, thus lived in an ideal and beautiful companionship, unfortunately but too rare in the lives of men of genius. Wordsworth's remaining years were passed at Rydal Mount, except when his tranquil existence was broken by short journeys on the Continent or elsewhere. As he advanced in life his work won its way in the public favour. He was made Poet Laureate in 1843, and died peacefully April 23, 1850, as his favourite clock struck the hour of noon.

As a poet Wordsworth was surpassingly great within that somewhat restricted sphere which he has made

Wordsworth as a poet. peculiarly his own. He is deficient in a sense of humour, he possesses but little dramatic force or narrative skill, and he fails in a broad and living sympathy with the diverse passions and interests of human life. These limitations will always tend to make

him the poet of the appreciative few. To him, indeed,
his own words are strikingly applicable:

> "He is retired as noontide dew,
>   Or fountain in a noonday grove;
> And you must love him, ere to you
>   He will seem worthy of your love." [1]

Yet he is as truly the poet of the mysterious world we
call Nature, as Shakespeare is the poet of the life of man.
He, more than all other poets, teaches us to enter into that
world and find in it the very temple of God, in which and
through which He himself will draw close to us.

For Wordsworth's mystical rapture in the presence
of the living world is very different from a merely sensuous
or æsthetic delight; it is, in his highest moods, a profoundly
religious emotion. In the intensity of his contemplation,
his own being is lost in the flood of universal life "that
rolls through all things," and in an ecstasy of aspiration
he is "laid asleep in body and becomes a living soul." [2]
Such a mood, unintelligible to more phlegmatic and
commonplace natures, is characteristic of those in whom
the apprehension of ideal or spiritual things is exceptionally
strong. Plato or Plotinus, the passive Brahmin of the
East, or the German *Tauler*, seeks, each in his own fashion,
to erect himself above himself by an ecstasy of thought or
emotion. "By ecstasy," said Plotinus, "the soul becomes
loosened from its material prison, separated from individual consciousness, and becomes absorbed into the
Infinite Intelligence from which it emanated." Now to
Wordsworth the path of escape from the "material prison,"
the avenue of access to the "Infinite Intelligence," lay
through communion with the informing life in Nature.
His assurance that the universe was not a mechanical
contrivance, like a huge piece of clockwork, whose motive

---

[1] *A Poet's Epitaph.*
[2] *Lines on Revisiting Tintern Abbey.*

power was law, but a something divinely alive, is the basis alike of his poetry and his philosophy. This seemingly stolid countryman, with somewhat the aspect of a benignant farmer, recognises the presence of a sentient life in brook and flower, with the poetic apprehension of the Greek in the dewy morning of the world. He teaches that if we will but pause in our perpetual quest, and let Nature work her will on us, active influences, at work within her, will go out to us.

> "Nor less I deem that there are Powers,
> Which of themselves our minds impress;
> That we can feed this mind of ours
> In a wise passiveness." [1]

In accord with this, is Wordsworth's reiterated teaching that Nature, and the deep joy in Nature, is, or should be, the great formative influence in the life of man. If in youth man lies on the lap of his great Earth-Mother, something passes into his life which later experience, and the worldliness which may come with years, can never "utterly abolish or destroy." [2] It seemed to Wordsworth that the secret of life was to hold fast youth's generous emotions, its high imaginings, its deep fountains of joy, as an antidote to the deadening and contaminating influences of the world. He believed that it was by a consistent fellowship with Nature that this precious conservation of our high emotions could best be accomplished. To see again in age some aspect of Nature which sank deep into the soul in youth; to hear again in age that cry of the cuckoo which enchanted us in boyhood, is to revive our youthful rapture, and "beget that golden time again." [3] Thus a "natural piety," binding our days each to each,[4] should inoculate us against the contagion of the world.

[1] *Expostulation and Reply.*   [2] *Ode on Intimations of Immortality.*
[3] *Lines to the Cuckoo.*   [4] *The Rainbow.*

Wordsworth celebrates the beauty, harmony, and sublimity of Nature; he is fortified by its calm and its **Limitations of Wordsworth's view of Nature.** unbroken order; sustained with eternal hopes by the unwearied renewal of the vernal earth, by the "cheerful faith" that "all which we behold is full of blessings." [1] But Nature is not all a May day; she has a harsh and terrifying side, of which Wordsworth was apparently oblivious. He is silent as to her mysterious discords of pain, cruelty, and death. So far as we can tell, he is unimpressed by any feeling of her magnificent indifference to man. To this extent his poetry of Nature is partial and incomplete. Nevertheless, in this very incompleteness lies one source of Wordsworth's tranquillising and uplifting power. We are refreshed and sanctified by the very unreservedness of his conviction that the whole world is but the temple of the living God. Of all the poets who in the eighteenth century came to lead a rouged and tired generation of intrigue and scandal back to that mother-world to which they had become as strangers, Wordsworth proved himself the greatest and most inspired guide. The murmur of the Derwent,[2] the clouds gathered about the setting sun, the splendours of lonely dawns, the solitude of mountain-peak and lake and forest, all these things had been his world, and consciously and unconsciously the amplitude and sublimity of that world, extending illimitably about us in its large patience and inscrutable repose, possessed and enlarged his soul. His life rises to the dignity of a great example, because it is so outwardly ordinary and so inwardly exceptional; because he showed us how to make a new use of those familiar sources of joy and comfort which lie open to all who have eyes to see and ears to hear. His life was severely simple, yet the world was his, even as, up to the measure of our power of receiving, we may make it ours.

[1] *Lines on Revisiting Tintern Abbey.*   [2] *V. The Prelude.*

It is this serene and noble simplicity of Wordsworth's life and character that sheds over certain of his poems an indescribable and altogether incomparable charm. Such short lyrics as *The Solitary Reaper*, the poems to *Lucy*, or *The Primrose of the Rock*, are filled with that characteristic and magical excellence which refuses to be analysed or defined. Wordsworth's sonnets are among the best in the literature; and his longer poems, such as *The Excursion*, while deficient in compactness and structure, are illumined by passages of wonderful wisdom and beauty. At times, as in those characteristic masterpieces, the great companion odes *To Duty* and *On the Intimations of Immortality from Recollections of Early Childhood*, his verse has an elevation and a large majesty of utterance unheard in English poetry since the deep-throated harmonies of Milton. In spite of frequent lapses, Wordsworth's poetic art is of a very high order, and places him with the greatest poets of England.

In a very real sense Wordsworth is the poet of the new democracy, as he is of the new love of Nature. The chosen characters of his poems are the simple and hardy peasants of his native Cumberland. Like the good Lord Clifford, in the *Song at the Feast of Brougham Castle*, he found love in "huts where poor men lie." Once it was a canon of literary art that the shepherd-hero should prove to be a prince in disguise, or the charming shepherdess, like Perdita, the lost daughter of a queen. But Wordsworth, speaking for a world that has outworn its feudalism, discards all such adventitious and once necessary means of enlisting our sympathy. "The man's the gowd for a' that," and it is the deep democratic feeling to which we have now grown so accustomed in our modern literature that gives the sorrows of Margaret or of the old shepherd Michael an equal place in the world's heart with the most royal of sufferers, recog-

The poet of democracy.

nising in the humblest a common humanity consecrated by the dignity of a great grief.

Matthew Arnold, himself a poetic disciple of Wordsworth, has thus summed up the peculiar greatness of his master's work: "Wordsworth's poetry is great because of the extraordinary power with which Wordsworth feels the joy offered to us in Nature, the joy offered to us in the simple primary affections and duties; and because of the extraordinary power with which, in case after case, he shows us this joy, and renders it so as to make us share it." [1]

SAMUEL TAYLOR COLERIDGE.

(1772–1834.)

Wordsworth lived out his long, blameless, and devoted life under conditions singularly favourable to the full development of his genius. Freed from the pressure of money difficulties, and enabled to live simply amid the loveliest of natural surroundings, happy in his home and in his friends, and blessed with health and energy, he has left us a shining example of a serene and truly successful life. The story of Coleridge, Wordsworth's friend and fellow-poet, is tragically different. It is the story of a man of rare and varied gifts, who, from whatever cause, could not, or did not, put forth his powers to the full. Carlyle has condensed this into one epigrammatic sentence: "To the man himself had Nature given, in high measure, the seeds of a noble endowment; and to unfold it had been forbidden him."

Samuel Taylor Coleridge, the youngest of a large family, was the son of the vicar and schoolmaster at the little town of Ottery St. Mary, Devonshire. Left an orphan in his ninth year, he was admitted to the Charity School at Christ's

[1] Introduction to *Selections from Wordsworth*.

Hospital, London, and began the unequal fight of life. Here he met Charles Lamb, who has recorded some of their joint experiences in one of his *Essays of Elia*.[1] From the first, Coleridge seems to have half lived in a dream-world, created by "the shaping spirit of Imagination," which, as he says, "Nature gave me at my birth."[2] As a little child he wandered over the Devonshire fields, slashing the tops off weeds and nettles in the character of one of the "Seven Champions of Christendom;" and in school at London he would lie for hours on the roof, gazing after the drifting clouds while his schoolfellows played football in the court below; or in the midst of the crowded Strand, he would fancy himself Leander swimming the Hellespont. A hopelessly erratic, inconsequent element runs through his whole life, depriving it of unity and steady purpose. At nineteen he went to Cambridge and furnished his rooms with no thought of his inability to pay the upholsterers; then, under the pressure of a comparatively trifling debt, he gave up all his prospects, fled to London, and enlisted in the Dragoons. He returned to Cambridge, but left there in 1794 without taking a degree. Visiting Oxford in this year, he met the youthful Southey, in whom he found a kindred spirit. Both were feeling that impulse from the French Revolution which was agitating Europe. They agreed that human society should be reconstructed, and decided to begin the reform by establishing an ideal community in the wilds of America. The new form of government was to be called a Pantisocracy, or the government by all, and the citizens were to combine farming and literature. The bent of the two poets at this time is shown by the subjects of their work. They composed together a poem on *The Fall of Robespierre*, and Southey's *Wat Tyler* (1794) is charged with the revolutionary spirit. In 1795 Coleridge married

---

[1] *Christ's Hospital, Five-and-Thirty Years Ago.*
[2] Coleridge's *Dejection; an Ode.*

Sarah Fricker, whose sister Edith became the wife of Southey a few weeks later. The pantisocratic scheme was given up for lack of funds, and Coleridge and his wife settled at Clevedon, on the Bristol Channel. It was about two years after this that he met Wordsworth at Alfoxden, contributing *The Ancient Mariner* to their joint venture, the *Lyrical Ballads*. In 1798 Coleridge left for Germany, where he remained about two years, receiving a fresh and powerful stimulus from the new intellectual and literary life on which that nation had just entered. An immediate result of the visit was a translation of Schiller's *Wallenstein*, but its effect on Coleridge's tone of thought was profound and lasting. Through him, and afterward through Thomas Carlyle, the influence of German literature began for the first time to tell on that of England.

Coleridge returned to England in 1800. He gave up an excellent opening in journalism to lead a life of quietness and study, settling near Keswick, in Cumberland, a district to which his friend Wordsworth had already retreated. Here he was full of great plans; life seemed growing easier; but his work was interrupted by illness, and to quiet the torments of gout and neuralgia, he unhappily resorted to a quack specific containing opium.

He thus gradually came under the power of this terrible drug, and for the next fifteen years he battled with a habit which was clouding his splendid intellect, and benumbing his energies and his will. To follow this melancholy story is like watching the efforts of some hurt creature struggling in the toils. Estranged from his family, he became, as he writes, "the most miserable of men, having a home, and yet homeless." Finally, under the care of a Mr. Gilman, a surgeon, at Highgate, London, he conquered his fatal habit.

Carlyle, who visited him at Mr. Gilman's, says that he "gave you the idea of a life that had been full of sufferings, a life heavy laden, half vanquished, still swimming pain-

fully in seas of manifold physical and other bewilderment." [1]
Once, with the sense of power strong within him, he had
looked forward to the composition of some mighty works
which should adequately express his genius; now, with so
much yet undone, he was beaten and disheartened, tired
by the long fight against himself and the world. His health
was shattered, his will weakened, while the sense of failure
weighed him down. In one of his later poems he pictures
himself as listless and inert in the midst of the glad young
vigour of the spring, idle while "all Nature seems at work"
about him, his sadness but deepened by the melancholy
sense of contrast. In him the motive power is extinct.

> "And would you learn the spells that drowse my soul?
>   Work without hope draws nectar in a sieve,
>   And hope without an object cannot live."

Such poems bring us closer to him than any intrusive
words of criticism. *Youth and Age* is even more beautiful
in its patient hopelessness and the pathos of its unavailing
look backward to a lost youth.

> "This breathing house not built with hands,
>   This body that does me grievous wrong,
>   O'er aery cliffs and glittering sands,
>   How lightly then it flashed along —
>   Naught cared this body for wind or weather
>   When youth and I lived in't together."

Now, when "no hope is,"

> "Life's a warning
>   That only serves to make us grieve,
>   When we are old;
>   That only serves to make us grieve
>   With oft and tedious taking-leave,
>   Like some poor nigh-related guest,
>   That may not rudely be dismist,
>   Yet hath outstayed his welcome while
>   And tells the jest without the smile."

[1] Carlyle's *Life of Sterling.*   [2] Coleridge's *Youth and Age.*

Hopeless as the sadness of this poem is, it is yet the sadness of a tranquil and quiet acceptance of a great loss. In nothing is the real sweetness and soundness of this man's nature more manifest than in the absence of all taint of bitterness, of peevish complaint or Byronic despair. What he deems his own failure does not prevent his genuine delight in Wordsworth's great achievements. And when at last — as in one of his own poems — Hope and Love, overtasked, at length give way, their mute sister, Patience,

"Both supporting, does the work of both." [1]

When Coleridge wrote his words of regret for the youth and life that seemed to have slipped away from him so fast, the corruptible body was already pressing heavily on the mind that mused upon so many things. Four years later, on July 25, 1834, he was delivered from the burden of the flesh. The world had let him die in his conviction of failure, but no sooner had the grave closed over him than England resounded with his praise.

If Wordsworth's was a life lived out in the still, high altitudes of thought, if it was heroic in its simplicity and austerity, it has in it a certain chill that seems to come from its very loftiness and isolation. But Coleridge, with his rare and lovely nature, is perpetually hurting himself against the rough places of an uncompromising world. He is struggling all his life with the crowd, stumbling, and beaten, and disheartened, and by the mysterious law of human suffering, he gains a tenderness that we miss in Wordsworth in spite of all his successes. If Wordsworth has the stimulating vigour of the stoic, Coleridge has the great compassion of the Christian.

For in spite of his inward conviction that he had failed, there is, especially in his later poems, the stillness of a great calm. In Henry Crabbe Robinson's *Diary* there is

[1] *Love, Hope and Patience in Education.*

this significant passage: "Last night he [Coleridge] concluded his fine development of the Prince of Denmark by an eloquent statement of the moral of the play. 'Action,' he said, 'is the great end of all; no intellect, however grand, is valuable, if it draw us from action and lead us to think and think till the time of action is passed by, and we can do nothing.' Somebody said to me, 'This is a satire on himself.' 'No,' said I, 'it is an elegy.'" [1]

Much of Coleridge's work is, like his life, fragmentary and incomplete; yet its range and variety bear witness to the broad scope and many-sided vigour of his genius. He was one of the great English talkers. On every hand we find testimony to his personal influence upon his distinguished contemporaries. As a converser he held somewhat the same place as that occupied by Samuel Johnson immediately before, and by Thomas Babington Macaulay immediately after, him.

Coleridge's work.

In Coleridge's full life the writing of poetry was but one interest, even perhaps a somewhat incidental one. His discursive energy spent itself in philosophy, in theology, in political journalism, and in criticism. He strove to infuse into the common-sense and materialistic English philosophy, the more ideal and spiritual character of contemporary German thought. He was the most profound and philosophic critic of his time. His *Biographia Literaria* contains an exposition of Wordsworth's poetic principles even superior to that put forth by that poet himself. His lectures on Shakespeare began an era in the history of English Shakespearean criticism.

As philosopher and critic.

Coleridge left but little poetry. Much of this is scrappy and unfinished, and no small proportion is obviously inferior in quality to his best poetic work. He seems to have required peculiar conditions for poetic composition; inspiration came to him suddenly,

As poet.

[1] *Diary*, etc., of H. C. Robinson, vol. ii. p. 235.

in mysterious gusts; but often before a poem was finished, it as suddenly left him, apparently as powerless as an ordinary mortal to complete what he alone could have begun. Thus, after writing the second part of *Christabel*, a poem born of the very breath of inspiration, he waited vainly until the end of his life for the return of the creative mood. He tells us that when writing *Kubla Khan*, a poem which came to him in his sleep as a kind of vision, he was interrupted "by a person on business from Porlock," and that on his return he was unable to complete it. He concludes with the pathetically characteristic words: "The author has frequently purposed to finish for himself what had been originally, as it were, given to him. Αὔριον ἄδιον ᾄσω; but the to-morrow is yet to come."

We should rather attribute the smallness and incompleteness of his poetic work to some defect of character or purpose, some outside limitation which clogged the free exercise of a great gift, than regard it as the result of any flaw in the quality of the gift itself.

While in mere bulk his contribution to poetry is comparatively small, its intrinsic value outweighs all the ponderous mass of poor Southey's laborious epics. When Coleridge's genius works freely and under favourable conditions, we are captivated by a music that places him with the lyrical masters of the literature, and impressed by the sense of his absolute originality of tone. His descriptions of Nature are often condensed and vivid, like those of Dante, showing the power to enter into the spirit of a scene and reproduce it with a few quick strokes:

> "The sun's rim dips; the stars rush out;
> At one stride comes the dark." [1]

In some poems, indeed, he seems to follow in the track of Wordsworth; but in *Christabel, The Ancient Mariner*,

[1] *The Ancient Mariner.*

and *Kubla Khan*, he stands alone. There have been many poets of the supernatural; but one province of the land of visions Coleridge rules as his demesne, and

"Within that circle none durst walk but he."[1]

The Ancient Mariner is connected with that revival of interest in native ballad-poetry which was one phase of romanticism. Not only is it a ballad in form; it is filled with those ghostly and mysterious elements which, in a cruder shape, enter so largely into the folk-song and legend of primitive superstition. Such elements were congenial to certain writers of the romantic school, both in Germany and England, representing as they did the "Renaissance of Wonder,"[2] the reaction against the matter-of-fact and rational spirit of the preceding period. In both *The Ancient Mariner* and *Christabel* the ghostly and the horrible lose much of that gross and physical terror which the ordinary literature of superstition is content with calling forth. Coleridge's more subtle art brings us into a twilight and debatable region which seems to hover between the unseen and the seen, the conjectural and the real. He invests us with nameless terrors, as when we fear to turn because of a fiendish something that treads behind.

The Ancient Mariner.

We are also to observe the skill with which this supernatural element is woven into a narrative of possible incidents, so realistically told as fully to persuade us of their truth. By such means Coleridge has carried out his professed object, and almost deluded us into a temporary belief in the whole story.

Coleridge has thus created a new thing out of the crude materials of vulgar superstition, but in doing this he has

---

[1] Dryden, *Prologue to the Tempest.*
[2] The phrase of Theodore Watts-Dunton.

employed other agencies than those already named. In
The moral significance of the poem. his shadowy world, as in that of Hawthorne,
we are haunted by the continual suggestion
of some underlying moral significance. How far
we should attempt to confine the spiritual suggestiveness of
The Ancient Mariner within the limits of a set moral is open
to question. To do this may seem to some like taking the
poem out of its twilight atmosphere to drag it into the
light of common day. Yet we can hardly fail to feel that
Coleridge has here written for us the great poem of *charity*,
that "very bond of peace and of all virtues" which should
bind together all created things. It is against this law of
love that the mariner sins. He wantonly kills a creature
that has trusted him, that has loved him, that has par-
taken of the sailors' food and come at their call. The
necessary penalty for this breach in the fellowship of
living things is an exclusion from that fellowship. His
"soul" is condemned to dwell alone, until by his compassion for the "happy living things" about the ship —
by the renewal of that love against which he has sinned —
he takes the first step toward his return into the great
brotherhood of animate creation. For *hate*, or wanton
cruelty, is the estranging power which, by an inevitable
law, forces a man into spiritual exile, just as *love* is the
uniting power which draws together all living things.
The very power to pray depends upon our dwelling in this
mystic fellowship of charity; and in the poem, praying
and loving are constantly associated. (See verses 14 and
15 in Part iv., also 22 and 23 in Part vii.)

The underlying meaning in this becomes apparent in
that verse which gives us the completest statement of the
thought of the poem:

> "He prayeth best who loveth best
> All things both great and small;
> For the dear God who loveth us,
> He made and loveth all."

The last couplet gives us the reason for the declaration contained in the first.   Not only is love the bond between all *created* things — it is the bond also between the Creator and his creatures.   It is the mysterious, underlying principle of creation because it is the essence of its Creator, and an outcast through his violation of love here is no longer able to approach the Source of all love.   For the loneliness of the mariner does not consist in his loss of human sympathy merely;   he seems to drift on that strange sea of isolation almost beyond the power of the Universal Love:

> "So lonely 'twas that God himself
> Scarce seemèd there to be."

Looked at from this aspect, *The Ancient Mariner* becomes the profoundest and perhaps most beautiful expression of that feeling of sympathy for all living things which we have found uttering itself with increasing distinctness in later eighteenth-century literature.

But Coleridge's place as a poet is far from resting entirely on his poems of the supernatural.   Like Wordsworth, although not perhaps so instinctively and habitually, he sees in nature the outward manifestation of a divine energy, and God is the "all-conscious presence of the Universe." But he realises, as Wordsworth did not appear to do, that to each man nature is but what his mood or his power of spiritual apprehension makes her.   To the dulled or jaundiced eye the world is obscured or discoloured; we endow Nature with that joy which is within our own souls, or darken her fairest scenes with the pall of our sorrow, so that we receive from her "but what we give." [1]   In the philosophical element of Coleridge's maturer poems we recognise the influence of that idealistic thought of contemporary Germany which was but the philosophic form of the rebound from the materialism of an earlier time.

[1] *Dejection; an Ode.* For this view of Nature see this poem and contrast it with Wordsworth's *Expostulation and Reply.*

As he watched the promise of the French Revolution depart in the license and frenzy of the Reign of Terror, Coleridge, like Wordsworth and Southey, aban-

A poet of man. doned his youthful hopes for a settled conservatism. Burke had written at the opening of the Revolution "that the effect of liberty to individuals is that they may do what they please; we ought to see what it will please them to do before we risk congratulations which may be soon turned into complaints."[1] Seven years later, during which he had looked on at the murderous riot of a nation from which all external forces of control had been suddenly withdrawn, Coleridge reaches in his "France" a similar conclusion. He sees that true liberty must rest upon obedience to a moral law, that the only foundation for the improvement of society is the improvement of the individual, without which a so-called liberty may but hand men over to the tyranny of evil habits and desires.

> "The Sensual and the Dark rebel in vain,
> Slaves by their own compulsion! In mad game
> They burst their manacles and wear the name
> Of Freedom, graven on a heavier chain!"[2]

In this conviction, that liberty is obedience to the highest, Coleridge is one with Wordsworth and with John Ruskin, the daring and impassioned social reformer of our own day.

[1] Burke, *Reflections on French Revolution.*
[2] Coleridge, *France; an Ode.*

SIR WALTER SCOTT.

(1771–1832.)

Burns was the lawful heir to the songs of Scotland, Walter Scott to her romance and her ballads. The peasant life of Scotland, as it then was, belonged preeminently to the Ayrshire ploughman; but the romantic past of Scotland, with its lawlessness, its wild heroism, its chivalric daring, its fascinating background of mountain, loch, and glen, belonged to Scott, the child of the best blood of the Scottish Border.

Scott and Burns.

Walter Scott was born in Edinburgh, in 1771. Edinburgh, picturesque and romantic in itself, stands in the midst of a region crowded with memorials of Scotland's past. When we look at the map of this historic region, the very names of the places — Tweedsdale, Eskdale, Teviotdale, the Cheviot Hills, Lammermuir, Yarrow, Stirling, the Trossachs, Melrose, Dryburgh, Hawthornden — are full of poetic suggestion, and all this was Scott's birthright.[1] He was born in this land, and the blood of men who had helped to make it famous was in his veins. "In Scott," writes Andrew Lang, "met the blood of Highlands and Lowlands, Celtic, Teutonic, and Norman." Scott himself took a genuine pride in the fact that he came of "gentle folk," and traced, in his *Autobiography*, his lineal descent from that ancient chief, Auld Wat of Harden, "whose name I have made to ring in many a Border ditty, and from his fair dame, the Flower of Yarrow; no bad genealogy for a Border Minstrel."

Life.

Scott's father was a Writer to the Signet (attorney); his mother, Anne Rutherford, was the daughter of a distinguished Edinburgh physician. When Scott was eighteen months old a serious illness left him incurably lame. He was a delicate child, and in his third year he was sent to his grandfather's farm at

Sandy Knowe.

Sandyknowe, in the valley of the Tweed. On a neighbouring crag was Smailholme Castle, the scene of Scott's ballad
The Eve of St. John; a few miles away

> ". . . fair Tweed flows round holy Melrose,
> And Eildon slopes to the plain."

Scott's conscious life began among these scenes; their
influence entered into him as a child and remained with
him until the end. He would lie on the grass, watching
the sheep, or listen eagerly to strange tales of Border forays
from the old shepherd, or "Cow Baillie," who had charge
of the flocks and herds. Much of his childhood was passed
at Sandyknowe, in familiar intercourse with the country-
people. He listened eagerly to scraps of old ballads and
ancient songs, to anecdotes of the great Jacobite risings of
1715 and 1745, and thus, while his education was irregular,
he came to know the past of his country as he only knows
it who learns it not from books but from the traditions of
the people themselves. So Darsie Latimer, in *Redgauntlet,*
heard from the lips of Wandering Willie the marvellous
tales of his ancient house.

To this knowledge of Scotland's history and romance
Scott added, as he grew to manhood, a minute acquaintance
with the scenes in which all this drama of the
past had been enacted. He knew the little-
travelled country roads, the nooks and corners of
Scotland, as only the man does who has explored
and reëxplored them, and has lain through whole sunny
days among the heather. He knew the people, as he only
does who enters the doors of many a lonely farmhouse.
Such knowledge gave life and truth to his stories and
his poems, when he retold in after life the

Knowledge of Scottish scenery and life.

> "tales that charmed *him* yet a child." [1]

[1] Epistle to William Erskine, prefixed to the third Canto of *Mar-
mion.* See the whole passage, and *cf. Marmion,* Canto iv., xxiv., where
Scott pictures himself "a truant boy" lying among the broom on
Blackford Hill.

By this direct knowledge and comprehensive sympathy, he was able, as it were, to absorb Scotland herself, the outward aspect of her valleys, glens, and lochs, her towns, her fishing villages and hamlets, her people's life, her history, spirit, and tradition, and lift them, by the simple force of his imaginative and poetic art, into the unchanging region of literature.

In 1778, when he was seven years old, Scott was sent to the high school of Edinburgh. He loved romantic literature, but he refused to learn Greek. In 1786 he entered his father's law-office, gaining there that acquaintance with the legal life of Edinburgh which he afterwards utilised in his novel of *Redgauntlet*, and in 1792 he was called to the bar. In 1796, the year of the death of Burns, Scott began his literary career by publishing his version of the ballads of the German romantic poet Bürger. For some time Scott had been diligently collecting the ballads of his own country, and two volumes of his *Minstrelsy of the Scottish Border* (1802) were the first result of his labours. But Scott was himself a Minstrel of the Scottish Border, —

Early translations.

> "The last of all the bards was he
> Who sung of Border chivalry."

After translating German ballads and collecting Scottish ones, it was but natural that he should take the further step and pass on to original composition. *The Lay of the Last Minstrel*, his first extended attempt in this direction, appeared in 1805. The strangeness, vigour, and beauty of the poem, the interest of its story, the buoyant and spirited movement of its verse, fascinated a public accustomed to Cowper's mild reflections, or Crabbe's realism.

The Lay of the Last Minstrel.

"He blew his bugle so loud and hoarse,
  That the dun-deer started at fair Craikcross;
  He blew again so loud and clear,
  Through the grey mountain-mist there did lances appear;
  And the third blast rang with such a din
  That the echoes answer'd from Pentoun-linn,
  And all his riders came lightly in." [1]

Scott's verse has lost its novelty, but in reading such lines as these, we can still feel the force of that magic which once enchanted the world. The *Lay* was followed by *Marmion* (1808), *The Lady of the Lake* (1810), and by other poems.

Scott was not a careful workman like the scholarly and fastidious Gray, but his writings were the overflow of a vigorous and capacious nature, the unstudied expression

Miscellaneous writings. of a full mind. We are too apt to think of him merely as a poet and novelist and forget the astonishing amount of miscellaneous literary work he somehow contrived to accomplish.[2] While he was writing his poems, for instance, he found time to write reviews, compose a life of Dryden, and carry through a great quantity of editorial work. Yet these enormous literary labours did not interfere with the performance of his professional and social duties. And in all this there was no apparent effort; all is done with that ease which suggests great power.

Meanwhile, Scott's poetry had found imitators, and had lost something of the charm of novelty. Byron, who had sprung into sudden fame by the publication of the first instalment of *Childe Harold* (1812), was the poetic sensation of the hour. Scott, who never thought himself a great poet, left the field open to his brilliant rival. He gave up

[1] *The Lay of the Last Minstrel*, Canto iv.
[2] So far as I am aware, there is no complete edition of Scott's works. His *Miscellaneous Prose Works* fill twenty-eight volumes.

writing poetry, he declared with a genuine frankness, because Byron "beat him," and in 1814 he published

Waverley and the Waverley novels.

Waverley. *The Lay of the Last Minstrel* made an epoch in English poetry, *Waverley* made an epoch in English fiction. Scott had conquered and captivated the public once by his poetry, he was now to conquer it a second time by his prose. It would, indeed, be almost as difficult to find a parallel for the variety and extent of Scott's successes as for the almost inexhaustible fertility of his genius. But *Waverley* rather marks a stage in the consistent development of Scott's powers, than his entrance into a new field. His poems had been "metrical romances," novels in verse; his novels were romances in prose; the form is changed, but the sources of the inspiration are, in many cases, essentially the same. In the novels, however, there is a greater breadth and reality, and, above all, the characters, are more individual and more clearly defined. *Waverley*, which had been published anonymously, was followed by novel after novel from the pen of the same mysterious author. After writing some of his best stories of Scottish life, — *Guy Mannering* (1815) and *The Antiquary* (1816) among the number, — Scott won his first triumph in the field of foreign history by *Ivanhoe* (1819), probably the most popular and in some respects the most fascinating of his romances. A few years later he published *Quentin Durward* (1823), the first of his novels in which he passed beyond the British Isles and laid the scene in foreign lands. Besides getting through an appalling mass of other work, Scott wrote over thirty novels and stories between 1814 and 1831, an average of about two a year. Some of these are naturally better than others, but there is not one (unless it be *Count Robert of Paris*) that has not some special claim upon our affection, not one that we would willingly spare. All things considered, it must be ad-

mitted that the average of excellence in the Waverley
novels is surprisingly high.

In 1812 Scott had bought land on the Tweed near
Melrose, and there he built for himself the great house
he called Abbotsford. For some years his life
Prosperity and failure. at Abbotsford was busy and successful. Scott
was Sheriff of Selkirkshire and Clerk of the Law
Courts; he was the country gentleman, the most hospitable
of hosts; he was antiquarian, poet, novelist, and man of
letters, and — to his sorrow — he was man of business also,
a silent partner in the firm of his friends and publishers the
Ballantynes. In 1820 Scott was made a Baronet, and two
years later he represented Scotland when the King visited
Edinburgh. In 1826, when he was at the height of his
fame, and when every ambition seemed gratified, Scott
found himself involved as secret partner in the failure of
the Ballantynes, and personally liable to the extent of
£117,000. Scott's goodness and strength were equal to
the emergency. He was no longer young, he had worked
terribly and his health was breaking, but he set himself to
the task with a steadfast courage.

In two years (1826–1828) he had earned nearly £40,000
for his creditors by his painful but unflinching toil. Shortly
before his sudden change of fortune Scott had begun to
keep a journal. This *Journal*, written for no eye but his
own, has now been published, and the reader can now live
through those years with Scott, and know him as he was.
The *Journal* is a noble book, the deepest and noblest, in
some respects, that Scott ever wrote. No one can read its
brief, manly record of that gallant fight with adversity, no
one can follow the story of that struggle, — saddened by
domestic losses, by failing health and by waning powers,
yet indomitably maintained until the last, — without knowing that here was indeed a man. Great as Scott was in
his prosperity, it was only in these years of scathing trial

that his latent greatness was fully revealed. But the strain on body and mind was not to be borne. After Scott's return from a Continental tour, undertaken in the vain hope of restoring health to mind and body, he died peacefully in his home at Abbotsford, September 21, 1832, "in the presence of all his children." "It was a beautiful day," writes Lockhart, "so warm that every window was wide open, and so perfectly still that the sound of all others most delicious to his ear, the gentle ripple of the Tweed over its pebbles, was distinctly audible as we knelt around the bed, and his eldest son kissed and closed his eyes."[1] He was buried in the ruined Abbey of Dryburgh, among the scenes and associations he had loved.

There is no need to dwell on Scott's character. A hundred years ago Byron declared that Scott was the only

Character and work. successful genius he ever knew who was "as genuinely beloved as a man" as he was "admired as an author." From that day to this the world has loved Sir Walter and honoured his manhood as well as read his books. Even Carlyle, who undervalued the Waverley novels, declared that Scott had no cant about him, and that he was "the soundest specimen of British manhood put together in this eighteenth century of time."

In Scott's works we possess a partial revelation of this healthy, strong, and manly nature. He wrote and edited a phenomenal number of books, but his literary labours, extensive as they were, absorbed only a part of his splendid energy. His life was more than his art; he was bigger than all his books; yet his books do truly although but partially represent him, and in them many of the sterling traits of his character survive.

The position of Scott in literature seems, when we begin to reflect upon the matter, a strikingly isolated one. Scott

[1] Lockhart's *Scott*, vol. x. 217.

did not preach; he did not analyse his own soul, or publish his deepest emotions to the world; yet his pre-

Relation to his time. decessors were didactic, while many of his contemporaries and successors were given over to introspection and self-revelation. The truth appears to be that Scott not only wrote about the past, but that in many respects he belonged to it rather than to our modern world. The poetry of the nineteenth century is intellectual, heavy with its burden of thought; Scott's poetry, spirited, rapid in movement, and often careless in execution, is the poetry of action. Scott, indeed, was by nature an old-time man of action, rather than a modern man of letters. Born of good fighting-stock, he had in him the stuff out of which soldiers and leaders are made. Modern poets are fond of insisting upon the supremacy and permanence of art; Scott set the doer of the deed higher than the poet who celebrated it in song. It was this quality that helped to make Scott one of the few really successful narrative poets of English literature. Byron, in some respects his follower, was self-centred, and made Europe the confidant of his woes; Scott was reticent, honestly interested in other people, in his characters, in the story he had to tell, and in the scenes he described. His pleasure in an heroic deed or a beautiful scene is the simple, almost childlike delight of a manly, direct, and unsophisticated nature. He has not that deep sense of the mystery of things which pervades the work of a Coleridge or a Hawthorne. He is not, like Wordsworth, a mystic or a philosopher.

It is obvious that Scott's poetry lacks some of the characteristic beauties of modern verse — its depth, subtilty, and finish: we should also realise that it possesses many old-time merits. It was the minstrel's office to sing the deeds of heroes, and Scott is preëminent among the modern poets of war. His descriptions of battles, it has been often said, are the most Homeric in English literature. His ballads, *The Eve of St. John, Red Harlaw,* and the rest, are not mere ingenious imitations, they have the force and fire of the native minstrel.

> "What would'st thou do, my squire so gay
> That rides beside my reyne,
> Were ye Glenallen's Earl the day,
> And I were Roland Cheyne?'
> . . . .
> 'Were I Glenallen's Earl this tide,
> And ye were Roland Cheyne,
> The spur should be in my horse's side,
> And the bridle upon his mane.'" [1]

Simple as this may seem, there is in it, as in so much of Scott's best verse, that thrill of the heroic, so often lost in the melodious refinements of recent poetry, that full-blooded manhood which all the dexterity of the anæmic modern cannot recapture. The same buoyancy and wholesomeness distinguish Scott's songs. No one would claim for him the lyrical genius of Shelley or Swinburne, but Scott's songs have a very positive excellence of their own. By all means let us delight in Shelley's *Indian Serenade,* or the Spring Chorus in Swinburne's *Atalanta,* but let us hold fast to our love of such songs as *March, march, Ettrick and Teviotdale, Jock o' Hazeldean,* or *Proud*

Novels. *Masie. Waverley* was not the earliest historical novel, but Scott may be called the first master of historical fiction. If we would measure the greatness of his work, we must compare the Waverley novels with some of the romances that preceded them, with *The Castle of Otranto, The Mysteries of Udolpho,* or even with *Thaddeus of Warsaw* (1803) and *The Scottish Chiefs* (1810). What is the vital distinction between Scott's romances and such stories as these? It is not

[1] Ballad of *Red Harlaw* in *The Antiquary.*

merely that he is a better antiquarian, — that he knows incomparably more about the costume or manners of the past, — it is, above all, because he was able to people those shadowy centuries for us with real, substantial men and women. Scott, like Shakespeare and many another, is not what is called "true to history," but, on the whole, he is surprisingly true to the fundamental and enduring facts of human life. Nor must we think of him solely, or perhaps even chiefly, as the great revealer of the past, as the predecessor of such picturesque and realistic historians as Macaulay or Froude. Scott is probably greatest when he puts aside the trappings of historical romance, and shows us the daily life of the Scottish people, — the fisher-folk, like the Mucklebackets, — in the smoke of its peat fires, in its humour, its poverty, its tragedy, and its homely toil. When we review the enormous range and the high average excellence of Scott's work in fiction, and remember the ease and rapidity with which it was produced, we feel that he exhibits a creative force rare even among the great geniuses of the literature.

Scott, then, stands at the entrance to Victorian England, with many of the virtues and some of the limitations of an earlier time. He works in the primary colours.

Summary. He is not intense, he does not question deeply, or analyse motives. He does not excel in that morbid anatomy of emotion which has become the fashion with many novelists of this present age of so-called superior culture and advanced ideas. He thinks that life is good and that there is wholesome enjoyment to be gained from action. He admires honour and courtesy and bravery among men, and beauty and gentleness and modesty among women. He has no "message;" he does not preach to us, but he was a kindly, high-minded gentleman, and it is good to be with him in his books. He rose to be great, "but he was always good," and his works bear witness to the breadth, sympathy, and purity of one of the great creative intellects of our literature, worthy indeed of a place among the immortals, side by side with Chaucer, and nearest to the feet of Shakespeare himself.

CHARLES LAMB.

(1775–1834.)

Charles Lamb — called by Coleridge the "gentle-hearted Charles" [1] — was born in London, 1775. He was the youngest of three children; his family were in poor circumstances, his father being little more than a servant to a Mr. Salt of the Inner Temple. From his eighth to his fifteenth year, Charles studied as a "blue-coat boy" at Christ's Hospital, and here there sprung up between him and his fellow-student Coleridge a friendship which proved lifelong. On leaving school he obtained a clerkship in the South Sea House, and two years later in the India Office. His father's health failed, and Charles became the chief support of the little family. But the quiet of their household was soon broken by a terrible event. Mary, Charles Lamb's sister, was seized with violent insanity, and killed their mother (1796). Mary was taken to an asylum, where she recovered, and Charles procured her release on his becoming responsible for her guardianship. Thenceforth, after his father's death, he devoted himself to the care of his afflicted sister. For intervals, which he called "between the acts," they lived quietly in the most devoted companionship, Mary aiding in her brother's literary work, and presiding at their little receptions, which Coleridge and sometimes Wordsworth attended. Then, again, Mary would "fall ill," and return for a time to the asylum.

Through all this strain and distress, with occasional

[1] See Coleridge's poem, *This Lime Tree Bower My Prison*, in which several references to Lamb occur.

fears for himself, Lamb's cheerful and loving nature saved him from bitterness and despair, and he found courage to work. He lived his "happy-melancholy" life, and died quietly at London in 1834. His sister, whose name is forever linked with his as the object of his care and partner of his literary work, survived until 1847.

In spite of daily work in the office, and of his domestic troubles, Lamb found time and heart for literature. As a boy he had spent many odd hours in the library of Mr. Salt, "browsing chiefly among the older English authors;" and he refers to Bridget Elia (Mary Lamb) as "tumbled early, by accident or design, into a spacious closet of good old English reading." This preference for Elizabethan writers endured through life, and their style and mode of thought became in some degree natural to himself. His first venture was a contribution of four sonnets to a book of poems on various subjects by his friend Coleridge (1796). After some minor works, he published *John Woodvil* (1801), a tragedy on the early Elizabethan model, which was severely criticised, and later a farce, *Mr. H——* (1806), which failed on the first performance.

His *Specimens of English Dramatic Poets who Wrote about the Time of Shakespeare,* with notes, aroused new interest in a great body of writers then largely neglected, and showed Lamb himself a critic of keen natural insight, his suggestions often being of more value than the learned notes of commentators. Thus Lamb, with William Hazlitt, another critic of the time, helped in bringing about that new era of criticism in which Coleridge was the chief mover. In 1807 appeared *Tales Founded on the Plays of Shakespeare,* the joint work of himself and his sister Mary. Lamb is best known, however, by his essays, first published, under the name of *Elia,* in the *London Magazine* (founded 1820). Written for the most part on trivial subjects, with no purpose but to please, they bring us close to the lovable nature of the man, full, indeed, of sadness, but full, too, of a refined and kindly humour, ready to flash out in a pun, or to light up with a warm and gentle glow the cloud that overhangs him. In these essays we see Lamb's conservative spirit and hatred of change. His literary sympathies lay with the past, and he clung with fondness to the memories of his childhood.

THOMAS DE QUINCEY.

(1785–1859.)

Thomas De Quincey impresses us as some being from another planet, who never entirely domesticated himself on our earth. We picture him as an alien crea-

Appearance and character.

ture, gliding timorously and obscurely among the mass of ordinary men, remote himself from their lives and ambitions, yet observing them with the curiosity of a stranger and retiring to meditate upon the meaning of their acts and ways. Even his appearance had something eccentric and elfish. He is described by those who knew him as frail, withered, and diminutive (he was scarcely more than five feet high), his garments often strangely assorted, his face lined with innumerable wrinkles gathered "thickly around the curiously expressive and subtle lips." [1] But the forehead was lofty, the eyes deep-set and gentle; for this fragile little body was the house of an acute and unwearying intellect, stored with curious spoils from a lifetime of varied reading.

The strangeness of his way of living sets him still more apart from other men. He was an opium-eater, a philosopher, with the impassive, deeply contemplative spirit

[1] For descriptions of De Quincey, see the account of "Papaverius" in *The Book Hunter*, by J. H. Burton; *Personal Recollections of De Quincey*, by J. R. Findlay, and Masson's *De Quincey* in English Men of Letters Series.

of an Oriental; much of his life slipped away in dreams.
His "natural inclination to a solitary life" was fostered
and increased by the use of that terrible drug, which
admitted him to the dreamlife of those trances, to that
inward life of vision, he has so vividly described. At times
he came out into the light and mixed with his kind, but
he seems to have required solitude for the shaping and
perfecting of his thought. "No man," he writes, "will
ever unfold the capacities of his own intellect, who does
not at least chequer his life with solitude. *How much
solitude so much power.*" [1]

An acquaintance with De Quincey's life but deepens our
impression of him as an eccentric dreamer and recluse.
We read of his morbid dread of being pursued; we follow
him in his solitary wanderings, and see him haunting the
streets of Edinburgh, when the town is asleep, thinking
his own unimaginable thoughts. The true life of De
Quincey is that wonderful inner life of thought and vision
into which we cannot penetrate; the outward events of
his singular history must be here passed over with the

De Quincey's life.

merest mention. Thomas De Quincey was the
son of a merchant of literary tastes, and was
born in Manchester in 1785. His father died
when De Quincey was in his seventh year. His mother
appears to have been a woman of high character and
intelligence, but inclined to be over-rigid and unsympathetic. He early distinguished himself in the classics,
becoming famous for his Latin verses, and being able, it
is said, to converse easily in Greek at fifteen. He ran away
from the Manchester Grammar School, to which he had
been sent in 1800, finding the commercial air of the town
"detestable," and the life of the school uncongenial and
monotonous. After some months of wandering in North
Wales he made his way to London, where he passed
about a year in an aimless, vagrant existence; haunting

[1] *Suspiria De Profundis :* "Dreaming."

the streets and city parks, and coming in contact with
the darker side of the great capital. Having become
reconciled to his family, he was sent to Worcester
College, Oxford, in 1803, where he remained for five
years. It was during his stay at Oxford that he began
the use of opium; taking it, however, in moderation
as an occasional means of mental exhilaration. He
also began a more systematic study of German and
English literature, his young enthusiasm fastening especially on Wordsworth and Coleridge, whom he recognised as having, in his own time, restored the ancient
greatness of English poetry. He longed to know Coleridge personally, and in 1807 succeeded in meeting him at
Bristol, making the acquaintance of Wordsworth later
in the same year. After leaving Oxford (1809), he settled
near Wordsworth in the Lake District at Town End,
Grasmere. Except for occasional intervals this continued to be his home for over twenty years. Here he
enjoyed the friendship of the "Lakists," especially Coleridge; pored over German metaphysics, and indulged his
passion for walking. In 1813, being "attacked by a most
appalling irritation of the stomach," he greatly increased
his use of opium, bringing down upon himself those terrible experiences which he has preserved for us in his
Confessions. In 1816 he married a young country girl,
Margaret Simpson, whose father owned a neighbouring
farm. He began to be embarrassed for money, and after
reducing his supply of opium by desperate efforts, he
became the editor of a provincial journal. His literary
Entrance   career really began, however, in 1821, with the
into liter-   appearance, in the *London Magazine,* of his
ature.   *Confessions of an English Opium Eater.* The
novelty of the subject, the unsparing frankness of these
self-revelations, and, we may assume, their wonderful style
and poetic imagery, secured for the new writer an imme-

diate success. From this time De Quincey was distinctively a writer for magazines, being connected during the forty years of his literary life with *Blackwood's Magazine*, *Tait's Magazine*, *Hogg's Weekly Instructor*, and others. His first contribution to *Blackwood's*, a translation of Lessing's *Laocoön*, appeared in 1826, and his relations with that magazine led to his settling in Edinburgh in 1830. He lived in various lodging-houses in the town itself, or in a cottage in the outskirts at Lasswade; a shy, obscure scholar, full of a winning grace and charm; a marvellous talker when he was in the mood; a lover of children; with all his oddities, a man of gentle and affectionate nature. The most important of De Quincey's last labours was the editing of a collected edition of his works which began to appear in 1853.[1] For the last two years of his life his strength was failing; the complete edition of his works was nearly finished when he was taken with his last illness, and died on the 8th of December, 1859.

In actual years De Quincey was just halfway between Wordsworth and Macaulay, and the fact is suggestive of his general relation to literary history. Early admiration and personal friendship connect him with Wordsworth and his great contemporaries. His affinity with Coleridge is especially close, and with Coleridge he was instrumental in bringing German literature and philosophy into England. On the other hand, he is associated with the rise of the new periodical literature, and in that movement Macaulay had an important place. Although De Quincey was fifteen years Macaulay's senior, the two men became contributors to the periodicals almost at the same time, for De Quincey was thirty-six when he published his *Confessions*, and Macaulay

De Quincey as man of letters.

---

[1] The first collected edition of De Quincey was published by Ticknor & Fields (now Houghton, Mifflin & Co.), and appeared in 1851–52. De Quincey furnished Mr. J. T. Fields, under whose supervision the work appeared, with some assistance for this edition.

but twenty-five when, three years later, his "Milton" appeared in the *Edinburgh Review*. De Quincey, therefore, while near in many ways to Wordsworth and Coleridge, is the immediate predecessor of the two great essayists, Macaulay and Carlyle. With Lamb, Hazlitt, Jeffrey, and Sydney Smith, De Quincey belongs to that group of essay-writers who were making an era in criticism. De Quincey's relation to this rising periodical literature may be compared to that which Addison held to the journals of his time, but between the work of the two essayists there is a difference, suggestive of the century of growth that lies between. De Quincey's essays are longer and more elaborate than those of Addison; more learned, often more impassioned and poetic, and, above all, they have a greater diversity of subject and of style. This diversity **His diversity.** may be due in part to the widening interests and growing cultivation of the reading public, but it is more directly and naturally attributable to the many-sidedness of De Quincey himself. He was at the same time a born student and book-lover and a close and inquisitive observer of life. He delighted in intellectual subtleties and fine-drawn analysis, and yet possessed all that passion for style, that pleasure of the artist in effects of word-melody, which is emphatically the endowment of the poet. Although these varied elements of De Quincey's genius are constantly intermingled in a single essay, yet one or the other of them commonly predominates, according to the nature of the subject, sometimes to the entire exclusion of the rest. Thus the reminiscences of the Lake poets, or the autobiographical sketches, are, for the most part, the outcome of De Quincey's power to observe; his essays on such widely separated subjects as theology, political economy, Greek poetry, English politics, and German metaphysics, attest the range of his scholarship; while still other sides of his nature are revealed in the fantastic humour of his *Mur-*

der Considered as one of the Fine Arts, in the narrative skill of *The Flight of a Tartar Tribe,* or in the prose-poetry of his *Levana and Our Ladies of Sorrow.* And in the essays, the style, adapting itself to the subject, ranges from simple, unadorned exposition to impassioned apostrophes or delicately modulated strains of melody, filled with a dim and visionary beauty, which, like the influence of poetry, evades the last analysis. This change, from the plainer and less inspired prose of the eighteenth-century essayists to De Quincey's more highly wrought and emotional manner, is analogous to that which had taken place in poetry at a somewhat earlier period. The difference between Addison and De Quincey is comparable to that between Pope and Collins, or Coleridge. Moreover, De Quincey shares with some latter eighteenth-century poets the tendency to skip over his immediate predecessors and take for his models Jeremy Taylor, Sir Thomas Browne, and the great masters of the yet earlier times.[1] Each of De Quincey's great successors in the history of English prose has added, in his own way, to its resources and capabilities; each has, perhaps, surpassed him in certain directions, yet he maintains undisturbed his supremacy in that " visionary dreamland," in which, says Leslie Stephen, " he is unrivalled." [2]

His place in English prose.

The appreciation of the peculiar flavour of De Quincey's writings must be gained from the sympathetic reading of his works. His *Murder Considered as One of the Fine Arts* is not a tragic masterpiece like Swift's *Modest Proposal,* with which it is usually compared, but, lacking the stifled wrath and pity which underlie that terrible arraignment, it is more buoyantly humourous, unweighted by the revolting elements which give to Swift's

De Quincey's works.

[1] *V.* Leslie Stephen's " Life of De Quincey" in *Dictionary of National Biography.*

[2] *Ibid.*

satire a painful and hideous incongruity. When De Quincey leaves his "admirable fooling," with its playful irony on the cant of æsthetic criticism, to tell the story of certain "memorable murders," the style becomes more simple and serious, and we come under the spell of his wonderful power of narrative. Then, as in *The Flight of a Tartar Tribe*, or the murder story of *The Avenger*, we feel that this great essayist was, within the brief limits he set himself, a master of the art of story-writing. But it is when De Quincey invades the province of the poet or of the musician, that his work becomes most distinctive. In his "dream-fugues," or dream-fantasies, he seems less anxious to impart certain definite ideas than to produce a positive emotional impression by the effect of his composition as a whole. Thus in parts of his *Confessions of an English Opium Eater*, or his *Suspiria de Profundis*, as in his *Dream-Fugue on the Theme of Sudden Death*, his appeal is not primarily to the understanding. And so marvellous is the power of melodious utterance, of imagery which excites and expands the imagination by its very vagueness, of words steeped in the odours of association, that De Quincey achieves this emotional effect with but little aid from exact thought.

Perhaps, on the whole, it is as a master of rhetoric that De Quincey is most admirable. Like a skilful organist he His style. knows all the stops and combinations of his wonderful instrument; yet so skilful is he that at times our attention wanders from the theme in our admiration of the dexterity of the performer. Even in dealing with such a subject as the story of Joan of Arc, consecrated beyond all the artifices of rhetoric by pathos, nobility, and wonder, he is able to indulge in passages, which, brilliant as they are as bits of rhetorical "bravura," are apt to impress us as a *tour de force*. This careful elaboration of the style tends to leave us admiring, but cold. Professor Masson remarks that the motive force in De

Quincey was intellectual rather than moral, and the distinction explains that touch of self-consciousness, that lack of the highest earnestness and sincerity, which at times we instinctively recognise in his work. Thackeray's loving-kindness and compassion, Carlyle's ardent singleness of purpose, when he is truest to himself, are the expressions of moral qualities, and those writers move us as De Quincey does not, because we respond to the language of a profounder and more genuine emotion. "From my birth," says De Quincey, "I was made an intellectual creature, and intellectual in the highest sense my pursuits and pleasures have been."

While this preponderance of the intellectual over the more purely moral side acts as a limitation on De Quincey's power to satisfy all our needs, few English prose-writers are more worthy of study. Delightful in his humour, fascinating in his narrative, wonderful in the intricate perfection of his sentences, influential as the reviver of an impassioned and musically modulated style, De Quincey has taken his place among the great masters of English prose.

The Later Poets of the Revolution.

BYRON AND SHELLEY.

The appalling plunge into murder and anarchy which followed hard upon the triumph of the Revolutionists in France, shocked into a sudden sobriety much of the vague enthusiasm for the cause of man. Thousands who, like Wordsworth and Coleridge, had joined in the contagious outcry for liberty and equality, recoiled like them in disgust from a revolution which had brought the dregs of society uppermost, and cast to the surface man's primitive baseness and cruelty. In France the towering genius and ambition of Napoleon were hurrying the nation back into despotism; in England, the government set its face against sorely needed reforms, through an unreasoning fear that change might prove the invitation to a Reign of Terror. Yet the Revolution had none the less begun a new epoch in the history of England and of the Continent; in spite of the efforts of conservative governments, its fires still smouldered everywhere beneath the surface, ready at a breath to burst into flame. After the battle of Waterloo (1815) the great powers of Europe met at Vienna and entered into a compact known as *The Holy Alliance.* The ostensible object of this alliance was to promote peace and good-will; its real purpose was to crush the spirit of democracy. It would have blotted the Revolution out of history, by reviving that older Europe which, in reality, no congress could restore. Austria, under her Prime Minister Metternich, threw her whole weight on the side of absolutism; but demonstrations among the students in the German universities (1817), insurrections in Spain and Naples, and the heroic struggles of the Greeks under Turkish oppression, showed that the revolutionary spirit was unextinguished.

England was passing through a critical period of popular distress and dangerous discontent. On the one hand a government set in its conservatism; on the other a people unsettled by new industrial conditions, impoverished by overtaxation, impatient to gain a voice in their own government, and brought at length by poor crops to the verge of actual starvation. The assembling of the people for free speech was pronounced illegal; and at a great meeting at Manchester, the cavalry charged upon the crowd, and answered their petitions for a vote in Parliamentary elections with the edge of the sword (1819). A year later a conspiracy was formed to murder the members of the Cabinet.

Four poets, — LORD BYRON (1788–1824), PERCY BYSSHE SHELLEY (1792–1822), THOMAS CAMPBELL (1777–1844), and

THOMAS MOORE (1779–1852), — all born during the last quarter of the preceding century, express in greater or less degree the spirit of this time. Each was, in his way, a poet of the Revolution, a lover of liberty, a believer in progress. When Wordsworth and Coleridge sang their first pæans to Liberty, her white robes were still stainless, her fame unspotted. The poets of this younger group in their early manhood had looked on at the crimes committed in her name; they had breathed in an atmosphere heavy with the sense of failure; they were confronted with an oppression and misery calculated to make them embittered and rebellious.

In some respects, Lord Byron, in the power and brilliancy of his genius, in his audacious and dramatic personality, thrusts himself forward as the most truly representative poet of this time. We see in his life, character, and work, a rebellious arraignment of life, a passionate, impotent complaint against the entire order of things.

George Gordon Byron was born in London, January 22, 1788. The same year saw the birth in Germany of **Byron.** Arthur Schopenhauer, destined to be the great preacher to modern times of a philosophy of despair. The Byrons, or Buruns, were thought to be descended from a Scandinavian settler in Normandy. The family had come into England with the Conqueror. They were a fighting race; we find them in the field at Creçy, at the siege of Calais, at Bosworth, at Edgehill. Ungovernable and proud, the spirit of the viking seemed to survive in them; and after long generations they produced a poet. Byron reminds us of the hero in some Greek tragedy, born to a heritage of guilt and suffering. His granduncle, "the wicked lord," was convicted of manslaughter, and, like some of his nephew's miserable heroes, was cast out from human society. The father of the poet, Captain John Byron, known as "Mad Jack," was a profligate and heartless spendthrift; his mother, Catherine Gordon, who traced her descent from James I., was a silly and impulsive woman, subject to furious paroxysms of temper. Having squandered his wife's fortune, Captain Byron left her in greatly straitened circumstance shortly after the birth of their son. The worse than fatherless child was thus left wholly at the mercy of an injudicious and passionate woman, who treated him, according to her passing whims, with alternate harshness and over-indulgence. Under these wretched conditions Byron's life began. He grew up a spoiled child, passionate, head-strong, sullen, and defiant. On all this was piled yet another misery — he was lame, owing to the deformity of one foot; and to his vain and morbidly sensitive nature this misfortune was a life-long torture. In 1798, by the death of "the wicked lord," he succeeded to the title and family estates. In 1801 he entered Harrow, where he was noted as a fighter, and acted as ringleader in a boyish rebellion against the authorities. Four years later he went to Trinity College, Cambridge, where he led the life of the idle and dissipated undergraduate. Here his "gyp," or college servant, spoke of him with respect as "a young gentleman of tumultuous passions." In 1807 he published his first book of poems, *Hours of Idleness*. An unfavourable review of this youthful venture, which had in reality but little merit, aroused his passionate temper, and he struck back fiercely in a satire on *English Bards and Scotch Reviewers* (1809). Revolutionist as he was by nature, Byron had a deep and genuine appreciation of the historic greatness of Europe, and after two years of Continental travel (1809–1811), he gave the world the splendid record of his impressions in the first two cantos of *Childe Harold* (1812). The result was one of the most sudden and memorable successes in English literary history; in his own familiar phrase, Byron awoke one morning and found him-

self famous. The poetic star of Scott, who had been en-
chanting the world with his vigorous ballads of romance
and chivalry, declined before the brightness of this new
luminary. The public turned from tales of Border warfare,
from the mailed knights and moated castles of mediævalism, to enter under Byron's guidance the unfamiliar
regions of the East. *The Giaour* (1813) is the first of a
succession of Eastern tales, in the metre of Scott, each
of which increased the fever of popular enthusiasm. In
these tales the Byronic hero, first outlined in *Childe
Harold*, reappears under different names and varying disguises, with significant persistence in all his solitary, joy-
less, and misanthropic personality.

In 1815 Byron married Miss Milbanke, but after about
a year they separated for reasons not fully known. The
public turned furiously upon the man it had so lately
idolised, and overwhelmed him with its sudden condemnation. Smarting under a sense of injustice, Byron
left England forever, pursued across Europe by the outcry against him. After spending some time at Geneva
under the stimulating influence of Shelley, he settled at
length on the "waves of the Adriatic, like the stag at bay
who betakes himself to the waters." During this time
he wrote with extraordinary power and rapidity, producing, among a great number of other poems, the remaining cantos of *Childe Harold, Cain, Manfred,* and *Don Juan.*
At length he seemed to weary of poetry, as he did of
everything, declaring that he did not consider it his "vocation," but that if he lived ten years, he was determined
to do something in new fields. His ardent and invincible
spirit found the way. He threw himself into the cause of
the Greeks, then struggling against Turkish despotism, and
in 1823 chartered a vessel and sailed from Genoa in their
aid. He reached Missolonghi, and was made commander-
in-chief of an expedition against Lepanto. But the pre-

sentiment of his approaching death was upon him. On his thirty-sixth birthday, while yet at Missolonghi, he composed some verses which seem touched with the spirit of prophecy:

> "If thou regret'st thy youth, *why live?*
> The land of honourable death
> Is here. . . .
> Then look around, and choose thy ground
> And take thy rest."

Death would not spare him for the soldier's grave he coveted. He was stricken with illness before he could take the field, and died at Missolonghi, April 19, 1824. In his delirium he imagined that he was leading his Suliotes at Lepanto, and cried out, "Forward, forward, follow me!" At length, as the last lethargy settled down upon his untamable and restless spirit, he said quietly to his attendant, "Now I shall go to sleep." He did not speak again.

The life and work of Lord Byron were an immense force not only in the history of England but throughout Europe.

Byron's work. His generation hailed him as the voice of their aspirations and complaints. He uttered for them, in verse of an indomitable and masculine vigour, full of a somewhat declamatory but magnificent rhetoric, their iconoclasm, their despairs, their unbeliefs; and he shares in both their weakness and their strength. Probably no other English poet ever won such admiration from contemporary Europe; he gave English literature a larger place on the Continent, and, in Mazzini's words, "led the genius of Britain on a pilgrimage throughout all Europe." [1] But while realising the importance of Byron in the large movement of democracy as a social and political force, our primary question is rather as to the permanence and value of his contributions to literature. The world has

[1] Essay on "Byron and Goethe."

moved rapidly away from the thoughts and tastes of
Byron and of his day, but it is the distinction of the great
poets to express not their own time merely, but that which
is common to all times. Has Byron done this? Even
when judged by the most liberal standards, it must be
admitted that Byron's poetry does not possess in any great
measure that "great antiseptic" a high excellence of
style. He is dashing, brilliant, unequal, effective, but
careless of finish and detail even to an occasional slip in
grammar. The movement of his verse is nervous, strong,
and free, but Shelley surpasses him in subtle lyrical quality,
and in his inspired instinct for the aptest word. Yet we
forget these shortcomings in his immense vitality and ease;
and when fairly caught in the rapids of his eloquence,
we are borne along by the power of the orator joined
to the power of the poet. In satire, by *The Vision of
Judgment* and *Don Juan*, he towers above the other mod-
erns as the successor of Dryden and of Pope. He has a
feeling for large results; his descriptions are bold, broad,
and telling, and the historic past of Europe lives in his
swelling lines. He is the poet of the mountain-peak, the
sea, and the tempest. A contempt for his fellow-men
mingles curiously with his love of Nature and her solitudes.
Unlike Wordsworth, he does not efface himself in her
presence, but finds a congenial spirit in her moods of
fierceness and of power.

For the rest, Byron's life and work are the memorial
of his imperious and colossal egotism. His demands on
His egotism. life were enormous, his disappointments correspondingly severe. Napoleon would have made
the world minister to his lust of power; Byron, to his lust
of pleasure. *I myself would enjoy, yet I suffer:* this is the
sum of his arraignment of life. He could create but one
type of hero, because he could not escape from the tyranny
of his own personality. His heroes never learn of suffer-

ing; they stand solitary in the midst of the sufferings of the world in the insatiate egotism of their own woes, sullen and defiant until the last.   There is a sublimity in the inveterate opposition of the individual will to the impassive fatality of things; but in Byron this is weakened by the strain of selfishness, and at least a suspicion of insincerity.   For Byron's romantic unhappiness and mad dissipations were more conducive to popularity than Wordsworth's placid contentment and sobriety.   Yet while we may be uncertain as to how much of Byron's demonstrative despair was "playing to the gallery," his devotion to liberty at least was genuine.   He could exclaim while others doubted:

> "Yet Freedom! yet, thy banner, torn but flying,
> Streams like a thunderstorm *against* the wind."[1]

His faith in freedom glows in his verse, and lends a parting and consecrating radiance to his unhappy life.   But his conception of freedom is shallow and unregulated; he confuses it with the license to every man to do what shall seem good in his own eyes.   "I have simplified my politics," he writes, "into an utter detestation of all existing governments."   His heroes are, for the most part, desperate men, in reckless revolt against the social and moral laws.   Haughty, unyielding, self-centred, they are rather the foes to society than its saviours.   Selim, in *The Bride of Abydos*, boasts of his love for freedom; but by freedom he means the unchecked license of the buccaneer, free to sail where he will, with a thousand swords ready to destroy at his command.   Byron is without a real social faith; impatient to pull down, he is powerless to lay hold on any rational or helpful law of life for himself or for others.   He fails to see, with Ruskin, that anarchy is eternally a law of death,

His devotion to liberty.

---

[1] *V.* this passage, *Childe Harold*, Canto iv., stanzas xcvi.–xcviii.

to realise Wordsworth's joy in the submission to the high-est. His *Cain*, in which the deepest and most serious side of his nature found expression, is the direct antithesis of Wordsworth's *Ode to Duty*. It is the pathos of such a life as that of Byron that it brings its own revenges. His mad revolt against things as they are becomes, as he grows older, but more furious and bitter, until it reaches its brilliant but terrible consummation in *Don Juan*.

The want in Byron's poetry lies deeper than any mere defect in manner. So far as it fails to present any reason-able and well-considered view of life; so far as it fails to be ennobling, helpful, and inspiring, just so far does it lack elements which make for permanence. For Byron himself, where we cannot admire, it is easy to pity and to excuse. Carlyle once likened him to a vulture, shrieking because carrion enough was not given him; he was rather a caged eagle, who in impotent protest beat out his life against the bars. The contest told even on his audacious energy. Young as he was, he could write, "The dead have had enough of life; all they want is rest, and this they implore." He would have two words put over his grave, and no more: *Implora pace*. The fascination of Byron's personality, the sadness of his story, will enshrine the memory of the man, a strong and tragic figure; while by many a poem, and still more by the superb vitality of many a brilliant passage, he has secured a lasting place among the poets of his country.

Percy Bysshe Shelley (1792–1822) stands with Byron as a poet of revolt; but his devotion to liberty is purer, his love for man readier to declare itself in deeds of help and sympathy, his whole life ennobled by loftier and more unselfish aims. In Byron we may see the masculine element of revolt audaciously interrogating earth and heaven, deficient in reverence and in faith, instant to destroy; in Shelley rather a feminine unworldliness, erring through its incapacity to adjust

Shelley.

itself to the ways of earth; we see in him a theorist and a dreamer, building in the air his shimmering palaces of clouds until he "falls upon the thorns of life." Trelawney describes him as "blushing like a girl" at their first meeting, and speaks of his "flushed, feminine, and artless face."[1] Strong yet slender in figure, with sensitive, almost girlish face, with deep-blue poet eyes, and a mass of wavy brown hair, early streaked with grey, Shelley in our imagination moves among other men as one apart. A daring independence of mind distinguished him from the first. It was his nature to accept nothing on the authority of others, but rather to question and prove all things for himself. He dreamed of what the world should be before life had taught him what it was, and in the fervour of his ideals of truth and righteousness, in his "passion for reforming the world,"[2] — young and confident, but too often hasty and mistaken, — he found himself misunderstood and at issue with the world. At Eton, where he was sent in 1804, he was solitary, shy, eccentric; he did not join in the cricket or football, and was commonly spoken of by the boys as "Mad Shelley." The petty tyranny of the fagging system moved him to protest, and he set on foot a conspiracy to suppress it. In his school days, in one of those sudden flashes of prophetic insight that sometimes illuminate the spirit in early youth, his ideal of life came to him with strange distinctness. He tells us how he then made this resolve, weeping:

> "I will be wise,
> And just, and free, and mild, if in me lies
> Such power; for I grow weary to behold
> The selfish and the strong still tyrannise
> Without reproach or check."

To a temperament so ardent, lofty, and ill-fitted for conformity to the routine thought and usage of ordinary

---

[1] Trelawney's *Recollections of Last Days of Shelley and Byron*, p. 26.
[2] Preface to *Prometheus Unbound.*

men, life was certain to prove but a hard matter at best, and Shelley's youth was passed under conditions which, for such a nature as his, were peculiarly unfortunate. His father, Sir Timothy Shelley, a country gentleman in Sussex, was the embodiment of commonplace and pre-judiced conservatism; limited and bound by the habits and traditions of his class, it was inherently impossible for him to understand his son's character or tolerate his aims. Shelley's loving and loyal nature made him sus-ceptible to influence, but his fiery zeal and independent temper would not brook authority, and any attempt to compel him to act against his convictions aroused in him the spirit of the martyr. His conflict with authority came but too soon. His active mind, prone to doubt and to inquire, hurried him into scepticism, and in 1811 he was expelled from Oxford, which he had entered five months before, for a pamphlet *On the Necessity of Atheism.* Shortly after quitting Oxford, he married Harriet Westbrook, a mere schoolgirl, who had excited his pity and sympathy, and who was decidedly his inferior in social position. Sir Timothy, who had been seriously provoked by his incom-prehensible son's disgrace at Oxford, was naturally incensed anew by this act of folly, and the two young creatures — Shelley was but nineteen and his girl-wife three years younger — were cast adrift. After an interval, a small allowance was granted to them by Sir Timothy and Harriet's father, and they wandered from place to place, Shelley absorbed in his theories, his poetry, and his projects for reclaiming the world. *Queen Mab*, a notable though im-mature production, was the work of this time, and was privately printed in 1813. Toward the close of the same year Shelley and his wife separated, and after her death in 1816 he married Mary Godwin, who proved herself more capable than the unfortunate Harriet had been, of giving his complex and delicately poised nature the sympathy and help he longed for. William Godwin, Mary Godwin's father, was a theoretical reformer, who preached the peaceable abolition, through the pure force of reason, of law, government, and religion; and Shelley, who had previously felt an enthusiastic admiration for his teachings, was now brought into closer relations with the advocate of these extravagant doctrines. He had thus, on the one hand, broken with authority and custom, by his expulsion from Oxford and his breach with his father, and on the other he had surrendered himself, in his impulsiveness and immaturity, to the guidance of a man who expressed the sweeping and unscientific notions of social reform then current among extremists. *Alastor* (1816), Shelley's next poem, in which he describes the lonely wanderings and death of a poet who pursues the unattainable and ideal beauty, discloses to us the springs of Shelley's own nature. Like Marlowe, Shelley was possessed by the "desire for the impossible," and his insatiable and buoyant spirit mounts into regions where we cannot follow. In the nobility of its verse and the beauty of its natural descriptions, *Alastor* shows a great advance in poetic power, and from this time the splendours of Shelley's genius steadily disclose themselves. In his next poem, *The Revolt of Islam* (1818), he poured out those hopes for the regeneration of the world, which are a vital force in his life and poetry. Shelley was less blindly destructive, less hopeless, than Byron. He saw that the disappointment which succeeded the failure of the Revolution had "unconsciously found relief only in the wilful exaggeration of its own despair," and he wrote *The Revolt of Islam* in the belief that men were "emerging from their trance."[1] His hero, Laon, is not a Lara or a Manfred, lost in selfish gloom and misanthropy, but a poet-prophet, aspiring after excellence, who falls a

Alastor and other poems.

[1] Preface to *The Revolt of Islam*. The passage first quoted apparently refers to Byron.

willing martyr to his love for men. In contrast to Byron's chaotic despondency, the poem strikes anew the note of hope and prophecy; it suggests to us that the interval of doubt and depression is passing; it proclaims a social faith. Mankind is to be saved by Love, and in the poem "Love is celebrated everywhere as the sole law which should govern the moral world." The whole poet-world of Shelley is transfigured and glorious in the radiance of this faith. The doctrine of *The Revolt of Islam* was but reiterated in one of the noblest of his poems, the lyrical drama of *Prometheus Unbound* (1820). There we see Prometheus, the type of humanity, or of the human mind, chained to the precipice by Jupiter, the personification of that despotic authority which clogs man's free development. The hour of liberation is at hand. Asia, the incarnation of that ineffable ideal which Shelley sought, the "life of life," and "shadow of beauty unbeheld," journeys to meet Prometheus. Jupiter is overthrown, the rule of despotism broken. Prometheus unbound is united to Asia, that is, the mind of man is wedded to its holiest aspirations, and the world enters upon the reign of universal love.

> "Love from its awful throne of patient power
> In the wise heart, from the last giddy hour
> Of dread endurance, from the slippery, steep,
> And narrow verge of crag-like agony springs,
> And folds over the world its healing wings." [1]

So in the closing chorus of *Hellas* (1822), a drama inspired by the Greek war for independence, the poet's vision sees in the coming Golden Age the return of "Saturn and of Love."

> "Not gold, not blood, their altar dowers,
> But votive tears and symbol flowers." [2]

---

[1] *V.* the speech of Prometheus to Asia, Act iii. Sc. 3, and the beautiful lyric "Life of Life, thy Lips Enkindle," Act ii. Sc. 5.
[2] *Hellas.*

In spite of his professed opinions, Shelley is in this poem one of the most intensely Christian of English poets. In Mrs. Shelley's words, he had "an exceeding faith in the spirit of Christianity," and he went about among men the embodiment of love and pity, the helper of the helpless and the poor.

In 1818 Shelley left for the Continent, travelling and writing among the most beautiful scenes. A number of poems composed in the year following show the deep effect produced upon him by the news of the Manchester massacre [1] and by the thought of the oppression and misery at home. Among these are *The Masque of Anarchy*, in which Murder appears as Lord Castlereagh and Fraud as Lord Eldon, with its passionate appeal to the people to rise against their oppressors; "England in 1819," and "The Song to the Men of England." In these poems the democratic sympathies of Shelley take a passionate and distinctly practical form. The brief space between 1818 and his untimely death in 1822 is the period of Shelley's greatest work. Year by year the fulness of his genius was revealing itself. He had learned of life and of suffering; his faith was deepening, his mind maturing through experience and incessant study. He was becoming a more consummate master of his art. That labyrinthine profusion of fancy and imagery, which dazzles and confuses us in many of his earlier poems by its very splendour and excess, is chastened and restrained in his later songs, which stand preeminent among the most exquisite creations of lyric art. But English poetry was to suffer a sudden and irreparable loss. In 1822, while sailing on the Gulf of Leghorn, Shelley was caught in a squall off the Via Reggia and perished. So swiftly and so terribly did that breath of the Eternal, whose might he had invoked in song, descend upon him.[2]

[1] *V.* p. 490, *supra.*
[2] *V.* last stanza of *Adonais.*

Criticism can do but little toward helping us to an appreciation of Shelley's character and work. We dare not attempt by any cold analysis to reach the secrets of a nature so intricately and exquisitely fashioned; to apportion praise and blame, or to reconcile real or apparent contradictions. He was denounced by his contemporaries for acts and opinions which were rightly considered immoral and hurtful to the order and happiness of society. No admiration for Shelley should lead us to think lightly of his faults or blind us to their disastrous consequences. How far he was morally responsible for erroneous principles sincerely held we need not here inquire; what we should realise is that his wrong actions were in conformity with what he himself believed to be right. To be just to him we must identify ourselves, for the time, with his view of life. We must realise also the nobility of many of his aims, his childlike purity and innocence, which shrank back pained and perplexed at the defilements of the world.

Character and work.

Shelley's poetry, like his nature, must be known through sympathy rather than through criticism. No English poet is more remote from those tangible facts of life which daily engross us, none has fewer points of contact with the average mental state of the average man. Like his Skylark, Shelley mounts from the earth as a cloud of fire; and his song reaches us from blue aerial heights. If we have an answering touch of his nature, if we have it in us to leave the ground, we shall be caught up likewise into those luminous and unfathomable spaces where he sings. To understand Shelley, we must recall those moments when some deep feeling has shaken the dominion of the ordinary in us, when the familiar has grown strange to us and the spiritual near, or perhaps when a vague desire for a something unguessed has possessed us: then, if we imagine those feelings intensified a hundredfold, we are within sight of the confines of Shelley's world. This, indeed, is more particularly applicable to his larger and more difficult works, as *The Witch of Atlas* and *Epipsychidion;* many of his shorter and more familiar poems are free from obscurity, yet full of Shelley's peculiar magic. In his purely lyrical faculty, his power to sing, Shelley is almost without a parallel in English poetry.

JOHN KEATS.

(1795–1821.)

The inclination to associate Keats with Byron and Shelley, his contemporaries in poetry, is natural, but in many Keats, ways misleading. It is true that the three poets Byron, and were not far apart in age, and that none of Shelley. them lived to be old. It is true that each in his own way expressed some phase or quality of youth: Byron, its ungoverned passions and ill-considered despairs; Shelley, its generous, if visionary, aspirations; Keats, its freshness of unquestioning enjoyment, its undulled and exquisite sensibility to the beauty of the things of sense. But the points of difference between Keats and the older members of the group greatly exceed these more accidental or external marks of resemblance. While Shelley's noble tribute to Keats's memory and genius in *Adonais* links the two poets together in our thoughts, the personal relations between them were extremely slight, and in the nature of their genius they were widely different. Byron and Keats were even more widely separated. Byron speaks contemptuously both of Keats and of his poetry; while Keats, on his part, shows no trace of Byron's influence. In truth, Keats was entirely apart from the democratic and revolutionary movement to which Byron and Shelley belonged. Those kindred impulses, the pity for human suffering and the "passion for reforming the world," which had been a growing inspiration and power in English poetry from Thomson to Shelley, are absolutely alien to the poetry of Keats. His genius draws its nourishment from widely different sources, and to understand his relation to literary history we must approach him as the bringer of a fresh impulse into English poetry, the force of which is not yet spent.

Byron and Shelley, the poets of democracy, were representatives of the aristocratic class; Keats was the son of the head hostler in a livery stable at Moorfields, London. The poet's father, Thomas Keats, had married the daughter of his employer, and succeeded to the management of the business at the Swan and Hoop. There John, the eldest child, was born October 31, 1795. As a boy he appears to have been at first chiefly remarkable for beauty of face, courage, and pugnacity. According to the painter Haydon, who knew him well in after years, he was, "when an infant, a most violent and ungovernable child." When about seven or eight years old he was sent to a school at Enfield, a small town some ten miles north of London. Here fighting — according to one of his schoolfellows — was "meat and drink to him." He is described as violent and generous, as "always in extremes," "in passions of tears or outrageous fits of laughter." [1] He was a general favourite, yet he was often morbidly miserable and given to groundless suspicions of his companions. In such descriptions we recognise that acute sensibility to joy and suffering, that subjection to moods and sensations, which characterised him in after life. "You tell me never to despair," he wrote to Haydon in 1817; "I wish it were easy for me to observe the saying — truth is, I have a horrid morbidity of temperament." [2] A year later he wrote to Baily, "I

---

[1] This schoolfellow was Edward Holmes; *v.* Colvin's *Keats,* pp. 7, 8
[2] *Letters,* edited by H. B. Forman, p. 17.

carry all matters to an extreme, so that when I have any little vexation it grows in five minutes into a theme for Sophocles."[1] During the earlier part of his school days Keats seemed destined for military success rather than for distinction as a poet; but when he was about thirteen the passion for study took possession of him, and he read with as much intensity as he had fought. He knew no Greek, and in Latin his classical attainments extended no further than the Æneid,[2] yet he found out a way to Greek mythology through the pages of Tooke's *Pantheon*, Lemprière's *Classical Dictionary*, and Spence's *Polymetis*. Seldom has the strength and trustworthiness of that instinct which leads genius to select and appropriate the material most suited to its development been more strikingly illustrated. In this introduction to literature Keats had the benefit of the friendship of Charles Cowden Clarke, the son of the head master and a young man of decided literary tastes.

During these years at Enfield, Keats lost his father and mother, and in 1810, when he was but fifteen, his guardian took him from school and apprenticed him to a Mr. Hammond, a surgeon at Edmonton. As this town is but a few miles from Enfield,[3] Keats was able to keep up his intimacy with the Clarkes. The influence of Charles Clarke on Keats thus continued uninterrupted. The two friends read together, and discussed their favourite poets, and, through Clarke, Keats found a new world of delight in the poetry of Spenser. There is a close affinity between the genius of Spenser and that of Keats, and in reading the *Faërie Queene* the younger poet, with his beauty-loving and romantic nature, must have felt that

---

[1] *Letters*, edited by H. B. Forman, p. 176.

[2] C. C. Clarke's chapter on Keats in his *Recollections of Writers*.

[3] Edmonton lies between London and Enfield, and about three or four miles from the latter place.

he had come into his inheritance. Clarke says that he went "ramping" through the poem "as a young horse would through a spring meadow." [1] It seems to have been this pure enjoyment of Spenser's poetry that first stirred in Keats the desire to write, and, according to good authority, his *Imitation of Spenser* was his earliest attempt at verse. In another early poem, full of boyish raptures over chivalry, he does homage to Spenser, and calls on his gentle spirit to hover about his steps:

> "Spenser! thy brows are arched, open, kind,
> And come like a clear sunrise to my mind." [2]

At eighteen Keats had thus gained access to those two enchanted regions — the world of Greek mythology and the world of mediæval romance — which were to give their especial colouring to much of his greatest work. In consequence of a quarrel with Mr. Hammond, Keats did not complete the term of his apprenticeship, but
Settles in London. came up to London in 1814, and continued his study of medicine in the London hospitals. He seems to have acquitted himself creditably in his professional duties, but the whole force of his nature went out more and more toward poetry, which rapidly became his one absorbing passion. Through Clarke, who had also settled in London, he read Chapman's translation of Homer, and celebrated his conquest of this new kingdom for his imagination in a sonnet which is one of the first revelations of the extent of his poetic power. Soon after he met
Leigh Hunt. Leigh Hunt, and began a friendship which was to exercise an important influence on his career. Hunt, who was about ten years Keats's senior, was an amiable, but somewhat volatile and superficial man, with a fine feeling for the beauty of a poetic phrase, but no great

---

[1] *Recollections of Writers,* "John Keats."
[2] *Specimen of an Induction to a Poem.*

strength or creative power. His poetry, while sometimes pleasing, had a tendency to mere prettiness, and was too apt to sink into a colloquial familiarity which he mistook for ease, but which was beneath the dignity of art. His literary essays were graceful and appreciative. Hunt was the head of what was derisively called the "Cockney School." He had aroused the bitter antagonism of the great Tory periodicals, *Blackwood's Magazine* and the *Quarterly*, by the position he had taken in politics as well as in literature, for circumstances had made him a hero of the young Liberals. When Keats came to London, Hunt was in prison, in consequence of certain unflattering comments on the Prince of Wales. After softening his captivity by procuring a flowered wall-paper and by much reading of Spenser and the Italian poets, Hunt became, to Liberals, a martyr to liberty, and to Tories an object of attack. He had, moreover, aroused the opposition of the Edinburgh critics by an attack on the poetry of Wordsworth and of Scott. By becoming a poetic disciple of Hunt, Keats consequently laid himself open to castigation from two of the leading critical periodicals of the day. Keats's first volume of poetry, indeed, which appeared in 1817, escaped notice. It was a thin volume of short poems, full of youthful crudities, and marred by a weak effusiveness and sentimentality of

Endymion and its critics. phrase. But the publication of his long poem of *Endymion* in the year following brought down upon the new adherent of the "Cockney School" the brutal abuse of the *Quarterly* and *Blackwood's*, or, as Landor named it, "Blackguard's" Magazine. We know now that the injustice and cruelty of these attacks were not the cause of Keats's early death, that Shelley was mistaken when he called the reviewers murderers, and Byron when he said that the poet of *Endymion* had been "snuffed out by an article." [1] Indeed, after the first shock, Keats showed

---

[1] *Don Juan*, Canto xi. stanza lx.

a real restraint and manliness. "Praise or blame," he declared, "has but a momentary effect on the man whose love of beauty in the abstract makes him a severe critic on his own works. . . . I never was afraid of failure; for I would sooner fail than not be among the greatest."[1] Keats himself spoke of *Endymion* as a "feverish attempt rather than a deed accomplished,"[2] and while it gives abundant evidence of high poetic power, it lacks the sustained excellence and the fine restraint which are found in the greatest works. Not only was the poem a failure in the eyes of hostile critics: Keats had failed to express in it the real capacity that was in him. He was without a profession (for he had abandoned medicine), and without adequate means of living. He had his genius, and his resolve to be among the great English poets after his death. He was twenty-three when *Endymion* was published; he was not twenty-six when he

Rapid development.

died. Yet in the three years that remained for him, darkened toward the close by mental and physical sufferings, he won a lasting place among the poets of England. It is not the precocity of Keats that surprises us; it is the rapidity of his poetic development; the fact that he passes at one stride from the relaxing and mawkish strain so recurrent in the earlier poems, and from the "indistinct profusion"[3] of *Endymion*, to such highly-wrought artistic masterpieces as *Hyperion, The Eve of St. Agnes*, and the *Ode on a Grecian Urn*. It argues well for Keats's manliness and for his whole-souled devotion to his art, that, in the face of hostile criticism, his genius could thus suddenly and triumphantly assert itself. At this time (1818), a rival passion began to take its place beside his love of poetry. He met Miss Fanny Brawne, and his

[1] *Letters*, p. 207, Forman's edition.
[2] Preface to *Endymion*.
[3] Shelley's phrase; *v.* Forman's edition of Shelley's *Prose Works*, vol. iv. p. 186.

first feelings of mingled attraction and disapproval gave way to a violent infatuation. It is a feverish and, on Keats's side, a pitiable love-story, and carries us rapidly to a tragic ending. Signs of ill-health had before this begun to show themselves, the chances of any immediate recognition as a poet were most slight, and to Keats's excitable and jealous temperament, love meant tumult and too often torment. He held to his work, but the uncertainties and vexations of his position preyed upon him. "I shall be able to do nothing," he writes. "I should like to cast the die for love or death."[1] A few months later (February, 1820), consumption declared itself, and from the first Keats had no hope of his own recovery. In the same year he collected and published most of the poems which he had written since the appearance of *Endymion*, and on these poems his fame chiefly rests. In the fall of 1820 it became evident that Keats could not survive another winter in England, and in September he sailed for Naples with his friend Joseph Severn. He lingered for a short time in what he called bitterly a "posthumous existence," and died in Rome February 23, 1821. His last words were to his faithful Severn, "Thank God, it has come."

The moving principle of Keats's life and poetry is the worship of beauty. Somehow there had been lodged in this son of a London hostler a seemingly miraculous power to know and love beauty and to embody this fine perception of it in a beautiful form. To him the exercise of this power to perceive and to create was the supreme, almost the sole, interest. It took the place of a religion. The first articles of his creed remain for us in two familiar passages; in his conviction that

> " A thing of beauty is a joy forever,"

[1] *Letters*, 19th October, 1819, p. 433, Forman's edition.

and that beauty and truth are one.[1] We may add to these his prose statement that "with a great poet the sense of beauty overcomes every other consideration, or rather obliterates all consideration," [2] and we may recall further his significant words to Miss Brawne, "Why may I not speak of your Beauty, since without that I could never have lov'd you?" [3] The delight in beauty in its outward manifestations depends partly on the soul and partly on the senses. Physically, Keats was endowed with so fine and pleasure-loving an organisation that his senses as well as his soul were delicately responsive to outward impressions. This peculiar freshness and openness to impression lies on the surface of his character and work. "The glitter of the sea," says Haydon, "*seemed to make his nature tremble.*" He luxuriates in sensations, he goes into raptures over the taste of claret or of fruit. In his work he communicates something of his keener susceptibility to our duller and more phlegmatic senses. That wonder of romance, *The Eve of St. Agnes*, for instance, is

The Eve of St. Agnes. a poem of sensuous impressions. We are made to feel the aching cold, or the "poppied warmth of sleep;" to hear the resonance of the silver trumpets, or the pattering of the "flawblown sleet;" to see the "carvèd angels, ever eager-eyed;" to taste the jellies "soother than the creamy curd." It is a poem of contrasts: the radiance of light and colour, the storm and darkness; the palsied crone and the ancient beadsman, beside the absorbing happiness and ecstasy of love and youth. It is this same fastidious susceptibility to beauty that declares itself in the almost unrivalled verbal felicity of Keats's best work. So rich are his best poems in this magical quality — as, for instance, his finest odes — that

[1] See opening of *Endymion* and the end of *Ode on a Grecian Urn.*
[2] Letter to his brother George, *Letters*, p. 57, Forman's edition.
[3] *Ibid.*, 351.

we linger over them, held by pure delight in the perfection of the phrase. This full felicity of expression, perhaps Keats's greatest distinction as a poet, is the quality he

As master of form.
seems to have admired most in the poetry of others. As a boy, he had gone into raptures over the epithet "sea-shouldering whales;" and in the numerous allusions to the works of his favourite poets which are scattered through his letters, his enthusiasm is always for the phrase, never, or rarely, for the idea. He wrote to his friend Bailey that he looked "upon fine phrases like a lover." [1] With his openness of nature to beautiful impressions and this fastidious felicity of phrase, Keats luxuriated in two great realms of beauty — the world of the classic Greek, and the world of mediæval romance. His fellowship with the one has given us such poems as *Hyperion* and the *Ode on a Grecian Urn;* his fellowship with the other, *St. Agnes' Eve* and *La Belle Dame sans Merci.* Shelley put his humanitarianism into his *Prometheus;* under Tennyson's classic poems is the undercurrent of modern ideas; the soul of Coleridge's *Ancient Mariner* is modern within its quaint old ballad-form. But Keats is remote, not merely from his modern surroundings, but from the spirit of his time; in his classic poems he is close to Swinburne, and in his mediævalism he is really the precursor of Rossetti and the Pre-Raphaelites. Besides such poems as those of which we have spoken, Keats has given us in many of his odes and sonnets specimens of his personal feelings and moods.

That Keats was an inspired interpreter of beauty; that he has enriched the literature with poems which, though few

His place as a poet.
in number, possess a fascination of their own, these things are beyond question. Yet after this is freely recognized, the place which Keats holds among the great poets of England remains still

[1] *Letters*, p. 364, Forman's edition.

undetermined. Our feeling on this matter will depend
largely upon our ideal of poetry and our convictions as to
its true aims. If we believe that the highest function of
the poet is to give pleasure through the creation of a beauty
that appeals primarily to the senses, the poetry of Keats
will come near to realising our ideal. If, on the other
hand, we believe that the highest and truest poetry, while
possessing this beauty, adds to it a beauty more purely
spiritual, a teaching and uplifting power, and an element
of thought, we shall find Keats's poetry distinctly in-
sufficient for our highest moods. It must be remembered,
His theory moreover, that the absence of the ethical and
of poetry. spiritual elements in the poetry of Keats is not
accidental, but is the result of his most settled
convictions in regard to poetry as an art. He was opposed
to the idea that the poet should be a teacher, a belief which
was the inspiration of Milton, Wordsworth, Shelley, Tennyson, and Browning. He condemned the philosophic element
in Wordsworth's poems; he condemned the love of humanity and the desire to serve it in Shelley's. The artist, he
declared, must have no purpose beyond that of the poetic
effect. Such a purpose is wrongly thought of as the god
of the work, "but," he adds, "an artist must serve Mammon." [1] This theory of poetry is plainly in keeping with
the tastes and character of Keats himself. Supreme in
one province, he is grievously lacking in the highest aspirations, in spirituality, and in the ardour for right and
truth. Apparently devoid of a religious sense, his perception of beauty grows less sensitive as beauty becomes less
physical and more abstract. Back of the work of the
greatest poets we recognise the tremendous force which
comes from the whole mind and nature of the man.
Keats's poetry, beautiful within its limits, is circumscribed
by the serious limitations of Keats himself. In *Lamia,*

[1] Letter to Shelley, *Letters,* p. 505, Forman's edition.

for instance, which has been pronounced "one of the most glorious jewels in the crown of English poetry,"[1] the luxurious emotions of the senses, the fascination of the Circe, are idealised and elevated into a superiority to thought and to truth. We are called upon to sympathise with Lamia, the serpent-temptress transformed into a beautiful woman; a fair illusion, destroyed by the eye of truth. Lamia beseeches her lover not to think, knowing that "a moment's thought is passion's passing bell." We cannot but recognise in this the spirit of Keats when he wrote, "Oh, for a life of Sensations, rather than of Thoughts!"[2] Lamia dies, but Truth, the philosopher who has wrought her destruction, ought, says the poet, to have his temples bound with "speargrass" and the "spiteful thistle." Contrary to his theory, Keats has here given us a poem with a teaching; but the teaching, while characteristic, is neither elevated nor true. It is possible that the shortcomings of Keats are the result of immaturity, and that, had he lived, his genius would have declared itself in other ways.[3] What he might have done is matter for conjecture; but we know that his later poems are not immature but highly finished, and it is clear that his advance toward a poetry of moral power and philosophic thought would only have been gained by a radical change in his views

Lamia.

[1] A. C. Swinburne, "Keats," in _Encyclopedia Britannica_, ninth edition.

[2] _Letters_, p. 53, Forman's edition.

[3] Matthew Arnold contends that, from what we know of Keats, it is _probable_ that his genius would have developed in "moral interpretation." He quotes from Keats's letter to show that he had a growing desire for study, and gives this as a proof of his intellectual possibilities. He omits, however, a later passage in which Keats declares that he prefers pleasure to study (_Letters_, p. 432). Probably Keats often expressed a passing mood, and too much weight should not be given to his often impulsive utterances

of poetry, and by not so much a growth as a total making over of the man himself. Judging him by what he has done, we are constrained, unless we adopt his views of poetry, to admire with certain reservations. His poetry is the song of the Sirens. It is weakened by a strain of effeminacy; and its atmosphere, often heavy as with sweet and cloying odours, is deliciously enervating. We miss in it the manly vigour of those mountain heights where, as in Wordsworth or Shelley, the air is pure and clear. We should lose much were we unable to yield ourselves to that spell of warm and abundant loveliness of which Keats is master, but if we rejoice in the life-giving air that blows on the high altitudes of poetry, we will not drift into that unthinking or wholesale adulation in which lovers of Keats are apt to indulge. The motto from his master Spenser which Keats prefixed to *Endymion* is the index to the spirit of all his work; it expresses Keats's ideal, but we may question whether that ideal is the highest:

Keats's poetic limitations.

> "What more felicity can fall to creature
> Than to enjoy delight with liberty?"

CHAPTER II.

VICTORIAN ENGLAND.

THE year 1832 may conveniently be regarded as the beginning of the latest literary epoch of England. Not only did many of the great authors who stand as representatives and exponents of the Victorian age, begin to write in or about that year, but many surrounding conditions in society or in thought which have helped to give form and color to their work, then began to impress themselves upon the tone of literary production. It is never easy to select, out of the complex and multifarious life of a time, those particular social conditions or current modes of thought which have done most toward giving to the literature of the epoch its special note or personality. But in dealing with a past epoch at least some of our difficulties have been removed by the mere lapse of time. Rightly or wrongly time has selected for us what we must assume to be the leading characteristics of the period. The confusion of innumerable voices has long ceased, thousands of daily happenings have passed out of mind, and the meaning and due relations of great events have grown more clear. Keeping in mind the obstacles to our gaining a just and comprehensive idea of that time to which we may be said to belong, we must try to understand its general meaning and personality, so far as our nearness to it will permit.

We can detect three forces at work in the life and thought of recent England, which have been potent factors in the contemporary literature.

516

(1) *The advance of democracy.*
(2) *The general diffusion of knowledge and of literature.*
(3) *The advance of science.*

These are not separate but interdependent forces; each has acted on the others, and their combined influence has done much to determine the distinguishing spirit of our epoch and its literature.

1. *The advance of democracy.* By the year 1830 the conservative reaction which had followed the meeting of the Congress of Vienna, had given way before a fresh outbreak of the revolutionary spirit. In this year the Bourbon king, Charles X., was driven by the liberals from the throne of France. The event awakened in Germany a responsive agitation, and the progress of democracy in Europe, which had but suffered a temporary check, was resumed. In England this tendency showed itself in changes so radical that they constituted in fact a peaceable and legal revolution. The period of prophetic anticipation, the period of disappointment and oppression, were past, and the nation entered upon an era in which the ideas of democracy were to be actually put into practice through a series of important reforms.

For centuries the landholding class had governed the country and monopolized the government offices. Many people were also excluded from a share in political power by reason of their religious views. By successive acts many of these religious disabilities were removed, dissenters and Roman Catholics permitted to hold certain town and government offices, and by the Emancipation Bill (1829) Romanists were allowed to sit in Parliament. Still more momentous was the overthrow of the political supremacy of the landowner. The passage of a Reform Bill in 1832 extended the franchise to the middle class, which during the industrial and commercial growth of the last century had increased in wealth and importance;

and by this and other changes Parliament became more
directly representative of the people's will. A second
Reform Bill in 1867 admitted the working class to a share
in political power, while a third and still more sweeping
act in 1884 still farther extended the right of suffrage
Within half a century the real governing power in England
has thus been peaceably transferred from an exclusive
upper class to the great bulk of the nation. William IV
found England practically an oligarchy. Under Victoria
it became an almost unadulterated democracy. The
widespread results of this transference of power are mat
ters of history. It has tended to weaken class distinctions
to better the condition of the working class, and to give
increased opportunities for popular education. It ha
been clearly related to that great growth of the reading
public and those wider means for the spread of knowledge
which are so intimately connected with the literature of
the time. The social changes and agitations of which
these Reform Bills are but a part are certainly one of the
greatest features in the history of our time. It has been
said that "The most impressive thing in Europe to-day
is the slow and steady advance of the British democracy."
Thus that wider human sympathy which we saw spring up
and increase during the eighteenth century, uttering itself
with gathering power and distinctness in a long succession
of poets from Thomson to Shelley, has taken in our time
an increasingly definite and practical form.

But these reforms have been far from satisfying many
who long for a yet more radical change. The philanthropi
efforts of Robert Owen (1771–1858) in behalf of the fac
tory operative and the poor were followed toward the
middle of the century by the Christian socialism of Charles
Kingsley (1819–1875) and Frederic Denison Maurice
(1805–1872), and later (in 1860) by the new economi

---

[1] *V.* Rae's *Contemporary Socialism.*

teachings of John Ruskin (1819-1900), the importance of whose work as a social reformer is but beginning to receive due recognition. Labor on its part has banded itself together in organizations which have become a distinctive feature in our modern society, and on every side there are signs of expectancy and social unrest. These aspirations and uncertainties have written themselves in the pages of the literature. They are echoed in our poetry; they have been a great formative influence in the novel, the distinctive literary form of the day, either directly, from Godwin's *Caleb Williams* (1794) to Besant's *All Sorts and Conditions of Men* (1882), and Mrs. Ward's *Marcella* (1894), or in less obvious and more subtle ways.

2. *The more general diffusion of knowledge and literature.*

The more general diffusion of education, the prodigious multiplication of cheap books and reading matter in every conceivable shape, is closely related to the democratic spirit of society and to the advance of applied science. Education, like political power, is no longer monopolized by an exclusive class; the readers are the people, and reading matter, if not literature in the stricter sense, is now produced by them and for them. This reading public has been widening since the days of Defoe and Addison. The early years of the eighteenth century gave birth to the periodical essay, and many of the great English newspapers — *The Morning Chronicle, The Times, The Morning Post, The Morning Herald,* founded during the last quarter of that century — began that wider influence of journalism which is one of the features of the present time. The rising literary importance of these great journals during the latter eighteenth and early nineteenth centuries is illustrated by the fact that Coleridge, Lamb, Thomas Campbell, and William Hazlitt, a noted English literary critic, were among their contributors. Newspapers have rapidly multiplied during the present century, and their circulation has enormously increased with the removal of the stamp and paper duties which were formerly levied upon them, and with the improved mechanical means for their production.[1] "A Preaching Friar," wrote Thomas Carlyle in 1831, "settles himself in every village and builds a pulpit which he calls Newspaper. Therefrom he preaches what momentous doctrine is in him, and dost not thou listen and believe?" Through the pages of his *Weekly Register* (established 1815) it was possible for William Cobbett, the son of a day-laborer in Surrey, to become one of the most powerful political writers of his time. The opening of the nineteenth century saw the introduction of another important agency in widening the power of literature, in the foundation of the great reviews. *The*

Periodical literature. *Edinburgh Review,* an organ of Whig or Liberal opinions, was started in 1802, nearly a century after the foundation of *The Tatler.* This provoked the establishment, in 1809, of *The London Quarterly,* which came forward as an advocate of opposite political views. Among the reviews and periodicals that followed were *Blackwood's Magazine* in 1817, *The Westminster Review* in 1824, and two weekly papers of a high order, *The Athenæum* and *The Spectator,* in 1828. These magazines had the support of many of the ablest and best known writers of the day, and many of them were immensely stimulating to the public interest in literature. Even the partisanship and ferocity of some of the book reviews were not actually without good result, as they tended to promote literary discussion. Thus Francis Jeffrey, the first editor of *The Edinburgh,* pronounced his sentence of condemnation on the poetry of Wordsworth; Coleridge defended his friend's poetic principles in his

[1] In 1827 there were 308 newspapers published in the United Kingdom, of which 55 were in London. In 1887 the number of newspapers published in the British Islands is given at 2125; 435 of which are published in London. *V.* Ward's *Reign of Victoria,* vol. ii. p. 509.

Biographia Literaria (1817); Wordsworth himself stated them in prefatory essays to his poems. Hazlitt, Lamb, Southey, De Quincey, and Walter Savage Landor were writing during these early years of the century on books and writers past and present, so that the time may be thought of as a *period of literary criticism.*

But literature and knowledge were passing even beyond these limits to leaven the poorer and more ignorant strata of society. A literature more especially devoted to the cause of popular education became important about the time of the first Reform Bill. Men like Charles Knight (1791–1873), the brothers William and Robert Chambers, George L. Craik, and Samuel Smiles consecrated their lives and energies to this work, the importance of which it is not easy to over estimate. In the year of the passage of the Reform Bill (1832) two cheap magazines were established. The first of these, *The Penny Magazine*, was established in London by Charles Knight; the second, *Chambers' Edinburgh Journal*, was started quite independently by the Chambers brothers. Both of these were enormously popular, the former reaching a circulation of two hundred thousand copies at the end of a year. Besides cheap and good periodical literature, there were penny cyclopedias, cheap editions of good authors, and the beginning of those means for the diffusion of literature and knowledge which have now become so familiar. By the legislative provision for popular education (Foster Education Act, 1870), and by private enterprise, Victorian England showed her deep sense of the duty and the necessity of a general education. Carlyle spoke in the best spirit of the time when he declared, "If the whole English people, during these 'twenty years of respite,' be not educated, . . . a tremendous responsibility before God and man will rest somewhere." [1]

Popular literature.

---

[1] *Past and Present*, Bk. iv. chap. iii.

3. *The advance of science.* Science, which has attracted
to its service a large proportion of the intellectual force of
the time, has conspicuously affected the life of modern
England in two distinct ways. First, by its application
to directly practical ends it has wrought a revolution in
the material conditions of civilized life. So far as his
physical surroundings are concerned, the civilized man of
to-day lives in a new earth which science has created for
him. And second, by its researches into the history and
nature of things, by theories which touch upon the problems of man's origin and destiny, science has been a disturbing or modifying element in almost all contemporary
thought, and in almost every department of intellectual
activity. In brief, it has both transformed life and altered
our conception of life; it has done much to change the
aspect of the world without, and it has penetrated the life
of the very soul within.

Many of those important changes in the outward conditions of daily life which have followed the practical
application of science to life, date from about
Science and that period which we have fixed upon as the
modern life.
beginning of the present literary era. In 1830
the Liverpool and Manchester Railroad went into operation, and six or seven years later a great period of railroad construction began. The first electric telegraph in
England was erected in 1837, the year of Victoria's accession, and steam communication with the United States
was begun in the following year. These new means of
locomotion and transportation, like those new means
of production which immediately preceded them, have
helped to create the modern spirit, the note of personality which marks the time. The facilities for quick and
easy intercourse meant the further breaking down of old
barriers between town and country, between section and
section; they meant the lessening of provincialism or

ignorant prejudice, and they meant the opportunity for the transmission of newspapers and of news; so in this, as in many other ways, modern science came as an ally of modern democracy. On the other hand these changes have rudely broken in upon seclusion and contemplation; modern industrialism, with its railroads and factories, has made the world uglier; intenser competition and greater chances of money-making have made man more selfish and sordid. Wordsworth lived to lament the invasion of the peaceful retirement of his beloved Cumberland by the railway and the tourist.

> " The world is too much with us, late and soon,"

at least twice a day it gets itself recorded in print, and insists upon thrusting in our faces the catalogue of its latest crimes and scandals. It is as though we lived in the street,

> " Jaded with the rush and glare
> Of the interminable hours,"[1]

and were unwilling or unable to take sanctuary in the dimness and coolness. All this has tended to foster in us that feverish haste and activity, that desire for the new thing, however ignorant we may be of the old, which seems hardly conducive to the creation of enduring masterpieces of literature. "Wherever we are, to go somewhere else; whatever we have, to get something more;" these, according to Ruskin's caustic aphorism, are the moving desires of the modern world.

The second effect of the advance of science, its modification or disturbance of thought or belief, is also to be taken into account in our study of recent literature. The year 1830, which witnessed a triumph of applied science, was also productive in purely scientific investigation. Sir Charles Lyell's *Prin-*

Science and modern thought.

---

[1] *The Buried Life,* Arnold.

ciples of Geology (1830), which revealed the vast extent of
earth's past, was one of the first of those many books of
science which, during the last half century, have combined to modify some of our fundamental ideas of life.
This book, says Professor Huxley, " constituted an epoch
in geological science," and also prepared the world for the
doctrine of evolution. This last named theory of the
beginning and the law of life, put forth by Charles Darwin
and Alfred Russell Wallace in 1859, steadily forced upon
those who accepted it a wholesale readjustment of their
ideas comparable to that which the discovery of Copernicus forced upon our forefathers. It struck at the root
of men's conceptions of existence; its influence reached far
outside the ranks of the specialist, into the whole world of
thought, moving men to utter again the old cry:

> "Ah me, ah me, whence are we or what are we?
> In what scene the actors or spectators? "

With new problems and aspirations, social, scientific, or
religious; with a world that seems to move with an ever-
accelerating rush and swiftness; our literature has been
heavy-laden with the burden of our seriousness and our
complaining. The childlike lightsomeness of Chaucer's
England, the young energy of Shakespeare's, the shallow
flippancy and finical polish of Pope's, all these have passed.
In Arnold's magnificent and melancholy lines, the England
of to-day is

> "The weary Titan, with deaf
> Ears and labor-dimmed eyes.
>   .   .   .   .   .   .
> Bearing on shoulders immense
> Atlantean, the load
> Well-nigh not to be borne,
> Of the too vast orb of her fate." [1]

This is the England whose voice is heard in the Victorian
literature.

[1] " Heine's Grave."

The new conditions of life and thought which thus took rise in England in or about the year 1832, found a group of young writers capable of interpreting them. By that year the extraordinary outburst of poetic genius which began during the closing years of the preceding century had spent its force. The year 1832 saw the death of Sir Walter Scott. Wordsworth, Coleridge, and Southey still lived, indeed, but their work was done; while the recent and untimely deaths of Keats, Shelley, and Byron had made a sudden gap in English poetry. Into the firmament thus strangely left vacant of great lights, there had risen a new star. In 1830, Alfred Tennyson, the representative English poet of our era, definitely entered the literary horizon by the publication of his *Poems, Chiefly Lyrical.* Macaulay and Carlyle, two writers who were to occupy a large space in the prose of the opening era, had entered literature a few years before the advent of Tennyson; and immediately after his coming many of the other great writers of the epoch crowd in quick succession. The next decade saw the advent of Robert Browning (*Pauline,* 1833); Elizabeth Barrett, afterward Mrs. Browning (*Prometheus Bound,* 1833); Charles Dickens (*Sketches by Boz,* 1834); William Makepeace Thackeray (*Yellowplush Papers,* 1837), and John Ruskin (*Salsette and Elephanta,* 1839).

It is not easy to form any general conception of the literary period thus begun. The sixty years which make up the Victorian era have been years of immense literary activity and productiveness; many, and often conflicting, elements have found expression in them, and even in this comparatively short space, so rapid has been the movement, so fierce and unremitting the pressure of the time, that successive phases of thought or style have followed each other with confusing swiftness. The general features of the Victorian literature will grow clearer to us through

The new era in literature.

a study of some of those authors who represent its diversified activity.

The practical and prosperous temper of an England that eighty years ago seemed entering upon a period of solid comfort and prosperity, is reflected in the work of the brilliant essayist and historian, THOMAS BABINGTON MACAULAY (1800–1859). From his first publication, an essay on *Milton* in the *Edinburgh Review*, 1825, Macaulay's career was one of unbroken and well-deserved success. Few writers have brought to their work more enthusiasm for literature, or more patient industry; few have ruled over a wider range of reading, or collected a store of information as diversified and exact. Macaulay was the born man of letters. Before he was eight he was an historian and a poet; having compiled a *Compendium of Universal History,* and written a romantic poem, *The Battle of Cheviot.* From the first he was an insatiable reader; from childhood he began laying up in his prodigious memory those ever-accumulating stores which were to constitute his magnificent literary equipment. His nurse said "he talked quite like printed books," showing a command of language which greatly amused his elders. When he was about four, some hot coffee was spilled on him while out visiting with his father. In answer to the compassionate inquiries of his hostess he replied: "Thank you, madam, the agony is abated."[1] As Macaulay grew to manhood his juvenile tastes were turned into solid acquirements, and there is something substantial and well-rounded in the life built on these good foundations. He was successful as statesman and as author. He was courted and admired in the most distinguished circles; and his wide reading, his phenomenal memory, his brilliant conversation, sparkling with spoils from many literatures, helped to make him a social and literary leader. He

T. B. Macaulay.

[1] Trevelyan's *Macaulay,* i. p. 40.

thoroughly enjoyed the world and the age in which he found himself ; finding it full of substantial comforts, and a sensible and rational progress. England with her ever-lengthening miles of railroads, with the smoke of her thousand factories, with her accumulating gains, delighted him with her tangible and visible successes. But to his shrewd and practical intelligence the spiritual hungers and alterations, the mysterious raptures and despairs of finer and more ethereal natures, must have seemed wholly unintelligible. After reading Wordsworth's *Prelude* he writes in his diary: "There are the old raptures about mountains and cataracts; the old flimsy philosophy about the effect of scenery on the mind; the old crazy mystical metaphysics; the endless wilderness of dull, flat prosaic twaddle; and here and there fine descriptions and energetic declamations interspersed." [1] Macaulay felt, to use his own oft-quoted phrase, that "an acre in Middlesex is better than a principality in Utopia." The very soul of genius looks out at us through Shelley's dreamy and delicate features; we know where his principality lies. Carlyle thought once, as he looked unobserved at Macaulay's sturdy, blunt features, with their traces of Scottish origin, "Well, anyone can see that you are an honest, good sort of a fellow, made out of oatmeal." [2] In truth Macaulay was as naturally and happily in accord with the average sentiment of the mass of men about him, as Shelley was out of tune with it; and his ability, unlike the mystical power of Shelley, differs from that of the average man less in kind than in degree. Not only has such a temperament a better chance of happiness than a more ideal one; not only is it better fitted for wordly success; in Macaulay's case it was this very glorified commonplaceness which qualified him for the great work he had to do. Robust, upright, manly, un-ideal, it was

[1] Trevelyan's *Macaulay*, ii. p. 239.
[2] Trevelyan's *Macaulay*, i. p. 23.

easy for the growing reading public to understand him, and to these popular qualities he added wide scholarship and a style of absolute clearness, of captivating movement, and unwearied brilliancy. We cannot wonder that Macaulay, following close on those means for widening the sphere of literature already noted, should have become to the growing circle of readers the great popular educator of his time. His essays, covering a wide range of subjects, brought history and literature to the people through the pages of the magazines. India came home to them in his *Clive* and *Hastings;* Italy in his *Machiavelli;* England in his *Chatham;* literature in his *Milton* and his *Johnson.* The comparative compactness with which these subjects were handled, the impetuous rush and eloquence of the style, their picturesqueness, richness, their sparkling antithesis, took the public by storm. And Macaulay has still another qualification as a missionary of learning: he was, in Lord Melbourne's neat phrase "cock-sure of everything." Such confidence hardly indicates power of the finest order, but none the less it is often grateful to untrained minds, which qualification and reservation tend to confuse. As an English writer [1] says, in an admirable bit of criticism on this point: "uninstructed readers like this assurance, as they like a physician who has no doubt upon their case."

The great work of Macaulay's later years was his *History of England from the accession of James II.* On this task he concentrated all the fullness of his powers: he brought to it a high standard of excellence, an infinite capacity for taking pains, a marvellous style, and the loving labor of a lifetime. More than a century before, Addison had declared that through *The Spectator* he would bring philosophy out of the closet, and make it dwell in clubs and coffeehouses. Macaulay, who is to be associ-

[1] Rev. Mark Pattison.

ated with Addison as accomplishing a similar work on a
far larger scale, wrote before the publication of his *History*,
"I shall not be satisfied unless I produce something which
shall for a few days supersede the last fashionable novel
on the tables of young ladies." [1]   The immense sale of his
book, absolutely unprecedented in a work of this character, is overwhelming testimony to Macaulay's position
as a popularizer of knowledge. "Within a generation of
its first appearance," writes his biographer, "upward of
one hundred and forty thousand copies of the *History*
will have been printed and sold in the United Kingdom
alone," while according to Everett no book ever had such
a sale in the United States, " except the Bible and one or
two school-books of universal use." [2]

We should be careful to estimate the importance of
Macaulay's work at its full value; we should appreciate
the soundness and manliness of his life and character; we
should realize his peculiar significance at a time when
literature was becoming more democratic. At the same
time we should feel that, great as his gifts were, they were
not of the highest order; excellent as his aims were, they
were not the loftiest nor the most ideal. If we compare
the two famous essays on Johnson, the one by Macaulay
and the other by Carlyle, we shall perceive that the first is
the brilliant, graphic production of a capable and highly
trained man of letters; that the second has the penetrative
insight, the more exquisite tenderness of the man of genius.

In passing from Macaulay, the versatile and accomplished man of letters, to THOMAS CARLYLE (1795–1881),
the great man whose Titanic energy and invigorating power sought an outlet through the making of books, we are impressed, at the very
outset, with a strong sense of dramatic contrast. Study

Thomas
Carlyle.

[1] Trevelyan's *Macaulay*, ii. p. 327.
[2] Trevelyan's *Macaulay*, ii. p. 327.

the portraits of the two men: Macaulay, as he looks out at us from the front of Trevelyan's biography, round-faced, unwrinkled, smooth-shaven, complacent; Carlyle, with his tumble of hair and shaggy beard, his gaunt face, worn and lined with innumerable wrinkles, his sunken cheeks and deep-set, wonderful eyes. It is the face of an inspired peasant; lit up at times, so those who knew him tell us, by a strong and passionate vehemence, expressive of scorn, of humor; expressive, too, of that infinite reserve of tenderness that lay in the deep places of his strong nature. To this man life was terribly and tragically earnest. He battled through it, with set teeth and iron purpose, as a strong man forces and shoulders his way through a tangled jungle. "Woe unto them," he said to his friend Sterling, and reiterated in his essay on Scott — "woe unto them that are at ease in Zion." He lives

"As ever in his great Task-master's eye;"

he adds to the stern and inflexible conception of duty characteristic of his Calvinistic ancestry, that indwelling sense of God's presence so strong in the Hebrew prophet, so rare in our modern Western world. To him as to Wordsworth the world is "the living garment of God," creation definable in one or another language as God's "realized thought." Standing thus in the porch of the infinite, he never loses that awe and wonder which the most of us never feel, or, feeling, so easily put by. A man who dwells with "the immensities and the eternities" is not likely to adapt himself to the world's ways, or agree with the world's judgments; rather like the risen Lazarus in Browning's *Epistle of Karshish*, he brings from other regions a standard which the world cannot understand. Hence, while Macaulay was in comfortable accord with an age of material progress, teaching, as Emerson said, "that 'good' means good to eat, good to wear, material com-

modity," Carlyle often stood apart in flat antagonism and
fiery denunciation. Uncompromising to himself, he was
habitually uncompromising toward others; crying out to
a faithless and blinded generation as some stern prophet
of the desert. Writing in *Sartor Resartus* of Teufels-
dröckh, the imaginary philosopher into whose mouth he
put his own teaching, and whose experiences in many
instances are but reflections of his own, Carlyle says:
" In our wild Seer, shaggy, unkempt, like a Baptist living
on locusts and wild honey, there is an untutored energy,
a silent, as it were, unconscious strength, which, except
in the higher walks of Literature, must be rare." [1] This
may stand, with certain reservations, as a picture of
Carlyle himself; in its spirit and broad outlines essentially
true.

Thomas Carlyle was born at Ecclefechan, a little village
in Dumfriesshire, Scotland, December 4, 1795. Froude
describes the place as "a small market town
consisting of a single street, down the side of
which, at that time, ran an open brook. The
aspect, like that of most Scotch towns, is cold, but clean
and orderly, with an air of thrifty comfort." [2] About
sixty miles to the northwest of Ecclefechan lay the district which had brought forth Burns, that other great
Scotch peasant, of whose life Carlyle was to be the truest
interpreter. Some thirty miles to the south, at the edge
of the Cumberland Hills, was the birthplace of Wordsworth. Carlyle's father, James Carlyle, was a thrifty,
hard-working stone-mason; a sterling, unapproachable,
reticent man, with strong religious convictions, and a
faculty of concise and vigorous speech. He possessed
"humor of a most grim, Scandinavian type," a quality
which notably characterized his son. James Carlyle was

Carlyle's
life.

---

[1] *Sartor Resartus*, Bk. i. chap. iv.
[2] Froude's *Carlyle*, i. p. 3.

one of five brothers, graphically described by an apprentice to one of them as "a curious sample of folks, pithy, bitter-speakin' bodies, an' awfu' fichters." According to Carlyle himself, they were remarkable for "their brotherly affection and coherence; for their hard sayings and hard strikings." When such a granite stock produces a genius — a man that can speak for it — we may look for originality, a strong accent, an iron grip, and a stroke like that from a sledge-hammer. There is little in the outward events of Carlyle's life that need detain us. In his childish years he led "not a joyful life," he tells us, "but a safe and quiet one." His home was the prudent, God-fearing household of the Scotch peasant; all the surroundings wholesome, perhaps, but somewhat rigid and repressing. "An inflexible element of authority," Carlyle writes, "surrounded us all." He ran barefoot with his brothers and sisters, all younger than himself, in the street of Ecclefechan; he was sent to the village school, and afterward to the grammar school at Annan, a town on the Solway Firth, some eight miles from home. His parents were proud of the ability he showed, and were anxious to fit him for the ministry of the Kirk, naturally the highest ambition of such a household; so at fourteen he entered the University of Edinburgh, having walked the eighty miles that lay between Ecclefechan and the capital. He succeeded in obtaining a place as teacher of mathematics in the Annan Academy, and left the university in 1814, before taking his degree, to enter on his duties. In 1816 he gave up his post to become master of a school in Kirkcaldy. But the drudgery of teaching became intolerable, and a change in his religious views had forced him to abandon the idea of entering the ministry. In 1818 he took his little savings and settled in Edinburgh, where he began the study of the law. But he had not yet found his work. Law lectures proved indescribably dull to him, "seeming to point toward nothing but money as wages for all that bog-post of disgust."

Already dyspepsia, his lifelong tormentor, had fastened upon him. He knew that he was "the miserable owner of a diabolical arrangement called a stomach," a bitter knowledge that never left him. These years of uncertain prospects and physical suffering were also a critical time of doubt, despair, and fierce spiritual conflict. He has told us in *Sartor Resartus* the story of this period of "mad fermentation," with its doubts of God, of the obligations of duty, of the reality of virtue. How he stood in those days of trial, "shouting question after question into the Sibyl-cave" and receiving for answer "an echo"; how he called out for Truth, though the heavens should crush him for following her; how he reached at length the appointed hour of deliverance when, in a mysterious flash of conversion, he came forth free, independent, defiant.[1] We must study this crisis of the spirit in the words of Carlyle himself, remembering the intensity of his nature, his passion for probing things to the centre, his sincerity, his capacity for faith.

Meanwhile Carlyle's aspirations had turned toward literature, and he had contributed a number of articles to the *Edinburgh Encyclopædia*. He also began to learn German, a study destined powerfully to affect his life and work. His German studies brought him into contact with a literature which seemed to reveal to him " a new heaven and a new earth." He became an enthusiastic student of Richter. His works give evidence of his absorption of the ideal philosophy of Fichte, and above all he came under the spell of Goethe. These studies did more than colour Carlyle's thought and help to produce the peculiar mannerism and eccentricity of his style. There was at that time a furor for German literature, and the literary results of Carlyle's studies thus fortunately happened to fall in

[1] *Sartor Resartus*, Bk. ii. chap. vii.

with the popular demand. Thus in 1822 he contributed an article on *Faust* to the *New .Edinburgh Review;* his translation of Goethe's *Wilhelm Meister* appeared in 1824, his *Life of Schiller*, which had previously come out in the *London Magazine*, was published in book form in 1825; and his *Specimens of German Romance* in 1827. The year before the publication of the book last named he married Miss Jane Welsh, the daughter of a provincial surgeon of good family and of considerable local reputation. On her father's death Miss Welsh had inherited a small farm at Craigenputtock, in Dumfriesshire, and there Carlyle and his wife settled in 1828. The little farmhouse was set solitary in the midst of a somewhat dreary tract of moorland, and here, shut out from the world, Carlyle threw himself at work with characteristic intensity. He had left behind him the time of hackwork and translations, and was reaching out toward something that should more truly represent him. He wrote a number of essays for the *Edinburgh*, among them his unapproachable study of Burns; and here he composed *Sartor Resar-*

Sartor Resartus. *tus.* This extraordinary book contains the germ of Carlyle's philosophy. His grievous uncertainties and hesitations were over. Much had been lived through to make this book, and into it Carlyle poured what he had gained, in good measure and running over. Carlyle's personality is always present in his writings, but never more strongly than here. Midway in this mortal life he delivered to us the deepest things that life and suffering had taught him, the essence of his message. In *Sartor Resartus*, with its indescribable compound of grim humour, abruptness, tenderness, grotesqueness, broken by overpowering torrents of eloquence, Carlyle reveals himself. It was his master passion to get at the heart of any object of thought, to tear away all the external and outward aspects through which any fact may reveal itself to us, and, discarding everything superfluous and accidental, lay bare its underlying meaning. In his studies of men he does not rest at the outward events of their lives; he would lay hold of their very souls, and it is this which gives to his judgment such an extraordinary truth and value. In the same way he sees that in every case there is the outward form in which a fact becomes apparent to us, its body; and there is its soul, its inner meaning and reality. "It is the duty of every hero," he declares in a later book, "to bring men back to this reality," to force them to penetrate beneath the surface, to teach them "to stand upon things and not upon the shows of things." *Sartor Resartus*, or the tailor re-tailored, is the philosophy of clothes, that is, the vesture or symbols of things; it aims to point us to the reality that underlies these outward forms or *clothes*, in which the underlying fact reveals itself. "Symbols are properly clothes — all forms whereby spirit manifests itself to sense, whether outwardly or in the imagination, are clothes; man's body is but his 'earthly vesture;' the universe itself, with its manifold production and reproduction, is but the living garment of God." Through all the book spirit is recognized as the true and enduring reality. With Carlyle it is the things which are unseen that are eternal, and in this he stood in absolute opposition to the material and scientific element in his time. Human history itself is but the clothing of ideas in acts, and the great man, or hero, is but the highest human revelation of the will and spirit of God.

In 1833 *Sartor Resartus* began to appear in *Fraser's Magazine*, finding but few readers among a bewildered or indifferent public. In the year following, Carlyle took a decisive step in leaving Craigenput-tock and settling in London. There he lived, during the forty-seven years that remained to him, in a house in Chelsea, which became the resort of many dis-

Settles in London.

tinguished men, and was thought of by many, says Professor Masson, "as the home of the real king of British letters." Up to this time Carlyle's life had been a stubborn fight with poverty. He had won recognition from the discriminating few; but he would write in his own way and in no other, and as yet he had gained nothing like a popular recognition. In a few years this was entirely changed. His popularity was begun by the appearance of his *French Revolution*, in 1837. About the same time he gave the first of several courses of lectures, which made his strange, rugged figure and impassioned earnestness familiar to London audiences. He "toiled terribly," bringing forth his great works with indescribable stress and effort. In 1866, shortly after he had fought his way through a mighty task — his *Life of Frederick the Great* — he was made Lord Rector of the University of Edinburgh, a post of great honour. At last his own country had honoured her prophet, but the triumph was shattered by the sudden death of Mrs. Carlyle, "for forty years the true and loving helpmate of her husband." Fifteen years longer Carlyle himself lingered on; wandering about the Chelsea Embankment or Battersea Park, living over in an old man's dreams that past which he recorded in his *Reminiscences*. Strength had altogether left him, and life was a weariness. He died, February 4, 1881, and was buried, according to his wish, beside his family in the little churchyard at Ecclefechan.

With all deductions, Carlyle remains one of the most influential and considerable figures in the literature of his century. He stands in the midst of its noise of traffic, its haste to get rich, the prophet of the spiritual and the unseen. Wordsworth had protested against that "custom," that daily pressure of the trivial, which deadens the higher side of our nature, and "lies upon us like a weight." Carlyle helped men to

Carlyle's work.

rid themselves of the burden of the petty and conventional, which was stunting the growth of their souls. He would have them do this, not by seeking refuge from the world of every day in some region of cloudy romance, but by realizing that, looked at rightly, this world of every day is essentially divine and miraculous. "Is not nature," he asks, "as eternal and immense in Annandale as she is at Chamouni? The chambers of the east are opened in every land, and the sun comes forth to sow the earth with orient pearl. Night, the ancient mother, follows him with her diadem of stars: and Arcturus and Orion call *me* into the infinitudes of space as they called the Druid priest or the shepherd of Chaldea." [1]

And great as is this miracle called nature, still greater is the wonder of that miracle called man. As Carlyle was opposed to modern science in his conception of the physical world, seeing in it a living divine revelation, and not a dead "world machine," he likewise became more and more at odds with that view of society which would regard it rather as a mechanism than as a living thing. He distrusted the democratic theories and reforms which marked his time. He sneered at the cry for "ballot boxes and electoral suffrages"; [2] believing that the saving of the world must come not through majorities, which were ignorant or confused; not through institutions, which were likely to become mere hollow, ineffectual contrivances, but through the personal element, the hero, or great man, who had been, and must continue to be, the largest factor in history. With Carlyle there is no patent political receipt for progress. He has no patience with that idea of history which regards human society as an organism developed according to fixed laws, an idea which reflects the scientific temper of our time. To him the history of

[1] Froude's *Life*, i. 244. *Cf.* passage on Miracles in *Heroes and Hero Worship*, lect. ii.
[2] *Heroes and Hero Worship*, lect. iv.

the world is at bottom the history of the great men who have worked here. This intense individualism, as opposed to merely governmental authority, may seem to suggest Byron and Shelley, but one must remember that with Carlyle the few are to command, the many to obey.

Without attempting to codify Carlyle's work into any set system, it is safe to say that a great proportion of it is closely related to this central theory of history. In the *Heroes and Hero Worship* (1841) the importance of the great man in history is enforced by a study of a series of heroes, representative of the different forms in which the hero has appeared. It aims to show that in all these cases the essential heroic qualities — earnestness, sincerity— have been the same. So the lives of *Frederick the Great* and of *Cromwell* are but more exhaustive studies of the great man as a historic factor. Carlyle's heroes were commonly taken from the strong men who had the power to compel the world to do their will. But we must not fall into the error of regarding him as a mere believer in brute strength. Right and might he believed were in the long run synonymous, not because might made right, but because in the large movement of history the strongest were ultimately the wisest, the most righteous. This thought of the ultimate triumph of right over wrong, and of strength over weakness, is the text of his *French Revolution*. The world is true and not a lie, and a sham government, grown too decrepit to govern, like that in eighteenth-century France, is a lie and cannot stand. Had the revolution failed to take place, Carlyle tells us, he would have despaired of the world. As it was, it demonstrated that though the mills of the gods grind slowly, injustice, misgovernment, and the sceptre of the strong in the hand of weakness, work at last the inevitable retribution. "Verily there is a reward for the righteous, doubtless there is a God that judgeth the earth."

We may differ in our estimate of the truth or value of Carlyle's doctrines; we may be convinced that hero worship is a vain dream, as a practical form of government in our modern society; but this need not at all interfere with our admiration for his books, as masterpieces of literary art. Carlyle's style is without parallel in the entire range of English prose. Often turgid and exclamatory, its lack of simplicity and restraint is relieved by a grim play of humor, or forgotten in the momentum of its terrific earnestness. Under all mannerisms we know that a strong man is speaking to us out of the depths of his soul, as one man seldom dares to speak to another in this solitary and conventional world. Its power is very different from that of mere literary dexterity. "I feel a fierce glare of insight in me into many things," Carlyle wrote in his Diary, "I have no *sleight of hand*, a raw, untrained savage, for every civilised man has that sleight." [1] His *French Revolution* having at length "got itself done" after incredible effort, Carlyle seems to fairly hurl it in the face of the public, which as yet would not know him. "You have not had for a hundred years," he thunders, "any book that comes more direct and flaming from the heart of a living man. Do with it what you like, you ——" [2]

This determination to speak what was in him to say, in his own fashion and without regard to any literary precedent, is another of the many traits which Carlyle and Wordsworth have in common. Both belong in this to that revolt against the formalism of the Augustan Age, and to both "conventionality was the deadly sin."

To the force of earnestness and unconventionality, Carlyle added a phenomenal descriptive power. He had the

---

[1] Froude's *Carlyle*, iii. p. 47.   [2] Froude's *Carlyle*.

poet's instinct for the picturesque and dramatic; by the intense concentration of his imaginative insight the past is alive not only for him but for us also; he both sees and makes us see. In his *French Revolution*, the "prose epic" of our century, the most dramatic episode in modern history has received its greatest interpretation in literature. The descriptions of the death of Louis XV., of the destruction of the Bastile, the twilight silence of a pastoral idyl after its noise and fury, of the flight and capture of the king — to find anything comparable to these and countless others like these, we must turn to the pages of our greatest poets. Or again, what can we find to set beside those pages in which the meaning and wonder of a great city are flashed on us, as though we had been suddenly caught up into the air and made to look down upon it with the comprehensive and penetrative gaze of a god.[1] Carlyle, too, is one of the greatest of word portrait-painters. Read his description of the face of Dante, with its "deathless sorrow and pain"; of Rousseau's, with his "narrow contracted intensity, bony brows, deep, straight-set eyes." Read, too, those unsparing characterisations of his contemporaries; they may be unfair, unjust, untrue, but what an instinctive and lavish power of characterisation they exhibit. Often carelessly uttered, and soon forgotten, every word goes home to its mark with the merciless power and precision of a well-directed javelin.

Descriptive power.

And finally Carlyle's style reflects his own humour and large-hearted tenderness; the pathetic gentleness of a strong, stern man who has suffered. It were better if we dwelt less on Carlyle's grumblings and dyspepsia, his irritability, his half-humorous vituperations, and thought more of his unobtrusive acts of kindness and of the compassion that was in him.

Humour and tenderness.

[1] See *Sartor Resartus*, Bk. i. chap. iii.

Surely it is no common pity that goes out to us in such a passage as this: "Poor, wandering, wayward man! Art thou not tried, and beaten with stripes, even as I am? Ever whether thou bear the Royal mantle or the Beggar's gabardine, art thou not so weary, so heavy-laden: and thy bed of Rest is but a grave. Oh, my Brother, my Brother! why cannot I shelter thee in my bosom, and wipe away all tears from thy eyes!"

Carlyle has helped his time not so much by the promulgation of any definite system of philosophy, for in his teachings he is often open to the charge of inconsistency and exaggeration, but by the fresh inspiration he has brought to its higher life. He is a great writer, but above all he has been a spiritual force, quickening and invigorating the moral and religious life. His work is to be associated in this with that of JOHN RUSKIN (1819–1900),

John Ruskin. another great exponent of the highest ideals of the century. In Ruskin, much that is best in contemporary life, thought, and art was combined and stamped with the seal of his own aggressive and dogmatic personality. On the right hand or on the left, he touches or supplements one or another of our great modern guides, rising at the same time distinct from them all in his own work and character. Like Keats he is exquisitely responsive to beauty, and has come as her priest and her revealer. In all his work as art critic, in his lifelong efforts to coax or scourge an obdurate British public to a more general and genuine love of beautiful things, he touches at one point the æsthetic element of the age. Like Wordsworth, he is the lover and interpreter of Nature, doing for her in his prose a work similar to that which Wordsworth and the other great Nature-poets performed in verse. And like Carlyle, Ruskin is a preacher and prophet to his generation; not rapt, like Keats, in

¹ *Sartor Resartus*, Bk. ii. chap. ix.

æsthetic delights; not wholly withdrawn, as Wordsworth, into the contemplation of nature, he throws himself into the noisy strifes and dissensions of his time, coming among the crowds of the market place to warn, to rebuke, and so far as he can, to help and to restrain.

Nothing but a loving study of Ruskin's work can give us any conception of the wonder and loveliness of his prose-poetry of Nature. Here the exquisite sensibility of the landscape painter to colour and form is joined to the poet's gift of language, his guiding instinct in the choice of words; here, too, something of the scientist's spirit toward the world of matter is tranfused and uplifted by the spiritual apprehension of the mystic. Ruskin's sense of colour is as glorious as Shelley's, his word-pictures often as luminous and as ethereal; indeed, so phenomenal is his descriptive power that he may be thought of as having created a new order of prose. Take, for instance, his description of the Rhone, and notice how alive it is with Ruskin's joy in colour and power; how the wonderful adjectives reveal his delight in the mighty river's crystalline purity and force. "For all other rivers there is a surface, and an underneath, and a vaguely displeasing idea of the bottom. But the Rhone flows like one lambent jewel; its surface is nowhere, its ethereal self is everywhere, the iridescent rush and translucent strength of it blue to the shore, and radiant to the depth. Fifteen feet thick, of not flowing but flying water; not water, neither — melted glacier, rather, one should call it; the force of the ice is with it, and the wreathing of the clouds, the gladness of the sky, and the continuance of time." After a few sentences we come upon this bit of pure poetry: "There were pieces of wave that danced all day as if Perdita were looking on to learn; there were little streams that skipped like lambs and leaped like chamois; there were pools that shook the sunshine all

Descriptions of Nature.

through them, and were rippled in layers of overlaid ripples, like crystal sand." [1]

Ruskin's descriptions of Nature affect us not merely because of their magical richness and flow of style; not because he piles up in them a shining structure of light and colour, but because to him, as to Wordsworth and Carlyle, the shows of earth and sky are far more than an empty pageant; because he, too, "sees into the life of things," [2] and reveals it to us. "External nature," he declares, "has a body and soul like a man; but her soul is the Deity." [3] And this doctrine that we are to regard Nature as the bodily or visible revelation of God, is not with Ruskin a mere philosophic theory; it is remarkable for its vitality and definiteness, it is intimately connected with his principles of æsthetics, and makes beauty illustrative

Ideas of beauty and art.

of the nature of God. He believes we are so made that, when we are in a cultivated and healthy state of mind, we must delight in beauty and be thankful. The apprehension of true beauty is, therefore, a test of our nearness to Him whom it expresses and reveals; and taste, the faculty by which this beauty is discerned and enjoyed, is, in its highest form, a moral or ethical quality. "The sensation of beauty is not sensual on the one hand, nor is it intellectual on the other, but is dependent on a pure, right, and open state of the heart, both for its truth and its intensity." Hence, in those attributes or qualities which enter into the beauty of Nature, Ruskin sees the types or symbols of "God's nature or of God's laws"; in the infinity of Nature, Divine incomprehensibility; in her unity, Divine comprehensiveness; in her repose, Divine permanence; in her symmetry, Divine justice; in her purity, Divine energy; "in her moderation,

---

[1] *Præterita*, vol. i. chap. v.

[2] Wordsworth, *Lines on Revisiting Tintern Abbey.*

[3] *Modern Painters.*

the type of government by law." [1] With these ideas of
Nature and Beauty, Ruskin's principles of art are naturally
connected. Just as the perception of Beauty is a moral
attribute, so the interpretation of Beauty, which is the
work of the artist, is likewise moral, the act of a pure soul.
Perhaps Ruskin gives the clearest and briefest statement
of this, his fundamental art principle, which has exposed
him to endless ridicule and misunderstanding, in a paragraph in *The Queen of the Air:* "Of course art-gift and
amiability of disposition are two different things; a good
man is not necessarily a painter, nor does an eye for
colour necessarily imply an honest mind. But great art
implies the union of both powers; it is the expression, by
an art-gift, of a pure soul. If the gift is not there, we can
have no art at all; and if the soul — and a right soul, too —
is not there, the art is bad, however dexterous." [2] On this
principle of the foundation of great art in morality, all
Ruskin's work as an art critic is built. He tells us, for
example, that in all his work as a critic of architecture his
aim has been, "to show that good architecture is essentially
religious — the production of a faithful and virtuous, not
of an infidel and corrupted people." [3] These ideas of Ruskin must be firmly grasped, because they are the keynote
not only to his work, but to his life also, making his whole
career consistent and intelligible. He is first of all a great
moral, or rather a great Christian, teacher. English-born,
he really belongs by descent to the land of Knox and Carlyle, and religious earnestness, the passion to convert, to
dogmatise, and to reform, go even deeper with him than
his love of beauty. Like Carlyle he was brought up on

[1] *Modern Painters,* vol. ii. pp. 263–319.

[2] *Queen of the Air,* § 106; *cf. Sesame and Lilies, Of Kings' Treasuries,
The Mystery of Life, and its Arts,* §§ 105–106; *v.* also, contra, Symonds'
Renaissance in Italy: Fine Arts, pp. 24–30.

[3] *Crown of Wild Olive, Traffic.*

the study of the Bible, reading it and committing long passages in it to memory in daily Bible lessons at his mother's knee. While Keats was first of all the worshipper of beauty Ruskin has been first of all the impulsive and passionate defender of convictions, the proselytiser and the knight-errant of unpopular truths. Shortly after his graduation from Oxford, he entered the lists in his *Modern Painters* (1st vol., 1843) as the champion of Turner, whose merit as one of the greatest landscape painters of all time had then

Literary Work.

received but scanty recognition. This work, although the outcome of a desire to vindicate the genius of Turner, far outgrew the limits of its original design, and became, as it progressed, a setting-forth in prose of unexampled splendour and purity, of Ruskin's theory of art. He contends for faithfulness to the object portrayed; he would have the painter go himself to Nature, "rejecting nothing, selecting nothing, and scorning nothing." This last saying is worthy of our especial regard, because it shows us that Ruskin's teaching but carries that love of truth and sincerity which Wordsworth and Carlyle exemplified, into the sphere of art. Ruskin's advice may be set side by side with Wordsworth's trust that he has avoided false descriptions in his poems, because he has "at all times endeavoured to look steadily at the subject." To "look steadily at the subject" — this chance phrase of Wordsworth defines the nature of a change in the art, the poetry, and the life of the English world.

For about twenty years from the publication of the first volume of *Modern Painters*, Ruskin gave his chief energies to the study and criticism of art. *The Seven Lamps of Architecture* and *The Stones of Venice*, besides the concluding volumes of the *Modern Painters*, are among the works of this time. But from about 1860, while Ruskin's deepest interests and purposes remained unchanged, his best effort was given to ethics and social reform. In his loving study of nature, art, and beauty, the cry of his century would not let him rest; the thought of the sordid ugliness of the world about him, of the sufferings, the problems of humanity, beset him, and he would not put them by. "I am tormented," he wrote, "between the longing for rest and lovely life, and the sense of the terrific call of human crime for resistance, and of human misery for help." In order to answer this call, Ruskin must leave his chosen sphere of work, and face a new task. He must attack, single-handed, the deep seated evils, the cherished prejudices of modern England, the very law by which it lived. Yet the call was answered, and whatever may be thought of the wisdom or practical value of Ruskin's economic doctrines, we cannot but feel a glow of honest admiration, on seeing his ardour, his audacity, his purity of purpose, realising as we must the greatness of his foe. Great as this break in Ruskin's life seems, from art to social science, in reality the work of his second period was the consistent and logical consequence of his first. For twenty years he had laboured for the cause of pure art, and the conviction had but grown stronger in him that pure art was the outcome of a just, pure, and believing community. He believed that it was idle to preach the love of art and of beauty to a nation whose standards of living were vulgar and dishonest, whose real worship was the worship of wealth and worldly success. To promote the cause of art, it became necessary to secure, by the establishment of nobler and truer ideals of living, that moral soundness out of which pure art is produced. Ruskin was thus brought by a different route to face those same insistent questions which had enlisted the efforts of Carlyle, of Maurice, and of Kingsley; questions which yet press upon us unanswered.

The industrial changes of the last hundred years had

brought not only an enormous increase of wealth, but had given new chances of acquiring it to people of almost every social class. The early part of the eighteenth century had witnessed the rise of the merchant class through the expansion of the colonial trade; the latter part of the century saw the rise of the manufacturing class. With golden prizes dangling before their eyes, the energies of the great mass of men had become more and more exclusively material. In their haste to get rich, men became more selfish and grasping; they were impelled to forget mercy and pity. The love of money thus became more and more the great temptation of the modern world. We have watched the growth of the new love of Nature; Nature's fairest scenes were scored by railroads and scorched and blackened by the soot and grime of factories. We have watched the growth of the new pity for man; in the early part of our century men, women, and little children were sacrificed to Mammon by labour in mills and factories so prolonged and severe that it stunted and twisted their miserable bodies and darkened their miserable souls.[1] When Ruskin began work as an economist many of these evils had indeed been removed, but the master passion of the age remained unchanged. This modern spirit has been often assailed, but no protest has been more direct and momentous than that of Ruskin. To discuss, or even to state, his economic theory, set forth in such books as *Unto This Last* (1862), the *Crown of Wild Olive* (1866), *Time and Tide* (1868), or *Fors Clavigera* (begun 1871), papers addressed to the workingmen of England, would take us beyond our proper limit. It may be said briefly that it is essentially an attempt to apply the ethical teachings of Christianity to the actual conduct of business and government. The competition on which the whole structure of our society is founded,

[1] See Gibbins' *Indust. History of England*, for account of passage of factory laws.

Ruskin declares to be "a law of death," to be set side by side with anarchy in its destructive power. The true foundations of a state are not liberty, but obedience; not mutual antagonism, but mutual help.[1] From the standpoint of the literary critic, the books in which these strange doctrines are unfolded are substantial additions to English prose. In the *Modern Painters*, and other early books, Ruskin had proved himself master of a style unprecedented in its wealth of poetry and beauty, but in these later books all adornment is severely subordinated to the strong utterance of the thought. The power of using what he called "pleasant language" had not, indeed, passed away, but we can perceive that a growing weight of thought and earnestness has brought a greater plainness and directness of speech. If Ruskin's later style lost something in pure beauty, it gained in simplicity, in intensity, in pure power. There is, as in the *Fors Clavigera*, directness, tenderness, strong outbursts of denunciation and scorn, with an undertone of satiric humour that recalls the power, but not the malignity, of Swift.

JOHN HENRY NEWMAN (1801–1890), stands apart from the other great prose-writers of his century, in his life, his strongly marked and impressive personality, his work, and his aims. Newman was above all a theologian. In his most familiar hymn "Lead, kindly Light," he asks for Divine guidance, and his work is largely the expression of his spiritual quest, his intellectual struggles and inward experiences, or it is prompted by his desire to combat and confute a public indifferent or hostile to him or to his cause. His most famous book, the *Apologia pro Vitâ Suâ* (1864) is a record of his spiritual experiences. In it he "spoke out," as he said, his "own heart," talking to us at times very simply and directly as though he were confiding in us as in a friend. Newman's books are thus a

J. H.
Newman.

[1] *Modern Painters*, vol. v. p. 205.

part of his life history. They are partial revelations of an extraordinary man.

The chief events of Newman's career were merely the outward results of that inner life of spiritual warfare and change which so absorbed him. Educated at Oxford, Newman began his work as a clergyman of the Church of England. For a time he was a leading spirit in a concerted effort, begun at Oxford in 1833, to make the English church more spiritual, and to bring it closer in doctrine and practice to the Church of the early and mediæval times. But while he taught others, Newman's own views were changing, and he soon began to think differently from his own followers. In 1843 he resigned his office as Vicar of St. Mary's near Oxford, and two years later, after vain efforts to find some "middle way," he found in the Roman Catholic Church "a home after many storms." In 1849 he founded a brotherhood, or monastic retreat, at Edgbaston, near Birmingham, and there the long remainder of his life was chiefly passed. He was made Cardinal in 1879, and died at Edgbaston Oratory in 1890.

Newman resembles some mediæval saint and ascetic mysteriously transported into the midst of our practical, scientific, and unbelieving modern world. Born only a year later than Macaulay, Newman was an alien and a pilgrim in that England which Macaulay regarded with complacent satisfaction. His life was lonely; he had friends but they came "unasked and unhoped" for. A man of searching, subtle intellect, a master of irony, a keen and dangerous disputant, he had yet the soul of the poet, with a deep reserve of tenderness and pity. The weight of the world's misery, coldness, and unbelief, pressed heavily upon him. He was passionately, almost fiercely, religious, and to him the things which were real were the things which were not seen.

Newman is among the greatest masters of English prose,

by the transparent clearness, the ease, beauty, and singular persuasiveness of his style. His prose is remarkable for the variety of its excellence. He could be plain, almost homely and colloquial, delicately ironic, eloquent, passionate, or pathetic. There is no sense of strain or effort, his sentences seem to flow from him with that ease which accompanies great power. But we feel, above all, that he is using this power over words, not for the pure pleasure of it, not to achieve certain artistic results, but always as a means and never as an end. He said of himself, "I think I have never written for writing's sake," and we are sure that, unlike some modern artists in words, Newman made style the servant of his purpose, that his end was not to please with rare or beautiful phrases, but to get his meaning into the mind of his reader and persuade him to see as he sees.

From the technical or special nature of his subjects, Newman's work often lacks that broad human interest which is usually characteristic of great literature. From the purely literary aspect this is a disadvantage which even the fine quality of his style cannot always entirely overcome.

Such writers as Macaulay, Carlyle, Ruskin, and Newman force us to realise the greatness of our modern literature in the sphere of prose. Since the time of Addison, **Other prose writers: the historians.** English prose has steadily broadened in range and increased in literary importance. Carlyle, Ruskin, and Macaulay, were surrounded by many other prose writers some of them of great importance and distinction; by scientists, scholars, historians, and literary critics, and by innumerable novelists who were busy supplying the rapidly increasing demand for works of fiction. The Victorian Age has probably surpassed any other period of English literature in the number and excellence of its historical writers, and in the importance of its contributions to historical research. Some of this historical work is learned and important rather than brilliant, and its gains in accuracy have been offset in some cases by a loss of dramatic power, picturesqueness, and literary charm. HENRY HALLAM (1777–1859), the father of Tennyson's chosen friend, was one of the most laborious and best equipped of the earlier historians; GEORGE GROTE (1794–1871) wrote a monumental *History of Greece* (12 vols. 1846–1856); HENRY HART MILMAN (1791–1868), a *History of Latin Christianity* (1854–1856), and ALEXANDER WILLIAM KINGLAKE (1809–1891) a brilliant and vivid account of the *Invasion of the Crimea* (1863–1887).

A little after the middle of the century, several writers came into prominence who did much to increase our knowledge of English history, especially during the earlier period. Foremost among these were WILLIAM STUBBS (1826–1901) and his friend EDWARD A. FREEMAN (1823–1892). Both were associated with Oxford, Freeman having succeeded his friend Stubbs (who was made a bishop in 1884) as Regius Professor of modern history in that university. Freeman was a profuse and often discursive writer, but he gave a marked impetus to historical study. His *History of the Norman Conquest* (1867–1876) is one of his best known works. Bishop Stubbs was among the foremost of this group of students who were enlarging and correcting men's understanding of the past by their patient and minute study of the original authorities. His *Constitutional History of England* (1874–1878) treats of the origin of the nation's government, and follows the growth of the English constitution from its obscure beginnings to the accession of Henry VIII. JOHN RICHARD GREEN (1837–1883), the friend and, to some extent, the disciple of Freeman and Stubbs, added to a well-directed industry a singular breadth of view, and the grace of a smooth, animated, and sometimes eloquent style. Green was a London curate with a fondness for historical and antiquarian research. Compelled by failing health to give up his parish, he turned to his favourite studies, and after five years published his *Short History of the English People* (1874). Probably no English history since Macaulay's had been received with such enthusiasm on both sides of the Atlantic, and probably no book since Macaulay's has done so much to make the past of England alive and real to the imagination of the general reader. Green's books on English history are inspired by a deep patriotism, and a sympathetic understanding of man. He is the historian "not of Kings or Conquests but of English People." His object is to enter into and depict the life of the whole nation through all its centuries of continuous evolution; to exhibit each factor in progress, each element of change, in its proper relations and in due proportion; to slight no social class from king to churl, to neglect neither economics nor law, neither wars nor literature. Green has succeeded as no other has done in this seemingly impossible task. He has "set Shakespeare among the heroes of the Elizabethan Age, and placed the scientific inquiries of the Royal Society side by side with the victories of the New Model."[1] Among Green's distinguished contemporaries in his historical writing were JAMES GAIRDNER, the greatest authority on the troubled period of the Civil Wars, and Protectorate, MANDELL CREIGHTON, JAMES BRYCE, the author of *The American Commonwealth*, W. E. H. LECKY, the historian of the eighteenth century, and JOHN ROBERT SEELEY. One great master of the art of historical narrative remains to be noticed, — JAMES ANTHONY FROUDE (1818–1894). This brilliant and forcible writer had little in common with the Dryasdust historians of the modern scientific school. He did not write history in the spirit of the scientist, who makes it his chief business to observe and accurately report facts, he wrote it in the spirit of the literary artist, with an instinctive feeling for dramatic

J. A. Froude.

[1] *Short History of the English People.* Preface to the first ed.

effects. In science, the important matter is, after all, the fact, not the observer of the fact; in the arts, the all-important thing is the personality of the artist, — the man who shows us life or nature as it appears to him. Froude did not believe that history was a science. He felt that it was difficult, probably impossible, to reach the absolute truth about the past. The historian, according to this view, is bound to have opinions; he is forced to tell the story as he is able to interpret the facts. Froude's most important work, the *History of England from the Fall of Wolsey to the defeat of the Spanish Armada*, appeared between 1856 and 1870. The lucidity and picturesqueness of its style, and its dramatic power in the portrayal of character, made it widely popular, but it was fiercely attacked by Freeman and others on the score of inaccuracy. Repeated assaults have certainly impaired the public confidence in Froude's fairness and reliability, but whatever may be his shortcomings as a scientific historian, there is no dispute about his eminence as a man of letters. One would as soon call the constitutional histories of Hallam and Stubbs romantic as pronounce Froude dull. Froude, like Macaulay and Carlyle, belongs to literature, and his place as one of the great prose writers in an age of great prose is secure.

During this period a great amount of force has been expended on the study of literature and literary criticism. The names of such leading critics as THEODORE WATTS-DUNTON, FREDERICK HARRISON, WALTER PATER, JOHN ADDINGTON SYMONDS, EDWARD DOWDEN, and LESLIE STEPHEN, will occur to every reader. Among such writers MATTHEW ARNOLD (1822–1888) occupies a high and peculiarly representative place. Arnold was the son of Dr. Thomas Arnold, the great headmaster of Rugby, and both his father and grandfather were clergymen of the Church of England. He was

Literary criticism: Matthew Arnold.

thus rooted and grounded in faith both by inheritance and early influences. But from these deeply religious surroundings of his boyhood, Arnold was plunged at Oxford into the the midst of that conflict of beliefs and no-beliefs, that jar of doubt and speculation, which marked a time of spiritual crisis. At Oxford, indeed, there were "great voices in the air," [1] the voice of Newman, pleading for a solution of all doubt by simple faith, a solution which Arnold afterward declared, "to speak frankly," was "impossible." [1] Arnold, who had thus abruptly passed from the shelter of his father's influence into the heat of the conflict of his time, seems to have had a certain power to sympathise alike with the teachings of Rugby and the doubts of Oxford. His nature had a positive and emotional, perhaps even a religious strain, but this ran through a temperament austerely and coldly intellectual. Emotionally he apparently felt the need of faith, but his intellect, as hard and keen as highly tempered steel, was inexorable in its demands for exact demonstration, for precision and lucidity of thought. A great part of Arnold's poetry is the reflection of this inward conflict between these incompatible elements in his nature. He looks backward with regret and longing, while he suffers himself to be borne along on the relentless current of his time. In his prose he rebukes, or reasons, or criticises, he builds up systems of conduct; but there remains within him a void which neither his sovereign remedy of "culture" nor any mere ethical system can fill. In his poetry he laments the loss of that which he discards, and half shrinks from conclusions which he feels constrained to accept.[2]

Yet we must not think of Arnold's poetry as a mere wail of regret or outburst of despair. On the contrary its

[1] Lecture on "Emerson," in *Discourses in America*.

[2] Stanzas from *The Grande Chartreuse*. See the passage beginning "Wandering between two worlds," etc.

prevailing note is self-reliance; help must come from the soul itself, for

> " The fountains of our life are all within."

He preaches fortitude and courage in the face of the mysterious and the inevitable — a courage indeed forlorn and pathetic enough in the eyes of some — and he constantly takes refuge in a kind of stoical resignation. He delights in showing us human sorrow, only to withdraw our minds from it by leading us to contemplate the infinite calm of Nature, beside which our transitory woes are reduced to a mere fretful insignificance. All the beautiful poem of *Tristram and Iseult* is built up on the skilful alternation of two themes. We pass from the feverish, wasting, and ephemeral struggle of human passion and desire, into an atmosphere that shames its heat and fume by an immemorial coolness and repose.

Arnold's poetry has an exquisitely refined, finished, and delicate beauty; it reveals the critic, the thinker, and, above all, the man of a fine but exclusive culture. Set almost wholly in a single key, there are times when we weary of its persistent and pathetic minor. It is often coldly academic rather than warm with human life and passion, and we are apt to miss in its thin, intellectual atmosphere, just that large-souled and broadly human sympathy which it is difficult to associate with Arnold himself. At times, as in the fifth of the series entitled *Switzerland*, we feel under the exquisite beauty of the verses an unwonted throb of passion, and then, as in the poem last mentioned, we touch the highest point of Arnold's poetic art.

In his work as literary critic, Arnold has occupied a high place among the foremost prose writers of the time. His style is in marked contrast to the dithyrambic eloquence of Carlyle, or to Ruskin's pure and radiant colouring. It is a quiet style, restrained, clear, discriminating, incisive, with little glow of ardour or passion.

As critic. Notwithstanding its scrupulous assumption of urbanity, it is often a merciless style, indescribably irritating to an opponent by its undercurrent of sarcastic humour, and its calm air of assured superiority. By his insistence on a high standard of technical excellence, and by his admirable presentation of certain principles of literary judgment, Arnold performed a great work for literature. On the other hand, we miss here, as in his poetry, the human element, the comprehensive sympathy that we recognise in the criticism of Carlyle. Arnold's varied energy and highly trained intelligence have been felt in many different fields. He has won a peculiar and honourable place in the poetry of the century; he has excelled as literary critic, he has laboured in the cause of education, and finally, in *Culture and Anarchy, St. Paul and Protestanism*, and certain later books he has made his contribution to contemporary social and religious thought.

In no direction has this development of prose been more remarkable than in that of the novel, the distinctive literary form of the modern world. Since the **The growth of the novel.** publication of Richardson's *Pamela*, in 1740, the range of the novel has immensely broadened, and its importance as a recognised factor in our intellectual and social life has surprisingly increased. WILLIAM GODWIN (1756–1836) employed the novel as a vehicle of opinion. His *Caleb Williams* (1794) was one of the earliest of those novels with a purpose, of which there are so many examples in later fiction. MARIA EDGEWORTH (1767–1849), the author of *Castle Rackrent, The Absentee, Helen*, and other novels, has been called the creator of the novel of national manners. By her pictures of Irish life she did somewhat the same service for that country that

Scott, on a larger scale, was soon to perform for his beloved Scotland; she gave it a place in literature. To Scott, the unexampled popularity of the novel in modern times is largely due, and many writers in England, as well as Dumas in France, carried on his work in historical romance. Conspicuous among Scott's literary descendants were G. P. R. JAMES (1801–1860), who wrote about one hundred novels and stories, most of them historical, between 1825–1850; W. HARRISON AINSWORTH (1805–1882), an unequal, but at times a vigorous writer; and EDWARD BULWER, LORD LYTTON (1805–1873), who, after producing *The Last Days of Pompeii* (1834) and other historical romances, turned to the realistic treatment of modern life in *The Caxtons* (1845–1849) and *My Novel* (1853). But while some writers were producing romantic tales, full of moving adventures and marvellous escapes, others were endeavouring to present the more ordinary and prosaic aspects of modern life. Shortly before the appearance of *Waverly*, JANE AUSTEN (1775–1817) had published *Sense and Sensibility* (1811), the first of her finished and exquisite pictures of the daily domestic life of the middle class. In these novels the ordinary aspects of life are depicted with the minuteness and fidelity of the miniature painter, while their charming and unfailing art saves the ordinary from becoming tiresome or commonplace. Miss Austen has found worthy successors, but no superior, in her chosen field. The *Cranford* of ELIZABETH GASKELL (1810–1866) is a masterly study of the little world of English provincial life, as are the *Chronicles of Carlingford* of MARGARET OLIPHANT (1820). Mrs. Gaskell is further remembered for work of a more tragic and powerful order than the quaint and pathetic humour of *Cranford*. Her first novel, *Mary Barton* (1848), laid bare before the reading world the obscure life and struggles of the poor who toiled in the great manufactories of Manchester.

Alton Locke, Tailor and Poet, of CHARLES KINGSLEY (1849), the story of a London apprentice who becomes involved in the Chartist agitations, shows the same sympathetic interest in the heavy burdens of the poor, and in that unhappy antagonism between employer and employed which remains one of the unsettled problems of our time.

But the life of the outcast and the poor has found its most famous if not its most truthful chronicler in CHARLES DICKENS (1812–1870), one of the greatest novelists of the epoch. Dickens was the second of eight children. His earliest associations were with the humbler and harsher side of life in a metropolis, as his father, John Dickens, a clerk in the Navy Pay-office was transferred from Portsmouth to London in 1814. The knowledge thus hardly gained through early struggles and privations, became a storehouse from which Dickens drew freely in his later work. The Marshalsea Prison, where John Dickens was confined for debt, is described in *Little Dorrit.* David's experiences as a wine merchant's apprentice in *David Copperfield,* the most autobiographical of the novels, may have been suggested by Warren's blacking factory, where Dickens worked as a boy; while Dickens' youthful struggles with shorthand and reporting are reflected in Copperfield's later history. Remembering the great novelist's early experience, it seems but natural that he should have chosen to let in the sun and air on some of the shabbier and darker phases of existence; depicting types of many social gradations; obscure respectability, the vagrants and adventurers in the outer circles of society, down, as in *Oliver Twist* (1837–1838), to the pick-pocket and the murderer. There is Jo, the London street waif of *Bleak House* (1852–1853), "allers a-movin' on"; Jingle, the gay and voluble imposter of *Pickwick* (1836–1837); and that questionable fraternity, the Birds of Prey, that flit about the dark places of the Thames in *Our Mutual Friend* (1864–1865). Through this portrayal of the under strata of society there runs a strong, perhaps a sometimes too apparent moral purpose; yet take us where he will, Dickens' art is always pure, sound, and wholesome.

It is as a humorist that Dickens is at his best. There is a whimsical and ludicrous extravagance in his humour, an irresistible ingenuity in the ridiculous, peculiar to him alone. From the time when a delighted people waited in rapturous impatience for the forthcoming number of *Pickwick*, to the publication of the unfinished *Edwin Drood* (1870), nineteenth century England laid aside her weariness and her problems to join in Dickens' overflowing, infectious laughter. When we are ungrateful enough to be critical of one who has rested so many by his genial and kindly fun, we must admit that Dickens was neither a profound nor a truthful interpreter of life and character. His is for the most part a world of caricature, peopled not with real living persons, but with eccentricities and oddities, skilfully made to seem like flesh and blood. We know them from some peculiarity of speech or manner, some oft-repeated phrase; they are painted from without; we are rarely enabled to get inside of their lives and look out at the world through their eyes. The result is often but a clever and amusing burlesque of life, not life itself. It may also be admitted that we feel at times, in Dickens, the absence of that atmosphere of refinement and cultivation which is an unobtrusive but inseparable part of the art of Thackeray. Without detracting from some famous and beautiful scenes, Dickens' pathos is often forced and premeditated, his sentiment shallow, while there are heights from which he is manifestly shut out. When he attempts to draw a gentleman or an average mortal distinguished by no special absurdities, the result is apt to be singularly insipid and lifeless. Notwithstanding these shortcomings, Dickens has won notable successes outside the field of pure humour. His *Tale of Two Cities* (1859) is a powerful story, quite different from his usual manner, and many scenes throughout his other books, as the famous description of the storm in *David Copperfield*, are triumphs of tragic power.

WILLIAM MAKEPEACE THACKERAY (1811–1863) was the keen but kindly satirist of that surface world of frivolity and William Makepeace Thackeray. fashion into which the art of Dickens so seldom penetrates. Thackeray was born at Calcutta, but was early sent to England for his education. He had something of that regular training which Dickens lacked, going to Cambridge from the Charterhouse School in London. He left college, however, shortly after entering, to study art on the Continent, and finally, losing his money, he returned to England, and about 1837 drifted into literature. After writing much for periodicals, he made his first great success in *Vanity Fair* (1847–1848). In this book, under its satiric and humorous delineation of a world of hollowness and pretence, runs the strong current of a deep and serious purpose. "Such people there are," Thackeray writes, stepping "down from the platform," like his master, Fielding, to speak in his own person — "such people there are living and flourishing in the world — Faithless, Hopeless, Charityless; let us have at them, dear friends, with might and main. Some there are, and very successful, too, mere quacks and fools; and it was to combat and expose such as these, no doubt, that laughter was made." [1]

The passage is better than any outside comment on the spirit of Thackeray's work. Only the shallow and undiscriminating reader fails to see that Thackeray's seriousness is deeper and more vital than his cynicism; that though the smile of the man of the world is on his lips,

[1] *Vanity Fair*, vol. i. chap. viii.

few hearts are more gentle, more compassionate, more tender; that though he is quick to scorn, few eyes have looked out on this unintelligible world through more kindly or more honest tears. Satirist as he is, he kneels with the genuine and whole-souled devotion of Chaucer, of Shakespeare, and of Milton, before the simple might of innocence and of goodness. In the midst of this world of *Vanity Fair*, with its pettiness, its knavery, and its foolishness, he places the unspoiled Amelia and the honest and faithful Major Dobbin. If in *Pendennis* we have the world as it looks to the idlers in the Major's club windows, we have also Laura, and "Pen's" confiding mother, apart from it, and unspotted by its taint. But more beautiful than all other creations of Thackeray's reverent and loving nature, is the immortal presence of Colonel Newcome, the man whose memory we hold sacred as that of one we have loved — the strong, humble, simple-minded gentleman, the grizzled soldier with the heart of a little child. In such characters, Thackeray, too, preaches to us, in his own fashion, the old lesson dear to lofty souls, that

> " Virtue may be assailed, but never hurt:
> Surprised by unjust force but not enthralled." [1]

So he reënforces Scott's dying injunction to Lockhart: "Be a good man, my dear," by showing us, in the corruption of much that is mean and vile, that beauty of holiness which can

> "redeem nature from the general curse,"

that fair flower of simple goodness which, blossoming in tangled and thorny ways, sweetens for us the noisome places of the earth.

In addition to his work as painter of contemporary manners, Thackeray has enriched the literature by two remarkable historical novels, *Henry Esmond* (1852), and

[1] Milton's *Comus*, p. 281, *supra.*

its sequel, *The Virginians* (1857–1859). In the first of these we have the fruits of Thackeray's careful and loving study of eighteenth century England, a period with which he was especially identified, and which he had treated critically with extraordinary charm and sympathy in his *Lectures on the English Humorists* (published 1853). *Esmond* is one of the greatest, possibly the greatest historical novel in English fiction. The story is supposed to be told by Esmond himself, and the book seems less that of a modern writing about the past than the contemporary record of the past itself. Nothing is more wonderful in it than the art with which Thackeray abandons his usual manner to identify himself with the narrator he has created. Yet in this, perhaps, we should rather see the real, tender-hearted Thackeray, his thin veil of cynicism thrown aside.

Thackeray's style is exceptionally finished and charming; light, graceful, and incisive, it places him among the greatest prose masters of English fiction.

So many able and distinguished writers of the Victorian period have chosen the novel as their favourite or exclusive form of literary expression, and so familiar is their work, that even a mere enumeration of them is here both impossible and unnecessary. Their works, with that of countless others whose books represent every shade of merit or demerit, and reproduce almost every ripple of thought or discussion, are among the best-known influences of our modern life.

Among the many women who have gained distinction as writers of fiction since the appearance of Miss Burney's *Evelina* (1778), one at least cannot be passed over, even in the briefest survey.

Mary Ann, or Marian Evans (GEORGE ELIOT) was born November 22, 1819, at South Farm, Arbury, a "small, low-roofed farmhouse" in Warwickshire. Her father, George

Evans, was agent to Sir Roger Newdigate, of Arbury Hall, within the boundaries of whose estate the farm lay.

George Eliot. Arbury Hall is in the northeastern corner of the county, some thirty miles from Stratford. It lies in the same rich and well-watered region that nourished the youth of Shakespeare; a sleepy, abundant land, prosperous, and steeped in drowsy centuries of quiet. In some part of this rich Midland district, at Griff House, near Nuneaton, at school in Coventry, or at Foleshill on its outskirts, the first thirty-two years of George Eliot's life were passed. She was identified with its local interests by birth and by daily contact; her earliest and tenderest recollections clustered round it, and the grace of its liberal beauty, sanctified by memory, remained with her until the end. Her early surroundings, she tells us,

> " Were but my growing self, are part of me;
> My present Past, my root of piety." [1]

This English provincial life, thus flowing in the very currents of her blood, became the living material of her art. She was at once of it, and, by the greatness of her genius, apart from it; able both to depict it from within, and to feel it from without. Birth and association thus qualified her to become its great painter, as emphatically as Dickens was the great painter of the slums and of the poor, or Thackeray of the London clubs and drawing-rooms. The rural or provincial background which is the setting of so many of her stories is painted from reality, and many of her best-known characters were drawn from or suggested by the Warwickshire people she had early known and loved.

Ordinary and uneventful as these early years in Warwickshire may seem at first, careful study will but strengthen our conviction of their importance in determin-

[1] Poems, *Brother and Sister.*

ing the broad character of her art. In a poem full of tender memories, in which she describes her early rambles with her brother, she lets us share the secrets of her childhood.

> " He was the elder, and a little man
> Of forty inches, bound to show no dread,
> And I the girl that puppy-like now ran,
> Now lagged behind my brother's larger tread.
> . . . .
> If he said ' Hush!' I tried to hold my breath;
> Wherever he said 'Come,' I stepped in faith." [1]

In *The Mill on the Floss*, in Maggie Tulliver's dim longings and spiritual growing-pains, we gain an insight into those years in which, with much stress and hunger of the spirit, the childish horizon widened. At sixteen George Eliot lost her mother and left school to keep house for her father, gaining some experience of farm-life which she afterward used in her description of the Poyser household in *Adam Bede* (1859). In 1841 she became intimate with a family named Bray, wealthy people who lived in the vicinity of Coventry, and under their influence abandoned forever her faith in Christianity as a divine revelation, seeing in it only a human creation of man's hopes and needs. Her nature, though prone to speculation, was by no means wanting in religious feeling, and the comparative suddenness of her loss of faith may impress us as unaccountable. In thinking of this we should remember her peculiar disposition. With all her masculine strength and activity of intellect, she was singularly susceptible to influence, and dependent to an unusual degree upon the help and encouragement of others. Strength of mind does not necessarily imply strength of character, although we are too apt to confuse the two, and this fact will help us to understand more than one incident in George Eliot's life. From the first her tastes

[1] *Brother and Sister.*

had been distinctly studious and scholarly, and in 1846 she began her literary career by translating a German work in harmony with the skeptical ideas she had adopted. Her home was broken up by her father's death in 1849, and two years later, after a short Continental tour, she settled in London as assistant editor of *The Westminster Review*, to which she had already contributed. Her Warwickshire life was over, and, like Shakespeare when he first turned his face toward London, she stood at the entrance to a new world. *The Westminster Review* numbered Herbert Spencer, James and Harriet Martineau, and many other distinguished writers among its contributors, and George Eliot's connection with it naturally gave her a place in literary circles.

Among others she met Mr. George Henry Lewes, a discursive, brilliant, but somewhat erratic writer, who combined keen literary sympathies with a distinctly scientific and philosophical bent. A deep attachment grew up between them, but marriage was impossible, as Mr Lewes' wife, from whom he was separated, was still alive, and through a technicality of the law a divorce could not be obtained. Believing the law unjust, George Eliot took a step which, even in its purely social or legal aspects, must be looked upon as a serious error. She entered upon a life-long union with Mr. Lewes, which, it must be remembered, was in her eyes a true marriage. It is no justification of this most unfortunate union that it proved a "marriage of true minds," most important in its effects upon George Eliot's literary career. It was at the suggestion of Mr. Lewes that George Eliot turned from her distinctly scholarly and critical labours as essayist and translator to begin that work in fiction on which her fame mainly rests. Heretofore her writing had represented chiefly the scholarly side of her mind; it had been the outcome of her studies of books. Now, under Mr. Lewes' encouragement, the other side of her genius declared itself by the publication in *Blackwood* of her first story, *Scenes of Clerical Life; The Sad Fortunes of the Rev. Amos Barton* (January, 1857). This sudden transference of energy into a totally new channel is one of the most surprising incidents of our literary history. From one aspect it is by no means without parallel: Scott abandoned poetry for romance writing; De Foe at sixty turned from journalism and pamphleteering and produced *Robinson Crusoe*. But the singularity in George Eliot's case is not that at thirty-eight she discovered within her a great gift that she had never dreamed herself possessed of, it is that it was left for another to make this discovery for her; that this critical change in her career was due not to an impulse from within, but to an influence from without. Thus again, as at the time of her contact with the Brays, we are impressed by her extreme dependence on others. From this "new era" in her life, as George Eliot called it, we are chiefly occupied in noticing the development of this strangely discovered gift, and in marking the establishment and growth of her fame. *Adam Bede*, her first long story, and one of the most powerful and spontaneous of her books, appeared in 1859, and it was felt "that a new power had arisen in English letters." *Adam Bede* was followed by masterpiece after masterpiece at intervals of one, two, or three years; thoughtful books of substantial workmanship, not fluently written, with Scott's easy joy in power, but with unspeakable effort, self-discipline, and toil. *The Spanish Gypsy* (1868), a dramatic poem, marked a new literary departure, but George Eliot's poetry, though thoughtful and mechanically correct, is distinctly inferior to her prose. Mr. Lewes died in 1878, and barely two years later the world was electrified by the news of George Eliot's marriage to a young London banker, Mr. John Walter Cross. At this time George Eliot was slightly over sixty and Mr. Cross some twenty years her junior. When the intensity of her devotion to Mr. Lewes is taken into account we are inclined to regard this second marriage as but another proof that George Eliot's nature was dependent rather than self-reliant. "In her moral development," writes Mr. Cross, "she showed from her earliest years the trait that was most marked in her all through life, namely, the absolute need of some one person who should be all in all to her, and to whom she should be all in all." In the fall of 1880 her health was failing, and in December of that year she died suddenly after a brief illness.

George Eliot stands easily in the front rank of English novelists; she must, moreover, be recognised as one of the most influential and distinctly representative writers of her time. Whatever views we may hold of the true scope and purpose of fiction as an art, we can hardly escape assigning to George Eliot's work a position of the highest significance and importance in the history of nineteenth century thought. The art of Thackeray may seem to us finer and less laboured; we may miss in such a novel as *Daniel Deronda* that great master's half playful cynicism and exquisite lightness of touch. Scott's spontaneous, instinctive power of telling a story for the story's sake may appeal to us more strongly, the romantic twilight, the old-world enchantment of the Waverley Novels may bring us more of that blessed rest from the burdens of the day which we may consider it is the true purpose of the novel to bestow. Yet, whatever we may find or miss in George Eliot's novels, we must admit that they reveal to us a profound and tragically serious student of life. Employing a literary form which, in less self-conscious and exacting days, was generally looked upon as a means of relaxation, George Eliot's place is rather with Ruskin, Darwin, Arnold, Browning, or Herbert Spencer, with "the teachers and seekers after light," the signs of trouble often written on their foreheads — than with Scott or Jane Austen, with Dickens or Wilkie Collins. Yet George Eliot is more than a thinker, precisely as Browning is more than a thinker; both are artists, and give us, not abstract doctrines, but a philosophy clothed in the language and embodied in the living forms of art. Both feel the burdens and obligations laid upon those who in our modern time think deeply or feel acutely, and both, in harmony with its analytic and questioning spirit, are constrained not only to depict but to moralise, to search into the motives and the consequences of conduct, to analyse the subtle constitution of the soul. But in this analysis George Eliot is an artist because she studies and interprets the soul not merely with her intellect but by her true human sympathy, by the intensity of her imaginative understanding. A scholastic flavour hangs about some of our modern guides, as, for instance, Matthew Arnold, which proclaims them as primarily readers of books. George Eliot was a scholar, but she was still more emphatically a student of life. It is life itself as she has seen it and known it, in the farmhouse or the field, life in the formative experiences of her own soul, which affords her the material for her thought. "I have always thought," she writes, "that the most fortunate Britons are those whose experience has given them a practical share in many aspects of the national lot; who have lived among the mixed commonalty, roughing it with them under difficulties, knowing how their food tastes to them, and getting acquainted with their notions and motives, not by inference, from traditional types in literature, or from philosophic theories, but from daily fellowship and observation." George Eliot herself was such a "fortunate Briton," and her work, like that of Shakespeare, of Burns, of Carlyle, and of Dickens, rests securely on her sympathetic understanding of the daily life of man. The truth of her insight into the most ordinary, and, as we might consider them, commonplace lives, her tenderness for them, her perception of the pathos and the wonder of their narrow world, is one of the finest traits in her character and her art. In her earliest story, after telling us that the Rev. Amos Barton, whose fortunes she is describing, was "palpably and unmistakably commonplace," she goes on to speak of commonplace people in words which may be taken as a text of all her work. The large majority of our fellow-creatures, she declares, are "simply men of complexions more or less muddy, whose conversation is more or less bald and disjointed. Yet these commonplace people — many of them — bear a conscience, and have felt the sublime prompting to do the painful right; they have their unspoken sorrows and their sacred joys; their hearts have perhaps gone out toward their first-born, and they have mourned over the irreclaimable dead. Nay, is there not a pathos in their very insignificance — in our comparison of their dim and narrow existence with the glorious possibilities of that human nature which they share?" [1]

Here is that democratic spirit of human brotherhood of which we have so often spoken, uttering itself again through literature. Reflecting on these words we measure again the distance that the England of Victoria has travelled from the England of Pope. It is not enough for us to appreciate that George Eliot shows us ordinary people under ordinary conditions; others have done this. Her distinction is that she feels and makes us feel a something in ordinary lives which before was not apparent. Perhaps when he looks into his own soul no man truly deems himself commonplace. George Eliot gives us such a glimpse into the souls of others. Hence her characters are substantial, living people, filling us with an intense sense of reality. Looking into our own lives we

[1] *The Sad Fortunes of the Rev. Amos Barton,* chap. v.

know that their secret vicissitudes are true. Such art is comparatively independent of plot and incident. In order to interest us in her characters George Eliot is not forced, as Dickens was, to depend upon outward eccentricities or cheat us into a conviction of reality by the minute accuracy of the stage setting. In Tom and Maggie Tulliver, in Dorothea Brooke, in Tito Melema, or in Gwendolen Harleth, we enter into and identify ourselves with the inner experience of a human soul. These, and the other great creations of George Eliot's genius, are not set characters; like ourselves they are subject to change, acted upon by others, acting on others in their turn; moulded by the daily pressure of things within and things without. We are made to understand the growth or the degeneration of their souls; how Tito slips half consciously down the easy slopes of self-indulgence, or Romola learns through suffering to ascend the heights of self-renunciation. This contrast between the human craving for happiness regardless of consequences, between the simple desire for pleasure so pathetically inherent in the young and undisciplined, and the stern obligation to sacrifice our pleasure to the common good, is eminently characteristic of George Eliot. She reiterates the hard lesson with inexorable earnestness, that the weakness which prompts us to thoughtless self-gratification is a wickedness which brings with it inevitable retribution. There are few downright villains in her books, but in almost every novel are characters that fail through selfishness or a weak inability to deny themselves the things that seem pleasant. Beside Tito Melema we naturally place the amiable and yielding Arthur Donnithorne, and in the same general group are Godfrey Cass, Grandcourt in his colossal and imperturbable egotism, and poor, desiccated Casaubon who, selfishly unconscious of the sacrifice, suffers Dorothea's fresh and ardent womanhood to be immolated to him and to his "Key to all Mythologies." In *Adam Bede* is Hetty Sorel, with her soft, girlish beauty, "seeing nothing in this wide world but the little history of her own pleasures and pains"; in *Felix Holt*, Esther Lyon, whom Felix declares to be "no better than a bird trimming its feathers and picking about after what pleases it"; in *Middlemarch*, Rosamond Vincy, who, we are told, "would never do anything that was disagreeable to her"; and in *Daniel Deronda*, Gwendolin Harleth, set between Grandcourt's selfishness and Deronda's self-sacrifice, "busy," at first, "with her small inferences of the way in which she could make her life pleasant." Contrasted with such characters, marring their own lives and those of others by their wrong ideas of life's purpose, are those who are strong enough with deliberate self-abnegation to choose "the painful right." Disciplined by suffering, their personal griefs are merged in the peace that comes from self-surrender. Yet self-sacrifice is insisted on by George Eliot, not because of an earthly peace or a future reward; right-doing is often a hard thing; wrong-doing is often a pleasant and an easy thing; but "because right is right," we are to follow it "in scorn of consequence." Fedalma exclaims at the crisis of her fate:

> "Oh, all my bliss was in my love, but now
> I may not taste it; some deep energy
> Compels me to choose hunger."

Such a moral tone is both lofty and in the highest degree austere and uncompromising. Not only are the inexorable claims of duty constantly forced home to us, but in the performance of duty George Eliot recognised no divine helper; she is strengthened by no hope of a reward hereafter. The individual loses that the race may gain. As surely as Byron stood for individualism, hurling his maledictions against the universe because it would not permit him to enjoy, so George Eliot stood for altruism, teaching that the death of selfishness is our road and the world's road to progress and to peace. Such doctrines place her with the great moral teachers of her century, but render her books preëminently exacting and almost sombre. Her novels move under a heavy weight of tragic earnestness; admirable as is their art, graphic and telling as is their humour, they are weighed down with a burden of philosophic teaching which in the later books, especially *Daniel Deronda*, grows too heavy for the story, and injures the purely literary value. "My books," she writes, "are deeply serious things to me, and come out of all the painful discipline, all the most hardly learned lessons of my past life." From the literary aspect, perhaps *Silas Marner* is her most artistically perfect story, and *Middlemarch* her greatest work. In the latter book, that hunger for an unattainable and far-off good, which George Eliot so frequently expresses, is set amid the stifling atmosphere of modern society. Trying to sacrifice their lives to others, both Dorothea and Lydgate are caught in the mesh of circumstances, and fail. "There is no sorrow," Dorothea exclaims, "I have thought more about than that — to love what is good, to try to reach it, and fail." And Lydgate feels that in her words he has "found room for the full meaning of his grief." But quite aside from their teaching, it is the art of these great books — their poetic beauty of style, their subtle understanding of the lives of men and women — that places them with the great imaginative productions of the literature.

In 1855 ANTHONY TROLLOPE (1815–1882) began in *The Warden* his restful and marvellously life-like studies of life in an English cathedral town, which he made famous under the name of "Barchester."

A. Trollope.

Trollope had very positive and obvious limitations as a novelist, and paradoxical as it may sound, it is probable

that without these limitations his work would lose much
of its charm. The little world to which he introduces
us in his best books is substantial, comfortable, and —
from one aspect — most soothingly commonplace. In this
sleepy place the strain and tension of our time is hardly
felt, and little happens which is not mildly agreeable or
amusing; there are no great problems, no tragic intensity,
no beating of the soul against the bars; the very dulness is
a grateful sedative. Trollope's humour is wholesome and
kindly, he does not preach to us as do some of his betters,
he has enriched English literature with the Bishop and
Mrs. Proudie, and in Barchester he has provided for us a
place of refuge.

It was during these middle years of the nineteenth century that two other novelists, CHARLES READE (1814–1884)
and WILLIAM WILKIE COLLINS (1824–1889), won
the popular favour. Reade was a rough but
forcible writer, who, like Dickens, wrote many of his novels
with the express purpose of exposing and correcting contemporary social abuses. *Christie Johnstone* (1853) shows
the weakness and folly of the idle aristocracy, by contrast-
ing the languid and aimless rich with the vigorous activity
of the Edinburgh fish-wives: *It is Never too Late to Mend*
(1856) attacked the English prison system, and *Put Your-
self in His Place* (1870) was directed against the trade-
unions. In these stories we sometimes lose the novelist
in the social reformer, but Reade when he chose was
master of a vigorous and vivid narrative style. His one
romance, *The Cloister and the Hearth* (1861), a wonderfully
careful and minute study of life in the fifteenth century,
has been placed by Swinburne "among the very greatest
masterpieces of narration." [1]

WILLIAM WILKIE COLLINS (1824–1889) showed a fertility
of invention and great ingenuity in the conception and

[1] Swinburne's *Miscellanies*, 1886.

elaboration of his plots. He knew how to make the most of a mystery, and his characters, although often **Wilkie Collins.** stagey and conventional, are sometimes distinctly amusing. On the whole, *The Woman in White* (1860), *Armadale* (1866), and *The Moonstone* (1868) must be placed with the most skilfully written and fascinating novels of plot and incident.

A few years before Trollope published *The Warden*, English readers had been thrilled by certain sombre and **The Brontës.** powerful stories at the farthest remove in their passionate intensity from the placid and uneventful existence which is pictured in the chronicles of Barsetshire. These stories were written by CHARLOTTE, EMILY, and ANNE BRONTË, the daughters of the parish clergyman of the little Yorkshire village of Haworth. The place was gloomy as well as remote. The parsonage overlooked a forlorn and crowded graveyard; a bleak and windy moorland stretched away at the back. Mr. Brontë, the father, was severe and unsympathetic: the outlook on life was contracted. There were heavy domestic sorrows. The genius of the Brontë sisters broke through this narrowness and repression, and an accumulation of pent-up emotion, a sense of rebellion against the barriers of circumstance, and a romantic delight in the mysterious and the terrible, were poured out into those extraordinary works of fiction which, after more than half a century, have not yet lost their charm. Charlotte Brontë (1816–1855) published *Jane Eyre* in 1847. In the same year Emily Brontë (1818–1848) published *Wuthering Heights*, a story which in its descriptions of nature, its sombre unreality, and its wild and stirring power, seems, in some respects, the most perfect incarnation of the Brontë genius.

Meanwhile the historical romance, although not the favourite form of fiction, was by no means abandoned.

Between the publication of *Vanity Fair*, in 1848, and the appearance of *Daniel Deronda*, in 1876, in those years when Thackeray, Dickens, Trollope, and George Eliot were revealing the life of contemporary England, CHARLES KINGSLEY found subjects for romance in the Alexandria of the fifth century (*Hypatia*, 1853), in the Elizabethan seamen (*Westward Ho!* 1855), and in the last struggle of the English against their Norman conquerors (*Hereward*, 1866). Towards the close of the same period R. D. BLACKMORE (1825–1900) published *Lorna Doone* (1869), a poetic story of life and love in the wild and beautiful scenery of North Devon. A little later, the year before the death of George Eliot, J. H. SHORTHOUSE (1834–1903), a scholarly Birmingham manufacturer, won the praise of the cultivated and discerning by the spiritual elevation, subtle thought, and delicate beauty of his *John Inglesant* (1881), a philosophical romance of the time of Charles I.

Romance.

While Shorthouse was following up his first success, writing dreamy, finely-wrought, and tranquil stories, remote from the real world of thought and action, the love of romance revived at the touch of a very different master. ROBERT LOUIS (BALFOUR) STEVENSON (1850–1894) was born in Edinburgh, that "romantic town" in which, some seventy years before, Walter Scott, his great predecessor in romance, had first seen the light. In many ways Stevenson was Scott's spiritual descendant. Both were born with the rare gift of telling a story. Among many points of resemblance we note certain material dissimilarities. Scott's range of sympathy was far wider, his work more varied, his genius more comprehensive. Stevenson was a most careful and laborious artificer in words, fastidious to the verge of over-refinement in the niceties of style; Scott, one of the most happy-go-lucky and careless of writers, did not

R. L. Stevenson.

pause to hunt for the magical or curious word; he put the thought down as it came.

Stevenson began his work in literature with sundry essays, sketches of travel, and short stories (cir. 1875–1883). These were followed in 1883 by *Treasure Island*, his first long story of adventure. *Treasure Island* is a boy's book — with a difference. We recognise the familiar materials of the sensational story-teller, for here are pirates, a lonely and mysterious island, a search for hidden treasure, much bad language, and a prodigious expenditure of blood. But these rather shabby stage properties have become a new thing under Stevenson's hand. He has lifted his theme into a higher region by his own genuinely romantic enjoyment of the story, and by his gift of a literary style. When we understand the nature of Stevenson's success in this book, we have gone a long way towards understanding him and the especial nature of his genius. He had, as Mr. Henry James has said, "the perpetual boy in him." He kept that zest in life and adventure, that fine sensibility to outward impressions, that love of mystery, that buoyancy and romance, which are the glorious gift of youth. Stevenson himself let us into the secret when he told us that a boy's poetic imagination survives in the man and becomes "the spice of life to (the) possessor." [1] In Stevenson this boyish love of adventure, this roving imagination, was joined to a mastery of style and to the literary conscience of the artist. For the most part Stevenson did not write his stories to reform anything or anybody; his business was not morals, religion, psychology, or social science, yet in his later books his view of life deepens and matures. We cannot follow his development here through *Kidnapped* (1886), *The Master of Ballantrae* (1889), *David Balfour* (or *Catriona*) (1893), up to his unfinished romance *Weir of Hermiston*. But one characteristic of his work cannot be

---

[1] *The Lantern Bearers.*

entirely passed over — its pictorial power. His stories abound in scenes which are indelibly stamped on the imagination; we see David and Allan Breck frizzling on the top of the rock in *Kidnapped*, we see the duel between the brothers in the *Master of Ballantrae*, in the cold of that "windless" night when the sky was a black roof overhead and the candles burned steady. Apparently it was often the scene, the appropriate setting for a story, that set his imagination to work. "To his ardent fancy," said Mr. Sidney Colvin, "the world was a theatre, glaring with the lights and bristling with the incidents of romance." Stevenson did not confine himself to fiction; he wrote a number of remarkable essays, some literary criticism, and spirited, clever or charming verse. A youthful joy in romance, and an æsthetic devotion to the refinements of style, were far from satisfying his whole nature. He had a tougher fibre in him; he had the force to think and the strength to endure. So we have the Stevenson of *Dr. Jekyll and Mr. Hyde*, of *Thrawn Janet*, *Will o' the Mill*, and *Æs Triplex*, the Stevenson who fought poverty, neglect, and ill health, with a gallant courage, and who could yet write for his own requiem:

> "Glad did I live and gladly die,
> And I laid me down with a will."

Preëminent among the recent novelists are GEORGE MEREDITH (1828–1909) and THOMAS HARDY (b. 1840). Meredith's position in contemporary fiction has been, and to a great extent still remains, an exceptional one. For many years his work was utterly ignored by the many, although greatly praised by the few; and when the public were at length made to understand that to slight Meredith implied a lack of culture, the feeling of many a timid reader towards his novels was less a hearty liking than a distant and bewildered respect. To-day his novels hold the place of certain classics in the

Meredith and Hardy.

popular estimation; like *Paradise Lost* and Gibbon's *Roman Empire* they are enveloped in a haze of traditional reputation; they are almost as much venerated as those immortal works and almost as little read. At least one reason for this will become clear if we turn to the first pages of *The Egoist* (1879). Mr. Meredith when he desires to befog his readers, is master of an almost unintelligible style. To the frequent difficulty of his manner must be added the difficulty of many of his themes. He is professedly the philosopher, who has chosen to communicate the results of his study of human life through the form of fiction. Like Browning, with whom he is often compared, he is interested primarily in what men think, and only secondarily in what they do; in the subtle psychologic analysis of the motives which produce and the consequences which follow the act, rather than in the act itself. Yet if there are difficulties in these novels, there is also much that repays the effort to overcome them. A recent writer well says: "Whatever one's impression of Mr. Meredith's novels as novels, they indubitably contain a great deal of apt, entertaining, and original comment upon the general subject of human nature." Most of us probably will go further than this; we shall probably find in these extraordinary novels not only wise, if often cryptic, comments on life, but also in the midst of much philosophy, certain memorable characters and scenes. But often, as in the justly famous love scene between Richard and Lucy in *The Ordeal of Richard Feverel*, the figure of the author pops out like some cynical showman from behind his puppets, and we seem to hear Puck's amused comment (the comment of one alien to human passions), "What fools these mortals be."

The sombre and impressive novels of Thomas Hardy are the work of a man of genius who is a poet at heart. The essentially poetic character of his mind is shown, not in any outward adornment of style, but in the tone and construction of his greatest books, and in his whole view of human life and nature. When the critics **Thomas Hardy.** attempt to define the spirit of his work they instinctively compare or contrast it with that of the great poets, — with the work of Æschylus, Lucretius, or Shakespeare. This does not prove Mr. Hardy the equal of these master poets, but it does show that he has at least a touch of their quality, that he has that desire for the fundamental fact, that breadth and seriousness, found in men of the first order of genius.

Born in an obscure hamlet, in the heart of a wooded region north of Dorchester, Mr. Hardy has passed the greater part of his life among the country scenes and the rustic life he has chosen to describe. He is "a peasant and a woodlander," a student and a thinker. At seventeen he began the study of architecture in Dorsetshire, and at twenty he came up to London to practise his profession. In 1871 he published his first novel, *Desperate Remedies*, and in 1874 won his first great popular success by *Far From the Madding Crowd*. He gave up the practice of his profession, retired to Dorsetshire, and devoted himself to literary work.

Mr. Hardy is one of the most subtle and sympathetic of the modern interpreters of Nature. His descriptions have the minuteness and accuracy born of long knowledge and close observation, and they show, what is even more than this, the power of entering into the mood of a scene, of making us feel the tone, or atmosphere, of a landscape, of identifying himself, as it would seem, with the very life of the natural objects he describes. These moors and farms and sheepfolds that he has revealed to us in storm and calm, in daylight, in darkness, or at dawn, he peoples with men and women of a strong, primitive type, the true children of the soil. He has written true pastorals, full of humour, and yet touched with an idyllic freshness and beauty; not suppressing homely or vulgar realities, but impressing us with a sense of the pathos and wonder in occupations that are as old, almost, as the life of men. In such books as *Far From the Madding Crowd,* we are brought near to that immemorial, and almost inarticulate peasant class, that lives close to the dumb creatures, and in the old vital dependence upon the earth. Mr. Hardy's peasants inevitably suggest comparison with Shakespeare's rustics, and every reader feels that Jacob Poorgrass and his fellows belong with that immortal company which produced Pyramus and Thisbe at the palace of Theseus.

But Mr. Hardy does not merely show us the tragedy and comedy of human life, played by men and women of strong passions, of simple and powerful natures, upon an ancient and majestic scene. He is not an impartial, dispassionate observer, he is an interpreter or critic of life; he shows us the pettiness, the defeats, the cruel misery and tragedy of man's lot, and forces us to ask why these things should be. The transitory and ineffectual life of man is contrasted — as in the poetry of Matthew Arnold — with the permanence and power of the physical universe. But in Mr. Hardy's view, Nature is not merely indifferent to man: at times there is something in the constitution of things almost positively malign. To pervert Arnold's phrase, Mr. Hardy sees in the world "a power not ourselves that makes" not "for righteousness" but for failure and iniquity. Man is not the captain of his soul, he is the helpless victim of ironic and malicious forces. At the critical moments the thing we call chance intervenes to ruin him; uncontrollable passion, implanted within him, defeats his best aims and drives him to death and failure. "As flies to wanton boys, so we to the gods, they kill us for their sport." In a

View of life.

word, Mr. Hardy's greatest and most earnest novels are written to illustrate and enforce a view of life analogous to that of Lucretius or of Schopenhauer.

Without inquiring into the correctness of such views, we may observe that the passionate sincerity of Mr. Hardy's convictions has apparently impaired his impartiality as an observer of the facts of life. Especially in some of his later books he resembles a scientist who, in his anxiety to prove a preconceived theory, observes and reports upon only one set of facts, unconsciously slighting or suppressing whatever militates against his conclusion. We are asked to concur in Mr. Hardy's verdict, but we must remember that his conclusion is based on data which he himself has carefully selected and arranged. There are, in fact, sources of consolation which he ignores, substantial mitigations of the miseries of existence which have absolutely no place in his world. This failure to view these eternal problems with the comprehensive or impartial intelligence of Æschylus, or of Shakespeare, this inability to weigh all the evidence and to see life fairly in all its aspects, is a flaw in Mr. Hardy's art. At the same time, his earnestness, his sincerity, his poetic genius, and dramatic power, entitle him to a high place among the masters of English fiction.

While the life and aspirations of our age find their most popular and influential interpretation in the novel, the Victorian era made some lasting additions to the great body of English poetry. Poetry was studied and practised as an art with a care which recalls the age of Anne, and even minor writers acquired an extraordinary finish and a mastery of novel poetic forms. This attention to form is commonly thought to have begun with Keats, and Tennyson proved himself one of the most versatile and consummate artists in the history of English verse. As is usual in periods of scru-

Recent poetry.

pulous and conscious art, this Victorian poetry was graceful or meditative, rather than powerful and passionate.
It excelled in the lyric rather than in the dramatic form;
it delighted in expressing the poet's own shifting moods,
and as a rule it left to the novel the vigorous objective
portrayal of life. It found a relief in escaping from the
confined air of our modern life into the freedom and simplicity of nature, and it never lost that subtle and inspired feeling for the mystery of the visible world which
came into poetry in the previous century. The supremacy
of science and the advance of democracy, the two dominant motive forces in recent English life and thought,
acted on modern poetry in different ways. There were
poets who thought themselves fallen on evil days; who,
repelled by the sordidness, ugliness, and materialism of a
scientific and mercantile generation, sought to escape in
poetry to a world less vulgar and more to their minds.
Like Keats, they ignored the peculiar hopes and perplexi-
ties of their age, to wander after the all-sufficient spirit of
beauty, and like Keats they found refuge and inspiration
in the romance and mysticism of the Middle Ages or in
the repose, restraint, and beauty of the world of the
Greeks. This æsthetic and neo-classic spirit in literature,
was associated with the rise of a new school of
The Pre-
Raphaelites. painters, known as the Pre-Raphaelite Brotherhood. This school was founded about 1848 by
three young painters, William Holman Hunt, Dante
Gabriel Rossetti, and John Everett Millais. A little later
Thomas Woolner, a sculptor, and others joined the movement. These men aimed to free English art from its
bondage to a formal or conventional manner, which as they
believed, hindered its progress. Their avowed object was
"to enforce and encourage an entire adherence to the
simplicity of nature." Painters were then taught to copy
Raphael; the Brotherhood went back for their models to

certain Italian painters before Raphael's time, which were then comparatively neglected. While they advocated truth and simplicity in painting, the Pre-Raphaelites often went back to the Middle Ages for their subjects, and much of their work was full of a mysticism and symbolic suggestion, characteristic of the mediæval spirit. From this aspect, therefore, the Pre-Raphaelite movement was but an additional manifestation of that sympathy with the Middle Ages which had already declared itself in other ways. The ideas of the Pre-Raphaelites found literary expression in a magazine called *The Germ* (1850). Rossetti was a poet as well as a painter. As he exerted a powerful influence on poets as well as on painters, and as he often expressed the same or similar conceptions in both colour and verse, a curiously close relation between poetry and painting became one of the characteristics of the movement. Pictures were suggested by poems, poems were written to illustrate or to interpret pictures, so that the ideals of this group of poets and painters were often embodied almost simultaneously in two arts. DANTE GABRIEL ROSSETTI (1828–1882), the son of an exiled Italian painter and scholar, was the leading spirit of the Pre-Raphaelite movement, at least on its poetic or literary side. The elder Rossetti was a poet and a student of Dante, and his children grew up in an atmosphere of Italian art and culture. One of his sons, WILLIAM MICHAEL ROSSETTI, became well known as a critic and translator, and his daughter, CHRISTINA ROSSETTI (1830–1894), stands with Mrs. Browning as one of the foremost women poets of her time. Dante Rossetti left school at fourteen and began the study of art. From early childhood he was both a reader and a writer of verse. *The Blessed Damosel*, one of the best known and most characteristic of his poems, was composed in his nineteenth year, and was first published in *The Germ*. In 1861 he published some masterly translations of early Italian poetry, but his public recognition as a poet dates from the appearance of his collection of *Poems* in 1870. This book, which was eulogistically reviewed by his friends, produced a sensation in the literary world hardly inferior to that created a few years earlier by Swinburne's *Poems and Ballads.* There was a morbid and neurotic strain in Rossetti's artistic and poetic temperament, and the last years of his life were both pitiable and tragic. He was sensitive, emotionally over-wrought, self-willed, and self-indulgent. Absorbed in his art, he was "physically indolent," and he had "practically no recreations." His health, naturally good, became impaired, and he suffered from neuralgia and insomnia. Unable to endure physical suffering he became addicted to the use of chloral, and lived for years a most unwholesome, secluded, and wretched life. He was subject to morbid delusions, but some of his best poems were composed during this time. There was something both winning and commanding about Rossetti's personality, and the devotion of his friends is the one redeeming feature in these painful and darkened years. He died in 1882.

Rossetti's poetry has called forth some severe criticism, and much unmeasured, perhaps extravagant, praise. His place among the English poets is still uncertain, but it is proper to observe that his most unbounded eulogists, such as Mr. Swinburne and Walter Pater, have been men who were bound to him by personal loyalty and affection, and who sympathised with his views of life and art. The æsthetic school of poetry embodied certain fundamental poetic principles of Keats', and upon the soundness of those principles its permanent value must, to a large extent, depend.[1]

Rossetti's poetry.

[1] It is but fair to remind the reader that there is no conclusive authority on these matters, and that any criticism of Rossetti and his followers must be of necessity a personal judgment.

Pater declared that Rossetti had "ever something about him of mystic isolation," and one of the most pronounced features of the Pre-Raphaelite poetry is its deliberate aloofness from actual life. Rossetti and his associates separated themselves from the activities and responsibilities of their time, from the ordinary interests, occupations, consolations, and desires of the men about them, and built a Palace of Art for their delight and their place of refuge. Such a retirement from the world into a Sanctuary of Beauty has its dangers for the artist as well as for the man. Poetry, divorced from any normal relation to life, is in grave peril of becoming effeminate, languorous, over-elaborated, morbid, and unreal. The poet, loving Beauty only and absorbed in a mere luxury of emotion, loses his vitality and poise of nature, and his art suffers.

Rossetti had great artistic gifts; his poetry is richly coloured, his verse is curiously and skilfully wrought, but his work is not entirely wholesome, manly, or sincere. His poetic world lies beyond the bounds of our ordinary experience, — a shadowy world, ruled by mystery, wonder, beauty and love, and lit by another light than that of common day. In his poetry something of the unearthly spirit of Blake and of the poet of *The Ancient Mariner*, something of the magic of Keats' *La Belle Dame Sans Merci*, survives. "The Renaissance of Wonder," says Theodore Watts-Dunton, "culminates in Rossetti's poetry as it culminates in his paintings." There can be no question that Rossetti's poems are beautiful; that they are full of pictures, like some illuminated missal, gorgeous in colour, and marvellously wrought. It is more doubtful whether, as has been often urged, this outward beauty in Rossetti's work is but the visible garment, or symbol of spirit. Rossetti, it has been said, is at heart a mystic. According to this view, all the mysteries of the world of spirit, all those realities above the reach of sense, were revealed to

Rossetti through beauty and emotion. The unseen reached him through the loveliness of colour and form, and he learned the secrets of the universe " from a woman's eyes." This view has probably an element of truth; nevertheless, Rossetti's poetry is not so much spiritual as unreal. It may be lit by a spiritual radiance, but if so the white light is changed by the many-coloured medium through which it has passed, and .split up into rich and gorgeous hues. In other words, while it may be that in Rossetti's poetry body is united with soul, yet in this union it is not the spiritualisation of the body which impresses us, it is the materialisation of things spiritual and unseen. In *The Blessed Damozel*, for instance, earthly love is carried into the very courts of heaven. Standing on " the ramparts of God's house," the gaze of the maiden is fixed, her longings are centred on the earth. With all its background of Christian imagery, admirably decorative as it is, from the pictorial point of view, the poem is essentially pagan. Rossetti has been often compared to Dante, but Dante believed in the spirit behind the symbol, while Rossetti, an avowed agnostic, found a certain æsthetic satisfaction in the beauty of Christian ritual and creed. The result in Rossetti's case was an inconsistency, a touch of insincerity, which injures the quality of his work. There are poems of Rossetti's not open to such objections, and in any case, it is beyond question that in such masterpieces as *The Burden of Nineveh*, *The King's Tragedy*, *The Last Confession*, and many of the *Sonnets* he has made an unique and considerable contribution to the poetry of his time.

Among the little band of devoted followers that Rossetti gathered around him in the earlier part of his career was **William Morris.** WILLIAM MORRIS (1834–1896), a man of restless energy and an extraordinary versatility of mind. Morris tried his hand at painting, architecture, and poetry. In 1863, in conjunction with Rossetti, Ford Maddox Browne, and Edward Burne-Jones, he founded an establishment for household decoration. Morris was the leading spirit, although by no means the greatest artist, in this enterprise, which was deservedly successful. But while Morris's energy expended itself in many directions, — while he made household furniture, stained-glass windows, curtains, rugs, and tapestry, or sought to improve the art of printing and book making, — one controlling motive gives a unity to his work. A true lover of beauty himself, he tried in innumerable ways to stimulate a national love of the beautiful, to refine the popular taste, and to mitigate the ugliness or commercialism of modern life.

In early manhood Morris was fascinated by the strange beauty of *The Blessed Damosel*, and a little later he met Rossetti and was strongly influenced by his magnetic and dominant personality. Like the other members of the little group, Morris was strongly attracted to the Middle Ages, and his first book, *The Defence of Guenevere and other Poems* (1858), consists of a series of remarkable mediæval studies. One of the poems in this collection, "The Haystack in the Flood," presents the passionate and savage side of mediæval life with truth and power, but many of the poems are purely pictorial. In these poems everything is studiously unreal; the knights, the maidens with large eyes and yellow hair and decorative figures, and all those objects and images which were the theatrical "properties" of the Pre-Raphaelites are freely introduced. "Tall damsels clad in white and scarlet walk in garths of lily and sunflower, or under apple boughs, or feed the swans in the moat."[1] Morris showed the same avoidance of the problems and vexations of modern life in his classic study *The Life and Death of Jason* (1867), and in *The Earthly Paradise* (1868–1870), containing the most popular

[1] Beers' *English Romanticism in the Nineteenth Century*, 327.

and possibly the best of his poems. *The Earthly Paradise* is a collection of twenty-four romantic narrative poems on classic or mediæval themes. A thread of connection, similar to that employed in the *Canterbury Tales*, holds these stories together. A company of adventurers, having left Norway in the time of pestilence in search of an earthly paradise where they may escape the fear of death, are hospitably received at a western city, founded by Greek exiles centuries before. For the space of a year the mariners and their hosts meet and beguile the time with telling the stories drawn from many sources which compose the main part of the poem. *The Earthly Paradise*, it has been said, "is fit reading for sleepy summer afternoons." We are transported to an enchanted region, a world of beautiful illusions, where everything seems shadowy and remote. Nothing here moves us very deeply; it is as though we saw life through a golden haze that dimmed and softened the harsh edge of reality. Our dreamy contentment is disturbed by no cry of human passion; it is interrupted by no real earnestness of mood, by no memorable thought; we are permitted to glide along on the smooth current of the even, melodious, and (it must be confessed) somewhat monotonous verse. Morris did not attempt to do more in *The Earthly Paradise* than bring a temporary repose and forgetfulness through art.

> "Dreamer of dreams, born out of my due time,
> Why should I strive to set the crooked straight?
> ' Let it suffice me that my murmuring rhyme
> Beats with light wing against the ivory gate,
> Telling a tale not too importunate
> To those who in the sleepy region stay,
> Lulled by the singer of an empty day." [1]

But even in *The Earthly Paradise*, a poem in which the "idle singer" deliberately seeks for relief in a world of the ideal, there is a subdued but unmistakable undertone of

[1] *The Earthly Paradise* (Prefatory verses).

sadness. Art such as this may be a sedative, but the poet knows that it is powerless to ease the real ills of life, that it cannot "make quick-coming death a little thing." [1] The spirit of Morris and Rossetti was essentially pagan; in their poetry, as in so much pagan literature, the love of life and beauty is quickened by the dread of death.[2] A philosophy and a mood familiar to the pagan is summed up in one of the refrains of Morris's songs:

> "Kiss me, love, for who knoweth
> What thing cometh after death?" [3]

But Morris, in spite of his poems, was no mere dreamer; he was a burly, robust man, full of vitality, a fighter and a reformer. In his later years, he faced, as Ruskin did, the pressing social questions of his time, and strove manfully to set the crooked straight. He abandoned the liberal party in 1880, and, a little later, actively espoused the socialistic cause. A belief in the possibility of social reform gave a new hopefulness and vigour to some of Morris's later verse, and entered largely into his prose-romance, *The Dream of John Ball* (1888). Morris's socialism, however, was largely the expression of his æsthetic and artistic ideals; it sprang rather from his desire to make the world more picturesque and beautiful than from any deep human sympathy. Shortly before he threw himself into socialistic work, Morris, who was deeply interested in Iceland, had brought out *Sigurd the Volsung and the Fall of the Niblungs* (1876), a fine poem of epic proportions, taken from Icelandic sources. Morris was a prolific writer both in poetry and in prose; he had unquestionably a strong influence upon the social, artistic, and literary life of his time, but there is a diffuseness in his poetry which is likely to tell

[1] *The Earthly Paradise* (Prefatory verses).
[2] See concluding paragraph of Pater's essay, "Æsthetic Poetry," in *Appreciations*.
[3] *Earthly Paradise*, "Ogier the Dane."

against its permanence. "Æstheticism," said Ibsen, "is as fatal to poetry as theology is to religion." Fluent and beautiful as Morris's poetry is, it is lacking in human sympathy; it extends over a wide area, but its forces are seldom concentrated in the living or memorable phrase.

Another poet associated with the Pre-Raphaelite Brotherhood was ALGERNON CHARLES SWINBURNE (1837-1909).

Swinburne. Swinburne, the eldest son of Admiral Charles Henry Swinburne, came of an old and honourable Northumbrian family. He was educated at Eton and at Oxford. He visited Landor in Italy whom he already passionately admired, and he began a long and close friendship with William Morris, Edward Burne-Jones, and Rossetti, who was nine years his senior. But while Swinburne, like Morris and Rossetti, has lived in an ideal world of art and beauty; while, like his brother poets, he has often chosen to write on classic or mediæval themes,—his temper, unlike theirs, is not gentle and dreamy, but stirring, rebellious, and defiant. The first book of Mr. Swinburne's to make a decided impression on lovers of poetry, was his noble classical drama, *Atalanta in Calydon* (1865). *Atalanta* is among the greatest reproductions of classical tragedy in English literature; without attempting to settle questions of precedence, we may safely class it with Milton's *Samson Agonistes* and with Shelley's *Prometheus Unbound*. Its pathos is true and restrained; and in its choruses, with their superb union of force and grace, with the exultant and impetuous lightness of their lyrical flight, the world heard for the first time the marvellous music of the great modern master of English verse. True to the spirit of Hellenic tragedy, *Atalanta* shows man helpless in the grasp of fate. Although the hero, Meleager, perishes through the act of his mother, he declares that he is really slain by that law which mixed death with his life from the beginning. But while the play is so far classical, Swinburne departs widely from the spirit of the great Greek tragedians in permitting the Chorus to hurl defiance and rebuke at the Ruler and Maker of the world. This bitter and passionate indictment of the ordering of the universe is more akin to the rebellion of Schopenhauer, Byron, or Hardy, than the deeply religious spirit of Æschylus or Sophocles. In 1866 the publication of Swinburne's *Poems and Ballads* awoke a tempest of mingled praise and condemnation. While the religious and moral sense of the nation was shocked and disgusted, lovers of poetry, and especially those who were young and enthusiastic, were in raptures over the new poet's consummate mastery of language and metre, and over the indescribable magic of his strange melodies. Swinburne has written much since the publication of this extraordinary book. He has produced *Bothwell* (1874), *Mary Stuart* (1881), and several other long historical dramas; he has written a second classical tragedy, *Erictheus* (1876), *Tristram of Lyonesse* (1882), a romantic narrative poem of great beauty, together with odes and other lyrics, and a very large amount of prose. We cannot but be impressed by this extraordinary mass of work. Its volume alone inspires respect, and as we read we find evidences on almost every page of the wealth of the poet's vocabulary and his technical skill. But astonishing as this work is, we can find in it, as a whole, no assurance of progress. Indeed, although forty years have passed since Swinburne's early triumphs, he has possibly never equalled, and almost certainly never surpassed, the supreme efforts of his youth.

Swinburne's ultimate place among the English poets is still uncertain. Every one admits his gifts of expression; every one agrees that he is "a born tamer of words," — "an absolutely consummate artist of word music of the current and tempestuous kind." But many feel that he is not merely fluent, but too often unrestrained and diffuse.

Many grow satiated with "this revel of rhymes" (as Swinburne himself described it); bewildered with the rush and
din of this unfailing torrent of words they long for more
matter and less art, for some solid basis of thought, some
inspiration that they can live by, for some evidence of the
philosophic mind. A few recent enthusiasts, indeed, have
pronounced Swinburne a profound and original thinker; if
this be so, he has concealed the fact from the great majority of his readers and critics.[1] Swinburne, in fact, is an
artist, not a philosopher. He is guided by impulse, by
feeling, not by careful thought, or a well-balanced judgment, and, when he essays to think, his highly emotional
nature combined, as it is, with an extraordinary volubility,
leads him into extremes. As a critic, his command of language is at once his distinction and his weakness; it betrays
him into reckless and unmeasured statements, and it has
made him preëminent as a master of exaggerated eulogy
or unmeasured vituperation. In spirit Byron and Swinburne, while separated by obvious differences in form, have
much in common. Both men show the same genuine, but
shallow ardour for liberty; the same impatience of restraint;
the same passionate rebellion against the order of things.
But the author of the *Hymn to Proserpine* and of the *Hymn
to Man* is more direct and daring than the author of *Cain*
and *Don Juan*. To Swinburne, life is bitterness; love a
consuming passion, an added misery; death a welcome
oblivion which shall cure and end all. Man, indeed, is the
one being in creation worthy of reverence, "the master of
things," and in the progress of man towards some unde-
fined goal, Swinburne finds, or attempts to find, a ground

[1] Mr. James Douglas writes: "In sheer intellectual power of the
imagination Mr. Swinburne is surpassed by none of his contemporaries
— in his best work the conquest of sense is as complete as the conquest of sound; the mastery of mind is as triumphant as the mastery
of music." Chambers' *Cyclopedia of English Literature*, iii. 677
(Revised Ed.)

of consolation and of hope. In such ideas there is nothing either original or profound. Swinburne's lack of philosophic insight should not blind us to the splendour of his poetic achievement, nor should the glorious melody, the profuse beauty of his verse, lead us to attribute to his poetry virtues which it cannot fairly be said to possess.

Swinburne's poetry is distinctly and vehemently anti-Christian; other poets of the period distressed by doubts, and unable to reconcile the old faith with the new knowledge of their time, have carried into their work that uncertainty and unbelief which was the moral disease of their generation. As we have said, the most characteristic poetry of Matthew Arnold is the outcome of this mood, having in its doubts a forlorn and pathetic bravery sadder than open despair. Somewhat the same tone is present, but animated by a strain of greater faith and hope, in the poems of Arnold's friend, ARTHUR HUGH CLOUGH (1819–1861), a man of genius and of promise, while JAMES THOMSON's *City of Dreadful Night* (1874) is the poetry of despair. It is chiefly by this poem, profoundly original, and burdened with a suffocating weight of gloom and terror, that Thomson is known. Beside the weary anguish of his cry from the abyss, the discontent of Byron seems the petulance of a spoiled child. But the pathos of Thomson's misery is heightened by a study of less familiar poems in which another side of his nature is disclosed. From them we learn to see in him a marvellous power of abandonment to joy, only surpassed by his capacity for despair. Few poems in our literature are gladdened with as keen a sensibility to beauty as the opening portion of *He heard Her Sing*. Here the rapture of the artist's temperament finds voice, and the verse leaps forward with a tumultuous delight in the joy of life. Two little idyls, *Sunday at Hampstead*, and *Sunday Up the River*, are very quiet and full of sunshine; but such poems only serve to intensify by contrast the blackness of Thomson's despair.

Happily, the two greatest and most representative poets of our epoch, Alfred Tennyson and Robert Browning, have neither preached "the religion of Beauty," nor taught the philosophy of despair. Differing widely in manner and in their theory of art, they have at least one point in common. Both face frankly and boldly the many questions of their age; neither evading nor succumbing to its intellectual difficulties, they still find beauty and goodness in the life of the world about them; holding fast the "things which are not seen" as a present reality, they still cherish "the faith which looks through death."

The poetry of faith and hope.

ALFRED TENNYSON (1809–1892) is already acknowledged as the representative English poet of his time. So far as contemporary judgment can foresee, his work will stand to posterity as the most rounded, melodious, and adequate expression in poetry of the soul of Victorian England. Singularly sensitive to the intellectual and spiritual perturbations of his time, he responded to its moods, entered into its passing phases of thought, and made them the very breath and animating principle of his work. He was a lover of beauty and his view of life was essentially spiritual, yet one great motive power in his work was that science which was the dominant intellectual force in his time.

Alfred Tennyson.

Close as he lived to his age in spirit, Tennyson dwelt in communion with Nature, holding himself consistently aloof from active participation in the restless and high-pressure life of his generation. Shy, morbidly sensitive, silent, except among an inner circle of chosen friends, the poet locked himself from his kind with books and Nature, a remote and keen observer of the conflicts in which he did not share; to whose eyes the whole battlefield lay disclosed.

Thus two great influences seem to have combined in Tennyson's life, to render him what he was: Nature and books. Like Wordsworth, he was country-bred, and shunned the air of cities; even to the last he "still was Nature's priest." But, unlike Wordsworth, who had but little of the book-lover or the scholar about him,[1] Tennyson lived close to his time, and to all times, through his love of books. On the side of scholarship, Tennyson claims kindred, not with Wordsworth, but with Milton, who was, perhaps, the poet of the library than of the field. Like Milton, he brought to the service of his art all that could be gathered by a lifelong study of the great productions of the past. His poetry represents the best traditions of literature, as truly as Browning's represents a distinctly radical element, and he constantly delights the scholar by reminiscences of his studies of the great poets of antiquity.[2] Through the printed page he felt with no less distinctness the pulse of the world of living men without. The force of these combined influences, books and Nature, grows clearer as we recall the story of the poet's secluded and uneventful life.

Alfred Tennyson was born August 6, 1809, at Somersby, a tiny village in the East Midland region of Lincolnshire, where his father, the Rev. George Clayton Tennyson, was rector. The country immediately about Somersby has a richness and beauty wanting in many parts of the county; there is no fenland, but the hills slope softly into rich valleys. Here and there are bits of woodland; near by there is a glen where the earth is

Tennyson's life.

[1] *V., inter alia,* the story of Wordsworth's cutting the pages of Burke with a knife which had been used to butter toast, in De Quincey's *Literary Reminiscences,* chap. xiii., "Wordsworth and Southey."

[2] *V.* E. C. Stedman's study of Tennyson and Theocritus, in his *Victorian Poets,* and the more recent work of J. Churton Collins on the classical element in Tennyson.

moist under the shadow of the pines.   It was into the depth
of this glen, while the world was mourning a great poet,
that the boy Tennyson stole away alone, and in the fullness
of his youthful despair cut in the sandstone the words,
"Byron is dead."   Tennyson's work bears witness to the
indelible impress of these early surroundings. The explorer recognizes here the brook

> "That loves
> To purl o'er matted cress and ribbed sand,
> Or dimple in the dark of rushy coves;" [1]

a grey, half-ruined grange which recalls the
desolate retreat of Mariana, or, from a neighbouring hill,
he looks out over the long sweep of the "ridged wolds"
which, rising from the low levels of the plain, stretch away
forty miles to the northward until they meet the distant
waters of the Humber.

> "Calm and still light on yon great plain
> That sweeps with all its autumn bowers,
> And crowded farms and lessening towers,
> To mingle with the bounding main." [2]

The grassy expanse of the Lincolnshire wolds, "wide,
wild, and open to the air," under a heaven of grey cloud, is
suggested in the opening lines of "The Dying Swan," while
an allusion like that to "the low morass and whispering
reed" carries us to the fenland that lay a short distance to
the south. We must think of the boy Tennyson wandering among such scenes, from the first reticent and undemon-
strative, but, we may be sure, living through those intense,
inward experiences which, often hidden or unintelligible
to those about, yet make up the true life-history of every
emotional and imaginative child. After some training at
home, and in the Grammar School at Louth, a town some
twenty miles from Somersby, Tennyson entered Trinity

[1] "Ode to Memory."   [2] *In Memoriam*, xi.

College, Cambridge, in 1828. Here, shy as he was, he showed that he had a rare and beautiful capacity for friendship. He joined a debating society which included among its members James Spedding, F. D. Maurice, R. C. Trench, and others,— the choicest spirits of the college.[1] Above all the others was one whose short life is indissolubly linked with the career of Tennyson, Arthur Henry Hallam, a young man of rare promise and singularly sweet and lovable nature. Long before he entered college Tennyson had written verses; he had even printed a volume in conjunction with his brother, Charles, in 1827; but at Cambridge he first made a decided impression by his prize poem, *Timbuctoo*. In 1830 Tennyson made his real entrance into the world of English letters by the publication of a slim volume, *Poems, Chiefly Lyrical*. We can see now, in this little book, the advent of a new poet. It is largely the work of an experimentalist in metre and melody, including as it does such tone-studies as "Claribel" and "Lilian." These are the preliminary studies of an artist with a fresh and exquisite feeling for beauty of form, who is bent on mastering the technique of his craft. Differing widely from Pope in his poetic manner, he had an equally scrupulous desire for technical excellence. He had something of Keats' sensuous delight in colour and melody, something of his magical excellence of phrase, yet even in this early effort we detect a characteristic note of divergence from those poets who, like Keats, loved "beauty only." He shows us his ideal poet,[2] "dowered with the hate of hate, the scorn of scorn, the love of love," whose melodies fling all abroad "the winged shafts" not of beauty but "of truth." In a remarkable and important poem, *The Palace of Art*, which

[1] Many of them became Tennyson's lifelong friends. For reminiscences of the society *v. In Memoriam*, lxxxvii.

[2] See "The Poet" and "The Poet's Mind," included originally in the edition of 1830.

appeared in a volume published in 1832, Tennyson defined his position on this point with extraordinary vigour and distinctness. Against Keats' reiterated poetic principle, that

"Beauty is truth; truth, beauty," [1]

Tennyson set the solemn allegory of the "sinful soul," which possessed all good things, merely that they might contribute to a mere selfish lust of æsthetic enjoyment. Stricken through at last with remorse, the soul, in the isolation of its gilded towers, hears afar off, with perception born of love, the call of humanity. To the fine æsthetic sensibilities of Keats, Tennyson thus added a moral earnestness in which, so far as appears, Keats was deficient. He remained unfaltering in his allegiance to the loftiest conception of the poet's mission. It is his distinction to have successfully combined the conscience of the man with the conscience of the artist, and to the last to have "followed the gleam." [2]

Tennyson lost his father in 1830, and in that year left Cambridge without taking a degree. In 1833 came the shock of a profounder sorrow in the loss of his more than brother, Arthur Hallam,[3] who died suddenly at Vienna. *In Memoriam*, that incomparable poem in which Tennyson long after gave to the world the record of this story of friendship and loss, admits us into the sacred places of this great grief. Tennyson's shy and morbidly reticent nature made him shrink from contact with the world at large, and he was all the more dependent for love and sympathy on the friendship of the tried and chosen few. Among them Hallam had held the first place, and his loss not only seemed to tear away part of Tennyson's life, but, if we may judge from *In Memoriam*, it set the

[1] Keats' *Ode on a Grecian Urn*.

[2] See "Merlin and the Gleam," in *Demeter, and Other Poems.*

[3] "More than my brothers are to me." — *In Memoriam*, ix., lxxix.

poet face to face with the everlasting and primal questions of existence. The secret vicissitudes of the soul within us, the hidden convulsions which shake the balance of life, the painful readjustment to changed conditions,—these things that constitute the essence of a true biography, are but a matter of surmise to those without. After Hallam's death Tennyson settled in London, living much to himself, writing constantly, but publishing almost nothing. He belonged to a select coterie, the "Sterling Club," where he met Carlyle, Thackeray, Landor, and other famous men. It was a time of preparation and growth, under the teaching of death and sorrow. Nearly ten years of silence were at last broken by the publication, in 1842, of two volumes of poems. The book included all of the earlier poems of which the author's maturer taste approved, revised with the Tennysonian fastidiousness, and about as much new matter. The new poems, among which were the "Morte d'Arthur," "Ulysses," "The Two Voices," and "Locksley Hall," showed a broadening and deepening power, and the volumes won Tennyson an enthusiastic recognition from both critics and readers. A year later the veteran Wordsworth pronounced him "decidedly the greatest of our living poets," [1] and from this time he took that leading place in the literature of his day which his astonishing vitality and productiveness so long maintained. The collected poems of 1842 showed plainly that distinguishing trait of Tennyson, his extraordinary mastery in widely different fields. His genius is eclectic. The classic world, as in "Ulysses" or "Lucretius"; the mediæval, as in "Stylites" or "Galahad"; the modern, as in "The Gardener's Daughter" or *Maud*, all are at his command. He is the consummate artist, as versatile in manner as he is varied in subject. He can pass at will

[1] Letter to Professor Henry Reed, quoted in Hallam Tennyson's *Life of Alfred Tennyson*, v. i. p. 210.

from the noble epic roll of the *Idylls* to the rough dialect of the "Northern Farmer"; from the pseudo-Wordsworthian simplicity of "Dora" to the somewhat Corinthian ornateness of *Enoch Arden*. In "The Voyage of Maeldune" he touches Rossetti and the Pre-Raphaelites, while in such stirring battle lyrics as "The Revenge" and the "Light Brigade" he invades the province of Drayton and of Campbell. Yet in all there is an indefinable flavour of individuality; the rough edges and sharp angles of fact are softened, and life is seen through a golden haze of meditative beauty. In the smooth flow of the verse, in its very turns and pauses, we recognise the trick of the Tennysonian manner. "Locksley Hall" is one of the poems which show the nearness of the poet to his time. It breathes the intensity, the exaggeration, the quick despair, the vast and unconquerable hopes of youth, and it sounded as a trumpet call to the young men of that generation. We are swept on in its buoyant movement by the prophetic enthusiasm of the new science which was transforming the world. The strain of personal complaining is overpowered by the deep pulsations of the "wondrous mother age." In its vision of the world that shall be, the very heavens are filled with the argosies of commerce. Then there comes that chant of a progressive humanity which is one of the recurrent motifs in modern literature. As Burns had discerned a time of universal brotherhood "comin' yet for a' that," so Tennyson sees afar off the era of a universal peace, the day of the parliament of man, when the whole world shall be one group of confederated states, when

"— the common sense of most shall hold a fretful realm in awe,
And the kindly earth shall slumber, lapt in universal law."

From 1842 until the time of his death, Tennyson lived a life of seclusion and steady industry: a life marked by few striking outward happenings, and chiefly remarkable for that progress of the soul within, of which the succession of his books is the lasting memorial. The year 1850 stands out from the rest as the year of his marriage to Miss Emily Sellwood, of the publication of *In Memoriam*, and of his appointment to the Laureateship. Three years later he settled at Farringford, in the Isle of Wight. With Farringford, and with a place at Blackdown in Sussex, which he bought in 1867 to avoid the curiosity of American tourists, his later life is chiefly associated. He bent all the fullness of his powers to win success in two great fields of poetry which in his earlier years he had left unattempted — the Epic and the Drama. Four of the *Idylls of the King* appeared in 1859, and others were gradually added until the work grew to the symmetry of its full proportions. In 1875 he published *Queen Mary*, the first of his series of drama. That a poet of sixty-six, with a lifetime of successes behind him in widely different lines, should leave them to struggle with the difficulties of a new and highly technical form of composition, and that he should persevere in this in spite of repeated discouragements, is worthy of especial notice. The purely spiritual side of Tennyson's genius, present almost from the first, grew with his growth. The merely sensuous delight in the tangible revelation of beauty, the luxury of eye and ear, yielded to a deeper perception of an underlying world of spirit, of which this world of sight and touch seemed but the shadow. The second "Locksley Hall" is full of a sense of the limitations of the new science, as the first is the pæan of its seemingly boundless possibilities. In "Despair" the issue raised by the scientific thought of the day is faced with a merciless and unflinching power. If the world is Godless, and man but a better brute, our life is a cheat and a curse, and endurance of it intolerable and purposeless. Face this and end it. Here the extreme but logical conclusion of those who see nothing in the universe but matter and law, is thrust home on us in poetry of passion and of terror. Meanwhile, in such poems as "De Profundis" and "The Ancient Sage," we see Tennyson's own conviction deepen that God and spirit are the eternal realities of the world. Poem after poem in *Demeter*, a book published just before the poet's death, turns on the mysterious relation of soul and body. It is the book of old age, written in the shadow of that night when no man can work. The servant body is falling into ruin, but everywhere the triumph of the undying spirit over the failing flesh is triumphantly proclaimed. The body is "foul at best"; it is but "the house of a brute let to the soul of a man," and its office done, the man "stands on the heights of his life, with a glimpse of a height that is higher." [1] When he wrote *Demeter*, Tennyson had passed the allotted threescore years and ten. He was awaiting with a beautiful tranquillity and confidence the time when the door of this "goodly prison" should be opened. Death came to him gently, as the gracious and fitting close to a lofty life. The white mist hung low over the earth, but the room in which the poet lay was glorious in moonlight. Illuminated in its white radiance, a volume of Shakespeare in his hand, his finger still marking the dirge in Cymbeline which he had lately read, the Laureate passed peacefully out of this "bourne of time and space" [2] as one prepared to depart.

Theodore Watts-Dunton has told us that there are poets of *energy* and poets of *art* [3] — poets, that is, whose predominant quality is original power, eruptive and irresistible as the volcanic discharge of molten lava, and poets

---

[1] "By an Evolutionist," in *Demeter, and other Poems*.

[2] "Crossing the Bar." *Ibid*.

[3] See the admirable and suggestive essay on "Poetry" in the *Encyclopædia Britannica*, ninth edition.

whose well ordered and less impulsive work bears the high finish of a refined and scrupulous art. In our day, Browning admirably represents the poet of energy, while Tennyson stands no less emphatically as the poet of art. As a craftsman Tennyson has few superiors in our literature; he approaches Milton in the perfection and excels him in the variety of his poetic workmanship. The Tennysonian style at its best has "an extreme subtlety and curious elaborateness of expression";[1] it has that intricacy of structure which points to extreme care and slowness in composition. While at times it can be terse and strong, or obtrusively simple and unadorned, its characteristic excellence is not compression or directness. Tennyson's gift is neither the sublime reticence and conciseness of Dante, nor the limpid and indescribably moving simplicity of Wordsworth when he is at his best. Graceful, melodious, and tender, Tennyson breathes through silver rather than blows through bronze. While in Browning's masculine and rugged utterance the thinker obtrudes himself, so that inconsiderate readers are often led to undervalue the purely poetic excellence, in Tennyson, through the very charm and perfection of his art, we are rather apt to underestimate the solid substratum of philosophic thought. We will therefore briefly consider Tennyson's poetry from this aspect in preference to dwelling on its obvious beauties. We will attempt to relate his work to those two new elements — the close communion with the life of Nature, the broader sympathy with the life of man — which we saw take their rise in the first quarter of the eighteenth century to become the motive force in the literature of modern times. As a poet of Nature Ten-

Tennyson's work. (margin note)

[1] Matthew Arnold, *On Translating Homer*, p. 285 (Macmillan's edition). The student is advised to read carefully the analysis of Tennyson's style in this passage. Note particularly the distinction between the *simplicité* of Wordsworth and Tennyson's *simplesse*, p. 289.

nyson is sometimes spoken of as the disciple of Wordsworth, but in fact, while he resembles the older poet in
Tennyson minuteness and accuracy of observation, in
as a poet of other respects his attitude is fundamentally
Nature. different. As we have said, to Wordsworth an
Infinite Power was perpetually revealing itself, not merely
through but in Nature. He believed that Nature possessed a conscious life, and that

> "Every flower
> Enjoys the air it breathes."

Tennyson, on the other hand, especially in his earlier
work, is impressed with the *order* underlying the processes
of Nature, with the "*law* which cannot be broken," and is
not insensible, as was Wordsworth, to the aloofness and
even apparent antagonism of Nature to man. In a word,
Wordsworth's view of Nature is essentially *mystical*, and
Tennyson's inherently *scientific*. To Wordsworth, moreover, as in "The Primrose and the Rock," Nature seems
the unbroken revelation of divine love, while Tennyson,
like Lucretius, Byron, and Leopardi, is not insensible to
the mystery of her seeming cruelty and indifference. To
the misanthropic hero of *Maud*,

> "— nature is one with rapine, a harm no preacher can heal;
> The Mayfly is torn by the swallow, the sparrow spear'd by the
> shrike," [1]

the "whole little world" is "a world of plunder and prey."
The conviction of Lucretius that man is but the puppet of
mighty and impersonal agencies, produced and destroyed
with equal indifference by the mechanical operation of
purposeless laws of life, is recognised and combated in *In
Memoriam* and "Despair." Tennyson quiets this paralys-
ing fear by his unshakable trust in the faith and lofty intui-
tions of man's soul, and by his assurance that the workings

[1] *Maud*, iv. stanza 4.

of Nature show an eternal purpose of progress, rather than the operation of blind and meaningless forces. He finds God

> "not in world or sun,
> Or eagle's wing, or insect's eye," [1]

nor in "the freezing reason," but in man's capacity to feel. He opposes to Nature's apparent indifference and cruelty the doctrine of evolution. This doctrine, the greatest contribution to thought of contemporary science, finds in Tennyson its poetic exponent; it is the very foundation-stone of his philosophy.

In his feeling for Nature, Tennyson is thus as truly the poet of modern science as Wordsworth and Coleridge were of the German philosophy of their day, but he accepts the dogmas of science only to interpret them according to his own poetic and spiritual insight.

Tennyson is no less distinctively the scientist in his views of human progress; he recognises a gradual and orderly development as the law alike of human society and of the material world. Byron's rebellious and ill-regulated clamour for liberty, Shelley's noble "passion for reforming the world" by some sweeping and unaccountable conversion of humanity, is succeeded by Tennyson's belief in that "moving upward" through the innumerable centuries whereby the beast in man is brought at length under the mastery of the spirit. In their youth Byron and Shelley saw liberty stricken down and bleeding through the reactionary power of conservatism; Tennyson, as a young man, witnessed the passage of the first Reform Bill (1832) and other hardly less important measures, by the strength of the reviving democracy; he beheld the peaceful advance of liberty by the modification and through the agency of existing institutions. This gradual, legal, and definite progress he has from first to last consistently

Tennyson as poet of man.

[1] *In Memoriam,* cxxiv.

represented. At the outset of his career he rejoices to see
Freedom

> "Slowly broaden down
> From precedent to precedent." [1]

At its close he pictures her as one who

> "like Nature, would'st not mar
> By changes all too fierce and fast
> This order of Her Human Star,
> This heritage of the past." [2]

Tennyson often touches on the social questions of his
time: in *The Princess* on the rights of women; in a large
group of poems, in which *Maud*, *Aylmer's Field*, and
"Locksley Hall" are included, on social distinctions as a
bar to marriage. But the noblest and most important exposition of his views of human progress is found in the
Idylls of the King.

The *Idylls of the King* has been called a quasi epic. Departing from the conventional epic form by its lack of a
The Idylls closely continuous narrative, it has yet that
of the lofty manner and underlying unity of design
King. which lead us to class it with the epics, at least
in the essentials. It consists of a series of chivalric legends,
taken chiefly from the *Morte d'Arthur* of Sir Thomas Malory,
grouped so as to exhibit the establishment, the greatness,
and the downfall of an ideal kingdom of righteousness
among men. "The Coming of Arthur," the ideal ruler,
shows us the setting up of this kingdom. Before this, was
disorder, great tracts of wilderness,

> "Wherein the beast was ever more and more,
> But man was less and less." [3]

Arthur slays the beast and fells the forest, and the old

---

[1] "You ask me why, tho' ill at ease."
[2] *Tiresias;* "Freedom." See also "Politics" in *Demeter*.
[3] "The Coming of Arthur."

order changes to give place to new. Then the song of Arthur's knights rises, a majestic chorus of triumph:

"Clang battleaxe and clash brand! Let the King reign."

In "Gareth and Lynette" the newly established kingdom is seen doing its work among men. Arthur, enthroned in his great hall, dispenses impartial justice. The knights

"Ride abroad redressing human wrongs."

The allegory shows us, in Gareth's contests with the knights "that have no law nor King," the contest of the soul with the temptations that at different periods of life successively attack it:

"The war of Time against the soul of man."[1]

Then follow the *Idylls*, which trace the entrance and growth of an element of sin and discord, which spreading pulls down into ruin that "fellowship of noble knights," "which are an image of the mighty world." The purity of the ideal kingdom is fouled, almost at its source, by the guilty love of Lancelot and the queen. Among some the contagion spreads; while others, in an extremity of protest, start in quest of the Holy Grail, leaving the duty at hand for mystical visions. Man cannot bring down heaven to earth, he cannot sanctify the mass of men by his own rapturous anticipations; he cannot safely neglect the preliminary stages of progress appointed for the race, he "may not wander from the allotted field before his work be done."[2]

So by impurity and by impatience the rift in the kingdom widens, and in "The Last Tournament," in the stillness before the impending doom, we hear the shrill voice of

[1] "Gareth and Lynette." Note the significance of the entire passage in which this line occurs.

[2] "The Holy Grail."

Dagonet railing at the king, who thinks himself as God, that he can make

> "honey from hornet-combs
> And men from beasts."

In "Guinevere," unequalled elsewhere in the *Idylls* in pure poetry, the blow falls; at length, in the concluding poem, Arthur passes to the isle of Avilion, and once more

> "The old order changeth, yielding place to new." [1]

Tennyson himself tells us that in this, his longest poem, he has meant to shadow "sense at war with soul," [2] the struggle in the individual and in the race, between that body which links us with the brute and the soul which makes us part of a spiritual order. But the mastery of the higher over the lower is only obtained through many seeming failures. Wounded and defeated, the king exclaims:

> "For I, being simple, thought to work His will,
> And have but stricken with the sword in vain;
> And all whereon I lean'd in wife and friend
> Is traitor to my peace, and all my realm
> *Reels back into the beast*, and is no more." [3]

But Arthur also half perceives the truth which it is the poet's purpose to suggest to us. It is short-sighted to expect the immediate sanctification of the race; if we are disheartened, striving to "work His will," it is because "we see not to the close." It is impossible that Arthur's work should end in failure — departing, he declares, "I pass, but shall not die," and when his grievous wound is healed, he will return. The *Idylls of the King* is thus the epic of evolution in application to the progress of human society. In it the teachings of *In Memoriam* assume a narrative form.

[1] "The Passing of Arthur."
[2] "To the Queen," epilogue to *Idylls of the King*.
[3] "The Passing of Arthur."

"Move upward, working out the beast,"

may be taken as a brief statement of its theme; and we
read in it the belief in the tendency upward and an assurance of ultimate triumph:

> "Oh, yet we trust that somehow good
>   Will be the final goal of ill,
>   To pangs of nature, sins of will,
> Defects of doubt, and taints of blood;
>
> That nothing walks with aimless feet;
>   That not one life shall be destroyed,
>   Or cast as rubbish to the void,
> When God hath made the pile complete." [1]

Tennyson, as the representative poet of modern England, is the poet of modern science. But he also represents
that intense spirituality which is conspicuously
present in these so-called mercantile and material times. With the scientist's deep perception
of the presence of *law*, he himself shared, as did Wordsworth, in the visionary rapture of the mystics. For him,
as for Arthur, the world of spirit veritably exists, more substantial than the world of sense, but the barrier to our
entrance is in our own limited powers. When the knights
report the result of their search after the Grail, Arthur
declares:

Tennyson and Science.

> "ye have seen what ye have seen " —

each as much as his spiritual sight permitted him. Those
with Gareth looking on the towers of Camelot, cry out in
the disbelief of the materialist:

> "Lord, there is no such city anywhere,
>   But all a vision."

But the warder tells them that the city is spiritual and
therefore real, seeing it

> "is built
> To music, therefore never built at all,
> And therefore built for ever."

[1] *In Memoriam*, 54.

Tennyson unites the modern grasp of physical truth with the apprehension of that spiritual element which permeates and sustains it, and to him, as his own Arthur, the

> "visions of the night or of the day
> Come, as they will." [1]

Appreciating, with the scientist, the law of the world of sense, he yet asks with the idealist:

> " The sun, the moon, the stars, the seas, the hills and the plains —
> Are not these, O Soul, the Vision of Him who reigns? " [2]

He yet points us to

> " — that true world within the world we see,
> Whereof our world is but the bounding shore." [3]

While no recent English poet is so versatile and so broadly representative as Tennyson, ROBERT BROWNING (1812–1889) has satisfied, as no other poet has done, some of the deepest spiritual needs of his generation. From the first his genius was more bold, irregular, and independent than that of Tennyson, and he was less responsive to the changing moods of his time. Indeed, he rather proved its leader, taking his own way, unmoved by praise or blame, and at last compelling many to follow him. His work is highly charged with an abounding vigour and audacity characteristic of Browning himself. Mrs. Orr tells us that "his consciousness of health was vivid;" Bayard Taylor speaks of his "vigour and elasticity;" his handshake has been compared to an electric shock; and Mr. Sharp speaks of his "intensely

Robert Browning.

---

[1] "The Holy Grail." See the curious account of Tennyson's trances, or visions, in Waugh's *Alfred, Lord Tennyson: a Study of His Life and Works.*

[2] "The Higher Pantheism."

[3] *De Profundis*, ii. 1. *Cf.*, also, "The Ancient Sage."

alive hand." Landor writes of him in lines crowded with suggestion:

> "Since Chaucer was alive and hale
> No man hath walked along our roads with step
> So active, so inquiring eye, or tongue
> So varied in discourse."[1]

Such allusions bring Browning before us as the keenly observant man of the world, alive to his very finger-tips, full of that robust and wholesome capacity for enjoyment which we associate with Chaucer and Shakespeare and Scott, but which among our modern men of letters is unfortunately rare. A knowledge of Browning's genial and aggressively active personality is of real value to one who would seize upon the spirit of his work. It is not an intrusive curiosity, but the spirit of the genuine student, which leads us to contrast Browning's superb equipoise with the lack of balance shown by so many of his contemporaries; to set his ready fellowship with men, his soundness of mind and of body, beside Rossetti's morbid life and imperfect human sympathies, his insomnia, and his disordered nerves. Matthew Arnold found a partial relief from the "something that infects the world" in the patient calm of Nature, yet to his melancholy fancy earth and sky seemed

> "To bear rather than rejoice."

But to Browning's inextinguishable hopefulness, God's "ancient rapture" in life and love and beauty is still visibly renewed in his world.[2] Like the happy child in *Pippa Passes*, he sings in our restless, doubting century, with its tired nerves and throbbing temples, the strange song of courage and of faith.

> "The year's at the spring
> And day's at the morn;
> Morning's at seven;
> The hill-side's dew-pearled;

[1] Sonnet to Browning.   [2] *Paracelsus*, Act **v.**

The lark's on the wing;
The snail's on the thorn;
God's in His Heaven —
All's right with the world."

We are refreshed by a wholesome delight in the simple joy of living, that in the thin intellectual atmosphere of our civilisation, comes with a delicious flavour of the antique world.

"O our manhood's prime vigour! no spirit feels waste,
Not a muscle is stopped in its playing, nor sinew unbraced.

. . . .

How good is man's life the mere living, how fit to employ
The heart and the soul and the senses forever in joy." [1]

This strain of manly confidence, this overflowing force and vitality, is not faltering or exceptional, it is part of Browning's masculine and powerful genius, and of his wholesome and happy life. Courage and cheerfulness are inseparable from his fine physique, his massive breadth of character, his wide sympathies with man and Nature, his hearty pleasure in physical and intellectual activity. He had a strange fellowship with all living things, reaching down to the tiny creatures of the grass; he loved music and painting and sculpture, with a love developed by long study and intimate knowledge. The beauty of Italy, his chosen land, that he declared was his "university," early entered into his life and art, and besides all this he found, what men of genius rarely find, a woman of fine nature and answering genius capable of responding to his highest moods.

There are few more beautiful love stories in our literature than this. In an exquisite series of *Sonnets*, probably her most perfect work, Mrs. Browning has told how Browning crossed the darkened threshold of her sick room, and how she knew that it was not death which

[1] *Saul*.

held her, but love.[1] And in *One Word More*, or *By the Fireside*, or in that exalted apostrophe in *The Ring and the Book*,[2] Browning pays an answering tribute to his "moon of poets." In thinking of Browning's unfaltering cheerfulness, we must remember that between his marriage to Miss Barrett in 1846 and her death in 1861, lay fifteen years, passed in the inspired air of Florence, of companionship as perfect as it was rare. Browning has been one of the most prolific of English poets. His work covers more than half a century of almost incessant production (*Pauline*, 1833 — *Asolando*, 1889), exhibiting in sheer bulk and intellectual vigour a creative energy hardly surpassed by any poet since Shakespeare. Written while England was passing through a time of spiritual despondency and fluctuating faith, Browning's poetry impresses us as some great cathedral, in which every part is duly subordinated to one symmetrical design, and consecrated to one ultimate purpose. It is independent and often eccentric in style; it is defiant of the prevailing theories of art; it rises solitary, abrupt, rugged, and powerful, from an age of fluent, graceful, and melodious verse.

Browning, like Milton and Wordsworth, comes before us as a teacher, but our first consideration is naturally not **Browning as artist.** the truth or value of his philosophy, but the poetic quality of his work. It is as a poet that he has chosen to appeal to us, and it is primarily as poet and not as philosopher that his work must take its place in literature. The salt of poetry may preserve a poem the philosophy of which is trite or fallacious, but it may be questioned whether any philosophy, however noble or invigorating, will secure it a permanent place in literature if it lack the poetic quality. Looked

---

[1] *Sonnets from the Portuguese*, i.
[2] See passage beginning "O lyric love," in *The Ring and the Book* at the close of Bk. i.

at simply from the art side, few dispassionate readers will deny that Browning's poetry has serious defects. In many instances, more especially in the longer poems, the fine gold is debased by an alloy of versified prose; and long philosophic arguments, ingenious, subtle, and sometimes wearisome, are thrust forward untransmuted by the poet's alchemy. It is probable that some such poems, for instance, the *Red Cotton Nightcap Country* (1873), while they may continue to hold a formal place in the literature, will cease to be read except by the curious or conscientious student. If Browning's verse is musical, its music is certainly different from that with which the masters have made us familiar. Habitually spirited, it is often jolting and abrupt; full of parentheses and ejaculations, and moving by sudden starts and jerks. To the casual reader Browning often seems impatient of form in his anxiety to get the thing said; thoughts and feelings seem crowding and jostling together for utterance, and he seems only anxious to "hitch the thing into verse," that he may turn to something new. His rhymes are apt to be fantastic and ludicrously ingenious to an extent unprecedented in serious poetry. The extravagances of *Hudibras*, of *Beppo*, and of the *Fable for Critics* in this direction, are fairly outdone by Browning in the *Old Pictures in Florence*, or in *Pacchiarotto*. The last-named poem in particular is an unparalleled exhibition of rhythmical gymnastics. English is racked and wrenched to the uttermost, and when it fails a Greek or Latin word is unceremoniously caught up and thrust in to take its place. It must further be admitted that Browning is at times obscure to a degree which even the difficulty of his subject does not justify; but this defect has been dwelt on to weariness, and usually with an unfortunate exaggeration. Indeed, a very large proportion of Browning's poetry presents no serious difficulty to an ordinarily attentive and unprejudiced reader; the complaint of obscurity comes most loudly from those whose knowledge of his work is slight, or from those who are so out of sympathy with his spirit that they

> "endure
> No light, being themselves obscure."

Such obvious features of Browning's art have exposed it to an unfavourable criticism in which there is undoubtedly a proportion of truth. On the other hand, many unacquainted with Browning's theory of art have been confident that he had missed his mark when he had only failed to hit their mark, at which, in fact, he had never aimed. In an age when finish, smoothness, and melody are made the primary requisites in poetry, our taste is naturally repelled by work distinguished by excellence of a very different order. We must remember that taste in such matters is largely influenced by custom, and that the generation trained to delight in the heroic couplet found even the blank verse of Milton intolerably harsh. In a word, Browning's artistic merits are those which, as they are novel, we have not been trained to appreciate; his defects are too often those to which training has made us the most sensitive. To enjoy Tennyson's work but little preparation was needed; the traditions of poetry were with him, and he completed or enlarged what others had begun. But Browning sought to conquer new regions for his art; like Wordsworth, he came distinctly as an innovator, and as such is within Wordsworth's rule, that every great and original poet must first create the taste by which he is to be enjoyed.

It is doubtful whether Browning's purely poetic merit is even yet fully appreciated. He has a marvellous accuracy of observation, painting the revealing details of a situation with a phenomenal truth and vividness. In much descriptive poetry, beauty is gained at the expense of truth and reality; in Browning, beauty is habitually subordinated to truth and power.

> "A tap at the pane, the *quick, sharp scratch*
> *And blue spurt of a lighted match,*
> And a voice less loud thro' its joys and fears
> Than the two hearts beating each to each." [1]

These lines may not impress us as beautiful, but we must recognise in them a precision in the use of words, a felicitous correspondence of sound and sense, which mark the master of style. Again, the description in *Christmas Eve* of the congregation in the Methodist chapel is no more beautiful than an interior by Teniers, but it has the same inimitable minuteness and fidelity. In the same way, Browning's metaphors, while unusually original and expressive, are often exact and striking rather than beautiful, being employed as an actual help to our understanding.[2] Many of Browning's longer poems, through the very wealth of his resources and through his erratic agility of mind, lack unity and directness; he is perpetually turned aside by the chance encounter with some tempting idea, so that we often leave the direct course for a kind of zigzag progress. On the other hand, he has given us poems, such, for instance, as "Martin Relph" and "Ivan Ivanovitch," which are masterpieces of strong and graphic narrative. In one province of poetry he is supreme — the dramatic monologue.[3] As triumphs of the poet's art such marvellous

---

[1] "Meeting at Night."

[2] See in illustration of this the metaphors in *The Ring and the Book;* see, also, conclusion to "Shah Abbas" in *Ferishta's Fancies,* where the difficulty of crossing a room in the dark without stumbling is likened to that in entering the heart of another without the lamp of love as a guide.

[3] A monologue or soliloquy, dramatic through the presence of some other person than the speaker, a presence inferred only from the words of the speaker himself.

productions as "My Last Duchess," "Andrea del Sarto," or "Fra Lippo Lippi" stand alone. It is as idle to say that such poems have not the sweetness or melody of Tennyson as it would be to complain that the "Lotus-Eaters" lacks Browning's invigorating power. On such a principle we might condemn Milton because he could not create a Fal-staff, or Shakespeare because he produced nothing similar to *Paradise Lost*. But above all we must remember that Browning's poems were written in accordance with what he regarded as the true function of art. In his view the high-est office of the poet, as of other artists, was to arouse, to sting into consciousness, the diviner side of man's nature. He teaches in "Andrea del Sarto" that something more than mere technical excellence is required for the produc-tion of the highest art; that it is better for the medium of expression to give way under the strain of thought and passion than for it to be coldly perfect because the soul is wanting.[1] The organist in "Master Hugues of Saxe-Gotha" turns dissatisfied from the intricate, technical excellence of a fugue, to Palestrina, the composer who emancipated music from pedantic trammels and breathed into it a new soul. In "Old Pictures in Florence" we are taught that it is the mission of art to tantalise by its very incomplete-ness, rather than to satisfy by its perfection and repose; that the aim of the true artist is to arouse a longing for an unseen and eternal perfection, which no earthly similitude can ever fully reveal. Without this moral, or spiritual, element and purpose, art sinks into a mere sensuous satis-faction in colour and form, such as that shown by the cor-rupt bishop who ordered his tomb at St. Praxed's. In the bishop's dying directions for the adornment of his tomb we see how a refined delight in the mere externals of beauty and culture may go hand in hand with the moral depravity of a "low-thoughted" spirit. One may prefer Tully's

---

[1] *Cf.* Ruskin's theory of art, p. 544, *supra.*

picked Latin to Ulpian, glory in the colours of marble and jasper, and design a frieze in which pagan nymphs dance through the most sacred scenes of Christian story, one may do all this and only demonstrate the radical insufficiency of the purely æsthetic view of art.[1]

Browning, then, does not set himself to manufacture "poetic confectionery"; strength and suggestiveness, rather than beauty, are his primary objects, and consequently his poetry is not cloying or relaxing, but bracing, instinct to an extraordinary degree with moral invigoration. It is not intended to be taken as a mild form of opiate, but to "sting," as Browning himself tells us, "like nettle-broth."[2] Looking, therefore, at his poetry apart from its moral or philosophic value, it appears that Browning's positive merits as an artist have been often undervalued because of the novelty of his methods and aims; because his peculiar excellences are distinctly different from those with which the tone of recent poetry has made us familiar.

Browning's optimism, of which we have already spoken, is not thoughtless but well grounded. Like Shakespeare, he does not seek to evade the melancholy and perplexing aspects of life, but confronts and conquers the spectres of the mind. Like his own "Cleon," his sense of the inadequacy of life is keen, while he sees a "world of capability for joy spread round us," "tempting life to take."[3] Even his buoyant and healthy nature is stirred to the depths by the bitter compulsion of his time. We have compared him to Chaucer, but he is Chaucer surrounded by the subtleties and searchings of nineteenth century thought; a profound and original

Browning as a teacher.

[1] "The Bishop orders his tomb at St. Praxed's."

[2] See Epilogue in *Pacchiarotto*, an important poem as a statement of Browning's view of his own work. Note especially last stanza.

[3] "Cleon."

genius, facing in deadly earnest men's "obstinate question-ings" of life and of death.

To Browning the only explanation of the mystery and the misery of this present life is to be found in its relation to a life to come. His view of life, like that of Carlyle, of Wordsworth, and of Tennyson, is essentially spiritual. To him God, the soul, and personal immortality are the fundamental and all-important facts.[1] Wordsworth found an intimation of immortality in certain ideas or sympathies innate in the soul; Browning found a similar intimation in the soul's inextinguishable longings and aspirations, which earth cannot satisfy and which witness to another life as the only adequate sphere of our activity. In a famous prose passage Browning has declared that nothing but the soul "is worth study." To him it is worth study because it only of things earthly will survive the temporal, because it sustains a definite relation to the eternal sphere of things. The development of the soul in this relation to the unseen is consequently the chief subject of Browning's work, as it is — in his judgment — the supreme interest of life. Familiar as this thought may seem to us, by making it the essence of his delineation of life, Browning has virtually created poetry of a wholly new order. Shakespeare is the unapproached interpreter of the life of man on earth, but in his dramas life is revealed in no vital or necessary relation to a hereafter; encompassed by darkness, it rather seems to us to be "rounded by a sleep." Milton, projecting himself in imagination into a world where Shakespeare did not enter, has, on the contrary, no real hold on the common or daily life of man.[2] Browning's purpose to show us the seen in the light of the unseen is, almost as truly as Milton's, a thing "unattempted

---

[1] See "La Saisaiz" — passage beginning, "I have questioned, and am answered," etc.

[2] See comparison of Milton and Shakespeare, pp. 185–186, *supra.*

yet in prose or rhyme." Shakespeare wrote in and for a bustling world, and his characters are shown to us in action. Browning wrote when life was outwardly more tame and conventional, and inwardly more complex; when the chief interest of man was not action but thought. Accordingly, as we might expect, Browning's dramatic power is of another order from that of the Elizabethans; he has a fine feeling for the striking elements of a situation, but his characters reveal themselves less through action than through thought. He is at his best when, in some moment of spiritual crisis, he makes a soul describe its inmost nature; he admits us to the inward struggle, intellectual or moral, often leaving us to infer its declaration in outward act. These words of George Eliot, who often worked like Browning in this hidden region of thought, help us to realise the peculiar difficulty of the task: "For Macbeth's rhetoric about the impossibility of being many opposite things in the same moment referred to the clumsy necessities of action, and not to the subtle possibilities of feeling. We cannot speak a loyal word and be meanly silent, we cannot kill and not kill in the same moment; but a moment is room wide enough for the loyal and mean desire, for the outlash of a murderous thought and the sharp backward stroke of repentance." [1]

An appreciation of Browning's skill as an interpreter of such dubious or complex moods must be gained by repeated study of his dramatic monologues. We can here only attempt to indicate some of the main points in his teaching.

As life here is to be looked at as a preparation for life hereafter, and this world as the divinely appointed forcing house of the soul, experiences are important chiefly as they forward or retard the soul's growth. Joy is one element in the soul's development, for Browning's whole view of life is essentially the reverse of ascetic; yet the more

[1] *Daniel Deronda*, vol. i. chap. iv.

fully we develop all our faculties, the more inherently inadequate life becomes. It is through this very inadequacy that the soul is taught to set its affections elsewhere. In Browning emotion is one great agency in breaking up our narrow and complacent contentment. He teaches us to prize moments of intense feeling and aspiration — moments like that in which "Abt Vogler" was enabled through music to transcend our temporal limitations — as times of escape when the soul learns to breathe in a purer air. It is the mission of the artist, the supreme expressor and interpreter of emotion, to awaken such aspiration, and hence the necessity — according to Browning's view — of soul, and stimulus to soul, in the truest art. So, earthly love may prove, as in "By the Fireside," a high emotion which shall forward the soul's progress; and so, too, as in "Youth and Art," the sacrifice of it to sordid ambition may stunt the spiritual progress of two lives. Browning is thus not only original and daring in method, but in aim; and whatever we may think of the poetic quality of his work, his view of life is the most spiritual and stimulating of any English poet, not excepting Milton.

The great mass of Browning's work makes any more specific criticism of it impossible here. It is doubtful whether in any one of Browning's dramas he really meets the requirements of the stage; yet, while he is not a dramatist, a large proportion of his poems, monologues, idyls, or lyrics, are as distinctly dramatic in spirit as in form. As closet dramas his plays have conspicuous merit, but as a rule his best work is found in his shorter poems. *Men and Women* (1855) contains many of the best of these, but characteristic masterpieces are scattered through his books, down to "Rephan" in *Asolando* (1889). *The Ring and the Book* (1868), a huge psychological epic of more than twenty-one thousand lines, remains, after all deductions, one of the most considerable and surprising poetic achievements of the century. We have spoken of this poem as an epic, but only for lack of an exacter word; in reality it is rather a series of dramatic monologues in which the same story is retold by different speakers; it is epic only by its length and by the underlying unity of its design. Browning's most ambitious, if not his greatest work, is thus a modification of his chosen poetic form.

With an intellectual force comparable to Dryden's, a moral ardour equal to that of Milton, Browning, too, is poet as well as thinker and teacher. He is no mere reasoner in verse, but the most profoundly passionate singer of his time. Through all his work there shines the noble spirituality, the marvellous subtlety, the strenuous earnestness of a great nature. Back of all stands the man, Robert Browning, who sings of himself in words which are at once an epitaph and a closing song of triumph as

> "One who never turned his back but marched breast forward,
>   Never doubted clouds would break,
>   Never dreamed, tho' right were worsted, wrong would triumph,
>   Held we fall to rise, are baffled to fight better, sleep to wake." [1]

Thus in this great English poet of our own day we find that deep religious earnestness, that astounding force, which we noted in those obscure English tribes who nearly fifteen centuries ago began to possess themselves of the island of Britain. It is, indeed, this sound and vigorous character of the English race, underlying all the long centuries of its literary history, which gives a profound unity to all it has created. Browning's "Prospice," that dauntless challenge to death from one who "was ever a fighter," repeats, in its cadence and spirit, poetry that comes to us from the dimly seen and far-off childhood of our race. If in the nineteenth century we have bartered and sold, and

---

[1] Epilogue in *Asolando*, Browning's last poem.

offered sacrifice to the Britannia of the market-place, it is still true that the great problems of existence have never been dwelt on with more earnestness, that the greatest voices of the literature have called us with a new ardor to the eternal and the unseen.

Henry Morley reminds us that the opening lines of Cædmon's *Creation*, the first words of English literature on English soil, are words of praise to the Almighty Maker of all things. After reviewing in outline the long and splendid history of the literature thus solemnly begun, we find in the two greatest poet voices of our own day, Alfred Tennyson and Robert Browning, the note of an invincible faith, an undiminished hope; we find them affirming, in the historic spirit of the English race,

"Thy soul and God stand sure."

Our survey of England's literary history naturally stops here. The nineteenth century and the reign of Queen Victoria ended together; with the coming of the twentieth century, England entered a new literary era, not in name merely, but in fact. During the closing years of the nineteenth century the great men of the era — Darwin, Rossetti, Arnold, Tennyson, Browning, Ruskin, and many more — ended their labours, and now the century, the queen, and nearly all the writers who have made her reign illustrious in literature, have passed into history.

The end of an era.

Already new writers are pressing forward, already we can see vaguely a new literary era taking form before our eyes. Everything is, as yet, indefinite and uncertain, but we see the promise, at least, of the revival of a literary and poetic drama in the work of STEPHEN PHILLIPS, HENRY ARTHUR JONES, and GEORGE BERNARD SHAW. We watch the progress of that

The present and the future.

concerted effort to bring back the Celtic spirit into literature, which is known as "the Celtic Revival." Foremost among the young poets of this movement is WILLIAM BUTLER YEATS. We see a poet like WILLIAM WATSON, continuing some of the best poetic traditions of the past, a poet like JOHN DAVIDSON searching for new methods and new themes. In the verse of HENRY AUSTIN DOBSON, inimitably graceful and delicate, dainty and pathetic, we find that the eighteenth century as well as the Middle Ages can be made a resting-place for an over-driven and over-practical generation. In RUDYARD KIPLING we already recognise the spokesman of the Colonies, of that "Greater England," which rejoices in its youth. As we study the work of Kipling, as we note the rise of innumerable colonial writers, and of English writers who deal with colonial themes, the widening range of English literature impresses us as a fact of the first magnitude. When we turn from Kipling's *Without Benefit of Clergy*, and his *Ballad of East and West*, to SIR GILBERT PARKER'S stories of Canada, or to the Australian poems of ADAM LYNDSAY GORDON and the Australian novels of MARCUS CLARKE, we see that the "Expansion of England" has brought with it the Expansion of English literature, and that an era has already begun in literary history the end of which is yet far distant.

And in Kipling, the poet of this Imperial England, we find again the vigour, the hopefulness, the reassuring courage of youth. After the beautiful but melancholy dream-world of Rossetti, Morris, or Walter Pater, the prose-poet of the Pre-Raphaelites, where men's spirits "falter in a mist," after the intellectual strivings of Clough and Arnold, after Hardy's pessimism, and Swinburne's bitter and stormy defiance, we come back in Kipling to the old cheery hardiness, the old zest in life. It is a call to action: —

"Go to your work and be strong, halting not in your ways " —.

Hardy, interpreting the life of a few counties, is over-whelmed by the thought of the innumerable generations that have lived and died there. The weight of the past is heavy on him, the past of an ancient land where the drama of life has been played so often. But Kipling's thought is not fixed on the past, not confined to Wessex, or to England: he looks forward to the future; his interests are spread over an empire.

> "Fair is our lot — O goodly is our heritage!
> (Humble ye, my people, and be fearful in your mirth!)
> For the Lord our God Most High
> He hath made the deep as dry,
> He hath smote for us a pathway to the ends of all the Earth!"

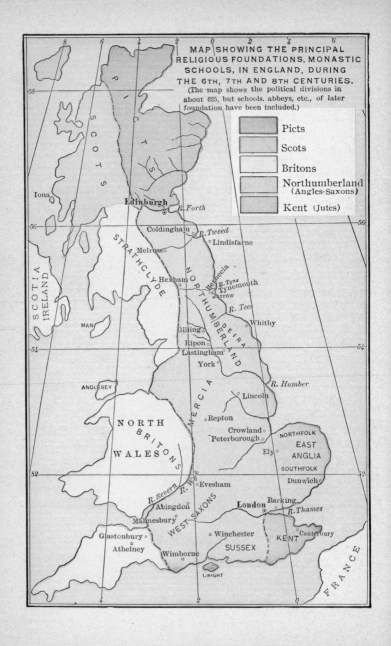

MAP SHOWING THE PRINCIPAL
RELIGIOUS FOUNDATIONS, MONASTIC
SCHOOLS, IN ENGLAND, DURING
THE 6TH, 7TH AND 8TH CENTURIES.
(The map shows the political divisions in
about 625, but schools, abbeys, etc., of later
foundation have been included.)

Picts
Scots
Britons
Northumberland
(Angles-Saxons)
Kent (Jutes)

PICTS

SCOTS

Iona

Edinburgh

R. Forth

Coldingham

R. Tweed

Lindisfarne

STRATHCLYDE

Melrose

Bernicia

Hexham

R. Tyne

Tynemouth

Jarrow

R. Tees

NORTHUMBERLAND

Whitby

SCOTIA
IRELAND

MAN

Giiling

DEIRA

Ripon

Lastingham

York

ANGLESEY

R. Humber

Lincoln

MERCIA

NORTH

BRITONS

Repton

Crowland

NORTHFOLK

WALES

Peterborough

EAST

ANGLIA

Ely

SOUTHFOLK

Dunwich

R. Severn

R. Wye

Evesham

WEST

Barking

Abingdon

London

R. Thames

Malmesbury

SAXONS

Glastonbury

Winchester

Canterbury

Athelney

SUSSEX

KENT

Wimborne

I. WIGHT

FRANCE

APPENDIX.

LIST TO ACCOMPANY MAP SHOWING PRINCIPAL RELIGIOUS FOUNDATIONS, ETC.

Iona: Founded (c. 563) by St. Columba from Ireland.

Coldingham: Double monastery of men and women (Celtic) founded by Ebba, sister of Oswiu of Northumbria, about the middle of the seventh century; *destroyed by Danes* **c**. 870.

Lindisfarne: Founded by Aidan, a Celtic monk from Iona, as a mission, c. 635.

Melrose: Founded c. 635 at old Melrose, two and a half miles east of present ruins, and burned by Kenneth MacAlpine, 839; first monastic home of St. Cuthbert.

Hexham: Founded by St. Wilfrid (674) and noted for its artistic beauty and magnificence.

Jarrow: Founded by Benedict Biscop, in 680, seven miles from his previous foundation of Wearmouth (674), the two houses, dedicated respectively to Peter and Paul, being made into one monastery, the home a little later of Bede (673–735).

Tynemouth: Chapel built (625) by Edwin, king of Northumbria; enlarged by Oswald, Edwin's successor; *burnt by Danes,* 865.

Whitby: Double monastery founded c. 657 by the Abbess Hilda, a pupil of the Celtic Aidan of Lindisfarne; home of Cædmon, 670.

Ripon: Monastery founded (660) by Abbot Eata of Melrose, a pupil of Aidan; afterwards bestowed on St. Wilfrid.

Lastingham: Founded c. 653 by Cedda (St. Chad), from Lindisfarne.

York: Church built for King Edwin of Northumbria by Paulinus (627); school founded by Egbert, first Archbishop of York (c. 750); Alcuin, 735–814.

Lincoln: Church built (c. 628) by Blaecca, a convert of Paulinus.

Repton: Double monastery founded about 660; *destroyed by Danes,* 870.

Crowland: Abbey founded, according to tradition, by Ethelbald of Mercia, c. 716; *destroyed by Danes,* 870.

Peterborough: The first Benedictine Abbey in the Fenland, founded (c. 655) by Sexulf, a Mercian thegn; *plundered by Danes,* 870.

Ely: Abbey founded by St. Etheldreda (St. Audrey) in 673; *destroyed by Danes,* 870.

Evesham: Abbey founded 709 and dedicated to the Virgin.

Abington: Monastery of St. Mary of Abington, founded by Hearn, nephew of Cissa, King of Wessex, c. 605 (Benedictine); *destroyed by Danes, rebuilt* 955.

Malmesbury: Abbey founded by Maelduib, a Scottish missionary and scholar, probably about 640. Aldhelm (640–709) studied under Maelduib before he entered the school at Canterbury; he returned to Malmesbury and became Abbot, 673.

Dunwich: School founded (633) by the Burgundian Felix, Bishop of Dunwich, after the model of the Gallic schools, his teachers being brought from Kent.

Barking: Double monastery founded (c. 666) by Earconwald, afterwards Bishop of London; *burnt by Danes,* 870.

Glastonbury: Abbey here a very early British foundation; monastery endowed by Ine, King of Wessex (d. 766). Archbishop Dunstan (924–985) educated here and became Abbot, 943.

Winchester: Cenwalh, King of Wessex, founded Old Minster of St. Peter and St. Paul, c. 648. King Alfred had a school attached to his court, and planned a New Minster which was built (903) by his son and successor Edward.

Canterbury: See, with three churches, a monastery and school founded by St. Augustine, 597–603. School reorganized and improved by Theodore of Tarsus and Hadrian, c. 670. Aldhelm studied here under Hadrian.

Athelney: King Alfred, defeated by Danes, took refuge here for a year, and founded a monastery and school (c. 879) in remembrance of the protection he had received.

Wimborne: Double monastery and school founded (c. 705) by Cuthburh, sister of King Ine of Wessex.

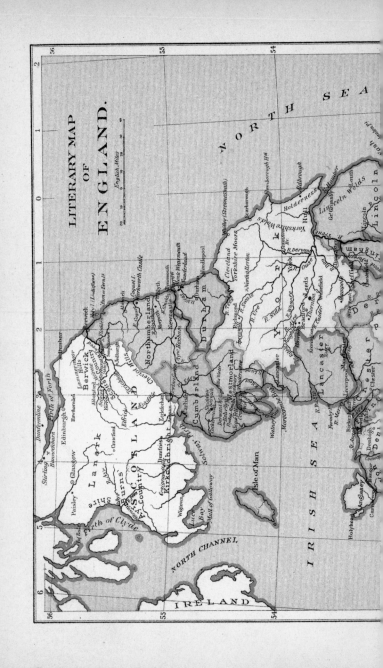

LITERARY MAP
OF
ENGLAND.

English Miles

LIST OF AUTHORS TO ACCOMPANY LITERARY MAP OF ENGLAND.

The following is a list of some of the most representative men in English literature. By referring to the accompanying map, the student will be able to find their birthplaces as well as some of the localities in which they have lived. Where the names of the smaller places have been omitted on the map, the county in which they are situated can be found from the following list, and their general situation on the map approximately determined.

Addison, Joseph, b. Millston, Wilts, l. London.
Alfred, King, b. Wantage, Berks, l. Winchester, Hants.
Arthurian Legends, chiefly located in Cornwall.

Bacon, Francis (Lord St. Albans), b. London, l. St. Albans, Hertford.
Bede, or Bæda, b. Monkwearmouth, Durham, l. Jarrow, Northumberland.
Beaumont, Francis, b. Grace-Dieu, Leicester.
Blake, William, b. and l. London.
Bolingbroke, Henry St. John (Lord), b. Battersea, Surrey, l. London.
Brontë, Charlotte, Anne, Emily, b. and l. Haworth, Yorkshire.
Browne, Sir Thomas, b. London, l. Norwich, Norfolk.
Browne, William, b. Tavistock, Devonshire, l. at Wilton and Dorking, in Surrey.
Browning, Elizabeth Barrett, b. Durham, l. London.
Browning, Robert, b. and l. London.
Bunyan, John, b. Elstow, near Bedford, Bedfordshire.
Burke, Edmund, b. Dublin, l. London, etc.
Butler, Samuel, b. Strensham, Worcester.
Burns, Robert, b. near Ayr, Ayrshire, Scotland.
Burton, Robert, b. Lindley, Leicestershire, l. Oxford.
Byron, Lord George Gordon, b. London, l. Newstead Abbey, Nottinghamshire.

Cædmon, b. (?), l. Whitby, Yorkshire.
Cambrensis, Geraldus, b. and l. Pembrokeshire, Wales.
Carlyle, Thomas, b. Ecclefechan, near Annan, Scotland.

Chatterton, Thomas, b. Bristol, Gloucester.

Chaucer, Geoffrey, b. and l. London.

Clough, Arthur Hugh, b. Liverpool, Lancashire.

Coleridge, Samuel Taylor, b. Ottery St. Mary, Devon, l. Keswick, Cumberland (Lake Country).

Collins, William, b. Chichester, Sussex.

Collins, William Wilkie, b. and l. London.

Cowley, Abraham, b. and l. London.

Cowper, William, b. Great Berkhampstead, Hertford, l. Olney, Bucks.

Crabbe, George, b. Aldborough, Suffolk.

Crashaw, Richard, b. and l. London.

Dekker, Thomas, b. and l. London.

Defoe, Daniel, b. London, l. London, Tilbury, etc.

De Quincey, Thomas, b. near Manchester, l. Grasmere, Westmoreland (Lake Country).

Dickens, Charles, b. Landport, Hampshire, l. London.

Donne, John, b. and l. London.

Drummond, William, b. Hawthornden, near Edinburgh.

Dunbar, William, b. and l. East Lothian, Scotland.

Dryden, John, b. Aldwinkle, All Saints, Northampton, l. London.

Eliot, George, b. Arbury Hall, Warwickshire, l. Nuneaton, Coventry, London.

Fielding, Henry, b. Sharpham Park, Somerset.

Fletcher, John, b. Northampton, l. Ryeland, Sussex.

Fuller, Thomas, b. Aldwinkle, Northamptonshire, l. London.

Gay, John, b. Frithelstock, Devon, l. Barnstaple, Devon.

Goldsmith, Oliver, b. Pallas, Ireland, l. London, etc.

Gray, Thomas, b. London, l. Stoke Pogis, Bucks, Cambridge.

Habington, William, b. Hendlip, near Worcester, Worcestershire.

Hall, Joseph, b. Bristow Park, Leicestershire.

Hardy, Thomas, b. Dorsetshire.

Herbert, George, b. near Montgomery, Wales, l. Bemerton, near Salisbury, Wiltshire.

Henryson, Robert, Dunfermline, Scotland.

Herrick, Robert, b. London, l. Dean's Prior, Devon.

Hogg, James, b. Ettrick, Selkirkshire, Scotland.

Hooker, Richard, b. at or near Exeter, Devon, l. London, Boscombe, Wilts, Bishopsborne, near Canterbury, Kent.

Howard, Henry (Earl of Surrey), b. (?) l. Surrey, Sussex.

Johnson, Samuel, b. Lichfield, Stafford, l. London.
Jonson, Benjamin, b. and l. London.

Keats, John, b. and l. London.
Kingsley, Charles, b. Holne Vicarage, Dartmoor, Devon, l. Eversley, Hampshire.

Lamb, Charles, b. and l. London.
Langland, William, b. Cleobury-Mortimer, Shropshire, l. Malvern Hills and London.
Layamon, b. North Worcestershire, l. Ernley Regis.

Macaulay, Thomas Babington, b. Rothley, Leicester, l. London.
Malmesbury, William of, b. in Somersetshire, l. Malmesbury, Wiltshire.
Map, Walter, b. Wales, l. Hertfordshire, Gloucestershire.
Marlowe, Christopher, b. Canterbury, Kent, l. London.
Marvell, Andrew, b. Winestead, near Hull, York, l. London.
Meredith, George, b. Hampshire, l. Box Hill, Surrey.
Milton, John, b. and l. London, and Horton, Bucks.
Monmouth, Geoffrey of, b. Monmouthshire, d. Llandaff St. Asaph, Wales.
More, Sir Thomas, b. and l. London.
Morris, William, b. Walthamstow, Essex, l. Kelmscott, Gloucester, London.

Peele, George, b. (?) l. London.
Pope, Alexander, b. London, l. London and Twickenham, Middlesex.

Raleigh, Sir Walter, b. Devon, l. London.
Ramsay, Allan, b. Lanarkshire, Scotland, l. London.
Richardson, Samuel, b. Derbyshire, l. London.
Rolle, Richard, b. Thornton, Yorkshire, l. Hampole, Yorkshire.
Rossetti, Christina, b. and l. London.
Rossetti, Dante Gabriel, b. and l. London.
Ruskin, John, b. London, l. London and Oxford and Brantwood, in Lake Country.

Sackville, Thomas (Lord Buckhurst), b. Buckhurst, Sussex, l. London.
Scott, Sir Walter, b. Edinburgh, l. Abbotsford, near Melrose.
Shakespeare, William, b. Stratford-on-Avon, Warwick, l. London.
Shelley, Percy Bysshe, b. Field Place, near Horsham, Sussex.
Shorthouse, Joseph Henry, b. and l. Birmingham, Warwickshire.
Sidney, Sir Philip, b. Penshurst in Kent.
Skelton, John, b. Norfolk, l. Cambridge.

Smollett, Tobias George, b. Dumbartonshire, Scotland.
Southey, Robert, b. Bristol, Gloucester, l. Keswick, Cumberland (Lake Country).
Steele, Richard, b. Dublin, l. London.
Stevenson, Robert Louis, b. Edinburgh, Scotland.
Suckling, John, b. Twickenham, Middlesex, l. London.
Surrey (Earl of), see Howard.
Swift, Jonathan, b. Dublin, l. London, Dublin, etc.
Swinburne, Charles Algernon, b. and l. London.

Taylor, Jeremy, b. Cambridge.
Tennyson, Lord Alfred, b. Somersby, Lincoln, l. Farringford House, Isle of Wight, and Blackdown, in Sussex.
Thomson, James, b. Ednam, Roxburgh, l. London.
Trollope, Anthony, b. London, l. Ireland, London, etc.

Vaughan, Henry, b. Brecknockshire, Wales.

Waller, Edmund, b. Coleshill, near Amersham, Hertford, l. London.
Walton, Izaak, b. Stafford, l. London, d. Winchester.
Wyclif, John, b. Hipswell (?), near Richmond, York, l. Oxford.
Wither, George, b. Brentnorth, Hampshire.
Wordsworth, William, b. Cockermouth, l. Grasmere and Rydal Mount (Lake Country).
Wyatt, Sir Thomas, b. Allington Castle, Kent.

Young, Edward, b. Upham, near Winchester, Hampshire.

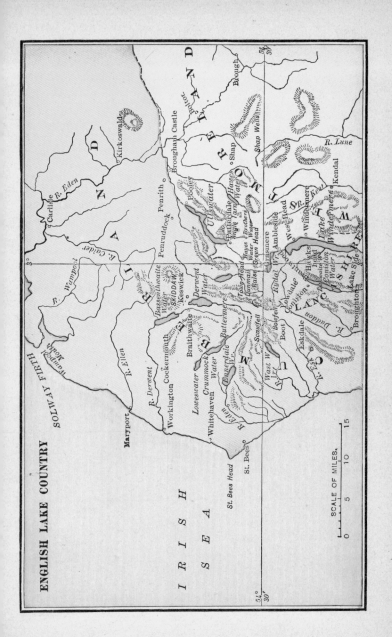

ENGLISH LAKE COUNTRY

SOLWAY FIRTH

I R I S H   S E A

St. Bees Head
St. Bees

SCALE OF MILES.
0   5   10   15

GENERAL TABLE OF ENGLISH LITERATURE.

I. THE FORMATION OF THE LANGUAGE, EARLY BEGINNINGS TO 1400.

1. THE BEGINNING TO THE NORMAN CONQUEST, — TO 1066.

597. Landing of St. Augustine.

A. CONTINENTAL AND PRE-CHRISTIAN ERA TO CIR. 670.

    1. Widsith.

635. Aidan introduces Christianity into Northumbria.

B. CÆDMON TO ALFRED (670–871).

670. Cædmon's Paraphrases.

    1. North $\left\{ \begin{array}{l} a. \text{ Cædmonian Poems.} \\ b. \text{ Beowulf.} \\ c. \text{ Bede.} \end{array} \right.$
    (Northumbria)

    2. South   Aldhelm.   640?–709.
    (Wessex)

C. ALFRED TO NORMAN CONQUEST (871–1066).

787–878. Invasions of the Danes.

    1. Revival of Prose under Alfred, 880.

        a. Anglo-Saxon Chronicle.
        b. Anglo-Saxon Translations from the Latin.

871. The Accession of Alfred.
878. The Peace of Chippenham.

    2. Later English Prose.
        Ælfric — cir. 950?–1016?

GENERAL TABLE OF ENGLISH LITERATURE — *Continued.*

2. THE NORMAN CONQUEST TO THE DEATH OF CHAUCER (1066–1400).

LITERATURE WAS WRITTEN IN

A. ENGLISH.	B. FRENCH.	C. LATIN.

1. Anglo-Saxon Chronicle to 1154.

Romances.

   (*a*) Song of Roland.
   (*b*) Arthurian Romances.

1. William of Malmesbury.
2. Matthew Paris.
3. Celtic legends enter English literature through Geoffrey of Monmouth's Historia Regum Britanniæ (1147).
4. Walter Map. Continues Arthurian legends (12th century).

2. English begins to gain ground in the 13th century.

   (*a*) Layamon's Brut. (cir. 1205).
   (*b*) French romances appear in English (13th and 14th centuries).

3. Triumph of English in the 14th century.

   (*a*) Chaucer (cir. 1340–1400).
   (*b*) Langland (cir. 1332–cir. 1400).
   (*c*) Wyclif (cir. 1324–1384).
   (*d*) Gower (1330–1408).

1204. Loss of Normandy by John of England.

1338–1453. Hundred Years' War.
1400. Death of Chaucer.

II. THE PERIOD OF ITALIAN INFLUENCE, 1400–1600.

A. THE REVIVAL OF LEARNING.

  1. In Education.

Colleges founded. Introduction of Printing, 1476. Greek at Oxford (Grocyn, 1491).

  2. In Literature.

   (*a*) Wyatt and Surrey.
   (*b*) The Elizabethan Period (Tottel's Miscellany to Death of Jonson, cir. 1557–1637). Shakespeare,

B. THE EXPRESSION OF REFORMATION IN LITERATURE (PURITAN ENGLAND).

1525– Tyndale's translation of Bible.
1642–1660. Civil War — Protectorate.
   a. Milton (1608–1674).
   b. Bunyan (1628–1688).

GENERAL TABLE OF ENGLISH LITERATURE — *Continued.*

III. THE PERIOD OF FRENCH INFLUENCE, 1660–CIR. 1750.

A. RESTORATION TO DEATH OF DRYDEN (1660–1700).

B. THE AUGUSTAN AGE (CRITICAL SCHOOL).

    1. Pope (1688–1744).
    2. Addison (1672–1719).
    3. Steele (1671–1729).
    4. Swift (1667–1745).

IV. THE MODERN ENGLISH PERIOD, CIR. 1750–1907.

A. THE REACTION AGAINST THE CRITICAL OR CLASSICAL SCHOOL (OR AUGUSTAN AGE).

    1. The New Sympathy with Nature.
      (a) Ramsay's *Gentle Shepherd*, 1725.
      (b) Thomson's *Seasons*, 1730.

    2. The New Sympathy with Man, Rise of Modern Democracy. The Influence of the French Revolution.
    1789. Fall of the Bastille.

    3. German Influence in Coleridge and Carlyle.

B. RECENT WRITERS, 1830–1907.

    1832. First Reform Bill.
      Macaulay.
      Carlyle.
      Ruskin.
      Thackeray.
      Tennyson.
      Browning.

STUDY LISTS.

NOTES AND REFERENCES.

THE following list is intended to be a practical working guide for the student or the general reader. As a rule, the references are to cheap and readily obtainable books, and (except in a few cases) works in foreign languages have been excluded, unless they can be had in an English translation. It has been found impracticable to include all the excellent school or college editions of standard texts. To have done this would have involved an unnecessary repetition of titles, and extended the list to an unwarrantable length. Many of them, however, have been omitted with reluctance. In some cases a method of approach to an author has been indicated by enumerating a few of his works in the order in which they are to be read. Books especially recommended are starred (*); this means that they are considered for some reason, indispensable, or particularly desirable; they do not, of necessity, possess the greatest intrinsic merit. The following abbreviations are used in the list: *E. M. L. = English Men of Letters Series; G. W. S. = Great Writers' Series; D. N. B. = Dictionary of National Biography; E. E. T. S. = Early English Text Society's Publications; S. P. C. K. = Society for the Promotion of Christian Knowledge.*

GENERAL REFERENCES.

I. HISTORY. * Green's *History of the English People*, 4 vols. (Harper); Green's *Short History of the English People* (Harper); Traill's *Social England*, 6 vols. (*Putnam*); Gairdner's *Students' History of England* (Longmans) is convenient and reliable for general reference.

ECONOMIC AND SOCIAL CONDITIONS. Cheyney's *Introduction to the Industrial and Social History of England* (Macmillan); Gibbins' *Industrial History of England* (Methuen).

II. LITERARY HISTORY. Taine's *History of English Literature*, 2 vols. (Holt), brilliant, but not always satisfactory or reliable; Jusserand's *Literary History of the English People*, Vol. I, 1905, Vol. II, 1907 (Putnam); Chambers' *Cyclopædia of English Literature* (new ed., 1902), 3 vols.; *Dictionary of National Biography*, 63 vols., Stephen and Lee (editors), Supplement, etc., 4 vols. (Macmillan); Warton's *History* *of English Poetry*, ed. by Hazlitt, 4 vols. (Tegg); Courthope's *History of English Poetry*, 4 vols., 1895–1903 (Macmillan); Howitt's *Homes and Haunts of the British Poets* (Routledge); Hutton's *Literary Landmarks of London* (Harper); * Baedeker's *Great Britain;* Emerson's *History of the English Language* (Macmillan); Lounsbury's *History of the English Language* (Holt); Parsons' *English Versification* (Leach); Alden's *English Verse* (Holt).

III. SELECTIONS. 1. *POETRY*. Ward's *English Poets*, 4 vols. (Macmillan). * Manly's *English Poetry*, 1170–1892 (Ginn), an admirable, convenient and comprehensive collection, includes many poems not readily accessible. *The Oxford Book of Verse*, 1250–1900 (Clarendon Press); Pancoast's *Standard English Poems* (Holt); Hale's *Longer English Poems* (Macmillan). 2. *PROSE*, etc. Craik's *Selections from English Prose*, 5 vols. (Macmillan); Pancoast's *Standard English Prose* (Holt); Cassell's *Library of English Literature*, ed. by H. Morley. Morley's *English Writers*, 11 vols. (Cassell), contains numerous translations of Early English and Celtic poems, paraphrases and abstracts of various works, etc. *The Oxford Treasury of English Literature* (Clarendon Press) Vol. I. "Old English to Jacobean" (includes poetry and prose with historical, critical, and biographical matter); Vol. II. "The Growth of the Drama" (1907).

IV. MISCELLANEOUS. * Ryland's *Chronological Outlines of English Literature* (Macmillan); Allibone's *Dictionary of Authors*, 5 vols. (Lippincott); Phillips' *Popular Manual of English Literature* (Harper); Ploetz's *Epitome of Universal History* (Houghton).

PART I.

FROM THE EARLIEST TIMES TO THE NORMAN CONQUEST.

(Pages 11-71).

1. **Celtic Literature.** — (Page 23.) For specimens of Celtic poetry, *v.* Morley's *English Writers*, Vols. I–XI, *passim*. See also "Shorter English Poems," in Cassell's *Library of English Literature;* Joyce's *Old Celtic Romances* (Longmans); Tennyson's "Voyage of Maeldune." Aubrey de Vere's poems, "The Children of Lir," "Cuchullin," etc., are based on Old Irish poems. * Lady Charlotte Guest's translation of the *Mabinogion* has been published in a cheap form by Dent & Co., London, and is also included in Everyman's Library. Skene's *Four Ancient Books of Wales*, 2 vols. (Edmonston and Douglas, Edinburgh), contains poems attributed to the bards of the sixth century. * *Cuchulain of Muirthemne; The Story of the Men of the Red Branch of Ulster, arranged and put into English by Lady Gregory* (Murray); * *Gods and Fighting Men: the story of the Tuatha de Danaan and of the Fianna of Ireland, arranged and put into English by Lady Gregory* (Scribner). *Irish Literature*, ed. by Justin McCarthy, 10 vols. (J. D. Morris & Co., Philadelphia), covers the whole field.

HISTORY AND CRITICISM. Hyde's *Literary History of Ireland*, Library of Literary History (Scribner); * Matthew Arnold's *Celtic Literature* (Macmillan); H. Morley's "The Celtic Element in English Literature," in *Clement Marot and Other Essays* (Chapman and Hall, London); Joyce's *Social History of Ancient Ireland* (Longmans).

2. **Early English.** (Pages 32–57.) (*a*) TRANSLATIONS; *Poetry. Beowulf:* * C. G. Child, prose (Houghton); Tinker, prose (Newson). * Earle, *The Deeds of Beowulf* (Clarendon Press); Garnett, verse, line-for-line translation (Ginn); Hall, rhythmical and alliterative (Heath). *The Cædmonian Cycle:* B. Thorpe, Metrical Paraphrase (London, 1832); Bosanquet, *Genesis* only (London, 1860). *Cynewulf:* * *Christ*, I. Gollancz, text and translation (Nutt); C. H. Whitman (Ginn); *Elene*, Garnett (Ginn); L. H. Holt, in Yale Studies in English, 1904 (Holt); *Juliana*, text and translation in Gollancz's *Exeter Book* (Kegan Paul). *The Phœnix:* I. Gollancz, text and translation in the *Exeter Book* (Kegan Paul); * Cook, in Cook and Tinker's *Select Translations from Old English Poetry* (Ginn). *Guthlac:* text and translation in Gollancz's

Exeter Book (Kegan Paul).   *Andreas:* text and translation in Gollancz's *Exeter Book* (Kegan Paul); R. K. Root, verse translation in Yale Studies in English (Holt).   *Judith:* Cook, text and translation (Ginn); Garnett, translation (Ginn); Morley's *English Writers,* Vol. II.

OTHER TRANSLATIONS. * Cook and Tinker's *Select Translations from Old English Poetry* (Ginn), a most convenient and useful collection. Good examples of Early English poetry are given in Longfellow's *Poets and Poetry of Europe.* * *The Seafarer,* * *The Fortunes of Man,* the opening of Cædmon's *Creation,* etc., will be found in Morley's *English Writers,* Vol. II.   See also, Morley's "Illustrations of English Religion," in Cassell's *Library of English Literature,* and Brooke's *Early English Literature,* appendix (Macmillan).

Prose.   (Page 57–71.) *Bede: Ecclesiastical History,* translated from the Latin by J. A. Giles (Bohn's Antiquarian Library).   *King Alfred:* Orosius' *History,* text and translation (Bohn's Antiquarian Library); * Boethius, translation by W. J. Sedgefield (Clarendon Press).

OLD ENGLISH CHRONICLE.   Giles' translation is published with his translation of Bede (*supra*) in Bohn's Antiquarian Library.

(*b*) LITERARY HISTORY AND CRITICISM.   * Ten Brink's *Early English Literature* (Holt); Brooke's *History of Early English Literature* (Macmillan); Azarias' *Development of English Literature,* Old English Period (Appleton); * Lewis' *The Beginnings of English Literature* (Ginn); Earle's *Anglo-Saxon Literature* (S. P. C. K.).   Henry Sweet in his Sketch of the History of Anglo-Saxon Poetry, in Hazlitt's ed. of Warton's *History of English Poetry* (Tegg), gives an excellent account of the early literature in a few pages.   Cook's Introduction to his edition of Cynewulf's *Christ* (Ginn) contains a valuable account of Cynewulf's life and writings.   White's *Ælfric, A New Study of his Life and Writings,* in Yale Studies in English (Holt).

(*c*) HISTORY.   Hodgkins' *Political History of England* (Longmans); Freeman's *Old English History* (Macmillan); * Green's *Making of England* and * *Conquest of England* (Harper).   Grant Allen's *Anglo-Saxon Britain* (S. P. C. K.) is an admirable summary of the entire period, including a brief survey of the language and literature.   De La Saussaye's *Religion of the Teutons* (Ginn), and Gummere's *Germanic Origins* (Scribner), contain much suggestive and curious information. *Biographical.*   William of Malmesbury's account of Aldhelm, and Cuthbert's *Letter on the Death of Bede,* are given in Morley's *Library of English Literature.*   Asser's *Life of Alfred,* Cook's translation (Ginn), or, translated by Giles in *Six Old English Chronicles* (Bohn's Antiquarian Library).   For *Cædmon* see Bede's *Ecclesiastical History.*

FROM THE NORMAN CONQUEST TO CHAUCER.

(Pages 72–103.)

Anglo-Latin Literature. (Page 75.) * Schofield, *English Literature from the Norman Conquest to Chaucer* (Macmillan). This is the best general survey of this period in English. Wright, *Biographia Britannica Literaria, Anglo-Norman Period* (London, 1846). Wright, *Anglo-Latin Satirical Poets and Epigrammatists of the Twelfth Century*, Rolls Series (London, 1872). Wright, *The Latin Poems commonly attributed to Walter Mapes*, text and translation (Camden Society, 1841). *Apocalypse of Golias* is given in translation in *Cassell's Library, Shorter English Poems*, ed. by Morley. Giles' *Six Old English Chronicles* (Bohn's Antiquarian Library) includes, in translation, the Latin histories of *Geoffrey of Monmouth, Gildas, Nennius*, etc. Translations of the Chronicles of *Matthew Paris, William of Malmesbury, Henry of Huntingdon*, etc., and the historical works, etc., of *Giraldus Cambrensis*, will also be found in Bohn's Antiquarian Library. Swan's translation of *Gesta Romanorum* is in the Knickerbocker Nugget Series. A. Jessopp's *Coming of the Friars* (Putnam) and * Ker's *The Dark Ages* (Periods of European Literature) (Scribner) relate to this period.

Norman-French Literature. (Page 80.) Toynbee's *Specimens of Old French* (ninth to fifteenth centuries) with Introduction, Notes, and Glossary (Clarendon Press), is a useful hand-book, and contains full bibliographical references, etc. Gaston Paris, *La Littérature Française au Moyen-Age* (Hachette, 1905); Gaston Paris, *Mediæval French Literature*, London, 1903 (Temple Primers); Saintsbury's *Short History of French Literature* (Clarendon Press), or Dowden's *History of French Literature*, Literatures of the World Series (Appleton). *The Song of Roland* has been translated into English prose by Isabel Butler in Riverside Literature Series (Houghton); A. Lang has translated *Aucassin and Nicolette* (Mosher). See also, for other French Romances, "Romance," section 4, below.

Romance Literature. (Page 81.) As a general guide in this field the student should consult: A. H. Billings' *Guide to the Middle English Metrical Romances* (Holt), and the article "Romance" in *Encyclopædia Britannica*, which gives a bibliography. Ellis, *Specimens of Early English Metrical Romances*, ed. by Halliwell, 3 vols. (Bohn); Ritson, *Ancient English Metrical Romances* (London, 1802), or, revised by Goldsmid (Edinburgh, 1884). * W. W. Newell, *King Arthur and the Table Round*, 2 vols. (Houghton), includes translations from *Crestien de Troyes*. *Syr Gawayn and the Grene Knyght*, ed. by Morris in E. E. T. S. * The same, "retold in modern prose," by J. L. Weston (New Amsterdam Book Co.). J. L. Weston has also published versions of the *Legend of Sir Launcelot du Lac* (1901), the *Legend of*

Sir Perceval (1906), and *King Arthur and his Knights,* 1899 (Scribner). *Sir Thomas Malory's Morte d'Arthur,* Globe Edition (Macmillan); selections from *Malory,* ed. by Mead (Ginn); *King Horn,* ed. by Hall (Clarendon Press); *Havelock the Dane,* ed. by Skeat (Clarendon Press); *The Squyr of Lowe Degre,* ed. by Mead (Ginn); Morley's *Early English Prose Romances,* seven specimens (Carisbrooke Library). A number of the important works of this period will be included in Heath's Belles-Lettres Series and in Ginn's Albion Series.

Celtic Literature. Thomas Stephens' *Literature of the Kymry,* tenth and twelfth centuries (Longmans); Fletcher, *Arthurian Materials in the Chronicles, especially of Great Britain and France,* Harvard Studies and Notes, Boston, 1906; Newell, *King Arthur and the Table Round* (Houghton); Nutt, *Studies on the Legend of the Holy Grail,* Folk-Lore Society Publications, 1888; Rhys, *Studies in the Arthurian Legend* (Clarendon Press, 1891); H. Maynadier, *The Arthur of the English Poets* (Houghton); Maccallum, *Tennyson's Idylls of the King and Arthurian Story from the Sixteenth Century* (Macmillan) contains an introduction dealing briefly with the earlier stages of the Arthurian legend.

English Literature. (Pages 84–103.) R. Morris, *Specimens of Early English,* Part I, 1150–1300 (Clarendon Press); Layamon's *Brut, or Chronicle of Britian,* ed. by Sir F. Madden, 3 vols., London, 1847. Morley's *English Writers,* Vol. III, includes extracts from the *Brut.* The *Ormulum,* ed. by R. Holt, 2 vols. (Clarendon Press). The *Nun's Rule, or Ancren Riwle* (modernised), ed. by Gasquet, is in King's Classics (De La More Press); *The Owl and the Nightingale* is included in Morris' *Specimens of Early English;* a selection from it is given in Manly's *English Poetry* (Ginn), together with selections from *King Horn,* the *Ormulum,* etc.; *Early Popular Poetry of Scotland,* ed. by Laing, revised edition by Hazlitt, 2 vols., London, 1895. BALLADS. F. J. Child, *The English and Scotch Popular Ballads,* 5 vols. (Houghton); * *English and Scottish Popular Ballads,* 1 vol., ed. by G. L. Kittredge, with an excellent introduction, from Professor Child's great collection; Gummere, *Old English Ballads,* Athenæum Press Series (Ginn); Kinard, *Old English Ballads* (Silver, Burdett), is a smaller collection, suited to less advanced students.

English History and Literature. *Norman Britain,* by Rev. W. Hunt, in Early Britain Series (S. P. C. K.); Jewett, *The Story of the Normans* (Story of the Nations' Series); Freeman's *Norman Conquest,* Vol. V, or the one-volume abridgment of it in the Clarendon Press; H. W. C. Davis, *England Under Normans and Angevins,* being second volume of *A History of England,* ed. by C. W. C. Oman (Putnam); Hall, *Court Life Under the Plantagenets* (Henry II) (Macmillan); Barnard, *Companion to English History,* — Middle Ages — (Clarendon Press); * Ker, *Epic and Romance* (Macmillan); Saintsbury, *The Flourishing* *of Romance and the Rise of Allegory*, in "Periods of European Literature" (Scribner); J. W. Hales, *Folia Literaria* (Macmillan), includes essays on "Old English Metrical Romances," "The Lay of Havelock the Dane," etc.; Chappell, *Popular Music of the Olden Time*, 2 vols. (Macmillan); Carlyle's *Past and Present* gives a good picture of a mediæval monastery; Gross, *The Sources and Literature of English History* (Longmans).

THE AGE OF CHAUCER.

(Pages 104-153.)

The Age of Chaucer. HISTORY, MANNERS, etc. Pauli, *Pictures of Old England* (Macmillan); Jusserand, *English Wayfaring Life in the Middle Ages*, fourteenth century (Putnam); Wright, *History of Domestic Manners and Sentiments in England During the Middle Ages* (Trübner, 1871); Cutt, *Scenes and Characters in the Middle Ages* (Virtue & Co., London, 1872); Brown, *Chaucer's England* (Hunt and Blackett, London, 1869); Jessopp, *Coming of the Friars and Other Essays* (Putnam); Schofield, *English Literature from the Norman Conquest to Chaucer* (Macmillan); Snell, *The Fourteenth Century* (Periods of European Literature, Scribner); Snell, *The Age of Chaucer* (Bell).

LITERATURE IN THE FOURTEENTH CENTURY.

(Pages 112-125)

Cursor Mundi (Page 112) has been edited in seven parts by R. Morris in E. E. T. S. * *Selections*, which give a fair general notion of the poem, are given in Morris and Skeat's *Specimens of Early English*, Vol. II (Clarendon Press), and in Manly's *English Poetry* (Ginn).

Richard Rolle, etc. (Page 113.) *Richard Rolle of Hampole and his Followers*, ed. by Horstman, 2 vols., in "Yorkshire Writers" (Sonnenschein); *English Prose Treatises of*, ed. by Perry in E. E. T. S. *The Prick of Conscience*, ed. by R. Morris for "The Philosophical Society," 1863. * *Selections from the Prick of Conscience* in Morris and Skeat's *Specimens of Early English*, Vol. II (Clarendon Press). This volume of Morris and Skeat's *Specimens* also contains some poems of *Lawrence Minot*, sundry lyrics, including "Alysoun," and will be found generally useful for this period. *Minot's Poems*, ed. by Hall, are published by the Clarendon Press.

Romance. (Page 116.) *Sir Gawain and the Grene Knight*, ed. by R. Morris in E. E. T. S. * A convenient English prose translation has been made by J. L. Weston (Nutt). *The Pearl* (Page 118) has been edited by Gollancz (Nutt), by R. Morris in E. E. T. S., and by Osgood in Belles-Lettres Series (Heath). *Selections* from *The Pearl* are given in Manly's *English Poetry*, and translations into modern

English verse have been made by Dr. S. Weir Mitchell (Century Co., 1896) and G. G. Coulton (Nutt, 1906).

John Gower. (Page 120.) *Confessio Amantis*, ed. by Macaulay, selections (Clarendon Press). *Confessio Amantis* in Morley's "Carisbrooke Library." A few *selections* are given in Ellis' *Specimens of the Early English Poets* (Washbourne, London, 1845). There is a very severe indictment of Gower's poetry in Lowell's *My Study Windows*, art. "Chaucer" (Houghton).

John Wyclif. (Page 122.) *Select English Works*, ed. by T. Arnold, 3 vols. (Clarendon Press). Selections from Wyclif's Bible are given in *Wycliffe's Bible* (Clarendon Press) Maynard, Merrill & Co.'s "English Classics," No. 107; and Morris and Skeat's *Specimens of Early English*, Vol. II. Brief selections from *Wyclif's English Works* (modernised) are given in the University of Pennsylvania's *Transactions and Reprints*, II, 5. For *Biography and Criticism, v. The Age of Wyclif*, by G. M. Trevelyan (Longmans); *John Wyclif* by Lewis Sergeant (Heroes of the Nation Series); *John Wyclif, his Life, Times, and Teaching*, by Rev. A. R. Pennington (S. P. C. K.).

Mandeville. (Page 124.) *The Travels of Sir John Mandeville* (Macmillan); *The Voyages and Travels of Sir John Mandeville*, ed. by Morley (Cassell's National Library); art. on *Mandeville* in D. N. B.

Langland. (Page 125.) WORKS. *The Vision of William concerning Piers the Plowman* (three texts) ed. by Skeat, 2 vols. (Clarendon Press); *William Langland's Piers the Plowman* (school edition) ed. by Skeat (Clarendon Press); * Langland's *Vision of Piers the Ploughman*, done into modern prose with an introduction by Kate M. Warner (Macmillan).

BIOGRAPHY AND CRITICISM. Jusserand's *Piers Ploughman, a contribution to the history of English mysticism* (Putnam); and for briefer treatment, his *Literary History of the English People*, Vol. I, Chap. IV.

Chaucer. (Page 132.) WORKS. *Works of Geoffrey Chaucer*, ed. by Skeat, 6 vols. (Clarendon Press). This is the standard edition, valuable for advanced work. * The Globe Chaucer, ed. by Pollard (Macmillan), or The Students' Chaucer, ed. by Skeat (Clarendon Press), are good editions, sufficient for all ordinary purposes. *Editions of Various Poems.* The *Prologue, The Knight's Tale*, and others of the *Canterbury Tales*, have been edited in a convenient form by Morris and Skeat (Clarendon Press), and by Liddell (Macmillan).

BIOGRAPHY, CRITICISM, etc. * A. W. Ward's *Chaucer*, E. M. L.; * Root's *The Poetry of Chaucer* (Houghton); or Pollard's *Chaucer*, in *English Literature Primers* (Macmillan), are excellent guides. Lounsbury, *Studies in Chaucer*, 3 vols. (Harper); Ten Brink, *The Language and Metre of Chaucer*, translated by Smith (Macmillan); Hempl, *Chaucer's Pronunciation* (Heath); * Lowell's essay on "Chaucer" in *My Study Windows* (Houghton); Hazlitt's lecture on "Chaucer and Spenser" in *Lectures on the English Poets* (Bohn); Snell's *Age of Chaucer*

(Bell); Ten Brink's account of Chaucer in his *English Literature*, Vol. II. (Holt). Saunders, *Canterbury Tales* (Macmillan), contains illustrations reproduced from the Ellesmere manuscript. See also, Palgrave's poem "The Pilgrim and the Ploughman," in his *Visions of England* (Cassell).

SUGGESTIONS FOR READING. "The Prologue," "Knight's Tale," "Clerk's Tale," "Man of Lawe's Tale," "Nonne Preste's Tale," "The Pardoner's Tale," Chaucer's "Tale of Sir Thopas," "The Prioresses Tale," "Ballad of Good Counseil," "Compleint to his Empty Purse," will serve as an introduction to a more extended knowledge of Chaucer's Works.

PART II.

1400–1860.

THE ITALIAN INFLUENCE.

Chaucerian School, etc.

(Pages 155–170.)

English Chaucerians. (Pages 155–159.) Selections from *Occleve Lydgate, Skelton*, or from some other writers of this period, will be found in Southey's *British Poets, Chaucer to Jonson* (Longmans); Fitzgibbon's *Early English Poetry*, in Canterbury Poets' Series (Walter Scott); Skeat's *Specimens of English Literature*, 1394–1579 (Clarendon Press, 1871); Ward's *English Poets;* Manly's *English Poetry*, etc.

Scottish Poets. (Pages 159–164.) *Barbour's Bruce* has been ed. by Skeat (E. E. T. S.). *R. Henryson, Fables*, ed. by Laing (Edinburgh, 1865). *The Testament of Cresseid* is included in Skeat's *Chaucerian and other Pieces* (Clarendon Press); *King James I of Scotland*, Poems ed. by Eyre-Todd in the "Abbotsford Series of Scottish Poetry" (Glasgow); *Henryson, Dunbar*, and *G. Douglas*, also appear in this series. See also, *Dunbar*, ed. by Arber, in "Selections from the British Poets" (Macmillan). The standard edition of Dunbar, including notes and memoir, is that of David Laing, 2 vols. (Edinburgh, 1834), Henderson's *Scottish Vernacular Literature* (Nutt), and J. H. Millar's *Literary History of Scotland* (Scribner), may be consulted with advantage for this period.

Ballads. See page 6, Study List, under English Literature.

Fifteenth Century Prose. (Page 168.) Sir Thomas Malory, *Le Morte d'Arthur*, 3 vols. (Nutt); a reproduction of the original edition, ed. with introduction and glossary by H. Oscar Sommer, and an essay on Malory's prose style by Andrew Lang. * *Morte d'Arthur*, Globe Edition (Macmillan); *Selections*, W. E. Mead (Ginn).

Beginning of the Renaissance.

(Pages 171–181.)

The Renaissance. History and Criticism. Symonds' *Renaissance in Italy*, 7 vols. (Holt); Burkhardt, *The Civilization of the Period of the Renaissance in Italy*, 2 vols. (Kegan Paul). L. F. Field's *Introduc-*

tion to the Study of the Renaissance (Scribner) is a short and convenient survey of the whole subject. * Symonds' art. "Renaissance," in the *Encyclopædia Britannica* (ninth ed.); Einstein, *The Italian Renaissance in England* (Macmillan); Denton, *England in the Fifteenth Century* (Bell); Moberly, *The Early Tudors*, in "Epochs of Modern History" (Scribner); Powers, *England and the Reformation* (Scribner); Froude, *History of England from the Fall of Wolsey to the Death of Elizabeth*, 12 vols. (Scribner).

Renaissance in England, 1400–1509. (Page 175.) *Caxton:* Blades, *The Biography and Typography of W. Caxton* (Trübner); *Golden Legend*, 7 vols. in "Temple Classics" (Macmillan).

The Oxford Reformers. (Pages 177–179.) * Seebohm, *Oxford Reformers* (Longmans) is the best general book on this group. *Erasmus, Concerning the Aim and Method of Education*, ed. by Woodward (Macmillan); *Select Colloquies*, ed. by Whitcomb (Longmans.); translations of *The Praise of Folly* and of the *Colloquies* are published by Reeves and Turner, London; *Desiderius Erasmus* by E. Emerton (Putnam); Froude, *Life and Letters of Erasmus* (Scribner); the two books last named contain many translations. *Colet:* Knight, *Life of Dean Colet* (Clarendon Press); *More: Utopia*, ed. by Collins (Clarendon Press); *Utopia*, "Temple Classics" (Macmillan); *History of King Richard III*, ed. by Lumby, Pitt Press Series (Putnam). Roper's *Life of More* is included in an edition of the " Utopia," published by Burt in Home Library. * See also for an admirable brief treatment, W. H. Shaw's *Lectures on the Oxford Reformers, Colet, Erasmus*, and *More*, Am. Soc. for Extension of University Teaching, Philadelphia.

The New Learning in Literature

(Pages 182–190.)

Wyatt and Surrey. (Page 183.) Wyatt, *Poems* (Aldine Edition); Surrey, *Poems* (Aldine Edition); Tottel's *Miscellany*, containing the "Songes and Sonettes," of Surrey, Wyatt, and "uncertain authors," is in Arber's "English Reprints."

Sackville. (Page 184.) *Gorboduc* is given in Manly's *Specimens of the Pre-Shakespearean Drama*, 2 vols. (Athenæum Press Series, Ginn). *The Mirror for Magistrates.* Sackville's *Induction* and *Complaint of Henry Duke of Buckingham* are given in Southey's *Early British Poets;* the *Induction* is in Skeat's *Specimens of English Literature*, 1394–1579; (Clarendon Press); *Works*, with memoir, etc., in "Library of Old Authors" (London, 1859).

Gascoigne. (Page 186.) *Works*, ed. by Hazlitt, 2 vols., Roxburghe Library (London, 1869), *The Steel Glass* is in Arber's Reprints, in Southey's *Early British Poets*, and is published in an inexpensive form by Macmillan; *Life and Writings*, by F. E. Schelling (Ginn).

Ascham. (Page 188.) Complete *Works,* ed. by Giles (London, 1884). *Toxophilus* and the *Scholemaster* are in Arber's Reprints.

Latimer. (Page 188.) *Seven Sermons, before Edward VI,* and the famous sermon on *The Ploughers,* are published in a cheap form by Macmillan.

CULMINATION OF THE RENAISSANCE.

(Pages 191–256.)

Elizabethan England. Creighton, *The Age of Elizabeth* (Longmans); Goadby's *The England of Shakespeare* (Cassell); Ordish, *Early London Theatres* and *Shakespeare's London* (Macmillan); * Stevenson, *Shakespeare's London* (Holt); Warner, *The People for whom Shakespeare Wrote* (Harper); Rye, *England as seen by Foreigners in the Days of Elizabeth and James I* (Jno. Russell Smith, 1865); Seccomb and Allen, *The Age of Shakespeare,* 2 vols. (Macmillan); Harrison's *Elizabethan England,* Camelot Series.

Spenser. (Page 202.) *Works* (Globe Edition, Macmillan); * *Faërie Queene,* ed. by Kitchen, Bks. I–II (Clarendon Press); *Shepheard's Calendar,* ed. by Herford (Macmillan).

BIOGRAPHY AND CRITICISM. * Church, *Life of Spenser* (E. M. L.); Craik, *Spenser and His Poetry,* 3 vols. (Griffin); Warton, *Observations on the Faërie Queene* (London, 1782); * Lowell, Essay on "Spenser," in *Among My Books* (Houghton); Dowden, essays on "Spenser the Poet and Teacher," and "The Heroines of Spenser," in *Transcripts and Studies* (Scribner); Landor's "Essay on Spenser," in *Imaginary Conversations* (given also in Pancoast's *Standard English Prose*). For a comparison of Chaucer and Spenser, see Hazlitt's *Lectures on the English Poets* (Bohn); *Outline Guide to the Study of Spenser* (Univ. of Chicago, 1894). See also portions relating to Spenser in Courthope's *English Poetry* and Jusserand's *Literary History of the English People.*

THE ENGLISH DRAMA.

(Page 211.)

Miracle Plays, Moralities, and Interludes, etc. (Page 214.) Pollard, *English Miracle Plays, Moralities, and Interludes,* gives specimens, with general introduction (Clarendon Press); Manly, *Specimens of the Pre-Shakespearean Drama,* 2 vols. (Ginn); *English Plays* in Cassell's *Library of English Literature,* Vol. III, ed. by Morley; *The York Mysteries,* ed. by Lucy Toulmin Smith (Clarendon Press); Gayley, *Representative English Comedies* (Macmillan).

History. A. W. Ward, *History of English Dramatic Literature to the Reign of Queen Anne,* 3 vols. (Macmillan); Chambers, *The Mediæval*

Stage, 2 vols. (Clarendon Press); Fleay, *A Biographical Chronicle of the English Drama,* 1559–1642, 2 vols. (London, 1871); Hazlitt, *Lectures on the Dramatic Literature of the Age of Elizabeth* (London, 1869); * Bates, *The English Religious Drama* (Macmillan); * Symonds, *Shakespeare's Predecessors in the English Drama* (Macmillan); Lowell, *The Old English Dramatists* (Houghton); Schelling, *The English Chronicle Play* (Macmillan); * Boas, *Shakespeare and his Predecessors in the English Drama* (Scribner) ; Schelling, *Elizabethan Drama,* 2 vols. (Houghton).

Shakespeare's Predecessors. (Page 222.) Manly, *Specimens of the Pre-Shakespearean Drama* (Ginn); * Thayer's *Six Best English Plays* (Ginn); Keltie, *The Works of the British Dramatists* (Edinburgh, 1872); * Lamb, *Specimens of the English Dramatic Poets* (Macmillan); Cunliffe, *The Influence of Seneca on Elizabethan Tragedy* (Macmillan); Simpson, *Scenes from Old Play Books* (Clarendon Press).

(*a*) GREENE. *The Plays and Poems of Robert Greene,* ed. by J. C. Collins, 2 vols. (Clarendon Press); *Marlowe's Dr. Faustus and Greene's Friar Bacon and Friar Bungay,* ed. by Ward (Clarendon Press); *Poems of Greene, Marlowe, and Ben Jonson* (Bohn).

(*b*) PEELE. *Works,* ed. by A. H. Bullen, 2 vols. (Scribner).

(*c*) KYD. *Works,* ed. by Boas (Clarendon Press); *Spanish Tragedy,* "Temple Dramatists" (Macmillan).

(*d*) LYLY. *Works,* ed. by Bond, 3 vols. (Clarendon Press); *Endymion,* ed. by Baker (Holt); *Euphues,* in Arber's Reprints; C. G. Child, *John Lyly and Euphuism,* Erlangen, 1894.

(*e*) MARLOWE. (Page 224.) *Works,* ed. by A. H. Bullen (Scribner); *Best Plays,* ed. by H. Ellis (Scribner); *Dr. Faustus,* with introduction and notes, "Temple Dramatists" (Macmillan); *Edward II,* with selections from *Tamburlaine* (Holt); For Criticism, see Dowden's essay on "Christopher Marlowe," in *Transcripts and Studies* (Scribner); "Marlowe," in Henry Kingsley's *Fireside Studies* (Chatto); A. W. Verity, *Marlowe's Influence on Shakespeare* (Macmillan and Bowes); Symonds, in *Shakespeare's Predecessors in the English Drama* (Scribner).

Shakespeare. (Page 229.) (*a*) WORKS. * Furness' *Variorum Edition* (Lippincott). This invaluable edition includes at present (1907) about one half of the plays. An extraordinary amount of material, carefully and skilfully selected, is brought together for the benefit of the student; in addition to the textual criticisms, there are general criticisms, both English and foreign. *Globe Edition,* ed. by Clark and Wright (Macmillan); *Cambridge Edition,* ed. by Wright, 9 vols. (Macmillan). There are many admirable editions of Shakespeare adapted for school use. Among these may be mentioned those of *Rolfe* (American Book Co.); *Hudson* (Ginn); *Verity,* "Pitt Press" (Putnam); *The Temple Shakespeare* (Dent), and the select plays ed. by W. G. Clark and W. Aldis Wright (Clarendon Press).

(*b*) GRAMMARS, LEXICONS, etc. Abbot's *Shakespearean Grammar* (Macmillan); Craik's *English of Shakespeare* (Ginn); Schmidt's *Shakespeare-Lexicon;* Nares, *A Glossary of Words, etc., in the Works of English Authors, particularly of Shakespeare and his Contemporaries* (London, 1888); Bartlett, *Shakespeare Concordance* (Macmillan); Mary Cowden Clark, *Complete Concordance to Shakespeare* (London, 1864); Furness' *Concordance to Shakespeare's Poems* (Lippincott); Skeat, *Shakespeare's Plays Illustrated by Selections from North's Plutarch* (Macmillan); * Dowden, *Shakespeare Primer* (American Book Co.); Lounsbury, *The Text of Shakespeare* (Scribner). See also the publications of the *Shakespeare Society* (43 vols.) and of *The New Shakespeare Society* (8 series).

(*c*) BIOGRAPHY. * S. Lee, *Life of Shakespeare* (Macmillan); Elze, *Life of Shakespeare* (Bohn); Halliwell-Phillips, *Outlines of the Life of Shakespeare*, 2 vols. (Longmans); Fleay, *Chronicle History of the Life and Work of Shakespeare* (Nimmo); Bagehot, "Shakespeare the Man," in *Literary Studies* (Longmans); Goldwin Smith, *Shakespeare the Man* (Doubleday).

(*d*) CRITICISM. * Brandes, *William Shakespeare* a critical study in translation (Macmillan); * Dowden, *Shakespeare: His Mind and Art* (Harper); an admirable and inspiring introduction to the study of Shakespeare. Coleridge, *Notes and Lectures on the Plays of Shakespeare* (Bohn); * Bradley, *Shakespearean Tragedy* (Macmillan); Jameson, *Shakespeare's Heroines* (Bohn); R. W. Emerson, "Shakespeare the Poet," in *Representative Men;* Carlyle, lecture on "The Hero as Poet," in *Heroes and Hero-Worship; Eighteenth Century Essays on Shakespeare*, ed. by Smith (Macmillan); Ulrici, *Shakespeare's Dramatic Art*, 2 vols. (Bohn); Ten Brink, *Five Lectures on Shakespeare* (Holt); Moulton, *Shakespeare as a Dramatic Artist* (Clarendon Press); Gervinus, *Shakespeare Commentaries* (Scribner); * Lowell, "Shakespeare Once More," in *Among My Books* (Houghton); * Wendell, *William Shakespeare, A Study in Elizabethan Literature* (Scribner). Bayne's article on "Shakespeare," in *Encyclopædia Britannica*, ninth edition, is valuable for the study of early environment. See also, for social conditions, etc., in Shakespeare's time, references on p. 12, Study List, under *Elizabethan England*.

ELIZABETHAN PROSE.

Hooker. (Page 247.) *Works*, with Walton's "Life," ed. by Keble and revised by Church and Paget, 3 vols. (Clarendon Press); * *Ecclesiastical Polity*, Bks. I–IV. (Morley's Universal Library); * Dowden's essay on "Richard Hooker," in *Puritan and Anglican* (Holt); * Walton's "Life of Hooker," in *Walton's Lives*.

Bacon. (Page 250.) WORKS. Among the numerous cheap and convenient editions of the *Essays*, Reynolds' edition (Clarendon Press), Abbot's edition (Longmans), and W. A. Wright's edition (Macmillan) may be mentioned. *Advancement of Learning*, ed. by Wright (Clarendon Press). Bohn's Library includes the important works of Bacon.

BIOGRAPHY AND CRITICISM. * Church's *Life*, in E. M. L. Spedding's *Letters and Life of Lord Bacon*, 7 vols. (London, 1862–1874), is the standard biography. * Macaulay, essay on "Bacon," in *Essays*.

THE DECLINE OF THE RENAISSANCE.

(Page 257–304.)

LATER ELIZABETHAN LITERATURE.

The Drama. (Page 261.)

Ben Jonson. (Page 264.) (*a*) WORKS, ed. by Cunningham, 3 vols. (Scribner); *Best Plays*, ed. by Nicholson, 3 vols. in Mermaid Series, (Scribner). Critical editions of the following plays have appeared in the *Yale Studies in English* (Holt): *The Alchemist, Bartholomew Fair, Poetaster, The Staple of News, The Devil is an Ass, Epicœne, or the Silent Woman*. The *Alchemist* is in the "Temple Dramatists," and *Every Man in his Humour* is published in convenient form by Macmillan and by Longmans. *Discoveries*, ed. by Schelling (Ginn); *Eastward Ho* and the *Alchemist*, edited by Schelling (Heath); *Dramatic Works and Lyrics*, ed. by Symonds, "Canterbury Poets."

(*b*) BIOGRAPHY AND CRITICISM. A. J. Symonds, *Life of Ben Jonson*, in "English Worthies" (Appleton); Swinburne, *A Study of Ben Jonson* (Scribner); Penniman, *The War of the Theatres* (Ginn).

Beaumont and Fletcher. (Page 266.) (*a*) WORKS. *Dramas*, ed. by Dyce, 11 vols. (London, 1846); *The Best Plays*, ed. by Strachey, in Mermaid Series (Scribner); *Philaster, The Faithful Shepherdess, The Knight of the Burning Pestle*, are in "The Temple Dramatists."

(*b*) BIOGRAPHY AND CRITICISM. G. C. Macaulay, *Francis Beaumont: a Critical Study* (Kegan Paul); *Beaumont and Fletcher and their Contemporaries* in *Edinburgh Review*, April, 1841.

THE POETS OF THE EARLY SEVENTEENTH CENTURY.

(1599 to 1660.)

Giles and Phineas Fletcher. (Page 268.) Giles Fletcher, *Christ's Victory and Triumph* (Dutton), also given in Southey's *Early British Poets;* Phineas Fletcher, *The Purple Island*, in Southey's *Early British Poets*.

William Browne. (Page 270.) *Britannia's Pastorals*, in Southey's *Early British Poets; Selections* in Manly's *English Poetry* and in Ward's *English Poets*.

Donne. (Page 270.) *Poems*, ed. by E. K. Chambers, **2 vols.** (Scribner). Gosse, *Life and Letters*, 2 vols. (Dodd), is the standard modern biography. Walton's "Life of Donne," in *Lives*, is a classic, but deals chiefly with one side of Donne's character.

Cowley. (Page 272.) *Works*, ed. by Grosart, in "Chertsey Worthies Library;" * Essays, Bayard Series (Scribner); * *Life*, in S. Johnson's *Lives of the Poets;* Gosse's essay on "Abraham Cowley," in *Seventeenth Century Studies* (Dodd).

Herbert. (Page 273.) *Poems*, in Aldine Poets (Macmillan); *The English Works of George Herbert, newly arranged and annotated and considered in relation to his life*, by G. H. Palmer (Houghton); Dowden, on Herbert and Vaughan, in *Puritan and Anglican* (Holt).

Crashaw. (Page 273.) *Poems*, ed. by A. R. Waller (Putnam); Gosse's essay on "Richard Crashaw," in *Seventeenth Century Studies* (Dodd), and Dowden's criticism of, in *Puritan and Anglican* (Holt).

Vaughan. (Page 273.) *Poetical Works* (Macmillan); *Silex Scintillans*, in "Temple Classics" (Macmillan); L. I. Guiney, article on "Henry Vaughan, the Silurist," in the *Atlantic Monthly*, May, 1894, and Dowden in *Puritan and Anglican.* See also selections from Vaughan, Herbert etc., in Pancoast's *Standard English Poems* (Holt), and notes.

The Cavalier Lyrists. (Page 275.) *The Minor Poets of the Caroline Period*, ed. by Saintsbury (Clarendon Press); *Cavalier Poets* (Maynard, Merrill); *A Book of Seventeenth Century Lyrics*, ed. by Schelling (Ginn).

Herrick. (Page 275.) *Works*, ed. by Pollard, 2 vols. (Scribner); *Poems*, 2 vols., in "Temple Classics" (Macmillan); *Chrysomela* (Macmillan); *Selections* from *Hesperides* and *Noble Numbers*, ed. with introduction by T. B. Aldrich, in "Century Classics" (Century). Gosse, essay on Herrick, in *Seventeenth Century Studies* (Dodd).

Milton. (Page 278.) (*a*) WORKS. *Poetical Works*, ed. by Masson, 3 vols. (Macmillan), is the standard edition. *Poetical Works*, Globe Edition (Macmillan). *The Cambridge Milton for Schools*, ed. by A. W. Verity (Putnam), containing nearly all of Milton's English poems, is published in ten small volumes, sold separately. There are numerous editions of Milton's selected poems, *Comus, Lycidas*, etc., adapted for school use. *Prose Works*, ed. by J. A. St. John, 5 vols. (Macmillan); *Selected Prose Writings* (Appleton); *Areopagitica*, ed. by Cotterill (Macmillan).

(*b*) BIOGRAPHY. The standard work on Milton is Masson's *Life of Milton, in connection with the History of his Time*, 6 vols. (Macmillan); Pattison, *Milton*, in E. M. L.; Garnett, *Milton*, in G. W. S.

(c) CRITICISM. * Raleigh's *Milton* (Putnam) and Trent's *Milton* (Macmillan) are excellent critical studies; Macaulay, "Milton" (in *Essays*, Vol. I); De Quincey, "On Milton" (in *Works*, Masson's ed. Vol. X); Lowell, "Milton" (in *Among My Books*, Vol. II); Maurice, "Milton" (in *The Friendship of Books and Other Essays*, Macmillan); * Arnold, "*Milton*" (in *Essays in Criticism*, 2d series, Macmillan); Bagehot, in *Literary Studies*, Vol. I (Longmans); * S. Brooke, *Milton*, in Students' Literary Series (Appleton); Dowden, "The Idealism of Milton," in *Transcripts and Studies* (Scribner); Addison, *Criticisms on Paradise Lost* (from *The Spectator*) ed. by Cook (Ginn).

SEVENTEENTH CENTURY PROSE.

(Page 289.)

Raleigh. *Poems*, with Sir Henry Wotton's (Macmillan); Selections from prose in Saintsbury's *Specimens of English Prose Style* (Kegan Paul) and Pancoast's *Standard English Prose* (Holt); Gosse, *Life of* (Appleton).

Jeremy Taylor. (Page 290.) * *Holy Living and Dying*, in Bohn's Library and " Temple Classics."

Burton. (Page 291.) *Anatomy of Melancholy*, 3 vols. (Bohn); *Life*, in Woods' *Athenæ Oxonienses*.

Sir T. Browne. *Works*, 3 vols. (Bohn); *Religio Medici and Urn Burial* in "Temple Classics;" *Hydriotaphia and the Garden of Cyrus* (Macmillan); Selections in Pancoast's *Standard English Prose* (Holt); L. Stephen, essay on, in *Hours in a Library* (2d series).

Fuller. (Page 293.) *Church History of Great Britain*, ed. by J. S. Brewer, 6 vols. (Clarendon Press); *Holy and Profane States; The Author and His Writings* (Sonnenschein); *Wise Words and Quaint Counsels of Thomas Fuller*, selected by Jessop (Clarendon Press); Coleridge on *Fuller* in *Literary Remains*.

Clarendon. (Page 293.) *Characters and episodes of the great rebellion* (*Selections*), ed. by Boyle (Clarendon Press).

Walton. (Page 294.) *The Complete Angler* in Bohn's Library, "Temple Classics," and in Everyman's Library (with introduction by A. Lang); *Lives*, of Donne, Hooker, etc., in Bohn's Library and "Temple Classics;" Lowell, essay on "Walton," in *Latest Literary Essays* (Houghton).

Bunyan. (Pages 295–304.) (a) WORKS. *Pilgrim's Progress* and *Grace Abounding*, ed. by Venables and Peacock (Clarendon Press). The *Pilgrim's Progress* may also be had in the " Temple Classics " and in Everyman's Library. *The Holy War and the Heavenly Footman.* ed. by Peacock (Clarendon Press) and in "Temple Classics;" *Life and Death of Mr. Badman* and *The Holy War* (Putnam).

(*b*) BIOGRAPHY. Froude, Life, in E. M. L.; Brown. *John Bunyan, his Life, Times, and Works* (Houghton); * Macaulay's life of Bunyan in *Encyclopædia Britannica* (also included in his *Essays*); W. H. White, *John Bunyan*, in "Literary Lives" (Scribner).

(*c*) CRITICISM. * Macaulay, essay on Southey's edition of the *Pilgrim's Progress*. in *Essays;* * Dowden, "Bunyan," in *Puritan and Anglican* (Holt); Foster, *Bunyan's Country; Studies in the Bedfordshire Topography of the Pilgrim's Progress* (Virtue & Co.); Royce, "The Case of John Bunyan," in *Studies of Good and Evil* (Appleton). See also, B. Wendell, *The Temper of the Seventeenth Century in English Literature* (Scribner).

PART III.

THE FRENCH INFLUENCE.
(Pages 305–321.)

THE ENGLAND OF THE RESTORATION.

HISTORY AND CRITICISM. Macaulay, *History of England*, Vol. I, Chap. III. Beljame, *Le Public et les Hommes de Lettres en Angleterre au XVIII Siecle* (1660–1744), Paris, 1881 (Hachette); Garnett, *The Age of Dryden* (Macmillan).

John Dryden. (Page 312.) *Works*, ed. by Walter Scott, and revised by G. Saintsbury, 18 vols. (Putnam); *Poetical Works*, ed. by W. D. Christie (Globe Edition); *Select Poems*, ed. by W. D. Christie (Clarendon Press); *Essays*, ed. by W. P. Ker, 2 vols. (Clarendon Press); *An Essay of Dramatic Poesy*, ed. by T. Arnold (Clarendon Press); *Select Satires*, ed. by Collins (Macmillan); Selections from the *Essays* and *Religio Laici* are to be found in Cassell's National Library; *Essays on the Drama*, ed. by W. Strunk, Jr. (Holt).

BIOGRAPHY. G. Saintsbury, *Life of Dryden* (E. M. L.); W. Scott, "Life," in Saintsbury's edition of the *Works*.

CRITICISM. W. Hazlitt, "On Dryden and Pope," in *Lectures on the English Poets* (Bohn); Macaulay, "Dryden," in *Essays*, Vol. I; Lowell, "Dryden," in *Among My Books;* M. Sherwood, *Dryden's Dramatic Theory and Practice*, Yale Studies in English, No. 4 (Holt).

SUGGESTED READINGS. "Absalom and Achitophel," Part I; "Mac-Flecknoe," "Under Mr. Milton's Picture," "Ode to the Memory of Mistress Ann Killigrew," "Alexander's Feast," "Veni Creator Spiritus," "Song for Saint Cecelia's Day." It will be found interesting and profitable to compare Dryden's modernised version of Chaucer's "Knight's Tale (Palamon and Arcite)," with the original, and analyse the respective merits of the two poetic styles. PROSE. "Essay of Dramatic Poesy," or selections in Strunk's "Dryden" or in Pancoast's "Standard English Prose."

OTHER RESTORATION WRITERS.

The Drama. (Page 319.)

(a) **Thomas Otway.** *Works*, ed. by Thornton (with biography), 3 vols., London, 1813; *Best Plays*, ed. by R. Noel (Mermaid Series); *Venice Preserved* and *Return from Parnassus* ("Temple Classics").

CRITICISM. Gosse, "Otway," in *Seventeenth Century Studies* (Dodd).

(*b*) **William Wycherley.** (Page 321.) *Complete Plays*, **ed.** by W. C. Ward (Mermaid Series).

(*c*) **William Congreve.** (Page 321.) *Complete Plays*, ed. by A. C. Ewald (Mermaid Series).

BIOGRAPHY. Gosse, *Life of William Congreve* (G. W. S.).

CRITICISM. Macaulay, "Comic Dramatists of the Restoration," in *Essays*, Vol. IV; Lamb, "On the Artificial Comedy of the Last Century," in *Essays of Elia*.

John Locke. (Page 321.) *Philosophical Works*, 2 vols. (Bohn); *Some Thoughts concerning Education*, ed. by R. H. Quick (Pitt Press Series); *An Essay concerning Human Understanding*, ed. by A. C. Fraser, 2 vols. (Clarendon Press).

BIOGRAPHY. T. Fowler, *Locke* (E. M. L.).

CRITICISM. Fraser, *John Locke as a Factor in Modern Thought* (Clarendon Press).

THE AGE OF POPE.

(Pages 322-392.)

HISTORY AND CRITICISM. * L. Stephen, *History of English Thought in the Eighteenth Century*, Chap. XII (Putnam); Beljame, *Le Public et les Hommes de Lettres en Angleterre au XVIIIᵉ Siecle* (Hachette); Perry, *English Literature in the Eighteenth Century* (Harper); Gosse, *History of English Literature of the Eighteenth Century* (Macmillan); W. J. Courthope, "Conservatism of the Eighteenth Century," in *The Liberal Movement in English Literature* (Murray); O. Elton, *The Augustan Ages* ("Periods of European Literature," Scribner); F. Harrison, "A Few Words About the Eighteenth Century," in *The Choice of Books* (Macmillan); Ashton, *Social Life in the Reign of Queen Anne* (Chatto); * Sydney, *England and the English in the Eighteenth Century*, 2 vols. (Macmillan); Mrs. Oliphant, *Historical Characters of the Reign of Queen Anne* (Century); * Lecky, *History of England in the Eighteenth Century*, Vol. I, Chap. IV; Vol. VI, Chap. XXIII (Appleton); Dennis, *The Age of Pope* (Hand-books of English Literature) (Macmillan); Morris, *Age of Anne*, and also his *Early Hanoverians*, both in *Epochs of History* (Scribner); * Thackeray, *English Humourists*, ed. by Phelps (Holt); Dobson, *William Hogarth* (Dodd); Spence, *Anecdotes and Observations of Books and Men from the Conversation of Mr. Pope*, 2d ed., 1858 (J. R. Smith); Dobson, *Eighteenth Century Vignettes*, 3 series (Dodd).

Alexander Pope. (Page 326.) *Works*, ed. by Elwin and Courthope, 10 vols. (Murray); *Poetical Works*, ed. by Ward (Globe Edition); *Essay on Man*, also *Satires and Epistles*, ed. by Pattison (Clarendon Press).

BIOGRAPHY. L. Stephen, *Alexander Pope* (E. M. L.); Courthope, "Life," in Elwin and Courthope's edition of *Works*, Vol. V; Carruthers, *Life, including Letters* (Bohn).

CRITICISM. Conington, "Poetry of Pope," in *Oxford Essays*, 1858; L. Stephen, "Pope as a Moralist," in *Hours in a Library*, Vol. I (Putnam); Essays in Lowell's *My Study Windows;* De Quincey's *Biographical Essays*, and also in his *Essays on the Poets;* Hazlitt, "On Dryden and Pope," in *Lectures on the English Poets* (Bohn).

SUGGESTED READINGS. "Spring," in *Pastorals;* "Windsor Forest," "Dying Christian to His Soul," "Elegy to the Memory of an Unfortunate Lady," "The Rape of the Lock," "An Essay on Man," "Epistle to Dr. Arbuthnot," "The Universal Prayer," "Ode on Solitude," Moral Essays, I.

SOME MINOR POETS OF POPE'S TIME.

Matthew Prior. (Page 336.) *Works,* ed. by Johnson (Aldine Poets); *Selected Poems,* ed. by Dobson (Scribner).

BIOGRAPHY. Dobson, "Matthew Prior," in *Eighteenth Century Vignettes* (Dodd); and also in the Introduction to his *Works,* ed. by Johnson.

John Gay. (Page 337.) *Poetical Works,* ed. by Underhill, 2 vols. (Scribner); *Poems,* Riverside edition (Houghton).

BIOGRAPHY AND CRITICISM. Life, in Underhill's edition of his *Works;* Essays in Dobson's *Miscellanies* (Dodd); *Westminster Review,* Vol. CXL, 1893.

Thomas Parnell. (Page 339.) *Poems,* ed. by Aitken (Aldine Poets); Goldsmith, "Life of Parnell," in *Works,* Vol. IV (Bohn).

AUTHORSHIP IN THE AUGUSTAN AGE.

Page 340. See general references to England of Pope (Study List, p. 20), and especially Beljame's *Le Public et les Hommes de Lettres en Angleterre au XVIIIe Siecle* (Hachette).

Richard Steele. (Page 344.) *Selections from Steele,* being papers from the *Tatler, Spectator, and Guardian,* ed. by Dobson (Clarendon Press); * *Selections,* ed. by G. R. Carpenter (Ginn).

BIOGRAPHY. Dobson, *Richard Steele* (E. W. S., Longmans); Aitken, *Life of Richard Steele,* 2 vols. (Scribner).

CRITICISM. John Forster, "Richard Steele," in *Biographical Essays* (Murray); Thackeray in *The English Humourists* (Holt).

Joseph Addison. (Page 351.) *Works,* ed. by Greene, 6 vols. (Macmillan); *Essays,* chosen and ed. by J. R. Green (Macmillan); *Criticisms on Paradise Lost,* ed. by Cook (Ginn); *Selections from Addison's papers in the Spectator,* ed. by Arnold (Clarendon Press); *Spectator,* ed. by Morley, 3 vols. (Routledge); * *Select Essays of Addison,* with Macaulay's essay on *Addison,* ed. by Thurber (Allyn & Bacon).

BIOGRAPHY. Courthope, *Addison* (E. M. L.); Lucy Aiken, *Life of Addison*, 2 vols. (London, 1843); Thackeray, *Henry Esmond* (*passim*).

CRITICISM. Hazlitt, "Periodical Essayists," in *English Comic Writers* ("Temple Classics"); Thackeray, in *The English Humourists;* Macaulay, essay on *Addison* (*supra*).

The History of the Novel. (Page 357.) Raleigh, *The English Novel from Its Origin to Sir Walter Scott* (Scribner); Simonds, *Introduction to the Study of English Fiction* (Heath); Cross, *Development of the English Novel* (Macmillan); Dunlop, *History of Prose Fiction*, 2 vols. (Bohn); Masson, *British Novelists and their Styles* (Lothrop); Tuckerman, *History of English Prose Fiction* (Putnam); Warren, *History of the Novel Previous to the Seventeenth Century* (Holt); Jusserand, *English Novel in the Time of Shakespeare* (Putnam); Stoddard, *Evolution of the English Novel* (Macmillan); Lanier, *The English Novel* (Scribner); Howells, *Criticism and Fiction* (Harper); Crawford, *The Novel; What It Is* (Macmillan); Matthews, *Historical Novel and Other Essays;* also his *Aspects of Fiction* (Scribner); Forsyth, *Novels and Novelists of the Eighteenth Century* (Appleton).

SUGGESTED READINGS. (Page 361.) Overbury's "Characters," in his *Works* (Library of Old Authors, Scribner); Earle, *Microcosmography* (Arber's English Reprints); *A Book of Characters*, selected from the writings of Overbury, Earle and Butler (Edinburgh, 1865). Compare these character-studies with the De Coverley papers.

Daniel Defoe. (Page 363.) *Works*, ed. by Aitken, 16 vols. (Dent); *Journal of the Plague Year* ("Temple Classics"); *Robinson Crusoe* (Everyman's Library); *History and Life of Colonel Jacque*, ed. by Aitken, 2 vols. (Dent); *Essay on Projects* (Cassell's National Library); *The Earlier Life and Chief Earlier Works*, ed. by Morley (Carisbrooke Library); *Selections from Defoe's Minor Novels*, ed. by Saintsbury (Macmillan).

BIOGRAPHY. Minto, *Defoe* (E. M. L.); Lee, *Life*, 3 vols. (London, 1869); Wright, *Life* (Coates); Forster, "Defoe," in *Historical and Biographical Essays* (London, 1860).

CRITICISM. *L. Stephen, "Defoe's Novels," in *Hours in a Library*, Vol. I (Putnam); Dennis, "Daniel Defoe," in *Studies in English Literature* (London, 1876); Forster, in *Historical and Biographical Essays*, Vol. II (London, 1858).

Jonathan Swift. (Page 372.) *Works*, ed. by Temple Scott, with Biographical Introduction by Lecky, 12 vols. (Bohn); *Gulliver's Travels* ("Temple Classics"); *Tale of a Tub, and Other Works*, ed. by Morley (Carisbrooke Library), includes selections from "Poems," and "Journal to Stella"; Stanley Lane-Poole, *Letters and Journals of Jonathan Swift* (Scribner). There are numerous expurgated editions of *Gulliver's Travels*, such as those published by Ginn & Co., and Maynard, Merrill & Co.

BIOGRAPHY. Craik, *Life*, 2 vols. (Macmillan); L. Stephen, *Swift* (E. M. L.).

CRITICISM. Collins, *Jonathan Swift; A Biographical and Critical Study* (Chatto); Moriarty, *Dean Swift and His Writings* (Scribner); Thackeray, in *The English Humourists* (Holt); Birrell, in *Men, Women and Books* (Scribner); Lecky, in *Leaders of Public Opinion in Ireland* (Appleton); Masson, in *The Three Devils* (Macmillan).

OTHER PROSE WRITERS OF THE EARLY EIGHTEENTH CENTURY.

John Arbuthnot. (Page 381.) Aitken, *Life and Works* (Clarendon Press).

Lord Bolingbroke. (Page 382.) *Works*, with *Life* by Goldsmith, 8 vols. (London, 1809); *Letters to Sir Wm. Wyndam and Pope* (Cassell's National Library); Selections in Pancoast's *Standard English Prose*.

BIOGRAPHY AND CRITICISM. Harrop, *Bolingbroke; a Political Study and Criticism* (Kegan Paul); * Collins, *Bolingbroke; an Historical Study* (Harper); Birrell, in *Essays About Men, Women, and Books* (Scribner); Sichel, *Bolingbroke and His Times*, 2 vols. (Longmans).

George Berkeley. (Page 385.) *Works*, ed. by Fraser, 4 vols. (Clarendon Press); *Selections from Berkeley*, ed. by Fraser (Clarendon Press).

BIOGRAPHY AND CRITICISM. *Life*, in Fraser's ed. of *Works:* * M. C. Tyler, "George Berkeley and his American Visit," in *Three Men of Letters* (Putnam).

RICHARDSON AND FIELDING.

Samuel Richardson. (Page 388.) *Works*, 20 vols. (Lippincott).

BIOGRAPHY. Dobson, *Samuel Richardson* (E. M. L); L. Stephen, in *Hours in a Library*, Vol. I (Putnam); Traill, in *The New Fiction* (New Amsterdam).

Henry Fielding. (Page 390.) *Works*, ed. by Saintsbury, 12 vols. (Dent); *Journal of a Voyage to Lisbon*, ed. by Dobson (Whittingham); *Tom Jones, Joseph Andrews*, and *Amelia*, in the Bohn Library.

BIOGRAPHY AND CRITICISM. Lawrence, *Life and Times of Henry Fielding* (London, 1855); Dobson, *Henry Fielding* (E. M. L.); Hazlitt, "On the English Novelists," in *Lectures on the English Comic Writers;* L. Stephen, in *Hours in a Library*, Vol. III (Putnam); G. B. Smith, "Our First Great Novelist," in *Poets and Novelists* (Smith and E.).

TOBIAS SMOLLETT.

Tobias Smollett. (Page 391.) *Works*, ed. with memoir by Saintsbury, 12 vols. (Lippincott); *Roderick Random, Peregrine Pickle*, and *Humphrey Clinker*, in the Bohn Library.

BIOGRAPHY AND CRITICISM. Hannay, *Life* (G. W. S.); Walter Scott, "Memoir," in *Biographical Memoirs;* Thackeray, in *The English Humourists* (Holt).

PART IV.

THE MODERN ENGLISH PERIOD.

(Pages 393–625.)

BEGINNING OF MODERN LITERATURE.   (Page 393–516.)

HISTORY AND CRITICISM. Mrs. Oliphant, *Literary History of England in the End of the Eighteenth and Beginning of the Nineteenth Century*, 3 vols. (Macmillan); * Saintsbury, *History of Nineteenth Century Literature*, 1780–1895 (Macmillan); Herford, *The Age of Wordsworth* (Handbooks of English Literature Macmillan); Saintsbury, *Essays on English Literature*, 1780–1860 (Scribner); Beers, *English Romanticism in the Eighteenth Century* (Holt); * Phelps, *Beginnings of the English Romantic Movement* (Ginn); Perry, *English Literature in the Eighteenth Century* (Harper); Gosse, *Eighteenth Century Literature* (Macmillan); Dowden, *French Revolution and English Literature* (Scribner); * Dowden, *Studies in Literature*, 1789–1877 (Scribner); Courthope, "The Revolution in English Poetry and Fiction," in *Cambridge Modern History*, Vol. X, Chap. XXII (Macmillan). See also Vol. IV of Brandes, *Main Currents in Nineteenth Century Literature* (Macmillan).

Samuel Johnson. (Page 401.) *Works*, 11 vols. (Oxford, 1823–25); *Lives of the Poets*, ed. by Hill, 3 vols. (Clarendon Press); *Rasselas*, ed. by Hill (Clarendon Press); *Vanity of Human Wishes*, ed. by Payne (Clarendon Press); *Selections*, ed. by Hill (Clarendon Press); *Lives of the Poets*, 3 vols. (Bohn); *Letters*, ed. by Hill, 2 vols. (Clarendon Press).

BIOGRAPHY. * Boswell, *Life*, ed. by Hill, 6 vols. (Oxford Wareh.); L. Stephen, *Johnson* (E. M. L.); Grant, *Life* (G. W. S.); * Macaulay, *Life*, 1856, in Encyclopædia Britannica, 9th ed.

CRITICISM. L. Stephen, "Dr. Johnson's Writings," in *Hours in a Library*, Vol. II (Putnam); Birrell, "Doctor Johnson," in *Obiter Dicta*, 2d series (Scribner); Hill, *Dr. Johnson; His Friends and His Critics* (Smith, Elder); Seccombe, *Age of Johnson* (Handbooks of English Literature, Macmillan); Landor, "Imaginary Conversations between Samuel Johnson and John Horne Tooke," in *Imaginary Conversations*, Vol. III (Dent); * Carlyle, "Samuel Johnson," in *Critical and Miscellaneous Essays;* Macaulay, "Samuel Johnson," in *Essays*, Vol. I (a review of Croker's ed. of Boswell).

SUGGESTED READINGS. "London," " The Vanity of Human Wishes," "Rasselas," "Letter to Lord Chesterfield," lives of "Pope," "Gray," and "Collins," or three or four other representative biographies, from the *Lives of the Poets;* Prologue spoken by Mr. Garrick, at the opening of Theatre Royal, Drury Lane.

Edward Gibbon. (Page 403.) Morison, *Gibbon* (E. M. L.); Autobiography, ed. by G. B. Hill (Putnam); Bagehot, "Gibbon," in *Literary Studies,* Vol. II. (Longmans).

THE WRITERS OF THE NEW SCHOOL.

Allan Ramsay. (Page 408.) *Poems,* with Life, 2 vols. (Paisley, 1877); *Poems,* with Biographical Sketch by J. L. Robertson (Canterbury Poets); *Gentle Shepherd* (Simpkin).
BIOGRAPHY. Smeaton, *Life* ("Famous Scots," Scribner).

James Thomson. (Page 410.) *Poems,* ed. by Tovey, 2 vols. (Aldine Poets); *Seasons,* and *Castle of Indolence,* ed. by Robertson (Clarendon Press); *Same,* ed. by Greene (Athenæum Press).
BIOGRAPHY. H. S. Salt, *Life* (London, 1889); Morel, *James Thomson, sa vie et ses œuvres* (Hachette); Bayne, *Life* ("Famous Scots," Scribner); Hazlitt, "Thomson and Cowper," in *Lectures on the English Poets* (Dodd); Johnson, in *Lives of the Poets* (Clarendon Press).

John Dyer. (Page 412.) *Poems,* ed. by Thomas (Welsh Library Unwin); Selections, with Essay by Dowden, in Ward's *English Poets,* Vol. III (Macmillan).
BIOGRAPHY. Johnson, in *Lives of the Poets* (Clarendon Press).

William Collins. (Page 412.) *Poems,* with Memoir, ed. by Thomas (Aldine Poets); Selections, with Essay by Swinburne, in Ward's *English Poets,* Vol. III (Macmillan).
BIOGRAPHY AND CRITICISM. Johnson, in *Lives of the Poets* (Clarendon Press); Swinburne, in *Miscellanies* (Scribner).

Thomas Gray. (Page 412.) *Works in Prose and Verse,* ed. by Gosse, 4 vols. (Macmillan); *Poetical Works,* ed. by Bradshaw (Aldine Poets); *Letters,* ed. by Tovey, 2 vols. (Bohn); *Selections,* ed. by Phelps (Athenæum Press).
BIOGRAPHY. Gosse, *Life* (E. M. L.); Johnson, in *Lives of the Poets* (Clarendon Press); Lowell, in *Latest Literary Essays* (Houghton); M. Arnold, in *Essays in Criticism,* 2nd series (Macmillan).

James Beattie. (Page 413.) *Poems,* ed. by Dyce (Aldine Poets).

Thomas Chatterton. (Page 419.) *Poetical Works,* ed. by Skeat, 2 vols. (Aldine Poets); *Poetical Works,* with Prefatory Notice by Richmond (Canterbury Poets); *Selections,* with Essay by Watts-Dunton, in *Ward's English Poets,* Vol. III (Macmillan).

BIOGRAPHY. Masson, *Life* (Dodd); Beers, in *History of English Romanticism in the Eighteenth Century* (Holt); R. Noel, in *Poetry and Poets* (Kegan Paul).

George Crabbe. (Page 413.) *Poetical Works*, with Life, ed. by his Son (Scribner); *The Borough* ("Temple Classics"); *Selected Poems* (Canterbury Poets).

BIOGRAPHY AND CRITICISM. Ainger, *Life* (E. M. L.); Kebbel, *Life*, in G. W. S. (Scribner); L. Stephen, in *Hours in a Library*, Vol. II (Putnam); Woodberry, in *Makers of Literature* (Macmillan); More, in *Shelburne Essays*, 2nd series (Putnam).

William Blake. (Page 416.) *Poems*, with memoir by W. M. Rossetti (Aldine Poets); *Poems*, with specimens of prose writings (Canterbury Poets).

BIOGRAPHY AND CRITICISM. Gilchrist, *Life* (Macmillan); Swinburne, *William Blake; a Critical Essay* (Chatto).

Oliver Goldsmith. (Page 422.) *Works*, with Life, ed. by Gibbs, 5 vols. (Bohn); *Poems, Plays, and Essays*, ed. by Aikin and Tuckerman (Crowell); *Miscellaneous Works*, ed. by Masson (Globe Ed.); *Vicar of Wakefield, Poems and Plays* (Morley's Universal Library); *Selections from Goldsmith*, ed. by Dobson (Clarendon Press); *Vicar of Wakefield*, ed. by Mary A. Jordan (Longmans); *Select Poems*, ed. by Rolfe (American Book Co.); *She Stoops to Conquer* (Cassell's National Library); *Plays* (Bohn).

BIOGRAPHY. Forster, *Life and Times of Oliver Goldsmith*, 2 vols. (Chapman and H.); Dobson, *Life* (G. W. S.); Black, *Life* (E. M. L.); Irving, *Life* (Putnam).

CRITICISM. De Quincey, in *Essays on the Poets;* Macaulay, in *Essays*, Vol. IV; Dobson, "Goldsmith's Plays and Poems," in *Miscellanies* (Dodd); *Thackeray, in *The English Humourists* (Holt); Howitt, in *Homes and Haunts of the British Poets* (Routledge).

Edmund Burke. (Page 429.) *Selections from Burke*, ed. by Payne, 3 vols. (Clarendon Press); *Works*, 6 vols. (Bohn); *Selections from Burke*, ed. by Perry (Holt); *Essay on the Sublime and Beautiful* ("Temple Classics"); *American Speeches and Letters on the Irish Question* (Morley's Universal Library); *Letter to a Noble Lord*, with Introduction and notes, ed. by Smyth (Ginn). Most of the important works are printed separately in the Bohn Library.

BIOGRAPHY. Prior, *Life* (Bohn); Morley, *Life* (E. M. L.).

CRITICISM. Dowden, in *The French Revolution and English Literature* (Scribner); L. Stephen, in *History of English Thought in the Eighteenth Century*, Vol. II (Putnam); Buckle, in *History of Civilization in England* (Longmans); Woodrow Wilson, "The Interpreter of English Liberty," in *Mere Literature* (Houghton); Morley, *Edmund Burke; an Historical Study* (Macmillan).

William Cowper. (Page 436.) *Works*, ed. by Benham (Globe Ed.); *Selections from the Poetical Works*, ed. by J. O. Murray (Athenæum Press); *Selections from Cowper, with Life,* ed. by Griffith, 2 vols. (Clarendon Press); *Selections from Poems*, ed. by Oliphant (Macmillan); *Letters*, ed. by Benham (Macmillan); *The Task* ("Temple Classics"); Selections from "The Task," in Pancoast's *Standard English Poems*; Selections in Cassell's National Library, and Canterbury Poets.

BIOGRAPHY. Goldwin Smith, *Cowper* (E. M. L.); Wright, *Life* (Unwin); *Life*, Southey, 2 vols. (Bohn); Benham, "Memoirs," in Globe Ed. of *Works* (Macmillan).

CRITICISM. Bagehot, "William Cowper," in *Literary Studies*, Vol. I (Longman); * L. Stephen, "Cowper and Rousseau," in *Hours in a Library*, Vol. III (Putnam), Brooke, "Cowper," in *Theology in the English Poets* (Appleton); Woodberry, "Three Men of Piety — Bunyan, Cowper, Channing," in *Studies in Letters and Life* (Macmillan); * Sainte-Beuve, "Cowper," in *English Portraits* (Translations from *Causeries du Lundi*, (Holt); Dobson, in *Eighteenth Century Vignettes* (Dodd).

SUGGESTED READINGS. Cowper's works will be found to repay close and repeated reading, both for their intrinsic merits and for their intimate relations to the literary and general history of his time. The student should make himself thoroughly familiar with the *Letters*, which can hardly be over-praised, and with *The Task;* he should know, of course, all the best of the shorter poems (*Lines on the Receipt of My Mother's Picture, The Loss of the Royal George, The Castaway, John Gilpin*, etc.), and he should have at least some acquaintance with the earlier poems (*The Progress of Error, Tirocinium,* etc.) which are often unduly neglected.

Robert Burns. (Page 444.)   *Poetical Works*, ed. by W. E. Henley (Houghton); *Complete Works and Letters*, ed. by Smith (Globe Ed.); *Poems and Songs*, 2 vols. "Temple Classics"; *Poems* (Canterbury Poets); *The Centenary Burns*, ed. by Henley and Henderson, 4 vols. (Whittaker); *Selections from the Poems*, ed. by Dow (Athenæum Press); *Life and Works*, ed. by Chambers, revised by Wallace (Chambers).

BIOGRAPHY. Shairp, *Burns* (E. M. L.); Blackie, *Life* (G. W. S.); Lockhart, *Life*, ed. by Douglass (Bohn).

CRITICISM. * Carlyle, (a) "Burns," in *Critical and Miscellaneous Essays;* (b) "Burns, The Hero as Man of Letters," in *Heroes and Hero Worship;* a convenient edition containing both essays is in Longmans' English Classics; Shairp, "Scottish Song and Burns," in *Aspects of Poetry* (Houghton); Stevenson, "Some Aspects of Robert Burns," in *Familiar Studies of Men and Books* (Scribner); Hazlitt, in *Lectures on the English Poets* (Dodd); Lang, "To Burns," in *Letters to Dead Authors* (Scribner); Henley, "Life, Genius, Achievement," essay in his edition of the *Works* (Houghton); Brooke, "Burns," in *Theology in the English Poets* (Appleton); Forster, "Burns," in *Great Teachers* (Redway); see also poems on Burns by Wordsworth and Whittier.

SUGGESTED READINGS. The following brief list contains only a few of Burn's more notable and familiar poems. It is intended as only an introduction to more extended study.

I Songs: "O Wert Thou in the Cauld Blast," "John Anderson, My Jo," "To Mary in Heaven," "Highland Mary," "Ye Banks and Braes o' Bonnie Doon," "Flow Gently Sweet Afton," "O, My Luve's like a Red, Red Rose," "Scots Wha Hae wi' Wallace Bled," "Is there for Honest Poverty," "Macpherson's Farewell," "Auld Lang Syne."

II. Sympathy with Nature and Animals: "To a Mountain Daisy," "To a Mouse on Turning up her Nest with a Plough," "On Scaring some Water-fowl in Loch Turit," "On Seeing a Wounded Hare Limp by Me."

III. "Address to the Deil," "Address to the Unco' Guid."

IV. "The Cotter's Saturday Night," "Tam o' Shanter," "The Twa Dogs," "The Brigs of Ayr," "The Jolly Beggars," "The Holy Fair."

William Wordsworth. (Page 450.) *Works of William and Dorothy Wordsworth*, ed. by Knight, 12 vols. (Macmillan); *Poetical Works*, ed. by Morley (Globe Ed.); *Selections from the Poems*, ed. by Dowden (Athenæum Press); *Selections*, ed. by M. Arnold (Golden Treasury Series); *Wordsworth's Prefaces*, ed. by George (Heath); *The Prelude*, *Sonnets*, and *The Excursion*, 3 vols. ("Temple Classics").

Biography. *Life*, Vols. IX, X, XI, of Knight's ed. of Wordsworth's *Works* (Macmillan); * Myers, *Life* (E. M. L.); Rawnsley, *Literary Associations of the English Lakes*, 2 vols. (Macmillan); * Legouis, *Early Life; a Study of the Prelude*, translated by J. M. Matthews (Dent).

Criticism. De Quincey, "On Wordsworth's Poetry," in *Works* (Masson's ed., Black); Saintsbury, "Wordsworth and Coleridge; Their Companions and Adversaries," in *History of Criticism*, Vol. III (Dodd); Hazlitt, (*a*) "On Wordsworth," in *Lectures on the English Poets* (Dodd); (*b*) "Wordsworth," in *Spirit of the Age* (Macmillan); Bagehot, "Wordsworth, Tennyson and Browning," in *Literary Studies*, Vol. II (Longmans); Shairp, (*a*) "Wordsworth, the Man and Poet," in *Studies in Poetry and Philosophy* (Houghton); (*b*) "The Three Yarrows," "The White Doe of Rylstone," in *Aspects of Poetry* (Houghton); Lowell, "Wordsworth," in *Among my Books*, Vol. II (Houghton); Hutton, "The Genius of Wordsworth," in Literary Essays (Macmillan); * L. Stephen, "Wordsworth's Ethics," in *Hours in a Library*, Vol. III (Putnam); * Arnold, "Wordsworth," in *Essays in Criticism*, 2d series (Macmillan); Courthope, "Wordsworth's Theory of Poetry," in *Liberal Movement in English Literature* (Murray); Lee, *Dorothy Wordsworth* (Dodd); C. F. Johnson, "Wordsworth," in *Three Americans and Three Englishmen* (Whittaker); Aubrey de Vere, in *Essays, Chiefly on Poetry* (Macmillan); Pater, in *Appreciations* (Macmillan); Vida D. Scudder, "Wordsworth and the New Democracy," in *Life of the Spirit in the Modern English Poets* (Houghton); * Swinburne, "Wordsworth and Byron," in *Miscellanies* (Scribner); Fields, in *Yesterdays with Authors* (Houghton); R. W. Church, in *Dante and other Essays* (Macmillan); Magnus, *A Primer of Wordsworth* (Methuen); Calvert, *Wordsworth* (Lee & Shepard).

SUGGESTED READINGS. " Ode on Intimations of Immortality from Recollections of Early Childhood," "Ode to Duty," "To the Cuckoo," "The Reverie of Poor Susan," "My Heart Leaps Up," etc., "The Daffodils," "Three Years She Grew," etc.; "Lines on Revisiting Tintern Abbey," "Laodamia." *Sonnets:* "The World is Too Much With Us," "Milton," "Composed upon Westminster Bridge. September 3, 1802." "They Dreamed Not of a Perishable Home," "Written in London, September, 1802 "; "When I Have Borne in Memory What Has Tamed." *Narrative:* "Hart-leap Well," "Ruth," "Michael," "The Brothers," "Rob Roy's Grave." *Lyrical:* "The Solitary Reaper," "The Primrose of the Rock," "The Grave of Burns," "She Dwelt among the Untrodden Ways," "She was a Phantom of Delight," "The Affliction of Margaret," "A Poet's Epitaph," "Expostulation and Reply," "The Tables Turned."

Samuel Taylor Coleridge. (Page 459.) *Poetical Works*, ed. by Campbell (Globe Ed.); *Friend, Biographia Literaria and Lay Sermons, Aids to Reflection and Confession of an Inquiring Spirit, Lectures on Shakespeare and other English Poets,* all in the Bohn Library; * *Selections from Prose Writings*, ed. by Beers (Holt); *Letters*, ed. by E. H. Coleridge, 2 vols. (Houghton).

BIOGRAPHY. * Campbell, *Life* (Macmillan); Traill, *Life* (E. M. L.); Caine, *Life* (G. W. S.); Allsop, *Letters, Conversations and Reflections of S. T. Coleridge*, 2 vols. (1836); Cottle, *Reminiscences of Coleridge and Southey* (London, 1847); Sara Coleridge, *Memoir and Letters* (Harper).

CRITICISM. Brandl, *Coleridge and the English Romantic Movement*, translated by Lady Eastlake (1887); Shairp, "Coleridge as Poet and Philosopher," in *Studies in Poetry and Philosophy*, 2d ed. (Houghton); Swinburne, in *Essays and Studies* (Scribner); Lowell, "Address in Westminster Abbey," in *Democracy and Other Addresses* (Houghton); C. F. Johnson, in *Three Americans and Three Englishmen* (Whittaker); Pater, in *Appreciations* (Macmillan); Woodberry, (*a*) " Coleridge and Sir George Beaumont," in *Studies in Letters and Life* (Macmillan); (*b*) "Coleridge," in *Makers of Literature* (Macmillan); Watson, "Coleridge's Supernaturalism," in *Excursions in Criticism* (Lane); Martineau, "Personal Influences on Our Theology — Coleridge," in *Essays Philosophical and Theological*, Vol. I (Holt); Tulloch, "Coleridge and His School," in *Religious Thought in Britain during the Nineteenth Century* (Scribner); Dowden, in *New Studies in Literature* (Scribner); Saintsbury, in *Essays in English Literature, 1780–1860* (Scribner); Hazlitt, in *The Spirit of the Age* (Macmillan); Brooke, in *Theology in the English Poets* (Appleton).

SUGGESTED READINGS. "The Ancient Mariner," " Christabel," " Kubla Khan," " Destruction of the Bastile," " To a Young Lady, with Poems on the French Revolution," " France, an Ode," " Youth and Age," " Complaint and Reply," " Work Without Hope," " Dejection, an Ode," " The Wanderings of Cain " (prose poem). The student should master at least as much of Coleridge's prose as is given in Beers' "Selections from Coleridge's Prose" (*supra*). Brief selections are given in Pancoast's "Standard English Prose" (Holt).

Sir Walter Scott (Page 470.) *Waverley Novels*, ed. by Lang (Estes); *Waverley Novels*, 25 vols. (Dryburgh Ed., Macmillan); *Poetical Works*, ed. by Lang 2 vols. (Macmillan); *Poetical Works*, ed. by Palgrave (Globe Ed.).

BIOGRAPHY. Lockhart, *Life* (Macmillan); *Journal of Sir Walter Scott, November*, 1825, *to April*, 1832, 2 vols. (Harper); Gilfillan, *Life* (Edinburgh, 1884); Hutton, *Life* (E. M. L.); Saintsbury, *Life* (Scribner); Lang, *Life* ("Literary Lives," Scribner).

CRITICISM. Jeffrey, (*a*) "Lay of the Last Minstrel," (*b*) "The Waverley Novels," in *Contributions to the Edinburgh Review* (Appleton); Carlyle, in *Miscellaneous Essays* (Scribner); L. Stephen, "Some Words about Sir Walter Scott," in *Hours in a Library*, Vol. I (Putnam); Lang, in *Letters to Dead Authors* (Scribner); Shairp, "Homeric Spirit in Walter Scott," in *Aspects of Poetry* (Houghton); Lang, in his Introduction to *Lyrics and Ballads of Sir Walter Scott* (Scribner); Bagehot, "The Waverley Novels," in *Literary Studies*, Vol. II (Longmans); Masson, in *British Novelists and Their Style* (Lothrop); Saintsbury, in *Essays in English Literature* (Scribner); Hazlitt, "Scott and Dumas," in *The Spirit of the Age* (Macmillan).

SUGGESTED READINGS. Any formal list of readings from Scott's works is, or ought to be, superfluous, but there is good reason to fear that Scott is neglected by readers of the present day to their great detriment. It should be a delight as well as a duty to read and re-read all of the "Waverley Novels," the "Journal" and at least "The Lay of the Last Minstrel," "Marmion," "The Lady of the Lake," "Rokeby" and the best of the shorter poems. A knowledge of Lockhart's "Life of Scott" (which, with Boswell's "Johnson" holds a foremost place in English biographical literature) is, of course, indispensable.

Charles Lamb. (Page 480.) *Works*, ed. by Ainger, 6 vols. (Macmillan); *Essays of Elia, Last Essays of Elia, Essays and Sketches*, all in "Temple Classics"; *Tales from Shakespeare*, ed. by Ainger (Macmillan); *Dramatic Essays*, ed. by Matthews (Dodd).

BIOGRAPHY AND CRITICISM. * Ainger, *Lamb* (E. M. L.); Lucas, *Life*, 2 vols. (Putnam); Annie Gilchrist, *Life of Mary Lamb* (Famous Women) (Little); Talfourd, *Memoirs of Charles Lamb* (Gibbings); Hazlitt, *The Lambs* (Scribner); Proctor (Barry Cornwall), *Charles Lamb* (Little); De Quincey, (*a*) "Recollections," (*b*) "C. Lamb," in his *Works*, ed. by Masson, Vols. III and V (Black); Swinburne, "Charles Lamb and George Wither," in *Miscellanies* (Scribner); Birrell,(*a*) in *Obiter Dicta*, 2nd Series (Scribner); (*b*) in *Res Judicatæ* (Scribner); Pater, in *Appreciations* (Macmillan); Harrison, "Lamb and Keats," in *Tennyson, Ruskin, Mill and Other Essays* (Macmillan); Woodberry, "Charles Lamb, or Elia," in *Makers of Literature* (Macmillan).

SUGGESTED READINGS. *Essays of Elia:* "Christ's Hospital Five and Thirty Years Ago," "The Two Races of Men," "The Old and New Schoolmaster," "Valentine's Day," "Modern Gallantry," "Dream Children; a Reverie," "Distant Correspondents," "A Dissertation upon Roast Pig," "A Bachelor's Complaint of the Behavior of Married People," "Captain Jackson." *Criticism and Poetry.* "On the Tragedies of Shakespeare," "Hester," "The Old Familiar Faces."

Thomas De Quincey. (Page 482.) *Works*, ed. by D. Masson, 14 vols. (Black); *Confessions of an Opium Eater* ("Temple Classics"); * *Joan of Arc and English Mail Coach*, ed. by J. M. Hart (Holt); * *Flight of a Tartar Tribe*, ed. by C. S. Baldwin (Longmans); *Selections*, ed. by Bliss Perry (Doubleday); *Selections*, ed. by M. H. Turk (Athenæum Press).

BIOGRAPHY AND CRITICISM. A. H. Japp (H. A. Page, pseud.), *Life and Writings* (Scribner); De Quincey *Memorials*, ed. by Japp, 2 vols. (Heinemann); Burton, "A Vision of Mighty Book Hunters," in *The Book Hunter* (Lippincott); * Masson, *Life* (E. M. L.); Findlay, *Personal Recollections of De Quincey* (A. and C. Black); L. Stephen, in *Hours in a Library*, Vol. I (Putnam); Saintsbury, in *Essays in English Literature, 1780–1860* (Scribner); Masson, "Prose and Verse — De Quincey," in *Wordsworth, Shelley, Keats and other Essays* (Macmillan).

SUGGESTED READINGS. The various books of selections from De Quincey, given above, form an admirable introduction to the more extended study of his work, and make a list of readings unnecessary. Mention must be made, however, of the papers on " Murder Considered as One of the Fine Arts," remarkable not only for their irony and humour, but also for their narrative passages. A most charming example of De Quincey's humour will be found in the third chapter of his *Autobiography.*

BYRON AND SHELLEY.

Lord Byron. (Page 491.) *Works*, ed. by Prothero and Coleridge, 12 vols. (Scribner); *Childe Harold*, ed. by H. E. Tozer (Clarendon Press); *Selections*, ed. by M. Arnold (Golden Treasury Series); *Selections*, ed. by F. J. Carpenter (Holt); *Letters* (Camelot Series); *Siege of Corinth* ("Temple Classics").

BIOGRAPHY. Roden Noel, *Life* (G. W. S.); Nichol, *Life* (E. M. L.); Elze, *Lord Byron* (Murray); Jeaffreson, *The Real Lord Byron* (Amsterdam); Thomas Moore, *Life* (Murray); R. C. Dallas, *Recollections of Lord Byron* (Philadelphia, 1825); Leigh Hunt, *Lord Byron and His Contemporaries* (Philadelphia, 1828); J. Kennedy, *Conversations with Lord Byron* (London, 1830); Trelawney, *Recollections of Shelley and Byron* (Frowde).

CRITICISM. Hazlitt, in *Spirit of the Age* (Macmillan); Macaulay, in *Essays*, Vol. I (Longmans); Mazzini, "Byron and Goethe," in *Life and*

Writings, Vol. VI (Smith, Elder), also in his *Essays* (Camelot Series); Morley, in *Miscellanies*, Vol. I (Macmillan); Swinburne, (*a*) in *Essays and Studies* (Scribner), (*b*) "Wordsworth and Byron," in *Miscellanies* (Scribner); M. Arnold, in *Essays in Criticism*, 2d series (Macmillan); Lang, in *Letters to Dead Authors* (Scribner); Roden Noel, " Lord Byron and His Times," in *Essays on Poetry and Poets* (Kegan Paul); Dawson, in *Makers of Modern English* (Whittaker); Trent, "The Byron Revival," in *Authority of Criticism* (Scribner); Woodberry, "The Byron Centenary," in *Makers of Literature* (Macmillan).

SUGGESTED READINGS. "The Prisoner of Chillon," "There's not a Joy the World Can Give," "Childe Harold " (Cantos III and IV), "Lines on Completing His Thirty-sixth Year," "She Walks in Beauty Like the Night," "The Destruction of the Host of Sennacherib," "Manfred," "Cain."

Percy Bysshe Shelley. (Page 497.) *Works*, prose and verse, ed. by H. B. Forman, 8 vols. (Scribner); *Poetical Works*, ed. by Forman, 5 vols. (Aldine Poets); *Poetical Works*, ed. by Dowden; (Globe Ed.); *Selections* (Golden Treasury Series, also Heath's English Classics); *Essays and Letters* (Camelot Series); *Select Poems*, ed. by W. J. Alexander (Athenæum Press); *Poems*, ed. by Brooke (Macmillan); *Prometheus Unbound*, ed. by V. D. Scudder (Heath).

BIOGRAPHY. Dowden, *Life* (Scribner); Shairp, *Life* (G. W. S.); Symonds, *Life* (E. M. L.); D. F. MacCarthy, *Early Life* (London, 1872); G. B. Smith, *A Critical Biography* (Edinburgh, 1877); W. M. Rossetti, "Memoir," in his edition of the *Poems* (Moxon); J. C. Jeaffreson, *The Real Shelley*, 2 vols. (Hurst and B.); Helen Moore, *Mary Wollstonecraft Shelley* (Lippincott); F. Rabbe, *Shelley: The Man and Poet*, 2 vols. (London, 1888); Leigh Hunt, in *Lord Byron and His Contemporaries* (Philadelphia, 1828); De Quincey, "Notes on Shelley," in *Works*, Masson's ed., Vol. XI (Black); T. J. Hogg, *Life* (to 1814), 2 vols. (London, 1858); Trelawney, *Recollections of Shelley and Byron* (Frowde); *Shelley Memorials*, ed. by Lady Shelley (London, 1859); Biagi, *Last Days of Shelley, New Details from Unpublished Documents* (Unwin).

CRITICISM. Bagehot, in *Literary Studies*, Vol. I (Longmans); Masson, in *Wordsworth, Shelley and Keats* (Macmillan); H. S. Salt, *A Shelley Primer* (Reeves and T.); Hutton, "Shelley's Poetical Mysticism," in *Essays Theological and Literary*, Vol. II (2d ed. 1877, Macmillan); Shairp, "Shelley as a Lyric Poet," in *Aspects of Poetry* (Houghton); C. F. Johnson, in *Three Americans and Three Englishmen* (Whittaker); Lang, "To Shelley," in *Letters to Dead Authors* (Scribner); Roden Noel. in *Essays on Poetry and Poets* (Kegan Paul); Dowden, (*a*) "Shelley's Philosophical View of Reform," (*b*) "Last Words on Shelley," in *Transcripts and Studies* (Scribner); M. Arnold, in *Essays in Criticism*, 2d series (Macmillan); Woodberry, in *Studies in Letters and Life* (Macmillan); Dawson, in *Makers of Modern Literature* (Whittaker);

Trent, "Apropos of Shelley," in *Authority of Criticism* (Scribner);
* Vida D. Scudder, "The Prometheus Unbound of Shelley," in *Atlantic Monthly*, Vol. LXX, 1892.

SUGGESTED READINGS. "Adonais," "The Sensitive Plant," "Alastor," "Prometheus Unbound." *Shorter Poems:* "The Skylark," "The Cloud," "Ode to the West Wind," "Arethusa," "Lines written among the Euganean Hills," "Stanzas written in Dejection, near Naples," "Mont Blanc," "Lines written in the Vale of Chamouni" (*cf.* Coleridge's "Mont Blanc"), "Mutability," "A Lament," " One Word is too often Profaned." In studying Shelley as a lyric poet the reader should turn, in addition to the above, to the choruses in " Prometheus Unbound" and "Hellas." Note particularly the "Life of Life, thy Lips Enkindle," from the former, and the last chorus from the latter of these two poems.

John Keats. (Page 504.) *Complete Works*, ed. by Forman, 5 vols. (Crowell); *Poetical Works*, ed. by Forman (Clarendon Press); *Poetical Works*, ed. by Lord Houghton (Aldine Poets); *Poems*, ed. by Palgrave (Golden Treasury Series); *Selections*, ed. by Arlo Bates (Athenæum Press).

BIOGRAPHY. * Colvin, *Life* (E. M. L.); W. M. Rossetti, *Life* (G. W. S.); *Love Letters of Keats to Fanny Brawne*, ed by Forman (Reeves and T.); *Letters of Keats to His Family and Friends*, ed. by Colvin (Macmillan).

CRITICISM. Masson, in *Wordsworth, Shelley and Keats* (Macmillan); Lowell, in *Among My Books*, 2d series (Houghton); * M. Arnold, in *Essays in Criticism*, 2d series (Macmillan); Swinburne, in *Miscellanies* (Scribner); Roden Noel, in *Essays on Poetry and Poets* (Kegan Paul); Woodberry, "The Promise of Keats," in *Studies in Letters and Life* (Macmillan); Hudson, in *Studies in Interpretation* (Putnam); Courthope, "Poetry, Music and Painting: Coleridge and Keats," in *Liberal Movement in English Literature* (Murray); M. Schuyler, "Centenary of Keats," in *Forum*, Vol. XX, 1895; Watson, "Keats and Mr. Colvin," in *Excursions in Criticism* (Macmillan).

SUGGESTED READINGS. 1. *Romantic and Mediæval:* "The Eve of St. Agnes," "The Eve of St. Mark," "La Belle Dame Sans Merci." *Classical Poems:* "Lamia," "Ode on a Grecian Urn," "Hyperion." *Personal Poems, Odes, Sonnets, etc:* "Ode to a Nightingale," "Ode to Autumn," "Ode on Melancholy," "Robin Hood." *Sonnets:* " On First Looking into Chapman's Homer," "Keen, Fitful Gusts are Whispering Here and There," "To One Who has been Long in City Pent," "On the Sea," "On Seeing the Elgin Marbles," "Bright Star, Would I Were Steadfast as Thou Art " (Keats' last sonnet).

VICTORIAN ENGLAND.

(Pages 516–625.)

I. HISTORY AND CRITICISM. *History of England.* Part III by T. F. Tout (Rivingtons); McCarthy, *History of Our Own Times from the Accession of Queen Victoria to 1880,* 2 vols. (Harper); McCarthy, *The Epoch of Reform,* 1830–1850 (Scribner); McCarthy, *England under Gladstone* (Scribner); Walpole, *History of England since 1815* (Longmans). *The Reign of Queen Victoria,* ed. by T. H. Ward, 2 vols. (Smith, Elder), includes a good chapter on Victorian literature. Oman, *England in the Nineteenth Century* (Longmans); Paul, *History of Modern England,* 5 vols. (Macmillan); Escott, *Social Transformations of the Victorian Age* (Seeley); Huxley, *Advance of Science in the Last Half Century* (Appleton).

II. LITERARY HISTORY AND CRITICISM. For general literary movements of the time, Dowden's *Studies in Literature* (Macmillan) and Dowden's *Transcripts and Studies* (Macmillan) will be found especially helpful. For a comparison of Elizabethan with Victorian poetry see J. A. Symonds, *Essays Speculative and Suggestive,* Vol. II (Chapman); Stedman, *Victorian Poets* (Houghton); F. Harrison, *Studies in Early Victorian Literature* (Lane); Beers, *English Romanticism in XIX Century* (Holt); Saintsbury, *History of Nineteenth Century Literature,* 1780–1895 (Macmillan); Saintsbury, *Essays on English Literature,* 1780–1860 (Dent, 1895); * Walker, *The Age of Tennyson* (Bell); Oliphant, *Victorian Literature* (Macmillan); Scudder, *Life of the Spirit in the Modern English Poets* (Houghton); Dawson, *Makers of English Prose, Makers of English Poetry,* and *Makers of English Fiction* (Revell); Traill in *The New Fiction and Other Essays* (Amsterdam).

Macaulay. (Page 526.) *Works,* edited by Lady Trevelyan, 8 vols. (Longmans); Essays on *Addison, Milton,* and the two essays on *Johnson,* are published in Longmans' English Classics. *The Historical Essays of Macaulay,* and the *Select Essays of Macaulay,* edited by S. Thurber (Allyn and Bacon); *Critical and Historical Essays,* 5 vols. ("Temple Classics"); *The Lays of Ancient Rome,* ed. by Rolfe (Harper).

BIOGRAPHY AND CRITICISM. Trevelyan, *Life and Letters,* 2 vols. (Harper), is the standard life. Morrison, *Life* (E. M. L.); Bagehot, Essay in *Literary Studies,* Vol. II (Longmans); J. Morley, in *Miscellanies,* Vol. I (Macmillan); M. Arnold, in *Mixed Essays* (Macmillan); F. Harrison, in *Studies in Early Victorian Writers* (Lane); L. Stephen, in *Hours in a Library,* Vol. III (Putnam).

Carlyle. (Page 529.) *Works,* Introduction by H.D. Traill, 30 vols., Centenary Ed. (Scribner); *Carlyle's Correspondence with Emerson,* 2 vols., ed. by C. E. Norton (Houghton); *Heroes and Hero-Worship,* also *Sartor Resartus,* ed. by MacMechan (Athenæum Press); *Essay* *on Burns*, ed. by Gore (Macmillan); *Critical and Miscellaneous Essays* (Appleton).

BIOGRAPHY. Froude, *Thomas Carlyle; A History of the First Forty Years of His Life*, 2 vols. (Harper); Froude, *Thomas Carlyle; A History of His Life in London*, 1834–1881, 2 vols. (Harper); Alex. Carlyle, *New Letters of Thomas Carlyle*, 2 vols. (Lane); Garnett, *Life* (G.W. S.); Nichol, *Life* (E. M. L.); *Letters and Memorials of Jane Welsh Carlyle*, ed. by Froude, 2 vols. (Scribner); Alex. Carlyle, *New Letters and Memorials of Jane Welsh Carlyle*, 2 vols. (Lane); Masson, *Thomas Carlyle Personally and in His Writings* (Macmillan); Macpherson, *Thomas Carlyle* ("Famous Scots," Scribner).

CRITICISM. Japp, *Three Great Teachers of Our Own Time* (Smith, Elder); John Morley, in *Miscellanies*, Vol. I (Macmillan); Lowell, in *Literary Essays*, Vol. II (Houghton); Peter Bayne, in *Lessons from My Masters* (Harper); Shairp, "Prose Poets, Carlyle," in *Aspects of Poetry* (Houghton); John Tulloch, "Thomas Carlyle as a Religious Teacher," in *Movements of Religious Thought in Britain* (Longmans); Birrell, in *Obiter Dicta*, Vol. I (Scribner); Hutton, in *Modern Guides of English Thought in Matters of Faith* (Macmillan); Arnold, "Emerson," in *Addresses in America* (Macmillan); Frederick Harrison, in *Studies in Early Victorian Writers* (Lane); Robertson, in *Modern Humanists* (Sonnenschein); Brownell, in *Victorian Prose Masters* (Scribner).

SUGGESTED READINGS. Among the most notable and representative of Carlyle's shorter works are: **Sartor Resartus, Heroes and Hero Worship, Past and Present*, the Inaugural address at Edinburgh *On the Choice of Books*, and the essays on **Burns, Johnson*, and *Richter*.

Ruskin. (Page 541.) Works, Brantwood Ed., 20 vols., ed. by C. E. Norton (Longmans); **Scudder, An Introduction to the Writings of John Ruskin* (Leach). [This consists of selections from Ruskin, admirably classified.] *Selected Essays and Letters*, ed. by Hafford (Ginn); *Sesame and Lilies*, ed. by Root (Holt).

BIOGRAPHY AND CRITICISM. **John Ruskin, Præterita, Scenes and Thoughts of My Past Life* (Wiley Sons); Collingwood, *The Life and Work of John Ruskin*, 2 vols. (Houghton); Geddes, *John Ruskin Economist*, ed. by Baildor (Simpkin); Mather, *John Ruskin, His Life and Teaching* (Warne); Waldstein, *John Ruskin, His Influence Upon Modern Thought and Life* (Harper); Hobson, *John Ruskin, Social Reformer* (Estes); Saintsbury, "Ruskin," in *Corrected Impressions* (Dodd); Frederick Harrison, "Ruskin as a Master of Prose," "Ruskin as a Prophet," "Ruskin's Eightieth Birthday," in *Tennyson, Ruskin, Mill* (Macmillan); and **Life in E. M. L.;* Brownell, in *Victorian Prose Masters* (Scribner); Robertson, in *Modern Humanists* (Sonnenschein).

SUGGESTED READINGS. *Sesame and Lilies* (fine in places, but full of exaggeration, false criticism, and inconsistency), **The Crown of*

Wild Olive, Unto This Last, Fors Clavigera, Letters V and VIII; *Modern Painters,* Part III, section 1, Chap. XV; "The Theoretic Faculty," *ibid,* section 2; "The Imaginative Faculty," Chaps. I–V.

J. H. Newman. (Page 548.) *Apologia pro vitâ suâ; Idea of a University* and *The Dream of Gerontius* (Longmans). * *Selections,* with introduction by L. E. Gates (Holt).

BIOGRAPHY AND CRITICISM. *Life,* by R. H. Hutton (Houghton) and by W. S. Lilly in D. N. B. Essays by * R. H. Hutton in *Modern Guides of English Thought* (Macmillan), and Shairp in *Aspects of Poetry* (Houghton). See also works of R. W. Church and others on "The Oxford Movement."

James Anthony Froude. (Page 552.) Paul, *Life* (Scribner).

Walter Pater and Literary Criticism. (Page 553.) Saintsbury, in *History of Criticism,* Vol. III, Bk. IX, Chaps. II–III (Dodd); Wright, Life of Walter Pater, 2 vols. (Putnam); Benson, *Walter Pater* (E. M. L.); H. F. Brown, *John Addington Symonds,* 2 vols. (Nimmo); Maitland, *Life and Letters of Leslie Stephen* (Putnam).

Matthew Arnold. (Page 553.) *Complete Works,* 14 vols. (Macmillan); *Poetical Works* (Globe Ed.); *Selected Poems* (Golden Treasury Series); *Selections from Prose,* ed. by L. E. Gates (Holt).

BIOGRAPHY AND CRITICISM. Paul, *Life* (E. M. L.); Russell, *Life* ("Literary Lives," Scribner); Saintsbury, *Life* (Dodd); Lang, in *Century Magazine,* Vol. I, p. 849, 1881–82; Hutton, (*a*) "Poetry of Matthew Arnold," in *Essays, Theological and Literary,* Vol. II (Macmillan); (*b*) "Arnold," in *Modern Guides of English Thought* (Macmillan); Brownell, in *Victorian Prose Masters* (Scribner); Woodberry, in *Makers of Literature* (Macmillan); Harrison, (*a*) in *Tennyson, Ruskin, Mill, and Other Essays* (Macmillan); (*b*) "Culture; a Dialogue," in *The Choice of Books* (Macmillan); Shairp, *Culture and Religion* (Houghton); Robertson, in *Modern Humanists* (Scribner); Jacobs, in *Literary Studies* (Scribner); Hudson, in *Studies in Interpretation* (Putnam); Forman, in *Our Living Poets* (Tinsley); Stedman, in *Victorian Poets* (Houghton); Swinburne, in *Essays and Studies* (Scribner); Amy Sharp, in *Victorian Poets* (Scribner).

SUGGESTED READINGS. *Poetry:* "Switzerland," "Isolation," "To Marguerite," "Absence," "Dover Beach," "The Scholar-Gypsy," "Thyrsis," "Stanzas from the Grande Chartreuse," "Tristam and Iseult," "Sohrab and Rustum," "The Forsaken Merman," "To a Gipsy Child by the Seashore," "Lines written in Kensington Gardens," "Stanzas in Memory of the Author of Obermann." *Sonnets:* "Shakespeare," "The Good Shepherd with the Kid," "East London," "Geist's Grave." *Prose:* "The Function of Criticism," in *Essays in Criticism,* 1st series; "The Study of Poetry," and "Milton," in *ibid.* 2d series: "Celtic Literature," "Numbers," in *Discourses in America.* Extracts from Arnold's prose, with admirable introduction, are given in Edward T. McLaughlin's *Literary Criticism* (Holt).

The Novel.

Maria Edgeworth. (Page 556.) *Castle Rackrent* and *The Absentee*, with an Introduction by Anne Thackeray Ritchie (Macmillan).

BIOGRAPHY. Hare, *Life and Letters*, 2 vols. (Houghton); Lawless, *Life* (E. M. L.); Ritchie, in *A Book of Sibyls* (Smith, Elder).

Jane Austen. (Page 557.) *Works*, ed. by R. B. Johnson, 10 vols. (Macmillan).

BIOGRAPHY AND CRITICISM. Goldwin Smith, *Life* (G. W. S.); Adams, *Life* (Lee and Shepard); *Memoir, by her Nephew, Austen Leigh* (Macmillan); Mrs. Ritchie, in *A Book of Sibyls* (Smith, Elder); Pollock, *Jane Austen, Her Contemporaries and Herself* (Longmans); Dawson, in *Makers of English Fiction* (Revell).

Charles Kingsley. (Page 558.) *Alton Locke*, with memoir by Thomas Hughes, *Hereward, Westward Ho!* (Macmillan).

BIOGRAPHY AND CRITICISM. *Letters and Memories of His Life*, ed. by His Wife, 2 vols. (Macmillan); Stubbs, *Charles Kingsley and the Christian Social Movement* (Stone); L. Stephen, in *Hours in a Library*, Vol. III (Putnam); Dawson, in *Makers of English Fiction* (Revell).

Charles Dickens. (Page 558.) *Biography and Criticism*, Forster; *Life*, 2 vols. (Scribner); Ward, *Life* (E. M. L.); Marzials, *Life* (G. W. S.); Mamie Dickens, *My Father as I Recall Him* (Dutton); Pierce and Wheeler, *The Dickens Dictionary* (Houghton); Gissing, *Charles Dickens, a Critical Study* (Dodd); F. Harrison, in *Studies in Early Victorian Literature* (Lane); Bagehot, in *Literary Studies*, Vol. II (Longmans); Lilly, in *Four English Humorists of the Nineteenth Century* (Murray).

William Makepeace Thackeray. (Page 560.) *Works*, Biographical edition, ed. by Anne Thackeray Ritchie, 13 vols. (Harper).

BIOGRAPHY AND CRITICISM. Trollope, *Life* (E. M. L.); Merivale and Marzials, *Life* (G. W. S.); Melville, *Life*, 2 vols. (Stone); G. B. Smith, in *Poets and Novelists* (Smith, Elder); Lilly, in *Four English Humorists of the Nineteenth Century* (Murray); Brownell, in *Victorian Prose Masters* (Scribner); F. Harrison, in *Studies in Early Victorian Literature* (Lane); Wilson, *Thackeray in the United States*, 1852–3, 1855–6; *including a Record of Thackerayana* (Dodd).

George Eliot. (Page 562.) *Works*, Personal ed., 12 vols. (Doubleday); *Adam Bede*, 2 vols., *Silas Marner* (" Temple Classics ").

BIOGRAPHY AND CRITICISM. Cross, *Life*, 3 vols. (Harper); L. Stephen, *Life* (E. M. L.); O. Browning, *Life* (G. W. S.); Cooke, *George Eliot; a Critical Study of Her Life and Writings* (Houghton); Blind, *Life* (Famous Women) (Little); Parkinson, *Scenes from the George Eliot Country* (Simpkin); Hutton, (*a*) "George Eliot as an Author," in *Modern Guides of English Thought in Matters of Faith* (Macmillan); (*b*) "George Eliot," in *Essays in Literary Criticism* (Coates); F. Harrison, in *Studies in Early Victorian Literature* (Lane); H. James, in *Partial Portraits* (Macmillan); Brownell, in *Victorian Prose Masters* (Scribner); Jacobs, in *Literary Studies* (Scribner); Lilly, in *Four English Humorists of the Nineteenth Century* (Murray); *Dowden, " George Eliot," "Middlemarch and Daniel Deronda," in *Studies in Literature* (Scribner); J. C. Brown, *Ethics of George Eliot's Works* (Blackwood); Lanier, in *The English Novel* (Scribner); Rev. Charles G. Ames, *George Eliot's Two Marriages* (Arnold & Co.).

Anthony Trollope. (Page 572.) *Chronicles of Barsetshire*, 13 vols. (Dodd).

BIOGRAPHY AND CRITICISM. *Autobiography* (Harper); Saintsbury, in *Corrected Impressions* (Dodd); F. Harrison, in *Studies in Early Victorian Literature* (Lane); H. James, in *Partial Portraits* (Macmillan).

The Brontës. (Page 574.) *Works of Charlotte, Emily, and Anne Brontë*, Haworth Edition, ed. by Mrs. Humphrey Ward, 7 vols. (Harper); *Jane Eyre*, 2 vols., *Shirley*, 2 vols., *Wuthering Heights and Agnes Grey*, 2 vols. (" Temple Classics ").

BIOGRAPHY AND CRITICISM: Mrs. Gaskell, *Life of Charlotte Brontë*, Haworth Ed. (Harper); Birrell, *Life of Charlotte Brontë* (G. W. S.); Swinburne, *Note on Charlotte Brontë* (Scribner); A. M. F. Robinson, *Life of Emily Brontë* (Little); Shorter and Nichol, *The Brontës and Their Circle* (Dodd); Mackay, *The Brontës in Fact and Fiction* (Dodd); W. W. Kinsley, "The Brontë Sisters," in *Views on Vexed Questions* (Lippincott); Swinburne, "Emily Brontë," in *Miscellanies* (Scribner); F. Harrison, "Charlotte Brontë," in *Studies in Early Victorian Literature* (Lane).

Robert Louis Stevenson. (Page 575.) *Works*, Biographical edition, ed. by Mrs. Stevenson, 25 vols. (Scribner).

BIOGRAPHY AND CRITICISM. Balfour, *Life*, 2 vols. (Scribner); Cornford, *Life* (Dodd); Raleigh, *Life* (Lane); *Letters to His Family and Friends*, ed. by Colvin, 2 vols. (Scribner); *Vailima Letters to Sidney Colvin*, 2 vols. (Stone); Mrs. M. I. Stevenson, *Letters from Samoa, 1891–95*, ed. by Marie C. Balfour (Scribner); Strong and Osbourne, *Memories of Vailima* (Scribner); Japp, *Robert Louis Stevenson ; a Record, an Estimate, and a Memorial* (Scribner); Kelman, *The Faith of Robert Louis Stevenson* (Revell); Genung, *Stevenson's Attitude to Life* (Crowell); Dawson, in *Makers of English Fiction* (Revell); Torrey, in *Friends on the Shelf* (Houghton); Baildon, "Robert Louis Stevenson; Essayist, Novelist, and Poet," in *Living Age*, Vol. CCXXI, 1899.

George Meredith. (Page 577.) *Works*, Boxhill Ed., 16 vols. (Scribner).

BIOGRAPHY AND CRITICISM. J. Lane, *Life* (Lane); Le Gallienne, *George Meredith, Some Characteristics* (Lane); Hannah Lynch, *George Meredith, a Study* (Methuen); Monkhouse, "Novels of George Meredith," in *Books and Plays* (Lane); Brownell, in *Victorian Prose Masters* (Scribner); Dawson, in *Makers of English Fiction* (Revell); Gosse,

"Historic Place of George Meredith and Thomas Hardy," in *International Monthly*, Vol. IV, 1901; G. M. Trevelyan, *Poetry and Philosophy of George Meredith* (Scribner).

Thomas Hardy. (Page 579.) WORKS (Harper).

BIOGRAPHY AND CRITICISM. Annie Macdonnell, *Thomas Hardy* (Dodd); * L. Johnson, *Art of Thomas Hardy* (Lane); Windle, *Wessex of Thomas Hardy*,(Lane); Dawson, in *Makers of English Fiction* (Revell); Vincent, in *The Bibliotaph* (Houghton); "The Novels of Thomas Hardy," in *Westminster Review*, Vol. CXIX, 1883; Gosse, "Historic Place of George Meredith and Thomas Hardy," in *International Monthly*, Vol. IV, 1901.

The Pre-Raphaelites. (Page 582.)

HISTORY AND CRITICISM. Beers, *History of English Romanticism in the Nineteenth Century* (Holt); Vida D. Scudder, *Life of the Spirit in the Modern English Poets* (Houghton); Bate, *English Pre-Raphaelite Painters* (Macmillan); Esther Wood, *Rossetti and the Pre-Raphaelite Movement* (Scribner); W. M. Rossetti, *Pre-Raphaelite Diaries and Letters* (Scribner); Holman Hunt, *Pre-Raphaelitism and the Pre-Raphaelite Brotherhood*, 2 vols. (Macmillan).

Dante Gabriel Rossetti. (Page 583.) *Poetical Works*, ed. by W. M. Rossetti, 2 vols. (Scribner); *Early Italian Poets. Vita Nuova* (Macmillan).

BIOGRAPHY AND CRITICISM. Knight, *Life* (G. W. S.); Benson, *Life* (E. M. L.); Swinburne, "Essays," in *Miscellanies* (Scribner); Forman, in *Our Living Poets* (Tinsley); W. Sharp, *Rossetti; a Record and a Study* (London, 1882); Caine, *Recollections of Rossetti* (Little); W. M. Rossetti, (a) *D. G. Rossetti; His Family Letters, with Memoir*, 2 vols. (Little); (b) *Ruskin, Rossetti, and Pre-Raphaelitism; Papers*, 1854–1861 (Dodd); Myers, "Rossetti and the Religion of Beauty," in *Modern Essays* (Macmillan); Pater, in *Appreciations* (Macmillan); Esther Wood, *Rossetti and the Pre-Raphaelite Movement* (Scribner).

SUGGESTED READINGS. "The Blessed Damozel," "Love's Nocturn," "The Burden of Nineveh," "A Last Confession," "Jenny," "The Ballad of Dead Ladies," "The Sea Limits," "Rose Mary," "The White Ship," "The King's Tragedy," "World's Worth" ; *Sonnets*, "Sibylla Palmifera," in *House of Life*, Sonnet XIX, and "The Choice," Sonnets LXXI, LXXII, *v.* also LXIII.

William Morris. (Page 586.) *The Earthly Paradise, Defence of Guenevere, Story of Sigurd the Volsung, Story of the Glittering Plain, Tale of the House of the Wolfings*, all published by Longmans; *Volsunga Saga* (Camelot Series); *Dream of John Ball* (Longmans).

BIOGRAPHY AND CRITICISM. Mackail, *Life*, 2 vols. (Longmans); Vallance, *William Morris; His Art, Writings and Public Life* (Macmillan); Swinburne, "The Life and Death of Jason," in *Essays and Studies* (Scribner); Saintsbury, in *Corrected Impressions* (Dodd); Pater, "Æsthetic Poetry," in *Appreciations* (Macmillan); Forman, in *Our Living*

Poets (Tinsley); Symons, in *Studies in Two Literatures* (Simpkin); Dawson, in *Makers of English Poetry* (Revell); Nordby, *Influence of Old Norse Literature upon English Literature* (Macmillan).

SUGGESTED READINGS. *The Earthly Paradise, A Dream of John Ball, Story of Sigurd the Volsung.*

Algernon Charles Swinburne. (Page 590.) *Poems,* 6 vols. (Harper); *Poetical Works,* Introduction by R. H. Stoddard (Crowell); *Atalanta in Calydon* (Chatto); *Erechtheus* (Chatto); * *Select Poems,* Introduction by W. M. Payne (Belles-Lettres Series, Heath).

BIOGRAPHY AND CRITICISM. Wratislaw, *Critical Study of Swinburne* (Wessels); Forman, in *Our Living Poets* (Tinsley); Saintsbury, in *Corrected Impressions* (Dodd); * Stedman, in *Victorian Poets* (Houghton); Dawson, in *Makers of English Poetry* (Revell); Lowell, "Swinburne's Tragedies," in *Literary Essays,* Vol. II (Houghton); Gosse, in *Century,* Vol. LXIV, 1902; G. Barlow, "On the Spiritual Side of Mr. Swinburne's Genius," in *Contemporary Review,* Vol.´ LXXXVIII, 1905; " Poetry and Criticism of Swinburne," in *Quarterly Review,* Vol. CCIII, 1905; More, in *Shelburne Essays,* 3d series (Putnam).

SUGGESTED READINGS. "Atalanta in Calydon; " "The Last Oracle," "A Forsaken Garden," "By the North Sea," "Hertha," "The Hymn to Proserpine," "Itylus," "The Pilgrims." *Essays:* "Poems of Dante Gabriel Rossetti," "Byron," in *Essays and Studies* (Scribner).

Alfred Tennyson. (Page 594.) *Life and Complete Works,* 10 vols. (Macmillan); *Works* (Globe Ed.); *Works* (Cambridge Ed.); *In Memoriam, Maud,* and *The Princess* ("Temple Classics "); *Select Poems,* ed. by Rolfe (Houghton); *Princess,* ed. by Cook (Ginn); *Idylls of the King,* ed. by Rolfe (Houghton).

BIOGRAPHY. *Memoir by his Son* (Macmillan); Waugh, *Study of Life and Work* (Macmillan); Lyall, *Life* (E. M. L.); Jennings, *Biographical Sketch* (Lippincott); Horton, *Life* (Dutton); Mrs. Ritchie, in *Records of Tennyson, Ruskin, Browning* (Harper).

CRITICISM. Luce, *Tennyson Primer* ("Temple Primers"); Luce, *Handbook to the Works* (Macmillan); *Tennyson Primer,* Dixon (Dodd); Chapman, *Companion to "In Memoriam"* (Macmillan); Gatty, *Key to "In Memoriam"* (Macmillan); Bradley, *Commentary on "In Memoriam "* (Macmillan); Tainsh, *Study of the Works* (Macmillan); Bagehot, "Wordsworth, Tennyson and Browning," in *Literary Studies,* Vol. II (Longmans); * Dowden, "Tennyson and Browning," in *Studies in Literature,* 1789–1877 (Scribner); Hutton, in *Literary Essays* (Macmillan); Bayne, in *Lessons from My Masters* (Harper); Genung, *Tennyson's "In Memoriam "* (Houghton); Roden Noel, in *Poetry and Poets* (Kegan Paul); Swinburne, "Tennyson and Musset," in *Miscellanies* (Scribner); Robertson, "Art of Tennyson," in *Essays Towards a Critical Method* (London, 1889); H. Van Dyke, *Poetry of Tennyson* (Scribner); Dawson, in *Makers of English Poetry* (Revell); Brooke, *Tennyson; His Art and His Relation to Modern Life*

(Putnam); Saintsbury, in *Corrected Impressions* (Dodd); Trent, "Tennyson and Musset Once More," in *Authority of Criticism* (Scribner); F. Harrison, in *Tennyson, Ruskin, and Mill* (Macmillan); Dixon, *Tennyson Primer, with a Critical Essay* (Dodd), contains useful bibliography and list of dates; * Masterman, *Tennyson as a Religious Teacher* (Knight and Millet); Littledale, *Essays on Idylls of the King* (Macmillan); Maccallum, *Tennyson's Idylls of the King* (Macmillan); Alford, "Idylls of the King," in *Contemporary Review*, Vol. XIII, 1870; Davidson, *Prolegomena to "In Memoriam"* (Heath).

SUGGESTED READINGS. 1. *Poems Illustrative of Tennyson's Art.* "Claribel," "Nothing Will Die," "Lilian," two songs on "The Owl," "Madeline," "The Northern Farmer," (old and new style), "Boädicéa," "The Charge of the Light Brigade," "The Revenge," "Tears, Idle Tears" and "The Splendour Falls on Castle Walls" (from "The Princess"), "Frater ave atque vale."

2. *Tennyson's Theory of Art.* "The Day Dream," "The Palace of Art," "The Flower," "The Poet," "The Poet's Mind," "Merlin and the Gleam."

3. *Tennyson as Poet of Nature: poems suggestive of particular localities.* "Mariana," "The Dying Swan," "The Brook," and the natural descriptions scattered throughout Tennyson's works. For interesting studies of this subject, see *The Laureate's Country*, by A. J. Church (Seeley); *In Tennyson Land*, by J. Cumming Walter (Redway), "Lincolnshire Scenery and Characters as Illustrated by Mr. Tennyson," in *Macmillan's Magazine*, November and April, 1873–1874, Howitt's *Homes and Haunts of the British Poets* (Routledge).

4. *Classical Poems.* "The Lotos-Eaters," "Ulysses " "Tithonus," "Œnone," "Demeter and Persephone."

5. *Arthurian Poems.* "The Lady of Shalott," "Sir Galahad," "Sir Launcelot and Queen Guinevere," *The Idylls of the King.* (The following *Idylls* are suggested if the entire series is not read, "Dedication," "The Coming of Arthur," "Gareth and Lynette," "The Holy Grail," "Guinevere," "The Passing of Arthur," "Epilogue").

6. *Dramas.* "Harold," "Becket."

7. *Tennyson as a Teacher.* (*a*) Ideas of democracy and social reform, class distinctions as a bar to marriage, etc. "The Gardiner's Daughter," "The Miller's Daughter," "Locksley Hall," "Aylmer's Field," "Lady Clara Vere de Vere," "The Beggar Maid," "Maud," "The Princess." (*b*) Political Poems. "You Ask Me Why tho' Ill at Ease," "Of Old Sat Freedom on the Heights," "Love Thou Thy Land," and for Tennyson's youthful and maturer feeling toward contemporary problems, "Locksley Hall" and "Locksley Hall Sixty Years After." (*c*) Religious and Philosophic Poems. "The Two Voices," *In Memoriam*, "Vastness," "The Higher Pantheism," "Despair," "The Ancient Sage," "By an Evolutionist," "Crossing the Bar."

Robert Browning. (Page 610.) *Poetical Works*, 12 vols., ed.

with introduction and notes by Porter and Clarke (Crowell); *Poetical Works*, ed. by Birrell (Globe Ed.); *Poetical Works* (Cambridge Ed.); *Selections*, ed. by Garnett (Endymion Series, Macmillan); *Selections*, ed. by Rylands (Bell's Miniature Series, Macmillan); *Dramatic Monologues, Men and Women, Paracelsus, Sordello, Pippa Passes* ("Temple Classics"); *Lyrical and Dramatic Poems*, ed. by Mason (Holt); *Letters of Robert Browning and Elizabeth Barrett Browning*, 2 vols. (Harper).

BIOGRAPHY. Mrs. Orr, *Life and Letters* (Houghton); * Sharp, *Life* (G. W. S.); Dowden, *Life* (Dutton); Mrs. Ritchie, in *Tennyson, Ruskin, Browning* (Harper); Cary, *Browning, Poet and Man* (Putnam); Marzials, *Life* (Macmillan); Waugh, *Life* (Westminster Biographies) (Small, Maynard).

CRITICISM. Mrs. Orr, *Handbook to the Works*, 3d edition (Macmillan); * Cooke, *Guidebook to Browning* (Houghton); Berdoe, *Browning Cyclopædia* (Macmillan); Alexander, *Introduction to Poetry of Browning* (Ginn); Corson, *Introduction to the Study of Browning's Poetry* (Heath); * Symons, *Introduction to the Study of Browning* (Cassell); Fotheringham, *Studies of Mind and Art of Browning* (Scribner); Berdoe, *Browning's Message to His Time* (Sonnenschein); Nettleship, *Robert Browning: Essays* (Matthews); Revell, *Browning's Criticism of Life* (Sonnenschein); Gosse, *Personalia* (Houghton); Bagehot, "Wordsworth, Tennyson, and Browning," in *Literary Studies*, Vol. II (Longmans); * Dowden, (*a*) "Tennyson and Browning," in *Studies in Literature, 1789-1877* (Scribner); (*b*) "Sordello," in *Transcripts and Studies* (Scribner); Hutton, in *Literary Essays*, 3d edition (Macmillan); Birrell, "On the Alleged Obscurity of Mr. Browning's Poetry," in *Obiter Dicta*, 1st series (Scribner); Roden Noel, in *Poetry and Poets* (Kegan Paul); Jacobs, in *Literary Studies* (Scribner); H. Jones, *Browning as a Philosophical and Religious Teacher* (Macmillan); Dawson, in *Makers of English Poetry* (Revell); Saintsbury, in *Corrected Impressions* (Dodd); Scudder, "Browning as a Humorist," in *Life of the Spirit in Modern English Poets* (Houghton); Chapman, in *Emerson and Other Essays* (Scribner); Stedman, in *Victorian Poets* (Houghton); Cooke, in *Poets and Problems* (Houghton).

SUGGESTED READINGS. 1. *Love Poems:* "Evelyn Hope," "By the Fireside," "One Word More," "The Last Ride Together," "Love Among the Ruins." 2. *Narrative:* "Martin Relph," "Muléykeh," "Ivan Ivanovitch," "The Flight of the Duchess," "Clive." 3. *Art Poems:* "My Last Duchess," "Andrea del Sarto," "Fra Lippo Lippi," "Pictor Ignotus," "Old Pictures in Florence," "A Toccata of Galluppi's," "Master Hughes of Saxe-Gotha," "Abt Vogler." 4. *Dramas:* "In a Balcony," "Pippa Passes," "Luria," "A Blot in the 'Scutcheon," "Paracelsus." 5. *Immortality and Religion:* "Rabbi Ben Ezra," "Epistle of Karshish," "Cleon," "Prospice," "Saul," "A Death in the Desert," "Christmas Eve," and "Easter Day," "Rephan." 6. *Longer Poems:* "The Ring and the Book."

INDEX.

INDEX.

Date Due